Remembering the Road to World War Two

'This is comparative history on a grand scale, skilfully analysing complex national debates and drawing major conclusions without ever losing the necessary nuances of interpretation.'

Stefan Berger, *University of Manchester, UK*

Remembering the Road to World War Two is a broad and comparative international survey of the historiography of the origins of the Second World War. It explores how, in the case of each of the major combatant countries, historical writing on the origins of the Second World War has been inextricably entwined with debates over national identity and collective memory.

Spanning seven case studies – the Soviet Union, Germany, Italy, France, Great Britain, the United States and Japan – Patrick Finney proposes a fresh approach to the politics of historiography. This provocative volume discusses the political, cultural, disciplinary and archival factors which have contributed to the evolving construction of historical interpretations. It analyses the complex and multi-faceted relationships between texts about the origins of the war, the negotiation of conceptions of national identity and unfolding processes of war remembrance.

Offering an innovative perspective on international history and enriching the literature on collective memory, this book will prove fascinating reading for all students of the Second World War.

Patrick Finney teaches in the Department of International Politics, Aberystwyth University, UK. He has published widely in the fields of twentieth century international history, history and theory and collective memory. Previous publications include (ed.) *Palgrave Advances in International History* (2005).

Remembering the Road to World War Two

International history, national identity, collective memory

Patrick Finney

Routledge
Taylor & Francis Group

LONDON AND NEW YORK

First edition published 2011
by Routledge
2 Park Square, Milton Park, Abingdon, Oxon OX14 4RN

Simultaneously published in the USA and Canada by Routledge
711 Third Avenue, New York, NY 10017

Routledge is an imprint of the Taylor & Francis Group, an informa business

Typeset in Garamond by Taylor & Francis Books

British Library Cataloguing in Publication Data
A catalogue record for this book is available from the British Library

Library of Congress Cataloging in Publication Data
Finney, Patrick, 1968–
Remembering the road to World War Two : international history, national
identity, collective memory / Patrick Finney. -- 1st ed.
p. cm.
Includes bibliographical references and index.
1. World War, 1939–1945--Causes--Historiography. 2. World War, 1939–1945--
Causes--Historiography--Case studies. 3. National characteristics--Case studies.
4. Collective memory--Case studies. I. Title. II. Title: Remembering the road
to World War II. III. Title: Remembering the road to World War 2.
D743.42.F565 2010
940.53'11--dc22
2010005313

ISBN 13: 978-0-415-23017-9 (hbk)
ISBN 13: 978-0-415-23018-6 (pbk)
ISBN 13: 978-0-203-84624-7 (ebk)

Contents

Acknowledgements

This book has been a very long time in the writing, and along the way I have received so much assistance from so many diverse people that I doubt my capacity to acknowledge it adequately here. I first studied international history at Leeds University, and would like to thank John Gooch, Phil Taylor, Geoff Waddington and above all Roy Bridge for fostering my development. This project began to take shape when I was working at the University of Wales, Lampeter, and I would particularly like to thank Colin Eldridge, Keith Robbins and Malcolm Smith for providing intellectual and material assistance during that time. The book was completed at the Department of International Politics, Aberystwyth University, and I would like to acknowledge diverse debts there to Martin Alexander, Will Bain, Ken Booth, Ian Clark, Campbell Craig, Graeme Davies, Jenny Edkins, Toni Erskine, Alastair Finlan, Mike Foley, Gerald Hughes, Peter Jackson, Milja Kurki, Andrew Linklater, Stephan Petzold, Andrew Priest, Len Scott, Roger Scully, Alistair Shepherd, Hidemi Suganami, Nick Wheeler and James Vaughan. I would also like to acknowledge financial support and sabbatical leave from the Department and the University. In the wider scholarly community, I have received useful advice, assistance and support from Antony Best, Susie Carruthers, Mick Cox, Oliver Daddow, Talbot Imlay, Keith Jenkins, Peter Lambert, Matt Levey, Spencer Mawby, Alun Munslow, David Reynolds, Geoff Roberts and Martin Thomas.

Routledge have provided a much better service to me as publishers than I probably deserve. Heather McCallum had a direct creative input when the project was first conceived, and it was guided to completion by the infinitely patient Victoria Peters. Thanks are also due to all the other professional and helpful people involved on the production side, and to Emily Kindleysides who was the last of many editorial assistants to work on the project. During its gestation, I profited greatly from the comments of a large number of readers on proposals, sample chapters and the final text. In addition to those that remained anonymous or who are named above, I would like to thank Richard Bosworth, Mark Donnelly, Bill Niven, Kevin Smith and Stuart Woolf. I am especially grateful to Stefan Berger who read the final manuscript in its entirety and made numerous insightful and helpful comments.

I have further benefited from presenting some of the ideas and material contained in this book at conferences and seminars. An exhaustive list would be far too unwieldy, but I would particularly like to express gratitude to audiences at the following meetings for their constructive comments: the Fourth European Social Science History Conference, The Hague, February 2002; a British International Studies Association Poststructural Politics Working Group Workshop, Manchester, May 2002; the International History Research Group, Aberystwyth, October 2004 and October 2007; the 'Defeat and Memory' Conference, Edinburgh, September 2005; Department of History and Welsh History Research Seminar, Aberystwyth, October 2005; Society for Historians of American Foreign Relations Annual Conference, Lawrence, Kansas, June 2006 (with particular thanks to Mark Bradley, Frank Costigliola and Walter Hixson); the Seventh European Social Science History Conference, Lisbon, February 2008; and the International Studies Association Annual Convention, San Francisco, March 2008. Students on my Special Subject on 'Great Britain and the Origins of the Second World War' at Lampeter and on the Master's programmes in International History at Aberystwyth also provided helpful feedback on some of my ideas.

Thanks are due to library staff at the University of Wales, Lampeter, the Hugh Owen Library and the National Library of Wales in Aberystwyth for facilitating my research.

This book has its origins in my thinking about the historiography of British appeasement, and a rather different version of chapter five was published as 'The romance of decline: the historiography of appeasement and British national identity', *electronic Journal of International History*, June 2000, http://www.history.ac.uk/ejournal/art1.html (accessed 5 March 2010). I am grateful for comments on it from the editors and three anonymous referees. Aspects of the arguments of other chapters were previewed in 'The stories of defeated aggressors: international history, national identity, and collective memory after 1945', in Jenny Macleod (ed.), *Defeat and Memory: Cultural Histories of Military Defeat in the Modern Era* (London, Palgrave, 2008), pp. 97–116.

All of those acknowledged here made this book possible, but any flaws or errors are entirely my responsibility.

On the personal front, I should like to thank my parents, Jack and Barbara, for their ongoing support. Above all else, I owe more than I can easily express to Laura Guillaume for her intellectual provocations and staunch emotional support, and for sharing in some excellent adventures. This book, at long last and with all my love, is for her.

Introduction

International history and the memory of the Second World War

> History is not and can never be a science in the current acceptation of this term. It would be better to recognize this and to consider the political and ethical implications of different modes of interpreting history than to hang on to a standard of objectivity and impartiality that has been more honoured in the breach than the observance throughout the history of historical writing.
>
> Hayden White[1]

In early June 2004, thousands of veterans of the D-Day landings converged on Normandy to mark the sixtieth anniversary of the largest amphibious assault in military history. Their ranks were much thinned from previous commemorations, and even those fit enough to make the journey were often so frail that this would be their final pilgrimage. The performance of personal acts of remembrance at military cemeteries was an important priority for these elderly travellers. Seventy-nine-year-old George Marsden paid his respects at the grave of childhood friend Fred Ambler, dismembered at his side by a German mine at the age of 19, leaving a small wooden cross with the simple inscription 'school-time pal, war-time buddy'.[2] Yet this was also a social occasion, as the veterans caught up with former comrades and chatted in cafes with members of the local population who fêted them as heroes. Indispensable, too, were visits to the beaches and landing grounds where old soldiers recalled in blazing sunshine what they had done and suffered there the best part of a lifetime ago. Some were eager to tell stories of the horror, terror and sacrifice they had witnessed; others were more reticent, either from natural reserve or lingering trauma: 'it was bad, very bad', recalled Maurice Cox of the 6th Durham Light Infantry, 'but it could have been worse'.[3]

Surrounding these poignant observances were a host of less elevated forms of remembrance. Memorabilia manufacturers had churned out 'a sourly impressive amount of laminated plasticky tourist dreck', and this was eagerly consumed by the hordes of tourists and 'grotesque medley of historical re-enactors' – 'car enthusiasts, costume fetishists and unhinged military wannabes' – who had flooded into northern France.[4] There were extensive formal commemorative ceremonies with political representatives from almost all the European combatant powers, including for the first time the Federal

Republic of Germany and Russia, a gesture of inclusivity that reflected a sincere desire to draw a definitive line under wartime (and Cold War) antagonisms. Yet there was brute political calculation here too. Every speech delivered refracted the events of D-Day through a different prism of national identity and contemporary political imperative, and the invitation to the Russians had also aimed to soothe their ruffled feathers following the eastward expansion of the European Union (EU) in May.[5] In this collision of authentic personal remembrance, debasing commerce, ersatz heritage experience, and the play of political capital, the D-Day commemorations perfectly encapsulated the ambiguity and complexity of a particular contemporary moment of war memory.

Over the following 15 months, the anniversaries of the remaining significant events in the closing stages of the war in Europe and the Far East were lavishly honoured. Particularly notable was the spectacular and elaborate Victory Day parade held in Moscow on 9 May 2005, at which Russian President Vladimir Putin hosted more than 50 world leaders and foregrounded the contribution of the Soviet Union, with its 27 million war dead, to the 'victory of good over evil'.[6] Memory also took more permanent form with the dedication of myriad new monuments. The American National World War II Memorial, a vast neo-classical edifice on the Mall in Washington DC, and the German Memorial to the Murdered Jews of Europe, a swelling sea of 2,711 concrete stelae in the heart of Berlin, were both eloquent statements about the contemporary salience of the war in the two nations' collective memories. Memory of the war was also intensely visible in the media. A cinematic landmark was Oliver Hirschbiegel's *Der Untergang*, a rendering of the last days of the Third Reich, and the first German film for decades to broach the representation of Hitler head-on.[7] War-themed television dramas and documentaries proliferated, bookshop shelves groaned under the weight of popular and scholarly tomes, and commentators endlessly dissected both the events of the war itself and its shifting significance across six post-war decades.

The war had certainly not ceased to fuel historical and political controversy. Within Germany, the legitimacy of remembering the suffering that Germans had experienced rather than inflicted was fiercely debated after neo-Nazis seized upon the anniversary of the destruction of Dresden in February 2005 to denounce this 'Holocaust of bombs'.[8] Putin's rousing celebration of the Soviet war effort was poorly received in the Baltic states: the presidents of Estonia and Lithuania snubbed the Victory Day celebrations, stressing that for them 1945 did not herald a liberation so much as the substitution of one brutal foreign occupation for another. Many other East European states, newly empowered by their recent admission to the EU, expressed similar reservations, and US President George W. Bush weighed in on their side denouncing the establishment of the Soviet empire in Europe as 'one of the greatest wrongs of history'.[9] In the Far East, Japanese Prime Minister Koizumi Junichiro's V-J Day expression of 'deep remorse and heartfelt apology' for wartime aggression did little to quell anger in China and South Korea over his government's approval earlier in the year of new school history textbooks that sanitised Japanese war crimes in Asia.[10]

Preserved in western public memory as an indubitably 'good war' – a status now secured by the enshrining of the Holocaust as its defining atrocity – the conflict also continued to serve as a potent analogical resource. In the wars of Yugoslav succession, Serbs and Croats had battled to portray each other as latter-day Nazis, and the Americans then liberally invoked the tropes of 'Munich' and 'Holocaust' to build support for their air campaign against Serbia in the 1999 Kosovo crisis.[11] On '9/11', the surprise bombing of Pearl Harbor had been 'the first frame of reference' within the US for the terrorist attacks, the comparison working both 'to rally patriotism' in the face of enemy perfidy and to 'promise eventual and righteous triumph to a nervous nation'.[12] Thereafter, representations of the Second World War were ubiquitously deployed to legitimise the 'War on Terror'. Prior to the 2003 invasion of Iraq, for example, Saddam Hussein was persistently represented as a new Adolf Hitler and anyone opposing the rush to war was tarred with hysterical accusations of appeasement.[13] The connection was then repeatedly reinscribed during the long cycle of anniversary commemorations. In his keynote speech to commemorate V-J Day in 2005, Bush declared that 'we are again a nation at war ... Once again, we face determined enemies who follow a ruthless ideology that despises everything America stands for ... And once again, we will not rest until victory is America's and our freedom is secure'.[14] Not that these comparisons went uncontested. Some critics lamented that the virtuous lustre of the 'good war' was being tarnished as it was harnessed to support manifestly bad ones.[15] Others objected that the 'good war' mythology was itself entirely pernicious, since it effaced Allied war crimes and atrocities inflicted on Axis civilians and had underwritten 60 years of subsequent western warmongering.[16]

Even as it recedes ever further from us, the Second World War thus remains vividly alive. The fiftieth anniversary commemorations in 1995 were widely interpreted as elegiac farewells to a war inexorably drifting out of contemporary consciousness, and yet ten years later it seemed that it had 'never been so important'.[17] As the round of seventieth anniversary commemorations is now playing out, that judgement remains defensible. The Russian–Estonian polemics over the Soviet 'Bronze Soldier' memorial in Tallinn in 2007 testify to the war's enduring capacity to provoke political contestation.[18] Novelist Nicholson Baker's idiosyncratic pacifist assault on the 'good war' myth in *Human Smoke*, in combination with a steady stream of filmic revisionings dealing with combat, resistance and post-war reckoning – and even Quentin Tarantino's baroque counterfactual romp *Inglourious Basterds* – demonstrate its continuing resonance in popular culture.[19] Memorialisation continues unabated, encompassing most recently in Germany the erection of monuments to the homosexual, Sinti and Roma victims of Nazi oppression.[20] The war also figured rhetorically in the 2008 American presidential election campaign as

Bush sought to damn Barack Obama as an appeaser for his professed willingness to talk without preconditions to the government in Teheran.[21] In academic culture, it also continues to enjoy a high profile. For historians of international relations, the study of contemporary and particularly Cold War topics may have recently become more modish, but this war and its origins nonetheless remain objects of considerable scrutiny.[22] As an historiographical study of debates on the origins of the war, this book intends both to contribute to this scrutiny and to comment upon it. Its specific ambition is to bring the international history literature into unwonted conversation with other bodies of work on national identity and collective memory.

Memory and history

The concept of memory has lately become 'the historical signature of our own generation'.[23] Projects of diverse yet overlapping kinds nestle together within the endeavour to uncover the work of memory. Some analyse the memories of individuals who have directly experienced particular – often traumatic – events; others explore specific vectors of memory, the media of films, museums, fictional literature, political rhetoric or public commemorations; yet others are concerned with the shared memories – the 'commingled beliefs, practices, and symbolic representations' – of social collectivities, whether they be ethnic, political, national or local; while a final cluster dissects the work of historians as authorised producers of disciplined historical knowledge. Uniting these disparate studies is a common concern with 'the ways in which people construct a sense of the past'.[24]

Commentators have identified varied roots for this scholarly preoccupation. On one level, there is an academic dynamic at work; methodological innovation (particularly the growth of oral history), the legitimisation and codification of contemporary history and the interdisciplinary opening towards anthropology, psychology and cultural studies.[25] But these structural changes need also to be contextualised within a broader cultural moment at which 'the fin-de-siècle world of the North Atlantic has been increasingly characterised by what the cultural critic Andreas Huyssen has called "mnemonic convulsions" expressed in cultural artefacts and experiences ranging from "museummania" and monumental art to personal memoirs, TV mini-series, and the nostalgia-laden products of retro-fashion'.[26] This saturation and obsession with memory are in turn due to processes of globalisation, geopolitical upheaval and dizzying technological transformations that have engendered an intense and multi-faceted 'insecurity about identity'.[27]

> The turning to memory is a 'nostalgia for the present' (to use Fredric Jameson's phrase), an anxiety about the loss of bearings and the speed and extent of change, in which representations of the past, the narration and visualizing of history, personal and collective, private and public, spell the desire for holding onto the familiar, for fixing and retaining the

lineaments of worlds in motion, of landmarks that are disappearing and securities that are unsettled.[28]

It remains a moot point whether this nostalgia should be construed in negative or positive terms, as indicative of 'an exhaustion of utopian energies' or of resistance to 'the synchronised "hyper-space" of globalisation'.[29]

Both in the present circumstances that have precipitated this reflection, and in the past phenomena that are its object, memory and identity lie intertwined. 'The core meaning of any individual or group identity, namely a sense of sameness over time and space, is sustained by remembering; and what is remembered is defined by the assumed identity';[30] indeed, it can be said that memory and identity are 'mutually constitutive'.[31] Underpinning this observation is a profound theoretical shift. The vast expansion over recent decades of the scope of historical studies ('which once had fairly clear tacit definition, largely as past politics') has been achieved through 'the ingenuity of ... authors in resituating object after object from the realm of the ostensibly natural to the realm of the ... socially constructed'.[32] This move is a precondition for studying anything historically, and in this instance memory and identity have both been reconceptualised, now regarded not as natural facts but as complex social processes and political constructs: 'highly selective, inscriptive rather than descriptive, serving particular interests and ideological positions'.[33]

The nature of the relationship between academic history and the broader currents of memory that have been the object of much of this work has been the focus of considerable theoretical debate.[34] For Pierre Nora, the *éminence grise* of the field, professional archive-oriented historiography and formalised social practices of memorialisation are yoked together, constituting the dominant modern, historical, way of knowing the past that contrasts unfavourably with more authentic, organic, spontaneous forms of living memory, now being snuffed out and supplanted. ('At the heart of history is a criticism destructive of spontaneous memory. Memory is always suspect in the eyes of history, whose true mission is to demolish it, to repress it'.)[35] A more prosaic definition reverses this hierarchy, and privileges proper 'historical awareness' – disciplined and disinterested reconstructive inquiry, aiming to get 'the story right', to 'value the past for its own sake' and 'to rise above political expediency' – over a 'social memory' that may lend groups 'a sense of identity and a sense of direction', but which is interested, fallible and prone to distortion.[36] Neither characterisation seems entirely satisfactory. The former, entailing 'a curious blend of a proclaimed avant-gardeism and a blood and soil, Heideggerian, nostalgia for a past allegedly based on genuine communities', exaggerates the artlessness and purity of memory.[37] The latter encapsulates historians' traditional claims to authority over the past, but oversimplifies and misconstrues their actual capacities.

It is altogether more plausible to render permeable the distinction between the two, rejecting both memory's 'arrogance of authenticity' and history's 'arrogance of definitiveness'.[38] Although each has its individual dynamic, grammar and conventions, both generate 'heavily constructed narratives with only institutionally regulated differences between them'.[39] They remain distinct enough to be said to mutually interrelate, but not necessarily in the manner commonly supposed. On the one hand, academic historiography would be a fairly vain activity if it did not, at least on some occasions, impact upon the meanings attributed to the past within the wider social world: the historian is certainly 'a "vector of memory" and a carrier of fundamental importance, in that the vision he [sic] proposes of the past may, after some delay, exert an influence on contemporary representations'. Yet, on the other hand, historical writing is itself profoundly conditioned by the understandings of the past prevalent outside the academy; the historian, 'like any other citizen, is influenced by the dominant memory, which may subconsciously suggest interpretations and areas of research'.[40] Competing formulations seek to encapsulate this relationship, from Emily Rosenberg's insistence that history and memory are 'blurred forms of representation whose structure and politics need to be analyzed not as oppositional but as interactive forms', through Marita Sturken's proposition that they are 'entangled', to Jay Winter's argument that they are 'braided together' in the processes of 'collective remembrance'.[41]

The cultural politics of historical knowledge

This perspective entails a certain scepticism about history's capacity to 'awaken us from the nightmare of memory' which is also grounded in recent theoretical debates within the discipline.[42] For the destabilising and decentring currents that precipitated the rethinking of memory and identity also impinged profoundly upon history. During the 1990s, a broad discursive turn naturalised the idea of historical knowledge as irredeemably perspectival just as a linguistic turn stressed the textualised nature of history, how its access to the past is heavily mediated and its representational adequacy compromised by its own literary form. Against the discipline's traditional quasi-scientific pretensions, it was asserted that an historical account was 'basically an act of the moral imagination ... a search for predecessors, an ordering of value, a conversation with the dead about what we should value and how we should live'.[43] Formerly dominant understandings of objectivity were undermined, and it is now utterly orthodox to concede that in research and writing historians are influenced 'by literary models, by social science theories, by moral and political beliefs, by an aesthetic sense, even by our own unconscious assumptions and desires'.[44]

This is not to say, however, that the prolonged and impassioned debates over theory concluded in consensus. The core critical ideas in play here were vehemently resisted, and through the later 1990s a dominant response coalesced, the essential thrust of which was to domesticate what was commonly dubbed 'postmodernism' by partially incorporating it. Partisans of this 'practical' or 'pragmatic realism' typically acknowledged some positive contributions – the opening up of new subjects for research, pluralisation of perspectives, and the sensitising of historians to the literary dimension and positioned character of their work – but ultimately rejected any threat to historians' capacity to generate authoritative knowledge about the past.[45] With no little rhetorical skill and strategic cunning, adherents of this position portrayed it as occupying a natural centre ground. Epistemologically, it eschewed both crude empiricism and nihilistic hyper-relativism. Methodologically, it promoted a democratic but bounded pluralism against both obsolete grand narrative and the chaos of unrestricted perspectivalism. Politically, it offered a reasonable liberal alternative to both hidebound conservatism and irresponsible radicalism. Moreover, it proved pragmatically effective in providing a basis upon which many practitioners could regroup and move forwards: hence the proliferation of explicit claims that the discipline's theoretical crisis is over and that history has emerged essentially unscathed.[46]

The underpinning premises here are somewhat different. It is undeniable that the theoretical debate no longer possesses its former configuration or polemical tone, but claims that the 'postmodern' challenge has been defeated belie the extent to which contestation about historical practice is continuing.[47] Moreover, even when this scholarship professedly locates itself beyond the linguistic turn, it remains shaped by the latter's potent insights.[48] Indeed, *contra* the logic of efforts to call time on theoretical ferment, much more generous assessments of the transformative impact 'postmodernism' has already had are possible.[49] Thus Gabrielle Spiegel, by no means a fanatical linguistic turn devotee, speaks of a 'profound change' in 'historiographical praxis': 'no one can doubt that it constituted a wholesale revision of the ways that historians understood the nature of their endeavour, the technical and conceptual tools deemed appropriate for historical research and writing, and the purpose and meaning of the work so produced'.[50] This text attempts to work certain ideas associated with the linguistic turn further, in the belief that their creative potential is not yet fully realised or exhausted.

A singular productive consequence of the linguistic turn, as it made historians 'more sensitive to the rhetorical conventions and ideological presuppositions which shape the books they write and the documents they study', was a 'boom in studies of past historiography'.[51] Moving beyond older modes of 'descriptive bibliography' to the more challenging task of 'trying to work out why historical writing looks as it does at the time and place of its composition', this new 'history of historical writing' tended to illuminate 'the degree to which positivist notions of history were self-deluding'.[52] Fruitful contributions to this project have been made from diverse theoretical positions; the author of one pioneering study on historical writing in the wake of the Second World War declared that 'the assumptions of this book owe more to E. H. Carr than Jacques Derrida'.[53] But in general 'practical realists' are not temperamentally inclined towards critical historiographical endeavour. Preoccupied with sources and facts, trusting in the operation of professional procedures and the preponderance of evidence to produce a single warranted interpretation, they cannot theorise historiographical pluralism satisfactorily.[54] Even in more sophisticated variants, acknowledging that divergent ideological presuppositions can generate irreconcilable but valid interpretations, their instinct is to close pluralism down, yearning in vain for ways to identify the most empirically adequate account.[55] Hence they remain more attached to an older historiographical discourse, wittily characterised by Michael Bentley as 'like theology': 'the study of error'.[56]

'Postmodern' resources (broadly defined) provide a more fruitful means for gaining a critical purchase upon historiographical reality, and particularly upon the politics of historical representation. Amongst a range of such inspirations, this study draws particularly upon the historical theory of Hayden White, with its core claim that 'there is an inexpungeable relativity in every representation of historical phenomena'.[57] When it comes to histor-iographical critique White highlights three inter-related issues of concern. First, he enjoins historians to respond to the textuality of histories – their status as 'verbal fictions, the contents of which are as much *invented* as *found*' – by putting questions to them that do not pertain only to their empirical basis and the specificities of the events with which they deal.[58] Second, proceeding from his understanding that 'stories are not lived' and that the historical record therefore does not determine them, he stresses that narrative emplot-ment entails fundamental aesthetic and political choices.[59] Third, he urges awareness of the broader ideological work that professional, disciplined, historical accounts perform, as they order reality in the service of particular political projects and interests.[60]

White's thought has heavily influenced the articulation of new critical historiographical practices. Robert Berkhofer, for example, calls on readers to move beyond 'the explicit arguments and narratives of histories' and to investigate their 'inner workings', 'how a text goes about constructing itself as a history'. This involves, *inter alia*, showing how 'a history is a multilayered text of evidential interpretation, argument, narrative, and Great Story', explicating 'stylistic figuration' and 'tropological prefiguration', exposing 'how discursive practices have both enabled the textualization and suppressed other representations', and uncovering 'implicit politicization as well as explicit politics'.[61] Emily Rosenberg expresses a similar sentiment in slightly more practical terms, when she urges historians to pose fresh historiographical questions:

> Who gets to tell the story of the past? What are the implications of where the story starts and stops; which characters and topics are included and excluded; what 'voice' is adopted; what metaphors provide structure? ... What dynamic relationship does each of us bring to the process of meaning and representation? Conscious or unconscious decisions about form, voice, and metaphor shape the content of historical stories, and many interpretive differences in historiography ... arise from this 'content of the form' and from inescapable issues of subjectivity and partiality.[62]

These approaches involve consideration of both text and context. Thus Geoff Eley has asserted that 'the fullest historiographical understanding' involves 'two distinct but complementary priorities': 'on the one hand, a close attention to the reading and explication of texts as such ... but on the other hand, an equally searching analysis of the social circumstances of their production, including the philosophical underpinnings of the relevant historiographical practices, the very specific institutional histories involved, and the range of political dynamics that may have impinged'.[63] There may sometimes be tensions between textualist and contextualist approaches, but 'historiography must be seen as a mutual dependence of text and context. The study of both is imperative in order to understand the production of historiographical meaning, and its changes'.[64]

It should be emphasised that construing historical writing through a Whitean lens does not reduce it entirely to ideology and interest. True, White contends that once historical events are narrated 'they enter a discourse that necessarily overlaps with the fictional'.[65] The transformation of facts into narratives – the attribution of meaning through emplotment – is an aestheticising act that endows historical accounts with 'fictive' properties.[66] Yet emphasising that historical narratives depend upon creative artifice does not reduce them simply to fiction.[67] It does not mean that 'all categories of truth are being dispensed with'.[68] Even for supposed arch-textualist Derrida, entirely collapsing the distinction between history and fiction would be 'silly'.[69] White affirms that historical narratives differ fundamentally from fictional ones since the events with which they deal 'can be assigned to specific time-space locations'.[70] Moreover, while meaning at the level of narrative always remains protean, it is a task of a quite different order to ascertain 'the truth-value of specific statements made about specific events'.[71] It in no way contravenes 'postmodern' shibboleths to assert that in order to qualify as a narrative interpretation, 'the individual statements that go to make up the narrative must be empirically confirmable'.[72]

Contrary to another common accusation, White's position also does not leave us adrift on a sea of hapless relativism, compelled to accept any and every historical account as equally valid. Those demonised as embodiments of idealist excess have in fact often devoted considerable thought to 'what makes one representation of the past better than others'.[73] The issue of how historians have negotiated the empirical record is certainly germane here. There are well-established and essentially uncontested generic conventions governing the technical processes involved in archival work, and the transformation of textual traces into evidence, and competing interpretations can be ranked according to how these have been followed. Equally, issues such as the range, volume and variety of sources consulted, and how well different types of evidence have been integrated, may be pertinent. Yet this scarcely exhausts the criteria for discrimination that can be brought to bear. There are also aesthetic factors – scope, originality, style, coherence, cogency – and questions about the political and ethical inspirations and implications of particular narrativisations. That texts should be empirically accurate is not unimportant, but this is essentially a minimum demand; the fruitfulness, interest and ideological import of texts at the level of meaning are ultimately more significant. These diverse criteria are always in play, implicitly if not explicitly, when assessing texts – flexible, interpretive, and contested, but nonetheless real, even if the boundaries between them are often blurred.[74]

This mode of engaging historiographical texts is therefore fuller than the approaches generally plied by 'practical realists'. The latter tend to charge 'postmodernism' with utterly discounting the role of empirical evidence, yet it is they who actually perpetuate an impoverishing caricature by system-atically repressing all but the empirical.[75] This is evident in their discomfort when trying to theorise those elements of historical practice that cannot easily be explained in technical terms: 'there is no training and there are no rules for the process of constructing a story out of the disparate pieces of evidence ... when it comes to creating a coherent account out of these evidential fragments, the historical method consists only of appealing to the muse'. Similarly, when it comes to ranking interpretations, other historians' conclusions are overwhelmingly debated narrowly in terms of the evidence: 'sources overlooked, misplaced emphasis, inappropriate categorization'. But the assumption that the choice and use of evidence determines an historian's perspective is flawed; in fact, 'the historian's perspective determines what counts as evidence, what "facts" best explain the evidence, and what plot structure is most useful and convincing'. So criticisms of this type cannot decisively 'demonstrate the superiority of one interpretation or story-type over another'.[76] Even if historians abide by all the relatively stable conventions of the discipline, they 'cannot produce a single uncomplicated version of events' because historical writing is a product not merely of empirical factors but also of context-grounded aesthetic, ideological and moral choices.[77]

Historiographical discussion should therefore proceed from the realisation that politicisation is not something that in certain unfortunate and untypical circumstances can befall history, but is rather its very condition of possibility. It should aim to read texts against the grain, to unfocus them 'in order to put into the foreground the constructed, rhetorical nature of our knowledge of the past, and to bring out the purposes, often hidden and unrecognised, of our retrospective creations'.[78] This allows us to engage historical writing as a site where multiple ideological forces and tensions are in play and to forge connections between disciplinary representations of the past and other discourses in the wider social world.

Writing the nation

One of the most fruitful issues to probe here is the interconnection between historiography and national identity. The academic study of nationalism has a long twentieth century pedigree, and it was sustained in the decades after the Second World War by the stubborn persistence of nationalist identification in defiance of liberal and Marxist expectations that it would gradually wither away. When the end of the Cold War heralded a marked recrudescence of both mildly devolutionary and virulently essentialist nationalisms, perversely confounding concurrent trends towards globalisation and regional integration, the field exploded with unprecedented vigour. Consequently, contemporary debates about the nature and dynamics of national identity are extremely complex with many different positions in play.[79] Essentialist views positing the enduring existence of natural national or ethnic entities with underlying characteristics, intrinsic capacities and clearly defined boundaries remain common currency within the discourse of fundamentalist nationalists; they also cling on tenaciously within the broader popular imagination and inflect much general scholarly analysis.[80] But the bulk of the specialist literature, conditioned by the general discursive turn within the human sciences, proceeds from the assumption that nations are both a phenomenon of relatively recent historical origin and 'best regarded as imaginative constructs'.[81]

Within this 'constructionist' consensus two broad camps can be discerned. On the one hand stand 'modernist' authors, who while accepting that nations are to an extent the results of inventive labour, nonetheless see them also as 'socially and politically determined', the necessary products of social processes integral to modernity. For these thinkers 'nations, once formed, were real communities of culture and power ... what [Emile] Durkheim would have called "social facts", with the qualities that he attributed to social facts: generality, exteriority, constraint'. On the other hand, a 'postmodernist' position emphasises 'the imagined quality of the national community and the fictive nature of unifying myths'. Far from being objectively determined, a nation is 'ultimately a specious community', an exercise in elite manipulation that 'has no existence outside its imagery and its representations'. A nation is a cultural construction, 'a "narrative" to be recited, a "discourse" to be interpreted and a "text" to be deconstructed': 'the nation is a communion of imagery, nothing more nor less'.[82] It is perhaps too crude to term nations 'fictions', since they are typically grounded in some kind of 'raw material' – a 'prior community of territory, language, or culture' – and they develop 'out of social and political experience'. But those communities must not be '"naturalized", as if they have always existed in some essential way, or have simply prefigured a history yet to come', and nations are 'the products of an imaginative ordering' of experience, 'not its revealed reality'.[83]

This second characterisation has most to recommend it, with suitable qualification and amplification to underline the nation's simultaneous power and intangibility. On the first count, for all that they are 'cultural artefacts', nations do command 'profound emotional legitimacy' and can inspire 'colossal sacrifices'.[84] They are immensely potent discursive formations 'ideologically, institutionally, culturally, practically in a thousand small ways'.[85] Although the conscious intervention of political and intellectual elites is typically important in their emergence, once established they are beyond the simple control of any individual agency or artifice. Yet paradoxically we should not be led by terming the nation a 'construct' (indeed denoting it with any noun) to endow it with too much unity, solidity or stability. The members of any particular national group are not bound together by a single, clearly bounded set of values, beliefs and memories. Rather, there are multiple notions of national identity in play at any given moment, not least because that identity co-exists with numerous other forms of social differentiation – such as class, gender, religion, political affiliation, regional loyalties – which all mutually construct each other.[86] National identity is the product of multiple over-lapping discourses that are themselves historically grounded and change over time as dominant conceptions are renegotiated: 'nations remain elusive and indeterminate, perpetually open to contest, to elaboration and to imaginative reconstruction'.[87] The fluidity and instability of national identity make it a never-ending process of becoming rather than a quality to be possessed or a state of being.

Historiography and national identity are intimately linked because the propagation of shared national pasts is crucial to the construction of national communities. Historical visions define who is included within or excluded from the nation, its territorial boundaries and its nature; through selective remembering and forgetting they establish a narrative trajectory that links national past, present and future in a continuum. The transmission of these narratives was never solely the work of professional academic historians, of course; even in the nineteenth century when the modern nation-state was born a whole gamut of invented traditions, symbolic representations and commemorative practices shared in this labour, and far more people would have been exposed to the nationalised past in the school room or army barracks than in the university seminar. But if academic historiography was primarily consumed by political, social and economic elites therein precisely lay its importance in the legitimatory endeavour. At the very moment that history was being professionalised, established in the universities and proclaiming its new scientific and objectivist credentials, much historiography was in fact written with a brazen patriotic cast and was clearly implicated in contemporary nation-building projects. Perhaps this was not surprising, given that in many countries state control over the funding of universities and appointments to them worked to ensure a high degree of political and social conformity on historians' part.[88] Thus the 'professionalization of history did not extricate historians from the needs and partisanship of their particular cultures; if anything, it strengthened it'.[89] Although the precise modalities differed from case to case, from Whig proclamations of the peculiar genius of the British constitution and English race, through the early delineations of American exceptionalism, to Prussian lauding of the nascent German Reich, historians proved remarkably eager to place themselves at the service of the nation-state, the new discipline's 'chief object of moral and political address'.[90]

This situation undoubtedly persisted well into the twentieth century; witness the heated debate over German war guilt in the inter-war period.[91]

But commentators typically assert that the emergence of social, economic and radical history, the democratisation and expansion of the profession, and the general discredit brought on nationalism by both world wars precipitated 'the almost complete disappearance of patriotic historiography in the West'.[92] While there is no denying that the terrain of history has vastly expanded over the last hundred years, and that cruder forms of racist propagandising lost their credibility within the mainstream discipline, this interpretation now seems difficult to sustain. First, the 1980s and 1990s demonstrated the undiminished potential for complicity between history and nationalist political projects; witness not just the overt nationalisation of the past in the newly-emergent republics of the former Soviet Union or Yugoslavia, but also conservative movements calling for a reassertion of nationalism in historio-graphy in Western Europe, whether in post-unification Germany, post 'First Republic' Italy or Margaret Thatcher's Britain. Second, there are good grounds to argue that 'the decline of nationalism in historiographical circles after 1945 has often been exaggerated'. Liberal and conservative forms of nationalism – visible, for example, in the tendency to deem recent authoritarian regimes '"parentheses" in the normal course of national history' – 'remained strong', the very use of the nation as an organising principle for historical work helped to reinscribe and naturalise national identity, and even when historians explicitly structure their work around alternative interpretive categories such as class or gender 'the national framework continues to condition their writing, sometimes openly, sometimes more subtly'.[93] The nation remains a ubiquitous presence, even if the forms that historiographical nationalism takes are now less essentialist and more pluralist than hitherto, with dominant discourses as likely to be resisted as internalised.[94] In Antoinette Burton's formulation, as a category of analysis for historians today it is simultaneously 'woefully inadequate' and yet 'indispensable'.[95]

This multiple intertwining of historical writing and discourses of national identity creates an obvious opportunity for critical historiography.[96] This can proceed along at least two, not mutually exclusive, axes; first, probing the role of historians as active propagandists, as 'constructors of national narratives'; second, exploring how they have themselves been written by the nation, how they have responded to 'the intellectual pressures, beliefs and cultural Weltanschauungen of their countries', and how prevalent understandings of national identity have conditioned their choices of subject matter, approach, methodology, emplotment and the basic assumptions through which they have figured the past. Of course, it is important to recognise the limitations inherent in this kind of inquiry. Whether professional historians ever were the pre-eminent producers of the national past is open to question, but today when they face increased competition from film, television, print and electronic mass media in representing the past, the limits of their influence are certain. Any inquiry that focuses exclusively on the political conditioning and implications of what historians produce without detailed exploration of how those texts are received and consumed must therefore necessarily remain circumscribed. Equally, it is crucial to remember that the lens of national identity is not the only fruitful one through which to analyse texts critically. Apart from the fact that national identification is itself not unitary, there are many other ideological and practical variables in play in the production of any piece of historical writing: hence it is important to avoid over-simplistic and reductive assertions about a putative hegemonic discourse of national identity, inexorably and mechanically generating historical narratives.[97]

Memories of World War Two

National identity is centrally at stake in the public collective remembering of war. By definition, war between nation-states often involves 'the threat of extinction, a threat that resonates long past the cessation of hostilities'.[98] Just as national identity is placed in question during conflict – when demarcating the national 'us' from 'them' becomes a matter of life and death – so after its conclusion, the sufferings, sacrifices and crimes of war must be retrospectively negotiated to secure a cohesive sense of national identity. This, at any rate, was the case after the Second World War according to the burgeoning literature on how diverse societies have historicised their experiences of it – a literature that has occupied an important place in the broader memory project of recent decades.[99] In different former combatant countries, particular versions of the wartime past, privileging certain values, characteristics, events or deeds and located within broader metanarratives, were propagated with greater or lesser degrees of conscious intentionality, and buttressed specific renderings of national identity in the present. These communal memories constituted 'subtle yet powerful mechanisms for generating and sustaining social solidarity'.[100] Narratives of heroism were fundamental to national recovery but these mingled with stories of victimhood and martyrdom – even in 'perpetrator' nations, both were needed to provide a mnemonic foundation for the restoration of national pride that yet approximated to lived experiences of the war.[101] Within this context, historians did not stand aloof from broader cultural and political debates but were rather deeply enmeshed in them. Their own writing contributed to this ideological labour and they were frequently captives of, or at least willing acolytes to, particular conceptions of the nation and broader collective memories.[102]

There has been much rumination on the appropriateness of the term collective memory, given that, strictly speaking, 'the collective does not possess a memory, only barren sites upon which individuals inscribe shared narratives, infused with power relations'.[103] Used alongside cognate terms such as cultural, national and public memory, collective memory needs to be understood as distinct from both individual and generational memory. In Thomas Berger's words:

> Collective memory differs from the other two forms in that it is based not
> on the direct experiences of individuals or groups of individuals in a

society, but rather the memories of the collectivity as a (necessarily fictitious) whole ... Collective memories serve an important practical function. They provide the collectivity with an identity and a common myth of origin. They endow it with emotional and normative underpinning. They simplify the task of organising collective action by providing its members with a common language and set of understandings about how the world functions and ought to function.[104]

Collective memory consists of narratives, symbols and images, embodied in a wide variety of cultural forms and circulating within society, forming a social framework, an 'organisational principle that nationally conscious individuals use to organise the national history'.[105] It is not a collective mental capacity so much as a field of contestation, 'the intersubjective outcome of a series of ongoing intellectual and political negotiations ... constantly subject to challenges and alternative interpretations'.[106] It is processual, unstable, partial and, perhaps somewhat ironically, by no means unified.[107] Moreover, it is quintessentially performative: 'in truth ... there is no such thing as memory; there is only the activity of remembering'.[108]

Numerous agents with claims to cultural authority – from governments to veterans' groups to social movements – will attempt to influence collective memory, but while malleable it cannot be manipulated entirely at will. On the one hand, even powerful institutional memories cannot constitute 'effective mental shackles'.[109] On the other, collective memory is forged within 'semantic and narrative parameters of social remembrance that inform and limit the historical imagination of the members of any given collective and that are inscribed in the media of communication as well as our bodies and minds'. For representations of the past to be transformed from potential into actual collective memories, they need to gain a purchase amongst those consuming them, to resonate meaningfully with their perceived experience: hence there is a constant interaction between would-be 'memory makers', selectively adopting and manipulating 'the intellectual and cultural traditions that frame all our representations of the past', and numerous different 'memory consumers', who 'use, ignore, or transform such artifacts according to their own interests'.[110]

It was only really in the 1980s that a reflective literature on the collective memory of the Second World War – what we might term a 'meta-memory' literature – began to emerge. Here, Henry Rousso's 1987 study of the 'Vichy Syndrome' was both path-breaking and paradigmatic. Surveying a broad range of memory discourses – from official commemorations, political rhetoric and war crimes trials, to film and other popular culture representations, to academic historiography – Rousso anatomised how the French had negotiated their wartime past and identified a series of discrete phases: an initial post-war period of retribution and reckoning followed by a prolonged interlude of collective repression dominated by the Gaullist myths of France as a nation of resisters and Vichy as a parenthesis, itself supplanted from the 1970s onwards as the grubby realities of collaboration and French complicity in the Holocaust were laid bare with accelerating obsession.[111]

Simultaneously, historians began to sketch out the discrete phases in West German efforts to master the Nazi past. During the immediate post-war era and height of the Cold War, dominant memories of the Third Reich were evasive and self-exculpatory, with a strong focus upon German suffering camouflaged by ritual cultivation of a diffuse sense of collective guilt; the Nazi regime was an aberration in German history and a handful of criminals were responsible for its atrocities. From the 1960s onwards, however, a leftward turn in German politics and the Cold War thaw precipitated a historiographical reorientation that sought the roots of Nazism in deep structural flaws in German society and critically confronted Nazi crimes and ordinary Germans' complicity in them. Conservative elements always resisted this movement, however, and in the 1980s when the political tide again turned a concerted neo-nationalist campaign began to slough off the stigma of guilt and to fashion new positive narratives of the national past. This led to the *Historikerstreit*, a fierce and protracted public debate between Germany's leading intellectuals about the legitimacy of conservative efforts to relativise Nazi crimes – including the Holocaust – and to normalise the national past, which itself then precipitated serious scholarly exploration of the politics of German memory.[112]

In the early 1990s, Richard Bosworth surveyed these and other national cases in an important comparative study exploring how societies involved in the Second World War had 'historicised and thus comprehended that experience'. He argued that in all the major combatant countries particular readings of the Second World War era had served as a kind of moral and political touchstone for decades after 1945, setting the parameters of political and cultural debate and exerting an overwhelming ethical force. In each case, he asserted, 'the initial traumatic effect of the war was to "freeze time" and thus to provide a simple historical explanation about what had recently happened'.[113] These explanations had a monumental quality of one sort or another: 'for the victors World War II was a "good war", the memory of which was to be handed down to succeeding generations; for the losers it was a "bad war" whose memory was painful and to be avoided'. Naturally, in each case the dynamics of memory were different. In the Soviet Union, where the mythology of the Great Patriotic War served a crucial legitimatory function for the regime, and in Japan, where a nationalist historical orthodoxy proved largely immune to critical revisionism, explanation remained static. In West Germany and Great Britain, in contrast, there were historiographical 'paradigm shifts' in the 1960s, but in each case these were progressive, and enhanced the conflict's ethical and political significance. Thus in Britain the rise of social history and the provocations of A. J. P. Taylor served to reaffirm the democratic promise of the 'People's War'.

Bosworth's central argument, however, was that by the early 1990s this 'long Second World War' was drawing to a close, as the war's geopolitical consequences were reversed or undone and its history was normalised: 'between 1945 and 1990 World War II was transformed in the historical consciousness of both victors and defeated, from a political and moral monument into a historical antiquity without any specific practical lessons for life'.[114] Beginning in Italy in the 1970s, with the crumbling of an erstwhile orthodox anti-fascist explanation of the wartime past, and moving through the demise of collectivism in Thatcher's Britain, the emergence of more vigorous conservative nationalist readings of the past in Germany and Japan, and the disintegration of the Great Patriotic War myth in the fragmenting Soviet Union, 'the ethical values of anti-fascism, the Resistance and the People's war were finally obscured or replaced'.[115] Historical debate would continue, of course: indeed, in many instances a fresh plurality of voices emerged. But its parameters had decisively shifted as once sacrosanct interpretations were demolished and hitherto inadmissible views openly canvassed, both indicative of a disconnection of the history of the war from ethical and political concerns. Although Bosworth welcomed the democratising dimension of these developments, he could not but regret the eclipse of broadly progressive interpretations that had contributed substantially to 'the spread of liberty, equality and fraternity', nor disguise his anxiety that truly profound and engaged reflection on the horrors of the Second World War might be on the wane.[116]

Bosworth's stimulating interpretation now requires qualification.[117] Of course, certain central post-war myths have waned and the character of meditation on the war has changed as it drifts out of lived experience and as contemporary political landscapes shift. Equally, the very emergence of a literature reflecting on the historicisation of the war might bespeak the presence of an ironic sensibility only conceivable once it had ceased to 'matter' so viscerally. But the case for viewing 1990 as some kind of watershed or decisive 'paradigm shift' is difficult to sustain given the salience of the war in subsequent years. Historiographical debate continues undiminished, progressive interpretations have not been banished from the field and in many instances remarkable continuity is evident with previous decades in terms of key themes, organisational parameters and crucial contested issues. Those debates also still engage with fundamental ethical and political concerns, as becomes obvious when they spill over into the public arena: witness the *Enola Gay* controversy at the Smithsonian Institution, the 'Goldhagen debate' about the role of ordinary Germans in the Holocaust, and the continuing polemics in Asia over Japan's wartime 'comfort women'. Indeed, in certain respects the post-Cold War years have witnessed a dramatic upsurge in the visibility of the war and its assumption of fresh meanings and valences.[118] Emblematic here is the case of the Holocaust, one of Bosworth's key reference points. This has become so ubiquitous across a plethora of cultural discourses in recent years that it has spawned its own meta-literature, sceptically dissecting an at times over-commercialised and debasing 'Shoah business'.[119] Moreover, in so far as it serves as ideological underpinning for a new militarised humanitarian interventionism, it persists as a powerful – if on this account troubling – ethical and political presence.[120]

Examination of particular national cases reinforces the point. True, writing in the early 1990s about the 'myth of the Blitz' in Britain, Angus Calder concluded that while 'still ideologically active – not yet, volcanically speaking, extinct' it no longer had 'anything like its old dominance'; and a subsequent study concurred that '1940' had 'passed into "proper history"'.[121] Yet the later 1990s arguably saw an 'explosion of Second World War commemoration'; and more recently Prime Minister Gordon Brown repeatedly invoked the spirit of the Blitz as he girded the country to weather its recessionary travails, a move in turn denounced by his opponents as arrogant faux-Churchillian posturing.[122] By the same token Bosworth's judgement that 'half a century after, France had, in most senses, settled its account with 1940' seems at the very least premature, in the light of the continuing Vichy-mania through the 1990s.[123]

In Germany, although unification initially encouraged an upsurge of neo-conservative efforts to normalise the past, Bill Niven has argued that ultimately it facilitated a much franker and fuller engagement with perpetration and atrocity in the Third Reich than was previously possible.[124] Even the more recent emphasis on non-Jewish German suffering, something that once generally connoted evasive self-pity, can be read as militating towards a more nuanced and capacious memory in which recognition of individual German suffering need not entail the displacement of the Holocaust. On this view, acknowledging that 'some Germans were victims, some Germans were perpetrators, and some Germans were both' does greater justice to the complexity of individual historical experience and undermines complacent 'good war' mythologizing.[125]

The example of the United States is even more striking. Bosworth excluded it from his account, partly on the grounds that its war experience was not sufficiently traumatic to engender a potent and distinctive collective memory of the type he identified elsewhere.[126] Yet in the 1990s a broad American public rediscovered the Second World War and the 'greatest generation' that had fought it, inserting it into the national consciousness with unprecedented force. Writing in 1999, Arthur Schlesinger wryly observed that post-war generations were seeking 'sustenance in the heroic past' in order to fill the 'psychic void' caused by the absence of existential challenges in their lives; nonetheless, he approved of a new readiness to confront the 'ghastly reality' of a war that now gripped the nation 'almost as intensely as it did when the world blew up 60 years ago'.[127] It may now be that this preoccupation has come to serve more dubious purposes, working to provide a moral basis for the assertion of global power in the 'War on Terror', but even so the war's pertinence and prominence seems undeniable.[128]

The sixtieth anniversary commemorations of 2004–5 engendered fresh claims from journalists about imminent 'final closure' on a conflict 'fading from memory into history ... as the number of surviving participants dwindles'.[129] Of course, it is simply a truism that the living link with the war will in due course be severed, but to assume that this will necessarily transform the character of collective memory is mistaken. (Indeed, these prognostications betray a failure to grasp not only the distinction between the dynamics of collective and individual memory but also the permeability of memory and history.) The trope of closure is satisfying and seductive, but it usually oversimplifies. After all, as Barbie Zelizer has pointed out: 'unlike individual memory, the power of collective memory can increase with time, taking on new complications, nuances, and interests'.[130] Consider as an example the 1389 battle of Kosovo: was this ever more alive in Serbian popular memory than in the 1980s and 1990s?[131] Alison Landsberg has recently argued that new mnemonic technologies make possible so-called 'prosthetic memories', deeply felt personal memories of events that were not directly experienced which, whilst neither organic nor natural, are not thereby false.[132] Even without this development, it is evident that collective memories commonly 'transcend the time and space of the events' original occurrence', taking on 'a powerful life of their own, "unencumbered" by actual individual memory'. This, so Wulf Kansteiner has argued, is the case in contemporary American society with the Holocaust, which has become part of the fabric of 'disembodied, omnipresent, low-intensity memory'.[133]

Yet commentators are divided on quite how we should conceptualise our current relationship to the war. For some, it was actually in the early years of the present century that the war finally lost its former centrality in 'the western moral imagination', its role becoming 'totemic rather than instructive'.[134] But others writing of the same period persuasively argued that the war still retained 'its grip on memory and myth'.[135] In 2000 Tony Judt was more inclined to agree that the decisive influence exerted by myths of the Second World War upon European politics was on the wane, and that the collapse of communism had precipitated a comprehensive rethinking of the place of the war in European history. But for him – *pace* Bosworth – this entailed on balance a more profound engagement with the murky ambiguities of the conflict and the selective amnesia that followed it.[136] Jan-Werner Müller offered the view that 'memories of the Second World War were "unfrozen" on both sides of the former Iron Curtain' after 1990, but highlighted nuanced differentiation rather than uniformity. In the West, he detected a movement towards 'closure' and a laying to rest of claims amidst ongoing controversies but in the East a persistence of unfinished business and new myths of nationalist salvation in the making. He concluded from this that historical narratives would have to be readjusted and collective memories recast if East and West were to be brought together in the project of a united Europe.[137]

Other observers also highlight the complex ways in which memories of the Second World War and the Cold War are simultaneously being renegotiated across contemporary Europe. 'The future of European solidarity', on this view, 'depends on a rethinking of the immediate European past', and the elaboration of narratives that more fully confront the suffering inflicted on Eastern Europe by the West in the Second World War, and the fact that 1945 there inaugurated communist subjugation rather than European integration. For Eastern Europeans 'to believe that they are full partners in Europe' will require the West further to rewrite some of its own post-war foundation myths.[138] On the one hand, tensions are particularly fraught along what was once the border between Cold War blocs, in the zone where former Axis powers abut the early objects of fascist expansionism, where new discourses of German and Italian suffering sit ill with their former victims.[139] On the other hand and more broadly, EU efforts to prescribe a respectful attitude towards the Holocaust as the foundation for a common European memory and identity – as 'the very definition and guarantee of the continent's restored humanity' – are generating considerable resentments in eastern Europe.[140] There, privileging the specific fate of European Jewry over other instances of suffering – particularly that inflicted by Soviet communism – is a mnemonic move of highly dubious legitimacy.[141] It is, however, arguably positive that across the continent for the first time 'competing myths are no longer being fostered in confinement, but in constant dialogue between neighbours, besides which in each country as well as being fostered they are also being debunked'.[142]

So Bosworth may well have mistaken what was – at least in some cases and in some respects – the end of a chapter for the end of the story. He captured the crucial role that particular myths of the Second World War played in politics and culture across several post war decades, but his broader claim that a 'long Second World War' came to a definitive close around 1990 is difficult to sustain. The unfolding process of mnemonic negotiation over the meanings of the 'long Second World War' did not conclude in 1990, but rather entered a new phase with the end of the Cold War and may well have entered yet another with the first eastern enlargement of the EU in 2004. The consequences of the war are still being worked through in a blizzard of compensation claims and rhetorics of victimhood, and reworking its memory is a crucial element in the evolution of contemporary political identities. Of course, it remains an open question whether these controversies signify a last gasp of contestation, 'the product of a particular transitional moment'.[143] Tony Judt has indeed recently prophesied 'a kind of closure': 'sixty years after Hitler's death, his war and its consequences are entering history. Postwar in Europe lasted a very long time, but it is finally coming to a close'.[144] Yet Susan Rubin Suleiman is more adamant that 'World War II and the Holocaust are clearly still with us'.[145] Richard Ned Lebow is even blunter in dismissing the notion that controversy will soon be stilled; given the impossibility of stabilising readings of the past, especially in the light of changing 'contemporary problems and needs', he predicts that 'the politics of memory will be a salient feature of the European landscape for many decades to come'.[146]

The continued proliferation of the 'meta-memory' literature has certainly contributed to these ambiguities by complicating the historical picture. The many different 'cultural forms that are implicated in the post-war processes of reworking and coming to terms with the events of 1933–45' have each been individually studied.[147] Pioneering work on France and Germany has been complemented by analyses of the memorialisation and instrumentalisation of the war in the other major combatant powers and in smaller states. Fine-grained analyses, often based on freshly opened archives or oral testimony and employing cultural history and anthropological methodologies, have begun to excavate the multiplicity of memory. Where earlier studies were primarily concerned with would-be dominant narratives and elite representations, attention has now turned to private memories and how different social groups consumed, negotiated and contested official readings. In view of the profound dissonance now identified between individual and official memory in Western as well as Eastern Europe, and the starkly competing memories of different social collectivities within countries, notions of homogeneous national remembering passing though unitary and discrete phases are now more difficult to sustain. This increasing specialisation makes it much more problematic to map the terrain in particular cases and even harder to formulate synthetic explanations of the trajectory of memories of the war in general.[148]

What does emerge clearly from this work, however, is the complicity of historians in the elaboration of these discourses of memory and the concomitant negotiation of national identity. Even leaving aside the issue of whether historical knowledge is irredeemably interested, the history of the Second World War in combatant countries was of such immediate political relevance that writing on it cannot be understood simply as the product of empirical factors and an internal disciplinary dynamic. Concluding his study of patriotic memories in post-war France, Belgium and the Netherlands, Pieter Lagrou enumerated countless instances where 'scholarly histories were no more than erudite derivatives of political memories'.[149] Recovery after the war required not merely material reconstruction but also political reconciliation and the reformulation of national identity, and historians played an important role by furnishing pasts usable for these purposes. But if they thus contributed to the elaboration of dominant discourses on history and identity, they also operated within them, subject to broader political, social and cultural pressures. Of course, their role differed from case to case: for example, Mary Fulbrook has contrasted the role of historians in the German Democratic Republic – where they were conscious and willing participants in the communist regime's nation-building project – with that in the Federal Republic where in a quite different institutional and political context they merely 'did little to dent, and quite a lot to contribute to' dominant attitudes towards the Nazi past.[150] Equally, shifts in these complex relationships can be discerned over time as variables change: for example, as one generation gives way to another or as historical research becomes more specialised or is transformed by methodological innovation. But given the political contexts in which interpretive traditions were founded during and after the war, that conflict's enduring contemporary significance, and the impossibility of detaching representations of the past from present day ideological positions and anxieties, history, memory and identity were indissolubly intertwined.

International history as a discourse of memory?

To date, international historians concerned with the Second World War era have remained doubly detached from these developments. The question of apportioning responsibility for the war, which of course embraces its diplomatic and political antecedents, has persistently figured in its historicisation, but it has understandably often been overshadowed by more highly charged issues such as wartime suffering, collaboration, war crimes and the Holocaust. Even when the question of 'war guilt' has come under discussion, historians of collective memory have not paid much attention to the contribution of international history as a vector: presumably, its reputation as one of the most barren and antediluvian of historical sub-disciplines has caused it to be passed over in favour of discourses that appeared potentially more significant or fruitful.[151] By the same token, international historians have been somewhat reluctant to turn a reflective critical gaze upon themselves and to conceive of their work as part and parcel of broader cultural discourses on memory.[152] (Bosworth's text – which appeared in a series dedicated to 'new international history' – was a partial exception to these generalisations. But his treatment ranged far beyond writing on international relations, and it is perhaps significant that some international historians of more conventional stripe took vociferous exception to his analysis and its theoretical implications.[153])

This is not to deny that memory has lately emerged as an explicit concern on international history's agenda. Over the last two decades, a significant minority of international historians have embarked on a cultural turn, enriching practice through exploration of transnational cultural transfer, the activities of non-state actors and the discursive construction of foreign policy, and thus palpably reconfiguring the sub-discipline's common sense.[154] Within this broad and ramified enterprise, memory has 'evoked much recent interest'.[155] Yet the bulk of this work – both by avowed culturalists and others sensitised to the thematic by its general prominence – has eschewed the opportunity for reflexive historiographical critique in favour of an over-riding focus on the interconnection between memory and policy-making.

Robert D. Schulzinger, for example, contributed an essay on memory to a landmark historiographical collection on the state of American foreign relations history. But he seemed primarily interested in exploring 'the role that memories play in determining how people conduct their affairs', thus simply giving a mnemonic twist to the venerable issue of the deployment of historical analogies and lessons in policy-making and propaganda. Although he also asserted that the processes and sites of collective cultural memory being explored in the emergent war memory literature could provide 'excellent evidence for historians of U.S. foreign relations', there was little acknowledgement that their work might already be implicated in them.[156] Similarly, Robert J. McMahon devoted his Society for Historians of American Foreign Relations presidential address to the contested memory of the Vietnam War in American society, insightfully dissecting the diverse ways in which the war had been represented in presidential rhetoric, the writings of political commentators and officials, and popular culture, and noting that what was essentially at stake in these fierce debates was 'American identity and purpose'. Yet it was only in his final paragraph that he mentioned how international historians as both teachers and authors were 'unavoidably participants in as well as observers of this evolving societal debate', and that the sub-discipline had itself been 'fundamentally reshaped' by the changed intellectual climate bequeathed by the conflict. Whilst urging international historians to contribute to the study of its memory, McMahon did not develop the idea that international history might itself be part of the story.[157]

Other diverse contributions have dealt with the propaganda value of mythicised representations of specific diplomatic exchanges, the 'memory diplomacy' conducted by governments and non-state actors seeking to put particular narratives of past conflicts into wider circulation, and the parallel cultural logic of popular culture representations of past conflicts and contemporary foreign policy.[158] This work is extremely stimulating, and its preoccupation with deploying memory to enrich our understanding of the sources and nature of foreign policy is entirely explicable given the sub-discipline's traditional explanatory mission.[159] Yet there remains considerable scope for developing memory work in a more reflexive direction. The foundations for such a project already exist in a more conventional literature concerned with how 'governments have tried to control historical research and writing' – through sponsored documentary publications, official histories and assistance to memoirists – 'in order to justify current policies'.[160] Moreover, some of this work does offer suggestive hints about the more diffuse and indirect means whereby interpretations of the past with specific political inspirations may be insinuated into the scholarly literature.[161] Yet realising the full potential of a turn to memory requires a more systematic analysis of how academic international history is intertwined with broader cultural discourses on the past.

It should be acknowledged that the critical approach advocated here is somewhat at odds with the prevailing historiographical temper of the field.[162] Not only has historiographical writing always been a rather undervalued pursuit within this robustly empiricist sub-discipline, but when indulged in it tends to take the restricted form characteristic of 'practical realist' approaches lamented above. (This is no great surprise, given the scepticism on display towards 'postmodernist' ideas such as those of White on the relatively rare occasions when international historians indulge in extensive metatheoretical reflection.[163]) Marc Trachtenberg recently demonstrated this in the methodological prescriptions contained within his important text on *The Craft of*

International History. Discussing the 'critical analysis of historical texts', Trachtenberg usefully outlined the necessity of identifying their core arguments, architecture and key claims, internal logic and the adequacy of their evidential grounding. Yet his basic assumption was that the weight of the empirical evidence, processed through rational professional discourse, would enable historians decisively 'to get to the bottom' of any historical problem. Hence his fundamental recommendation that 'when authors disagree, as they usually do on important issues, you ask: who's right?' Trachtenberg's approach thus suppressed the inevitable pluralism of historical writing, and how divergent underpinning assumptions and conceptualisations generate multiple, competing and at times contradictory interpretations of the past.[164]

Some existing historiographical studies of the origins of the Second World War can serve as further illustration of an ingrained antipathy to the idea that historical knowledge is necessarily interested. Robert J. Caputi's *Neville Chamberlain and Appeasement* is a classic of descriptive historiography, offering a compendious recapitulation of the arguments advanced by scholars over several decades, but explicitly eschewing any probing of the extra-empirical factors that shaped them. Caputi draws a sharp distinction between 'a review of the relevant historiography' and 'discussion of the postwar historical zeitgeist', lauding the progressive triumph of 'empiricism' over 'emotion' in a manner that lends the whole text a rather sterile air.[165] David Dutton's *Neville Chamberlain* is much more sophisticated, alive to the influence of historians' 'generation, perspective, preoccupations and prejudices' and the fact that 'precisely the same documentation' can be 'used as the basis of radically different analyses'. Yet it is also fraught with tension, since it simultaneously indulges in an untenable idealisation of 'objective scholarly analysis' – asserting its discreteness from political polemic, self-serving memoir and otherwise interested writing – that the material considered cannot actually support. Moreover, the logic of the text is clear as it concludes with a chapter offering the author's own privileged interpretation.[166] This reflects a wider tendency within international history to combine ritualistic acknowledgement of the mutability, pluralism and tentativeness of interpretation with a rhetorical mode – both in historiographical and 'substantive' practice – that reinscribes faith in the capacity of traditional historical methodology to deliver secure narratives of the past.

Of course, this kind of historiographical treatment still serves a useful function in mapping the terrain of debate. Moreover, other interventions offer more positive intimations of the form of historiographical sensibility being advocated here. International historians are for the most part little inclined to look beyond the details of conflicting interpretations or their evidential basis to ask structural questions about the kinds of stories being told. In his best-selling synthesis of *The Origins of the Second World War*, however, Philip Bell explores how the field has always been structured around certain sets of interpretive dichotomies (that could perhaps be correlated to classic narrative archetypes), such as the thesis of an inevitable war versus that of an unnecessary war or arguments stressing ideology and intention against those emphasising power politics and structural determinants. He briefly canvasses these positions, asserting that they have all 'flourished during the whole period since the 1930s' even though they have not 'all been continuously and equally prominent'. Granted this remains a rather stunted form of narratology, absent interrogation of the roots of these options in broader cultural repertoires of narrative resources (whether national or sub-disciplinary) or the politics of their promulgation at particular conjunctures (how, when and why particular arguments 'have come and gone, flared up and faded').[167] Yet it does at least begin to open up pertinent questions.

Other contributions are more attuned to the politics of historiography, both in terms of the inspirations and entailments of particular strategic interpretive preferences and the role of contextual political, cultural, social and disciplinary factors in promoting the emergence of certain arguments and their acceptance as plausible. These issues are partially broached in some of the monographic essays and edited collections on the historiography of the origins of the war.[168] There are also a number of more specialist studies which have demonstrated the possibilities of this kind of inquiry. Here one might invoke Peter Jackson's stimulating exploration of how generations of commentators came to frame the fall of France as the product of *décadence*, a profound political, economic and social malaise in the Third Republic. Jackson discusses the general prevalence within modern French political culture of narratives of decline, fall and renewal, how the deployment of the particular *décadence* paradigm suited the strategic purposes of post-1940 regimes in France and the diverse incentives that caused historians in France and abroad so long to subscribe to it.[169] Similarly, David Reynolds' exhaustive study of the fashioning of Winston Churchill's history of the Second World War tracks not only how his arguments were forged against the context of the nascent Cold War and battles with other memoirists to secure his reputation for posterity, but also how they both drew upon and influenced the national myths about the war that were coalescing in the later 1940s.[170] These studies — together with examples dealing with other conflicts in modern international history — are not premised on precisely the same assumptions in play here, but they evince something of a similar spirit.[171]

Two more directly inspirational exemplars from the existing literature can be mentioned in closing. The potential fruitfulness of pushing culturalist concern with memory further in a reflexive direction is demonstrated by Emily Rosenberg's highly instructive analysis of Pearl Harbor in American memory. Here Rosenberg considers academic historiography alongside numerous other memory discourses, including popular history, political rhetoric, feature films, documentaries and memorials. She explores the mutual interactions between these media, and how certain basic discursive traditions were established, reproduced and contested within them by the work of memory activists and intertextual repetition. For Rosenberg Pearl Harbor is 'a figurative site of contested meanings where power is exerted and challenged', and her aim is 'not to stabilize some truth about this iconic event but to investigate its instability and to see what can be learned from the terms of contestation'. She explores the persistence of two core emplotments, the one depicting the surprise attack on Pearl Harbor as an act of infamy, and the other portraying it as an act of presidential deception, a means to engineer the United States into war in Europe via the back door. Each was potent because it drew on familiar patterns and narrative structures already circulating in American culture: in the former case, other examples of alleged surprise attack, such as the sinking of the *Maine* in 1898, and in the latter a tradition of suspicion towards executive authority and penchant for conspiracy theories. Moreover, through changing circumstances, each served identifiable political purposes in sustaining notions of national identity and rationalising particular policy options at home and abroad.

The potency of this analysis lies not only in its identification of the structures and roots of the competing narratives, but also in its vision of academic history as but one amongst many memory discourses, distinct in its conventions but always thoroughly saturated with ideology and not necessarily privileged. History, Rosenberg writes, is 'inevitably selective, mediated, and structured', arising 'situationally from particular times, places, and interpretive communities': empirical evidence is crucial, 'but its selection and interpretation remain so contingent, so dependent upon questions asked and upon diverse narrative and metaphorical frames', that closure is an elusive goal.[172]

Louis A. Pérez's trenchant critique of historical writing on the 1898 war over Cuba, in slight contrast, testifies to the benefits to be gleaned from a critical practice fully alive to the politics of historiography. Pérez explores how US foreign relations historians adopted modes of explaining the conflict that originated in the political rhetoric of contemporary US policy-makers, and which served to rationalise decades of American domination over Cuba and sustain a self-serving image of national altruism and virtue. As he puts it, 'popular narratives and political pronouncements seemed possessed of the capacity to validate themselves and passed directly into the collective memory and thereupon proceeded to inform the assumptions from which historical scholarship was derived'. Thus this literature 'assumed unabashedly self-congratulatory tones, as the dominant historiographical discourse commemorated selflessness and sacrifice, magnanimity of intention and generosity of purpose, as the source of the U.S. policy'. Like Rosenberg, Pérez assumes the mutual imbrication of politics, history, memory and identity:

> The telling of 1898 – in historical discourses both popular and professional, repeated and refined – has served as a means of self-affirmation of what the nation is, or perhaps more correctly what the nation thinks itself to be, as past and present have been conjoined in the service of self-revelation. Representations of 1898 were early invested with the ideals by which Americans wished to define and differentiate their place in the international system.

Yet Pérez is more keen to launch an indictment. Through close textual analysis he shows how interpretations conveyed particular messages through their choice of explanatory factors, chronological framing, presences and absences, and attributions of motive and agency, and how once set in place the dominant discursive framework was almost impervious to revision in the light of fresh evidence. Failings here were not merely professional; Pérez is also conscious of the ideological functions that these interpretations performed within a series of domestic and international political contexts, working 'to form and inform notions of nation, to foster a sense of past and place congruent with the normative structures around which the nation defines itself'. Thus international historians were complicit not only in the perpetuation of particular forms of power relations in the Caribbean but also in the longer term trajectory of twentieth century American imperialism. Pérez's study demonstrates how a sub-discipline with intense pretensions to scholarly objectivity, which consequently disdains reflexive interrogation of the ideological baggage with which contemporary writing is freighted, can unwittingly become embroiled in diverse political projects.[173]

Remembering the road to World War Two

Building upon these diverse mnemonic and historiographical foundations, this text essays a critical reading of some key debates about the road to the Second World War of each major combatant country. It discusses the evolution of interpretations and the archival, disciplinary, cultural and political factors that have contributed to the construction of shifting historical understandings. Its central purpose is to locate this process in the context of concurrent political and cultural debates over national identity and collective memory. Though the precise modalities of the relationship differ from case to case, it will explore how international history has been inextricably entwined with these debates, at times almost completely in thrall to broader collective memories, at others simply underpinned by unacknowledged claims about national identity, and at yet others conveying political implications through choice of subject matter, framing and emplotment, by virtue of location within a specific mnemonic terrain. Its approach may be too conventional to qualify as a Foucauldian genealogy, but its concern is certainly to focus on 'the conditions of possibility that enabled various claims to be made at different times, how claims, once made, came to be regarded as tenable, and what the political result of that outcome was'.[174]

This text aims to speak to readers with diverse interests in national identity, war memory, the origins of the war and historical theory, though given its rationale and scope none of these is treated exhaustively.[175] I do not offer a comprehensive account of debates over national identity in these various countries, and international history writing would in any case not necessarily figure prominently therein. (On balance my argument is concerned much more with how such debates have shaped international history rather than *vice versa.*) Equally, how the Second World War has been historicised across myriad cultural discourses in the various combatant countries is the context for rather than central concern of this treatment, and I draw on the extensive 'meta-memory' literature as a guide here, necessarily eliding certain nuances. When it comes to the historiography of the origins of the war, my key concern is to make the case that it possesses a politics, and in doing so I offer only a limited exploration of certain key themes within the field rather than a full bibliographical panorama. By the same token, although this exercise is premised upon the theoretical assumption that the texts discussed have ideo-logical effects in the real world, I am more concerned with reading a politics out of them than with examining precisely how they were consumed. (Not least because for some international historians the first premise – that these texts were not ideologically innocent – may still be rather hard to swallow.)

Forging connections between international history writing and the 'meta-memory' literature on the Second World War brings profit to both. On the one hand, stitching the historiography of the origins of the war into that literature contributes to the ongoing work to thicken understandings of the multiple ways in which the war was remembered and instrumentalised across post-war decades; in some cases it also disrupts or nuances existing under-standings of the broad contours of memory. On the other hand, confronting international history with memory adds a fresh dimension to historiographical debates about the origins of the war, by making the case that this historio-graphy cannot be satisfactorily understood without serious consideration of a range of cultural and ideological factors. It also stimulates broader reflection on the story that the sub-discipline tells itself about what international historians produce and why, which in turn has theoretical implications for the nature of history *per se*.

Notes

1 H. White, 'An old question raised again: is historiography art or science? (Response to Iggers)', *Rethinking History*, vol. 4, no. 3, 2000, p. 402.

2 J. Wilson, 'Keeping the flame of memory alight', *The Guardian*, 7 June 2004, p. 7.

3 T. Hunt, 'One last time they gather, the Greatest Generation', *The Observer*, 6 June 2004, http://www.guardian.co.uk/secondworldwar/story/0,14058,1232606,00.html (accessed 21 October 2005).

4 E. Ferguson, 'On the beaches', *The Observer*, 9 May 2004, http://www.guardian.co.uk/second worldwar/story/0,14058,1223737,00.html (accessed 21 October 2005); Hunt, 'Greatest Generation'.

5 A. Langenohl, 'State visits: internationalised commemoration of World War II in Russia and Germany', *Eurozine*, May 2005, http://www.eurozine.com/articles/2005-05-03-langenohl-en. html (accessed 21 October 2005).

6 'Putin salutes war veterans', *The Guardian*, 9 May 2005, http://www.guardian.co.uk/ secondworldwar/story/0,14058,1479684,00.html (accessed 21 October 2005).

7 O. Hirschbiegel (dir.), *Der Untergang [Downfall]* (2004).

8 M. Sontheimer, 'Why Germans can never escape Hitler's shadow', *Spiegel Online*, 10 March 2005, http://service.spiegel.de/cache/international/0,1518,druck-345720,00.html (accessed 14 March 2005).

9 T. Hunt, 'Bush: U.S. erred after World War II', *Northwest Herald*, 8 May 2005, http://www.nwherald.com/MainSection/331216789090506.php (accessed 21 October 2005); on East European sensibilities, see A. Krzeminski, 'As many wars as nations: the myths and truths of World War II', *signandsight*, 6 April 2005, http://www.signandsight.com/features/96.html (accessed 21 October 2005).

10 J. McCurry, 'Koizumi apologises for wartime wrongs', *The Guardian*, 16 August 2005, http://www.guardian.co.uk/international/story/0,1549740,00.html (accessed 21 October 2005).

11 D. B. MacDonald, *Balkan Holocausts? Serbian and Croatian Victim-Centred Propaganda and the War in Yugoslavia* (Manchester, Manchester University Press, 2002); R. Paris, 'Kosovo and the metaphor war', *Political Science Quarterly*, vol. 117, no. 3, 2002, pp. 423–50.

12 E. S. Rosenberg, *A Date Which Will Live: Pearl Harbor in American Memory* (Durham, NC, Duke University Press, 2003), pp. 174–75.

13 S. Milne, 'The opponents of war on Iraq are not the appeasers', *The Guardian*, 13 February 2003, http://www.guardian.co.uk/comment/story/0,3604,894422,00.html (accessed 21 October 2005).

14 'President commemorates 60th anniversary of V-J Day', White House press release, 30 August 2005, http://www.whitehouse.gov/news/releases/2005/08/20050830-31.html (accessed 1 September 2005).

15 M. Kettle, 'Bush's war has nothing to do with the spirit of D-Day', *The Guardian*, 1 June 2004, http://www.guardian.co.uk/secondworldwar/story/0,14058,1228618,00.html (accessed 22 October 2005).

16 R. Drayton, 'An ethical blank cheque', *The Guardian*, 10 May 2005, http://www.guardian.co.uk/comment/story/0,3604,1480178,00.html (accessed 24 October 2005); D. Barnouw, *The War in the Empty Air: Victims, Perpetrators, and Postwar Germans* (Bloomington, IN, Indiana University Press, 2005).

17 'European histories: towards a grand narrative?', *Eurozine*, May 2005, http://www.eurozine.com/articles/2005-05-03-eurozine-en.html (accessed 21 October 2005).

18 K. Brüggemann and A. Kasekamp, 'The politics of history and the "war of monuments" in Estonia', *Nationalities Papers*, vol. 36, no. 3, 2008, pp. 425–48.

19 N. Baker, *Human Smoke. The Beginnings of World War II, the End of Civilization* (New York, Simon and Schuster, 2008); S. Lee (dir.), *Miracle at St. Anna* (2008); B. Singer (dir.), *Valkyrie* (2008); S. Daldry (dir.), *The Reader* (2008); Q. Tarantino (dir.), *Inglourious Basterds* (2009).

20 N. Kulish, 'Germany confronts Holocaust legacy anew', *New York Times*, 29 January 2008, http://www.nytimes.com/2008/01/29/world/europe/29nazi.html (accessed 19 February 2008).

21 I. Chotiner, 'Appeasement's taint is all in hindsight', *New York Times*, 25 May 2008, http://www.nytimes.com/2008/05/25/weekinreview/25chotiner.html (accessed 30 May 2008).

22 'The future of World War II studies: a roundtable', *Diplomatic History*, vol. 25, no. 3, 2001, pp. 347–499.

23 J. Winter, 'The generation of memory: reflections on the "memory boom" in contemporary historical studies', *Bulletin of the German Historical Institute, Washington DC*, no. 27, Fall 2000, http://www.ghi-dc.org/bulletin27F00/b27winterframe.html (accessed 23 November 2005).

24 A. Confino, 'Collective memory and cultural history: problems of method', *American Historical Review*, vol. 102, no. 5, 1997, pp. 1386–89.

25 G. Eley, 'Foreword', in M. Evans and K. Lunn (eds), *War and Memory in the Twentieth Century* (Oxford, Berg, 1997), pp. viii–ix.

26 D. James, 'Meatpackers, Peronists, and collective memory: a view from the south', *American Historical Review*, vol. 102, no. 5, 1997, p. 1404.

27 A. Megill, 'History, memory, identity', *History of the Human Sciences*, vol. 11, no. 3, 1998, pp. 37–62, quote at p. 39

30 *Introduction: history and memory of war*

28 Eley, 'Foreword', p. vii.
29 J-W. Müller, 'Introduction: the power of memory, the memory of power and the power over memory', in J-W. Müller (ed.), *Memory and Power in Post-War Europe: Studies in the Presence of the Past* (Cambridge, Cambridge University Press, 2002), pp. 15–16.
30 J. R. Gillis, 'Memory and identity: the history of a relationship', in J. R. Gillis (ed.), *Commemorations: The Politics of National Identity* (Princeton, NJ, Princeton University Press, 1994), p. 3.
31 Müller, 'Introduction', p. 3.
32 H. Kellner, 'Introduction: describing redescriptions', in F. R. Ankersmit and H. Kellner (eds), *A New Philosophy of History* (London, Reaktion, 1995), p. 18.
33 Gillis, 'Memory and identity', p. 4.
34 See G. Cubitt, *History and Memory* (Manchester, Manchester University Press, 2007), which also canvasses the various criticisms of the scholarly turn to memory.
35 P. Nora, 'General introduction: between memory and history', in L. D. Kritzman (ed.), under the direction of P. Nora, *Realms of Memory: Rethinking the French Past: Vol. I: Conflicts and Divisions* (New York, Columbia University Press, 1996), p. 3.
36 J. Tosh, *The Pursuit of History: Aims, Methods and New Directions in the Study of Modern History* (London, Longman, 1999, 3rd edn), pp. 1–4.
37 R. J. B. Bosworth, 'Film memories of fascism', in R. J. B. Bosworth and P. Dogliani (eds), *Italian Fascism: History, Memory and Representation* (London, Macmillan, 1999), p. 103.
38 Megill, 'History, memory, identity', p. 57.
39 R. Starn and N. Z. Davies, 'Introduction', *Representations*, no. 26, 1989, p. 2.
40 H. Rousso, *The Vichy Syndrome: History and Memory in France since 1944* (Cambridge, MA, Harvard University Press, 1991), p. 4.
41 Rosenberg, *A Date Which Will Live*, p. 5; M. Sturken, *Tangled Memories: The Vietnam War, the AIDS Epidemic, and the Politics of Remembering* (Berkeley, CA, University of California Press, 1997), p. 5; J. Winter, *Remembering War: The Great War between Memory and History in the Twentieth Century* (New Haven, CT, Yale University Press, 2006), p. 6.
42 Quote from Müller, 'Introduction', p. 23.
43 D. Harlan, *The Degradation of American History* (Chicago, University of Chicago Press, 1997), p. 105.
44 R. J. Evans, *In Defence of History* (London, Granta, 1997), p. 249.
45 Evans, *In Defence of History*, can stand as a representative example from a considerable literature.
46 E. Breisach, *On the Future of History: The Postmodernist Challenge and its Aftermath* (Chicago, University of Chicago Press, 2003); D. Cannadine (ed.), *What is History Now?* (London, Palgrave, 2002).
47 J. H. Arnold, 'Responses to the postmodern challenge; or, what might history become?', *European History Quarterly*, vol. 37, no. 1, 2007, pp. 109–32.
48 G. M. Spiegel (ed.), *Practicing History: New Directions in Historical Writing after the Linguistic Turn* (New York, Routledge, 2005).
49 S. Berger, H. Feldner and K. Passmore (eds), *Writing History: Theory and Practice* (London, Arnold, 2003).
50 G. M. Spiegel, 'Revising the past/revisiting the present: how change happens in historiography', *History and Theory*, vol. 46, no. 4, 2007, p. 3.
51 K. Thomas, 'New ways revisited', *Times Literary Supplement*, 13 October 2006, p. 4.
52 M. Bentley, 'Island stories', *Times Literary Supplement*, 13 October 2006, p. 6.
53 R. J. B. Bosworth, *Explaining Auschwitz and Hiroshima: History Writing and the Second World War, 1945–1990* (London, Routledge, 1993), p. 30.
54 W. Kansteiner, 'Mad history disease contained? Postmodern excess management advice from the UK', *History and Theory*, vol. 39, no. 2, 2000, pp. 218–29.
55 M. Fulbrook, *Historical Theory* (London, Routledge, 2002).
56 M. Bentley, 'General introduction: the project of historiography', in M. Bentley (ed.), *Companion to Historiography* (London, Routledge, 1997), p. xiii. It should be acknowledged,

however, that I have drawn liberally on historiographical work by Richard Evans, Mary Fulbrook and numerous other 'practical realists' in the chapters which follow.

57 H. White, *Figural Realism: Studies in the Mimesis Effect* (Baltimore, MD, Johns Hopkins University Press, 1999), p. 27.

58 Quote from H. White, *Tropics of Discourse: Essays in Cultural Criticism* (Baltimore, MD, Johns Hopkins University Press, 1978), p. 82 (emphasis in original).

59 Quote from H. White, *Figural Realism*, p. 9.

60 See, in particular, H. White, *The Content of the Form: Narrative Discourse and Historical Representation* (Baltimore, MD, Johns Hopkins University Press, 1987), pp. 58–82.

61 R. F. Berkhofer, *Beyond the Great Story: History as Text and Discourse* (Cambridge, MA, Harvard University Press, 1995), p. 281.

62 E. S. Rosenberg, 'Considering borders', in M. J. Hogan and T. G. Paterson (eds), *Explaining the History of American Foreign Relations* (Cambridge, Cambridge University Press, 2004, 2nd edn), p. 192.

63 G. Eley, 'The profane and imperfect world of historiography', *American Historical Review*, vol. 113, no. 2, 2008, pp. 427–28.

64 D. Stone, *Constructing the Holocaust: A Study in Historiography* (London, Vallentine Mitchell, 2003), pp. 18–19.

65 J. Young, 'Toward a received history of the Holocaust', *History and Theory*, vol. 36, no. 4, 1997, p. 25.

66 White, *Tropics of Discourse*, p. 98.

67 K. Jenkins and A. Munslow, 'Introduction', in K. Jenkins and A. Munslow (eds), *The Nature of History Reader* (London, Routledge, 2004), p. 3.

68 Stone, *Constructing the Holocaust*, p. 15.

69 J. Derrida, 'Following theory', in M. Payne and J. Schad (eds), *life.after.theory* (London, Continuum, 2003), p. 27.

70 White, *Tropics of Discourse*, p. 121.

71 White, 'An old question raised again: is historiography art or science? (Response to Iggers)', p. 402.

72 Stone, *Constructing the Holocaust*, p. 16.

73 F. R. Ankersmit, *Historical Representation* (Stanford, CA, Stanford University Press, 2001), p. 21.

74 R. Torstendahl, '"Correct" and "fruitful" as bases for historiographical analysis', in R. Torstendahl and I. Veit-Brause (eds), *History-Making: The Intellectual and Social Formation of a Discipline* (Stockholm, Kungl. Vitterhets Historie och Antikvitets Akademien, 1996), pp. 77–94.

75 Evans consistently opposed facts and politics, implying that empirical evidence must either be absolutely sovereign or count for nothing: *In Defence of History*, pp. 191–253.

76 E. Somekawa and E. A. Smith, 'Theorizing the writing of history or, "I can't think why it should be so dull, for a great deal of it must be invention"', *Journal of Social History*, vol. 22, no. 1, 1988, pp. 152–53.

77 J. Arnold, *History: A Very Short Introduction* (Oxford, Oxford University Press, 2000), p. 116.

78 H. Kellner, 'Language and historical representation', in Jenkins (ed.), *Postmodern History Reader*, p. 134.

79 For an overview, see G. Day and A. Thompson, *Theorizing Nationalism* (London, Palgrave, 2004).

80 M. Fulbrook, *German National Identity after the Holocaust* (Oxford, Polity, 1999), pp. 8–12.

81 G. Cubitt, 'Introduction', in G. Cubitt (ed.), *Imagining Nations* (Manchester, Manchester University Press, 1998), pp. 2–3.

82 A. D. Smith, 'Gastronomy or geology? The role of nationalism in the reconstruction of nations', *Nations and Nationalism*, vol. 1, no. 1, 1995, pp. 4–9.

83 G. Eley and R. G. Suny, 'Introduction: from the moment of social history to the work of cultural representation', in G. Eley and R. G. Suny (eds), *Becoming National: A Reader* (New York, Oxford University Press, 1996), p. 9; Cubitt, 'Introduction', p. 3.

84 B. Anderson, *Imagined Communities: Reflections on the Origin and Spread of Nationalism* (London, Verso, 1983), pp. 14, 16.

85 Eley and Suny, 'Introduction', p. 18.

86 S. Woolf, 'Introduction', in S. Woolf (ed.), *Nationalism in Europe, 1815 to the Present: A Reader* (London, Routledge, 1996), pp. 28–32.

87 Cubitt, 'Introduction', p. 3.

88 See, for example, S. Berger, *The Search for Normality: National Identity and Historical Consciousness in Germany since 1800* (Oxford, Berghahn, 1997), especially pp. 1–55.

89 Arnold, *History*, p. 55.

90 Quote from P. Joyce, 'The return of history: postmodernism and the politics of academic history in Britain', *Past and Present*, no. 158, 1998, p. 224. For case studies, see S. Berger, M. Donovan and K. Passmore (eds), *Writing National Histories: Western Europe since 1800* (London, Routledge, 1999) and D. Deletant and H. Hanak (eds), *Historians as Nation-Builders: Central and South-East Europe* (London, Macmillan, 1988).

91 K. Wilson (ed.), *Forging the Collective Memory: Government and International Historians through Two World Wars* (Oxford, Berghahn, 1996), chs. 3–5.

92 P.M. Kennedy, 'The decline of nationalistic history in the west, 1900–1970', *Journal of Contemporary History*, vol. 8, no. 1, 1973, pp. 77–100, quote at p. 99.

93 K. Passmore with S. Berger and M. Donovan, 'Historians and the nation state: some conclusions', in Berger, Donovan and Passmore (eds), *Writing National Histories*, pp. 281–304, quotes at p. 292.

94 S. Berger, 'A return to the national paradigm? National history writing in Germany, Italy, France, and Britain from 1945 to the present', *Journal of Modern History*, vol. 77, no. 3, 2005, pp. 629–78.

95 A. Burton, 'Introduction: on the inadequacy and the indispensability of the nation', in A. Burton (ed.), *After the Imperial Turn: Thinking With and Through the Nation* (Durham, NC, Duke University Press, 2003), p. 8.

96 For example, S. Berger (ed.), *Writing the Nation: A Global Perspective* (London, Palgrave, 2007); S. Berger and C. Lorenz (eds), *The Contested Nation: Ethnicity, Class, Religion and Gender in National Histories* (London, Palgrave, 2008).

97 S. Woolf, review of Berger, Donovan and Passmore (eds), *Writing National Histories*, in *Institute of Historical Research Reviews in History*, May 2000, http://www.history.ac.uk/reviews/paper/berger.html; see also the authors' response at http://www.history.ac.uk/reviews/paper/berger1.html. (both accessed 10 November 2005).

98 W. Schivelbusch, *The Culture of Defeat: On National Trauma, Mourning, and Recovery* (London, Granta, 2003), p. 5.

99 For orientation in the vast literature see, for example, Evans and Lunn (eds), *War and Memory in the Twentieth Century*; J. Winter and E. Sivan (eds), *War and Remembrance in the Twentieth Century* (Cambridge, Cambridge University Press, 1999).

100 D. Bell, 'Introduction: memory, trauma and world politics', in D. Bell (ed.), *Memory, Trauma and World Politics* (London, Palgrave, 2006), p. 5.

101 A. Confino, 'Remembering the Second World War, 1945–65: narratives of victimhood and genocide', *Cultural Analysis*, vol. 4, 2005, pp. 47–65.

102 Berger, 'A return to the national paradigm?'.

103 J. Bourke, 'Introduction: "remembering" war', *Journal of Contemporary History*, vol. 39, no. 4, 2004, p. 474.

104 T. Berger, 'The power of memory and memories of power: the cultural parameters of German foreign policy-making since 1945', in Müller (ed.), *Memory and Power*, p. 80.

105 T. Snyder, 'Memory of sovereignty and sovereignty over memory: Poland, Lithuania and Ukraine, 1939–99', in Müller (ed.), *Memory and Power*, p. 39. This is not to imply that national memory is the only form of collective memory, or that it is ever uncontested: Winter, *Remembering War*, pp. 183–200.

106 Berger, 'The power of memory and memories of power', p. 83.

107 B. Zelizer, 'Reading the past against the grain: the shape of memory studies', *Critical Studies in Mass Communication*, vol. 12, no. 2, 1995, pp. 218–34; A. Rigney, 'Plenitude, scarcity and the circulation of cultural memory', *Journal of European Studies*, vol. 35, no. 1, 2005, pp. 11–35.

108 J. K. Olick, *In the House of the Hangman: The Agonies of German Defeat, 1943–1949* (Chicago, University of Chicago Press, 2005), p. 20.

109 R. N. Lebow, 'The memory of politics in postwar Europe', in R. N. Lebow, W. Kansteiner and C. Fogu (eds), *The Politics of Memory in Postwar Europe* (Durham, NC, Duke University Press, 2006), p. 15.

110 W. Kansteiner, 'Finding meaning in memory: a methodological critique of collective memory studies', *History and Theory*, vol. 41, no. 2, 2002, pp. 179–97, quotes at pp. 196, 180.

111 Rousso, *The Vichy Syndrome*, is a translation of the 1990 French second edition. É. Conan and H. Rousso, *Vichy: An Ever-Present Past* (Hanover, NH, University Press of New England, 1998) continues the treatment into the 1990s.

112 For example, C. S. Maier, *The Unmasterable Past: History, Holocaust, and German National Identity* (Cambridge, MA, Harvard University Press, 1988).

113 Bosworth, *Explaining Auschwitz and Hiroshima*, quotes at p. 3.

114 C. Lorenz, review of Bosworth, *Explaining Auschwitz and Hiroshima*, in *History and Theory*, vol. 35, no. 2, 1996, pp. 234–52, quotes at p. 236.

115 Bosworth, *Explaining Auschwitz and Hiroshima*, p. 4.

116 Bosworth, *Explaining Auschwitz and Hiroshima*, quote at p. 189.

117 Bosworth himself reflected further on the question in relation to Italy in 'Explaining "Auschwitz" after the end of history: the case of Italy', *History and Theory*, vol. 38, no. 1, 1999, pp. 84–99, admitting that 'a debate over the meaning of the "long" Second World War continues unabated almost a decade after the end of history' (p. 86).

118 M. Evans, 'Memories, monuments, histories: the re-thinking of the Second World War since 1989', *National Identities*, vol. 8, no. 4, 2006, pp. 317–48; H. Fleischer, 'The past beneath the present: the resurgence of World War II public history after the collapse of communism: a stroll through the international press', *Historein*, vol. 4, 2003/4, pp. 45–130.

119 T. Cole, *Images of the Holocaust: The Myth of the 'Shoah Business'* (London, Duckworth, 1999).

120 D. Levy and N. Sznaider, *The Holocaust and Memory in the Global Age* (Philadelphia, PA, Temple University Press, 2006).

121 A. Calder, *The Myth of the Blitz* (London, Jonathan Cape, 1991), p. xiv; M. Smith, *Britain and 1940: History, Myth and Popular Memory* (London, Routledge, 2000), p. 9.

122 N. Hewitt, 'A sceptical generation? War memorials and the collective memory of the Second World War in Britain, 1945–2000', in D. Geppert (ed.), *The Postwar Challenge: Cultural, Social, and Political Change in Western Europe, 1945–58* (Oxford, Oxford University Press, 2003), p. 91; J. Kirkup, 'Gordon Brown speaks of optimism for 2009 in New Year's message', *Daily Telegraph*, 1 January 2009, http://www.telegraph.co.uk/news/newstopics/politics/labour/4045579/Gordon-Brown-speaks-of-optimism-for-2009-in-New-Years-message.html (accessed 2 January 2009).

123 Bosworth, *Explaining Auschwitz and Hiroshima*, p. 113.

124 B. Niven, *Facing the Nazi Past: United Germany and the Legacy of the Third Reich* (London, Routledge, 2001).

125 R. G. Moeller, 'Germans as victims? Thoughts on a post-Cold War history of World War II's legacies', *History and Memory*, vol. 17, no. 1/2, 2005, pp. 147–94, quote at p. 182; M. M. Anderson, 'Crime and punishment', *The Nation*, 17 October 2005, http://www.thenation.com/doc/20051017/anderson (accessed 14 November 2005).

126 Bosworth, *Explaining Auschwitz and Hiroshima*, p. 193.

127 A. Schlesinger, 'Searching for a heroic past: the rediscovery of World War II', *AARP Bulletin*, May 1999, http://www.aarp.org/bulletin/may99/wwii.html (accessed 6 June 2001).

128 D. H. Noon, 'Operation enduring analogy: World War II, the war on terror, and the uses of historical memory', *Rhetoric and Public Affairs*, vol. 7, no. 3, 2004, pp. 339–65.

129 'Lessons yet to be learned', *The Guardian*, 7 June 2004, http://www.guardian.co.uk/secondworldwar/story/0,14058,1232925,00.html (accessed 14 November 2005); I. Black, 'World watch', *The Guardian*, 11 July 2005, http://www.guardian.co.uk/comment/story/0,3604,1525715,00.html (accessed 21 November 2005).

130 Zelizer, 'Reading the past against the grain', p. 217.

131 F. Bieber, 'Nationalist mobilization and stories of Serb suffering: the Kosovo myth from 600th anniversary to the present', *Rethinking History*, vol. 6, no. 1, 2002, pp. 95–110.

132 A. Landsberg, *Prosthetic Memory: The Transformation of American Remembrance in the Age of Mass Culture* (New York, Columbia University Press, 2004).

133 Kansteiner, 'Finding meaning in memory', p. 189.

134 C. Caldwell, 'World War II in the west's political imagination', *Financial Times*, 18 September 2004, http://hnn.us/roundup/entries/7533.html (accessed 27 September 2004).

135 D. Reynolds, 'World War II and modern meanings', *Diplomatic History*, vol. 25, no. 3, 2001, p. 469.

136 T. Judt, 'Preface' and 'The past is another country: myth and memory in postwar Europe', in I. Deák, J. T. Gross and T. Judt (eds), *The Politics of Retribution in Europe: World War II and its Aftermath* (Princeton, NJ, Princeton University Press, 2000), pp. vii–xii, 293–323. This said, Judt also shared with Bosworth a sense of regret that certain taboos inherent in the post-war myths had been lost as the price for a new pluralism (pp. 314–15).

137 Müller, 'Introduction', pp. 3–13, quotes at pp. 6–7.

138 T. Snyder, 'Balancing the books', *Eurozine*, May 2005, http://www.eurozine.com/articles/2005-05-03-snyder-en.html (accessed 21 October 2005).

139 See, for example, P. Ther, 'The burden of history and the trap of memory', *Eurozine*, August 2006, http://www.eurozine.com/articles/2006-08-21-ther-en.html (accessed 14 October 2006); 'Memories of wars: Italy and her Eastern Adriatic neighbours since 1989', theme issue, *Journal of Southern Europe and the Balkans*, vol. 6, no. 2, 2004.

140 T. Judt, *Postwar: A History of Europe since 1945* (London, Pimlico, 2007, pb. edn), pp. 803–31, quote at p. 804.

141 C. Leggewie, 'A tour of the battleground: the seven circles of pan-European memory', *Social Research*, vol. 75, no. 1, 2008, pp. 217–34.

142 Krzeminski, 'As many wars as nations'.

143 N. Gregor, 'The legacy of National Socialism: introduction', in N. Gregor (ed.), *Nazism* (Oxford, Oxford University Press, 2000), pp. 336–37.

144 Judt, *Postwar*, p. 10. Judt here evinces faith in the capacity of academic history to banish myth, and implies that the fuller historical disclosure now finally underway will facilitate a salutary moving on from the wartime past (pp. 829–31).

145 S. R. Suleiman, *Crises of Memory and the Second World War* (Cambridge, MA, Harvard University Press, 2006), p. 4.

146 Lebow, 'The memory of politics in postwar Europe', p. 36.

147 Quote from G. Bartram, 'Reconstruction of the past in post-war European culture: a comparative approach', in G. Bartram, M. Slawinski and D. Steel (eds), *Reconstructing the Past: Representations of the Fascist Era in Post-War European Culture* (Keele, Keele University Press, 1996), p. 12.

148 Cf. the brief attempt to apply the 'Vichy Syndrome' model to other European cases in H. Rousso, 'History of memory, policies of the past: what for?', in K. H. Jarausch and T. Lindenberger (eds), *Conflicted Memories: Europeanizing Contemporary Histories* (Oxford, Berghahn, 2007), p. 29.

149 P. Lagrou, *The Legacy of Nazi Occupation: Patriotic Memory and National Recovery in Western Europe, 1945–1965* (Cambridge, Cambridge University Press, 2000), p. 305. Lagrou posits the existence of a rather short 'long Second World War', ending in the mid-1960s when the myths that had grounded post-war reconstruction began to be challenged (p. 15).

150 Fulbrook, *German National Identity after the Holocaust*, p. 103.

151 See, for example, the historiographical material in Rousso, *The Vichy Syndrome*, pp. 241–71.

152 Witness the diverse contributions in 'The future of World War II studies' (see note 22).

153 For example, M. Kitchen, review of Bosworth, *Explaining Auschwitz and Hiroshima*, in *International History Review*, vol. 16, no. 1, 1994, pp. 189–91. Throughout this book, I generally define 'international history' broadly as 'historical writing on international relations', whether or not the author would primarily identify themselves as an 'international historian'. On the instability and permeability of the generic category of 'international history', see P. Finney, 'Introduction: what is international history?', in P. Finney (ed.), *Palgrave Advances in International History* (London, Palgrave, 2005), pp. 1–35.

154 J. C. E. Gienow-Hecht and F. Schumacher (eds), *Culture and International History* (Oxford, Berghahn, 2003).

155 D. Reynolds, *From World War to Cold War: Churchill, Roosevelt, and the International History of the 1940s* (Oxford, Oxford University Press, 2006), p. 343, and more widely pp. 331–51.

156 R. D. Schulzinger, 'Memory and understanding U.S. foreign relations', in Hogan and Paterson (eds), *Explaining the History of American Foreign Relations*, pp. 336–52, quotes at pp. 352, 343. See also R. D. Schulzinger, *A Time for Peace: The Legacy of the Vietnam War* (Oxford, Oxford University Press, 2006).

157 R. J. McMahon, 'Contested memory: the Vietnam War and American society, 1975–2001', *Diplomatic History*, vol. 26, no. 2, 2002, pp. 159–84, quotes at pp. 183–84.

158 See, respectively, T. G. Otte, 'A "German paperchase": the "scrap of paper" controversy and the problem of myth and memory in international history', *Diplomacy and Statecraft*, vol. 18, no. 1, 2007, pp. 53–87; B. C. Etheridge, 'The Desert Fox, memory diplomacy, and the German question in early Cold War America', *Diplomatic History*, vol. 32, no. 2, 2008, pp. 207–38; E. A. Martini, *Invisible Enemies: The American War on Vietnam, 1975–2000* (Amherst, MA, University of Massachusetts Press, 2007).

159 It should also be noted that while 'postmodernist' theory was one of the original inspirations for culturalism, its theoretical and political edge is now less apparent; focus on cultural issues is often chiefly justified on empirical grounds, as simply a means to produce a fuller picture of how things actually were.

160 Reynolds, *From World War to Cold War*, p. 344.

161 A. Best, 'The "ghost" of the Anglo–Japanese alliance: an examination into historical myth-making', *Historical Journal*, vol. 49, no. 3, 2006, pp. 811–31.

162 The following discussion draws on P. Finney, 'Hayden White, international history and questions too seldom posed', *Rethinking History*, vol. 12, no. 1, 2008, pp. 103–23.

163 See, very diversely, C. Elman and M. F. Elman (eds), *Bridges and Boundaries: Historians, Political Scientists, and the Study of International Relations* (Cambridge, MA, MIT Press, 2001); J. L. Gaddis, *The Landscape of History: How Historians Map the Past* (Oxford, Oxford University Press, 2002); G. Roberts (ed.), *The History and Narrative Reader* (London, Routledge, 2001).

164 M. Trachtenberg, *The Craft of International History: A Guide to Method* (Princeton, NJ, Princeton University Press, 2006), quotes at pp. 51, 107, 79.

165 R. J. Caputi, *Neville Chamberlain and Appeasement* (Selinsgrove, PA, Susquehanna University Press, 2000), quotes at pp. 234, 115.

166 D. Dutton, *Neville Chamberlain* (London, Arnold, 2001), quotes at pp. 185, 75.

167 P. M. H. Bell, *The Origins of the Second World War in Europe* (London, Longman, 2007, 3rd edn), pp. 43–54, quotes at p. 45.

168 See, for example, P. Grosser, *Pourquoi la Seconde Guerre Mondiale?* (Brussels, Éditions Complexe, 1999) and (at least some of) the contributions in R. Boyce and J. A. Maiolo (eds), *The Origins of World War Two: The Debate Continues* (London, Palgrave, 2003) and G. Martel (ed.) *The Origins of the Second World War Reconsidered: A. J. P. Taylor and the Historians* (London, Routledge, 1999, 2nd edn). Note also my earlier reader: P. Finney (ed.), *The Origins of the Second World War* (London, Arnold, 1997).

169 P. Jackson, 'Post-war politics and the historiography of French strategy and diplomacy before the Second World War', *History Compass*, vol. 4, no. 5, 2006, pp. 870–905.

170 D. Reynolds, *In Command of History: Churchill Fighting and Writing the Second World War* (London, Allen Lane, 2004).

171 Other, diverse, examples include S. Hurst, *Cold War US Foreign Policy: Key Perspectives* (Edinburgh, Edinburgh University Press, 2005); A. Mombauer, *The Origins of the First World War: Controversies and Consensus* (London, Longman, 2002); J. Winter and A. Prost, *The Great War in History: Debates and Controversies, 1914 to the Present* (Cambridge, Cambridge University Press, 2005).

172 Rosenberg, *A Date Which Will Live*, quotes at pp. 6, 156.

173 Louis A. Pérez Jr, *The War of 1898: The United States and Cuba in History and Historiography* (Chapel Hill, NC, University of North Carolina Press, 1998), quotes at pp. 39, 42, x, 68.

174 J. Edkins, *Trauma and the Memory of Politics* (Cambridge, Cambridge University Press, 2003), p. 46.

175 This study is based primarily, though not exclusively, on sources in English. Doubtless this imposes certain limitations, but I am confident that translations and secondary commentaries provide a sufficient basis for sound judgement. Equally, in a comparative project of this nature the relentless accumulation of nuance is not an unmitigated good.

1   On virtue

Stalin's diplomacy and the origins
of the Great Patriotic War

> This attitude of the Soviet Union is predetermined by its general policy of struggling
> for peace, for the collective organisation of security and for the maintenance of one of
> the instruments of peace – the existing League of Nations. We consider that one
> cannot struggle for peace without at the same time defending the integrity of inter-
> national obligations, particularly such as have direct bearing on the maintenance of
> existing frontiers, on armaments and on political or military aggression.
>
> Maxim Litvinov, Soviet Commissar for Foreign Affairs, address
> to the Council of the League of Nations, 17 March 1936[1]

The signature of the Nazi–Soviet pact on 23 August 1939 was one of the
most dramatic diplomatic coups of the inter-war years, signifying a rapprochement between bitter ideological enemies who had rained invective and
scorn upon each other for years. Where the Soviet Union was concerned, the
pact raised fundamental questions about the nature of General Secretary Josef
Stalin's foreign policy. Since the mid-1930s, with the indefatigable Litvinov
to the fore, the Soviets had been ardent advocates of collective security,
pursuing a Popular Front policy to concert all anti-fascist elements in Europe
against Nazism. Now, Stalin and German Foreign Minister Joachim von
Ribbentrop clinked glasses of vodka and Crimean champagne to toast their
non-aggression treaty and the incipient partition of Poland, joking cynically
about the Soviet Union joining the Anti-Comintern pact. In Britain, the
Labour Party *Daily Herald* encapsulated the dismay of the left as it damned
Stalin for 'one of the most indefensible and shocking reversals of policy in
history'; in the Soviet Union itself, there was equal bewilderment: 'we felt
that we did not understand something as we should have ... Yesterday, we
were taught to hate fascism but today to take it for a friend'.[2]

From the very outset, the apparent incongruity between the previous
path of Soviet policy and the pact was reconciled in diverse ways. Soviet
propaganda insisted that the collective security policy had been sincere and
genuine, but had been confounded by the western powers' refusal to agree
terms in the alliance talks that had been proceeding for months. In the words
of Vyacheslav Molotov, Litvinov's successor, negotiations 'had come to a
deadlock owing to insuperable differences and had ended in failure through

the fault of the ruling classes of Britain and France'.[3] The dilatory manner and contradictory demands of the western powers had raised suspicions that their real aim was to divert Nazi expansionism eastwards, thus embroiling the Soviet Union in war. The pact was therefore justified as a *realpolitik* necessity to ensure Soviet security whereby Stalin had skilfully 'out-Muniched' them.[4] The British government, having largely discounted the value of a Soviet alliance, reacted to the pact with relative equanimity, while the French were more disconcerted by its strategic implications; yet both predominantly viewed it as an act of *realpolitik*, of either a defensive or imperialist kind.[5] An alternative but at this point marginal interpretation imputed a much more sinister character to Stalin's policy and blamed excessive and ever-escalating Soviet demands for the failure of talks with the West. On this view, Soviet collective security rhetoric had been mere verbiage, camouflaging the true aim of seeking an agreement with Germany in order to plunge the capitalist world into internecine conflict, thus furthering revolutionary expansionist goals.[6]

These two starkly opposing interpretations marked out the terrain on which the subsequent historiographical debate on Soviet policy in the 1930s has been conducted. Existing in many different variants with diverse nuances, the two arguments have remained in play in continual contestation. Historians often attribute this to the congenital secrecy of the Soviet regime and its reluctance (shared to a lesser extent by its post-Soviet successors) to open its archives to historical scrutiny; 'gaps in the evidence', it is asserted, mean debate has been 'locked in the realm of speculative interpretation and political polemic'.[7] But while it is undeniable that documentation is lacking for some crucial facets of Soviet diplomacy, a more fundamental reason for the persistence of this pluralism is that interpretations are inextricably bound up with a larger set of political and moral questions about the legitimacy and capacity for virtue of the Soviet system as a whole, questions that the demise of communism has done little to still or resolve.

'Persistent and prolonged struggle': Soviet historiography and the origins of the war

Within the Soviet Union and its successor states, the development of narratives of the origins of the war has to be understood within two broader contexts. The first is the overt politicisation of Soviet historiography. Within all political systems, it has been argued, historiography functions 'to socialize the coming generation, to legitimate political institutions, to perpetuate established mores and mythology, and to rationalize official policies', but in the post-war Soviet Union – 'because of a unique blend of ideological, historical, and political factors' – it was 'charged with these functions to an unprecedented degree'.[8] At the heart of Marxism-Leninism lay an explicit metanarrative: an interpretation and periodisation of human history which offered an overarching theory of how historical change occurred, complete with a teleology, namely the realisation of human potential and freedom under communism.

Since the Bolsheviks who made the revolution of 1917 conceived of themselves as acting within this broader framework, it was scarcely surprising that the regime should have devoted careful attention to scripting its own history. More pragmatically, the legitimacy of a political system founded in violent revolution depended on the inculcation of belief that the seizure of power had been 'law-governed', popular and the inevitable product of prodigious leadership.[9] So, from the first, the Bolsheviks averred that history was 'a sphere of acute ideological struggle' and a means to inspire the masses with loyalty, confidence and pride in the new political order.[10]

In the first decade after 1917, although the state did work to foster ideologically secure historiographical foundations for itself, bourgeois historians were not entirely eradicated and there was healthy debate within the Communist Party about the utility of history in general and the true meaning of the revolution in particular. But this relative pluralism was foreclosed in the 1930s after Stalin's rise to power and launch of the 'Second Bolshevik Revolution'; tighter institutional and ideological controls were imposed and the new climate of intellectual sterility was exemplified by the promulgation of a simplistic (and in many respects mendacious) master narrative of Soviet history in the *History of the Communist Party of the Soviet Union (Bolsheviks), Short Course*, published in 1938. Stalin's death in 1953 and the subsequent onset of 'de-Stalinization' saw renewed liberalisation. Access to archives became easier and the publication of primary source material more frequent, so interpretations acquired a firmer grounding in documentary reality; simultaneously, debates became more sophisticated and diverse and historians acquired an unprecedented sense of constituting a self-regulating professional community.[11] But if history regained something of an autonomous dynamic, becoming more than simply the handmaiden of politics, nonetheless the broad tenets of Marxism-Leninism continued to govern scholarship, state and Party supervision remained close, and the vicissitudes of contemporary politics were closely reflected in the nature and content of historiographical output. Nor was this surprising, since if anything the abandonment of terror laid even greater importance on history as a means of manufacturing consent; hence Nikita Khrushchev's famous aphorism: 'historians are dangerous people ... They must be directed'.[12] Indeed, the two decades of conservative stagnation that followed Khrushchev's ouster in 1964 saw the pendulum swing once more back towards repression with a further crackdown on independent thinking amongst historians.

The second context is the cataclysmic impact of the Second World War upon the Soviet Union and the particular nature of its subsequent public historicisation. The Soviet experience of the war was unparalleled in terms of psychological trauma and physical destruction. Estimates of casualties vary widely and are politically charged, but deaths are now estimated at 27 million, with over 70,000 villages, 1,700 towns and 32,000 factories devastated.[13] Even though the war had been fought to victory and had delivered tangible gains in a sphere of influence in Eastern Europe and incipient superpower status, the mammoth costs compelled the regime to promulgate positive authorised readings of it: this was an effort 'to impose a single meaning onto a complex and diverse human experience', effacing crimes, blunders and ambiguities 'in favor of a narrative that celebrated an unmitigated communist heroism and universal suffering'. This narrative portrayed victory in the war as the ultimate vindication of the Soviet system, and emphasised the signal contribution made to it by the particular institutions and interest groups that were central in the post-war political order. Thus, 'Soviet official memory of the war advanced a simplified tale aimed at the mobilization of the past in the service of the present and the future'.[14] For four decades after 1945, such representations of the war, in academic historiography, popular culture and a host of public commemorative practices, were the regime's crucial mnemonic technologies for instilling and securing a sense of Soviet identity amongst the disparate peoples of a sprawling empire.

A conflict that had rapidly been dubbed the Great Patriotic (or Great Fatherland) War – a designation imputing a unique nature to the Soviet dimension of the broader global hostilities yet also carrying resonances from Russia's national past and the first 'Patriotic War' against Napoleon in 1812[15] – over time acquired a full-blown cult. This did not emerge fully formed immediately after the war was won, nor was it monolithic or immutable, but from 1945 onwards the historicisation of the Second World War served as a crucial means of ensuring cohesion in Soviet society. Nor was this simply a work of historical engineering: for all its excesses the cult would not have endured so long had it not achieved 'an effective fusion of personal and public imagination' as Soviet 'citizens, politicians and historians ... consistently placed the war at the center of their private and public worlds'.[16] The Soviet case is thus a natural starting point for this study: because of the traumatic impact of the war upon almost every Soviet citizen, and the political task of legitimation with which representations of it were entrusted, the war loomed much larger in post-war consciousness here than in most other combatant countries and its memory was explicitly intertwined with the negotiation of national identity.

In these circumstances, Soviet historians writing on the origins of the war were clearly implicated in the regime's wider political purposes.[17] They elaborated a narrative extending and modifying the view first adumbrated in wartime propaganda, defending Stalin's diplomacy in the 1930s. The precise shape that this orthodox interpretation acquired, moreover, was very much dependent upon the political exigencies of post-war reconstruction and the nascent Cold War.

Stalin established the basic parameters of the general war myth in a keynote address in February 1946 which, with rhetorical excess that betrayed the gravity of what was at stake, elucidated the lessons to be drawn from victory. The war, he prescribed, had proven the viability, popularity and relative superiority of both the Soviet system and of the multi-national Soviet state. The armed forces had certainly played a crucial part in the triumph, but the fundamental material foundations had been laid by the pre-war programmes of collectivisation and industrialisation, and by the purges that had accompanied them. This speech was integral to a general 'memory project from above' that aimed simultaneously to 'establish myths' justifying the brutalities of the 1930s, 'erase memories of the nearly fatal defeats and divisions of World War II', and 'justify the future rule of the Communist Party' as the country geared up for the massive task of reconstruction. Yet it also reflected Stalin's personal priorities. As he abandoned the partial and forced liberalisation of the war years and attempted to reassert fuller autocratic control, he needed to efface alternative focuses for loyalty and encourage unquestioning obedience to his leadership; hence, the stress upon the wisdom of the Party and the durability of the system and the downplaying – compared to wartime rhetoric – of the contribution of the military and the general populace.[18]

In discussing the outbreak of the war, Stalin reaffirmed Lenin's theory of imperialism and identified the contradictions of capitalism as its root cause. Some contemporary western observers interpreted this as an aggressive reassertion of the inevitability of conflict between capitalism and communism, and thus as tantamount to the 'declaration of World War III'.[19] Subsequent commentators have sometimes concurred, arguing that where previous propaganda had presented the pre-war diplomacy of the western powers in relatively benign terms (as misguided and pusillanimous rather than duplicitous), now Stalin aimed 'actively to transform the image of the Allies from partners in the anti-Hitler coalition into crypto-enemies of the Soviet Union and virtual allies of Hitler'.[20] Yet another reading might stress how, with post-war Soviet foreign policy still in flux, Stalin was actually careful at this juncture to distinguish between the 'freedom-loving' democratic capitalist states and fascist ones and to concede that the war had had an anti-fascist character even before the Soviet Union entered it.[21] However, as Cold War tensions intensified, the gloomy prophecies of western conservatives proved to be self-fulfilling, and the Soviet myth did indeed come to stress affinities between the fascist and democratic capitalist powers, resurrecting the image of a monolithic capitalist imperialism as minatory external other.

The first key historical text enunciating this harsher interpretation was *Falsifiers of History*, published in 1948.[22] Jointly authored by Stalin himself, this became 'the single most important source of Soviet historical writing on the war period and provided a definitive framework for the interpretation of the Western role in the war'.[23] It was directly prompted by the appearance in January 1948 of *Nazi-Soviet Relations, 1939–1941,* an edited collection of captured German diplomatic documents sponsored by the American State Department. As Grand Alliance cooperation transmuted into Cold War confrontation, American opinion decisively shifted to view Stalin's present-day foreign policy as revolutionary, expansionist and threatening; a natural corollary was that negative interpretations of Soviet pre-war diplomacy that had previously lurked on the margins suddenly acquired much greater plausibility.[24] The documents within *Nazi-Soviet Relations* – including the secret protocol to the Nazi–Soviet pact delineating spheres of influence in Poland, the Baltic states and Bessarabia – were thus selected and arranged so as to highlight pre-war cooperation and contacts between the Hitler and Stalin regimes, undermining the argument that the Soviet Union had consistently opposed fascism, and implying that agreement with Hitler was not so much a regrettable necessity as the ultimate aim of Stalin's diplomacy.[25] Thus, in a mirror image of the interpretive manoeuvre about to be performed by Stalin, the underlying similarities between Nazi Germany and Stalinist Russia were emphasised; each camp claimed itself the legitimate heir of the just cause of the previous war as they girded themselves to fight another.[26]

Falsifiers of History insistently equated the behaviour of the western democracies with that of the Nazi dictatorship.[27] First, its narrative focused on how the western powers had facilitated 'the reconstruction and development of ... war-industrial potential' in Germany after the First World War, particularly through the 'golden rain of American dollars' which fell on Germany from the 1924 Dawes Plan onwards. Having thus provided 'the first and principal pre-requisite of Hitler aggression', the Allies compounded their crimes in the 1930s by appeasing Nazism: 'it should be clear to everyone that it was this ... connivance with Hitler Germany's aggressive demands, that led to the Second World War'. Where the Soviet Union waged a 'persistent and prolonged struggle' to 'maintain and consolidate collective security', the western powers, sacrificing smaller countries, tried to direct Hitler's aggression to the east 'and utilise it as a weapon against the USSR'. This led inexorably to the 'unheard-of act of treachery' of the Munich conference in September 1938, and although negotiations were held between the Soviets, the British and the French through 1939, these offered no hope of agreement; the western powers were utterly insincere, attempting to bind the Soviets with definite obligations while accepting none themselves, and simultaneously conducting 'back-stage negotiations with Germany' to which they 'attached incomparably greater importance'. Fortunately, these machinations were 'exposed by J. V. Stalin' who perceived that the Anglo-French 'war provocateurs' were trying to engineer a Soviet–German conflict, just as the Soviets also faced a threat from the Japanese in Asia. Hence, 'the Soviet Government found itself compelled to make its choice and conclude the Non-Aggression Pact with Germany'. Skilfully exploiting inter-imperialist contradictions, this was 'a wise and far-sighted act of Soviet foreign policy under the conditions that then obtained' which strengthened borders and defences and eventually facilitated victory.[28]

While grounded in the historical record, this denunciation was concocted through a highly selective focus on certain episodes and pieces of evidence, construed in very particular ways. For example, there was no mention of the secret protocol, of Soviet–German diplomatic contacts through the 1930s or of the purges in the armed forces that arguably made the Soviet Union of dubious value as an alliance partner for the West. Moreover, relatively anodyne British aspirations in 1937 and 1938 for a general European settlement were interpreted as concrete evidence that London desired an anti-Soviet alliance with Berlin. (*Falsifiers* also initiated the elevation of the United States to the role of 'chief culprit in the Soviet historical indictment of the Allied role in the war'.) But the text was skilfully crafted to project a positive image of the regime for domestic and foreign consumption and to construct an external capitalist menace that might justify domestic hardship and renewed Stalinization. Lingering traces of pluralism in writing on this subject were eradicated by about 1950, as rigid Party discipline and the *Falsifiers* line were imposed upon the historical profession through the public denunciation of maverick scholars by their peers. Simultaneously, in broader terms, historians were discouraged from probing sensitive areas of recent history at all.[29] All this memory work contributed to buttressing a late-Stalinist sense of Soviet identity.

(The questions of how the regime decided to structure memory in this way and to what extent it succeeded in marginalizing counter-memories in its legitimation project are beyond the scope of this study. The former question, in any case, remains intractable for want of empirical evidence. The latter is being explored by a new generation of cultural historians that has made the fashioning of identity – class, national, gender, 'Soviet' – under socialism one of its chief preoccupations.[30] The idea of the Soviet Union as an omnipotent totalitarian state, able to manipulate an atomised population at will, no longer passes muster in the light of this work. It is equally implausible to contend that the myth of the Great Patriotic War was just a cynical sham, so at variance with private memories that it was utterly hollow. Much current scholarship stresses the significance of genuine ideological belief amongst Soviet leaders, and given its longevity and puissance the cult must also have resonated widely on an individual level. One important recent study stresses how 'the supra-class, cross-ethnic aspect of the myth provided the polity with a previously absent integrating theme and folded large groups previously excluded into the body politic': this success being achieved in large part because the myth left open 'symbolic space for the articulation of particularistic, albeit nonantagonistic' identities, and could thus be made to work for diverse social groups.[31])

Broadly speaking, *Falsifiers of History* provided the parameters and even much of the phraseology of all subsequent Soviet accounts: 'the consistency of the pre-1953, post-1953 and post-1964 versions is astonishing'.[32] Later renderings did, however, introduce new nuances as political priorities changed, for example after Khrushchev became the dominant figure in the post-Stalin leadership. Khrushchev harboured ambitious visions of achieving communism within a generation through modernising the Soviet system, stripping away its Stalinist excrescences and reinspiring the people with enthusiasm for Leninist ideals. But how could the Party confront and explain existing problems without undermining its own authority and legitimacy? Khrushchev's solution entailed rewriting the master narrative of Soviet history, hence his denunciation of Stalin in his 'secret speech' to the Twentieth Party Congress in February 1956.[33] In this address, he attacked Stalin's political record and character and the 'cult of personality' that had allowed him free rein to abuse power, but also argued that he had only strayed off the true Leninist path after 1934 (once collectivisation and crash industrialisation had established the fundamental features of the system), thus blaming the state's woes on Stalin while exonerating the system itself and the current generation of political leaders.[34]

The Great Patriotic War was one of the chief targets of this revisionism. Khrushchev savagely criticised Stalin's tendency to hog the credit for the final victory while shirking blame for the setbacks that had preceded it, and enumerated a catalogue of crimes and errors. Stalin had failed to take the true measure of fascism; almost fatally weakened the military through the purges; made poor use of the breathing space purchased by the Nazi–Soviet pact; ignored countless warnings of the imminent German attack in 1941; delayed mobilisation at the cost of countless lives; and persistently either failed to make timely decisions or ineptly intervened in the conduct of military affairs. The victory, Khrushchev argued, was due not to Stalin but to the whole Soviet nation, under the guiding leadership, of course, of the Party, and with a prodigious contribution from the military. According greater freedom of expression to the masses to unleash previously stifled energies and initiatives was a crucial plank in Khrushchev's reform programme, and the 'secret speech' clearly intimated that the ideological shackles on historical scholarship would now be loosened.[35]

Subsequently, the main lines of the established narrative remained in place but it was amended and supplemented. The military, angry at their marginalisation by Stalin, were in the van here; a host of memoirists documented the former leader's blunders, reaffirmed the significance of commanders and soldiers in the successful war effort and rehabilitated comrades purged in the 1930s.[36] Historians of international relations essayed similar revisions which culminated from 1960 onwards in the publication of the first major multi-volume official history of the war, embodying the Khrushchev era interpretation. Its treatment of the Nazi–Soviet pact, for example, was much more extensive and much more 'closely tied to a set of facts' than any previous account, even if it continued to present the familiar rationalisations and justifications, and to deny the existence of the secret protocol.[37] Aided by increased access to key western works on the war era, and the publication of more Soviet documentary material, the trend was towards a more open and deeply textured treatment.[38] The basic thrust was still to celebrate the achievement of the Soviet state, but this was no longer a litany of unrelieved perfection; errors and setbacks could be confronted, though they were largely blamed on Stalin, in accordance with the political exigencies of the Khrushchev era.

There always remained definite limits to this revisionism, however, and the latitude granted in these years proved temporary. Conservative vested interests, anxious that reform was indeed threatening Party authority, forced

Khrushchev from office in 1964. A collective leadership ultimately dominated by Leonid Brezhnev succeeded him, and steered a new consensual course of consolidation, eschewing dramatic innovation and the attainment of communism as an urgent goal. In retrospect, the shift towards lauding 'actually existing socialism' has been deemed portentous, proving the system was essentially unreformable and dooming it to sclerosis and collapse. It certainly represented a decision to maintain the essence of the Stalinist system in terms of rule by a privileged bureaucratic class, the militarised command economy, and police state control. The historiographical analogue to this policy shift was a further adjustment of the master narrative to offer a more uniformly positive, if somewhat anodyne, vision of the national past. Criticism of Stalin thus became much more muted, and contentious issues such as the Great Terror once more faded from view. If Stalin was not quite rehabilitated in the 1960s there was certainly an end to the anti-Stalin campaign, and by the 1970s it could be argued that 'he had been restored as an admirable leader'.[39] Though it took some time for the new line to be disseminated amongst the historical profession, and while all the gains made during the thaw could not be clawed back, there was a perceptible tightening of the ideological screws to ensure future conformism.

The concrete implications of this for writing on the origins of the war are illustrated by the Aleksandr Nekrich affair. Nekrich was a war veteran and respected member of the Academy of Sciences Institute of History who in October 1965 published *June 22, 1941*, a study of the domestic, diplomatic and military antecedents of the war and its disastrous first phase.[40] It might well be difficult for a casual reader to appreciate why this text caused a controversy. It had been approved by state, Party and military censors, was replete with ritualistic Stalinist phraseology and indicted the western powers for inciting Germany against the Soviet Union and thus frustrating hopes for the formation of an anti-fascist coalition. It did not broach deeply taboo issues such as the secret protocol and it defended the territorial annexations in the Baltic and elsewhere on security grounds. Even the sections heavily critical of Stalin and Soviet preparations for war were broadly in line with Khrushchev's own pronouncements. For example, Nekrich argued that 'the cult of personality led to serious mistakes in the decision of a number of political and strategic questions on the eve of war and in the course of military operations against Hitler's Germany', but he quoted from official sources to support this statement while also admitting some positive contributions from Stalin and praising the progressive domestic developments that had led to the creation of a superior 'state of a new kind'.[41] He further concluded that despite setbacks victory was ultimately achieved thanks to 'the military and economic might of the state', 'the mass heroism of the Soviet soldiers' and the 'inexhaustible bravery, unprecedented heroism, and supreme readiness for self-sacrifice' of the people, 'unified and directed' by the Party.[42]

Whether Nekrich actually transgressed the Khrushchev-era orthodoxy remains a moot point, but it was also ultimately irrelevant since by the time his book was published the ideological climate had hardened. Moreover, it was the reception the book enjoyed as much as anything that marked this out as an exemplary case through which a new line could be promulgated. In February 1966 leading historians and military figures in the Division of the History of the Great Fatherland War of the Institute of Marxism-Leninism held a roundtable discussion on the book. Many participants insisted that Nekrich had not gone far enough; one argued that, taking Stalin's errors as given, it was chiefly necessary to 'analyze the process which allowed Stalin, who was not equal to his task, to become head of the party and the state, with unlimited powers'.[43] Thus, as Nekrich later recalled, the discussion in effect served as 'a critique of the functioning of the Soviet system in both normal and exceptional circumstances, and of its political and military leaders', and as evidence that 'historians were realizing that the main reason for our unpreparedness for the war was the system of unlimited arbitrary power'.[44] Some of the charges Nekrich made in his text – such as when Stalin's failure to heed myriad warnings of Hitler's aggressive intentions was attributed to his 'unrealistic concept of international relations' – certainly could be read as attacks on the system itself, even upon the precepts of Marxism-Leninism.[45] When transcripts of this discussion subsequently appeared in the western media and such implications were drawn out by commentators, Nekrich was subject to a disciplinary investigation and ultimately expelled from the Party for 'deliberate distortion' in a text 'used by foreign reactionary propaganda for anti-Soviet purposes'.[46]

In 1967 Nekrich was assailed in the pages of one of the most authoritative Soviet historical journals, and the parameters for future work were laid down with pointed reference to recent political edicts interpreting the Soviet past. The fundamental charge was indicated by the title given the denunciation, 'in the ideological captivity of the falsifiers of history'. Nekrich had 'betrayed the scientific principles of Marxist historiography' by confining his treatment to the antecedents and early disastrous period of the war, without any counter-balancing discussion of the later successes leading to victory or sufficient analysis of the building of socialism in the 1930s. This decision was not politically neutral since it focused attention on negative factors of a 'temporary character', whilst neglecting positive ones 'of decisive significance'; failing to acknowledge how the superiority of the Soviet system and the operation of objective historical laws eventually 'made the victory of the USSR inevitable' was quite inadmissible. Beyond this, and as testimony to the more sophisticated state of post-1953 Soviet historiography, numerous detailed points were addressed: Nekrich had misrepresented the nature of the Nazi–Soviet pact (as offering no real benefit to Moscow); interpreted the policy of Britain and the United States too positively (that is, 'from a non-class position'); and failed to appreciate the good reasons that Stalin had for doubting intelligence about the imminent German invasion (largely relating to the dubious *bona fides* of its British sources). But there were also meaningful silences as, for example, no reference at all was made to Nekrich's arguments about the purges or their effect on the military.[47] Although Nekrich was not deprived of his post at the Institute of History, he was subsequently harassed to such an extent that in 1976 he went into exile.

This third, Brezhnevite, variant of the orthodox interpretation remained dominant until the 1980s. The war was still caused by the contradictions of capitalism – 'imperialism was the true culprit' – and Soviet policy had '"persistently worked for a system of collective security which could have bridled the aggressors and prevented a second world war"' while Britain and France 'continued to pursue a policy of collusion with the aggressive states, dubbed the Munich policy'.[48] But, on the one hand, the errors that had been confronted under Khrushchev were airbrushed out of the picture, and the best possible gloss was once more placed on the Nazi–Soviet pact, subsequent territorial annexations and the Red Army's performance in the early part of the conflict (as achieving a 'result of paramount importance: they frustrated the strategic concept of the Nazi leadership – to effect a lightning-like rout of the Soviet Union').[49] On the other hand, there was no return to 1940s hagiography: Stalin drifted much more into the background in comparison to the central part as hero or villain that he had previously played. This interpretation was encapsulated in authoritative official publications dealing with the history of Soviet foreign policy (often co-authored by policy-makers such as long time Foreign Minister Andrei Gromyko) and in a new multi-volume history of the Second World War supplanting the previous one produced under Khrushchev.[50]

True, this period was marked by cross currents. It has been argued that 'the trend towards elaborating a more sophisticated historiography of the origins of World War II and the publication of more archival material continued unabated'. Many works appearing during these years were more detailed than anything previously published, the major series *Dokumenty Vneshnei Politiki SSSR* progressed to revealing material on the 1930s, and it was complemented by other collections, including in 1971 a two-volume edition detailing *Soviet Peace Efforts on the Eve of World War II*, though these were of course edited to buttress the official line.[51] But this progress was both tightly circumscribed and apt to be interrupted. *Dokumenty Vneshnei Politiki SSSR* abruptly ceased publication after the 1977 volume that covered the year of Munich, leaving the delicate and sensitive events of 1939 comparatively obscure, while a second edition of *Soviet Peace Efforts* appearing in 1976 was much truncated;[52] moreover, archival access was 'considerably restricted', with access 'to higher party and government archives ceas[ing] altogether'. The basic line established in official works was sacrosanct: not only was it impermissible for historians or memoirists dealing with the war to deviate from it in matters of interpretation, but 'authors were even told that they could not publish information about the war unless it had already been published or stated elsewhere'.[53]

The conformity imposed upon historians of this subject made perfect sense within the broader context of the Brezhnev regime's legitimation strategies. It was during these years that there emerged the full-blown cult of the Great

Patriotic War. In 1965 Victory Day was designated a full public holiday for the first time since 1946, museums and gargantuan memorial statues sprang up across the country, and the reiteration of the lessons of the war was stitched into the activities of youth organisations and schools. Newly-wed couples were even encouraged to make obeisance at their local memorial on the journey from wedding ceremony to reception. Generational change and incipient disenchantment with the politics of stagnation compelled the regime to exploit all possible sources of legitimacy to forestall apathy and cynicism. Having abandoned the dynamic pursuit of heroic future goals, it sought to capitalise on a putatively glorious past and the inspirational deeds of earlier generations as the ideological glue to hold the empire together; thus the cult of history became the prime means to instil faith and loyalty in the population.[54] Writers on the origins of the war had their part to play in this project, as evidenced not least by the frequency with which their texts found contemporary parallels with the 1930s and issued hortatory warnings about the continuing threat from imperialism.[55]

'Not only an illegal document, but an amoral one': glasnost and the Nazi-Soviet pact

The accession to power of Mikhail Gorbachev in 1985 signalled the beginning of the end for the Soviet cult of the Great Patriotic War. Gorbachev embarked on a bold reform project to modernise, restructure and reinvigorate the Soviet system and to overcome the dire consequences of two decades of stagnation, and even if the precise goals of his programme were inconsistent and apt to change over time, reform necessarily entailed further adjustment of authorised readings of the past. By the later 1980s, he had gone even further than Khrushchev in rejecting the legacy of Stalinism, and in harking back to the 1920s – construed as an era of humane democratic socialism and the mixed economy of the New Economic Policy (NEP) – as the model to which the polity should aim to return. Simultaneously, he encouraged the filling in of 'blank pages' in the historical record and more open discussion of previous crimes and errors in order to mobilise popular enthusiasm for Leninist ideals and to break the power of conservative vested interests. This unleashed a ferment of historical controversy about all the sensitive aspects of the Soviet past and for several years fundamental political questions about the state's future were articulated through historical arguments. (Historians for some time lagged behind novelists, filmmakers and other cultural commentators in exploring these newfound freedoms, but eventually did make a distinctive contribution.)

Ultimately, Gorbachev proved unable to control either the consequences of reform or the parameters of historical revisionism. In both realms, he sought to construct and hold a centre ground between Stalinist conservatives, resisting both socio-economic and political change and the destruction of positive evaluations of the Soviet past, and free market democrats, advocating wholesale transformation of the system and rejecting not just Stalin but Lenin and the entire 'socialist choice' of October 1917. But as the country lurched into economic crisis, the viability of Gorbachev's mooted reformed socialism was cast into serious doubt just as the positive Leninist lineage that he sought was washed away by the torrent of historical revisionism. To the very end, the legitimacy and fate of the regime were intimately bound up with its capacity to control readings of its own past. As Gorbachev's centre ground evaporated and nationalist discontent from the constituent republics led to their secession, in 1991 the Soviet Union simply ceased to exist.[56]

Contested memories of the Great Patriotic War and its origins occupied a central place in the historical controversies of these years. In May 1985 Victory Day was celebrated with the now customary parades and pomp, and in his speech Gorbachev did not depart from the established formulae in explaining the sources of Soviet triumph, even according Stalin personally a share of credit.[57] But over the next two years as reform began to make headway, understandings of the conflict 'changed radically'.[58] The criticisms of Stalin's political and military conduct of the war canvassed under Khrushchev were resuscitated in even stronger form; the experiences of ordinary soldiers began to be discussed in a much grimmer and more realistic light than hitherto; and critics argued that victory, far from vindicating the system, had actually been achieved in spite of Stalinism, not least because of the disastrous effect of the pre-war purges. Countervailing arguments were not entirely absent; Stalinist conservatives, Russian nationalists not necessarily attached to communism but keen to retain a sense of pride in the past achievements of state and people, and senior historians with a vested professional interest all spoke up for orthodox views, but constituted a definite rearguard action.[59]

The key issue over which the war cult came to be challenged was that of the Nazi–Soviet pact. This had always been one of the most vulnerable points in the orthodox narrative, not because of the way in which it was presented as necessary for Soviet security and forced upon Stalin by western intransigence (an interpretation defensible in the light of the evidence), but rather because the suppression of the very existence of the secret protocol involved a denial of facts that had been well known in the West since at least the Nuremberg trials. Once greater freedom of expression was permitted to historians and information began to flow a little more freely between East and West, this act of concealment was almost bound to be subject to scrutiny. Yet revelation of the secret protocol would be explosive. On the one hand, it would expose the regime's mendacity and the hollowness of its claim to be the champion of a consistent anti-imperialist foreign policy, thus providing grist to the mill of Russian reformers anxious to undermine Soviet legitimacy. On the other hand, it would cast doubt on the legality of the incorporation of the Baltic states and Bessarabia (the then Soviet Republic of Moldavia) into the Union, which would strengthen the hand of nationalist groups in those and other constituent republics eager to assert their autonomy from Moscow. This episode thus illustrates not just debates between pro- and anti-reform elements in the

Russian centre, but also how a plurality of new nationalist readings arose in the republics as the Soviet master narrative fragmented.[60]

During protest demonstrations on 23 August 1987, the anniversary of the pact, nationalist groups in the Baltic states began to demand publication of the secret protocol and revelation of the true circumstances surrounding their 'annexation' by the Soviet Union. Given what was at stake, this was one of Stalin's acts that Gorbachev was extremely reluctant to abjure.[61] On the seventieth anniversary of the October revolution later that year, in a speech generally regarded as 'a breathtakingly critical review of the Soviet regime's troubled history', he robustly defended the pact (as having thwarted western plans to turn Hitler eastwards) and continued implicitly to deny the existence of the protocol.[62] Within the Baltic states, however, historians and journalists 'systematically picked apart the standard interpretation of the events of 1939–40' in a manner that had revolutionary implications; whereas in Moscow it was possible to separate socialism from Stalin by turning back to Lenin, if Soviet absorption of the Baltic states in 1940 was shown to be rooted not in indigenous socialist revolution, but in a Stalinist bargain with Hitler and Red Army brute force, then socialism itself would be profoundly discredited there.[63]

In August 1988 Baltic reformist newspapers published the texts of the secret protocol for the first time on Soviet soil, and the forty-ninth anniversary was marked by massive popular demonstrations. Although the state-controlled press in the wider Union did not publicise these events, historians did enter the lists. The reform minded, such as Mikhail Semiriaga, decried the whole settlement with Hitler using what had always been the most plausible counter-argument to the official line: not only was the secret protocol morally reprehensible, the non-aggression pact itself was a political miscalculation that adversely affected the Soviet Union's strategic position and foreclosed the genuine alternative of alliance with the West ('the Soviet leadership ... shut the wrong door'). Conversely, conservatives such as Aleksandr Orlov and Stephan Tiushkevich continued to discount the existence of the protocol (intoning familiar charges of falsification) and to defend the pact as a regrettable necessity forced on Stalin by the behaviour of Britain and France ('there was no alternative').[64] These arguments tended to correlate with their proponents' views not just on domestic reform but also on foreign policy, the former camp supporting Gorbachev's 'common European home' openings towards the West, the latter viewing them as capitulationist.[65] In the space between these poles numerous compromise positions emerged, including that of Dimitrii Volkogonov, one of the most important historians during and after the transition to post-communism as he himself mutated from loyal establishment propagandist into hardened critic of all things Soviet. In his landmark 1989 biography of Stalin, he argued that the secret protocol 'gave a distinctly negative character to an otherwise forced and perhaps necessary step'.[66]

By 1989 maintenance of the orthodox line was becoming untenable. Historians were boldly discussing the secret protocol and pressure from the

Polish government and Baltic nationalists – particularly the vocal delegates to the new Congress of People's Deputies elected in March 1989 – was intensifying. The regime had already conducted an internal archival investigation, but in June a special commission for the 'political and legal assessment of the Soviet–German Pact' was appointed by the Congress. The proceedings of the commission were heated, since its members reflected the full spectrum of opinions, and when it finally reported in December 1989 its overall conclusion – approved by the majority in the Congress and probably shared by Gorbachev – was a compromise; the secret protocol (officially acknowledged for the first time) was condemned as illegal and immoral, but the pact was deemed justified in the circumstances then prevailing. Many historians shared this position at this point, but it was nonetheless contentious. Conservatives within the Congress were reluctant to cast any doubt on the legitimacy of Stalinist diplomacy, while the more radical reformers believed that to seek justification for the pact in geopolitical exigency was to whitewash Stalin's true imperialist ambitions. By this point, in any event, copies of the texts of the agreements had already been reproduced in the official journal *International Affairs*, and during 1990 extensive new documentary material on the last year of peace was published (though it was not until 1992 that the original Soviet texts were unearthed in the archives).[67]

The regime's authority over the past was now slipping away. In the Baltic states, Moldavia and many of the other republics anti-Soviet nationalist narratives were emerging to ground new senses of separatist consciousness. (Thus when asked at a reform movement conference in October 1988 what would be the new face of Lithuanian historiography, one historian replied that 'in the future readers would know that the authors were Lithuanian'.[68]) Within Russia, Gorbachev's efforts to treat the late Lenin of the NEP as a guiding light proved increasingly vain, as radicals like Boris Yeltsin argued that better models were 'the semiconstitutional czarism of 1905' and the last Tsar's famous reforming Prime Minister Pyotr Stolypin,[69] while embattled conservatives became increasingly vociferous in their resistance to modification of the orthodox Soviet account.

On Victory Day 1990, Gorbachev attempted to stabilise the disintegrating war cult. In an unprecedented fashion, his speech stressed the tragic dimensions of the war and its colossal costs, invoking patriotism rather than socialism, and focusing on the experiences and contributions of ordinary Soviet citizens rather than the Party. He critiqued Soviet diplomatic and military preparations for war, and admitted to many setbacks and mistakes, thus vainly attempting to rework the myth for his own ends and to rally what he praised as a people 'capable of overcoming any difficulties and resolving any problems' behind his reform programme.[70] In a similar vein, establishment historians continued to attempt to hold onto a compromise position: hence the attempt to explain the (defensible) pact and the (criminal) secret protocol as products of two separate strands in foreign policy at the time, 'on the one hand, the Soviet Union's policy which reflected the socialist substance of this state, an open diplomatic line taken over from Lenin's period ... on the other hand, Stalin's anti-people policy oriented towards collusion and perfidy'.[71]

But the general trend was towards a polarisation and radicalisation of the debate. In March 1991, the first volume of a projected new (third) multi-volume history of the war that had been prepared by Volkogonov was the subject of an extraordinary critique in a meeting at the Ministry of Defence. Volkogonov's treatment encapsulated an increasingly critical reformist denunciation of Stalin's pre-war diplomacy. Such an account was anathema to the conservative military and political establishment, and Volkogonov was abused as a traitor and his work condemned as containing the 'outlines for an indictment' for a 'Nuremberg II on the Communist Party'. (Several of the participants in this meeting were to be prominent in the August 1991 conservative coup that in retrospect sealed the fate of communism.)[72] Moreover, the views of even moderate historians at this time became steadily radicalised as the legitimacy of the regime waned. Aleksandr Chubarian, for example, who in the late 1980s had held to the centrist line, criticising errors in Stalin's diplomacy whilst abjuring the more thoroughgoing criticisms of Semiriaga, was by the early 1990s prepared to bluntly characterise the Nazi–Soviet pact as 'not only an illegal document, but an amoral one as well'.[73]

The precise role that rethinking the Great Patriotic War and Soviet history generally played in the demise of the regime is open to debate. A perceptive journalist has argued that 'intellectually, politically, and morally' Gorbachev's 'history' speech of November 1987 played 'a critical role in undermining the Stalinist system of coercion and empire'.[74] Historians might prefer a more measured verdict that acknowledges the destabilising impact of the destruction of cherished historical assumptions but nonetheless recognises that 'contemporary experience of Soviet politics and economics was no doubt more important' in determining events and attitudes.[75] But since the regime had used representations of the past so overtly to instil loyalty for decades, it was scarcely surprising that debate about the future should be conducted using this same language. Each interest group – conservative, 'democratic socialist', radical free marketeer, nationalist – grounded its political programme in a distinctive historical vision, expressing attitudes towards the existing system and preferences for alternative forms of social and political identity through contrasting readings of key episodes in the Soviet past. So while historians were emancipated from the shackles of Marxism-Leninism in these years, the result was not the emergence of a simple truth to supplant a distorted and falsified Soviet master narrative (however much partisans of particular positions tended, for emotional and strategic reasons, to present matters in this way); rather, the loosening of ideological control permitted the articulation of a range of interpretations, each no less interested than the former hegemonic one.[76]

International historians were entirely implicated in this broader process. Since the 1940s, the regime had imposed a single narrative of the origins of the war and the pact that emphasised *realpolitik* necessity, Stalin's wisdom and the essential righteousness of a Soviet regime operating in an antagonistic capitalist world, and this position continued to be maintained by Stalinist conservatives. The denial of the existence of the secret protocol was always a hostage to fortune, however, and once freer debate was conceded it was naturally the point of departure for those wishing to unpick the Soviet narrative. Gradually, reformist and nationalist opposition turned to the most obvious alternative reading which, like a photographic negative, stressed instead the utter immorality of the pact, the folly of Stalin's diplomacy in the 1930s and thus, by extension, the criminality of the Soviet system as a whole. By the early 1990s, debate was polarised between these two extremes, as efforts to articulate a compromise between them (an analogue to Gorbachev's reformed socialism) were rendered untenable. Historians with pronounced political views, or active in the debates over reform, quite naturally evolved interpretations congenial to their own politics. But even those who conceived of themselves simply as disinterested scholars were shaped by these vibrant debates and their writings certainly exercised some agency within them during these last few years of the Soviet state, when the mass public was consuming history on an unprecedented scale 'with an animal hunger'.[77]

'The means of Soviet survival in a hostile world': the western gaze on the Soviet 1930s

Of course, it is no great revelation that historiography in the Soviet Union was in thrall to politics, that the regime made strategic use of representations of the war era and that a multiplicity of counter-histories with specific political connotations arose in the later 1980s. But it would be erroneous to suppose that in contrast historical scholarship in the West was value-free. Through this same period, western writing on the Soviet Union and the origins of the war was also shaped by identifiable political tensions. Moreover, it insistently engaged, albeit perhaps a little more subtly, with the problematic of Soviet identity that was centrally at stake in the Great Patriotic War myth. Granted, it was produced under quite different political, social and disciplinary conditions to Soviet scholarship, but it was structured around the same set of narrative options and was, *inter alia*, a debate about the nature and legitimacy of the Soviet state. Implicitly invoking Nazism as the reference point for twentieth century evil, what was essentially contested in arguments about the character of Stalin's diplomacy was the possibility of anti-fascist virtue in the Stalinist system.

The western gaze upon Russia has for centuries been freighted with ideological baggage. Far from simply gathering knowledge, western political, literary and academic observers have projected their own 'morbid fears, suppressed phobias and febrile imaginings' onto that territory, creating multiple stereotypical constructs of 'Russia' as an external other that simultaneously served to secure senses of self.[78] This was certainly evident during the early Cold War when foreign policy 'discourses of danger' about the Soviet East played a crucial role in fixing the internal and external dimensions of western identity.[79] It was at this point that the modern discipline of Russian/Soviet studies in the United States – the world powerhouse of the subject – was effectively invented, when federal government and private foundations poured money into this budding branch of academe, ensuring that the production of 'usable scholarship ("applied research") in America's national interest' lay at the heart of its mission. This did not of course mean that every scholar in the field was a doctrinaire lackey of the military-industrial complex, but it did make it 'a highly politicized profession imbued with topical political concerns, a crusading spirit, and a know-the-enemy raison d'être'.[80]

Little wonder that the dominant interpretive paradigm in post-war Soviet studies so suited the political interests of the West in the Cold War. The concept of totalitarianism yoked fascist, Nazi and communist states together as exemplars of a particular type of modern revolutionary regime, characterised by a chiliastic and expansionist ideology, political dominance of a single mass party, monopoly of mass communications and armed force, centralised command economy and terroristic police control. It was codified in the post-war years in political and academic discourse and did not merely reflect but also helped to shape ideological Cold War confrontation. On this view, Stalin was rapacious and evil, a kindred spirit to Hitler, and driven to restless expansion by the need for external enemies to excuse harsh domestic repression and the 'indefinite deferral of the utopian promises of Marxism'. This interpretation offered ample justification for a robust policy of containment abroad (as defensive of threatened democratic freedoms) and the creation of the national security state at home, as anti-Nazi energies were channelled into waging a new conflict.[81] 'Totalitarianism was the great mobilizing and unifying concept of the Cold War ... It provided a plausible and frightening vision of a Manichaean, radically bifurcated world in which the leaders of the free world would have to struggle (until victory was won) or perish.'[82] (Simultaneously, in the United States, the objectivity paradigm was vigorously reasserted within history after a prolonged inter-war flirtation with 'relativism'; this too contributed to fortifying the West by positing a sharp distinction between 'our' scientific truth and 'their' debased ideological practices.[83]) 'Utilizing the concept of totalitarianism was thus a patriotic, political gesture as well as a methodological preference'.[84]

While not slavish adherents to the totalitarianism model, historians of the Soviet Union nonetheless partook of its critical perspective upon communism. According to their post-war consensus, October 1917 was a terroristic *coup d'état* and Bolshevik leaders with unbroken continuity from Lenin to Stalin had ruthlessly established a dictatorship according to an inexorable political logic that naturally culminated in the cruel excesses of Stalinism. This sensibility dominated the field until the 1970s when a new generation of historians emerged, inspired by *détente*, internal developments in the Soviet Union that seemed incompatible with 'totalitarianism' and the cultural climate of the post-Vietnam United States. These revisionists were armed with new methodological tools derived from social history and essayed a 'history from below', arguing that the Soviet experiment could not be comprehended solely in terms of elite manipulation and terror (probing the extent of popular support for the October Revolution was a characteristic preoccupation), and explored alternative paths of development that were not taken, casting doubt on the presumed ineluctable affinity between Lenin and Stalin. These two perspectives were clearly predicated not only upon different methodological and philosophical commitments, but also upon drastically contrasting beliefs about the nature of the Soviet system, as was at least implicitly acknowledged by their proponents during often fiercely polemical debates in which the epithets 'cold warrior' and 'fellow traveller' were apt to be bandied about. (In the 1990s, the collapse of the USSR gave a considerable fillip to totalitarianist interpretations, though the now cutting-edge cultural historians challenge the assumptions of both previous schools of thought.)[85]

International historians working on Soviet policy in the 1930s were, to an extent, institutionally and intellectually detached from these mainstream Soviet studies debates; but the two opposing narratives around which their deliberations revolved had similar political inspirations and entailments. First, there was the thesis of the 'German school', given one of its initial full articulations in *Nazi–Soviet Relations*, itself a foundational text of totalitarianism. On this view, Stalin's eventual alignment with Hitler was not merely strategically wrongheaded and immoral: it was the consummation of a profoundly Machiavellian, expansionist and revolutionary ideological project. The Popular Front line was never more than a feint or an insurance policy, concealing the persistent prime goal of securing agreement with Nazi Germany in order to plunge the capitalist world into enervating internecine conflict from which the Soviet Union could profit. Ranged against this view was the 'collective security school' interpretation, in substance a more moderate and empirically secure version of the orthodox Soviet narrative. Although Stalin was obviously a communist, he pursued a pragmatic defensive line through the 1930s, and sincerely laboured to concert an anti-fascist coalition; the vacillation and pusillanimity of Britain and France in refusing such cooperation ultimately compelled him to turn with regret to the German option, which he did only in July or August 1939.[86] Of course, within these two schools of thought many different viewpoints can be discerned; equally, there is scope for compromise between them, as in the work of an 'internal politics school' that interprets conflicting strands in Soviet policy as evidence of dispute between pro-German and pro-western policy-makers.[87] But the conflict between these two starkly opposed interpretations has nonetheless structured the field for six decades.[88]

The politics of these two perspectives can easily be elucidated. 'German school' authors approach their subject with a profoundly negative and (at least weakly) totalitarianist image of the communist experiment, in terms of its unrelieved internal wickedness and external affinity with Nazi Germany. Hence Robert Tucker's argument that 'Stalin's German orientation was not rooted in anything personal. It belonged to his Bolshevik political culture and the legacy of Lenin ... August 1939 represented the fruition of Stalin's whole complex conception of the means of Soviet survival in a hostile world and emergence into a commanding international position'.[89] It was no coincidence that some adherents to this view were exiles from the Soviet bloc with personal experiences that made them antipathetic towards communism, such as Jiri Hochman, 'a veteran of the "Prague Spring" who emigrated to avoid further imprisonment after the Soviet crackdown';[90] nor that others were prominent as conservative commentators on contemporary Soviet affairs such as the ubiquitous diplomat, historian and pundit, George Kennan.[91]

'Collective security school' interpretations, conversely, are predicated upon a much more positive image of the Soviet state. Rather than casting it as an inherently threatening antagonist, doomed to partnership with Hitler by its barbarous ideology, this perspective countenances the possibility that Stalin's approach to statecraft, 'when stripped of its Marxist-Leninist jargon, was the traditional balance of power policy': thus the Soviet Union was potentially available as a partner in an anti-Nazi alliance but for the anti-communist prejudices of western policy-makers.[92] This argument, in turn, was not uncommonly advanced by left-leaning, liberal or radical authors, including A. J. P. Taylor.[93] (The image underpinning the 'internal politics school' is similarly relatively positive, as it stresses defensive motivations, rejects the totalitarianist notion of Soviet policy-making as monolithic and presumes that elements within it advocated working with the West against Hitler, thus implying at least the possibility of anti-fascist integrity.) But even where it is not possible to correlate authors' arguments with their life histories or overt political investments, all western historians through the Cold War were here working within a discourse that was ideologically radioactive.[94]

This point can be better appreciated if we consider the implications of their arguments. Of course, this scholarship was not directly involved in the sustaining or undermining of identity amongst the Soviet people, though it did speak precisely to the question of how justified Soviet leaders were in grounding their self-understanding and domestic legitimacy in an anti-fascist heritage. But the conflicting views of the Soviet Union built into these interpretations did carry prescriptions for contemporary western policy that were part and parcel of broader discourses about western identity and the values by which we should live.[95]

From the perspective of the mid-1980s, after the rhetoric of a resurgent neo-conservatism had once more branded the Soviet Union as totalitarian, if not 'the focus of evil in the modern world', this seemed self-evident.[96] The historical argument that Soviet policy in the 1930s had been aggressive, treacherous and ideological (in the pejorative sense) fit the image of that state in the present as '*by nature* expansionist, armed to the teeth, disposed to violence, fond of diplomatic tests of will, and ... hard to deter and harder to beat'. Policy preferences flowed from this mode of thinking, specifically a conservative domestic social and economic agenda and 'ambitious strategic nuclear counterforce ("warfighting") postures' abroad to counter a Soviet

Union 'willing to take high risks for the sake of expansion'. Conversely, the argument that Moscow had in the face of Hitler been motivated far more by defensive considerations complemented the image of it as 'a fairly typical great power whose behaviour in international politics can be explained by the mixture of fear, greed, and stupidity that has characterised most great powers in the past as they have tried to secure their borders and pursue their interests in a world without law'. This Soviet Union, 'more conservative than reckless', could thus be countered with a more liberal strategy, namely 'deterrence based largely on a policy of countervalue retaliation', since it would not be likely 'to bet that a collapse of Western will would neutralize the huge retaliatory destructive power that could survive any Soviet nuclear offensive'.[97]

'Purblind ideologue' or 'cautious and pragmatic'? The postcommunist Great Patriotic War

It could be argued that the highly politicised state of the historical writing discussed above was anomalous. Perhaps the contentious nature of the Soviet experiment and its universalist emancipatory claims, the political urgencies generated by Cold War confrontation, and the relative paucity of available Soviet primary sources conspired to make this a field peculiarly prone to ideological partisanship and the proliferation of conflicting, self-interested, interpretations? Comparative exploration of how writing on the war's origins in other cases was also bound up, albeit in different ways, with the politics of collective memory and national identity, follows in subsequent chapters. But the impact of the dramatic changes attendant on the end of the Cold War on these historiographical debates also suggests that such an argument would be too simplistic.

The fading of Cold War division between Soviet and western traditions, together with increasing access to Soviet bloc documentation in published editions and archives, may one day perhaps lead to a decisive 'paradigm shift' or the absolute resolution of some long contentious questions. Equally, despite 'the enormous accretion of knowledge that has resulted from the opening up of the Soviet archives', much crucial material remains unavailable.[98] But at an interpretive level there has been remarkable continuity over the last 20 years, with archival revelations often serving chiefly to perpetuate old arguments that still carry their Cold War charge. Claims that the collapse of the Soviet Union has taken the ideological and ethical heat out of its historiography by making 'the question of being "for" or "against" it irrelevant' are at the very least premature, on the evidence of writing on Soviet foreign relations.[99] Similarly, changing perspectives and new archival evidence may be said to have created 'an extraordinarily unstable historical landscape' where the literature on 'Russia's war' in general is concerned;[100] but in writing on the origins of that conflict, although it has become ritualistic for authors to privilege their own accounts by asserting that with Cold War polemics a thing of the past we – or rather they – can now arrive at more definitive and less politicised explanations, 'the basic lines of interpretation and the debates among them have not been fundamentally altered'.[101]

On the one hand, strong 'German school' arguments were given a perceptible fillip as part and parcel of a general upsurge of triumphalist conservative commentary after 1991.[102] For example, R. C. Raack has argued that the policy of Stalin – 'the Soviet Fuhrer' – was 'utterly ruthless and in no way defensive', with the Molotov–Ribbentrop pact designed 'as the first step in a Bolshevik *Drang nach Westen*' since the lengthy Anglo-Franco-German war it presaged would breed revolutionary ferment that the Red Army could then exploit.[103] In a similar vein, Aleksandr Nekrich has dubbed the assumption that the Soviet Union would only enter the fray – to revolutionary effect – once the capitalist powers had exhausted themselves, the 'Stalin doctrine'. For Nekrich, Stalin's preference was always for an arrangement with Germany, and dabbling with collective security was intended to pressurise Hitler, provide a measure of insurance lest he failed to modify his anti-Soviet attitude, and envenom relations between the western powers and Germany, thus making a debilitating inter-imperialist war all the more likely. In explaining Stalin's pro-German orientation, Nekrich adduced a certain sort of trade unionist affinity between autocrats ('the thinking and behaviour of a German dictator probably seemed more comprehensible than the mentality of politicians from democratic states') and, in classic totalitarianist mode, 'the genetic bonds between the Soviet and Nazi regimes'.[104] The political positioning of individual authors such as Nekrich, exemplifying the perennial phenomenon of émigré hostility, is fairly transparent; but the prominence of these arguments in western historiographical discourse after 1991 demonstrates more generally that the end of the Cold War has not diminished the potential for sustaining conservative political identities through unsympathetic engagement with the Soviet past.

On the other hand, the 'collective security school' case has also been vigorously restated. Gabriel Gorodetsky's authoritative study of the two years before the launch of Operation Barbarossa is empirically rich, drawing on a number of East European and Russian archives, and indicative of how new materials are thickening our knowledge. For Gorodetsky, 'Stalin was little affected by sentiment or ideology in the pursuit of foreign policy': 'it would be a mistake to attribute Soviet foreign policy in the wake of the Molotov–Ribbentrop pact either to the whims of a tyrant or to relentless ideological expansionism', for it was rather 'an unscrupulous *Realpolitik* serving well-defined geopolitical interests', expansionist but in line with the traditional goals of Tsarist foreign policy (responding 'to imperatives deep within its history'). Gorodetsky's treatment is not uncritical of Stalin, since his misapprehensions and miscalculations on the eve of the German invasion constitute the 'grand delusion' of the book's title; but it is in this context broadly positive: 'and yet, even with hindsight, it is hard to devise alternatives which Stalin could have safely pursued'.[105] Similarly, Michael Carley has published a study of Anglo-Franco–Soviet relations before the war that identifies visceral western anti-communism as the chief impediment to the creation of an effective, war fighting anti-Nazi alliance, making it one of the most important causes of the Second World War. Carley's work has proved controversial, partly because of its brisk plain-speaking narrative form, but also because of its unwavering moralistic tone; it is a story 'about moral depravity and blindness, about villains and cowards, and about heroes who stood against the intellectual and popular tides of their time' (that is, in advocating a multilateral alliance against Nazism).[106]

The debate engendered by Carley's text revealed that the central issue between these two schools remained how to correctly perceive the nature of the Soviet Union. For Carley and his supporters, Stalin was 'not a purblind ideologue', 'not driven by ambitions for world communist domination', but 'cautious and pragmatic', fearing general war as likely to unleash counter-revolutionary forces that would destroy Soviet socialism.[107] For critics, this view misrepresents the 'inescapable ideological straitjacket' within which Stalin operated, ignores his conviction that 'collective security was bound to fail according to the Marxist laws of historical development' (that foresaw inexorably rising contradictions within the capitalist and fascist camps),[108] and disregards the evidence that Stalin signed the Nazi–Soviet pact in order to precipitate European war and social revolution. So, while for Carley Stalin was available as an alliance partner against fascism, for his critics – such as Igor Lukes, another Czech émigré – this view rests on 'an extremely idealistic portrait of the Stalinist Soviet Union': 'it was the nature of the Soviet Union, the values it stood for, its domestic and international *modus operandi*, and the conduct of its leader ... that ... rendered an alliance between Great Britain, France, and the Soviet Union impossible'.[109]

For all the complexity of the interpretive points at issue, and the recent expansion of our factual knowledge, this is an argument that has echoed down the years from the 1930s. At bottom, what is still in dispute is whether it was Carley's Grand Alliance-advocating heroes or his appeasing villains who had the better measure of Stalin, but that issue is then overlaid with layers of sedimented Cold War argument about the Soviet state. In classic 'practical realist' mode, the protagonists tend to express their disagreements with reference to the evidence: 'collective security school' partisans accuse Carley's 'German school' critics of ignoring the 'THOUSANDS of Soviet diplomatic documents' that support his argument, while those same critics charge that Carley relies too much on untrustworthy – because tendentiously edited – published Soviet documentary collections.[110] The issue of authors' political investments haunts these exchanges, with all perceiving ideological blinkers as a problem for their opponents. For Lukes, Carley's arguments are invalid not least because they simply reproduce the self-serving and obfuscating rhetoric of Soviet diplomats in the 1930s and of 'all Stalinist and Brezhnevite pamphlets [produced] during the Cold War'.[111] For Carley, Lukes' arguments are 'perhaps explained by the desire of a Czech émigré to carry on the cold war against the Czech communist left'.[112] In effect, both sides accuse the other of treating as deficient or inadequate any evidence that does not accord with their prejudices, or of indulging in readings that are 'self-serving in [their] reaffirmation of pre-existing ideological and political preconceptions'.[113]

An external observer is apt to conclude that every judgment about the empirical record of Soviet diplomacy in the 1930s involves ideological considerations, and is conditioned by assumptions external to that evidence about the nature of the Soviet Union and the communist experiment.[114] In that sense, both sides are simultaneously right – and wrong. Smoking guns are very seldom found in archives, and the capacity of empirical evidence to determine interpretations is sorely limited when historians are approaching it with widely divergent ideological assumptions. Consequently, narrowly conceived iterations of what 'the documents' may or may not legitimately be held to mean will never resolve this dispute, since broader historiographical and philosophical issues and indeed personal political and emotional investments are actually at stake. At bottom, 'German school' authors are simply not prepared to countenance the possibility of anti-fascist virtue in either the Soviet system or its foreign policy; conversely, while 'collective security school' historians by no means whitewash the brutalities and crimes of Stalinism, they can conceive that Stalin pursued a virtuous foreign policy. The fact that this field is still structured around these two opposing politicised views strongly suggests that, for many international historians at least, Cold War antagonisms remain alive.[115]

This point holds despite numerous recent efforts to articulate compromise positions that transcend the ideology-*realpolitik* binary. Professing a desire to slough off 'presentist' concerns and rejecting the notion of 'pure *Realpolitik*', these authors also embody the quotidian scholarly dynamic whereby interpretive progress and professional kudos are sought via the synthesis of prevailing dichotomised interpretations. From such a perspective, 'Soviet policy is seen to stem from an ideological view of the world, but an ideology with sufficient flexibility in its practical implementation to enable Moscow to pursue many possible lines of action'.[116] Communism must be taken seriously as a determinant of Stalin's foreign policy – since, for example, he assumed the pervasive hostility of all the capitalist powers and the need to keep them divided, as well as 'the inevitability of capitalist crises and imperialist wars' – without consequently deeming him the prisoner of an irrational and fanatical world view; 'complex and contradictory', Stalin 'was a realist and a pragmatist as well as an ideologue'.[117] His desire to avoid entanglement in a European war produced the Nazi–Soviet pact, 'the result of a combination of ideology and realism in Soviet political culture: an ideological view of the outside world centred on the idea that historical events would repeat themselves on the pattern of World War I; and a realistic approach to great-power policy essentially following the blueprint of the nineteenth-century struggle for mastery in Europe'.[118] Yet this synthetic gesture is unlikely to allay debate, since its iterations are by no means entirely congruent and it remains unclear yet how far they really do more than nuance the 'collective security school' line. Moreover, the temper and tenor of some robust responses betray an ingrained resistance to any form of positive revisioning of Soviet foreign policy, with the issues of the iniquities of Stalinism and responsibility for the Cold War still lurking at its heart.[119]

Developments in the former Soviet Union over this same period illustrate even more explicitly how debating that state's nature through writing its history remained a means for advancing political projects and grounding identity. Within Russia, the years immediately after 1991 were characterised by 'a euphoric and total repudiation of the Soviet past', a natural analogue to the optimistic belief that a rapid painless transition to capitalist democracy was possible.[120] Simultaneously, the concept of totalitarianism, imported from the West, enjoyed a substantial vogue as commentators struggled to historicise the Soviet experience within broader contexts in Russian and European history, and comparisons of communism and Nazism became commonplace.[121] A natural corollary was that in writing on the origins of the war, highly critical, extreme 'German school' interpretations found growing favour.[122] In the other post-Soviet republics, of course, new nationalist, often profoundly essentialist and anti-Soviet, histories continued to be elaborated at an accelerating pace to ground independence; nor were these necessarily unitary, since different political factions negotiated the Soviet past in diverse ways to further their particular programmes for the national future.[123]

Bluntly anti-Soviet interpretations have continued to be an important element in debates about the war. Over time, however, a greater plurality of views emerged. The massive and intractable political and economic difficulties that emerged within the Russian polity a few years into the postcommunist period created a greater measure of political pluralism and engendered, if not a general mellowing of views upon the Soviet past, at least the crystallisation of a series of more nuanced relationships with it in politics and historiography. To oversimplify, free market democrats tended to remain most critical of the Soviet period, while the reformed Russian communists were the most positive, even if what they found chiefly appealing there were the traditions of a strong state, military might and empire rather than the socialist spirit of October. To an extent, there was overlap here with some strands of Russian nationalist thought: although virulently anti-communist in domestic terms, some expansionist nationalists were apt to praise 'the Soviet development of Siberia, the intervention in Poland in 1939, the post-war Warsaw Pact, and Soviet success in developing atomic weapons'.[124] Indeed, the Soviet wartime past began to serve as a source of multiple contradictory lessons from which 'advocates of opposing visions of the post-Soviet future' could select at will: pro-western democrats could appropriate the memory of wartime alliance and cooperation in order to reintegrate the war experience into 'an eventual liberal narrative of Russia's past'; nationalist and anti-western conservatives could emphasise the traditional orthodox themes of Allied perfidy and the virtues of an authoritarian political order in withstanding external threats; while the far right might even find a positive history in Nazi–Soviet collaboration against 'the bourgeois democracies and international Zionist conspiracies', whose machinations in their minds still bedevilled Russia.[125]

Subsequently, however, these divisions were blurred and reformulated as Russia witnessed the strange revivification of the myth of the Great Patriotic War. From the mid-1990s onwards, partly in response to shifting public opinion, President Boris Yeltsin began to modify his erstwhile dogmatic anti-communism by subtly appropriating elements of the mythology of the war to forge a new positive sense of Russian national grandeur.[126] The Museum of the Great Fatherland War, opened in Moscow in 1993, eschewed extensive criticism of Stalin and glossed over the grubbier episodes of Nazi-Soviet collaboration, reproducing the Soviet view of the German invasion as 'a bolt from the blue, a sudden attack on an unsuspecting, peace-loving country by an evil power bent on conquest'.[127] In 1995, the official celebrations of the fiftieth anniversary of Victory Day were also characterised by relatively uncomplicated patriotic commemoration and – to the chagrin of Yeltsin's communist opponents whose metaphorical garments were being purloined – the uncritical usage of much of the rhetoric and symbolism of the Soviet war myth, as evidenced by the issuing of a stamp featuring Stalin's image for the first time in 40 years.[128] The following year, with fears of Chechen terrorism mounting, the celebrations were even more elaborate and militaristic: 'Stalin's war, with its victorious military imagery and underlying story of continued national danger, was used in an attempt to redeem Boris Yeltsin, just as twenty years before it had been used to rejuvenate Leonid Brezhnev'.[129]

This strategy was deployed with even greater intensity by Yeltsin's presidential successor Vladimir Putin. During the Victory Day celebrations in May 2000, Putin extravagantly praised those who had 'defended the great Soviet Motherland', urging that the ingrained national habit of victory might 'help our generation to build a strong and flourishing country [and to] raise high the Russian banner of democracy and freedom'. Simultaneously, Stalin acquired an even higher profile, appearing on a specially minted coin for the first time ever and being granted pride of place on a commemorative victory plaque.[130] Subsequently, Putin indulged more generally in such revivalism, restoring the Soviet-era national anthem (albeit with new lyrics) and the red star as the official symbol of the armed forces. Similarly, his government exerted influence over school history textbooks, downplaying, even rationalising, Stalinist repression in order to inculcate patriotism amongst the young. That said, there were limits to Putin's veneration of the Soviet past; he resisted, for instance, persistent calls for Volgograd to once more be named Stalingrad. Equally, he also drew discriminatingly on symbols from Russia's imperial past, endorsing the tsarist-era white, red and blue flag and double-headed eagle as official emblems of the Russian Federation. Moreover, in 2005 the annual public holiday celebrating the anniversary of the October 1917 revolution was replaced with one marking the victory over Polish occupiers in 1612 following which the Romanov dynasty was founded.[131] Putin was thus less a simple unreconstructed Soviet-nostalgic than an adept nationalist *bricoleur*, selectively appropriating and adapting iconography and rhetoric from the entire Russian past in accord with his own political priorities, specifically his predilection for returning to tough, centralised, even authoritarian government in order to rebuild Russia's great power status.

That said, the centrality to his nation-building endeavours of a slightly modulated version of the mythology of the Great Patriotic War was plain enough. This was graphically illustrated during the 2005 commemorations of the sixtieth anniversary of the end of the war, with the grandiose parade held in Moscow on Victory Day vividly 'conjuring up a massive display of military might and discipline reminiscent of the Brezhnev era'.[132] Putin also stirred controversy with a state of the nation address just prior to Victory Day when he described the collapse of the Soviet Union as 'the biggest geopolitical catastrophe of the century'.[133] In press interviews, Putin expounded his carefully crafted attitude towards the Soviet past, on the one hand disdaining as 'absolute rubbish' the suggestion that he wanted to turn the clock back, yet on the other maintaining that there were dimensions to Soviet history of which contemporary Russians could still be proud. When pressed on the territorial annexations following the Nazi–Soviet pact, Putin acknowledged that these had had tragic consequences, but deprecated the persistent demands from the Baltic states for an apology. Such an apology had already been forthcoming, he averred, when the Soviet government in 1989 had acknowledged the illegitimacy of the secret protocol. In quoting that statement, he implicitly endorsed its very telling formulation that the protocol was the product of 'a personal decision by Stalin which contradict[ed] the interests of the Soviet people'.[134]

Trends in Russian historiography closely paralleled this political rapprochement with the orthodox Soviet interpretation. By the later 1990s the majority of post-Soviet historians tended to present Stalin's search for collective security against Germany as genuine, and the Nazi–Soviet pact as designed to procure a defensive buffer zone.[135] School textbooks similarly described the pact and protocols as the outcome of a 'difficult choice', forced on a reluctant Soviet Union by the fact that Germany was about to attack Poland.[136] In 1998 a new multi-volume history of the war was published, produced under the auspices of the Defence Ministry and the Russian Academy of Sciences, and suggestively entitled *The Great Patriotic War, 1941–1945*. This new history was very different in content from that aborted in 1991, since it skated over possibly contentious episodes in pre-war diplomacy, focused on Soviet triumphs rather than setbacks, and offered overall a rather celebratory interpretation harking back to that ascendant before 1985; thus it effectively attempted to co-opt and integrate what was formerly a great Soviet achievement into a positive narrative of Russian national history: 'whilst the Party may be mentioned increasingly infrequently in post-Soviet writing on the war, the cult of the Party is increasingly being replaced by what might be termed the cult of the "Motherland". Essentially, where previously the Party was beyond criticism, now the patriotism of the Soviet people, in particular the Russians, is beyond doubt'.[137]

Broadly pro-Soviet accounts never disappeared from the debate, but in this new climate they proliferated, with the 'Russian academic establishment and media' particularly keen to remind both the peoples of the former Soviet Union and the wider world of the debt that they owed to those Soviet citizens who sacrificed themselves to defeat Nazi barbarity.[138] A western author from the 'German school' recently decried the fact that defence of 'Stalin and the punitive organs on which he and his system depended has become more widespread in Russia', directly implicating Putin in this drive 'to forget the crimes of the past'. He further lamented that the argument justifying the Nazi–Soviet pact on the basis of western perfidy, which was once 'advanced by Soviet propaganda', again 'enjoys wide support in official circles in Russia today'.[139]

Evidence from public opinion surveys suggested that Putin's efforts have borne fruit. The number of Russians citing victory in the Great Patriotic War as the event in history that made them most proud doubled between 1996 and 2003, from 44 per cent to 87 per cent. Positive perceptions of Stalin, closely related to his role as wartime leader, rocketed over the same period: in 2003 over a quarter of those surveyed said they would vote for Stalin as president if he were still alive. 'Unpleasant facts' like the purges and Nazi–Soviet pact 'have been repressed from mass consciousness'. (It is revealing that in 2003 only 23 per cent of those polled knew what the Molotov–Ribbentrop pact was; it is probably even more significant that many more – 40 per cent – were nonetheless prepared to endorse it as justified.) One commentator has therefore gone so far as to claim that victory in the war 'is the most potent symbol of identification in present-day Russia, and the sole prop for national self-belief', its commemoration now serving above all 'the centralist and repressive social order that has been imposed in the post-totalitarian culture and society under Vladimir Putin'.[140] Another observer, noting that the profile of the war has grown even further since 2005, has concurred that it serves as 'Russia's national shibboleth, the proof of its collective strength and virtue in the modern age'.[141]

The evidence also indicates that adherence to the war myth is far from being confined to the elderly generations who were for long its most obvious core constituency. The vast majority of respondents did not cite personal involvement or lost relatives as their reason for acknowledging the contemporary significance of Victory Day, but rather its historical and political importance for the nation. Thus the vitality of the collective memory of the war is not dependent upon residual living memory.[142] James Wertsch has argued that the Great Patriotic War myth partakes of a schematic narrative template with deep roots in Russian culture, whereby a peaceful Russian people is assailed by an aggressive outsider, leading to a period of existential danger and suffering before an eventual rousing heroic triumph. Repeatedly employed to explain successive foreign invasions, this 'triumph-over-alien-forces'plotline is arguably '*the* underlying story of Russian collective remembering'.[143] This may explain the secular puissance of the myth and the continuity in Russian memory culture – remarkable in view of the apparent rupture around the time of the collapse of communism – over many decades. In any event, with the titanic conflict of 1941–45 being invoked in an explicit attempt to ground a new Russian state and national identity, no representation of it can be devoid of contemporary political ramifications. In contemporary Russia, it would seem, the long Second World War is very far from over.

Notes

1 J. Degras (ed.), *Soviet Documents on Foreign Policy: Vol. III: 1933–1941* (Oxford, Oxford University Press, 1953), p. 170.
2 D. C. Watt, *How War Came: The Immediate Origins of the Second World War, 1938–1939* (London, Mandarin, 1990, pb. edn), pp. 457–65, quote at p. 465; anonymous Soviet citizen, quoted in A. Weiner, *Making Sense of War: The Second World War and the Fate of the Bolshevik Revolution* (Princeton, NJ, Princeton University Press, 2001), p. 371.
3 Speech by Molotov, 31 August 1939, in Degras (ed.), *Soviet Documents*, p. 370.
4 *New York Times*, 23 August 1939, quoted in P. Brendon, *The Dark Valley: A Panorama of the 1930s* (London, Pimlico, 2001, pb. edn), p. 584.
5 Watt, *How War Came*, pp. 463–70; M. J. Carley, *1939: The Alliance that Never Was and the Coming of World War II* (Chicago, Ivan Dee, 1999), pp. 207–14.
6 For American responses, see E. Mark, 'October or Thermidor? Interpretations of Stalinism and the perception of Soviet foreign policy in the United States, 1927–47', *American Historical Review*, vol. 94, no. 4, 1989, pp. 944–45.
7 G. Roberts, *The Soviet Union and the Origins of the Second World War: Russo–German Relations and the Road to War, 1933–1941* (London, Macmillan, 1995), pp. 62–63.
8 N. W. Heer, *Politics and History in the Soviet Union* (Cambridge, MA, MIT Press, 1971), p. vii.
9 E. Acton, *Rethinking the Russian Revolution* (London, Edward Arnold, 1990), quote at p. 49.
10 *Pravda*, 28 January 1988, quoted in J. Hochman, 'The Soviet historical debate', *Orbis*, vol. 32, no. 3, 1988, p. 369.
11 R. Markwick, *Rewriting History in Soviet Russia: The Politics of Revisionist Historiography, 1956–1974* (London, Macmillan, 2001).
12 Quoted in Heer, *Politics and History*, p. 11.
13 S. Linz (ed.), *The Impact of World War II on the Soviet Union* (Totowa, NJ, Rowman and Allanheld, 1985); C. Merridale, *Night of Stone: Death and Memory in Russia* (London, Granta, 2000), pp. 269–306.
14 A. Weiner, 'In the long shadow of war: the Second World War and the Soviet and post-Soviet world', *Diplomatic History*, vol. 25, no. 3, 2001, p. 455.
15 N. Schleifman, 'Moscow's Victory Park: a monumental change', *History and Memory*, vol. 13, no. 2, 2001, pp. 8–9.
16 Weiner, 'In the long shadow of war', pp. 443, 456.
17 For a suggestive account of writing on the war in Asia – largely bracketed here – see J. T. Sanders, 'Moscow on the Pacific: Soviet historians and the war in the Pacific, 1941–45', in R. W. Love Jr (ed.), *Pearl Harbor Revisited* (London, Macmillan, 1995), pp. 75–91.
18 F. Costigliola, 'The creation of memory and myth: Stalin's 1946 election speech and the Soviet threat', in M. Medhurst and H. Brands (eds), *Critical Reflections on the Cold War: Linking Rhetoric and History* (College Station, TX, Texas A & M University Press, 2000), pp. 38–54, quotes at p. 41.
19 W. Douglas, quoted in Costigliola, 'The creation of memory and myth', p. 38.

20 M. Gallagher, *The Soviet History of World War II: Myths, Memories, and Realities* (New York, Praeger, 1963), p. 23.

21 J. Stalin, *Speeches Delivered at Meetings of Voters of the Stalin Electoral District, Moscow* (Moscow, Foreign Languages Publishing House, 1950), pp. 21–24.

22 Soviet Information Bureau, *Falsifiers of History (Historical Information)* (London, Soviet News, 1948).

23 Gallagher, *The Soviet History of World War II*, p. 60; for Stalin's role, see G. Roberts, 'Stalin, the pact with Nazi Germany, and the origins of postwar Soviet diplomatic historiography', *Journal of Cold War Studies*, vol. 4, no. 4, 2002, pp. 93–103.

24 Mark, 'October or Thermidor?', pp. 951–62.

25 R. Sontag and J. Beddie (eds), *Nazi–Soviet Relations, 1939–1941: Documents from the Archives of the German Foreign Office* (Washington D.C., Department of State, 1948).

26 F. Furet, *The Passing of an Illusion: The Idea of Communism in the Twentieth Century* (Chicago, University of Chicago Press, 1999), p.398.

27 *Falsifiers* was accompanied by an alternative compilation of German documents to lend it authority.

28 *Falsifiers of History*, quotes at pp. 9, 11–13, 15–16, 26, 41, 27, 44.

29 Gallagher, *The Soviet History of World War II*, pp. 60–63 (quote at p. 63), 79–102.

30 S. Fitzpatrick (ed.), *Stalinism: New Directions* (London, Routledge, 2000); J. Fürst (ed.), *Late Stalinist Russia: Society between Reconstruction and Reinvention* (London, Routledge, 2006).

31 Weiner, *Making Sense of War*, p. 385; see also the nuanced reflections on veterans in C. Merridale, *Ivan's War: The Red Army, 1939–1945* (London, Faber and Faber, 2006, pb. edn), pp. 321–35.

32 M. Light, 'The Soviet view', in R. Douglas (ed.), *1939: A Retrospect Forty Years After* (London, Macmillan, 1983), p. 74.

33 T. H. Rigby (ed.), *The Stalin Dictatorship: Khrushchev's 'Secret Speech' and Other Documents* (Sydney, Sydney University Press, 1968), especially pp. 52–61.

34 Khrushchev, however, presented himself and other de-Stalinizers in a better light than his conservative rivals: Rigby (ed.), *The Stalin Dictatorship*, p. 17.

35 Markwick, *Rewriting History in Soviet Russia*, pp. 47–51.

36 S. Bialer (ed.), *Stalin and his Generals: Soviet Military Memoirs of World War II* (New York, Pegasus, 1969).

37 Gallagher, *Soviet History*, pp. 153–75, quote at p. 169; V. Aspaturian, 'Diplomacy in the mirror of Soviet scholarship', in J. Keep (ed.), *Contemporary History in the Soviet Mirror* (London, Allen and Unwin, 1964), pp. 243–85, especially pp. 258–63.

38 The major series of *Documents on Soviet Foreign Policy – Dokumenty Vneshnei Politiki SSSR* (*DVP*) – began to appear in 1957. O. Pick, 'Who pulled the trigger? Soviet historians and the origins of World War II', *Problems of Communism*, vol. 9, no. 5, 1960, pp. 64–68 discusses published Soviet documents.

39 S. Cohen, *Rethinking the Soviet Experience: Politics and History since 1917* (New York, Oxford University Press, 1985), pp. 119–21.

40 V. Petrov (ed.), *'June 22, 1941': Soviet Historians and the German Invasion* (Columbia, SC, University of South Carolina Press, 1968) contains the translated text, reviews and other materials.

41 Petrov (ed.), *'June 22, 1941'*, pp. 37–245, quotes at pp. 100, 112; Rigby (ed.), *The Stalin Dictatorship*, p. 49.

42 Petrov (ed.), *'June 22, 1941'*, pp. 228–30.

43 Petrov (ed.), *'June 22, 1941'*, pp. 250–61, quote from V. M. Kulish at p. 257.

44 A. Nekrich, *Forsake Fear: Memoirs of an Historian* (Boston, MA, Unwin Hyman, 1991), pp. 159–60.

45 Petrov (ed.), *'June 22, 1941'*, p. 182; Heer, *Politics and History in the Soviet Union*, pp. 253–56.

46 Nekrich, *Forsake Fear*, p. 203.

47 Petrov (ed.), *'June 22, 1941'*, pp. 277–304, quotes at pp. 277, 302, 279, 286.

48 I. K. Koblyakov, *USSR: For Peace, Against Aggression, 1933 – 1941* (Moscow, Progress, 1976), pp. 5, 236 (quoting Brezhnev).

49 'Foreword', in V. M. Falin *et al.* (eds), *Soviet Peace Efforts on the Eve of World War II (September 1938–August 1939): Documents and Records: Part I* (Moscow, Novosti, 1973), p. 36.

50 For example, A. A. Gromyko and B. N. Ponamarev (eds), *Soviet Foreign Policy, 1917–1980*, 2 vols (Moscow, Progress, 1981, 4th edn).

51 T. J. Uldricks, 'Evolving Soviet views of the Nazi–Soviet pact', in R. Frucht (ed.), *Labyrinth of Nationalism, Complexities of Diplomacy: Essays in Honor of Charles and Barbara Jelavich* (Columbus, OH, Slavica, 1992), p. 339; see also G. Roberts, *The Unholy Alliance: Stalin's Pact with Hitler* (London, Tauris, 1989), pp. 14–15.

52 J. Herman, 'Soviet peace efforts on the eve of World War Two: a review of the Soviet documents', *Journal of Contemporary History*, vol. 15, no. 3, 1980, pp. 577–602. Extensive publication of material on 1939 only came in the 1990s, when *inter alia* this DVP series was revived.

53 R. W. Davies, *Soviet History in the Gorbachev Revolution* (London, Macmillan, 1989), pp. 4, 101.

54 Weiner, *Making Sense of War*, pp. 343–48; N. Tumarkin, *The Living and the Dead: The Rise and Fall of the Cult of World War II in Russia* (New York, Basic, 1994), pp. 125–57.

55 See, for example, Koblyakov, *USSR*, pp. 240–44. J. Erickson, 'May 1945: the Soviet view', *History Today*, vol. 35, no. 5, 1985, pp. 10–14 offers an overview.

56 R. W. Davies, *Soviet History in the Gorbachev Revolution* and *Soviet History in the Yeltsin Era* (London, Macmillan, 1997); W. Laqueur, *Stalin: The Glasnost Revelations* (New York, Scribner's, 1990). Gorbachev posited a fundamental discontinuity between Lenin and Stalin while his opponents argued for continuity, of a positive kind in one case and negative in the other. Equally, Gorbachev tended towards an 'intentionalist' explanation of the rise of Stalinism, whereas his opponents emphasised structural factors: M. von Hagen, 'Stalinism and the politics of post-Soviet history', in I. Kershaw and M. Lewin (eds), *Stalinism and Nazism: Dictatorships in Comparison* (Cambridge, Cambridge University Press, 1997), pp. 285–310.

57 Davies, *Soviet History in the Gorbachev Revolution*, p. 129.

58 Davies, *Soviet History in the Gorbachev Revolution*, p. 103; cf. H. Phillips, '"Glasnost" and the history of Soviet foreign policy', *Problems of Communism*, vol. 40, no. 4, 1991, p. 68.

59 Davies, *Soviet History in the Gorbachev Revolution*, pp. 100–114 and *Soviet History in the Yeltsin Era*, pp. 6–36; Laqueur, *Stalin*, pp. 203–25; L. Siegelbaum, 'Historical revisionism in the USSR', *Radical History Review*, no. 44, 1989, pp. 32–61.

60 On nationalism, see R. G. Suny, *The Revenge of the Past: Nationalism, Revolution, and the Collapse of the Soviet Union* (Stanford, CA, Stanford University Press, 1993). Stephen Kotkin has characterised the Union's demise as 'national in form, opportunist in content': *Armageddon Averted: The Soviet Collapse, 1970–2000* (Oxford, Oxford University Press, 2001), p. 105.

61 Uldricks, 'Evolving Soviet views of the Nazi–Soviet pact', pp. 344–46.

62 Roberts, *Unholy Alliance*, pp. 7–8; cf. Hochman, 'The Soviet historical debate', pp. 369–83.

63 A. E. Senn, 'Perestroika in Lithuanian historiography: the Molotov–Ribbentrop pact', *The Russian Review*, vol. 49, no. 1, 1990, pp. 46–47.

64 Uldricks, 'Evolving Soviet views of the Nazi–Soviet pact', pp. 345–47, quoting Semiriaga writing in early October 1988; Roberts, *Unholy Alliance*, pp. 21–22, quoting the riposte three weeks later.

65 M. von Hagen, 'From "Great Fatherland War" to the Second World War: new perspectives and future prospects', in Kershaw and Lewin (eds), *Stalinism and Nazism*, p. 244.

66 D. Volkogonov, *Stalin: Triumph and Tragedy* (London, Weidenfeld and Nicolson, 1995, pb. edn), pp. 355–66, 384–87, quote at p. 356.

67 L. Bezymensky, 'The secret protocols of 1939 as a problem of Soviet historiography', in G. Gorodetsky (ed.), *Soviet Foreign Policy, 1917–1991: A Retrospective* (London, Cass, 1994), pp. 75–85; Roberts, *Soviet Union and the Origins of the Second World War*, pp. 186–87; Uldricks, 'Evolving Soviet views', pp. 347–50; 'Half a century ago. Europe enters the war', *International Affairs {Moscow}*, no. 9, 1989, pp. 13–48; 'Around the non-aggression

pact (Documents of Soviet–German relations in 1939)', *International Affairs {Moscow}*, no. 10, 1989, pp. 81–116.

68 Senn, 'Perestroika in Lithuanian historiography', p. 56.

69 R. Daniels, 'Was communism reformable?', *The Nation*, 3 January 2000, http://www. thenation.com/doc/20000103/daniels (accessed 3 February 2006).

70 Tumarkin, *Living and the Dead*, pp. 196–99, quote at p. 198.

71 'The Baltic states join the Soviet Union: Documents on the USSR's relations with the Baltic countries in 1939–40', *International Affairs {Moscow}*, no. 3, 1990, p. 135.

72 D. Remnick, *Lenin's Tomb: The Last Days of the Soviet Empire* (London, Penguin, 1994, pb. edn), pp. 398–411, quoting Soviet Defence Minister D. Yazov at p. 404.

73 Quote from A. O. Chubarian, 'Politics and morality in Soviet foreign policy', in Gorodetsky (ed.), *Soviet Foreign Policy*, p. 184; R. H. Johnston, *Soviet Foreign Policy, 1918–1945: A Guide to Research and Research Materials* (Wilmington, DE, Scholarly Resources, 1991), p. 192; Uldricks, 'Evolving Soviet views of the Nazi–Soviet pact', pp. 348–53. Cf. the contributions of Soviet scholars to a conference held in Paris in September 1989, collected in D. W. Pike (ed.), *The Opening of the Second World War* (New York, Peter Lang, 1991), especially pp. 34–67.

74 Remnick, *Lenin's Tomb*, p. 51.

75 Davies, *Soviet History in the Yeltsin Era*, pp. 39–40.

76 For primary evidence on this process, see J. Boyer and J. Kirshner (eds), 'Roundtable, Moscow, January 1989: Perestroika, history, and historians', *Journal of Modern History*, vol. 62, no. 4, 1990, pp. 782–830.

77 Remnick, *Lenin's Tomb*, p. 59.

78 J. Erickson, 'A mental illness called Russia', *The Times Higher*, 3 March 2000, p. 24, reviewing M. Malia, *Russia under Western Eyes: From the Bronze Horseman to the Lenin Mausoleum* (Cambridge, MA, Harvard University Press, 1999); see also D. S. Foglesong, *The American Mission and the 'Evil Empire': The Crusade for a 'Free Russia' since 1881* (Cambridge, Cambridge University Press, 2007).

79 D. Campbell, *Writing Security: United States Foreign Policy and the Politics of Identity* (Manchester, Manchester University Press, 1992).

80 Cohen, *Rethinking the Soviet Experience*, pp. 3–37, quotes at pp. 10–11. W. Welch, *American Images of Soviet Foreign Policy: An Inquiry into Recent Appraisals from the Academic Community* (New Haven, CT, Yale University Press, 1970), for example, assumes scholars 'should be fashioning a solid body of knowledge about Soviet external conduct' to assist 'the officials of our government responsible for dealings with the Soviets' (p. ix).

81 Mark, 'October or Thermidor?', pp. 958–59.

82 A. Gleason, *Totalitarianism: The Inner History of the Cold War* (Oxford, Oxford University Press, 1995), p. 3.

83 P. Novick, *That Noble Dream: The 'Objectivity Question' and the American Historical Profession* (Cambridge, Cambridge University Press, 1988), pp. 281–319.

84 G. D. Rosenfeld, 'The reception of William L. Shirer's *The Rise and Fall of the Third Reich* in the United States and West Germany, 1960–62', *Journal of Contemporary History*, vol. 29, no. 1, 1994, p. 107.

85 S. Fitzpatrick, 'Revisionism in Soviet history', *History and Theory*, vol. 46, no. 4, 2007, pp. 77–91 surveys these developments, stressing how small a part new data played in them. M. Malia, 'Clio in Tauris: American historiography on Russia', in A. Molho and G. Wood (eds), *Imagined Histories: American Historians Interpret the Past* (Princeton, NJ, Princeton University Press, 1998), pp. 415–33 concedes that western writing was conditioned by value judgements, but then implies that conservative ones were accurate whereas revisionist ones were not.

86 These two views thus depend upon a dichotomous opposition between Stalin as ideologue (meaning a revolutionary expansionist) or pragmatic *realpolitiker* (meaning a defensive-minded guardian of the Russian national interest). This reflects a pervasive tendency on the part of international historians to conceptualise ideology as the antithesis of an

idealised *realpolitik*, even though 'realism' is as ideological a position as any other: A. Stephanson, 'Stalin's hyper-realism', *Diplomatic History*, vol. 25, no. 1, 2001, pp. 136–39.

87 See, for example, J. Haslam, *The Soviet Union and the Struggle for Collective Security in Europe, 1933–39* (London, Macmillan, 1984) and 'Soviet–German relations and the origins of the Second World War: the jury is still out', *Journal of Modern History*, vol. 69, no. 4, 1997, pp. 785–97.

88 These categorisations are taken from Roberts, *The Soviet Union and the Origins of the Second World War*, pp. 1–8. T. J. Uldricks, 'Debating the role of Russia in the origins of the Second World War' in G. Martel (ed.) *The Origins of the Second World War Reconsidered: A. J. P. Taylor and the Historians* (London, Routledge, 1999, 2nd edn), pp. 135–54 offers another excellent overview.

89 R. Tucker, 'The emergence of Stalin's foreign policy', *Slavic Review*, vol. 36, no. 4, 1977, p. 576, and more extensively *Stalin in Power: The Revolution from Above, 1928–1941* (New York, Norton, 1990).

90 Uldricks, 'Debating', p. 142. Hochman's key work is *The Soviet Union and the Failure of Collective Security, 1934–1938* (Ithaca, NY, Cornell University Press, 1984).

91 G. Kennan, *Russia and the West under Lenin and Stalin* (New York, Mentor, 1961, pb. edn), pp. 276–327.

92 T. J. Uldricks, 'Stalin and Nazi Germany', *Slavic Review*, vol. 36, no. 4, 1977, p. 599.

93 A. J. P. Taylor, *The Origins of the Second World War* (London, Penguin, 1964, pb. edn).

94 This is not to deny, of course, that these debates also had an empirical dimension: for example 'German school' authors often prioritised German documents over Soviet ones.

95 That 'thousands of people in one country (the United States) could earn a living by observing another (Russia) will doubtless be of interest to future generations trying to make sense of the twentieth century'; 'nowhere else did perceptions of Russia constitute so integral a part of the national fabric' (S. Kotkin, '1991 and the Russian revolution: sources, conceptual categories, analytical frameworks', *Journal of Modern History*, vol. 70, no. 2, 1998, p. 385).

96 Gleason, *Totalitarianism*, p. 197.

97 B. Posen, 'Competing images of the Soviet Union', *World Politics*, vol. 39, no. 4, 1987, pp. 579–80 (emphasis in original).

98 G. Roberts, *Stalin's Wars: From World War to Cold War, 1939–1953* (New Haven, CT, Yale University Press, 2008, pb. edn), p. xiii. The story of the opening of Soviet archives is too intricate to be related here, but the process has been very much influenced by political considerations: for an overview see A. Banerji, *Writing History in the Soviet Union: Making the Past Work* (New Delhi, Social Science Press, 2008), pp. 225–57. Arguably, under Vladimir Putin 'the era of openness is coming to an end' and 'the flow of new archival material from Russia is slowing to a trickle': C. Pleshakov, *Stalin's Folly: The Secret History of the German Invasion of Russia, June 1941* (London, Weidenfeld and Nicolson, 2005), p. 277.

99 S. Fitzpatrick, 'Introduction', in Fitzpatrick (ed.), *Stalinism*, p. 6; cf. Kotkin, '1991 and the Russian revolution', p. 386.

100 R. Overy, *Russia's War* (London, Allen Lane, 1998), p. xiii; but cf. Weiner, *Making Sense of War*, pp. 12–21.

101 R. Daniels, 'The Soviet Union in post-Soviet perspective', *Journal of Modern History*, vol. 74, no. 2, 2002, p. 391.

102 For the mood of the early 1990s, see the symposium on 'The Russian revolution: seventy-five years on', *Times Literary Supplement*, 6 November 1992, pp. 3–9. The contributors include A. Ulam, author of a standard text on Soviet foreign policy – *Expansion and Coexistence: The History of Soviet Foreign Policy, 1917–1967* (London, Secker and Warburg, 1968) – espousing a variant of the 'German school' view.

103 R. C. Raack, 'Stalin's plans for World War II', *Journal of Contemporary History*, vol. 26, no. 2, 1991, pp. 225, 222, 216 and *Stalin's Drive to the West, 1938 – 1945: The Origins of the Cold War* (Stanford, CA, Stanford University Press, 1995).

104 A. Nekrich, *Pariahs, Partners, Predators: German–Soviet Relations, 1922–1941* (New York, Columbia University Press, 1997), quotes at pp. 63–66. A. Weeks has more recently written of the 'totalitarian kinship' between Stalin and Hitler: *Stalin's Other War: Soviet Grand Strategy, 1939–1941* (Lanham, MD, Rowman and Littlefield, 2003, pb. edn), p. 50.

105 G. Gorodetsky, *Grand Delusion: Stalin and the German Invasion of Russia* (New Haven, CT, Yale University Press, 1999), quotes at pp. 316, 323.

106 Carley, *1939*, quote at p. xiii. Radical critiques echoing the orthodox Soviet narrative's emphasis on western anti-communism have formed a persistent strand in the debate on British appeasement: see, for example, A. Finkel and C. Leibovitz, *In Our Time: The Chamberlain–Hitler Collusion* (New York, Monthly Review Press, 1998). As 'collective security school' views fit with critical attitudes towards appeasement, so 'German school' views complement sympathetic ones: see, for example, G. Weinberg, 'The Nazi–Soviet pact: a half century later', reprinted in K. Eubank (ed.), *World War II: Roots and Causes* (Lexington, MA, D. C. Heath, 1992, 2nd edn), pp. 272–83.

107 This particular debate was conducted on the H-DIPLO discussion list in February–March 2000. Discussion logs can be searched at http://www.h-net.msu.edu/~diplo/ (accessed 2 Janaury 2009). Quotes from M. J. Carley, H-DIPLO post, 21 February 2000.

108 P. Konecny, H-DIPLO post, 23 February 2000.

109 Quotes respectively from I. Lukes, H-DIPLO post, 25 February 2000, and Lukes, H-DIPLO review, 21 February 2000. Lukes' work includes 'Did Stalin desire war in 1938? A new look at Soviet behaviour during the May and September crises', *Diplomacy and Statecraft*, vol. 2, no. 1, 1991, pp. 3–53, and 'Stalin and Czechoslovakia in 1938–39: an autopsy of a myth', *Diplomacy and Statecraft*, vol. 10, nos 2/3, 1999, pp. 13–47.

110 Quote from G. Roberts, H-DIPLO post, 1 March 2000; cf. I. Lukes, H-DIPLO post, 25 February 2000 and P. Konecny, H-DIPLO post, 2 March 2000.

111 I. Lukes, H-DIPLO post, 25 February 2000.

112 Carley, *1939*, p. 272.

113 G. Roberts, H-DIPLO post, 1 March 2000.

114 Witness the exchange between Carley and G. B. Strang, following Strang's passing reference to 'Lenin's mass murders' (Strang, H-DIPLO posts, 11 and 17 March 2000; Carley H-DIPLO post, 14 March 2000). Carley finds the descriptor inappropriate, and implies that anyone who would employ it suffers from bias that renders their views on Soviet foreign policy in the 1930s deeply suspect.

115 Cf. R. Jervis, 'Political science perspectives', in R. Boyce and J. A. Maiolo (eds), *The Origins of World War Two: The Debate Continues* (London, Palgrave, 2003), pp. 208–9.

116 K. Neilson, *Britain, Soviet Russia and the Collapse of the Versailles Order, 1919–1939* (Cambridge, Cambridge University Press, 2006), quotes at pp. 318, 38–39.

117 Roberts, *Stalin's Wars*, quotes at pp. 38, xii–xiii.

118 S. Pons, *Stalin and the Inevitable War, 1936–1941* (London, Cass, 2002), p. xiii.

119 W.F. Kimball (ed.), roundtable review of Roberts, *Stalin's Wars*, H-DIPLO, July 2007, http://www.h-net.org/~diplo/roundtables/PDF/StalinsWars-Roundtable.pdf (accessed 24 October 2007).

120 Davies, *Soviet History in the Yeltsin Era*, pp. 2–3.

121 Gleason, *Totalitarianism*, pp. 211–16.

122 Weeks, *Stalin's Other War*, draws approvingly on this literature.

123 See, for example, V. Kuzmenko, 'Belarus during World War II: some aspects of the modern view of the problem', *Journal of Slavic Military Studies*, vol. 11, no. 2, 1998, pp. 98–112; and W. Jilge, 'The politics of history and the Second World War in post-communist Ukraine (1986/1991 – 2004/2005)', *Jahrbücher für Geschichte Osteuropas*, vol. 54, no. 1, 2006, pp. 50–81.

124 Davies, *Soviet History in the Yeltsin Era*, p. 68.

125 Von Hagen, 'From "Great Fatherland War" to the Second World War', pp. 249–50.

126 P. Duncan, 'Contemporary Russian identity between east and west', *Historical Journal*, vol. 48, no. 1, 2005, pp. 286–87.

127 B. Keys, review of Nekrich, *Pariahs, Partners, Predators*, in *H-NET Reviews*, March 1998, http://www.h-net.org/reviews/showrev.php?id=1863 (accessed 6 February 2006).

128 Davies, *Soviet History in the Yeltsin Era*, pp. 73–75; D. Hearst, 'Coming to the aid of the Party', *The Guardian*, 1 May 1995, *G2*, p. 9; Schleifman, 'Moscow's Victory Park', pp. 17–29.

129 C. Merridale, 'War, death, and remembrance in Soviet Russia', in J. Winter and E. Sivan (eds), *War and Remembrance in the Twentieth Century* (Cambridge, Cambridge University Press, 1999), p. 80.

130 *BBC Monitoring*, 'Russia's Putin addresses participants of victory parade' and P. Henderson, 'Russia marks end of World War II with parades and pomp', *Reuters*, in *Johnson's Russia List (JRL)*, #4290, H-DIPLO post, 9 May 2000; 'Stalin depicted on Russian money for first time', *Agence France Presse*, in *JRL*, #4288, H-DIPLO post, 8 May 2000; *BBC Monitoring*, 'Kremlin victory plaque gives prominence to Stalin', in *JRL*, #4295, H-DIPLO post, 14 May 2000.

131 V. Isachenkov, 'Soviet-era red star gets rehabilitated', *Associated Press*, in *JRL*, #6574, 27 November 2002, http://www.cdi.org/russia/johnson/6574.htm (accessed 13 February 2006); D. W. Benn, 'The teaching of history in Putin's Russia', *International Affairs*, vol. 84, no. 2, 2008, pp. 365–70; N. Adler, 'The future of the Soviet past remains unpredictable: the resurrection of Stalinist symbols amidst the exhumation of mass graves', *Europe–Asia Studies*, vol. 57, no. 8, 2005, pp. 1093–1119.

132 N. P. Walsh, 'Soviet flags fly as Russia remembers', *The Guardian*, 10 May 2005, http://www.guardian.co.uk/world/2005/may/10/secondworldwar.russia (accessed 12 March 2010).

133 C. Bigg, 'Was Soviet collapse last century's worst geopolitical catastrophe?', *Radio Free Europe/Radio Liberty*, in *JRL*, #9135, 30 April 2005, http://www.cdi.org/russia/johnson/9135-11.cfm (accessed 13 February 2006).

134 'President Putin's interview with German television channels ARD and ZDF', *www.kremlin.ru*, in *JRL*, #9143, 5 May 2005, http://www.cdi.org/russia/johnson/9143-21.cfm (accessed 13 February 2006).

135 A. Hill, 'Stalin and the west', in G. Martel (ed.), *A Companion to International History, 1900–2001* (Oxford, Blackwell, 2007), pp. 260–63.

136 J. V. Wertsch, 'Blank spots in collective memory: a case study of Russia', *Annals of the American Academy of Political and Social Science*, no. 617, 2008, pp. 63–65.

137 A. Hill, 'Recent literature on the Great Patriotic War of the Soviet Union 1941–45', *Contemporary European History*, vol. 9, no. 1, 2000, pp. 169–79, quote at p. 175.

138 Weiner, 'In the long shadow of war', p. 448. Cf. A. Litvin, *Writing History in Twentieth-Century Russia: A View from Within* (London, Palgrave, 2001), pp. 130–31.

139 D. Murphy, *What Stalin Knew: The Enigma of Barbarossa* (New Haven, CT, Yale University Press, 2005), pp. 247, 251, xii. For a more recent discussion, see T. J. Uldricks, 'War, politics and memory: Russian historians reevaluate the origins of World War II', *History and Memory*, vol. 21, no. 2, 2009, pp. 60–82.

140 L. Gudkov, 'The fetters of victory: how the war provides Russia with its identity', *Eurozine*, May 2005, http://www.eurozine.com/articles/2005-05-03-gudkov-en.html (accessed 21 October 2005).

141 C. Merridale, 'Haunted by Stalin's ghost', *History Today*, vol. 59, no. 9. 2009, p. 34.

142 V. Krayev, 'Victory Day gives hope', *Rosbalt*, in *JRL*, #7178, 12 May 2003, http://www.cdi.org/russia/johnson/7178-79.cfm (accessed 9 December 2003).

143 J. V. Wertsch, *Voices of Collective Remembering* (Cambridge, Cambridge University Press, 2002), quotes at pp. 93–94 (emphasis in original).

2   On guilt

The Federal Republic of Germany and Nazi aggression

> Never forget that the rulers of present-day Russia are common blood-stained criminals ... Furthermore, do not forget that these rulers belong to a race which combines, in a rare mixture, bestial cruelty and an inconceivable gift for lying, and which today more than ever is conscious of a mission to impose its bloody oppression on the whole world ... *In Russian Bolshevism we must see the attempt undertaken by the Jews in the twentieth century to achieve world domination* ... Germany is today the next great war aim of Bolshevism.
>
> Adolf Hitler, *Mein Kampf*, 1925–26[1]

At the 1937 Paris International Exhibition the pavilions of Nazi Germany and the Soviet Union stood face to face on the banks of the Seine, graphically representing inter-war Europe's ideological fractures. Boris Iofan's multiplanar Soviet pavilion was crowned with Vera Mukhina's massive sculpture 'Industrial Worker and Collective Farm Woman' depicting two archetypal Soviet citizens, jointly holding hammer and sickle aloft and striding forward 'symbolic of the irreversible momentum propelling the socialist worker and peasant into the future'.[2] Across the Place de Varsovie, Albert Speer's austere neoclassical German pavilion – 'a study in rigid calm' – was fronted by a 60 metre tall rectilinear tower looming over Mukhina's figures, itself topped by a huge bronze eagle grasping a swastika in its talons. Where the Soviet pavilion gave an impression of forward and even offensive momentum, Speer's tower and the statues that guarded its entrance gave the German pavilion the defensive mien of 'a solid fortress'. This was not accidental. Speer had illicit sight of the blueprints for the Soviet building while on a preliminary visit to Paris to survey the exhibition grounds and subsequently amended his own design to ensure that the German edifice was the taller and appeared to be curbing the Soviet onslaught.[3] Observers' judgements were inevitably conditioned by their ideological predispositions, but conservative opinion was not slow to grasp how Speer's structure projected 'all impending aggression ... onto the Soviets'.[4]

The German pavilion thus concretised a key trope of Nazi propaganda, portraying the regime as a defensive entity and specifically as a bulwark of European civilisation against Bolshevism. Nazism was far from unique amongst nationalist movements in constructing an aggressive foreign policy on the foundation of an acute sense of victimhood, 'that morally exculpatory excuse for intolerance, persecution and violence in the modern world'.[5] But the consequences were abnormally devastating, especially in this instance for European Jewry and the peoples of the Soviet Union. From the coalescence of Hitler's worldview in the early 1920s, the Jews and the Bolsheviks were fused together as forces of pernicious evil threatening the purity and survival of Germandom. Thereafter a sense of Nazi aggression as responsive, even pre-emptive, was one of the most insistent themes in the regime's propaganda and self-understanding. In 1939 Hitler infamously warned that 'the annihilation of the Jewish race in Europe' would follow 'if the international Jewish financiers in and outside Europe should succeed in plunging the nations once more into a world war'.[6] The genocidal war in the East from 1941 was presented both tactically as a pre-emptive strike against an impending Soviet assault and strategically as a preventative crusade to preserve civilisation from Asiatic barbarism.[7] Even in his final political testament, Hitler continued to deny responsibility: 'it is untrue that I, or anybody else in Germany, wanted war in 1939. It was wanted and provoked exclusively by those international politicians who either came of Jewish stock, or worked for Jewish interests'.[8]

Since 1945, negotiating the wartime past in order to fashion contemporary national identity has been at least as central a problem in the political and historical culture of the Federal Republic of Germany (FRG) as it was in the Soviet Union.[9] But rather than instrumentalising a momentous though costly triumph, the issue here was how to negotiate devastating defeat and a burden of guilt. In losing the war the Germans suffered terrible destruction from aerial bombardment and advancing Soviet forces, and then saw their country occupied and partitioned, with ancient German communities across Eastern Europe uprooted and expelled. That German aggression had precipitated the war, and the Nazis visited upon diverse racial and political others genocidal iniquities infinitely more terrible than whatever the average German had suffered, compounded the fruits of defeat. Constructing a narrative that accommodated these uncomfortable facts and yet provided a workable foundation for post-war German national identity was a formidable task. Although responses have been extremely diverse at any given point and over time, it is nonetheless possible to locate them on a broad spectrum ranging between two opposed tendencies. On the one hand, there have been agonised liberal efforts to confront candidly and work through the implications of this heritage, accepting Nazism as a fundamental rupture that means Germany can never be a 'normal' nation, and even advocating post-national forms of identity. On the other hand, conservative and nationalist elements have been more inclined to dissociate contemporary Germans from Nazism and its crimes, insisting that these should not be the central elements in the national story and advocating a more or less continuous and positive sense of historical identification with a German nation stretching back at least to 1871.[10]

Within this context, historical literature even of the most resolutely empiricist stripe cannot avoid implication in broader philosophical, moral and ideological issues.[11] This is certainly true of writing on foreign policy. While not as ethically charged as Holocaust historiography, it nonetheless speaks directly to the question of responsibility for the war and thus to the meaning of Hitler's aggression within the longer run of German history. Reviewing this literature, it is possible to discern persistent conservative interventions, albeit often fiercely contested, to displace or evade German responsibility and thereby recuperate a positive nationalist identity. Over more than six decades a range of overlapping narrative strategies have been deployed in order to explain away, sanitise or even justify Nazi aggression.

'Satanic genius': war origins in the early FRG

Any brief discussion of the historiography of Nazi foreign policy, especially one contextualising it against the literature on war memory and national identity in the FRG, must be highly selective. But focusing on these conservative tendencies can be justified by the recent coalescence of more critical perspectives on West German efforts to master the Nazi past. Conventional wisdom long held that these had been broadly successful, with the establishment of a healthy democratic culture in which the war and its crimes were 'not only remembered' but 'actively worked on, labored, rehearsed', in contrast to the baneful 'historical amnesia' that prevailed in the other major Axis power, Japan.[12] The terrain of war memory was mapped as progressing from a phase of psychically necessary forgetfulness in the 1950s through a painful critical engagement with the reality of Nazi atrocities from the 1960s to a situation in the 1980s in which the wartime past was the subject of mature, vigorous and pluralist debate. Recent work, however, has advanced a more disparaging judgement.

The contradictory currents of memory post-unification underpin this reorientation. One catalyst has been the conservative voices, increasingly vocal from the mid-1980s, urging a renationalisation of German history and an end to masochistic obsession with an era for which ample apology and reparation have allegedly long since been made. This disturbing and tenacious chorus testifies to the persistence of a continuous thread of staunchly nationalist opinion stretching back to the war years and indeed beyond.[13] But it is a minority view that has had an unintended salutary effect in spurring more searching analyses of the balance sheet of memory; in consequence, assessments of the earlier candour of historians, politicians and populace in settling accounts with Nazism have in fact become increasingly negative. Against the yardstick of a post-unification present in which debates about the Nazi past reached an unprecedented pitch and where memory has become much more inclusive, previous generations have been found wanting. The commemorations of war's end in 1995, the 'Goldhagen debate' over the role of ordinary Germans in the Holocaust, the controversies over the 'Crimes of the *Wehrmacht'* exhibition and the agonizing over a national Holocaust memorial all indicated that the focus of memory was now squarely where it ought to be: on German perpetrators and the whole panoply of victims of Nazism. By the turn of the century there had emerged a greater willingness than ever to make 'critical memory of German crimes a cornerstone of German national identity' and to come frankly to terms not only with complicity in National Socialism but also with the 'second guilt' of having failed retrospectively to confront it.[14] The tenor of war commemorations in 2005 demonstrated that this point still held, despite the renewed and pronounced emphasis in the last few years on German suffering in the expulsions and air war; when Germans are discussed as victims today it is arguably as 'victims as well as, not instead of ... perpetrators'.[15] In this context, it is not inappropriate to analyse key strands in the international history literature with a sceptical eye towards their politics.

The 1940s and 1950s have been a central focus of revisionist work on memory. It is now contended that the Germans did not so much repress recollection of Nazism as actively remember it with extraordinary selectivity, prioritising their own loss and suffering and marginalizing its crimes and true victims.[16] Internal and external factors conspired to preclude greater contrition.[17] Although the occupying powers were initially committed to thorough de-Nazification predicated upon attribution of collective guilt, this process was aborted through widespread amnesties because of the imperatives of reconstruction, specifically the need to establish an indigenous administration and stable political order. 'The price for post-war integration of those [many] Germans compromised by their beliefs and actions in the Third Reich', Jeffrey Herf has argued, 'was silence about the crimes of that period. Memory and justice might produce a right-wing revolt that would undermine a still fragile democracy'. The electoral victory of Konrad Adenauer's conservative Christian Democrats in 1949 meant 'justice delayed – hence denied – and weakened memory' as the price for building a new democracy.[18] Adenauer's stance was one of 'public penance and strictly limited liability'.[19] Apology and restitution were made, as in the 1952 settlement with Israel giving compensation to Holocaust survivors; but admissions that 'unspeakable crimes have been committed in the name of the German people' were carefully formulated to elide agency and responsibility.[20]

The dominant view was that only a handful of perpetrators had really been culpable for Nazi crimes and that, if anything, the Germans had been victims of Nazism too. 'We've been led by criminals and gamblers', lamented a celebrated Berlin diarist in the last desperate days of the war, 'and we've let them lead us like sheep to the slaughter'.[21] Punishment and reparation were consequently rather token in character, and undertaken in a self-righteous, and impatient spirit. Indeed, they often seemed to be regarded as necessary but tiresome precursors facilitating an over-riding prioritisation of German suffering, particularly that inflicted by the Soviet Union which had been the prime mover behind the expulsions from Eastern Europe and still held tens of thousands of prisoners of war. When Adenauer went to Moscow in 1955 to negotiate over these captives, his implication that there was a moral equivalence between German war crimes and the Red Army's conduct infuriated Khrushchev, but was suggestive of a mindset that utterly refused to grasp the unique character of German guilt. The context of the Cold War also encouraged these sentiments since the imperative of integrating the FRG into the anti-Soviet Western bloc underpinned the actions of both Adenauer and the western Allies. It was therefore less a matter of choosing between memory and democracy than of remembering the war in a very specific way in order to ground a particular kind of conservative order.[22]

This strategy obscured less comfortable issues, principally the Holocaust and responsibility for the war itself. Where the outside world was concerned, the authoritative reckoning of the latter was embodied in the Nuremberg war crimes trials. Here the Allies sought to establish German guilt beyond per-adventure, precluding a replay of the post-Versailles revisionist debates, by indicting leading Nazis for conspiring to wage an aggressive war, 'planned and prepared for over a long period of time and with no small skill and cunning'.[23] Through a forensic if somewhat narrowly conceived reconstruction of German political and military planning, the prosecution presented aggression as 'the criminal core of Nazism' and its foreign policy as calculated and programmatic.[24] Copious documentary evidence from *Mein Kampf* to the 1937 Hossbach Memorandum was tabled to prove that an expansionist blueprint to destroy the Versailles settlement and carve out *lebensraum* for Germans in the East had been elaborated at the founding of the Nazi party in the 1920s and then 'remained unaltered until the party was dissolved in 1945'.[25] Outside Germany, the Nuremberg judgement merely reinforced pre-existing common sense perceptions. Thus eminent historian Lewis Namier who helped edit captured German diplomatic documents for publication remarked in 1953: 'we were determined to do this work on their archives with the utmost impartiality and with impeccable scholarship. But we did not doubt that it would turn out a formidable indictment'.[26] Similar assumptions about the 'predetermined deadly course' of Nazi conquest were reproduced in influential contemporary histories such as wartime British Prime Minister Winston Churchill's 1948 memoir, *The Gathering Storm*.[27]

The Nuremberg proceedings were obviously conditioned by political expediency, and within Germany they were resented as an imposition of victor's justice. But the verdicts did not necessarily disturb dominant modes of viewing the recent past; although the intention was to hand down exemplary punishment, as elsewhere these trials were simultaneously exculpatory, effectively offering amnesty to all those not indicted. Indeed, such German support as there was for the trials derived in large measure from an expectation that a few scapegoat guilty verdicts would swiftly close the book on retribution.[28] The final judgement contained 'not the slightest imputation of blame for the German people or German traditions' and focused exclusively on the role of a criminal elite of conspiratorial Nazi party zealots that 'controlled the destiny' of the nation.[29] As the senior French judge feared, it could thus easily be read as refuting the notion that 'Hitlerian crimes [had] their roots deep in the German people'.[30]

This was certainly an argument that German historians, suffused with nationalist values, were primed to run. The profession evinced a remarkable degree of continuity from Weimar through the Third Reich and beyond, and judgements on how far it was compromised have recently become much harsher.[31] A few mostly liberal or Jewish historians emigrated and another minority offered overt intellectual justification for racist territorial expansion. But if the discipline thus escaped intensive 'Nazification', this was largely because most German historians 'had long cultivated their own brand of cultural and political nationalism which proved to be largely compatible with the biological nationalism of the Nazis';[32] so they tended to be, for example, broadly in sympathy with Nazi anti-communism and foreign policy aims through the early war years. Philosophical and methodological commitments further inhibited oppositional historiography. The historicist tradition valorised political and diplomatic history and the promotion of identification with the nation-state through empathetic narrative reconstruction of the ideas and actions of political leaders. Marginalizing social, economic and structural factors, asserting the primacy and autonomy of foreign policy, and eschewing law-bound explanation, historicism inevitably tended to justify and rationalise national policy.[33] Reverence for the nation-state together with an attachment to 'success' as a criterion for historical judgement meant that 'most historians greeted the Nazis as the latest victors whose history they, by the very nature of their profession, had to write'.[34] Simultaneously, a commitment to idealised value-free inquiry and scholarly standards as guarantees of integrity deprived them of the moral and political resources needed to prevent creeping incorporation. So although Nazi ideology was not fully or uncritically accepted, collectively the profession 'overwhelmingly legitimated the national socialist regime'.[35]

After the war, the discipline remained largely unreconstructed; few émigrés returned, only a handful of historians were purged, and historicist traditions were not radically reassessed.[36] (Intensely patriarchal structures of academic appointment and promotion, making younger scholars dependent upon powerful patrons for advancement, also helped perpetuate conservative values.) Of course, there was a certain amount of 'critical stock-taking', but much of it 'was little more than a rhetorical smoke-screen of lament, behind which the same old national apologias, somewhat turned down in volume, could and did continue'. Angst over the perceived 'international conspiracy to blacken the whole of German history' at Nuremberg further rallied historians 'to the defence of the nation'.[37] War origins were not a particularly favoured subject in this climate where 'the consequences, not the causes' of the war preoccupied the nation.[38] But nonetheless a series of key ideas about Nazi foreign relations emerged, evincing a remarkable coherence despite their individual nuances, and clearly partaking of the 'ready lexicon of exculpation' already put into circulation by the Nuremberg defendants and other, more respectable, public figures.[39]

Two central interlocking arguments were the restriction of guilt to a few elite conspirators, pre-eminently the demonic genius of Hitler, and the presentation of Nazism as an aberration in German history, engendered by broader European trends.[40] In *The German Catastrophe*, published in 1946, one of the profession's elder statesmen Friedrich Meinecke characterised Hitler's accession to power as the result of 'a very singular and in no small degree a chance chain of causes', not the product of any 'pressing necessity' inherent in the unfolding historical process in Germany. Hitler had organised 'a band of criminals ... which fastened upon the German people and sucked them dry'. Meinecke reproduced approvingly the verdicts of earlier conservative observers that Hitler '"really does not belong to our race at all"', even that '"this fellow has no Fatherland"'. Together with repeated references to Hitler's 'demonic self', these characterisations rendered him an almost inexplicable accident. Meinecke admitted that Nazism was in part a product of Prussian militarism and pan-German nationalism but immediately insisted that it was 'not a phenomenon deriving from merely German evolutionary forces' but one that had 'certain analogies and precedents in the authoritarian systems of neighboring countries'. It was a result of 'the optimistic illusions of the Age of Enlightenment and the French Revolution', of the 'mistaken striving after the unattainable happiness of the masses of mankind, which then shifted into a desire for profits, power, and a general striving for living well'.[41] On this reading Nazism was a pathology of modernity, a product of 'western materialism and utilitarianism' against which positive German values – such as the 'Idealist notion of the state providing a political order free of social and political conflict' – could even be juxtaposed.[42]

Gerhard Ritter, first chair of the FRG historical association, advanced similar arguments more strongly. The negative elements in Nazism, he claimed, were all foreign imports; racism was an Austrian trait, nationalism a product of the French Revolution, social Darwinism was British while Machiavellianism was Italian. Socialism and mass politics were again European phenomena that had been imposed with dramatic adverse consequences upon the German nation. (Ritter's work constituted a conservative defence of authoritarian government insofar as it identified the volatility and suggestibility of the masses as the key precursor of 'the totalitarian possibility in Europe'.[43]) Meinecke had enthusiastically supported the early stages of Nazi expansionism, but in his text passed over in silence Hitler's political and foreign policy successes before 1939, deeming them now irrelevant (crimes against humanity were alluded to but briefly).[44] Ritter was bolder, bluntly defending efforts to throw off the shackles of Versailles and assert the German right to self-determination (as recognised at Munich). It was only in March 1939, with the occupation of rump Czechoslovakia, that things began to go awry as a demonic force turned German policy onto a new and deeply dangerous track.[45] This interpretation not only served to dissociate Hitler from German history but also legitimated those actions that the Nazis had committed before supernatural forces supposedly intervened.[46]

The argument that Hitler was not really of the German people ineluctably led to portraying them as his victims. Golo Mann, though a former exile and amongst the more democratically minded in the profession, nonetheless in 1958 advanced a patriotic view of German innocence and suffering. He too asserted that Nazism was not properly 'a chapter in German history'; Hitler had risen from nowhere – again like a demon – to beguile a peace-loving people into supporting the Nazis who then behaved towards them like 'foreign conquerors'. The war had been Hitler's war, and as the German people's resistance to him grew so he increasingly waged war on them, massacring thousands. This victimisation was compounded by the Allies who committed atrocities against the Germans quite equivalent to those of Hitler, for example with the 'insane' forced division of their country. These pleas were coupled with efforts to spread blame for the war – French attempts to control Germany through a policy of alliances, incessant British appeasement, American neutrality and Stalin's rapacious pact with the Nazis should not be forgotten in explaining its outbreak.[47] Such arguments came close to reproducing the self-justifications of Nazi policy-makers in displacing blame onto those whom the Germans attacked.

Most of these interpretations rested upon the idea that modernity had spawned a novel, totalitarian, form of state. Totalitarianism was invoked more explicitly in an overlapping strand of explanations advanced by, amongst others, the Swiss Walther Hofer, which characterised the Third Reich as but one exemplum of a dictatorial state where society was subject to total control by terror and propaganda and where relentless expansion was inherent in an ideology of permanent revolution. Although Hitler's responsibility for the war was usually affirmed, his anti-communism was minimised and a fundamental affinity posited between the Third Reich and Soviet Russia; indeed, in some cases Hitler and Stalin were presented as jointly responsible for launching a war to destroy the European order in 1939.[48] This was hardly surprising given that totalitarianism virtually constituted the official ideology of the FRG, underpinning the constitution and ultimately being enshrined by government fiat in school curricula. The concept was extraordinarily useful in the Adenauer era: if the Third Reich was essentially both a European phenomenon and a regime which held an atomised society in terrorised thrall then ordinary Germans were relieved of complicity; simultaneously, affirming damnable similarities between Nazism and communism facilitated the FRG's integration into the Cold War western alliance and provided a weapon with which to beat the totalitarian successor GDR. It also enabled conservative Germans to carry anti-communist prejudices seamlessly over from the Third Reich into the post-war world.[49]

A further mode of exoneration focused on the impersonal machinations of geopolitics. Ludwig Dehio was very far from a dyed in the wool nationalist, and in essays in the 1950s rejected simplistic ideas that the Third Reich could be bracketed off, instead treating the world wars together as twin efforts by Germany to achieve European supremacy. This framing transgressed a basic taboo in associating the statesmen of Imperial Germany with the Nazis and foreshadowed later continuity arguments, but here content blunted radical potential as Germans were again absolved of real responsibility for Hitler's crimes. For Dehio, the last war was a product of 'the daemonic nature of power' in international relations that impelled states to seek hegemony, and of the tragic accidents of geopolitical contingency that allotted Germany the physical location, means and opportunity to play this doomed part. After the shock of the First World War the inherent flaws and iniquities of the Versailles system together with internal convulsions generated by economic crisis, communist agitation and mass disenchantment inevitably drove Germany along the path to war. The situation was exacerbated by the fact that 'Germany's warders' – the other powers of Europe – 'turned out to be cowardly or irresponsible, helpless or short-sighted'; catastrophe then became certain once the state was seized by the 'Satanic genius' of Hitler, the apotheosis, 'the very incarnation', of 'the daemon of the total struggle for hegemony'.[50] This argument relativised Nazi actions in the context of an amoral international system where recourse to aggression was not unprecedented and almost eradicated human (and German) agency by focus on structural factors. Thus it complemented other formulations in which Nazism was 'a perversion, a plague, a catastrophe, and finally a tragedy' that simply befell Germany.[51]

These narrative strategies were not inherently illegitimate. After all, few would dispute that Hitler was uncommonly evil, his ideology and actions fiendishly irrational and central to the course of politics in the Third Reich. Many accounts of the inter-war crisis seek the roots of Nazism in dislocations engendered by broad long-term processes of economic, social and political change. Anglo-American scholarship in the 1950s was also largely preoccupied with exploring the responsibility of systemic factors and powers other than Germany 'for allowing war to break out in 1939'.[52] Moreover, despite their political entailments it would be unwise to declare empirical comparisons between Nazism and communism entirely impermissible.[53] But the cumulative deployment of these arguments in this context almost entirely marginalised the issue of German liability for Nazism and the war; as Hans Kohn lamented in 1954, 'the troubling problem is not the personality of Hitler nor the phenomenon of mass civilization, but the fact that the Germans in their overwhelming majority fell for their worst features'.[54] Coupled with the near absence of the Holocaust and the incipient heroicisation of the conservative nationalist bomb plot resisters of 20 July 1944 and even the *Wehrmacht* as guardians of an 'other Germany' untainted by Nazism, this was a thoroughly apologetic discourse. But of course it fitted the public mood: as Hannah Arendt noted ruefully in 1950, 'the average German looks for the causes of the last war not in the acts of the Nazi regime, but in the events that led to the expulsion of Adam and Eve from paradise. Such an escape from reality is also, of course, an escape from responsibility'.[55]

In generating a 'simple historical explanation' as a first retrospective understanding of the Second World War, Germans were scarcely unusual amongst the combatants.[56] Equally, these evasive and superficial formulations conformed closely in certain respects to generic archetypes, which figure persistently in the response of nations more generally to defeat. Thus 'all blame [was] transferred to the deposed tyrant' so that the losing nation might feel 'cathartically cleansed, freed of any responsibility or guilt'; equally, in so far as 'the path that led to war and defeat' was admitted as 'an error', this was construed as a 'mistaken detour' in the national narrative.[57] Yet it would be wrong to attribute these explanations simply to the absence of sufficient empirical evidence to ground more profound accounts, or to the influence of recurring structural or psychological factors inhibiting reflection. As Donald Bloxham has argued in relation to the Holocaust, franker and fuller reckonings may have eluded the contemporary legal and political imagination, but the material basis for them was nonetheless in place.[58] Equally, these interpretations were forged in the course of extensive and wide-ranging political, philosophical and even theological debates that constituted a 'vibrant public discourse' on the recent past. Moreover, for all the political expediency of these dominant narratives, they were less the product of cynical calculation than of genuine 'conviction and perception'.[59]

Beyond Germany diverse interpretations flourished.[60] Totalitarianism was scarcely a German invention and through the tense Cold War decade of the 1950s interpretations dependent upon it – and compatible with the dominant indigenous discourse of victimhood – proliferated. But another very powerful strain in Anglo-American and émigré writing not only took for granted the Nuremberg view that Nazi aggression had caused the war but also located it within a continuum of German history marked by flawed national character and deformed political and cultural development.[61] (Classics of this genre include A. J. P. Taylor's *The Course of German History*.[62]) The responses to American journalist William Shirer's best selling *The Rise and Fall of the Third Reich* published in 1960 neatly illustrate what was at stake between these two antagonistic positions. For Shirer, Nazism was 'but a logical continuation of German history' which had run from 1871 to 1945 'in a straight line'. In the United States, the book was praised by reviewers sharing Shirer's prejudices and suspicion about how securely rooted democracy was in the FRG. But many historians castigated it for hysterically rehashing essentialist wartime propaganda and for conceptual poverty, specifically failing to appreciate the nature of the modern totalitarian state and the relationship of Nazism to wider European trends. These criticisms shaded into political objections to the book's supposedly pro-communist sub-text and the damage it could do to the FRG's place in the western alliance. Needless to say, German reviewers treated a 1961 translation with unremitting hostility, damning Shirer as a German-hater lacking an historian's objectivity and for completely passing over 'the core of the problem – totalitarianism in its specifically National Socialist form'. Underpinning these responses too, in the aftermath of the Berlin wall crisis, were anxieties about potential repercussions on American attitudes at a point when the Bonn government felt in acute need of friends.[63]

In the space between these polarised interpretations, other historians struggled to bring key interpretive issues into focus. Alan Bullock's landmark 1952 biography of Hitler meticulously reconstructed the course of Nazi diplomacy, relying largely on the mass of documentary evidence presented at Nuremberg, and discerned consistent objectives, formulated in the 1920s, to overthrow Versailles and acquire living space in the East. But whilst this was very much in tune with the Nuremberg view, he simultaneously gestured towards the 'demon' theorists by presenting Hitler as an unprincipled opportunist animated solely by a relentless nihilistic lust for power. By the same token, he both described Hitler as the *reductio ad absurdum* of powerful German political and cultural traditions and stressed that the malaises of which he was a symptom were not confined to a single country.[64] Given these tensions, it was scarcely surprising that Bullock was criticised both for underestimating Hitler's unswerving convictions – presenting him in Hugh Trevor-Roper's phrase as simply a 'mountebank dictator' – and for attributing to him a systematic plan that simply did not exist.[65] But the issues he broached of the relative significance of Hitler's ideas and intentions in the Third Reich, the nature of his foreign policy programme, and the extent to which he was the avatar of continuous traditions in German history were to be central in the fervent debates that erupted during the 1960s.

'Racist war of annihilation': Nazi foreign policy from the 1960s

From the 1960s, historical writing on Nazism mushroomed and reached a new plane of sophistication, even if there was considerable continuity in some of the core issues at stake.[66] A concatenation of political, social and disciplinary factors of a kind that precipitated the emergence of a scholarly historiography on the Second World War era in most European countries at this point was responsible. Politics in the FRG shifted leftwards; the Social Democrats repositioned themselves, broadly accepting the market economy and a pro-western orientation, and broke the Christian Democrat stranglehold on power, joining them in coalition in 1966 then forming their own government with the liberal Free Democrats in 1969. Simultaneously, geopolitical changes including the tentative growth of détente and accelerating doubts about the identity of interest between Western Europe and the Vietnam-embroiled United States undermined the totalitarianist verities of the Adenauer era. Social Democrat Chancellor Willy Brandt contributed to this through his *Ostpolitik*, establishing fresh contacts with the Soviet Union and gingerly advancing towards recognition of the GDR. Generational change underpinned this new political topography. The counter–cultural protests that culminated in Europe-wide unrest in 1968 acquired a particular character in the FRG as neo-Marxist critiques focused on potential fascist continuities with the Third Reich and thus articulated a 'deep-seated sense of unease' at the founding generation's failure to confront the past candidly.[67] Political transformation was thus imbricated with the coalescence of more critical attitudes towards the Nazi past. A spate of war crimes trials beginning in 1958, the prosecution of Adolf Eichmann in Israel in 1961 and the Frankfurt Auschwitz trial convened in 1963 were landmarks; even if sentences were too often paltry, the process of judicial reconstruction shattered complacency and self-delusion by bringing the crimes of Germans under Nazism into unprecedented focus.

Shifts in academic interpretations of the national past fed on and fuelled these processes. A. J. P. Taylor's *The Origins of the Second World War* and Fritz Fischer's work on German policy in the era of the First were particularly influential. Taylor's vigorous if ultimately incoherent interpretation was primarily controversial for portraying Hitler as a supreme improviser in international affairs, thus challenging the Nuremberg line that his programmatic aggression was the prime cause of the war. But though this was widely deemed exculpatory, Taylor's assertion that Hitlerite expansion was not ideologically motivated – not specifically 'Nazi' – but rather in tune with longer-term German foreign policy traditions was in essence a more sophisticated reprise of his earlier argument about negative continuity.[68] Simultaneously, Fischer attacked the orthodoxy that Germany bore no particular responsibility for the First World War by arguing not only that the Imperial elite had engineered its outbreak but also that it had done so in pursuit of expansionist goals not dissimilar to those of the Nazis. This interpretation too was not utterly novel – a minority of German historians had challenged the nationalist consensus through the 1950s – but appearing in conjunction with Taylor's it propelled the issue of continuity to centre stage.[69]

A new generation of historians, influenced by social science methods and known as the 'Bielefeld school', now pioneered the idea of the German *Sonderweg* ('special path'). This metanarrative inverted proud historicist presumptions of political, cultural and moral superiority, asserting that Germany had followed a disastrous course through deviating from the normal pattern of European development.[70] The weakness of its liberal tradition meant that during the nineteenth century economic development had not been matched by political modernisation. In attempting to contain the resulting socio-political tensions, the authoritarian governments of Imperial Germany had resorted to expansionist 'social imperialism' which had ultimately precipitated the First World War. The attenuated nature of the 1918–19 revolution then ensured that liberal democracy was insecurely rooted in the Weimar Republic and unable to flourish. The rise of the Nazis accordingly followed, but Hitler's regime too was inherently unstable and thus the internal contradictions of the German state triggered another catastrophic conflict. It was only with utter defeat that the *Sonderweg* came to an end and the conditions were established, in the FRG at least, for the co-existence of modern social and economic structures and liberal democracy. (In pointing to the tragic consequences that had followed 1871, the *Sonderweg* thesis thus chimed perfectly with Brandt's tentative moves to accept post-1945 partition as legitimate, even necessary.) Liberal advocates of 'historical social science' urged interdisciplinary innovation and the critical exploration of negative continuity in the national past as a means to democratic renewal. This represented a stark methodological and political challenge to previously dominant historicist thinking which, while not vanquished, was placed on the defensive by the idea of Hitler as the culmination of German historical development.

The rise of 'historical social science' expanded the parameters of writing on modern German history and Nazism. The growing sense of urgency about interrogating the Nazi past also coincided with significant expansion in German universities that created 'both opportunity and necessity for successive waves of doctoral candidates to embark on intensive monographic research projects'.[71] Simultaneously, significant fresh primary documentary material became available, including Hitler's so-called *Second Book*, first published in 1961 and containing his geopolitical thinking from the late 1920s, and the accumulating volumes of captured material edited by American, British and French historians in the series *Documents on German Foreign Policy, 1918–1945*.[72] The thrust of the resultant research in international history was influenced by the claims of 'historical social science' and the provocations of Taylor and Fischer, not only as regards continuity but also with respect to the roots and nature of foreign policy. On the one hand, in asserting that German diplomacy before 1914 was in large part a product of elite anxieties about internal social and economic tensions, Fischer opened up the question of its domestic roots and structural determinants. On the other, for all Taylor's revisionist élan, his picture of the 1930s was very much that of an old-fashioned diplomatic historian, reducing 'the international relations of the period to the obsolete formula of independent states pursuing intelligible interests with varying degrees of diplomatic skill' and marginalizing issues of ideology, economics and domestic determinants.[73] Historians contesting his arguments were therefore drawn to engage precisely these structural and thematic realities behind and beyond the narrow confines of diplomacy.

Despite these developments, authors who remained closely wedded to the historicist tradition made the most enduring contributions to the literature on foreign policy. From the late 1960s until well into the 1980s, the main conceptual debate within the historiography of Nazism was between so-called 'intentionalist' and 'functionalist' approaches.[74] 'Intentionalists' prioritised human agency and specifically the consistent dictatorial will of a leader at the head of a coherent power structure seeking to implement carefully formulated ideological goals. 'Functionalists', conversely, argued that policy emerged as a function of structural social and economic pressures and competition between different agencies in a polycratic regime. This resulted in its unplanned cumulative radicalisation, as the most pernicious elements within the Nazi worldview were successively selected for implementation.[75] Leading international historians such as Andreas Hillgruber, Klaus Hildebrand and Hans-Adolf Jacobsen were pioneers of the former approach, more traditional in its methodology and conservative in its political entailments, responding in a guarded manner to the new interpretative agenda. Although prepared to countenance the possibility of continuities in patterns of German foreign policy, they consistently opposed the Bielefelders' contention that it was an expression of domestic pressures. Equally, while keen to elucidate the ideological forces that Taylor had discounted, they resisted the notion that structural or thematic factors should be prioritised in analysis above policy-makers' ideas and actions. This defence of method was also a defence of subject matter, insofar as both Bielefelders and 'functionalists' tended to be much more interested in internal than external affairs, while the 'intentionalists' insisted that 'the high politics of states and classic diplomatic history had ... to retain their proper place in German historiography'.[76]

Central to 'intentionalist' scholarship was the identification of an ideological programme of expansion, conceived by Hitler in the 1920s, systematically pursued and, in the dominant variant, aimed at global domination.[77] This entailed successively restoring Germany's great power status, establishing pre-eminence in central Europe, attaining continental hegemony and *lebens-raum* through the conquest of the Soviet Union, imperialist expansion in Africa and the Middle East, and finally at some distant date a titanic conflict with the United States for 'world dominion'.[78] These geopolitical ambitions were interlinked with an anti-Semitic and racist agenda to conduct a '"biological revolution"' by breeding 'a superior, Germanic elite' – indeed a 'new human being' – and to eradicate the Jewish–Bolshevik archenemy.[79] 'Intentionalists' reaffirmed the centrality of Hitler posited at Nuremberg; he personally took major decisions and imposed his will upon policy-making agencies advocating alternative strategies. But in the scale of the aspirations delineated and the prominence accorded to Hitler's ideological motivations and exterminatory racism, this programme went considerably beyond that previously outlined. Similarly, the 'intentionalists' were careful to distance themselves from the notion of a rigid blueprint, unfolding mechanically to timetable, since in their more textured account external contingencies and internal pressures inevitably intervened. Thus Hitler's original aim of building his continental empire with at least the acquiescence of Great Britain was confounded by unanticipated Anglo-French stubbornness over Poland in September 1939, which left him confronting general war years earlier than intended. Subsequent miscalculation embroiled him in a drawn out conflict with the Soviet Union without having settled with Britain in the West, and then also precipitated him into confrontation with the United States; attempting to realise the final three stages of his plan simultaneously doomed the Third Reich to destruction.

'Functionalists' rarely essayed similarly detailed reconstructions of foreign policy, but nonetheless certainly challenged this paradigm. Hans Mommsen asserted that Hitler's foreign policy did not consist of 'an unchanging pursuit of established priorities'; its aims, 'purely dynamic in nature, knew no bounds' – the description '"expansion without object"' was 'entirely justified' – and 'to interpret their implementation as in any way consistent or logical [was] highly problematic'.[80] For Martin Broszat, ideological concepts such as *lebensraum*, anti-Semitism and anti-Bolshevism were originally functional, designed to integrate the diverse antagonistic forces within the state, but ultimately the plebiscitary social dynamic of the Nazi movement pushed Hitler into turning such metaphors into reality and policy ever further from rational control.[81] Thus 'the disruption of the unified bureaucratic state order, the growing formlessness and arbitrariness of legislation and of decision-making, and of transmitting decisions, played a part in speeding up the process of radicalisation which was every bit as important as any ideological fixity of purpose'.[82] The direction of policy was determined by the restless dynamism of an unstable regime, the dictates of propaganda, and bureaucratic social Darwinist competition. Finally, a Marxist variant emphasised social and economic tensions generated by the attempt to combine rapid rearmament with protection of living standards which in 1939 forced Hitler into a war of plunder to stave off internal revolt.[83]

From the 1980s, the general trend in the historiography of Nazism was towards transcendence of the overdrawn dichotomy between intention and structure, typically through the invocation of Hitler's 'charismatic authority'.[84] In international history 'functionalism' served a useful purpose in problematising over-rigid schematisation, but generally it was deemed unconvincing and so with some modifications 'intentionalist' scholarship stands at the heart of contemporary understandings.[85] Denying the existence of intelligible goals in Nazi foreign policy and the power of ideology seems unsustainable, given the durability of Hitler's core ideas about domestic revolutionary change and the implementation of an Aryan world order, and the correspondence between his expressed ambitions and what he (almost) achieved. Of course, realising these goals involved improvisation, opportunism and tactical manoeuvring, not least because the Third Reich was indeed a polycratic state, but 'intentionalists' demonstrated that these insights were not incompatible with the ultimate supremacy of Hitler's will. Foreign policy was the area of government in which Hitler was 'most passionately interested', where he 'set markers and involved himself at decisive points', such that he constituted its 'central determinant'. Although structural factors such as political, economic and social tensions were in play, these often reinforced Hitler's resolve to pursue a course of action rather than imprisoning him. But satisfactory conceptualisations of Nazi foreign policy must encompass both intention and structure; ideological aims were an important determinant but they fused inseparably with strategic, power–political and economic considerations, just as Hitler's functional role as Führer was crucial in integrating the desires of party cadres, *Wehrmacht*, diplomats, industrialists and masses as policy progressively radicalised.[86]

Elucidating the politics of 'intentionalism' and 'functionalism' is complicated. *Prima facie*, 'intentionalism' was aligned through its historicist methodology and its advocates' conservative political inclinations with the nationalist tradition, whereas 'functionalism' was an expression of nascent critical attitudes towards Nazism. This was the self-understanding of 'functionalists' who construed their polycracy paradigm as a riposte to totalitarianist notions of the Third Reich as omnipotent monolith and averred that 'Hitlercentric' interpretations were inherently apologetic in glossing over the complicity of other political forces that collaborated in his rise to power and rule. Conversely, in contrast to earlier discourses of exoneration, 'intentionalism' had the definite merit of bringing Nazism's racist and genocidal dimensions into clear focus. Indeed, 'intentionalists' were apt to accuse 'functionalists' in turn of underrating 'the capacity of Nazi leaders for premeditated evil' and thus 'making the regime appear less monstrous than it was'. 'Decision-making procedures, administrative structures or the dynamics of organizational rivalries ... were at best secondary. To make them a vital part of a general interpretation of National Socialism is to trivialise the subject, to write morally incompetent history. What really matters is the distinctive murderous will of the Nazi leadership'. On this reading, it was the 'functionalist' elision of agency, through displacement of explanation to the level of process, that had exculpatory implications.[87] Underpinning these controversies were disagreements about how far documentary evidence could or should be read literally, the nature of objectivity, and the validity of rationalising the criminal excesses of Nazism through historical discourse. But both 'intentionalism' and 'functionalism', depending on context and the precise formulation offered, were potentially conducive to exculpation. Indeed, this is the central thrust of a landmark controversial study of Holocaust historiography which has indicted this whole generation of historians – 'intentionalists' and 'functionalists' alike – for intellectual and political failings.[88]

The politics of 'intentionalism' deserve further consideration, however, given its relatively greater significance. The other crucial issue here is continuity, whether and how far Hitler was the inheritor of older traditions in German statecraft. Jacobsen's work exploring the diverse state and Party agencies involved in policy-making argued strongly that the Third Reich represented radical discontinuity. With a view to rebutting Taylor's theses on improvisation and continuity, Jacobsen argued that there was an unwavering inner consistency behind Hitler's foreign policy in the search for racial renewal and the destruction of the Judeo–Bolshevik enemy.[89] Although in its early stages it resembled a traditional revisionist policy this was merely a 'convenient smokescreen' for his true, fanatical goals.[90] Foreign policy development from 1933 'should be seen less in the light of the continuity of German history, and rather more under the aspect of a revolutionary change'.[91] This formula harked back to apologetic historicist formulations of the 'demon theory' of Hitler's rise to power and of Nazism as parenthesis; though Jacobsen did not second Ritter's argument that Nazi policy took a decisive turn in 1938–39 (with its concomitant defence of revisionist achievements before that point), he sharply differentiated Hitler from his predecessors and from conservative nationalist currents in German foreign policy.

Other leading 'intentionalists' adopted more nuanced positions. In Hillgruber's words, 'on the one hand, continuities certainly exist, while on the other hand deep breaches and important new departures can be identified'.[92] Hildebrand noted a series of respects in which Hitler was rooted in German history. First, 'the continental and overseas demands of Hitler's Programme place it completely within a particular tradition of power politics such as is observable in Prussian–German history since the days of Bismarck'. Second, that programme 'integrated all the political demands, economic requirements and socio-political expectations prevailing in German society' since 1871. Third, 'Hitler's dictatorship was the culmination of and surpassed the caesaristic tradition in Prussian–German history'. But set against this were elements of 'revolutionary discontinuity'. Although anti-Semitism was not unknown in German history (hence it functioned well for Hitler as an integrative tool), the fanatical racist dogma that lay at the heart of his project – envisaging genocide, 'world domination' and a biologically-engineered 'master race' – was 'new and revolutionary'. Over time, and especially after the beginning of the 'racist war of annihilation' in the East in 1941, the traditional, 'rational', elements in Hitler's thinking began to be undermined and eclipsed by the 'ideological': 'racist dogma had finally triumphed over the political cunning in his Programme'.

Conservative elites had initially welcomed Hitler and supported his use of revisionist diplomacy and the integrative motifs of anti-Semitism, anti-Bolshevism and *lebensraum*; but when 'the racist dogma shed its cloak of mere propaganda and entered the phase of its implementation', it not only 'torpedoed the policy of cunning calculation' but also made clear that Hitler's interests were manifestly inimical to theirs since he intended to destroy existing racial, political and social arrangements and thus their positions within Germany.[93] (Hence, 'Prussian–German conservatism gave birth unawares to a revolutionary who pretended to be its servant but proved to be its murderer'.[94]) Here lay a second major breach with the past. There could be no question of Hitler as the culmination of a *Sonderweg* in which foreign policy-makers had risked 'social imperialist' wars in order to stave off internal threats and preserve the domestic order, because Hitler's prime motivation derived from a bellicose ideology valorising foreign expansion and actively seeking the revolutionary destruction of that order.

This presentation of Hitler's programme as combining traditional geopolitical goals and novel racist dogma conveys ambiguous political messages. Acknowledging fundamental continuities in the former entails a rupture with pure apologetic discourses that sought to bracket Hitler off completely; but that which is identified as the criminal core of the Nazi project – Hitler's 'racist war of extermination' – is categorically presented as 'a "new" feature in the history of Prussia-Germany'. A clear distinction is thus drawn between the 'rational' element of 'pragmatic political calculation' that was in the

German tradition and the 'irrational' racism that was a fundamental 'intrusion' (with the former implicitly coded positive). Thus although 'intentionalists' garnered kudos for confronting the enormity of Nazi racism, they simultaneously established an exculpatory distance between it and mainstream currents in German history. By the same token, the conservative elites that had collaborated with Hitler and shared his earlier goals were presented as ultimately victims too, insofar as he aimed to supplant them with a 'new Nazi elite'. Responsibility for the war and its atrocities did not lie with them since by its outbreak they had 'long since been forced into political submission by the Führer'; moreover, as they 'found themselves more and more in opposition to him' they became fully tragic figures unable to 'find anyone among the enemy powers who would listen to their "alternative" plans' because Hitler's conduct had determined the latter to fight for unconditional surrender.[95]

Coupled with the explicit rejection of the *Sonderweg* thesis, these 'intentionalist' arguments posit a circumscribed continuity that preserves a broadly positive image of traditional German foreign policy goals and conservative nationalist elites. Hence one can see the full force of the 'functionalist' criticism that to stress the singular character of a regime 'devoted to an utterly novel principle for the public order, scientific racism' and characterise National Socialism primarily in terms of 'Hitlerism' risks obfuscating key questions of continuity and complicity.[96] This was a common strategy in FRG public discourse even in these decades of supposed critical engagement: profusely 'acknowledging the shame of anti-Semitism and maintaining an attenuated view of Nazism's social and political context' – thus ducking 'the more difficult and disturbing questions of Nazism's structural rootedness in German society at large' – could be 'different sides of a single coin'.[97] Conservative political investments and methodological preferences valorising historical specificity and 'great men' jointly conduced towards such an argument, which also worked to preclude any suggestion of fascist continuities after 1945. The changing climate had rendered flat denial of continuity implausible, but Hillgruber and Hildebrand still elaborated a narrative of the Third Reich that rested upon an equivocation and thus permitted a generally positive story of the German past.[98] Thus where the *Sonderweg* thesis developed in a more sophisticated form the continuity arguments of an earlier generation of Germanophobe authors, so 'intentionalism' carried over some key tropes of exculpatory 'demon theory' interpretations – in which Hitler figured as an interloper in German history – into the era of document-based historical scholarship.

Moreover, in positing a fundamental dualism between power politics and racism, 'intentionalism' incarnated a key post-war mnemonic manoeuvre of 'ultraconservatives' who – according to Jeffrey Olick – 'often claimed that it was precisely this addition of biological racism to a more defensible core of political values that [had] baffled them and contributed to their turn away from National Socialism'. This is not to say, of course, that these 'intentionalist' authors were as personally implicated in Nazism as Martin Heidegger or other figures discussed by Olick.[99] But it is nonetheless tempting to see their interpretations, buttressed by reference to – but not essentially derived from – the documentary record, as an historiographical expression of this generic conservative response.

This is neither to denigrate the empirical achievements of the 'intentionalists' nor to deny that their insights still dominate debates in the field.[100] Indeed, the argument that Nazi foreign policy was 'a combination of traditional military and political goals dating back to the pre-1914 Wilhelmine Empire and the new ideology of Nazism as expressed especially by Hitler' with its open-ended racial and spatial ambitions is now utterly orthodox.[101] Moreover, it is widely agreed, the key point where Hitler's policy was – 'both qualitatively and quantitatively' – 'uniquely different from that of preceding regimes' was in the 'appalling ruthlessness of the Nazi extermination campaign in Russia' against which Imperial German plans for the domination of Eastern Europe 'pale into insignificance'.[102] Indeed, it could even be argued that the 'intentionalist' emphasis upon Nazi biological politics was prescient given that by the 1990s 'the centrality of race to all areas of National Socialist policy and practice had been established'.[103] But subsequent authors have been less ready to treat racism as an extraneous interpellation, instead tracing its roots in longer-term trends in German nationalist thinking and posing questions about perpetration that these earlier 'intentionalists' evaded.[104] Similarly, although it is evident that in the later 1930s Nazi foreign policy radicalised to an extent that disconcerted traditional conservative opinion, the complicity of nationalist elites is nonetheless more strongly emphasised, in accord with recent inclinations to probe how myriad socio-political groups were implicated in the Nazi project.[105]

That said, in comparison to the historiography of the Holocaust, what is striking about the literature on foreign policy is its relatively static character over recent decades.[106] Christian Leitz has recently observed that it has been marked by a 'comparative silence', and his own limpid synthesis of the current mainstream position demonstrates the lack of fundamental movement since it could have been penned 20 years or more ago. He writes very much in the 'intentionalist' tradition, prioritising political and diplomatic transactions above profound forces and systemic factors, with chapters framed around Hitler's foreign policy pronouncements from *Mein Kampf* onwards. Moreover, his account demonstrates how the 'intentionalist' paradigm continues to depend upon a core distinction between geopolitical and racial elements, with problematic consequences. He is writing explicitly against what he sees as a disturbing tendency for emphasis on the Holocaust to overshadow all else in the study of Nazi Germany. Indeed, he decries the incipient emergence of a mirror image of the Nuremberg view; if the Allied prosecutors balefully subsumed the Holocaust within Nazi plans to commit aggression, now foreign policy is sometimes almost viewed as a mere function of Hitler's genocidal racist drive.

Leitz accordingly sets out to make a case for the continued significance of the power-political dimension, on the grounds that from 1933 to 1941 this 'outweighed everything else in Hitler's mind, including deliberations on racial matters'. Leitz is scarcely alone in voicing anxieties about the over-whelming salience of the Holocaust in contemporary consciousness, and he acknowledges that Hitler's worldview was thoroughly racialised. But even if he is writing to correct an imbalance in the broader literature, given the contemporary landscape of memory there is something not merely old-fashioned but troubling about an account of Nazi expansionism that prioritises *realpolitik* whilst almost bracketing off the racial. In other words, Leitz inadvertently underlines the persistent ambivalence within the 'intentionalist' acknowl-edgment of Nazi racism, which must on some level be attributable to a continued historicist insistence on the autonomy and distinctiveness of foreign policy.[107] The centrality of war to the Nazi project is undeniable, but other recent accounts are more successful in 'integrating political, economic, social, and military history' and in fusing the analysands of race and power politics as they explicate the 'core' of Nazism as 'racially conceived struggle and war'.[108] By the lights of such texts, writing on foreign policy from within the 'inten-tionalist' tradition remains positioned towards the conservative end of the spectrum of historiographical responses to Nazism.

'Preventive war'? The 1980s, unification and beyond

The focus adopted here perhaps gives too negative an overall impression of German historiography during these decades. Other critical discourses were apparent, notably wide-ranging arguments about whether Nazism was a manifestation of generic fascism. Heavily influenced by Marxism, and tracing roots back to contemporaneous analyses, this proposition was anti-totalitarianist in associating Nazism with other right wing movements rather than the Soviet Union. In viewing fascism as a perennial product of crisis-ridden capitalism such arguments also suggested continuity – principally between the Third Reich and the FRG – but liberal historians tended to join con-servatives in repudiating them 'for being too politicised or too abstract, in either sense too distant from the "real" history of Nazi Germany'.[109] (Fascism approaches were also little interested in Nazi foreign policy, beyond char-acterising it as imperialist and inevitably entailing war.[110]) Furthermore, through to the 1980s 'historical social science' flourished and other critical perspectives (including feminist history, the history of everyday life, and a steadily developing Holocaust historiography) proliferated. But there was never an absolute 'paradigm shift', more a pluralisation of perspectives because older conservative approaches remained potent within both academic and popular historical consciousness. Moreover, from the early 1980s the climate changed again as nationalist thinking enjoyed a renaissance and brought into public debate a range of openly apologetic arguments to buttress the reasser-tion of a revitalised, positive national identity. These included an audacious strategy for displacing blame for Nazi aggression, the claim that at bottom the Second World War had been not merely defensive, but pre-emptive.

In 1982 the Christian Democrats returned to office under Chancellor Helmut Kohl as part of the broader shift that saw advocates of fiscal conservatism and a more robust policy towards the Soviet Union attain power across Western Europe and in the United States. Kohl encouraged conservative desires to 'normalise' German history, not least through sanitising and relativising the crimes of the Third Reich. Critical historians advocating 'post-nationalist' identities rooted in 'constitutional patriotism', attachment to western liberal values and insistent meditation on 'Auschwitz' were placed on the defensive. The visit Kohl orchestrated with American President Ronald Reagan to lay wreaths at a military cemetery at Bitburg during the May 1985 commemorations of the end of the war betrayed his intent. Reagan's overriding concern with the FRG's anti-Soviet potential in the 'Second Cold War' inclined him to prioritise reconciliation: 'I want to focus on the future', he intoned, 'I want to put that history behind me'.[111] The ceremony uniting former enemies was thus conceived as 'an act of symbolic resolution, a closing of the books on the past, the consummation of Germany's long-earned return to normalcy'.[112] But when Reagan spoke of those interred at Bitburg, including members of the *Waffen-SS*, as 'victims of Nazism also ... just as surely as the victims in the concentration camps' he aroused a storm of controversy, especially given his initial reluctance to make a compensatory visit to Bergen-Belsen.[113] This skewed approach to wartime suffering recalled the memory politics of the Adenauer era, and Kohl was keenly aware how resuscitating totalitarianist anti-communism could ground a more assertive German identity that would also prove acceptable to the West.

Kohl gathered conservative historians around him to advise on new museums in Bonn and Berlin to promote national historical consciousness, partly through marginalizing Nazism. Like-minded commentators urged that it was time to 'emerge from the shadow of the Third Reich'; German history should not be presented 'as an endless chain of mistakes and crimes'.[114] It was 'morally legitimate and politically necessary' to restore self-confidence by cultivating a positive identification with the national past.[115] True, the landscape of memory was complex. During a state visit by the president of Israel in 1984 Kohl declared fulsomely that he would 'resist every attempt to suppress or play ... down' Nazi crimes; yet he also stressed 'the mercy of being born too late' which freed his generation of direct guilt.[116] A few days after Bitburg, Federal President Richard von Weizsäcker gave a counterbalancing address marking the end of the war. He referred in standard conservative terms to 'the war started by Hitler' and to 8 May 1945 as 'the end of an aberration in German history' but also sensitively canvassed the panoply of victims of Nazism and urged his compatriots to 'face up as well as we can to the truth'.[117] As Bitburg demonstrated, the left and Jewish groups were also vocal in opposing the reorientation of German memory and identity. Indeed, what was most striking here was the overt contestation between contrasting memories and desires for normalisation or frankness; witness, further, the debates around Edgar Reitz's 1984 film *Heimat*, focusing on a single German community across the century and presenting Nazism as a transitional and remote experience, and French director Claude Lanzmann's 1985 *Shoah*, still acclaimed as the most searching filmic exploration ever of perpetration and suffering.[118] But overall critical perspectives were at bay. The *Sonderweg* metanarrative drifted out of favour because of exposure of its conceptual flaws and political attack from the right, and previously inadmissible arguments began to find open public expression.

This was the context for the eruption in 1986 of the *Historikerstreit*, an intense and multi-faceted controversy about the place of Nazism in German history, provoked by two prominent conservative intellectuals: international historian Andreas Hillgruber and historian of ideas Ernst Nolte. The central issues at stake in this 'historians' quarrel' were the singularity of the Holocaust and whether Nazism had been a defensive response to 'Asiatic' Bolshevism. Hillgruber published a pair of essays dealing respectively with the suffering of the German army and population in the East under Soviet onslaught in the final months of the war and the Nazi genocide against the Jews. Simply juxtaposing these in a volume entitled *Two Kinds of Demise* was provocative enough in its suggestion of equivalence, but Hillgruber also evoked empathy for the fate of soldiers and civilians in the former case while treating the Holocaust with dry detachment. Moreover, as in his pioneering work in the 1960s, he rather subtly elided the questions of perpetration and the strength of anti-Semitism amongst the German armed forces, political elites and indeed general populace.[119] Nolte was more inflammatory, though his arguments were not unfamiliar to readers of his work over the two previous decades. On a general level, he asserted that 'the demonization of the Third Reich is unacceptable', and that it should be viewed in less black and white terms, not as something apart from the rest of human history. Specifically he argued that, the technicalities of industrialised gassing aside, the Holocaust was not unique but merely one instance of modern mass murder amongst many others, such as the Turkish genocide against the Armenians and Pol Pot's crimes. Moreover, he claimed that Nazism in essence was a defensive reaction to communism – 1917 being 'its logical and factual prius' – and that the Holocaust was a response to Bolshevik extermination of class enemies: 'was the Gulag Archipelago not primary to Auschwitz?' Did the Nazis 'perhaps commit an "Asiatic" deed merely because they and their ilk considered themselves to be potential victims of an "Asiatic" deed?'[120]

Although the battle-lines were complex, Nolte and Hillgruber were supported by conservative sympathisers, including other 'intentionalists' like Hildebrand, while ranged against them – behind social philosopher Jürgen Habermas who led the critical counterblast – were an array of broadly left-wing figures including 'functionalists' like Mommsen and Broszat, and other luminaries of 'historical social science'. The disturbing implications of these revisionist endeavours were obvious. Nolte was resurrecting the claim that Nazism was simply of a piece with other modern authoritarian regimes and lending credence to the Nazi assertion that their actions, genocidal atrocities included, were justified by a prior Bolshevik menace. Effectively, this meant displacing racism and anti-Semitism from the heart of understandings of Nazism and replacing them with anti-communism, which made it possible to encode Hitler's war in the East in positive – or at the very least in tragic – terms. Redefining the Nazis as fellow-strugglers (albeit ones prone to regrettable excesses) in a conflict with communism that still continued could help stimulate 'a revitalized patriotism that would allow the Federal Republic to be proud of a German past not irredeemably tainted by National Socialism'. 'By divesting the Nazi crimes of their singularity and by making them at least partially understandable as a response to the Bolshevik threat', Nolte and others 'were seeking to create a nationalist pedigree for the Federal Republic which would not be prevented by the Nazi interlude from reaching back to the glories of the Imperial period'.[121] Vehement debate about the empirical and political dimensions of these arguments continued for well over a year.

Within these broad contexts, the resurgence in international history of the narrower claim that Operation Barbarossa had been launched as a pre-emptive strike had a direct political relevance. Like much of the neo-conservative case this originated in Nazi propaganda, and had subsequently been offered in mitigation by the defence at Nuremberg.[122] Thereafter it was a persistent presence in the military memoir and historical literature, even if its dubious associations rendered it somewhat marginal during the 1960s and 1970s.[123] But in the 1980s it once more gained visibility in academic discourse and the highbrow press. Contrary to the 'intentionalist' orthodoxy that Barbarossa was carefully planned from at least July 1940 as 'the realization of Hitler's ideologically based program of conquering *Lebensraum* in the East', this view implied that it was rather an almost improvised reaction to Soviet troop movements and diplomatic pressure that gave Hitler good reason to believe Stalin was about to realise his long-standing threat to advance communism westwards.[124] (Whether Stalin actually was planning an attack in 1941, or at some later date, remained a somewhat moot point.[125]) Barbarossa thus instigated a war to defend Europe from Stalin's revolutionary ambitions, and Hitler was (in somewhat Taylor-esque fashion) a conventional *realpolitiker* impelled into action by the agency of another. Nolte cleaved to this view and, though it was too extreme for most 'intentionalists' including Hillgruber, Hildebrand did flirt with it in presenting 1941 as the inevitable consequence of a clash between two totalitarianist programmes of expansion.[126] Stronger versions made a Machiavellian Stalin the 'key figure' in 1941, with Hitler simply his 'useful tool' and 'dupe', provoked into attacking as part of a master plan to destroy capitalism using him as a 'military surrogate'.[127] In displacing prime responsibility for the war from Hitler and his ideology onto Stalin, these arguments overlapped with certain variants of 'German school' thinking on Soviet foreign policy: historiographical anti-communism could serve the diverse purposes of both German nationalists and critics of the Soviet regime. Crucial here was Viktor Suvorov, a defector who had served in Soviet military intelligence, who became the most tireless proponent of the thesis across Europe, particularly with his much publicised book *Icebreaker*.[128]

Though scorned by most mainstream scholarly opinion, such arguments nonetheless increasingly became established as a pole in the debate, as in the multi-authored volume dealing with Barbarossa published in 1983 by the state-funded Research Institute for Military History in the series *Germany and the Second World War*.[129] Massively authoritative, this monumental 30 year endeavour effectively represents the authorised FRG version of the war, though its traditional Rankean scholarship has proved not uncontroversial: Omer Bartov, for example, has criticised the political entailments of its conservative methodology, disregard for social and cultural history and marginalisation of the Holocaust.[130] The introductory paragraphs of this particular volume delineated a debate between 'two diametrically opposed views'; on the one hand, a 'programmatic', 'intentionalist' explanation, and on the other the argument that 'Stalin's aggressive policy in Eastern central Europe ... provoked Hitler into reacting' by launching a 'preventive war'.[131] Accordingly, both views were canvassed within. Joachim Hoffmann painted Stalin's actions in the blackest possible colours, with the Nazi–Soviet pact inaugurating an 'imperialist partnership' built upon 'offensive aspirations', and Soviet expansionism between 1939 and 1941 both abetting German 'acts of aggression' and unjustifiably warlike in itself. Substantial evidence of belligerent Soviet intent in 1941 was also presented, including movements of massive military forces into Western provinces, the aggressive configuration of their deployment, diplomatic intimations, and Stalin's speech to military academy graduates on 5 May declaring that the peace policy was over and that it might soon be necessary to seize the offensive initiative. Granted, Stalin knew the Red Army was under prepared and wished to delay war until 1942, but nonetheless Barbarossa anticipated his sedulously prepared and skilfully concealed aggressive plans.[132] Other contributors vigorously contested Hoffmann's thesis and the editorial verdict came down decisively against it; after all, it depended upon tendentious exegesis of ambiguous evidence and was undermined by the more concrete indications that the Nazis privately did not fear a Soviet offensive. But its very presence in this arena and the cries from right-wing critics that the volume overall was too negative in its portrayal of the *Wehrmacht* were worrying testimony to a changing climate.[133]

Even so, at the end of the turbulent 1980s a sanguine view was warranted since preventative war partisans remained a small minority and the *Historikerstreit* burnt out with left-liberal historians having fended off the reassertion of a narrow national identity. But then the collapse of the Eastern bloc and advent of unification unexpectedly intervened. The wave of triumphalist conservative commentary triggered by the disintegration of the Soviet Union sought to cast the crimes of communism – hitherto allegedly airbrushed by liberal academic opinion – in their true perspective; which in effect often meant pronouncing them quantitatively if not qualitatively more evil than those of Nazism.[134] This rhetoric was very widespread, with blanket condemnation of the communist past bolstering conservative identities in the United States and Western Europe, as well a variety of political positions, nationalist and free market democrat alike, in the former Soviet bloc. In the FRG, it eminently suited the relativising purposes of both a new right – the self-styled 'generation of '89' – and a swathe of more moderate nationalist conservatives. Moreover, whereas the existence of a united nation from 1871 to 1945 had previously been widely portrayed as a disastrous aberration, unification now reframed matters and offered an unprecedented opportunity to lift the burden of German exceptionalism. The left was placed in a quandary, torn between either upholding 'post-nationalist' values or reaching an accommodation with the nation in an effort to imprint resurgent national consciousness with a democratic and liberal character. The result was a complex series of intertwined debates on national identity, history and the politics of memory, characterised by continuing pluralism but nonetheless with 'nationalising' perspectives disturbingly evident.[135]

Conservative historiographical challenges to established views on each phase of German history since 1871 soon emerged. The right was keen to rehabilitate Bismarck's Second Reich as a suitable point of departure for national identity, and so began to portray it in a much more flattering light. This involved denial of a negative *Sonderweg* linking Bismarck to Hitler and of German responsibility for the First World War; that conflict was once more portrayed as a tragic accident, product of Germany's unfortunate geopolitical situation as a powerful yet vulnerable state at the continent's heart. Simultaneously, the old FRG was attacked as a provincial diversion from the norm of a unified nation-state, and for its masochistic preoccupation with the Nazi past, subservience to western values and the North Atlantic alliance, and the treachery and moral blindness of *Ostpolitik*. Research into the GDR also flourished, largely within the framework of totalitarianism and therefore negative in import. Comparing the GDR and the Nazi dictatorship made it possible to bracket both off from the 'true' course of national history, and stridently emphasising the urgency of coming to terms with the iniquities of GDR communism meant 'removing the Nazi period from public sight or ... belittling its importance in modern German history'. But in addition to attempting to displace the Third Reich from centre stage, nationalist scholars sought to reinterpret it. Often this entailed the revival of old tropes, such as the lionisation of the conservative resistance. More daring was the stress on the positive modernising aspects of Nazism found in the work of new right luminary Rainer Zitelmann; characterising the Nazis as 'technological innovators, social revolutionaries, ... economic innovators in the Keynesian tradition, and pioneers of the welfare state and mass consumerism' was to emphasise peripheral elements in their project, and thrust anti-Semitism and 'the horrendous inhumanity of National Socialism to the sidelines'.[136]

This revisionism also touched on the Second World War era in predictable ways. The suffering of German soldiers, POWs and expellees, usually at the hands of the Red Army, gained renewed prominence, often accompanied by disingenuous plaints that it had hitherto been erased from post-war memory.[137] In a monumental history of German external relations from 1871 to 1945, Klaus Hildebrand refined his thesis that 'the blend of race and space that drove Hitler's diplomacy was "sui generis, something qualitatively new in the history of German foreign policy"'; Hitler and Bismarck '"had nothing in common"', and though German history did lead to Hitler 'it need not have done so'.[138] Hildebrand's analysis made much of the German Reich's perennial geopolitical predicament: 'too strong not to upset the balance of power on the Continent, and too weak to exercise hegemony over Europe', it was inevitably prey to 'the dangers of living under permanent pressure'. Yet 'the destructive excess of [Hitler's] historical vision' marked Nazi foreign policy out as unique; indeed, what 'was truly diabolical' about it was the manner in which 'seemingly familiar historical phenomena apparently continued to exist' but in fact 'forfeited their historical, and not least their moral dignity to a dogma which took over everything and finally proved to be utterly destructive'.[139] Others echoed this idea of a radical break with German diplomatic traditions, sometimes by resuscitating notions of Hitler as '"the incarnation of evil"'. Moreover, although Germany's ultimate responsibility for launching the Second World War was generally accepted, familiar caveats crept in with allusions to the joint culpability of western appeasers and the causal link between the flaws of Versailles and the collapse of Weimar.[140]

Despite the potentially dubious implications of asserting Hitler's detachment from German traditions, there remained significant ground between such liberal-conservative views and those of more extreme figures like Nolte. He continued to characterise the conflict as a European civil war in which Nazism was (somewhat perversely) an ally of western liberalism against the common communist enemy; on this reading, anti-Bolshevism constituted the 'rational centre' of Nazism, with anti-Semitism and Judeocide mere by-products. (A view that rather bizarrely echoed the Stalinist interpretation of fascism and the Holocaust.) Nolte's arguments, and the succour that they gave to disreputable far right elements including Holocaust deniers, in many ways rendered him a marginal academic figure; on the other hand, in 2000 he was awarded the conservative Konrad Adenauer Foundation's prestigious annual literature prize which occasioned a controversial encomium from prominent historian Horst Möller, who asserted that Nolte's interventions were important and legitimate even though he did not personally endorse their central thesis.[141]

Drawing strength from and reinforcing this overarching characterisation of Nazism, preventative war arguments became more numerous and extravagant. Hoffman now portrayed Germany as having been in a 'critical', 'exceedingly vulnerable' and 'increasingly more difficult' position by the autumn of 1940, with insufficient resources to survive a protracted war, Britain undefeated and the United States looming menacingly. Hence Stalin confidently began to apply diplomatic pressure with 'provocative' demands to extend the Soviet Union's sphere of influence in Northern and Eastern Europe which left the

Germans 'only one alternative: to submit to subjugation or to fight' (in another formulation, making these concessions would have left the Reich encircled). Confident of increasing Soviet strength, Stalin used his speech on 5 May 1941 to reveal his 'aggressive intentions', as 'he worked militarily, politically, and through propaganda, with all his might, to begin a war of conquest'. The Soviet armed forces were already numerically superior to those of Germany, Soviet military doctrine favoured the offensive, and specific operational plans were prepared and presented to Stalin on 15 May. Deployment of a gigantic army proceeded apace for a projected strike some time between July and September, deepening the anxieties of the Germans who had feared a Red Army offensive since the spring of 1941. Given Stalin's conviction that conflict with capitalism was inevitable, and his concrete plans to instigate a 'revolutionary war of liberation', it was clear that 'Hitler under high pressure only barely preempted an attack planned by Stalin'.[142]

In his determination to present Stalin as the 'principal warmonger' whose agency was paramount, Hoffman focused quite lopsidedly on (alleged) Soviet plans, and sidestepped rather than confronted the 'intentionalist' case about the internal and ideological roots of German aggression. So Hitler's decision-making remained opaque, though Hoffman had to concede implicitly that plans for Barbarossa were in train independently of Soviet deployments in May and June 1941 – indeed, it was part of his case that the Germans underestimated precise Soviet capabilities and intentions such that pre-emption in fact occurred almost 'by accident'. Yet on a more fundamental level, Hitler's actions were presented as a response to Soviet diplomatic pressure in 1940 and his perceptions of 'the rapidly increasing superiority and strength of Soviet armaments'. The fact that Hoffman now firmly insisted, in accord with Suvorov's central argument, that the Germans had only beaten the Soviets to firing the first shot by a matter of days or weeks also illustrated how his views had hardened since the 1980s. Furthermore, in focusing attention on the alleged atrocities committed by the Red Army during 'Stalin's war of extermination', Hoffman also perceptibly minimised the significance of the Holocaust, referring dismissively to 'anti-Jewish excesses' and asserting that 'these actions had no precedent in German tradition, and they were carried out without the knowledge or even approval of the German population'.[143] Weighty monographs by other German scholars pursued the same themes, multiply reinforcing perceptions of German victimhood.[144]

Through this same period the preventative war thesis also proliferated in Russia, with further works by Suvorov and a host of other authors.[145] German and Russian scholars – and their counterparts elsewhere – drew validation from each other's work, tending equally 'to accept the most negative (that is, bellicose) readings of often ambiguous Soviet military and political documents'. They thus forged a somewhat curious alliance since there was very little common political ground between, on the one hand, Germans seeking to justify the Nazi war effort in order to buttress a more assertive nationalism and, on the other, these Russians damning Stalin and debunking the whole

Great Patriotic War myth, who often tended to be liberal and reform-oriented. But both groups were 'so alienated from the Soviet past' that they were 'ready to believe the worst of it in every instance', and the argument that Stalin's machinations were chiefly responsible for the slaughter of 1941–45 suited their diverse purposes equally well.[146] Where the historiography of Nazism was concerned, rebutting it entailed the reiteration by 'intentionalists' of the well-established and amply documented case that Barbarossa was the product of Hitler's enduring determination to destroy Judeo-Bolshevism, which impelled him forward relatively heedless of external circumstances. There was a little more scope for novelty when it came to probing Stalin's motives since, although established modes of emplotment were not transcended, post-communist archival releases did make pertinent new evidence available.[147]

Russian and western authors drawing on this material, often with the avowed aim of refuting nationalist apologetics, have concluded that 'the balance of evidence still shows that Stalin's outlook was defensive and reactive', even fearful.[148] Any plans he might have entertained for taking revolutionary advantage of an inter-imperialist war were confounded by the overwhelming German victories of 1940, and thereafter he strained every sinew to avert confrontation with Hitler until the Soviet armed forces were stronger. Fuller and more reliable accounts of the infamous May speech suggest it was less a call to arms than an attempt to boost morale. The offensive military plans presented to Stalin were not only in line with the prevailing Soviet doctrine of 'aggressive defence' but also essentially a response to what German troop movements suggested was an imminent attack. In any event, Stalin refused to countenance pre-emptive action since he was determined to offer the Germans no provocation and the Red Army was consequently left badly deployed without a coherent defensive strategy; Stalin's delusion to the last that he could prevent war thus doomed the Soviet Union to months of catastrophic defeat.[149] (Another leading 'collective security school' author has even essayed that Soviet foreign and domestic policy through the 1930s – including the Great Terror – has to be understood as a reaction to the 'fascist war threat', thus mirroring Nolte's central claim.[150]) The Soviet Union was certainly planning for the eventuality of conflict with Nazi Germany, but given Hitler's infamous and ingrained antipathy towards Bolshevism this was no more than prudent. Equally, doctrine dictated that such plans would entail offensive operations, but this hardly serves as proof that Stalin intended a revolutionary war of conquest. Most importantly, the 'information currently available' strongly suggests that Stalin did not approve the May war plan or intend to put it into effect: 'he was prepared to stand on the Rubicon but not to cross it, and that ambiguous stance was to have disastrous consequences'.[151]

The tendentious nature of preventative war accounts is manifest. Constantine Pleshakov – a Russian historian now working in the United States – recently confidently asserted that 'Stalin was indeed preparing a pre-emptive strike against Germany', whilst simultaneously admitting that it 'remained a researched option, not a definitive plan' and relying on speculative reconstruction in lieu of concrete evidence.[152] Such techniques make crystal clear how the preventative war paradigm depends largely upon extra-empirical suppositions about Stalinist iniquity, its existence testament ultimately to 'a political and psychological need for an "Evil Empire" of Machiavellian cunning, totalitarian cohesion, and omnivorous geopolitical appetite'.[153] Reviewers have hailed key rebuttals as conclusively demolishing the preventative war thesis, yet in the case of the Soviet Union it has been insinuated into the textbook literature as an argument to be seriously considered.[154] Moreover, its marginality and implausibility have been constantly vaunted since the 1980s, but it has nonetheless enjoyed uninterrupted visibility. Once more, this testifies to the difficulty inherent in banishing interpretations from the field by weight of argument or the invocation of 'evidence' without simultaneously addressing the political work they do and the ideological investments that underpin them.

That said, whether preventative war arguments thrive or fade away in the FRG will depend on the shifting terrain of collective memory. One pertinent point here is that the focus of scholarly research and public fascination in the new century is increasingly upon the war years, and in particular the closing stages of the war, rendering issues of foreign policy and war origins of less pressing interest.[155] This has generated delicacies, of course, since the insistent salience of German victims of the air war and expulsions in contemporary public discourse can seem in tension with the memory of Germans as perpetrators, as incarnated by the 'Crimes of the *Wehrmacht*' exhibition, reparations payments to forced labourers and the opening of the Memorial to the Murdered Jews of Europe.[156] This might seem even more problematic as a new discourse of 'normal' patriotism licenses not only the enthusiastic flag-waving of German football fans at the 2006 World Cup but also escalating German military deployments abroad. These facts might easily support the view that German collective memory has been reconfigured in an ethically problematic fashion, or even that a moment of 'mnemonic closure' is imminent, as the German relationship with Nazism loses 'its original sense of urgency' and becomes 'less emotionally fraught'.[157]

More optimistic assessments are, however, eminently tenable. Stefan Berger has recently argued that, in retrospect, the threat of a radical right-wing revisioning of national identity had passed by the end of the 1990s, and that 'the new right has been frozen out of ... respectable scholarship'.[158] Moreover, it is precisely because confrontation with German crimes is now so firmly entrenched – and the problem of individual perpetration squarely faced after decades of ritualised sublimation under the banner of symbolic collective guilt – that space has been opened up for German mourning and recognition of loss. As Robert Moeller has put it, the discourse on victimhood no longer carries 'a subtext of moral equivalency in which Jewish and German suffering [is] compared, justifying demands that the ledger of suffering be permanently closed'. The Holocaust memorial, on this view, 'is quite literally concrete evidence that the past of German crimes will long remain part of German political culture'.[159] The 'either-or dichotomy' between victimhood and perpetration is being subject to 'rapid eroding and new synthesis', albeit 'in ways that we are only beginning to understand'.[160] Breaking down the 'Manichean divide' between loss and guilt will thus lead to a more capacious remembrance of a complex past, forming the foundation for new forms of positive identification with the nation.[161] In such a landscape, the blatant apologetics of the preventative war thesis might appear not only undesirable but obsolete.

Across the decades, writing about Nazi foreign policy has been intimately implicated in wider discourses of collective memory and national identity. Initially, it was entirely of a piece with the dominant national discourse of exculpation, troping the Nazi past in ways that both echoed archetypal responses to defeat and shared in an overriding conservative tendency to deflect responsibility for aggression away from the German nation. When a mature historiography subsequently emerged, the dominant tradition did give voice to a more engaged reflection on the nature of Nazi expansionism, yet also – as a result of political persuasion and methodological preference – evinced a persistent evasiveness. In retrospect, this commingling of disparate elements was also not untypical of the broader moment of collective memory in the 1960s and 1970s. In new circumstances from the 1980s, mainstream international history retained this coding of moderate conservatism. 'Intentionalist' authors played a part in resisting partisans of the preventative war thesis who pushed the exculpatory possibilities of writing on international relations to their farthest extent. Yet strident calls through the 1990s urged the revivification of the great historicist traditions of diplomatic and political historiography, as the only forms of writing that could accustom Germans to a future in which the state could be a practitioner of power politics.[162] Simultaneously, it was other strands in the historiography of Nazism that confronted continuity, complicity and perpetration with unprecedented frankness. Hence, in broad terms it seems fair to conclude that international history has generally contributed a conservative thread to the complex yarn of German war memory.

Notes

1 A. Hitler, *Mein Kampf* (London, Hutchinson, 1969, rev. edn), pp. 604–5 (emphasis in original).

2 S. Peer, *France on Display: Peasants, Provincials, and Folklore in the 1937 Paris World's Fair* (Albany, NY, State University of New York Press, 1998), p. 44.

3 G. Lenz, 'Totalitarian propaganda in France: French planners and the Paris exhibition of 1937', unpublished paper delivered at the Southern Historial Association annual conference, Louisville, Kentucky, November 2000.

4 J. Herbert, *Paris 1937: Worlds on Exhibition* (Ithaca, NY, Cornell University Press, 1998), pp. 36–37.

5 M. Burleigh, *The Third Reich: A New History* (London, Macmillan, 2001, pb. edn), p. 268.

6 Speech by Hitler, 30 January 1939, in J. Noakes and G. Pridham (eds), *Nazism 1919–1945: Vol. 3: Foreign Policy, War and Racial Extermination* (Exeter, University of Exeter Press, 1997, rev. edn), p. 1049.

7 Ribbentrop justified Barbarossa as a pre-emptive measure to the Soviet ambassador in Berlin on 22 June 1941: R. Sontag and J. Beddie (eds), *Nazi-Soviet Relations, 1939–1941: Documents from the Archives of the German Foreign Office* (Washington D.C., Department of State, 1948), pp. 356–57.

8 Quoted in H. Trevor-Roper, *The Last Days of Hitler* (London, Macmillan, 1987, 6th edn), p. 209.

9 Constraints of space preclude consideration of war memory in the German Democratic Republic (GDR). This is regrettable since the two memory cultures were closely inter-twined, indeed in many ways mutually constitutive. GDR war memory had a relatively dogmatic 'anti-fascist' character echoing, *mutatis mutandis*, the Soviet line: see M. Fulbrook, *German National Identity after the Holocaust* (Oxford, Polity, 1999); and J. Herf, *Divided Memory: The Nazi Past in the Two Germanys* (Cambridge, MA, Harvard University Press, 1997).

10 Cf. the distinction between 'redemptive' and 'integrative republicans' in A. D. Moses, *German Intellectuals and the Nazi Past* (Cambridge, Cambridge University Press, 2007).

11 Witness the diverse historiographical treatments of P. Ayçoberry, *The Nazi Question: An Essay on the Interpretations of National Socialism (1922–1975)* (London, Routledge and Kegan Paul, 1981); I. Kershaw, *The Nazi Dictatorship: Problems and Perspectives of Inter-pretation* (London, Arnold, 2000, 4th edn); and J. Lukacs, *The Hitler of History* (New York, Knopf, 1997).

12 I. Buruma, *The Wages of Guilt: Memories of War in Germany and Japan* (London, Vintage, 1995, pb. edn), pp. 8–9.

13 S. Berger, *The Search for Normality: National Identity and Historical Consciousness in Germany since 1800* (Oxford, Berghahn, 1997).

14 B. Niven, *Facing the Nazi Past: United Germany and the Legacy of the Third Reich* (London, Routledge, 2001), quote at p. 5.

15 M. Nolan, 'Germans as victims during the Second World War: air wars, memory wars', *Central European History*, vol. 38, no. 1, 2005, p. 21.

16 Landmark works include N. Frei, *Adenauer's Germany and the Nazi Past: The Politics of Amnesty and Integration* (New York, Columbia University Press, 2002); and R. G. Moeller, *War Stories: The Search for a Usable Past in the Federal Republic of Germany* (Berkeley, CA, University of California Press, 2001).

17 J. K. Olick, *In the House of the Hangman: The Agonies of German Defeat, 1943–1949* (Chicago, University of Chicago Press, 2005).

18 Herf, *Divided Memory*, pp. 6–7.

19 Fulbrook, *German National Identity after the Holocaust*, p. 59.

20 Moeller, *War Stories*, p. 25, quoting a speech by Adenauer, 27 September 1951.

21 Anonymous, *A Woman in Berlin: Diary 20 April 1945 to 22 June 1945* (London, Virago, 2005), p. 155.

22 Moeller, *War Stories*, pp. 1–122. The apogee of relativisation was reached when some commentators explicitly drew on the wartime fate of Europe's Jews as 'a framework for understanding' the suffering of (non-Jewish) Germans: Olick, *In the House of the Hangman*, p. 175.

23 Quote from *The Trial of German Major War Criminals by the International Military Tribunal Sitting at Nuremberg, Germany (Commencing 20th November, 1945): Opening Speeches of the Chief Prosecutors* (London, HMSO, 1946), p. 7.

24 M. Marrus, *The Nuremberg War Crimes Trial, 1945–46: A Documentary History* (Boston, MA, Bedford, 1997), p. 122. This emphasis on the minutiae of military planning down-played the deeper impulses underlying Nazi aggression but reflected the approaches then dominant within diplomatic history and the trial's purpose (i.e. proving guilt rather than probing motives). On the deleterious consequences of this conceptual framework for the

historical profile of the Holocaust, see D. Bloxham, *Genocide on Trial: War Crimes Trials and the Formation of Holocaust History and Memory* (Oxford, Oxford University Press, 2001).

25 Quote from *The Judgement of Nuremberg, 1946* (London, TSO, 1999), p. 8. Modifications at the level of detail were admitted.

26 Quoted in D. C. Watt, 'British historians, the war guilt issue, and post-war Germanophobia: a documentary note', *Historical Journal*, vol. 36, no. 1, 1993, p. 181.

27 W. S. Churchill, *The Second World War: Vol. 1: The Gathering Storm* (London, Penguin, 1985, pb. edn), quote at p. 148.

28 Bloxham, *Genocide on Trial*, pp. 129–53.

29 Marrus, *The Nuremberg War Crimes Trial, 1945–46*, p. 227; *Judgement of Nuremberg, 1946*, p. 7.

30 Quoted in Marrus, *The Nuremberg War Crimes Trial, 1945–46*, p. 231.

31 In the later 1990s controversy focused on the tainted Nazi pasts of the pioneers of left-of-centre social and structural history approaches, and the collusion of their protégés in a conspiracy of silence: W. Kansteiner, 'Mandarins in the public sphere: *Vergangenheitsbewältigung* and the paradigm of social history in the Federal Republic of Germany', *German Politics and Society*, vol. 17, no. 3, 1999, pp. 84–120.

32 Berger, *The Search for Normality*, p. 38.

33 R. Schwok, *Interprétations de la Politique Étrangère de Hitler: Une Analyse de l'Historiographie* (Paris, Presses Universitaires de France, 1987), pp. 18–19; J. Caplan, 'The historiography of National Socialism', in M. Bentley (ed.), *Companion to Historiography* (London, Routledge, 1997), p. 546.

34 Berger,*The Search for Normality*, p. 30.

35 H. Schleier, 'German historiography under National Socialism', in S. Berger, M. Donovan and K. Passmore (eds), *Writing National Histories: Western Europe since 1800* (London, Routledge, 1999), p. 187.

36 Under the Nazis, methodologically innovatory 'folk history' had challenged the dominance of political history but it was subsequently marginalised as ideologically compromised: J. van Horn Melton, 'Continuities in German historical scholarship, 1933–60', in H. Lehmann and J. van Horn Melton (eds), *Paths of Continuity: Central European Historiography from the 1930s to the 1950s* (Cambridge, Cambridge University Press, 1994), pp. 6–9.

37 Berger, *The Search for Normality*, pp. 39–41.

38 S. Behrenbeck, 'Between pain and silence: remembering the victims of violence in Germany after 1949', in R. Bessel and D. Schumann (eds), *Life After Death: Approaches to a Cultural and Social History of Europe during the 1940s and 1950s* (Cambridge, Cambridge University Press, 2003), p. 62.

39 Olick, *In the House of the Hangman*, p. 115.

40 Unless otherwise indicated, the following discussion is based on Schwok, *Interprétations de la Politique Étrangère de Hitler*, pp. 61–72, 143–47 and É. Husson, *Comprendre Hitler et la Shoah: Les Historiens de la République Fédérale d'Allemagne et l'Identité Allemande depuis 1949* (Paris, Presses Universitaires de France, 2000), pp. 29–47.

41 F. Meinecke, *The German Catastrophe: Reflections and Recollections* (Boston, MA, Beacon, 1963, pb. edn), quotes at pp. 93, 96, 58–59, 1.

42 Berger, *The Search for Normality*, p. 44.

43 A. Gleason, *Totalitarianism: The Inner History of the Cold War* (Oxford, Oxford University Press, 1995), p. 159.

44 G. Iggers, *The German Conception of History: The National Tradition of Historical Thought from Herder to the Present* (Middletown, CT, Wesleyan University Press, 1983, rev. edn), p. 223.

45 For a more sympathetic view of Ritter, see K. Schwabe, 'Change and continuity in German historiography from 1933 into the early 1950s: Gerhard Ritter (1888–1967)', in Lehmann and van Horn Melton (eds), *Paths of Continuity*, pp. 83–108.

46 See also the arguments in FRG school history textbooks in the 1950s that the essential problem with the brutality of German conduct of the war in the East was that it was

counterproductive: B. von Borries, 'The Third Reich in German history textbooks since 1945', *Journal of Contemporary History*, vol. 38, no. 1, 2003, p. 51.

47 Quoted in Schwok, *Interprétations de la Politique Étrangère de Hitler*, pp. 66–70.

48 Schwok, *Interprétations de la Politique Étrangère de Hitler*, pp. 121–29, 151–53, 173–77.

49 Gleason, *Totalitarianism*, pp. 157–60.

50 L. Dehio, *Germany and World Politics in the Twentieth Century* (London, Chatto and Windus, 1959), quotes at pp. 12, 30–32.

51 Olick, *In the House of the Hangman*, p. 161; this pervasive rhetoric of 'infection' had also been 'a staple of Nazi ideology' (p. 169).

52 A. Bullock, 'Hitler and the origins of the Second World War', in E. M. Robertson (ed.) *The Origins of the Second World War: Historical Interpretations* (London, Macmillan, 1971), p.189.

53 See, recently, M. Geyer and S. Fitzpatrick (eds), *Beyond Totalitarianism: Stalinism and Nazism Compared* (Cambridge, Cambridge University Press, 2009); and H. Rousso (ed.), *Stalinism and Nazism: History and Memory Compared* (Lincoln, NE, University of Nebraska Press, 2004).

54 H. Kohn, 'Introduction', in H. Kohn (ed.), *German History: Some New German Views* (London, Allen and Unwin, 1954), p. 14.

55 Quoted in Y. M. Bodemann, 'Eclipse of memory: German representations of Auschwitz in the early postwar period', *New German Critique*, no. 75, 1998, p. 61.

56 R. J. B. Bosworth, *Explaining Auschwitz and Hiroshima: History Writing and the Second World War, 1945–1990* (London, Routledge, 1993), p. 3.

57 W. Schivelbusch, *The Culture of Defeat: On National Trauma, Mourning, and Recovery* (London, Granta, 2003), pp. 13, 31.

58 Bloxham, *Genocide on Trial*, p. 219.

59 Olick, *In the House of the Hangman*, pp. 139, 10.

60 Schwok, *Interprétations de la Politique Étrangère de Hitler*, pp. 43–55.

61 Caplan, 'The historiography of National Socialism', pp. 553–54. On the wider role of émigré historians, see H. Lehmann and J. Sheehan (eds), *An Interrupted Past: German-Speaking Refugee Historians in the United States after 1933* (Cambridge, Cambridge University Press, 1991).

62 A. J. P. Taylor, *The Course of German History: A Survey of the Development of Germany since 1815* (London, Hamish Hamilton, 1945). For commentary, see R. J. Granieri, 'A. J. P. Taylor on the "Greater" German problem' and N. J. W. Goda, 'A. J. P. Taylor, Adolf Hitler, and the origins of the Second World War', *International History Review*, vol. 23, no. 1, 2001, pp. 28–50 and 97–124 respectively.

63 G. D. Rosenfeld, 'The reception of William L. Shirer's *The Rise and Fall of the Third Reich* in the United States and West Germany, 1960–62', *Journal of Contemporary History*, vol. 29, no. 1, 1994, pp. 95–128, quotes from Shirer at p. 102 and M. Broszat at p. 116.

64 Schwok, *Interprétations de la Politique Étrangère de Hitler*, pp. 73–76, 147–50. In a second edition of *Hitler: A Study in Tyranny* (London, Penguin, 1962, 2nd edn), Bullock firmed up the notion of a foreign policy programme and emphasised racist ideology over a simple thirst for power.

65 R. Rosenbaum, *Explaining Hitler: The Search for the Origins of his Evil* (London, Macmillan, 1999, pb. edn), pp. 63–96, quote at p. 69; A. J. P. Taylor, *The Origins of the Second World War* (London, Penguin, 1964, pb. edn), p. 98. Trevor-Roper was a pioneer of 'intentionalist' approaches, evidenced in his 1960 article on 'Hitler's war aims' reprinted in H.W. Koch (ed.), *Aspects of the Third Reich* (London, Macmillan, 1985), pp. 235–50.

66 Continuities from contemporary observers of Nazism through to later scholarship are highlighted in N. Gregor (ed.), *Nazism* (Oxford, Oxford University Press, 2000).

67 M. Roseman, 'Division and stability: the Federal Republic of Germany, 1949–89', in M. Fulbrook (ed.), *Twentieth Century Germany: Politics, Culture and Society, 1918–1990* (London, Arnold, 2001), pp. 188–92, quote at p. 190.

68 For Taylor, see G. Martel (ed.), *The Origins of the Second World War Reconsidered: A. J. P. Taylor and the Historians* (London, Routledge, 1999, 2nd edn); and K. Burk, *Troublemaker. The*

Life and History of A. J. P. Taylor (New Haven, CT, Yale University Press, 2000) pp. 280–95.

69 A. Mombauer, *The Origins of the First World War: Controversies and Consensus* (London, Longman, 2002), pp. 119–74.

70 G. Steinmetz, 'German exceptionalism and the origins of Nazism: the career of a concept', in I. Kershaw and M. Lewin (eds), *Stalinism and Nazism: Dictatorships in Comparison* (Cambridge, Cambridge University Press, 1997), pp. 251–84.

71 Caplan, 'The historiography of National Socialism', p. 564.

72 C. M. Kimmich, *German Foreign Policy, 1918–1945: A Guide to Research and Research Materials* (Wilmington, DE, Scholarly Resources, 1981), especially pp. 114–23. The captured documents were gradually repatriated and German historians took over the leading editorial role in this series; the volumes (from an eventual total of 62) covering the Weimar period and 1941–45 appeared only in German.

73 T. W. Mason, 'Some origins of the Second World War', in Robertson (ed.), *The Origins of the Second World War*, p. 104.

74 The following discussion draws on Ayçoberry, *The Nazi Question*, pp. 215–25; J. Hiden and J. Farquharson, *Explaining Hitler's Germany: Historians and the Third Reich* (London, Batsford, 1989, 2nd edn), pp 110–29; Kershaw, *The Nazi Dictatorship*, pp. 134–60; T. W. Mason, 'Intention and explanation: a current controversy about the interpretation of National Socialism', in J. Caplan (ed.), *Nazism, Fascism and the Working Class: Essays by Tim Mason* (Cambridge, Cambridge University Press, 1995), pp. 212–30; and Schwok, *Interprétations de la Politique Étrangère de Hitler*, pp. 83–103, 131–40.

75 On the deep roots of the polycracy concept, see Gregor (ed.), *Nazism*, pp. 146–52.

76 Berger, *The Search for Normality*, p. 78.

77 On the extent of his aims, see Kershaw, *The Nazi Dictatorship*, pp. 154–59; and N. J. W. Goda, *Tomorrow the World: Hitler, Northwest Africa, and the Path toward America* (College Station, TX, Texas A & M University Press, 1998).

78 A. Hillgruber, *Germany and the Two World Wars* (Cambridge, MA, Harvard University Press, 1981), p. 50.

79 K. Hildebrand, *The Foreign Policy of the Third Reich* (Berkeley, CA, University of California Press, 1973), pp. 97, 21–22.

80 H. Mommsen, 'National Socialism: continuity and change', in W. Laqueur (ed.), *Fascism: A Reader's Guide* (London, Penguin, 1979, pb. edn), p. 177.

81 Kershaw, *The Nazi Dictatorship*, p. 139.

82 M. Broszat, *The Hitler State: The Foundation and Development of the Internal Structure of the Third Reich* (London, Longman, 1981), p. 359.

83 Caplan (ed.), *Nazism, Fascism and the Working Class*, especially pp. 104–30, 295–322.

84 See, for example, C. Browning, 'Beyond "intentionalism" and "functionalism": a reassessment of Nazi Jewish policy from 1939 to 1941', in T. Childers and J. Caplan (eds), *Reevaluating the Third Reich* (New York, Holmes and Meier, 1993), pp. 211–33; on 'charismatic authority', see I. Kershaw, 'Hitler and the uniqueness of Nazism', *Journal of Contemporary History*, vol. 39, no. 2, 2004, pp. 239–54.

85 Militärgeschichtliches Forschungsamt (ed.), *Germany and the Second World War: Vol. I: The Build-up of German Aggression* (Oxford, Oxford University Press, 1990), published in German in 1979, enshrines the sophisticated 'intentionalist' view.

86 The substance of this summary is drawn from Kershaw, *The Nazi Dictatorship*, pp. 159–60; quotes from C. Leitz, *Nazi Foreign Policy, 1933–1941: The Road to Global War* (London, Routledge, 2004), pp. 145–46. There is greater mileage in 'functionalist' arguments on the Holocaust claiming, for example, that policy initiatives came from periphery as well as centre or that the goal of extermination only crystallised at a late stage.

87 Mason, 'Intention and explanation', pp. 217–18.

88 N. Berg, *Der Holocaust und die Westdeutschen Historiker: Erforschung und Erinnerung* (Göttingen, Wallstein, 2003).

89 Schwok, *Interprétations de la Politique Étrangère de Hitler*, p. 44.

90 W. Carr, 'National Socialism: foreign policy and Wehrmacht', in Laqueur (ed.), *Fascism*, p. 122.

91 H-A. Jacobsen, 'The structure of Nazi foreign policy 1933–45', a 1978 article reprinted in C. Leitz (ed.) *The Third Reich: The Essential Readings* (Oxford, Blackwell, 1999), p. 93. The subsequent concession that 'obvious parallels are to be drawn between some objectives and previous German policies in the nineteenth and twentieth centuries' reads as an afterthought.

92 Hillgruber, *Germany and the Two World Wars*, p. 41.

93 Hildebrand, *The Foreign Policy of the Third Reich*, quotes at pp. 81, 146, 144, 135–36, 106–7, 126, 140.

94 K. Hildebrand, *The Third Reich* (London, Allen and Unwin, 1984), p. 97.

95 Hildebrand, *The Foreign Policy of the Third Reich*, quotes at pp. 97, 106–7, 114, 98. E. Jäckel, *Hitler's World View: A Blueprint for Power* (Cambridge, MA, Harvard University Press, 1981) – published in German in 1969 – also pioneered the delineation of Hitler's programme while giving little consideration to its roots in the German past.

96 Mason, 'Intention and explanation', p. 218.

97 G. Eley, 'Nazism, politics and the image of the past: thoughts on the West German *Historikerstreit* 1986–87', *Past and Present*, no. 121, 1988, p. 174.

98 Schwok argues that by stressing how Hitler did not desire the particular conflict that he precipitated over Poland in their treatment of 1939, these 'intentionalists' flirt with the thesis of far right Anglo-American authors like David Hoggan that war was 'forced upon' Hitler: *Interprétations de la Politique Étrangère de Hitler*, pp. 157–61, 184–86.

99 Olick, *In the House of the Hangman*, p. 174, and pp. 270–320 for the broader discussion.

100 P. Grosser, *Pourquoi la Seconde Guerre Mondiale?* (Paris, Éditions Complexe, 1999), pp. 95–161; R. Overy, 'Misjudging Hitler', in Martel (ed.), *The Origins of the Second World War Reconsidered* (2nd edn), pp. 93–115. Particular conceptions of German national identity were not, of course, the only determinants of the 'intentionalist' view; many scholars abroad partook of this emplotment and worked it further: for example, N. Rich, *Hitler's War Aims: Ideology, the Nazi State, and the Course of Expansion*, 2 vols (London, Deutsch, 1973–74); and émigré G. L. Weinberg's, *The Foreign Policy of Hitler's Germany*, 2 vols (Chicago, University of Chicago Press, 1970–80).

101 O. Bartov, 'Germany's unforgettable war: the twisted road from Berlin to Moscow and back', *Diplomatic History*, vol. 25, no. 3, 2001, p. 411.

102 D. Kaiser, 'Hitler and the coming of war', in G. Martel (ed.), *Modern Germany Reconsidered, 1870–1945* (London, Routledge, 1992), p. 179; W. Carr, *Arms, Autarky and Aggression: A Study in German Foreign Policy, 1933–1939* (London, Edward Arnold, 1972), p. 8.

103 N. Gregor, 'The National Socialist regime: introduction', in Gregor (ed.), *Nazism*, p. 128.

104 For discussions, see R. J. Evans, 'The emergence of Nazi ideology', in J. Caplan (ed.), *Nazi Germany* (Oxford, Oxford University Press, 2008), pp. 26–47; N. Gregor, 'Hitler', in S. Casey and J. Wright (eds), *Mental Maps in the Era of Two World Wars* (London, Palgrave, 2008), pp. 177–202; M. Mazower, *Hitler's Empire: Nazi Rule in Occupied Europe* (London, Allen Lane, 2008); and H. Walser Smith, *The Continuities of German History: Nation, Religion, and Race across the Long Nineteenth Century* (Cambridge, Cambridge University Press, 2008). Note also the implications of recent work on pre-Nazi military culture: K. Cramer, 'A world of enemies: new perspectives on German military culture and the origins of the First World War', *Central European History*, vol. 39, no. 2, 2006, pp. 270–98.

105 This is a key theme in J. Wright, *Germany and the Origins of the Second World War* (London, Palgrave, 2007).

106 On the comparator, illustrating growing awareness of the extent of complicity and the deeper roots of Nazi racism, see D. Stone (ed.), *The Historiography of the Holocaust* (London, Palgrave, 2004).

107 Leitz, *Nazi Foreign Policy, 1933–1941*, quotes at pp. 139, 5.

108 R. Bessel, *Nazism and War* (London, Phoenix, 2005, pb. edn), quotes at p. 5. See also R. J. Evans, *The Third Reich in Power, 1933–1939* (London, Allen Lane, 2005) and *The*

Third Reich at War, 1939–1945 (London, Allen Lane, 2008); and A. Tooze, *The Wages of Destruction: The Making and Breaking of the Nazi Economy* (London, Allen Lane, 2006).

109 Caplan, 'The historiography of National Socialism', p. 565.

110 Schwok, *Interprétations de la Politique Étrangère de Hitler*, pp. 105–19.

111 Quoted in G. Hartman (ed.), *Bitburg in Moral and Political Perspective* (Bloomington, IN, Indiana University Press, 1986), p. xiii.

112 Eley, 'Nazism, politics and the image of the past', p. 176.

113 Hartman (ed.), *Bitburg in Moral and Political Perspective*, p. 240.

114 R. J. Evans, *In Hitler's Shadow: West German Historians and the Attempt to Escape from the Nazi Past* (New York, Pantheon, 1989), pp. 18–19, quoting F. J. Strauss.

115 M. Stürmer, in *Forever in the Shadow of Hitler? Original Documents of the Historikerstreit, the Controversy Concerning the Singularity of the Holocaust* (Atlantic Highlands, NJ, Humanities Press, 1993), p. 17.

116 Quoted in Evans, *In Hitler's Shadow*, p. 17, and Buruma, *The Wages of Guilt*, p. 244.

117 Hartman (ed.), *Bitburg in Moral and Political Perspective*, pp. 267, 263, 273.

118 Fulbrook, *German National Identity after the Holocaust*, pp. 172–74.

119 O. Bartov, *Murder in our Midst: The Holocaust, Industrial Killing, and Representation* (New York, Oxford University Press, 1996), pp. 71–88; Evans, *In Hitler's Shadow*, pp. 47–65. Others more charitably claimed that Hillgruber could not 'be suspected of harboring apologetic intentions toward Nazism': C. S. Maier, *The Unmasterable Past: History, Holocaust, and German National Identity* (Cambridge, MA, Harvard University Press, 1988), pp. 19–25, quote at p. 19.

120 E. Nolte, in *Forever in the Shadow of Hitler?*, pp. 15, 22; Evans, *In Hitler's Shadow*, pp. 24–42, 66–91. Contextualising the Holocaust against other genocides is legitimate, of course, but entails intellectual, ethical and political risks: D. Stone (ed.), *The Historiography of Genocide* (London, Palgrave, 2008).

121 P. Baldwin, 'The *Historikerstreit* in context', in P. Baldwin (ed.), *Reworking the Past: Hitler, the Holocaust, and the Historians' Debate* (Boston, MA, Beacon, 1990), p. 6.

122 Marrus, *The Nuremberg War Crimes Trial, 1945–46*, pp. 142–48; M. Messerschmidt, 'Forward defense: the "Memorandum of the Generals" for the Nuremberg court', in H. Heer and K. Naumann (eds), *War of Extermination: The German Military in World War II, 1941–1944* (Oxford, Berghahn, 2000), pp. 381–99.

123 R-D. Müller, 'Introduction: policy and strategy', in R-D. Müller and G. Ueberschär (eds), *Hitler's War in the East, 1941–1945: A Critical Assessment* (Oxford, Berghahn, 2002, 2nd edn), pp. 3–41.

124 G. Ueberschär, 'Hitler's decision to attack the Soviet Union in recent German historiography', *Soviet Union/Union Soviétique*, vol. 18, nos 1–3, 1991, pp. 297–315, quote at p. 315.

125 Partly for this reason, the crucial distinction between 'pre-emption' and 'prevention' is blurred in much of this literature.

126 Evans, *In Hitler's Shadow*, pp. 42–46. Confusingly, this argument that Barbarossa was a reaction to unfolding external contingencies was sometimes dubbed 'functionalist': H. W. Koch, 'Part II: introduction', in Koch (ed.), *Aspects of the Third Reich*, pp. 181–95.

127 E. Topitsch, *Stalin's War: A Radical New Theory of the Origins of the Second World War* (London, Fourth Estate, 1987), quotes at pp. 4, 6, 40, 135.

128 V. Suvorov, *Icebreaker: Who Started the Second World War?* (London, Hamish Hamilton, 1990), previewed in his 'Who was planning to attack whom in June 1941, Hitler or Stalin?', *RUSI Journal*, vol. 130, no. 2, 1985, pp. 50–55. For fuller references, see T. J. Uldricks, 'The *Icebreaker* controversy: did Stalin plan to attack Hitler?', *Slavic Review*, vol. 58, no. 3, 1999, pp. 626–43.

129 Translated as Militärgeschichtliches Forschungsamt (ed.), *Germany and the Second World War: Vol. IV: The Attack on the Soviet Union* (Oxford, Oxford University Press, 1998).

130 O. Bartov, *Germany's War and the Holocaust: Disputed Histories* (Ithaca, NY, Cornell University Press, 2003), p. 69. Later volumes in the series dilate more extensively on the

Holocaust and move further beyond a narrow military history approach – for example, Militärgeschichtliches Forschungsamt (ed.), *Germany and the Second World War: Vol. IX/1: German Wartime Society, 1939–1945: Politicization, Disintegration and the Struggle for Survival* (Oxford, Oxford University Press, 2008) – but the criticism of the enterprise as a whole retains some validity.

131 M. Messerschmidt, 'Introduction', in Militärgeschichtliches Forschungsamt (ed.), *The Attack on the Soviet Union*, p. 1.

132 J. Hoffmann, 'The Soviet Union up to the eve of the German attack', and 'The conduct of the war through Soviet eyes', in Militärgeschichtliches Forschungsamt (ed.), *The Attack on the Soviet Union*, pp. 52–117 and pp. 833–940, quotes at pp. 96–97.

133 Messerschmidt, 'Introduction', and J. Förster, 'Operation Barbarossa in historical perspective', in Militärgeschichtliches Forschungsamt (ed.), *The Attack on the Soviet Union*, pp. 1–9, 1245–55; Evans, *In Hitler's Shadow*, pp. 44–46.

134 Bartov, 'Germany's unforgettable war', p. 420.

135 From a vast literature see, for example, J-W. Müller, *Another Country: German Intellectuals, Unification and National Identity* (New Haven, CT, Yale University Press, 2000).

136 Berger, *The Search for Normality*, pp. 111–97, quotes at pp. 151, 129–30.

137 R. G. Moeller, 'Sinking ships, the lost *Heimat* and broken taboos: Günter Grass and the politics of memory in contemporary Germany', *Contemporary European History*, vol. 12, no. 2, 2003, pp. 147–81.

138 J. Sheehan, 'The birth and death of two Reichs', *Times Literary Supplement*, 13 October 1995, pp. 7–8, reviewing and quoting K. Hildebrand, *Das Vergangene Reich: Deutsche Aussenpolitik von Bismarck bis Hitler 1871–1945* (Stuttgart, Deutsche Verlags-Anstalt, 1995).

139 K. Hildebrand, *Reich – Nation-State – Great Power: Reflections on German Foreign Policy 1871 – 1945* (London, German Historical Institute, 1995), quotes at pp. 6, 22–23.

140 Berger, *The Search for Normality*, p. 136, quoting M. Stürmer.

141 Berger, *The Search for Normality*, pp. 124–27, quoting Nolte at p. 126; Geoffrey Wheatcroft, 'Let's mention the war', *The Guardian*, 1 July 2000, http://www.guardian.co.uk/Archive/Article/0,4273,4035706,00.html (accessed 20 February 2006). There are perceptible affinities between nationalist/revisionist writing displacing responsibility for Nazi aggression to other powers and Holocaust denial: Lukacs, *The Hitler of History*, pp. 223–39.

142 J. Hoffmann, *Stalin's War of Extermination 1941–1945: Planning, Realization and Documentation* (Capshaw, AL, Theses and Dissertations Press, 2001), first published in German in 1995, quotes at pp. 31–32, 39, 51, 86–87. See also the summary in J. Hoffmann, 'The Soviet Union's offensive preparations in 1941', in B. Wegner (ed.), *From Peace to War: Germany, Soviet Russia and the World, 1939–1941* (Oxford, Berghahn, 1997), pp. 361–80.

143 Hoffman, *Stalin's War of Extermination 1941–1945*, quotes at pp. 30, 29, 330, 333–34.

144 K. Schmider, 'No quiet on the eastern front: the Suvorov debate in the 1990s', *Journal of Slavic Military Studies*, vol. 10, no. 2, 1997, pp. 181–94.

145 For examples in English, see V. A. Neveshin, 'Stalin's 5 May 1941 addresses: the experience of interpretation', *Journal of Slavic Military Studies*, vol. 11, no. 1, 1998, pp.116–46; B. V. Sokolov, 'Did Stalin intend to attack Hitler?', *Journal of Slavic Military Studies*, vol. 11, no. 2, 1998, pp. 113–41; and V. Suvorov, *The Chief Culprit: Stalin's Grand Design to Start World War II* (Annapolis, MD, Naval Institute Press, 2008).

146 Uldricks, 'The *Icebreaker* controversy', pp. 636–37.

147 J. Förster and E. Mawdsley, 'Hitler and Stalin in perspective: secret speeches on the eve of Barbarossa', *War in History*, vol. 11, no. 1, 2004, pp. 61–103.

148 R. Overy, *The Dictators: Hitler's Germany and Stalin's Russia* (London, Allen Lane, 2004), p. 443, and more generally pp. 490–93.

149 Recent summaries include C. Bellamy, *Absolute War: Soviet Russia in the Second World War* (London, Pan, 2008, pb. edn), pp. 99–135; and E. Mawdsley, *Thunder in the East: The Nazi-Soviet War, 1941–1945* (London, Arnold, 2007, pb. edn), pp. 3–54.

150 G. Roberts, 'The fascist war threat and Soviet politics in the 1930s', in S. Pons and A. Romano (eds), *Russia in the Age of Wars, 1914–1945* (Milan, Feltrinelli, 2000), pp. 147–58.

151 E. Mawdsley, 'Crossing the Rubicon: Soviet plans for offensive war in 1940–41', *International History Review*, vol. 25, no. 4, 2003, p. 865.

152 C. Pleshakov, *Stalin's Folly: The Secret History of the German Invasion of Russia, June 1941* (London, Weidenfeld and Nicolson, 2005), quotes at pp. 13, 57.

153 Uldricks, 'The *Icebreaker* controversy', p. 640.

154 R. Sakwa, *The Rise and Fall of the Soviet Union, 1917–1991* (London, Routledge, 1999), pp. 234–54.

155 R. J. Evans, *The Coming of the Third Reich* (London, Penguin, 2004, pb. edn), pp. xxviii–xxix.

156 See the diverse views in B. Niven (ed.), *Germans as Victims: Remembering the Past in Contemporary Germany* (London, Palgrave, 2006).

157 G. D. Rosenfeld, 'A looming crash or a soft landing? Forecasting the future of the memory "industry"', *Journal of Modern History*, vol. 81, no. 1, 2009, pp. 142–44.

158 S. Berger, 'A return to the national paradigm? National history writing in Germany, Italy, France, and Britain from 1945 to the present', *Journal of Modern History*, vol. 77, no. 3, 2005, p. 663.

159 R. G. Moeller, 'The Third Reich in post-war German memory', in Caplan (ed.), *Nazi Germany*, p. 266.

160 E. Langenbacher, B. Niven and R. Wittlinger, 'Introduction: dynamics of memory in twenty-first century Germany', *German Politics and Society*, vol. 26, no. 4, 2008, p. 8.

161 D. Barnouw, *The War in the Empty Air: Victims, Perpetrators, and Postwar Germans* (Bloomington, IN, Indiana University Press, 2005), p. 52.

162 Berger, *The Search for Normality*, p. 217.

3 On complicity

Italian foreign policy, Fascist ideology and the Axis

Firmly united by the inner affinity between their ideologies and the comprehensive solidarity of their interests, the German and Italian nations are resolved in future also to act side by side and with united forces to secure their living space and to maintain peace. Following this path, marked out for them by history, Germany and Italy intend, in the midst of a world of unrest and disintegration, to serve the task of safeguarding the foundations of European civilization.

Pact of Friendship and Alliance between Germany and Italy
('Pact of Steel'), 22 May 1939[1]

On 28 September 1937, the Italian *Duce* Benito Mussolini addressed an 800,000 strong crowd assembled on the Berlin *Maifeld* at the climax of his state visit to Germany. Amidst a tumultuous thunderstorm that created a truly Wagnerian atmosphere, but unfortunately also slowly dissolved his sheaf of notes, Mussolini extolled the close ties between the two countries that had in the previous year proclaimed themselves the Axis around which European diplomacy would henceforth revolve. National Socialism and Fascism, he declared, 'have in common many elements of our *Weltanschauung*' and 'conceptions of life and history', similar goals in economic, foreign and cultural policy, even the 'same enemies' in the shape of Bolshevism and capitalist plutocracy. The 'German rebirth' was inspired by the same 'spiritual force' that underpinned the 'resurrected Roman Empire' and bound the two nations 'in a single unshatterable determination', prepared to march together 'to the end'.[2] Similarly fulsome evocations of mutual solidarity accompanied Italian adherence to the Anti-Comintern Pact in November 1937 and acquiescence in the *Anschluss* in March 1938, the signature of a military alliance in May 1939, and finally Mussolini's declaration of intervention at the side of his 'great ally' in June 1940.[3] Moreover, Mussolini and – in the shape of the puppet Salò republic – Fascism (if not the better part of the Italian nation that repudiated them in and after July 1943) did indeed remain true to Hitler until the last when both met bloody common ruin.

These same years, however, also provided ample evidence of friction and suspicion that unsettled the public representation of intensifying cooperation grounded in intimate affinity of ideology and interest. Mussolini bridled that he was given only scant warning of Hitler's intention to seize Austria in March 1938, and was more generally irritated by Nazi German economic and political penetration of the Danubian and Balkan regions, supposedly earmarked as Fascist Italy's spheres of hegemonic influence. His invasion of Albania in April 1939 was partly motivated by pique at the Nazi occupation of Bohemia–Moravia in March. Hitler had neglected to inform Rome until the last minute of this annexation, even though it entailed the destruction of the Munich settlement that Mussolini proudly regarded as a product of his own mediation, and publicly relegated him to humiliating subordination within the Axis.[4] The binding military commitment signified by the 'Pact of Steel' in May 1939 was for the Italians hedged by the caveat that they could not contemplate fighting for at least three years; hence their utter dismay when Hitler precipitated war in September, compelling the adoption of a 'non-belligerence' ill-fitting with Fascist boasts that warfare alone placed 'the seal of nobility on those people who have the courage to face it'.[5] Once Italy finally joined the conflict Axis military operations were uncoordinated and, on the part of the Italians in Greece and North Africa, disastrously executed. Consequently Germany assumed almost complete control over the relevant theatres, dashing Mussolini's 'fantasy' of conducting a glorious 'parallel war'.[6]

Even for contemporary observers, apparent tensions between 'myth' and 'reality' nurtured diverse explanations of the nature of the Axis and therefore of Fascist foreign policy.[7] Some doubted that there was any political substance behind the elaborate façade of propaganda bluster, pondering whether Mussolini's visit to Berlin signified anything other than 'a piece of showmanship conjured up by "two of the world's master magicians in mass control"'.[8] Others similarly refused to accept the verbiage of immutable Fascist solidarity at face value but suspected that it camouflaged a pragmatic, even cynical, *realpolitik* strategy; Italy's national interest and geopolitical position dictated that Mussolini manoeuvre between the great powers, employing his 'customary opportunism' to play one off against the other in order to extract maximum advantage.[9] Such an understanding (spiced perhaps with wishful thinking) underpinned persistent British efforts to detach Mussolini from Hitler with judicious concessions, culminating in Winston Churchill's letter of 16 May 1940 urging that 'the joint heirs of Latin and Christian civilisation must not be ranged against one another in mortal strife'.[10] Yet others, increasingly numerous once Mussolini and Hitler had become co-belligerents, upheld the view that ideological bonds and the compelling 'parallelism' of their revisionist foreign policy programmes genuinely bound them together with indissoluble 'permanence'. When Mussolini proclaimed that '"for me Enemy No. 1 is and always has been the Anglo-Saxon"' such observers read him literally, believing that only German high-handedness and the ineptitude of Italian diplomacy and strategy sometimes rendered Axis co-operation less than complete.[11]

These three interpretations of Mussolini's diplomacy – as mere propaganda, as pragmatic *realpolitik* or as fanatical ideological expansionism – have lain at the heart of the historiographical debate ever since.[12] Their diverse positive and negative verdicts upon its wisdom and efficacy carry a political charge because since the ousting of Mussolini 'debate on Italy's future has been driven by reinterpretation of its past'.[13] More specifically, they speak to a question fiercely contested within post-war Italian politics and culture: should national identity be grounded in anti-Fascist readings of the Second World War era?[14] Initially, a consensus developed that Mussolini had indeed been no more than an 'artist in propaganda', an interpretation that sustained a range of anti-Fascist positions but which also suited fellow travellers wishing to elide critical interrogation of the recent past.[15] This view has never been banished from the field, but over time as scholarship became more sophisticated interpretations have come to focus rather on how far *realpolitik* or ideology was the essence of Fascist diplomacy. Advocates of the former position view Mussolini as a moderate expansionist, pursuing goals broadly in line with longer-term Italian nationalist traditions, an argument that generally casts him in a relatively charitable light and is congenial to conservative politics. For adherents to the latter view, in contrast, he rather incarnated a rupture with the national past because of his novel revolutionary ideology and rapacious ambitions, and his association with Hitler was immanent in his political project rather than an accident of diplomacy or geopolitics. Firmly asserting Fascism's complicity with Nazism, the epitome of twentieth century evil, this argument thus implicitly or explicitly supports anti-Fascist positions.

'Fascism was a fraud': the Sawdust Caesar

The demise of Fascism was protracted and divisive. After the Allied invasion of Sicily, the king, military leaders and dissident Fascists overthrew Mussolini in a palace coup on 25 July 1943. In September, the new government botched the conclusion of an armistice with the Allies and German troops surged southwards to occupy the majority of the country. In the south, a royal government exerted some nominal authority under the auspices of the occupying Allies; in the centre and north, the Germans established the Italian Social Republic based at Salò under Mussolini, triggering the emergence of a vigorous resistance movement comprising adherents of a wide spectrum of anti-Fascist parties. Thus began 'the most savage and destructive conflict which Italy had known since the Thirty Years' War', concurrently a patriotic liberation struggle against German occupation, a class war pitching peasants against landowners and workers against capitalists, and a civil war against residual Fascist sympathisers.[16] Since the Nazis were simultaneously conducting stubborn resistance against the invading Allied armies, deporting tens of thousands of conscript workers and hastening to ensnare the Jewish population in the Holocaust, by the time liberation was declared on 25 April 1945 the nation was lacerated and prostrate.

Italy's position was also laced with ambiguity. 'The country emerged beaten from the war, but without the stain of having maintained the Fascist regime to the end'; indeed the resistance experience provided narrative capital to sustain a claim that Italy should rank amongst the war's victors.[17] This had certainly been the thrust of the 'intensive propaganda effort' mounted by anti-Fascist elements towards the Allies after the 1943 armistice. Manoeuvring to avoid a punitive peace, this had presented Italians as victims of Fascism, the war as having been willed solely by Mussolini and his 'detested ally Germany', and the resistance as a 'struggle for national liberation' mounted by 'the entire Italian people'.[18] This mnemonic labour to present anti-Fascism as the true face of the nation bore some fruit, as the Allies, in contrast to the German case, largely left the business of purging Fascists and their sympathisers to the Italians themselves.[19]

Domestically, the post-war settlement partially embodied an anti-Fascist reading of the recent past. The abolition of the monarchy in 1946 was attributable not only to public disgust at the king's pusillanimity in abandoning Rome to the Germans in September 1943, but also to his long standing association with Mussolini. Similarly, the republican constitution of 1948 clearly reflected the resistance ideals of democracy, equality and the rule of law, and created a weak executive and strong legislature with numerous checks and balances to prevent any possible restoration of Fascism. The influence of anti-Fascism was felt more diffusely as well, for instance with the general discrediting of assertive nationalism in favour of a constitutional patriotism which contributed to staunch Italian support for European integration in the 1950s and the abandonment of imperialist aspirations.[20] Thus, 'antifascism became – at least in official rhetoric and enshrined in the Constitution – the foundation of the Italian Republic'.[21]

As these caveats betray, however, the break with the past was incomplete. Despite the formal proscription of Fascism, a neo-Fascist Italian Social Movement (MSI) was established and exerted a perceptible influence upon centrist conservative parties.[22] Moreover, the need to re-establish a functioning administration, the huge extent of collaboration during Fascism's long rule, and an understandable desire to move forward rather than dwell on the harrowing past led to the curtailing of purges and considerable continuity in state bureaucracy, police and judiciary. The latter were subsequently 'instrumental in hamstringing the most progressive items of the constitution' and through the early post-war years made liberal use of repressive Fascist legislation that remained on the statue book.[23] The key factor in curtailing the radical potential of the post-war settlement, however, was the nascent Cold War. An alliance between conservative political elements and the Roman Catholic Church, encouraged by unsubtle interference from the United States, secured the exclusion of the left from government by 1948. This brought into being a paternalistic political order, dominated for over four decades by the Christian Democrats (DC), and over time increasingly scarred by clientelism and corruption as the vices of *partitocrazia* attenuated democracy.[24] Hence the oft-expressed view that the republic was born of the resistance requires serious qualification. Anti-communism was a more pervasive value in the early republic than anti-Fascism; the left – pre-eminently the communists – attempted to establish the memory of the resistance as the republic's 'foundation myth', but this remained a sectional endeavour since the conservative establishment, mass media and educators generally preferred to pass over it with at best perfunctory recognition.[25]

In gauging the politics of this settlement, the comparison with the Federal Republic of Germany is helpful. Italy also witnessed a resurgence of conservative opinion in the 1990s, proclaiming the need to redress the alleged dominance of excessively critical myths about the wartime past. The anti-Fascist values that had prevailed during 'fifty years of Marxist hegemony', so prominent neo-conservative Silvio Berlusconi claimed, had perniciously distorted Italians' sense of their national past and alienated them from republican institutions.[26] Such interventions were manifestly intended to legitimise new political forces of the right, including Berlusconi's *Forza Italia* (FI) and the 'post-Fascists' of Gianfranco Fini's National Alliance (AN) – a reconstituted MSI – and to support an 'anti-anti-Fascist' renegotiation of the constitution and, indeed, national identity. This neo-conservative challenge is far more potent historically and politically than its German counterpart, but it too has called forth a fruitful critical response in a new wave of work on the memory of Fascism. This contends the notion that anti-Fascism achieved a hegemonic position after the war is actually the real myth, one that elides not only the multiplicity of memory but also the profoundly conservative nature of mainstream republican politics and culture. Moreover, from our contemporary perspective, even denunciatory anti-Fascist rhetoric seems often to have obfuscated crucial issues of complicity and criminality.

After 'the initial preoccupations and excitations of 1945–48' when the post-war settlement was being debated, the Fascist past was generally met 'with "silence", a forgetting and an obscuring of the regime and its disasters'.[27] The conservative establishment naturally preferred to avoid a past that could only unhelpfully divide, given that its electoral constituency had either been indifferent to, accepted, or believed in Fascism, and to focus energies on the more comforting anti-communist present. When conservative discourse did bring Fascism into focus, it tended to draw on the venerable stereotype of Italians as *brava gente*, fundamentally decent if unheroic folk, fatalistically enduring a dictatorship imposed upon them, 'without opposition and without enthusiasm', adopting an attitude of passivity that could nonetheless be coded positively as essential to survive 'events that defy understanding'.[28] If anti-Fascists were keener to keep this past prominent, their representations often depended upon a not dissimilar trope, contrasting the deeds of 'good Italians' and 'wicked Germans'. While explicable in the context of the propaganda struggles of the civil war period, this anti-Fascist rhetoric nonetheless constituted 'a largely self-absolving collective memory' in which popular support for Fascism and Italian perpetration of aggressive war and war crimes were conveniently absent.[29] In common with most other combatants, Italians in general tended to view themselves primarily as victims, which in this instance often meant focusing on what they had suffered between 1943 and 1945 rather than what they had done (or failed to do) between 1922 and 1943. This strategy displaced collective responsibility for Fascism, shifting culpability for the horrors of dictatorship and war onto external others (especially the Germans) and a scapegoated Mussolini.[30] Simultaneously, it decisively marginalised the experiences of those who had primarily suffered from Fascist violence, racism and imperialism, including the Jews.[31]

Historians broadly shared this disinclination to interrogate the recent past. 'Until the beginning of the 1960s', one authority has noted, 'Italian historiographers showed minimal interest in the study of fascism'.[32] Instead, 'the Risorgimento or Liberal Italy proffered more worthy and more illuminating areas of study'.[33] Was Fascism just 'a wound as yet too fresh', revulsion at a repugnant regime precluding the effort at historical understanding?[34] Perhaps, yet important too were traditional Rankean prejudices against contemporary history, where primary documentation and scholarly detachment might both be wanting; moreover, this methodological conservatism was inextricably intertwined with the political, for historians' role under Fascism had been 'less than valorous'.[35] Apart from a few pronounced anti-Fascists who fled into exile, an historical profession composed predominantly of conservative nationalists generally had few difficulties reaching an accommodation with the regime: it 'was not in any sense purged. Nor, very likely, was it in any profound fashion fascistised'. Continuity in personnel and values characterised the post-war period, reproduced by the patriarchal machinations of patronage in university appointments: since they had mostly not been ideological zealots – even if they had found much to admire in the regime – and had turned against Fascism before its end, historians' fellow-travelling was not particularly difficult 'to disavow in the ostensibly changed world of the Republic'.[36]

Of course, some historical writing was devoted to the Fascist era and this generally had a staunchly anti-Fascist character.[37] Emblematic was the work of liberal–conservative philosopher and historian, Benedetto Croce, who had become one of the most prominent opponents of the regime.[38] Croce scorned Fascism, yet his writings invoked a cluster of tropes familiar from Meinecke's indictment of Nazism with similarly ambiguous and exculpatory implications.[39] First, he defined it as a European rather than an Italian phenomenon, a pathological intellectual and moral sickness that had infected and enthralled Italians (and others) after the exceptional trauma of the First World War. Second, it was an aberration, a 'parenthesis', 'a complete and inexplicable break with Italy's previous history', and an episode decisively closed now that the republic had restored the positive traditions of the *Risorgimento* and Liberal Italy. 'Fascism should be condemned as tyrannous and destructive, but there was no need to be too obsessed with the condemnation, since the Fascist moment in human history had been brief and would not return'.[40] Third, no particular social group or class had conceived or desired Fascism, which had gained control 'thanks to illusions, tricks, and threats' on the part of a criminal elite.[41] Domestic recriminations were therefore inappropriate; whatever guilt could not be transplanted abroad was reserved for those wicked leaders who had imposed dictatorship on an unenthusiastic people and who were now largely dead or sufficiently punished. On this view, Fascism had been 'illegal, corrupt, and anti-Italian'.[42] It was also an 'historical negativity', with 'neither a vitality of its own, nor an ideology, nor mass support', nothing more, indeed, 'than a terroristic dictatorship'.[43]

The visceral emotional appeal for triumphant liberal anti-Fascists of this contemptuous dismissal is obvious, and it seemed warranted by the contrast between Fascism's grandiose rhetoric and scant achievements. Equally, it was clearly fit for the political purposes of rehabilitating Italy internationally in the post-war world and grounding a new republic resurrecting the best of pre-1922 values. Yet for all that contemporaries lauded Italian scholarship for its fulsome 'repudiation' of Fascism, this paradigm begged crucial questions.[44] The complicity of the mass of Italians with Fascism over 20 years was elided by the double move of externalising its origins and locating agency and responsibility only with an elite leadership. Similarly, the 'parenthesis' argument foreclosed consideration not only of the roots of Fascism within Italian national history and political culture but also of possible Fascist continuities across 1945. Finally, refusing to take Fascism seriously as a political movement implicitly minimised the gravity of the murderous deeds that it (or rather, of course, Italians acting on its behalf) had committed both at home and abroad. Since this apparently strident anti-Fascist critique also performed these acts of distancing and exoneration, it was actually not unpalatable to much mainstream conservative opinion.

It is true that other voices could be discerned. Some on the right cleaved to a version of totalitarianism, a move that once more located the origins of Fascism outside Italian national traditions, whilst simultaneously delegitimating communism.[45] Equally, some former Fascists wrote defences of a regime that they claimed had offered a genuine third way between capitalism and socialism. Typically such memoirs were as keen to malign the former leadership as were anti-Fascist accounts: professing nostalgic faith in the ideals and revolutionary potential of Fascism, they lamented that it had been allowed to degenerate into mere 'Mussolinism'.[46] Critical voices on the left were more significant, not least communist historians who were somewhat keener to explore the history of Fascism than their liberal or conservative counterparts. Such commentators posed searching (one might say, *Sonderweg*-style) questions about continuity, developing inter-war Italian Communist Party (PCI) leader Antonio Gramsci's ideas about Fascism's roots in liberal Italy and urging radical purging and structural reform after the war to ensure a decisive break with unhealthy national traditions.[47] Such interpretations, however, failed to gain traction beyond the political factions whose policies they underpinned. The architects of the conservative post-war settlement rather framed 1945 as the beginning of a second *Risorgimento*: thus the republic simultaneously incarnated an 'epochal break' (with the aberration of

Fascism) and 'the realization of a submerged [positive] national continuity (Risorgimento – post-war Republic)'.[48]

Historians specialising in international relations were never likely to challenge the comforting myth of Fascism as mere past parenthesis. Diplomatic history in Italy was steeped in historicist and Rankean values that had long made it a handmaiden of the state's nationalist aspirations; moreover, under Fascism 'a greater stress on diplomatic history' was arguably the 'major innovation' in historiography and academic barons 'stimulated a huge attention to foreign policy issues'.[49] Doubtless the inter-war years were simply interesting times in international affairs, but this work also vindicated the pursuit of power politics and of particular irredentist and imperialist goals. Despite the persistence of a measure of pluralism and respect for scholarly standards, it was generally assumed that diplomatic history 'could and should be harnessed to drive the nationalist dynamo of Fascist foreign policy'.[50] After the war, there was marked continuity. Diplomatic historians did not just do ideological work through the production of patriotic historiography rationalising national policy, they were often more literally in state service, combining university appointments, curatorial work in state archives and the editing of official documentary collections (even much of their teaching was for the benefit of those seeking careers as diplomats). Hence it is hardly surprising that just as before the war, 'very few diplomatic historians either questioned the fundamental soundness of the national project of their state or objected to the main lines of its international actions since the Risorgimento'.[51]

The dominant post-war image of Mussolini as international statesman partook of the broader discourse of derision.[52] Through the 1930s, the anti-Fascist left across Europe had represented Mussolini in relentlessly hostile terms as a 'Sawdust Caesar', part gangster, part clown, presiding over a hollow if tyrannical regime. While foreign conservative opinion had once admired him as a force for order, after the advent of Hitler cast him increasingly as dictator minor and following the brutality of Fascist warmongering in East Africa and Spain, it increasingly came to share this perception.[53] While conservatives within Italy had once been inclined to support Mussolini because his foreign policy goals largely overlapped with their traditional nationalism, they too turned against him as the Fascist regime became mired in escalating ideological extremism and – perhaps more damningly – military defeat. In these circumstances, conservative nationalists could find a representation that was contemptuous, stridently 'intentionalist' in its focus on a few elite leaders, and at least potentially parenthetical, just as usable as did those anti-Fascists who had predominantly crafted it, and so it was cemented in place post-war.

This belittlement of Mussolini also incorporated a particular characterisation of the 'tortuousness and inconsistency' of his foreign policy.[54] The most influential articulation of this position came from Gaetano Salvemini, a liberal democrat, distinguished historian, and prominent anti-Fascist exile. He made a signal contribution to pre-war denigration of Mussolini in several works that mocked the 'fairy-tale' pretensions of corporatism, the fatuous nature of his claims to be enacting a social revolution, and his sometimes murderous yet also absurd and petty tyranny.[55] Salvemini's fullest statement on international affairs came in his 1953 *Prelude to World War II*, an extended version of a critique first published in the 1930s, as pithy in its phrasemaking as it was patchy in its coverage. Salvemini declared that Mussolini 'was never the great statesman many believed him to be', but rather 'always an irresponsible improviser, half madman, half criminal, gifted only – but to the highest degree – in the arts of "propaganda" and mystification'. 'He always lived from day to day', pursuing but two ends, 'first and foremost, to catch the public eye' and then 'to keep Europe in a constant state of uncertainty which would permit him some day to grab something somewhere'. His 'real genius as a showman' – 'he was unsurpassed in the art of putting up a front behind which there was nothing but economic misery and moral degradation' – enabled him to retain power for decades but his vacuous policy was ultimately doomed to fail as eventually 'the military disasters of World War Two called his bluff'.[56]

Alternative interpretive possibilities lurked within Salvemini's repudiation. On the one hand, there are occasional glimpses of Mussolini as a pragmatic *realpolitiker*, 'using Germany to wrest concessions from France and vice versa', playing one camp off against the other very much in the style of the traditional Italian strategy of the 'decisive weight'. On the other, there are hints of an ideological Mussolini, the 'apostle of violence', who 'did his wicked utmost to follow Hitler's footsteps, his evil-doing being limited solely by his inability to do worse'. Yet both these remain undeveloped, overshadowed by Mussolini the 'gangster', pursuing 'a policy of improvisation without definite goal', mixing the pursuit of empty propaganda victories with incoherent outbursts of violence.[57]

For all its withering ridicule, and granting the understandable desire to minimise the historical significance of Fascism, 'reducing it to a grand comic opera with a cast of outlandish buffoons' was just as much an act of 'political escapism' as representing Hitler as a demonic genius.[58] Salvemini's apportioning of blame for what Fascism wrought underlines the point. Adamant that Mussolini was 'not the only villain in this book', Salvemini identified Hitler as the 'arch-criminal' who 'consciously, wilfully, and maliciously planned and unleashed' the war, but also directed considerable ire at appeasing Anglo–French conservative politicians who for too long 'worked more or less hand in glove' with Mussolini.[59] These arguments reflected contemporary historiographical common sense, but in this context also deflected attention from Fascist Italian aggression. Similarly, if Salvemini was more radical than Croce in suggesting that others within the Italian establishment – including the military, big business, imperialist politicians, civil servants, intellectuals, and the king – must also stand indicted, the exploration of complicity was not carried through; these 'indispensable' supporters amounted to 'less than 1 per cent of the population' and in general rhetoric and emplotment personalised responsibility squarely upon Mussolini.[60]

Salvemini's account drew almost entirely on press sources, but works by those with firsthand knowledge of Fascist diplomacy, or based more solidly on primary documentation – made available either through the Nuremberg process or privileged access to Italian materials – generally accepted the view that 'no long-range Fascist foreign policy existed', it being simply a 'series of improvisations' dictated by 'personal whims'.[61] Diplomatic historians of more conservative political bent could profess this view without discomfort. Prominent here was the extremely patriotic Mario Toscano, whose career had begun under Fascism and who served post-war as an historical adviser to the foreign ministry and vice-president of the commission overseeing the publication of Italian diplomatic documents.[62] Toscano produced a series of narrative diplomatic history studies, largely based on unpublished Italian sources. Works in this classic, densely reconstructive, vein tend inevitably to marginalise profound forces and ideology, and though the sober Toscano's Mussolini was no hapless buffoon, 'his actions were regulated by events and the will of others' in stark contrast to a Hitler who 'wanted war and prepared for it methodically'. Distance or friction between the Axis partners was highlighted in diverse ways, not least through the suggestion that 'fear' of Germany was a prime cause behind the 'Pact of Steel'.[63] Here again, casting Mussolini as a relative lightweight served exculpatory purposes.

The chief dissent from this broad consensus actually came from Mussolini's defenders on the far right, including former Fascist propagandist Luigi Villari who lionised him as a staunch anti-communist nationalist. Villari relativised Fascist crimes by stressing 'the most heinous infamies' inflicted on Italy during its 'so-called liberation' by the Allies and the 'butcheries' perpetrated by communist resisters. Regarding foreign policy, he too displaced blame abroad. All Mussolini had sought was peaceful revision of the Versailles *diktat*, but the British and French had refused to work constructively to this end or to restrain Hitler: their unreasonable harshness meant that he was ultimately 'forced into the Axis'. 'If Britain and France had stood with him in [the Four Power Pact of 1933], Hitler would have been kept on leash and there would have been no World War II in 1939, and perhaps none at all'. As it was, even once war broke out Mussolini had struggled manfully in the cause of peace but his hand was ultimately forced 'because Italy was being strangled economically by the unneutral economic actions of Britain' – the same British who had been responsible for 'tricking Italy's ally Hitler, into war in September, 1939'.[64]

The Cold War environment lent credibility to certain aspects of this argument, and of course it chimed with prevailing Italian sentiments of self-pity. But the assertion that Mussolini's regime had been a legitimate and popular one that 'any good Italian patriot' might have served with pride was too extreme at a moment when the preferred nationalist strategy was to forget Fascism as an aberration.[65] Moreover, Mussolini's utility as a scapegoat for recent ills was so wide-ranging that the attempt at rehabilitation was premature. The Salveminian interpretation of Fascist foreign policy prevailed through to the 1960s, not because an absence of documentation mandated a superficial treatment or because of its advocate's influential stature, but rather because its evasions and omissions gave 'comfort to a society that did not want to confront its expansionist, imperialist, and sometimes racialist past'.[66]

Similar interpretations held sway abroad. Wartime polemics had extended the pejorative readings put into circulation during the 1930s. In late 1943 a British leftist tract conducted a mock *Trial of Mussolini*, arraigning the *Duce* for his 20 year criminal spree at home and abroad. Mussolini had 'enslaved' an unwilling Italian people, and his Fascism 'was a fraud': 'the garish façade of a rejuvenated nation' may have fooled many, but its essential 'rottenness' was exposed by the popular revolt that so suddenly toppled it.[67] (It is tempting to see this as the inspiration for A. J. P. Taylor's more famous 1961 claim that 'everything about Fascism was a fraud', and Mussolini 'a vain, blundering boaster without either ideas or aims'.[68]) The trope of a dissociating distance between the Italian people and Mussolini was a staple of Allied war propaganda aiming to stimulate dissension on the Italian home front. In 1944 British journalist Maxwell Macartney picked up the theme in his *One Man Alone*, portraying a 'jerry-built', 'gimcrack Fascist regime', mired in 'incompetence and miscalculations'. Responsibility for its aggression was located firmly with Mussolini himself (and a handful of other elite leaders); this was definitely a '"Fascist" war' into which Mussolini had 'dragged' a recalcitrant nation. Macartney drew out the implication that this proved Italians had come through dictatorship relatively unscathed and that consequently 'no great effort will be required for the elimination of the Fascist virus'.[69]

Although such works occasionally discerned some consistency or method in Mussolini's foreign policy, the dominant view construed it as purely opportunistic. In 1959 esteemed British historian of Italy Denis Mack Smith deemed Fascism a movement that 'possessed no firm principles, no novel or consistent ideas, no new institutions that withstand serious examination', and Mussolini merely 'a stupendous poseur', master of pretence and the *volte-face*, 'the perpetual oscillation and unseriousness of his opinions' permeating the whole regime. Where Hitler possessed 'a genuine policy, however crazy and misguided', Mussolini 'simply accommodated his policy to whatever line his instinct told him would make good propaganda'. He was obsessed with style to the virtual exclusion of substance, but if this 'bent for propaganda' for a while masked the impracticality and inefficiency of the regime, the preference for a 'cosy, but counterfeit, world' ultimately proved disastrous in foreign and strategic affairs. He 'knew in his more lucid intervals that war might expose his bluff; but he could not extricate himself from the effects of twenty years' propaganda about war being beautiful and beneficial. Propaganda thus dictated policy, not *vice versa*'. 'Duped by his own phrases', he 'helped to precipitate a war for which he had prepared no armaments'. Devoid of principles in foreign policy – he 'would have fought against Germany at any time up to 1940 if she had ever seemed to be a loser' – he was simply 'lured' and 'inveigled' into Hitler's war and the catastrophic defeat that destroyed them both.[70]

The harmony between Italian and foreign interpretations can be partly explained by their common roots in a cohesive international anti-Fascist tradition. Equally, there was also at this point an overarching ideological goal shared between mainstream Italian and western opinion in the rehabilitation of Italy and the integration of the new democracy into the (West) European family of nations, ends to which this representation was highly conducive. Yet where foreigners were concerned, longer standing ethnocentric assumptions may also have contributed to this interpretive predilection. The suggestion that Anglo-Saxons have sometimes evinced a 'sense of moral superiority' over Mediterranean peoples that could easily slide into 'fatuous racism' is certainly worth considering.[71] When Elizabeth Wiskemann described Mussolini as embodying 'traditional continuity', since being 'theatrical, vain, hypersensitive, and sceptical', he was 'like a malicious caricature of his own people', it is hard not to detect a whiff of essentialist disdain.[72] Alan Cassels has speculated that the censorious character of much British scholarship derived from a sense of resentment that modern Italians, mired in dictatorship and corruption, had betrayed the glorious traditions of classical and renaissance civilisations which generations of intellectuals were schooled to revere.[73] Relatedly, Edward Ingram has suggested that British scorn may represent an act of psychological transference: in thus denigrating 'the only enemy the British could beat in the Second World War', perhaps historians were working through their own sense of humiliation at British decline?[74]

Whatever its varied roots, in post-war circumstances this 'Sawdust Caesar' paradigm served multiple diverse constituencies. It remained clearly visible in memoir and historical accounts into the 1960s and indeed beyond, established as a potent narrative tradition; thus in 1969 an authority such as Wiskemann could confidently affirm that 'from 1936 until the end nothing can be discerned that deserves the name of Italian foreign policy, nothing but a surrender to the pressure from Hitler with no regard for Italy's interest or capacity'.[75] In the 1960s, however, scholarship on Fascism entered a new and more mature phase, fuelled by an expansion of available documentary material and the emergence of new generations of scholars. Representations of Mussolini as clownish gangster came to seem increasingly inadequate as scholars inclined to take Fascism more seriously and brought into focus alternative, more sophisticated, interpretations that had already been glimpsed on the margins. Underpinning these developments were shifts in the landscape of politics and collective memory that led new questions to be posed, and lent a very particular ideological charge to the decision to choose one mode of emplotment over another.

'Elements of planning and a purposive will': taking Fascism seriously

Conservative monopoly over political power was loosened in the détente era as the left gained partial legitimation. In 1960 popular protest forced the DC to abandon plans to rule with the parliamentary support of the MSI and to launch an 'opening to the left', forming successive coalitions with the Italian Socialist Party (PSI) until the mid-1970s. During the later 1970s, even the PCI edged closer to national power as its electoral support surged and it gave parliamentary backing to a DC-led government of 'national solidarity' in the so-called 'historic compromise'. Political life was, however, extremely turbulent. Widespread protest movements persisted long after 1968 and the 'hot autumn' of 1969, extracting liberalising reforms from a recalcitrant establishment; the oil-crises of the mid-1970s engendered protracted economic difficulties; and terrorist campaigns from both right and left proliferated. 'Black' terrorism, abetted by elements in the state security apparatus, aimed to disconcert public opinion into opposing the leftward drift of politics and society. 'Red' terrorism, conversely, was animated by discontent with the meagre fruits of reformist parliamentarism and sought to mobilise the working class into revolution through kidnappings and assassinations. The republic overcame these travails, though the Red Brigades' murder of DC elder statesman Aldo Moro in 1978 ended the tentative legitimation of the PCI and, in retrospect, also ended hopes for the fruitful renewal of the political system. During the 1980s Italy took another conservative turn, governed by multi-party coalitions typically dominated by the moderate (and idiosyncratic) PSI leader Bettino Craxi, its politics increasingly marred by stagnation and corruption.[76]

The 'opening to the left' was accompanied by an anti-Fascist turn in collective memory. All those pro-republican political parties sheltering under what became known in the 1970s as the 'constitutional arch' publicly repudiated Fascism and subscribed to a myth of the resistance, symbolised by the elevation to the presidency in 1978 of Sandro Pertini, 'an independent and incorruptible socialist who had opposed Mussolini without hesitation or equivocation'.[77] Where the resistance had previously only been prominent in the sectional memory of the communists, it now gained much greater visibility as its heritage was generalised and promoted by the state. Thus these years witnessed a boom in the construction of publicly funded resistance monuments, the extension of the higher school history curriculum to cover the war years, greater critical coverage of the Fascist period on television, and a far more pronounced visibility of anti-Fascist and Marxist readings of the past across popular culture, for example in the cinema where Bernardo Bertolucci's epic *1900* was emblematic. If this signified a generally more extensive and critical engagement with Fascism, however, it had definite limitations. The dominant representation of the resistance was rather banalised, downplaying the particular contribution of the communists, the Italian roots of Salò and dashed hopes for radical social and political change, instead portraying the whole population rising up in a national redemption struggle against the Nazis.[78] The communists countenanced what was often 'a patriotic ritual emptied of its radical and participatory message' as the mnemonic analogue of the 'historic compromise' and price for their growing legitimation, since it was only on this basis that the conservative establishment was prepared for the first time to establish anti-Fascism as the ethical and political underpinning of the republic.[79]

The late coming of this turn and the domesticated nature of mainstream representations within it are not the only reasons why claims about the alleged post-war hegemony of anti-Fascism require serious qualification. The communists and their allies may have gained greater influence in 'the world of the intellect' – 'a place of immense and, to an Anglo-Saxon, almost incomprehensible prestige' – but the DC and its collaborators always remained dominant in 'the world of "real power"'.[80] Accommodation around the new myth was also fraught with tension. Alessandro Portelli has exquisitely evoked the ambivalences of resistance commemorations where DC dignitaries on the podium and communist veterans on the ground were divided within a shared ceremony, 'a metaphor for all the tensions and balances of public space in a republic "born of Resistance" and uneasy about this birth'.[81] Neither left nor right entirely abandoned their incompatible, partisan readings of the wartime past; indeed the more extreme elements never accepted this putatively unifying myth on any level. As the polarising political crises of the 1970s wore on, these conflictual histories came to the fore once more in strident public controversies. Hence this anti-Fascist moment would also prove to be a very fleeting conjuncture.

Despite these various caveats, it was nonetheless a positive innovation that anti-Fascism became 'a touchstone for much of the politics of contestation' in these years.[82] Moreover, academic study of the Fascist past blossomed. Growing temporal distance soothed Rankean qualms about the legitimacy of contemporary history which became established as 'the most prestigious and the most contested arena of historical research'. The gradual opening of archives to scholars was another pertinent factor, and documentary availability encouraged a particular focus on Fascism's seizure of power and the earlier years of the regime. The direction of inquiry was also – and again as elsewhere – shaped by methodological developments in the broader discipline. Thus social science influences stimulated innovative non-Marxist analyses of fascism as a generic phenomenon, while the rise of social history engendered regional studies and exploration of Fascism's impact upon diverse social groups, such as the working class; these complemented without supplanting more traditional studies of politics, diplomacy and administration.[83] Generational change was important here too, as much of this work was conducted by a cohort of younger scholars (both within Italy and abroad) who had 'not experienced Fascism directly' and so believed themselves 'able to confront it more freely, without revisionistic preconceptions or psychological inhibitions'.[84]

The overall thrust of this diverse and voluminous work is not easy to summarise. While it largely remained underpinned by broadly anti-Fascist assumptions, there was now a perceptible tendency to seek to understand rather than simply denounce Fascism, and to accord it the dignity of at least a certain substance. Thus scholars characteristically tended to stress 'the degree to which fascism was a political movement driven by clear yet often competing political and economic interests, rather than an exercise in mere political eclecticism, opportunism and chicanery'.[85] Despite a consequent thickening of understandings, however, it took some time for a new interpretive terrain replete with competing positions to emerge. Thus in the case of generic fascism studies, a profusion of stimulating work dissected its ideological content in unprecedented fashion, but by the mid-1970s there was still a marked 'lack of consensus' on even a bare definition.[86] More explicitly historical work was initially slow to move beyond established interpretations. Mussolini remained at the centre of inquiry, 'even if lower down the scale of political, economic and social power lay a tangle of forces' – the 'old order' of Liberal Italy – 'with a vitality of their own'. Fascism seemed 'an adaptable political movement', its 'more revolutionary pretensions' ultimately proving 'hollow indeed', as 'evil ambition' was 'conditioned by practical failure'. By the later 1970s, however, distinctive, fresh and antagonistic perspectives began to materialise. Anti-Fascist historians, increasingly stressing the 'murderousness' of a reactionary regime, more stridently proclaimed it as the product of profound negative continuities in national history and averred its affinities with Nazi Germany. But they were opposed by conservative voices who, if not necessarily sympathetic to Mussolini, nonetheless desired to present the Fascist episode as something other than an unrelievedly bleak chapter in the national story.[87] Scholarship on both sides drew inspiration and energy from the disputatious course of Italian politics; moreover, it directly contributed to the contestation of politics, memory and national identity, not least because these debates were given extensive coverage in the print media and on television.

The most important contribution here was made by Renzo De Felice, until his death in 1996 the foremost Italian historian of Fascism, chiefly because of his colossal multi-volume biography of Mussolini published between 1965 and 1997. Dense, sprawling and stylistically convoluted, this biography was arguably profoundly inconsistent both within individual instalments and across its vast 6,416-page span, yet it was also extraordinarily rich empirically and its successive volumes set the agenda for historical debate through three decades; hence even its harshest detractors deem it 'a work as indispensable as it is unlikely to find imitators'.[88] The early volumes proved relatively uncontroversial, since they presented Mussolini as a cynical and adroit political operator, lacking in long-range ideological objectives, and Fascism as 'an essentially reactionary force' (though on this last point there was a latent 'fuzziness').[89] This changed, however, with the publication in 1974 of the fourth tome covering the period 1929–36, coupled with the 1975 appearance of the text of an interview in which De Felice summarised his entire perspective on the *Duce*.[90] This latter pithy and bestselling work was in effect De Felice's core 'manifesto' ('from which his followers have never resiled') and his Mussolini was now a very different and hugely contentious beast.[91] Coming at a moment of acute political crisis with the DC apparently in disarray and the PCI, achieving its best ever election results, potentially on the brink of power, De Felice's interventions unleashed an intense public furore.[92]

De Felice's position contained several crucial elements. He argued that Fascism's core support was a dynamic emerging middle class, thus striking at the heart of the Marxist *doxa* that it stood for declining social elements threatened by modernity. Moreover, he claimed in consequence that far from being simply reactionary, Fascism always possessed an authentic revolutionary drive. Its manifest contradictions derived from the simultaneous existence of multiple Fascisms: 'Fascism as regime' involved compromises with the establishment in Italy (such as the king, Pope and military), but alongside it there was always 'Fascism as movement', a radical and dynamic force exerting a revolutionary influence. De Felice portrayed Mussolini as a serious, far-sighted thinker committed to a modernising project that would 'create a new kind of Italian' – a 'new fascist man' – and a third way between capitalism and communism. He stressed that by the mid-1930s this project had enjoyed considerable success, and that the Ethiopian war won Mussolini unparalleled broad support across the nation, indeed the 'consensus' alluded to in the biographical volume's subtitle. These claims were naturally controversial, given current anti-Fascist assumptions about the public's perpetual hostility towards the regime, the superficial impact of Fascist ideology, and the criminal folly of the Ethiopian war. Two further related assertions were similarly tendentious; first: that Fascism was *sui generis* and that it represented 'a closed chapter' – it 'is dead, and it cannot be revived' – blocking off all questions of continuity; second, that there was a 'fundamental difference' between the 'vitalistic optimism' of a progressive Fascism and the tragic, pessimistic and retrogressive force of Nazism. Thus De Felice sought with renewed determination to deny any potential link between the two creeds and remove any responsibility for Nazi crimes and racism from Italian shoulders.[93]

De Felice's genius was to deliver an intensely political intervention cloaked in the garb of 'an objective, scientific kind of historical analysis'. He stressed that he had approached Fascism 'with the greatest critical serenity possible', rooting himself solely in the archival evidence, thus to transcend the myths of 'communist cultural hegemony'. Yet despite the disingenuous claim that Mussolini was 'in many ways destroyed by my work', De Felice's *Duce* was a much more original and accomplished politician, and a far more human, even indeed, humane, figure than in any previous historical representation.[94] Moreover since his assiduously propagated argument contradicted the core tenets of anti-Fascist readings, at a time when they were central to the incipient legitimation of the PCI, it obviously had direct political implications. Some detractors questioned the veracity of De Felice's interpretation, critiquing particular substantive claims and alleging that he read Fascist documents too literally, always giving Mussolini the benefit of the doubt. Others were more exercised by the political legitimacy of his whole project, stressing the evils of Fascism and polemically condemning him for striking a pose of neutrality that rendered him 'objectively philo-fascist'.[95]

Since these critics were predominantly of the left, however, they were vulnerable to the charge that they were *parti pris*, their ferocious assault simply underlining the stranglehold communism had on intellectual life. Given the massive empirical resources De Felice had marshalled, it was easy to accept his claim that he was offering scholarly truth as an antidote to political misinformation. Moreover, his argument posed alluringly as a 'nonconformist counternarrative', an alternative to the imposed 'official' history of the republic, whilst in fact availing itself 'of the institutional power of agencies, parties, and media, which are far from marginal or subaltern in the nation's public life'.[96] He was also in tune with 'the spirit of the times' and as the Moro murder 'closed the Left's window of political opportunity in Italy' his views were gradually entrenched as a new orthodoxy.[97] (Albeit that the dominant popular understanding, constructed and disseminated through the mass media, rather simplified his position, 'airbrushing out his ambiguities and qualifiers'.[98]) Thus when his next volume appeared in 1981, extending coverage into the crucial pre-war years of 1936 to 1940, there was little public controversy and far less scholarly debate.[99] If Fascism had not quite been depoliticised, the De Felice affair – as a kind of lower key and reverse Fischer controversy – had demolished the notion that it could only legitimately be viewed through anti-Fascist lenses.

The literature on Fascist foreign policy shadowed the trajectory of the broader field, as more sophisticated representations were elaborated by both Italian and foreign scholars but with a transitional period before fully articulated interpretive options came into focus. (That said, a perennial lament holds that this historiography remains conceptually underdeveloped compared to that on Nazi foreign policy, concurrently in the midst both of the Fischer-Taylor triggered controversy on continuity and the burgeoning 'intentionalist-functionalist' debate.[100]) The key Italian archives 'remained closed longer than their counterparts elsewhere', with access then hampered by organisational problems and a certain bureaucratic caprice, but by the 1970s they had begun to open to (at least some favoured) scholars.[101] Moreover, from 1952 onwards volumes of the official edited documentary series charting Italian foreign policy from 1861, *I Documenti Diplomatici Italiani*, gradually made available a considerable quantity of material on the Fascist period.[102] These resources obviously provided a material base for the elaboration of more complex interpretations, even if the emplotments actually developed had been present in embryo in earlier commentary.

Most scholars now rejected the conventional wisdom that Mussolini's foreign policy consisted of no more than propagandist improvisation; despite his proclivity to bluster and undoubted instances of opportunism, they increasingly detected an underlying substance and direction or, in Jens Petersen's words, the 'much stronger presence of elements of planning and a purposive will ... than Salvemini had supposed'.[103] Thus Esmonde Robertson acknowledged that 'to all outward appearances Mussolini wanted action for its own sake and restlessly switched from one objective to another', but concluded that despite these 'apparent contradictions' his policy did indeed possess 'some system' in its drive towards the acquisition of true great power status.[104] Similarly, Italian scholars like Giorgio Rumi began to argue that Mussolini had definite goals, both revisionist – to overturn 'the order established by the diplomats at Versailles' – and imperialist – proclaiming 'the necessity for expansion in the Mediterranean and in Africa' – from the time of the March on Rome.[105] Although this work departed from the 'Sawdust Caesar' interpretation that had previously been *de rigueur* amongst anti-Fascist authors, the dominant sensibility was initially still critical: hence the reassurance proffered by Alan Cassels that 'to find coherence in [Mussolini's] foreign policy is not necessarily to applaud it'.[106]

Considerable attention was paid to charting the different phases in Fascist foreign policy. Research into Mussolini's early diplomacy, revealing that there had always been something of 'the ideologue and trafficker in revisionism' about him, undermined the notion that the 1920s had really been 'a decade of good behaviour' and hinted at more unswerving fundamental ambitions.[107] Yet it was also apparent that policy had assumed a more stridently revisionist character in the 1930s, with imperialist adventure, the formation of the Axis and eventual co-belligerence with Hitler, and the nature of this shift naturally demanded explanation. Many scholars thus sought to identify the process whereby and the point at which 'the healthy or commonplace traditions of Liberal Italy were ousted by a maleficent process of "fascistisation"'.[108] In the formulation of Enrico Serra, diplomats and more moderate Fascists had 'tried in vain to put into effect a traditional policy' but eventually Mussolini succeeded in imposing one 'based on ideology with the results which we know'.[109] (Though this argument has some plausibility, it is not entirely devoid of exculpatory overtones. It focuses on individual agency to the occlusion of structural factors and risks legitimising the achievements of Fascist policy in its allegedly pre-ideological, nationalist and *realpolitik*, phase; equally, it is not entirely incompatible with the 'parenthesis' paradigm.)

The motives behind the apparent radicalisation of policy with the Ethiopian adventure and intervention in the Spanish civil war were much debated. Italian Marxists naturally stressed the economic and structural motives behind Fascist imperialism, but others too contended that external policy might have internal sources and that the deleterious effect of the Depression on the Italian economy and public opinion pushed Mussolini down the road to aggression and intervention. A variant position advocated a more fully-fledged 'social imperialist' line, claiming that he turned to militarist expansion in the mid-1930s explicitly to reinvigorate popular support for a stagnating regime (a view not entirely dissimilar to 'Sawdust Caesar' arguments about the propagandistic essence of his policy). Yet others laid greater emphasis on international contingencies and the fact that from the mid-1930s conditions within Europe were unpropitious for the achievement of diplomatic success, thus inclining Mussolini towards Africa as the proving ground for Fascist dynamism. The role of ideology was also contentious. Jens Petersen's 1973 study of the origins of the Axis stressed the importance of ideological affinity, and Alan Cassels concurred that in the mid-1930s Mussolini's embrace of 'rigid, ideological diplomatic thinking' caused an 'irrevocable breach with democratic Britain and France'. Yet simultaneously, John Coverdale contended in a 1975 study of Italian intervention in Spain that strategic considerations far outweighed ideological factors (or domestic considerations), and that Mussolini's policy continued in all essentials that of Liberal Italy. A number of crucial larger interpretive issues were thus broached. Was Fascism's foreign policy a mere means to an end or its very *raison d'être*? Did its radicalisation in the later 1930s signify a qualitative change or merely the realisation of long nurtured ambitions? How did it relate to traditional Italian policy? Yet it often remained difficult in these very specialised studies, with their dense detail and fresh documentation, to discern any clearly delineated over-arching conceptualisation of Mussolini's foreign policy.[110]

The De Felice affair played a key role in bringing incipient contrasting interpretations into focus and revealing their politics. As it crystallised through the 1970s and early 1980s, De Felice's distinctive representation of Mussolini coupled a modernizing revolutionary ideologue on the home front with 'a Machiavellian realist who continually sought to find compromises and avoid confrontations' abroad.[111] Preoccupied in the 1920s with establishing his regime, after 1929 he placed increasing emphasis on 'the formulation of a foreign policy that sought to exploit Italy's "decisive weight" in the European balance and the possibility it offered for Italy to maneuver between the Anglo–French and the Germans – all in order to give Italy a "true" colonial empire and Mediterranean hegemony'.[112] It followed that the Axis was emphatically not the result of 'a presumed affinity or, even worse, an ideological identity', but was essentially a tactical alignment. Frustrated by Anglo–French opposition over Ethiopia, Mussolini nonetheless 'prolonged the formula of the "pendulum" policy' but found it increasingly difficult to effect: western anti-Fascism meant that 'the arc of the pendulum became narrower and narrower' and he was pushed ever closer to a Germany of whom he was actually 'suspicious and fearful'.[113]

True, there was a certain inconsistency here: whilst stressing the *Duce's* 'innate political realism', De Felice also contended that after 1936 he 'underwent a decisive phase of ideological evolution and involution', seeing foreign policy as a means to enact his domestic totalitarian cultural revolution and convinced that internationally Italy 'had to participate in the great historic struggle that would usher in the "new civilization"'.[114] Lamentably, on occasion thereafter, ideology overpowered Mussolini's 'political sense'. But De Felice's dominant line stressed the continued striving for equidistance, even for a general agreement with the western powers through the later 1930s. The 'Pact of Steel' was a product of Anglo–French intransigence over this design, but was intended by Mussolini to postpone war and keep Germany in check, and even when Hitler wrecked this hope Mussolini sought to continue his role as mediator between the blocs. Finally in 1940 he felt compelled – for reasons of prestige, territorial advantage and fear of Germany and isolation – to enter the war, but this again was intended to achieve for him the position of 'arbiter *super partes*' and was an 'almost platonic taking up of arms'.[115] The initial attempt to fight an 'autonomous and distinct' 'parallel war' yet again, for De Felice, underlined the distance and tension between Italy and Nazi Germany.[116]

De Felice's Mussolini *diplomatico* thus combined three key elements (leaving aside, for the moment, its inconsistencies).[117] First, he was no brutal or callous warmonger, but rather at most a moderate expansionist who 'excluded the possibility of a European war to concentrate on local successes in the name of revisionism'.[118] Second, the essential substance of his policy was not novel, since he sought merely 'to achieve the perennial diplomatic aspirations of the Italian monarchy and the liberal elite for great-power status and limited colonial expansion', *via* the venerable strategy of the 'decisive weight'.[119] Third, and relatedly, his association with Nazi Germany was a matter of contingency and reluctance (Mussolini 'found himself increasingly tied to Germany'), as much the result of Anglo–French myopia and hostility, as it was of his own positive agency or desire.[120] De Felice thus picked up on a number of tropes that had long been visible in the literature but he incorporated them into a comprehensive revisioning. Where conservative nationalists had previously chosen to forget Mussolini – or to sideline him within the derisive 'Sawdust Caesar' paradigm – temporal distance, new documentary resources, and above all the changing political climate now facilitated the construction of a more positive and respectful representation. Thus De Felice signalled the desire of conservative opinion to break with anti-Fascist orthodoxy and instead develop an anti-anti-Fascist perspective. Within this paradigm, taking Mussolini seriously on the domestic front involved seeing him as an innovatory politician intent on carrying through a radical modernising project, but in foreign affairs it meant reinventing him as a traditional Italian statesman. Instead of historicising Mussolini away as a parenthesis, or lamenting that at some point foreign policy had fallen prey to perverse 'fascistisation', this much bolder strategy entailed identifying positive elements of continuity from Liberal to Fascist Italy and, implicitly, beyond.

The most sustained counter-blast to De Felice's normalisation of Mussolini came from Denis Mack Smith, principally in a 1976 study of Fascism's wars and a concise 1981 biography.[121] Against De Felice's moderate *realpolitiker*, driven into conflict almost by force of circumstances, Mack Smith offered a serial bungler who 'deliberately and even carefully steered his fascist movement into imperialism and into a succession of wars which eventually left Italy prostrate'. Yet although it was highly usable for many Italians on the left, this scathing indictment of a shallow propagandist 'living in cloud-cuckoo-land' whose policy sometimes stemmed simply 'from the desire to cut a figure' now seemed not a little dusty, and superficial when set against De Felice's massive erudition.[122] In Italy, diplomatic historians were – predictably, given their intellectual and political investments – far more inclined to follow the latter's lead. Emblematic was Rosaria Quartararo, who in 1980 published a study of pre-war Anglo–Italian–German relations that presented Fascist foreign policy as ultra-realist, unswervingly committed to the strategy of the 'decisive weight', and in tune with the noblest national traditions. This was emphatically patriotic historiography, thoroughly Italocentric in presenting the Mediterranean theatre as central in the origins of the war and lauding the potency and capability of the Italian armed forces.[123] Quartararo's key warmongers were the British, senescent imperialists dismayed at the challenge of the virile rising powers, who not only 'coldy rejected' efforts for a peaceful revisionist settlement meeting Italy's legitimate demands for equal status, but sought to encircle their enemies and even contemplated preventative war to achieve 'the destruction of the Nazi regime and the Fascist one'.[124] As Richard Bosworth ruefully noted, this amounted in crucial respects to 'a revival of the Fascist–nationalist view of Italian foreign policy expressed by Villari' or even by Mussolini himself.[125] Thus in an increasingly conservative climate, an interpretation that had formerly been deemed beyond the pale became legitimate and potent in mainstream Italian historical thinking.

By the early 1980s, international historians of anti-Fascist bent were somewhat on the defensive. The De Felicean view now occupying centre stage within Italy, with its heavy overtones of 'apologetic nationalism', certainly did not appeal to them. Yet the leading anti-Fascist position advocated by Mack Smith seemed merely to substitute 'sarcasm' for analysis.[126] By the lights of contemporary scholarship, it focused with anachronistic narrowness on Mussolini's individual agency, obfuscating crucial questions about the well-springs and nature of policy, the role of structural factors and other actors, and Mussolini's relationship to Italian national traditions. Consequently its overall political message was 'strangely exculpatory', for all its vitriol.[127] The challenge was therefore to find a means of responding to De Felice's provocation that would build on the recent thickening of knowledge about Fascism and yet also be congenial to critical anti-Fascist politics. Such intellectually and politically satisfying narrative options were, in truth, already coalescing, and the next phase in the debate would see contestation fully joined between very starkly contrasting interpretive positions.

'Overtly and insistently ideological': the 'Pope of Anti-Democracy'?

Although Craxi was nominally a socialist, his dominance over Italian politics in the 1980s did not mean the ascendancy of progressive values. Rather, he coupled a distinctive brand of managerial reformist socialism with 'a modernist and strongman rhetoric that proved extremely popular with the new middle classes'.[128] He also consciously promoted the revivification of national pride, lauding Italian sporting successes, asserting a new independence in foreign affairs, and appropriating Garibaldi as his project's founding father.[129] His concrete achievements were, however, attenuated by the corruption and immobility increasingly afflicting the republic. Then, in the early 1990s, a political earthquake caused the whole post-war party system to collapse. One major cause was the demise of communism across Europe which not only delegitimated the PCI but also robbed the DC of its traditional anti-communist rationale. Another was the launch in 1992 of judicial investigations into corruption, which finally began to expose its phenomenal pervasiveness across the whole political spectrum. The subsequent disappearance (or rather fragmentation and reformulation) of all the major political parties, together with electoral reforms, led commentators to declare 'the unlamented death of the First Republic' and the emergence of a second.[130]

As new party groupings coalesced, the landscape of politics slowly changed; older ideological antagonisms faded somewhat in the face of a pervasive populist neo-liberalism, embodied above all in Silvio Berlusconi, controversial media magnate and entrepreneur turned politician. In 1994 Berlusconi became prime minister heading a coalition chiefly comprising his own FI, the xenophobic and separatist Northern League and the newly moderate 'post-Fascists' of the AN. This grant of respectability to Mussolini's spiritual heirs was hugely symbolic; as one commentator wrote, 'the whole climate in Italy has altered ... A ban has been removed, and a taboo has been broken'.[131] Although this administration was short lived, Berlusconi returned to power in 2001, with the AN again prominent coalition partners, and for the bulk of the present century he has remained prime minister at the head of a mutating centre–right bloc (in 2009 FI and the AN formally merged). Constantly beset by allegations of graft and cronyism, exploiting his control over the media in dubiously undemocratic ways, and preaching a rather anachronistic anti-communism, the autocratic advocate of neo-liberal freedoms Berlusconi is the charismatic emblem of the new conservative politics of the 'Second Republic'.[132]

Shifts in the collective memory of Fascism were inextricably imbricated with these political changes. The dominant tendency was not so much the overt rehabilitation of Fascism as its banalisation, part of a broader 'de-ideologisation' or 'pacification' of the past.[133] Indicative of this was a spectacular exhibition on 'The Italian Economy between the Wars' held in Rome in 1984 which told an apolitical story of modernisation and consumerism, omitting Fascist oppression and war and inciting not ethical engagement but apathetic, 'deracinated contemplation'.[134] Polemical interventions from De Felice and other public intellectuals continued the effort to demolish the pernicious supposedly official ideology of the state, with such success that even before the collapse of the 'First Republic' Richard Bosworth could lament the definitive 'eclipse of anti-Fascism'.[135] In the mid-1990s, the Fascist past once more became highly visible as the fiftieth anniversaries of the resistance and liberation coincided with the entry of Berlusconi and his 'post-Fascist' partners into government. Revisionist commentators assaulted anti-Fascist shibboleths about the virtue and patriotism of the partisans by publicising their alleged murderous score-settling around the conclusion of formal hostilities, and stressing their loyalty to Moscow and a totalitarian ideology. Simultaneously, those who fought for Salò were reinvented as honourable patriots, suffering alongside all other Italians during the tragic events of 1943–45, now predominantly represented in relativising terms as a civil war.[136] Thus it was that in 1994 a campaign could be launched 'to re-script the April 25 commemoration of the liberation of Italy – which has traditionally been an occasion to remember and honour the deeds of antifascist partisans ... as a holiday honouring the soldiers who fought for the Republic of Salò as well'.[137] ('The dead are all equal', according to a former Salò loyalist featured in the controversial television documentary, *Combat Film*.[138])

This neutralisation of the past was intended to facilitate 'national reconciliation' (one of the most insistent revisionist rhetorical themes), 'leaving behind the dichotomy between Fascism and anti-Fascism'.[139] For Berlusconi, this was to underpin a 'Second Republic' that 'would have a different constitutional base and owe little or nothing to the example of the Resistance'.[140] The 'post-Fascists' pursued a similarly supple mnemonic strategy. Transforming the MSI into the mainstream AN meant abandoning pure unreconstructed nostalgia for Fascism, deprecating the *Duce's* post-1938 extremist turn towards anti-Semitic legislation and alliance with Hitler, even while praising his modernising achievements before that date. Yet while elaborating this more palatable Mussolini, the AN simultaneously advocated transcendence of a divisive past and the consignment of Fascism 'to the history books'.[141] There was, of course, opposition to this revisionist tide. In 1994 300,000 demonstrators took to the streets in Milan on 25 April in protest at the AN, while some establishment figures such as former partisan Carlo Ciampi, president from 1999 to 2006, were 'zealous in defence of the memory of the Resistance'.[142] Yet this was now a rearguard action. After Berlusconi's return to power in 2001, proposals were tabled to give the ministry of education a role in vetting school history textbooks to eliminate ideological bias – meaning, in Berlusconi's words, 'Marxist deviations'.[143] In 2006 his government introduced a bill to accord Salò veterans – even irregulars – 'full military honours, pensions, and a general rehabilitation in recognition of their "good faith"', thus making explicit their equivalence with former resisters.[144] Together with a media predilection for presenting the Fascist past as 'just another part of a cheerful and marketable heritage', with an emphasis on surface image and sanitised spectacle, this powerful discourse of depoliticisation served very particular political purposes.[145]

Developments in the historiography of Fascism closely shadowed this broader memory politics, not least because of the extensive involvement of historians in media debates. The war years and the resistance struggle were the main focus of attention, with De Felice's final biographical tomes of 1990 and 1997, together with another popularising interview published in 1995, occupying centre stage. De Felice turned the communists' exclusivist variant of the 'myth of the resistance' back upon them by arguing that active resistance was the preserve only of an ideologically committed minority, with the vast majority of the population standing by passively; there was little to choose morally between the partisans and Salò, and indeed Mussolini's decision to head the republic reflected a patriotic desire to shield the nation from the worst excesses of German occupation. Moreover, the frailties and flaws of the 'First Republic' owed much to its origins in the self-interested machinations of the parties rooted in the resistance, and to the subsequent attempts to hegemonise an anti-Fascist ideology that was too sectarian to serve as the underpinning for genuine national unity.[146] Other commentators developed this idea that the resistance should no longer be considered the 'First Republic's original virtue' but rather 'the post-war nation's original sin'. This scholarship evidently chimed with the efforts of new political forces on the right to legitimate themselves against the reformulated leftist parties – still identified with the resistance heritage – but also to locate readings of the 'First Republic' and Fascism that would permit 'the construction of an Italy truer to its original but lately betrayed liberal values'; in some variants, building a 'Second Republic' in which neo-liberalism would be politically and culturally dominant entailed conceiving the whole period from 1922 to the 1990s as a vast parenthesis.[147]

Despite his death in 1996, De Felice's anti-anti-Fascist paradigm still remains influential, indeed orthodox, even if his followers have split into different schools. Perhaps the most important, headed by Emilio Gentile, explores the political culture and symbolic universe of Fascism, its pretensions as a secular religion and to effect a genuine cultural revolution. Conceptually innovative and empirically rich, this work has 'led to real advances in our understanding of the fascist period'.[148] That said, it has also been criticised for tacitly accepting De Felice's theses about the novelty and dramatic extent of Mussolini's domestic ideological ambitions and the reality of consensus.[149] (In the historiography of Nazi Germany, explorations of consensus connote frank and critical engagement with the uncomfortable truth of complicity. In Italy, however, the argument that Fascism was 'chosen and supported spontaneously by the people' is deployed to sustain the myth of an 'essentially innocuous', 'rosewater dictatorship' and thus discredit the anti-Fascist tradition. So 'collective guilt (if it was ever felt) turns into collective absolution'.[150]) Equally, for all the modish radicalism of its culturalist methodology, a tendency to downplay the coercive aspects of the regime and to read it superficially on its own terms have also been construed as congruent with 'apolitical' anti-anti-Fascist historiography.[151]

Historians with anti-Fascist intent have certainly not, however, been banished from the field. Especially significant here is recent work uncovering the racist brutality of Fascist colonialism, war crimes committed by Italian occupation forces, anti-Jewish repression, and the mechanisms of denial whereby post-war judicial and historical reckoning with these realities was evaded. These issues had been studied previously by a few scholars, but nonetheless remained amongst the 'hidden pages of contemporary Italian history' and on the margins of collective memory.[152] Collectively, this literature seriously undermines the tenacious myth of the Italians as *brava gente* even under Fascism, and often strongly implies that Fascism and Nazism were 'two variations of the same geopolitical and cultural project to reorganise the world, beginning with Europe'.[153] Yet for all its vigour, it remains to be seen how far it will impinge on broader consciousness given that the prevailing discourse probably makes the public less receptive to its message than ever before. The portents here are unpromising: on a rare occasion when Berlusconi decided to commemorate victims of atrocity and institute a national 'Day of Memory' on 10 February 2005 – solemnly intoning that in this instance 'we cannot and should not forget' – the victims concerned were (non-Jewish) Italians, killed by communist partisans around Trieste.[154]

Foreign policy did not figure prominently in these struggles over collective memory or in the general historiographical debate. De Felice's last two biographical instalments presented Mussolini's wartime diplomacy in a generally charitable light, especially his vain efforts to inject some moderation and wisdom into an Axis strategy increasingly deranged by Hitler's fanaticism. Yet as Mussolini's autonomy and influence were steadily eroded, this story became progressively less consequential, especially in relation to De Felice's inflammatory and therefore much more eye-catching treatment of the resistance.[155] As regards the origins of the war, Italian diplomatic historians generally hewed to the De Felice 'decisive weight' line articulated in the 1970s. In a study of Italian–Soviet relations, Rosaria Quartararo reiterated her view that in foreign policy Mussolini 'gave no heed to ideological dogma, but rather searched exclusively to identify what was useful to the nation', selecting partners 'with total independence from ideological considerations'; consequently, she argued, even in joining Operation Barbarossa, Mussolini's aim was to limit German conquests in the hope of facilitating a compromise peace.[156]

This broad interpretation was also espoused by some non-Italians. Richard Overy emphasised 'political realism, not ideology' as Mussolini's motive force.[157] Richard Lamb castigated British statesmen for persistently rebuffing Mussolini's sincere attempts to restore good relations after the Ethiopian war; with greater tact and consideration in London, 'Mussolini could have been kept out of Hitler's camp and the balance of power in Europe preserved'.[158] Similarly, Nicholas Farrell's recent biography of 'a great man who failed' – 'he certainly was not an evil man' – replayed familiar De Felicean themes. Mussolini was a 'realist and an opportunist', who 'had not intended to abandon Italy's traditional foreign policy objective of playing one set of nations off against another'. The 'Pact of Steel' was an attempt to 'control' Hitler, increasingly feared and despised by Mussolini, and to avoid war, even if in retrospect this proved a 'fatal error'. Fascism and Nazism were 'like chalk and cheese' and Mussolini in no way intended that they should 'march together to conquer the world'. The utility of these views within the contemporary project to normalise Fascism is manifest: Farrell writes explicitly to redeem Mussolini from western liberal and Marxist calumnies and 'set the record straight'.[159]

While foreign policy remained a low profile thematic, it nonetheless provided the occasion for a potent challenge to the De Felicean orthodoxy. Out of the archival labour, historiographical controversy and political travails of the 1970s, and taking a cue from the 'intentionalist' literature on Nazism, a coherent anti-Fascist position emerged presenting Mussolini's policy neither as buffoonish opportunism nor traditional *realpolitik* but as 'overtly and insistently ideological'.[160] Dino Grandi, foreign minister from 1929 to 1932, had despairingly observed that Mussolini considered himself the crusading '"Pope of anti-democracy"', and that he had an utterly '"*unreal* conception of diplomacy"' premised on '"revolutionary ideology"'. The largely non-Italian proponents of this view concurred, and asserted that the unrealism was moreover 'fundamental, irremediable, and programmatic'.[161] Reacting against the simplistic dismissals of the 'Sawdust Caesar' paradigm, they held that the ignominious defeat 'that doomed Mussolini, his regime, and Italy's great power aspirations cannot cancel out the magnitude of his purpose'.[162] Equally, they believed De Felice's contention that Mussolini discarded ideological considerations when turning to foreign affairs to be inherently implausible, and designed to dignify the *Duce* far too much by airbrushing out the bellicosity and criminality of his regime.

The staunchest advocate of this view has been American historian MacGregor Knox, from the landmark exposition of his 1982 monograph, *Mussolini Unleashed* – a book roundly criticised by Italian diplomatic historians, but translated by the publishing house of the PCI, grateful for any succour from abroad – through numerous subsequent essays and books.[163] For Knox, Fascism meant war 'and the force that propelled it along that path was above all the force of ideas'. Mussolini had by 1926–27 devised 'an integrated programme premised on the use of force both internally and externally'.[164] Revolutionary transformation at home – the remaking of the Italian people, national integration, and the destruction of the traditional establishment – was both to facilitate and to be achieved through revisionist and imperialist war, creating an Italian *spazio vitale* in the Mediterranean, the Balkans, Africa and the Middle East and delivering true great power status. 'Fascist wars and Fascist revolution were dialectically intertwined in an upward spiral of violence'.[165] These goals could only be achieved at the expense of the *status quo* powers Britain and France, which held Italy imprisoned in the Mediterranean, and in association with a revisionist Germany. The Axis alliance was thus no chance contingency, but rather a product of shared enemies as well as ideological affinity; indeed, in an oft repeated phrase, it was a matter of 'common destiny'.[166] True, Fascist diplomacy sometimes followed a rather tortuous path, but this was only because Mussolini had to trim in light of domestic opposition, economic and military weakness and unfavourable international circumstances; if he occasionally espoused a 'pseudo-pacifism', this did not make him any less 'a fanatic steering by ideology and set upon a course ever closer to National Socialist Germany' and to an inevitable war with the West. The 'Pact of Steel' was thus undeniably 'intended as a step toward war rather than a diplomatic manoeuvre'.[167]

Knox did not deny that Mussolini's thinking was related to longer term Italian nationalist traditions (his 'ideological lunacy had deep roots') which had also aimed at securing great power status through expansion in the Mediterranean, the Adriatic and Africa.[168] Yet his foreign policy incarnated decisive elements of discontinuity in its fusion of domestic and foreign revolutionary goals ('unique to his regime and that of his German ally'), its ideological fixations and its 'blindly and dogmatically geopolitical' nature.[169] This last was crucially exemplified in Mussolini's infamous February 1939 memorandum to the Fascist grand council: with its insistence that Italy 'march to the ocean' against the western powers, this was for Knox 'a sort of Mussolinian *Mein Kampf*, a lapidary statement of a geopolitical vision the dictator had entertained since at least the mid-1920s'.[170] Knox also detailed the brutality that accompanied Fascist bellicosity, in the repression of domestic opponents, ruthless colonial rule, fierce wartime occupation policy and the persecution of Italy's Jews, all intimately linked to the effort to transform Italians into 'a cruel and domineering master race'.[171] (There are, indeed, perceptible affinities between this international history literature and that on the darker sides of Fascist rule alluded to above.[172]) In this and other respects, and whilst not seeking to deny the greater extent of Hitler's ambitions and criminality, Fascism and Nazism were closely comparable and their histories inextricably interlinked.[173] This portrait of Mussolini clashed dramatically with the normalising discourse that gained in strength through the 1980s and beyond; in taking Fascism seriously yet insisting on its dangerous ambitions and essential malignancy, it suggested that the ethical lessons of anti-Fascism still possessed validity and force and mandated continued attention to Fascism as an historic phenomenon.

With nuanced variants, this interpretation of Fascist policy became the dominant view in the English language scholarship. Alan Cassels concurred with Knox that 'the Duce's methods and goals comprised a radical and alarming experiment' in Italian foreign policy.[174] John Gooch argued that periods of warm relations between Fascist Italy and the western powers were 'aberrations', and that co-belligerency with Germany represented a 'destiny' that was Mussolini's 'choice', 'the culmination of a process that had begun when he came into office in October 1922'.[175] In the same vein, Brian Sullivan has written of the Axis that 'while Nazi foreign policy complemented Fascist imperial aims, the ideological similarity of the two regimes made their alliance almost inevitable'.[176] Significantly, this view has also been vigorously propagated by a new generation of scholars. Thus Robert Mallett has analysed Fascist naval policy to demonstrate that 'Mussolini did indeed have a predetermined programme for war against the Western powers alongside Germany, a war whose ultimate objective was to wrest control of the Mediterranean from Anglo–French hands'; subsequently he essayed a general analysis of the 'extreme and fanatical radicalism' governing Italian diplomacy in the 1930s.[177] G. Bruce Strang similarly centred his study of Italy's road to war on Mussolini's *mentalité*, a heady and irrational blend of ultranationalism, social Darwinism, militarism, racism and imperialism, inevitably directed against the Anglo–French demoplutoracies.[178] Reynolds Salerno's study of the 'Mediterranean origins of the Second World War' also explored how 'war against the democracies became an ever more fundamental aspect of Mussolini's formula for Italian greatness'.[179] Moreover, in a comparative study Aristotle Kallis detected considerable similarities between the Fascist quest for a *spazio vitale* and the Nazi search for *lebensraum*, and the manner in which the two regimes 'blended radical elements of each country's nationalist tradition with a specific novel commitment to a fascist *new order*'.[180] Finally, this paradigm has also found expression in Italian scholarship, though it remains a decidedly minority position there.[181]

Although the contemporary historiographical debate is organised around the interpretations associated with Knox and De Felice, these are not the only narrative options in play. Crudely, they might be said to constitute opposite ends of a spectrum, with one pole emphasising ideology, revolutionary discontinuity and expansive imperialist ambitions, and the other stressing *realpolitik*, enduring national traditions and modest expansionist goals. However, alternative permutations can be devised simply by taking up intermediate positions. Indeed, Cassels, for example, is less persuaded of the over-riding and consistent explanatory power of ideology. His assertion that it was only in the early 1930s that Mussolini embarked on 'the reorientation of national methods and goals in the great game of world politics', and that he was 'impelled to radicalize Italian foreign policy ... by domestic factors', establishes some distance between himself and Knox.[182] A sustained attempt to capture the 'middle ground' has been made by H. James Burgwyn, who depicted Mussolini's policy as an amalgam of 'traditional Realpolitik', 'ideological prejudice', 'his volcanic and contradictory personality', Italian weakness and the force of circumstances. This Mussolini had 'expansionist goals that remained constant', drawn largely from 'the legacy of Italian nationalism' but also shaped by ideological antipathy to the democracies, yet he was also 'too much a believer in action based on expediency and day-to-day interests for any preordained doctrine or fixed program to dictate his diplomacy' and prone to fall 'victim to his own propaganda'. After 1936 ideological sentiment increasingly 'distorted and perverted Mussolini's understanding of Italian national interest and undermined his own policy of equidistance'. Yet Burgwyn still has Mussolini attempting with the 'Pact of Steel' to recapture 'a balancing role'. This effort to synthesise elements of the competing interpretations suggests that the price of compromise may be incoherence.[183]

Efforts were also made to step outside the De Felice–Knox dichotomy. Richard Bosworth has ploughed one such furrow for over 30 years in his work on Liberal and Fascist Italy. Seeking inspiration from the historiography of Nazism, Bosworth took his cues from the *Sonderweg* thesis and the posing of 'functionalist'-type questions about the relationship between regime and society.[184] He concurred with De Felice that Fascist foreign policy embodied continuity with Liberal Italy, but denied that this was reason to level a benign judgement upon it. Rather, policy-makers under both regimes had recklessly indulged in base nationalist manoeuvring and opportunistic imperialist expansionism; moreover, exaggerated public expectations and grandiose national myths – of a new Rome and the Mediterranean as *mare nostrum* – had long been in tension with the actual capabilities of the least of the great powers. Thus continuity certainly existed, but only in negative form, since 'Liberal foreign policy was as absurd and disastrous as was Fascist diplomacy'.[185] What was different in the more bellicose Fascist policy 'was not the aim, but the method (and even that only partially so)'.[186] Bosworth also argued that greater explanatory stress should be placed on enduring structures within Italy (including region, family and gender, influential traditional elites and patterns of political behaviour) and in the international system (including relative weakness and the habit of inconstancy), rather than on Mussolini's ideology and agency. When it came to explaining Mussolini's decision for war in June 1940, for example, he averred that 'no imaginable Italian leader, who accepted the myths around which Italian society had been organised since the Risorgimento' (and specifically 'Italy's pretensions to be a Great Power'), 'would not have entered a Great Power war at a time when it seemed plain that one side had won a total victory'. In this sense, Italy's belligerency was 'the natural result of Italian history', and far from being the work of 'one man alone' responsibility was shared by the whole Italian political class.[187]

Bosworth's biography of Mussolini portrayed him as a cynical misanthrope, full of crass Darwinist assumptions, an agnostic careerist and opportunist, and an inveterately pragmatic tactician: 'whatever else he was Mussolini was no Hitler impelled by a credo to act in one way and one way only'. He was a fundamentally weak dictator, indeed 'to a considerable degree Mussolini did not even dictate, but, rather, was swept along by a destiny ... which ended in squalid and deserved death'. Bosworth denied that Mussolini achieved much in modernising Italy or that there was any substance to his ideology or putative totalitarianism: it might even be said that 'Italy mastered him' rather than *vice versa*. Foreign policy was equally devoid of novelty. 'His empire in Africa was of the old-fashioned, ramshackle, costly variety, familiar from the nineteenth century', very different from the Nazi racial *imperium*, and the conquest of Ethiopia was certainly not the first stage in any long-desired revolutionary programme'.[188] After 1936, bellicosity 'acquired a momentum of its own'.[189] 'Fascist Italy drifted deeper into her alliance relationship with Germany', but 'the Axis was never really firm (and certainly was not dependent on a shared fascist ideology)'.[190] The ensuing events were best described as a process of 'lurching into war'.[191] 'Certainly there are no grounds for believing that Italy would have proved *treue* to Germany in 1940 had it been France or Britain which were the experts in *blitzkrieg*, in war on the cheap'.[192]

Gauging the relative political merits of Bosworth's deeply textured account is a complex matter, precisely because he is challenging both the dominant anti-anti-Fascist and anti-Fascist perspectives. He writes as 'an Anti-Fascist biographer', and evidently believes that stressing the *Duce's* 'Italianness' and the shared culpability of a whole political class – both diachronically and synchronically – facilitates the most searching contemporary reckoning with Italian complicity.[193] For him, a narrow 'intentionalism' that emphasises an exceptional ideology and locates guilt primarily with a few leading Fascists risks letting too many actors off the hook, and ironically conferring a form of great (if bad) man status upon those indicted. Bosworth seems intent rather on cutting Mussolini down to size, asserting that many of his flaws were common human ones even as he damns him as 'a bully, a coward and a failure'.[194] But presenting Mussolini as a careerist master of spin rather than a serious ideologue flirts with a reversion to exculpation *à la* the levities of Mack Smith, and it is a matter of interpretation whether Bosworth entirely defuses this charge through his careful efforts to articulate the place of Mussolini in Italian society and history. By the same token, for all his concern to explore the nuanced similarities as well as differences between Fascism and Nazism, and to bring into focus the crimes, aggression and racism of a 'vicious and retrograde tyranny', Bosworth's downplaying of ideology may seem to align him with conservative apologists who deny any affinity between the regimes; one reviewer, for example, has equated his treatment of Fascist foreign policy with that of De Felice.[195] Similarly, his invocation of an Italian people who 'both under the dictatorship and after, were more suspicious than believing', and who refused to 'become the fervent adepts and peerless warriors of a new political faith', could be appropriated to reinscribe the *brava gente* myth.[196] So, even this thoughtful attempt to step outside the coordinates of other accounts is not entirely free of suspect political connotations.

The debate in the literature on Fascist foreign policy has not closely followed the twists and turns of Italian politics or collective memory since the 1980s. Indeed, it has in some respects been rather static: the competing interpretations associated with De Felice and Knox (and, indeed, Bosworth) were all in play by the early 1980s and have simply remained in contestation ever since, even if they have been refined and developed. But if the relationship with collective memory has thus been in one sense rather loose, each of these positions on the interpretive terrain speaks to the legitimacy of the broad neo-conservative project to normalise the Fascist past. Of course, historiographical discussion is usually couched in relentlessly documentarist terms. As previously noted, De Felicean historiography presents its own readings as impartial correctives to leftist myths and foreign calumnies. Thus an American devotee writing on the Italian war effort has lamented the persistence of 'the stereotype of the cowardly and incompetent Wop' in the disparaging critiques of Anglo–Saxon scholarship: at worst, he claimed, such work is 'racist fiction'.[197] In more measured tones, Luciano Cafagna and Ernesto Galli della Loggia have argued that the intervention of 'foreign scholars in the Italian historical debate has not always favoured the purifying conflict of ideas': 'indeed, it is our impression that sometimes non-Italian historians permit themselves to write Italian history with an emphatic ideological and political bias that they would disdain in histories about their own countries'.[198]

International historians advocating anti-Fascist interpretations generally talk in similar terms. Mallett, for example, writes that 'historical facts, as contained within the primary documentary sources of official repositories, remain historical facts' and the 'balanced and intelligent scholar' will be led by them to only one conclusion. That most Italian historians are 'strangely unwilling' to accept this he finds illogical, but he does not pursue the issue.[199] Strang is slightly more forthcoming, noting that 'it is very convenient for Italian scholars to write history that absolves Italians of responsibility for the origins of the Second World War and minimizes Italy's expansionist and imperialist past on which Fascism built'.[200] Yet there is no substantial appetite to discuss ideological positioning, even as a problem for one's antagonists. Thus Knox has alluded to the 'intriguing' fact that the legitimacy of the AN is at stake in the controversy over Fascism, but then lamented that 'the debate's casting as a political struggle between Right and Left has impeded its ostensible purpose, the achievement of historical clarity'.

There are, of course, sensible things that can be said about empirical matters. Knox, for example, has criticised De Felice for 'the almost complete absence of military, naval and colonial archival documentation' in his work. Omitting these sources has important interpretive consequences in downplaying Fascist bellicosity, airbrushing out 'the extensive and bloody colonial warfare' in which it indulged and concealing the intimate links between foreign policy, military policy and the nature of the regime.[201] Other scholars have noted how lack of access to military and colonial archives, 'the fruit of protectionist impulses' and 'chronic (one might also say strategic) underfunding', has helped to forestall 'the writing of histories that challenge official or convenient views of the past'.[202] But none of this entails a decisive blow against the De Felicean interpretation: some subsequent Italian scholars have paid greater attention to Fascist strategy but nonetheless have continued to neglect Mussolini's expansionist thinking in arguing for 'the essentially defensive nature of Italian policy'.[203] If this suggests the improbability of decisively resolving the interpretive dispute on empirical grounds, Knox's other criticisms reinforce the point. When he charges De Felice with failing to produce a 'satisfyingly cohesive' or 'persuasive interpretation', and offering instead one lacking in 'interpretive coherence', he is rendering aesthetic judgements as much as empirical ones.[204]

In negotiating the complex phenomenon of Fascist foreign policy historically, scholars confront a voluminous and varied body of evidence that can be read in diverse ways and selectively appropriated to sustain competing interpretations. However much international historians might conceive of their interpretations as simple products of a technical dialogue with the documents, these readings have been intertwined ever since the 1940s with the evolving collective memory of Fascism in Italy and abroad, and with struggles over which political values should predominate within the Italian republic and nation. So in choosing one interpretive option over another, international historians are intervening in a political struggle. The issue of whether Fascism should be an object of unceasing critical meditation, a component of a positive national heritage or merely a fading element in an anodyne past remains of urgent relevance. The right has lately focused much energy on the need for constitutional reform, to purge 'anti-Fascist biases, to enhance the power of the executive and diminish – in particular – the role of Parliament and the judiciary', thus recasting 'the very basis of the relationship between legitimacy and legality'.[205] 'At a time like this', Alessandro Portelli has opined, 'the struggle over memory not only concerns the debates among historians or factional recriminations over the past but becomes the ground on which the very identity of our Republic and our democracy, born out of those events, stands or falls'.[206]

Notes

1 P. Sweet *et al.* (eds), *Documents on German Foreign Policy, 1918–1945: Series D, Vol. VI* (London, HMSO, 1956), p. 562.
2 C. Delzell (ed.), *Mediterranean Fascism, 1919–1945* (London, Macmillan, 1971), pp. 202–5; E. Wiskemann, *The Rome-Berlin Axis: A Study of the Relations between Hitler and Mussolini* (London, Fontana, 1969, rev. edn), pp. 105–6.
3 Quote from speech by Mussolini, 10 June 1940, in Delzell (ed.), *Mediterranean Fascism, 1919–1945*, p. 215.
4 B. R. Sullivan, 'More than meets the eye: the Ethiopian war and the origins of the Second World War', in G. Martel (ed.), *The Origins of the Second World War Reconsidered: A. J. P. Taylor and the Historians* (London, Routledge, 1999, 2nd edn), pp. 183–86.
5 J. Pollard, *The Fascist Experience in Italy* (London, Routledge, 1998), pp. 89 (quoting the 1932 *Enciclopedia Italiana*), 99–100.
6 A. Cassels, 'Mussolini and the myth of Rome', in Martel (ed.), *The Origins of the Second World War Reconsidered* (2nd edn), p. 69.
7 D. C. Watt, 'The Rome–Berlin Axis, 1936–40: myth and reality', *Review of Politics*, vol. 22, no. 4, 1960, pp. 519–43.
8 P. Brendon, *The Dark Valley: A Panorama of the 1930s* (London, Pimlico, 2001, pb. edn), p. 483, quoting *New York Times*, 26 September 1937.
9 I. Kirkpatrick, *Mussolini: Study of a Demagogue* (London, Odhams, 1964), p. 318.
10 Quoted in R. Overy, *The Road to War* (London, Macmillan, 1989), p. 143.
11 M. H. H. Macartney, *One Man Alone: The History of Mussolini and the Axis* (London, Chatto and Windus, 1944), quotes at pp. 19, 26, 8.
12 R. J. B. Bosworth, *The Italian Dictatorship: Problems and Perspectives in the Interpretation of Mussolini and Fascism* (London, Arnold, 1998), especially pp. 82–105.
13 J. A. Davis, 'Modern Italy – changing historical perspectives since 1945', in M. Bentley (ed.), *Companion to Historiography* (London, Routledge, 1997), p. 591.
14 Prominent conservatives in the 1990s argued that it was impossible to ground a healthy identification with the nation on 'alien' anti-Fascist values. But this wilfully begged the question of which values and orientations towards the past should be privileged within national identity (S. Patriarca, 'Italian neopatriotism: debating national identity in the 1990s', *Modern Italy*, vol. 6, no. 1, 2001, pp. 21–34).

15 D. Mack Smith, 'Mussolini, artist in propaganda: the downfall of Fascism', *History Today*, vol. 9, no. 4, 1959, pp. 223–32.

16 Quote from A. Lyttelton, 'Epilogue', in A. Lyttelton (ed.), *Liberal and Fascist Italy 1900–1945* (Oxford, Oxford University Press, 2002), p. 249.

17 E. Agarossi, *A Nation Collapses: The Italian Surrender of September 1943* (Cambridge, Cambridge University Press, 2000), p. 131.

18 F. Focardi, 'Reshaping the past: collective memory and the Second World War in Italy, 1945–55', in D. Geppert (ed.), *The Postwar Challenge: Cultural, Social, and Political Change in Western Europe, 1945–58* (Oxford, Oxford University Press, 2003), pp. 41–52, quotes at pp. 42, 47.

19 M. Battini, *The Missing Italian Nuremberg: Cultural Amnesia and Postwar Politics* (London, Palgrave, 2007).

20 Pollard, *Fascist Experience*, pp. 129–33; N. Doumanis, *Italy* (London, Arnold, 2001), pp. 156–62.

21 S. Pugliese, 'Introduction', in S. Pugliese (ed.), *Italian Fascism and Antifascism: A Critical Anthology* (Manchester, Manchester University Press, 2001), p. 21.

22 R. Chiarini, 'The "Movimento Sociale Italiano": a historical profile', in L. Cheles, R. Ferguson and M. Vaughan (eds), *Neo-Fascism in Europe* (London, Longman, 1991), pp. 19–31.

23 C. Duggan, 'Italy in the Cold War years and the legacy of Fascism', in C. Duggan and C. Wagstaff (eds), *Italy in the Cold War: Politics, Culture and Society, 1948–58* (Oxford, Berg, 1995), pp. 4–6, quote at p. 5.

24 Doumanis, *Italy*, pp. 164–66. *Partitocrazia* 'in its most negative and widely understood form referred to routine plunder and distribution of public resources and jobs among the mainstream political parties and their supporters' (p. 166).

25 D. Sassoon, 'Italy after Fascism: the predicament of dominant narratives', in R. Bessel and D. Schumann (eds), *Life after Death: Approaches to a Cultural and Social History of Europe during the 1940s and 1950s* (Cambridge, Cambridge University Press, 2003), pp. 265–72, quote at p. 266.

26 Quoted in A. Portelli, *The Order has been Carried Out: History, Memory, and Meaning of a Nazi Massacre in Rome* (London, Palgrave, 2004), p. 250.

27 Bosworth, *The Italian Dictatorship*, p. 236.

28 Sassoon, 'Italy after Fascism', pp. 267–68, 272–75, quotes at p. 273.

29 Focardi, 'Reshaping the past', pp. 41–52, quotes at pp. 45, 47.

30 R. Ben-Ghiat, 'Liberation: Italian cinema and the Fascist past, 1945–50', in R. J. B. Bosworth and P. Dogliani (eds), *Italian Fascism: History, Memory and Representation* (London, Macmillan, 1999), pp. 83–101.

31 R. Ben-Ghiat, 'The secret histories of Roberto Benigni's *Life is Beautiful*', *The Yale Journal of Criticism*, vol. 14, no. 1, 2001, pp. 253–66.

32 E. Gentile, 'Fascism in Italian historiography: in search of an individual historical identity', *Journal of Contemporary History*, vol. 21, no. 2, 1986, p. 180.

33 R. J. B. Bosworth, 'Italy's historians and the myth of Fascism', in R. Langhorne (ed.), *Diplomacy and Intelligence during the Second World War* (Cambridge, Cambridge University Press, 1985), p. 104.

34 R. De Felice, *Interpretations of Fascism* (Cambridge, MA, Harvard University Press, 1977), pp. 160–61.

35 Sassoon, 'Italy after Fascism', p. 267.

36 Bosworth, 'Italy's historians and the myth of Fascism', pp. 85–105, quotes at pp. 88, 101.

37 E. P. Noether, 'Italy reviews its Fascist past: a bibliographical essay', *American Historical Review*, vol. 61, no. 4, 1956, pp. 877–99.

38 D. Mack Smith, 'Benedetto Croce: history and politics', *Journal of Contemporary History*, vol. 8, no. 1, 1973, pp. 41–61.

39 De Felice, *Interpretations of Fascism*, pp. 14–30.

40 Mack Smith, 'Croce', quote at p. 51; Bosworth, *The Italian Dictatorship*, pp. 45–46, quote at p. 46.

41 De Felice, *Interpretations of Fascism*, p. 14, quoting Croce.

42 Noether, 'Italy reviews its Fascist past', p. 883.

43 Gentile, 'Fascism in Italian historiography', p. 180.

44 C. Delzell, 'Italian historical scholarship: a decade of recovery and development, 1945–55', *Journal of Modern History*, vol. 28, no. 4, 1956, p. 374.

45 Bosworth, *The Italian Dictatorship*, pp. 53–57; A. Gleason, *Totalitarianism: The Inner History of the Cold War* (Oxford, Oxford University Press, 1995), pp. 143–46, 156–57.

46 Noether, 'Italy reviews its Fascist past', pp. 884–85.

47 Bosworth, *The Italian Dictatorship*, pp. 47–52; De Felice, *Interpretations of Fascism*, pp. 30–54, 120–28, 145–53.

48 C. Fogu, '*Italiani brava gente*: the legacy of Fascist historical culture on Italian politics of memory', in R. N. Lebow, W. Kansteiner and C. Fogu (eds), *The Politics of Memory in Postwar Europe* (Durham, NC, Duke University Press, 2006), p. 152.

49 M. Clark, 'Gioacchino Volpe and Fascist historiography in Italy', in S. Berger, M. Donovan and K. Passmore (eds), *Writing National Histories: Western Europe since 1800* (London, Routledge, 1999), pp. 200, 198.

50 Bosworth, 'Italy's historians and the myth of Fascism', p. 89.

51 Bosworth, *The Italian Dictatorship*, pp. 82–84 and quote at p. 92.

52 C. Delzell, 'Benito Mussolini: a guide to the biographical literature', *Journal of Modern History*, vol. 35, no. 4, 1963, pp. 339–53.

53 Bosworth, *The Italian Dictatorship*, pp. 68–78. A 1936 book by American journalist George Seldes put the epithet 'Sawdust Caesar' into wider circulation.

54 Noether, 'Italy reviews its Fascist past', p. 885.

55 For example, G. Salvemini, *Under the Axe of Fascism* (London, Gollancz, 1936), quote at p. 119.

56 G. Salvemini, *Prelude to World War II* (London, Gollancz, 1953), quotes at pp. 10, 34, 118–20.

57 Salvemini, *Prelude to World War II*, quotes at pp. 156, 43, 510, 486, 118. On the traditional policy, see B. R. Sullivan, 'The strategy of the decisive weight: Italy, 1882–1922', in W. Murray. M. Knox and A. Bernstein (eds), *The Making of Strategy: Rulers, States, and War* (Cambridge, Cambridge University Press, 1994), pp. 307–51.

58 Duggan, 'Italy in the Cold War years and the legacy of Fascism', pp. 7–8.

59 Salvemini, *Prelude to World War II*, quotes at pp. 8, 510.

60 Salvemini, *Prelude to World War II*, quotes at pp. 7–8.

61 Noether, 'Italy reviews its Fascist past', p. 887.

62 Bosworth, *The Italian Dictatorship*, p. 83; L. B. Namier, 'For and against Italian responsibility', in J. Snell (ed.), *The Outbreak of the Second World War: Design or Blunder?* (Boston, MA, D. C. Heath, 1962), p. 46.

63 M. Toscano, *The Origins of the Pact of Steel* (Baltimore, Johns Hopkins University Press, 1967), quotes at pp. 330, 399 (originally published in Italian in 1948).

64 L. Villari, *The Liberation of Italy, 1943–1947* (Appleton, WI, Nelson, 1959), quotes at pp. 246, x, viii, xvii, 60–61.

65 Villari, *The Liberation of Italy*, p. 52.

66 G. B. Strang, *On the Fiery March: Mussolini Prepares for War* (Westport, CT, Praeger, 2003), p. 2.

67 'Cassius' [M. Foot], *The Trial of Mussolini: Being a Verbatim Report of the First Great Trial for War Criminals Held in London Sometime in 1944 or 1945* (London, Gollancz, 1943), quotes at pp. 72, 70.

68 A. J. P. Taylor, *The Origins of the Second World War* (London, Penguin, 1964, pb. edn), p. 85.

69 M. H. H. Macartney, *One Man Alone: The History of Mussolini and the Axis* (London, Chatto and Windus, 1944), quotes at pp. 115, v, 88, 63–64, 159.

70 Mack Smith, 'Mussolini, artist in propaganda', quotes at pp. 224, 227, 230–32.

71 R. J. B. Bosworth, 'Denis Mack Smith and the Third Italy', *International History Review*, vol. 12, no. 4, 1990, p. 786.

72 E. Wiskemann, *The Rome–Berlin Axis: A Study of the Relations between Hitler and Mussolini* (London, Fontana, 1969, rev. edn), p. 397.

73 A. Cassels, 'Switching partners: Italy in A. J. P. Taylor's *Origins of the Second World War*', in G. Martel (ed.), *The Origins of the Second World War Reconsidered: The A. J. P. Taylor Debate after Twenty-Five Years* (London, Unwin Hyman, 1986), pp. 73–74.

74 E. Ingram, 'Epilogue: a patriot for me', in Martel (ed.), *The Origins of the Second World War Reconsidered*, p. 249.

75 E. Wiskemann, *Fascism in Italy: Its Development and Influence* (London, Macmillan, 1969), p. 65.

76 P. Allum, 'Italian society transformed', and G. Pasquino, 'Political development', in P. McCarthy (ed.), *Italy since 1945* (Oxford, Oxford University Press, 2000), pp. 29–30, 69–81.

77 R. J. B. Bosworth, 'Explaining "Auschwitz" after the end of history: the case of Italy', *History and Theory*, vol. 38, no. 1, 1999, p. 88.

78 Fogu, '*Italiani brava gente*', pp. 153–57.

79 Portelli, *The Order has been Carried Out*, p. 11.

80 R. J. B. Bosworth, 'Italian foreign policy and its historiography', in R. J. B. Bosworth and G. Rizzo (eds), *Altro Polo: Intellectuals and their Ideas in Contemporary Italy* (Sydney, Frederick May Foundation, 1983), p. 68.

81 Portelli, *The Order has been Carried Out*, p. 240.

82 C. Levy, 'Historians and the "First Republic"', in Berger, Donovan and Passmore (eds), *Writing National Histories*, p. 275.

83 Bosworth, *The Italian Dictatorship*, p. 109; Davis, 'Modern Italy', pp. 598–603.

84 De Felice, *Interpretations of Fascism*, p. 161.

85 Davis, 'Modern Italy', p. 602.

86 R. Griffin, 'Introduction', in R. Griffin (ed.), *International Fascism: Theories, Causes and the New Consensus* (London, Arnold, 1998), p.8. For more on the 'generic fascism' literature, see also A. Kallis (ed.), *The Fascism Reader* (London, Routledge, 2003).

87 Bosworth, *The Italian Dictatorship*, quotes at pp. 117, 119, 236.

88 M. Knox, 'In the Duce's defence', *Times Literary Supplement*, 26 February 1999, p. 4, reviewing R. De Felice, *Mussolini l'Alleato, 1940–1945: Vol. 2: La Guerra Civile, 1943–1945* (Turin, Einaudi, 1997).

89 Bosworth, *The Italian Dictatorship*, pp. 110–19, quotes at p. 113.

90 R. De Felice, *Mussolini il Duce: Vol. 1: Gli Anni del Consenso, 1929–1936* (Turin, Einaudi, 1974) and *Fascism: An Informal Introduction to Its Theory and Practice: An Interview with Michael Ledeen* (New Brunswick, NJ, Transaction, 1976).

91 Bosworth, *The Italian Dictatorship*, p. 123.

92 For contrasting accounts, see R. J. B. Bosworth, 'In the green corner, Denis Mack Smith, in the red? black? corner Renzo De Felice: an account of the 1976 contest in the historiography of Italian Fascism', *Teaching History*, vol. 11, no. 2, 1977, pp. 29–43; and M. Ledeen, 'Renzo De Felice and the controversy over Italian Fascism', *Journal of Contemporary History*, vol. 11, no. 4, 1976, pp. 269–83.

93 De Felice, *Facism: An Informal Introduction*, quotes at pp. 44, 67, 77, 64, 26, 56, 104.

94 De Felice, *Facism: An Informal Introduction*, quotes at pp. 25, 115, 112, 103.

95 B. W. Painter Jr, 'Renzo De Felice and the historiography of Italian Fascism', *American Historical Review*, vol. 95, no. 2, 1990, pp. 392–99, quote at p. 396.

96 Portelli, *The Order has been Carried Out*, p. 3.

97 Bosworth, *The Italian Dictatorship*, p. 123.

98 A. L. Cardoza, 'Recasting the Duce for the new century: recent scholarship on Mussolini and Italian Fascism', *Journal of Modern History*, vol. 77, no. 3, 2005, p. 727.

99 R. De Felice, *Mussolini il Duce: Vol. 2: Lo Stato Totalitario, 1936–1940* (Turin, Einaudi, 1981); Painter, 'Renzo De Felice and the historiography of Italian Fascism', pp. 400–403.

100 S. C. Azzi, 'The historiography of Fascist foreign policy', *Historical Journal*, vol. 36, no. 1, 1993, pp. 202–3.

101 A. Cassels, 'Introduction', in A. Cassels, *Italian Foreign Policy 1918–1945: A Guide to Research and Research Materials* (Wilmington, DE, Scholarly Resources, 1981), p. 2. For a more recent assessment, see L. Nuti, 'Sources for the study of Italian foreign policy, 1861–1999', *Cold War History*, vol. 2, no. 3, 2002, pp. 93–110.

102 For details, see http://www.esteri.it/MAE/IT/Ministero/Pubblicazioni/DocumentiDiplomatici/ Documenti_diplomatici.htm (accessed 6 February 2009). The Fascist period is covered in three series, comprising 39 volumes, the last of which only appeared in 2006.

103 J. Petersen, 'La politica estera del fascismo come problema storiografico', in R. De Felice (ed.), *L'Italia fra Tedeschi e Alleati: La Politica Estera Fascista e la Seconda Guerra Mondiale* (Bolonga, Mulino, 1973), pp. 11–55, quote at p. 24.

104 E. M. Robertson, *Mussolini as Empire-Builder: Europe and Africa, 1932–36* (London, Macmillan, 1977), quotes at p. 17.

105 Quoted in Azzi, 'The historiography of Fascist foreign policy', p. 190.

106 A. Cassels, 'Was there a Fascist foreign policy? Tradition and novelty', *International History Review*, vol. 5, no. 2, 1983, p. 263.

107 A. Cassels, *Mussolini's Early Diplomacy* (Princeton, NJ, Princeton University Press, 1970), p. 397.

108 Bosworth, *The Italian Dictatorship*, p. 93.

109 Quoted in Bosworth, 'Italian foreign policy and its historiography', p. 74.

110 This paragraph primarily draws on Azzi, 'The historiography of Fascist foreign policy', pp. 190–202 (alluding explicitly to J. Petersen, *Hitler-Mussolini: Die Entstehung der Achse Berlin-Rom, 1933–1936* (Tübingen, Max Niemeyer, 1973) and J. F. Coverdale, *Italian Intervention in the Spanish Civil War* (Princeton, NJ, Princeton University Press, 1975)), and G. Schreiber, 'Italy's entry into the war', in Militärgeschichtliches Forschungsamt (ed.), *Germany and the Second World War: Vol. III: The Mediterranean, South-East Europe, and North Africa 1939–1941* (Oxford, Oxford University Press, 1995), pp. 110–26. Quotations from A. Cassels, *Fascist Italy* (London, Routledge and Kegan Paul, 1969), pp. 89–90.

111 Quote from Cardoza, 'Recasting the Duce for the new century', p. 726. See further R. De Felice, 'Alcune osservazioni sulla politica estera mussoliniana', in De Felice (ed.), *L'Italia fra Tedeschi e Alleati*, pp. 57–74.

112 R. De Felice, 'Mussolini, Benito', in P. V. Cannistraro (ed.), *Historical Dictionary of Fascist Italy* (Westport, CT, Greenwood, 1982), p. 361.

113 De Felice, *Facism: An Informal Introduction*, pp. 80–82.

114 De Felice, 'Mussolini, Benito', pp. 361–62.

115 M. Knox, 'The Fascist regime, its foreign policy and its wars: an "anti-anti-Fascist" orthodoxy?', *Contemporary European History*, vol. 4, no. 3, 1995, pp. 354–56, quoting R. De Felice, *Lo Stato Totalitario*, and *Mussolini l'Alleato, 1940–1945: Vol. 1: L'Italia in Guerra, 1940–1943* (Turin, Einaudi, 1990).

116 De Felice, 'Mussolini, Benito', p. 363.

117 On the inconsistencies, see Knox, 'The Fascist regime, its foreign policy and its wars', pp. 347–65; and D. Mack Smith, 'Mussolini: reservations about Renzo De Felice's biography', *Modern Italy*, vol. 5, no. 2, 2000, pp. 193–210.

118 De Felice, *Gli Anni del Consenso*, quoted in Azzi, 'The historiography of Fascist foreign policy', p. 193.

119 Cardoza, 'Recasting the Duce for the new century', p. 726.

120 R. De Felice, *Facism: An Informal Introduction*, in Cannistraro (ed.), *Dictionary*, p. 213.

121 D. Mack Smith, *Mussolini's Roman Empire* (London, Longman, 1976) and *Mussolini* (London, Granada, 1983, pb. edn).

122 Mack Smith, *Mussolini's Roman Empire*, quotes at pp. v, 252, 83.

123 R. Quartararo, *Roma tra Londra e Berlino: La Politica Estera Fascista dal 1930 al 1940* (Rome, Bonacci, 1980), previewed in her 'Imperial defence in the Mediterranean on the eve of the Ethiopian crisis (July–October 1935)', *Historical Journal*, vol. 20, no. 1, 1977, pp. 185–220.

124 Quartararo, quoted in Azzi, 'The historiography of Fascist foreign policy', p. 201; Bosworth, *The Italian Dictatorship*, p. 95.

125 Bosworth, 'Italian foreign policy and its historiography'', p. 81.

126 M. Knox, *Mussolini Unleashed, 1939–1941: Politics and Strategy in Fascist Italy's Last War* (Cambridge, Cambridge University Press, 1982), pp. 1–2.

127 Bosworth, 'In the green corner, Denis Mack Smith, in the red? black? corner Renzo De Felice', p. 38.

128 J. Foot, *Modern Italy* (London, Palgrave, 2003), p. 177.

129 T. Mason, 'The great economic history show', *History Workshop Journal*, no. 21, 1986, pp. 22–24.

130 D. Sassoon, '*Tangentopoli* or the democratization of corruption: considerations on the end of Italy's First Republic', *Journal of Modern Italian Studies*, vol. 1, no. 1, 1995, p. 126.

131 B. Spinelli, quoted in G. Crainz, 'The representation of Fascism and the resistance in the documentaries of Italian state television', in Bosworth and Dogliani (eds), *Italian Fascism*, p. 136.

132 On Berlusconi, see D. Lane, *Berlusconi's Shadow: Crime, Justice and the Pursuit of Power* (London, Penguin, 2005, pb. edn).

133 R. J. B. Bosworth, *Mussolini* (London, Arnold, 2002), p. 425.

134 Mason, 'The great economic history show', quote at p. 17.

135 R. J. B. Bosworth, *Explaining Auschwitz and Hiroshima: History Writing and the Second World War, 1945–1990* (London, Routledge, 1993), pp. 118–41.

136 D. Ellwood, 'Introduction: the never-ending liberation', *Journal of Modern Italian Studies*, vol. 10, no. 4, 2005, pp. 385–95; S. Neri Serneri, 'A past to be thrown away? Politics and history in the Italian resistance', *Contemporary European History*, vol. 4, no. 3, 1995, pp. 367–81. It was a centre-left scholar, Claudio Pavone, who most notably put the term 'civil war' into scholarly circulation in a landmark 1991 book on the resistance. His effort to produce a more deeply textured and nuanced account of the Salò period, questioning aspects of the 'anti-Fascist' myth from a progressive perspective, was subsequently exploited by the right for relativising purposes (Bosworth, *The Italian Dictatorship*, pp. 34–36).

137 R. Ben-Ghiat, 'Fascism, writing, and memory: the realist aesthetic in Italy, 1930–50', *Journal of Modern History*, vol. 67, no. 3, 1995, pp. 629–30.

138 J. Miller, 'Who chopped down that cherry tree? The Italian resistance in history and politics, 1945–98', *Journal of Modern Italian Studies*, vol. 4, no. 1, 1999, pp. 38–39.

139 S. Monticelli, 'National identity and the representation of Italy at war: the case of *Combat Film*', *Modern Italy*, vol. 5, no. 2, 2000, p. 145.

140 D. Ward, 'Fifty years on: resistance then, resistance now', *Journal of Modern Italian Studies*, vol. 4, no. 1, 1999, p. 61.

141 J. Follain, 'Italy needed fascism, says the new Duce', *Sunday Times*, 11 May 2008, http://www.timesonline.co.uk/tol/news/world/europe/article3908192.ece (accessed 12 May 2008), quoting the AN mayor of Rome.

142 Focardi, 'Reshaping the past', p. 62.

143 P. Willan, 'Italian MPs threaten to censor textbooks', *The Guardian*, 18 December 2002, http://www.guardian.co.uk/international/story/0,3604,861809,00.html (accessed 15 May 2006).

144 Ellwood, 'Introduction: the never-ending liberation', p. 391; P. Morgan, *The Fall of Mussolini: Italy, the Italians, and the Second World War* (Oxford, Oxford University Press, 2007), pp. 8–9.

145 Bosworth, *The Italian Dictatorship*, p. 16.

146 Bosworth, *The Italian Dictatorship*, pp. 16–20, 180–204.

147 Ward, 'Fifty years on', pp. 59–64, quotes at pp. 60–61.

148 S. Luzzato, 'The political culture of Fascist Italy', *Contemporary European History*, vol. 8, no. 2, 1999, pp. 317–34, quote at p. 318.

149 Cardoza, 'Recasting the Duce for the new century', pp. 735–37.

150 P. Corner, 'Italian Fascism: whatever happened to dictatorship?', *Journal of Modern History*, vol. 74, no. 2, 2002, pp. 325–51, quotes at pp. 350, 325–26.

151 Bosworth, *The Italian Dictatorship*, pp. 21–29.

152 'The hidden pages of contemporary Italian history: war crimes, war guilt and collective memory', theme issue, *Journal of Modern Italian Studies*, vol. 9, no. 3, 2004, See also K. von Henneberg, 'Monuments, public space, and the memory of empire in modern Italy', *History and Memory*, vol. 16, no. 1, 2004, pp. 37–85; S. Luconi, 'Recent trends in the study of Italian antisemitism under the Fascist regime', *Patterns of Prejudice*, vol. 38, no. 1, 2004, pp. 1–17; R. Ventresca, 'Mussolini's ghost: Italy's *Duce* in history and memory', *History and Memory*, vol. 18, no. 1/2, 2006, pp. 86–119; and J. Walston, 'History and memory of the Italian concentration camps', *Historical Journal*, vol. 40, no. 1, 1997, pp. 169–83.
153 C. Pavone, 'Introduction', *Journal of Modern Italian Studies*, vol. 9, no. 3, 2004, p. 277.
154 Morgan, *The Fall of Mussolini*, p. 231.
155 Bosworth, *The Italian Dictatorship*, pp. 96–98, 126–27.
156 R. Quartararo, *Italia-URSS, 1917–1941: I Rapporti Politici* (Naples, Edizioni Scientifiche Italiane, 1997), quoted in review by R. J. B. Bosworth, *Modern Italy*, vol. 6, no. 2, 2001, pp. 248–49.
157 Overy, *The Road to War*, p. 144.
158 R. Lamb, *Mussolini and the British* (London, John Murray, 1997), quote at p. 7.
159 N. Farrell, *Mussolini: A New Life* (London, Phoenix, 2004, pb. edn), quotes at pp. xix, 255, 327–28, 313, xviii, 242, xvii.
160 M. Knox, *Common Destiny: Dictatorship, Foreign Policy, and War in Fascist Italy and Nazi Germany* (Cambridge, Cambridge University Press, 2000), p. 146.
161 M. Knox, 'Fascism: ideology, foreign policy, and war', in Lyttelton (ed.), *Liberal and Fascist Italy*, p. 113, quoting Grandi (emphasis in original).
162 Knox, *Mussolini Unleashed, 1939–1941*, p. 290.
163 Bosworth, *The Italian Dictatorship*, pp. 98–101.
164 Knox, 'Fascism: ideology, foreign policy, and war', pp. 105, 109.
165 Knox, *Common Destiny*, pp. 112–47, quote at p. 146.
166 Knox, 'Fascism: ideology, foreign policy, and war', pp. 110–12, 128, latterly quoting Fascist Foreign Minister Ciano.
167 Knox, *Common Destiny*, p. 130 and 'The Fascist regime, its foreign policy and its wars', pp. 362–63.
168 Knox, 'Fascism: ideology, foreign policy, and war', p. 137.
169 Knox, *Common Destiny*, p. 146.
170 Knox, *Mussolini Unleashed, 1939–1941*, pp. 39–40.
171 Knox, *Mussolini Unleashed, 1939–1941*, quote at p. 289.
172 See, especially, D. Rodogno, *Fascism's European Empire: Italian Occupation during the Second World War* (Cambridge, Cambridge University Press, 2006).
173 See in particular Knox, *Common Destiny*, pp. 53–110.
174 Cassels, 'Was there a Fascist foreign policy?', pp. 255–68, quote at p. 268.
175 J. Gooch, 'Fascist Italy', in R. Boyce and J. A. Maiolo (eds), *The Origins of World War Two: The Debate Continues* (London, Palgrave, 2003), pp. 32–51, quotes at pp. 39, 48; see also J. Gooch, *Mussolini and his Generals: The Armed Forces and Fascist Foreign Policy, 1922–1940* (Cambridge, Cambridge University Press, 2007).
176 Sullivan, 'More than meets the eye', pp. 178–203, quote at p. 196.
177 R. Mallett, *The Italian Navy and Fascist Expansionism 1935–1940* (London, Cass, 1998), quote at p. 2; R. Mallett, *Mussolini and the Origins of the Second World War, 1933–1940* (London, Palgrave, 2003), quote at p. 222.
178 Strang, *On the Fiery March*, especially pp. 13–38.
179 R. Salerno, *Vital Crossroads: Mediterranean Origins of the Second World War, 1935–1940* (Ithaca, NY, Cornell University Press, 2002), quote at p. 216.
180 A. Kallis, *Fascist Ideology: Territory and Expansionism in Italy and Germany, 1922–1945* (London, Routledge, 2000), quote at p. 9 (emphasis in original).
181 R. Mallett, 'The Fascist challenge dissected', *Historical Journal*, vol. 44, no. 3, 2001, pp. 859–62; see also R. J. B. Bosworth, 'Benito Mussolini: bad guy on the international block?', *Contemporary European History*, vol. 18, no. 1, 2009, pp. 123–34.

182 Cassels, 'Was there a Fascist foreign policy?', p. 259.
183 H. J. Burgwyn, *Italian Foreign Policy in the Interwar Period 1918–1940* (Westport, CT, Praeger, 1997), quotes at pp. xii–xvii.
184 Bosworth, *The Italian Dictatorship*, pp. 99–100; *Mussolini*, pp. 4–11.
185 R. J. B. Bosworth, *Italy: The Least of the Great Powers: Italian Foreign Policy before the First World War* (Cambridge, Cambridge University Press, 1979), quote at p. ix. Note that in the German case 'continuity' arguments were generally coded as frank and critical and 'discontinuity' ones as evasive and exculpatory, the reverse of the situation with the arguments of De Felice and Knox.
186 Bosworth, 'Italian foreign policy and its historiography', p. 73.
187 Bosworth, 'Italian foreign policy and its historiography', pp. 78–79; 'In the green corner, Denis Mack Smith, in the red? black? corner Renzo De Felice', p. 38.
188 Bosworth, *Mussolini*, quotes at pp. 8, 11, 245.
189 R. J. B. Bosworth, *Italy and the Wider World 1860–1960* (London, Routledge, 1996), p. 51.
190 Bosworth, 'Italian foreign policy and its historiography', p. 78.
191 R. J. B. Bosworth, *Mussolini's Italy: Life Under the Dictatorship 1915–1945* (London, Allen Lane, 2005), p. 431.
192 Bosworth, 'In the green corner, Denis Mack Smith, in the red? black? corner Renzo De Felice', p. 39.
193 Bosworth, *Mussolini*, quote at p. 11; 'In the green corner, Denis Mack Smith, in the red? black? corner Renzo De Felice', pp. 38–39.
194 Bosworth, *Mussolini*, p. xv.
195 Bosworth, *Mussolini's Italy*, quote at p. 1; A. De Grand, 'Working towards the Duce: five recent books on Mussolini', *Journal of Modern Italian Studies*, vol. 11, no. 4, 2006, pp. 551–62.
196 Bosworth, *Mussolini's Italy*, quotes at pp. 571–72.
197 J. Sadkovich, *The Italian Navy in World War II* (Westport, CT, Greenwood, 1994), p. xv.
198 L. Cafagna and E. Galli della Loggia, in R. Ben-Ghiat *et al.*, 'History as it really wasn't: the myths of Italian historiography', *Journal of Modern Italian Studies*, vol. 6, no. 3, 2001, p. 419.
199 Mallett, *Mussolini and the Origins of the Second World War, 1933–1940*, p. 15.
200 Strang, *On the Fiery March*, p. 7.
201 Knox, 'The Fascist regime, its foreign policy and its wars', pp. 347–49. See, in contrast, M. Knox, *Hitler's Italian Allies: Royal Armed Forces, Fascist Regime, and the War of 1940–1943* (Cambridge, Cambridge University Press, 2000).
202 R. Ben-Ghiat, 'A lesser evil? Italian Fascism in/and the totalitarian equation', in H. Dubiel and G. Motzkin (eds), *The Lesser Evil: Moral Approaches to Genocide Practices* (London, Routledge, 2004), p. 147.
203 Strang, *On the Fiery March*, p. 11.
204 Knox, 'The Fascist regime, its foreign policy and its wars', quotes at pp. 352, 347, 357.
205 Ellwood, 'Introduction: the never-ending liberation', p. 393.
206 Portelli, *The Order has been Carried Out*, p. 16.

4 On decadence

French foreign policy and the fall of the Third Republic

Today ... Europe has its 'sick man'. Formerly, it was the Ottoman Empire; today, despite certain probably ephemeral appearances to the contrary, it is France. The causes of this sickness are the same. In both cases, a disproportion between declining strength (of which population is the index for France) and an overextended territory, which by a kind of senile megalomania still tends to be increased. Above all, in both cases, a decline in the spiritual force that constituted the power of the state; religious spirit in the case of Turkey, cult of individual liberty in the case of France.

Robert Aron and Arnaud Dandieu, *Décadence de la Nation Française*, 1931[1]

The acclaimed medieval historian Marc Bloch was called up from the army reserve in August 1939 at the age of 53 and thereafter endured a peripatetic ten months as a firsthand participant in France's defeat. Posted variously in Strasbourg and Picardy through the Phoney War, after the German invasion Bloch retreated with the First Army to Dunkirk in May 1940, was evacuated under fire to England and then shipped almost immediately back to Cherbourg. His campaign ended in June in Rennes where he escaped capture by changing into civilian clothes and reassuming the civilian identity of gentleman academic; after the armistice he was reunited with his family at their home in Guéret in the unoccupied southern zone. Desperately saddened by the tragedy that had befallen his country, Bloch spent that summer composing a statement of evidence about his experiences which became a searing indictment of those he held responsible for France's shattering reverse.[2] He lambasted 'the utter incompetence' of the French military command, but in seeking to illuminate the underlying causes of the disaster he spread blame across all sectors of French society; peasants, workers and bourgeoisie, politicians, teachers and journalists, all played their part in dooming the nation to its *Strange Defeat*. Even though Bloch remained convinced of the 'deep-seated vitality' and capacity for recovery of the French people, his remorseless analysis attributed the catastrophe to a fundamental structural and spiritual malaise that had sapped France's will and ability to resist the Axis challenge.[3] Bloch did not live to see the 1946 publication of the book. Seeking to make his own contribution to France's rebirth he joined the resistance, was captured, tortured and eventually executed by the Nazis in June 1944. According to resistance legend, his dying words were 'vive la France!'.[4]

This sturdy patriot's vivid sketch embodied a pervasive interpretive impulse. The shock of 1940 had revolutionary consequences, precipitating not only the demise of the Third Republic but also the inauguration of the collaborationist Vichy regime and years of humiliating occupation and shameful complicity. Defeat on such a monumental scale invited a comparably grand explanation, which it found with the elaboration of this paradigm of 'decadence'. On this view, the Third Republic 'had been rotten at its core. The civilian and military leadership of pre-war France, along with the deeply flawed security policies that they pursued, were products of this endemic moral decay. Consequently, the military disaster and subsequent political collapse were the inevitable culmination of a long process of decline'.[5] This rather determinist explanation proved remarkably enduring, remaining dominant for at least three decades within France and (to a lesser extent) beyond. This was in no small part because a negative image of the Third Republic as mired in demoralisation and division served the leaders of successive later regimes – from Vichy itself through to the Fourth and Fifth Republics – as a foil for the construction of alternative, positive senses of national identity. Moreover, with the nation as a whole in thrall to the 'Vichy Syndrome' – persistently evading confrontation with the more uncomfortable aspects of the wartime past – historians had little professional or personal incentive to challenge this instrumentalization.[6] Even though changing circumstances from the 1970s eroded the hegemony of decadence, as a range of nuanced and competing explanations emerged to occupy the interpretive terrain, it nonetheless remains 'very much in the historical mainstream': Bloch still serves as 'the starting-point for most historians in their search to understand the causes of the defeat'.[7]

The political inspirations and entailments of this emplotment, and of the historiography on France's road to war more generally, have been broached previously.[8] Yet this literature has not been located explicitly on the wider terrain of war memory whose contours and evolution Henry Rousso delineated in his landmark work. French collective memory was fraught with ambiguity in a manner not dissimilar to that of Italy. On the one hand, the war presented a hugely problematic legacy to negotiate in the shape of the defeat of 1940, collaboration and internecine division. But on the other, there was positive capital to draw upon in the shape of the resistance struggle and the contribution of the French to the eventual triumph over Nazi Germany. Even during the war itself, General Charles de Gaulle, the leader of the Free French movement, had realised that 'to reunite the nation and restore its self-respect' mnemonic politics would need to focus on national agency, unity and resistance while the murkier dimensions of the war experience were obscured. Hence his famous declaration in August 1944 at the liberation of Paris, which blithely effaced the role of the Anglo-Saxon Allies, internal division and collaboration: "'Paris liberated! Liberated by herself, by her own people with the help of the armies of France, with the support and aid of France as a whole, of fighting France, of the only France, of the true France, of eternal France'".[9]

After the war, the desire to restore French prestige and great power status in the international arena only reinforced these internal imperatives and, broadly speaking, until the 1970s the dominant themes in French collective memory were evasive: the 'sublime half-lie' of the 'myth of the resistance' posited that the nation had been united in heroic defiance of an external enemy, and entirely obscured the realities of collaboration.[10] (There was also a strong undercurrent stressing French victimhood, even martyrdom, especially in the suffering of deportees and prisoners of war.[11]) Yet in the early 1970s 'the glacier of official memory' began to fragment as a result of generational change and the awakening – on a global scale – of Jewish memory of the war.[12] Amidst the faltering of the post-war economic boom and the erosion of grandiose Gaullist notions of national identity, France witnessed what Rousso characterised as a 'return of the repressed': the comforting myth of a nation pristine in resistance was challenged by increasing emphasis on collaboration under Vichy, and in particular on French complicity in the Holocaust.[13] Thus self-exculpatory evasion was replaced with an obsessive self-flagellatory insistence on probing the darker aspects and ambivalences of the wartime past which continued into the new century.[14] (In this sense, of course, the trajectory of French memory differs significantly from the Italian comparator.)

This chapter maps the development of the international history literature against this terrain of national identity and collective memory, tracing the initial hegemony of the decadence paradigm, early and tentative contestation from within and without France, and then the upsurge of revisionist scholarship from the 1970s which has produced a plurality of competing interpretations. Reading this literature as a discourse on identity and memory reveals that it has been somewhat marginal. The issues that have excited the fiercest political and moral passions and which have lain at the heart of the 'Vichy Syndrome' – first resistance and then collaboration – concern the period of occupation rather than the origins and early stages of the war. Hence Andrew Shennan has argued that the memory of 1940 has been successively eclipsed by first 'consoling' and then 'painful' memories; the defeat has never 'received the kind of intense historical and journalistic scrutiny directed at the Occupation experience'.[15] Similarly, Stanley Hoffmann has opined that 'a book about the debacle-syndrome ... would probably be brief'.[16] There is undeniably some truth in this observation, and it is perhaps supported by opinion poll evidence that, from the 1940s to the 1980s (and despite the tumultuous scandals raging around the legacy of Vichy at the latter moment), the vast majority of French people unproblematically accepted some variant of the decadence explanation for the defeat.[17]

Yet this should not obscure the fact that there is, of course, a very respectable body of scholarship on the origins of the war and 1940 which can certainly be read for its politics. Moreover, to dismiss debates over the memory of 1940 as peripheral perhaps risks eliding the complexity and multiplicity of collective memory, which is not reducible to the issues that figure most prominently within it. Richard Golsan has recently discussed how, for all Rousso's unparalleled contribution in excavating French memory and mapping its evolution through successive phases, his schema should not be taken as definitive: in particular, his reliance on 'a straightforward chronological progression in which all discourses are fused into one' can obscure the extent to which different vectors or media of memory operated according to distinctive dynamics, patterns and rhythms. Separating out these discourses 'enables a somewhat more composite picture of the memory of the war in France while making it possible to analyze more closely the ways in which these multiple memories coincide with, overlap, and, on occasion, contradict each other'.[18] (To be fair to Rousso, as Golsan notes, he has himself opened up this issue in his subsequent work.[19]) Exploring the international history literature as one such discourse can certainly contribute to this project of thickening our understanding of French collective memory.

'A morally divided France': decadence and repression

Interpretations of the causes of the French defeat were conditioned by the political circumstances that prevailed following the armistice of 22 June. On 10 July the National Assembly, sitting at Vichy, voted extraordinary powers for constitutional revision to Marshal Philippe Pétain, the First World War hero of Verdun and last premier of the Third Republic; after the subsequent inauguration of the Vichy regime Pétain enjoyed almost untrammelled executive and legislative power as 'Head of the French State'. Successive Vichy governments sought to enact a National Revolution, a reactionary programme for the regeneration and reunification of society and polity, encapsulated in the tripartite slogan 'work, family, fatherland'.[20] The National Revolution was internally generated in the sense that it had its roots in pre-war ideological currents on the French right and was a spontaneous and autonomous initiative: it was not foisted on France by the German invaders.[21] Yet Vichy was, of course, also a collaborationist regime that was deeply complicit in the wider purposes of the Nazis, especially after the extension of the occupation over the whole country in November 1942. Most damningly, the Vichy authorities zealously cooperated in the Holocaust, which claimed almost 80,000 Jewish victims in France.[22] The legitimacy of Pétain's claim to represent France and the insidiously nostalgic values inherent in his mission to 'reconstruct the national soul' were contested from the very first.[23] The resistance abroad and at home – in the shape of De Gaulle's Free French and the heterogeneous domestic movements increasingly dominated by the communists – not only continued the national armed struggle against the Germans but also offered a range of alternative, progressive political prescriptions.[24] Vibrant and clamorous debates over the shape of the 'new

France' continued well past the vanquishing of Vichy in August 1944; the euphoria of liberation 'concealed very different interpretations of the past and very different visions of the future'.[25]

Given its seismic consequences, readings of the meaning of 1940 not surprisingly constituted a crucial mnemonic dimension of these wartime struggles. New political forces naturally attempted to legitimise themselves through narratives of the national past and this generally entailed locating responsibility for the defeat firmly with a decadent Third Republic, a forlorn counterpoint to their own vigour and promise. Such characterisations of the republic had in fact been commonplace in the anxious and turbulent inter-war years: 'by 1939 the perception that France had become the new "sick man of Europe" had taken deep root and had propagated a set of frightening stereotypes of national decay'. Contemporary observers readily tallied the components of the problem: a sagging birth-rate and population (with a marked gender imbalance) following the sanguinary catastrophe of the Great War; a corrupt, inefficient and unstable political system; a stagnating economy; and a society increasingly divided, polarised between extremes of left and right with sectional interests universally elevated above the common good.[26] In this sense, the defeat was scripted as the ineluctable product of secular national decay even before it occurred. Hence Jean-Paul Sartre's lament in February 1940 that 'our epoch is busy constructing an image of itself to cut the ground from beneath the historians' feet: it wants at least to have had the glory of judging itself, and to hand them ready made work'.[27]

This emplotment had deep roots. Theories of national decline, and narratives of degeneration, fall and renewal, had been endemic in French political culture from 1789. Dramatizing the present as embodying a process of deterioration from some past golden age leading to an inevitable collapse, actors on all sides of the political spectrum prophesied a national renewal that would restore French grandeur and allow the reborn nation once more to play a leading, exemplary role in international affairs. The strategic utility of this emplotment as 'an emotive political device' for those seeking 'to undermine the legitimacy of political opponents, multi-party politics and often even parliamentary institutions' explains its ubiquity in political narratives of French history.[28] That said, it should also be noted that the idea that 'war, death, and rebirth are cyclically linked' is by no means unique to France, or the modern era, being common rather to the narrative imaginaries of 'all the world's great cultures'. Moreover, interpreting the specific experience of defeat 'as a national crisis of infirmity and decadence from which the nation, having purged itself, emerges' (or may emerge) 'healthier and stronger than before' is to employ a very common consolatory troping.[29]

Supporters of Vichy readily turned to the decadence theory as France collapsed. Typically this entailed lamenting spiritual failings or the conspiratorial intrigues of socialists and Jews, often with great bitterness. In at least one prisoner of war camp at the demise of the republic, conservative French officers joined with their German captors to toast the death of 'the whore'.[30] The rhetoric and propaganda of the National Revolution was replete with references to the 'weaknesses', 'defects' and 'impotence' of the old regime, stressing the need to learn from the lesson of 1940 and 'rebuild France on a heap of ruins'.[31] Cementing in place 'the "decline and fall" narrative that undermined the legitimacy of the republican regime and bolstered that of Pétain's government', and establishing new state structures went hand in hand.[32] 'Vichy representations of the defeated nation stressed not just its decrepitude but its insalubrity ... France was an ugly sight – intoxicated (literally) by alcohol and (figuratively) by materialism and self-indulgence, gradually losing its vitality and creativity'. Thus while defeat was portrayed as a punishment for past sins, it simultaneously offered an opportunity to create a better future.[33]

Vichy sought to concretise this anathematisation of the Third Republic by putting numerous key figures of the regime on trial at Riom in 1942. These included Édouard Daladier, Radical premier from 1938 to 1940 and long-serving Minister for National Defence, Léon Blum, socialist Popular Front premier from 1936 to 1937, and General Maurice Gamelin, army Commander in Chief in 1940. The ostensible charge was that these leaders had failed to prepare the nation adequately for war between 1936 and 1940, but the wider purpose was to condemn the entire former political system. However, since the defendants adroitly both vindicated their conduct of policy in the 1930s – pointing, for example, to the major rearmament programme initiated by the Popular Front – and 'relentlessly associated some of the key officers of the Vichy regime – notably Pétain himself [a former Minister of War] – with the decision-making of the 1930s', the strategy in fact proved unsuccessful and the trial was abandoned.[34] The Riom proceedings thus demonstrated how alternative interpretations, confounding the assumption of decadence, always lurked on the margins of the dominant discourse. Equally, they illustrated how in practice headline accusations of decadence often concealed a rather more sectarian and restricted distribution of blame – in this case scapegoating the leftist elements associated with the Popular Front after 1936. (Significant continuities meant Vichy 'could only put part of the past on trial'.) Yet if the failure of the Riom trial demonstrated how difficult it was to prove the guilt of the republic in a judicial setting, nonetheless the general notion of decadence remained plausible and pervasive.[35]

As Bloch's testimony demonstrates, opponents of Vichy who had more cause to regret the defeat also turned instinctively to this interpretive framework. De Gaulle stridently condemned the 'anarchic abuses', 'chronic paralysis' and 'moral subsidence' of the republic: 'the loss of the Rhine in '36, the abandonment of the Austrians in '37, and of the Czechs in '39, the incoherence of the policy and the mediocrity of the strategy, were effects before they became causes. The nation was tottering for many years'.[36] That said, the resistance faced a challenge to craft an interpretation of 1940 that did not simply align it with Vichy. Resistance critiques therefore tended to allot prime culpability to the failure of the bourgeoisie as a ruling class. Timid, egoistic and defeatist, it had placed sectional interest above the national and comprehensively bungled preparations for war; moreover, these bourgeois elites now formed a core element of Vichy's constituency, which actually constituted the most damning evidence of their guilt. Thus lumping the Third Republic and Vichy together allowed the resistance both to distinguish its decadence critique from Pétain's and to valorise and legitimise the reformed and reinvigorated republicanism that coalesced as its core political prescription: discrediting all political alternatives was a means of claiming the right to leadership in post-war France.[37]

For de Gaulle, this interpretation also nestled within a distinctive variant of the larger declinist metanarrative. This, as he would phrase it in his memoirs published in the 1950s, conceived of France as 'endlessly vacillating from greatness to decline, but revived, century after century, by the genius of renewal!'.[38] Two thousand years of French national history were here construed as a long-term cyclical alternation between catastrophe and recovery, with a strong, predestined, paternal leader emerging at moments of crisis to reunite quarrelsome factions and lead the nation forward to a brighter future.[39] (Though Gaullist narratives naturally portrayed him as this providential man, Pétain was actually idealised in a similar fashion by his partisans.[40])

Journalists and other commentators produced a prodigious volume of histories during the war which worked the decadence narrative in diverse ways, often in the service of identifiable political projects. An influential and scathing representative was *The Gravediggers of France*, penned by the conservative émigré journalist André Géraud under the pseudonym Pertinax and first published in 1942, which indicted both Third Republic figureheads like Daladier and Gamelin and the men of Vichy such as Pétain. Pertinax's treatment was focused, as his title suggests, on the inadequacies and errors of individual statesmen, but this was against the backdrop of 'a morally divided France', 'a nation cut to its depth by political and social quarrels'. Compounding the flaws of policy-makers, the selfish attitudes of sectional groups on the left and right precluded the adoption of a vigorous policy and produced 'a terrible deficit in the country's moral and material preparation'. Thus the cumulative picture was of a France doomed to defeat by inexorable structural weaknesses; moreover, there were no Cassandras in the wings advocating preferable alternative policies. Indeed, Pertinax fused agency and structure when he opined of Daladier: 'the only strength of this spineless man was that he represented fairly well the average Frenchman of his time'. Ultimately, in line with the dominant resistance narrative, Pertinax placed the chief blame for defeat on the liberal bourgeoisie that had traditionally produced France's rulers. The 'impact of socialism' so unsettled 'the propertied classes' that they had shirked the challenge of public service, and drifted into servile appeasement and defeatism: 'France was betrayed by its supposedly conservative classes rather than by the democratic process'. Although in the revised edition of 1944 Pertinax was chary of explicitly invoking the term decadence – presumably fearful that it might inculcate hopelessness rather than resolve for the future at a critical time – he nonetheless urged that to revive the institutions of the Third Republic after victory 'would mean, for the people, going back to its own vomit'.[41]

After liberation, fierce debates about the constitutional settlement raged for two years before the promulgation of the Fourth Republic following a referendum in October 1946. This regime 'has never had a very good press', not least because 'its record of political crisis and ministerial instability ... was worse than that of the Third Republic'. Yet it was arguably a valiant attempt to construct a viable parliamentary regime avoiding the perceived 'twin evils' of communist revolution and Gaullist dictatorship. Accordingly, the republic was generally governed by coalitions of centrist parties with the communists and Gaullists in opposition on their respective flanks. It enjoyed some notable achievements, including inaugurating France's post-war economic recovery and pioneering European integration. Yet tentatively resuscitated national grandeur was severely dented by travails in the empire, as France became embroiled in a series of wars of decolonisation, especially in Indochina and then much more traumatically in Algeria. The refusal of hard line elements in the army to countenance concessions to the Algerian nationalists unleashed a crisis in which democratic government in France was imperilled. A solution was only found when de Gaulle emerged once more as national saviour, affecting to the right wing extremists 'that he was their man, ready to set up a strong government to save French Algeria, while to the political classes in Paris he pretended that he was the sole guarantor of the liberties of the republic against military dictatorship and fascism'. (The former claim was the more misleading, as de Gaulle moved towards recognising self-determination for Algeria once secure in power.) He engineered the adoption of a new constitution, endorsed in a referendum in September 1958, and thus the establishment of the Fifth Republic in which the president enjoyed much stronger powers *vis-à-vis* both parliament and government. Regarding himself as the embodiment of both the republic and France, President de Gaulle headed a 'highly personal and presidential regime' with relative serenity until the further eruption of revolutionary discontent in the disturbances of 1968.[42]

The first post-liberation decade – characterised by Rousso as a period of 'unfinished mourning' – witnessed genuine French efforts to come to terms with the wartime past that were hampered by continuing internal divisions. Naturally, 'rival political forces attempted to exploit an ambivalent heritage to their own advantage' and there was an extensive purge of collaborationist politicians, bureaucrats, businessmen, journalists and intellectuals. Moreover, politics in the early Fourth Republic was the almost exclusive domain of individuals who could claim some form of resistance credentials. Yet the purges themselves proved intensely divisive, and by 1953 – in the shadow of the Cold War – a widespread amnesty had been declared in the interests of reconstruction and national unity. Elections in the early 1950s consequently saw the return in significant numbers of right-wing deputies to parliament, and there was a notable resurgence of neo-Vichyite sentiment, 'despite the fact that the Vichy era had once been presumed permanently discredited'. Public veneration of Pétain after his death in a remote island prison in 1951 demonstrated how problematic it was to found a consensual national memory on candid repudiation of collaboration.[43]

As the 1950s wore on a more settled rendering of the wartime past did, however, become established as pre-eminent in public memory. In part this was because other preoccupations in Indochina and Algeria 'imposed themselves more urgently on the national conscience', allowing the memory of Vichy to become 'less insistent and less visible'.[44] Yet in part too it was because of the elaboration of a mnemonic vision that was suited to smoothing over wartime schisms. The Gaullist 'myth of the resistance' had originated in the 1940s, but only became firmly established much later, and particularly after 1958. This presented a somewhat abstract picture of a whole nation united in resistance to the Germans from 1940 onward and almost entirely effaced collaboration (apart from recognising a small handful of traitors). Although it did not go uncontested, this heroicising and redemptive representation did command wide assent. Thus communists might regret the marginalisation of their own singular contribution, but the lionisation of resistance nonetheless 'reinforced their own legitimacy'. Even former Vichy partisans were not necessarily that discomfited by a vision that focused attention on foreign enemies and draped the wartime civil war in soothing oblivion. (The functional equivalence of this myth with the one established in Italy in the 1960s should be apparent.) This anodyne representation both obscured national divisions and airbrushed the crimes of collaboration – hence Rousso's characterisation of the later 1950s and 1960s as a time of 'repressions' – but this was in keeping with its unifying purpose, and the restoration of national pride. (In Stanley Hoffman's rendering, de Gaulle became 'the nurse of France's self-respect'.) Within this Gaullist framework, the resistance 'became a common theme of films, novels, and historical treatises, while Vichy and collaboration fell under a taboo that was rarely violated'.[45]

Given these diverse preoccupations with the events following the armistice, the defeat and its antecedents became rather marginalised in political rhetoric. In the purge trials, prosecutions generally focused on how defendants had connived with the Nazi regime after 1940 rather than on their machinations and errors in the 1930s. Conspiracy theories about treasonous Fifth Column intrigues abounded in this milieu but were not susceptible to juridical proof and, in any case, threatened to have the counter-productive consequence of rehabilitating the Third Republic; conversely, mere incompetence was problematic to criminalise. The causes of defeat no longer aroused grand public passions, and while occasional references were made to it in debates over post-war reconstruction and during the final crisis of the Fourth Republic, these moments were untypical. In crucial respects it proved difficult to make the memory of defeat resonate with contemporary problems of decolonisation, economic modernisation and Cold War rivalry, or readily to instrumentalise it in a potent partisan fashion.

A parliamentary commission of inquiry, charged with investigating the political, economic, diplomatic and military events that had occurred in France between 1933 and 1945, sat from 1947 and demonstrated how the defeat had been relegated to 'a footnote in French politics'. It proceeded in a somewhat unsystematic fashion and was prematurely truncated, concluding in 1951 with a two volume report and nine volumes of supporting testimony which narrated a broadly familiar tale of decadence. Considerable emphasis was placed upon the failure of the military establishment to innovate and anticipate, but political and economic elites were also charged with allowing France to stagnate and fall behind its rivals. Ultimately, the report concluded, the republic '"had been drained of its spiritual content, its creative dynamism"'.[46] According to Robert Young, 'the blurred but powerful impression left by the report ... was that responsibility for the collapse was so widespread as to be indeterminate. It was a condemnation with which almost anyone could live, suggestive as it was of a discredited but mercifully defunct collective past'. On this reading, the decadence paradigm served a similar function to the 'myth of the resistance', as a technology for 'national reconciliation under the new Fourth Republic'.[47]

Despite the intervention of other preoccupations, the claim that the fall of the Third Republic had ceased to be politically meaningful should not be over-stated. It was true, for example, that de Gaulle's rhetoric after the war sometimes tended to sideline the defeat by talking of the two global conflicts as forming a 'thirty years' war' against German aggression. As a crucial component of his 'myth of the resistance' this had the double effect of diverting attention from internecine quarrels to foreign invasion and relativising the setback of 1940 through the teleology of final victory in 1945.[48] Yet on a deeper level, de Gaulle's whole post-war political philosophy was forged in the crucible of that defeat. Albeit that he interpreted the world through the prism of a pre-existing vision of French history, his predilection for a strong state and determination to preserve national independence – central elements in his political doctrine and enduring legacies to French political culture – were born of the lessons of 1940.[49]

Equally, the fall did retain a certain salience across the broader culture. True, it was not a subject that particularly attracted professional historians, and very few full-scale histories of the subject appeared in France in the three decades after the war. This reflected a transnational suspicion of contemporary history, sharpened in the French case by the post-war historiographical predominance of the *Annales* school, with its characteristic fondness for the medieval and early modern periods, prioritisation of economic, social and cultural phenomena over the political, and preference for the *longue durée* over the event. Indeed, *Annaliste* disdain for the event has itself been interpreted as symptomatic of a collective repression of the trauma of 1940 and a national refusal to confront the full horror of the dark years of occupation.[50] (The post-war *Annales* doyen Fernand Braudel spent five years as a prisoner of war in Germany, and later admitted that 'my vision of history took on its definitive form ... partly as a direct existential response to the tragic times I was passing through ... I had to believe that history, destiny, was written at a much more profound level'.[51]) There were active contemporary historians, especially those grouped in the Committee for the History of the Second World War, but their work was disproportionately devoted to exploring the phenomenon of resistance. There was little incentive for historians to open up the murky episode of defeat when the broad thrust of collective war memory so overwhelmingly focused on celebrating this more positive lineage.[52]

This said, however, a range of memoirists and commentators – including a few historians – did generate interpretations of the causes of 1940. Surveying this corpus of work in 1959, a Canadian historian taxonomised the key emplotments. Talk of 'conspiracy and general political skulduggery' proved impossible to still, but the notion of defeat as an inevitable product of spiritual decline, poor leadership and decrepit state institutions – even as an act of divine retribution for moral turpitude – stood centre stage.[53] While in a broad sense the decadence paradigm worked to legitimise the Fourth Republic and bind the post-war nation together, it also transpired that almost every faction and individual could devise a variant that served to validate their particular position. This widespread utility was demonstrated in the rash of memoirs that appeared in the later 1940s and 1950s from Third Republic luminaries such as Paul Reynaud, its penultimate premier, Gamelin and Georges Bonnet, Daladier's notoriously appeasing foreign minister during the last year of peace. The prime purpose of these authors was naturally self-exculpatory, to defend their own decision-making record; but typically this entailed not only sloughing responsibility off onto each other but also broad contextualisation, spreading the blame for defeat as widely as possible throughout the political system and nation. Thus Bonnet invoked the military weakness bequeathed by previous governments and the debilitating slackness induced in the economy by Popular Front social reforms as determinants of French policy at Munich.[54] (His memoirs were regarded as particularly untrustworthy on publication: reviewing them the historian Maurice Baumont implied that 'cowardice' was a better explanation for Munich.[55]) As much as any particular iteration, it was the cumulative impact of the inculpatory elements in these accounts that 'left something nearly indelible – the image of a sick, divided and demoralized France'.[56]

The ubiquity of the decadence framework, as well as the scope for partisan variations, can be appreciated by comparing notable communist, Gaullist and Vichyite accounts. Building on their wartime rhetoric, communist authors such as Maurice Thorez, pre- and post-war leader of the French party, natu-rally identified the selfish interests of capital and the bourgeoisie as the prime agents of French decadence and thus the debacle. Their suggestion that a conspiracy had subverted the republic found some echoes in the writings of Gaullist authors, including the war memoirs of the general himself. Yet the post-war Gaullist critique was in general much more concerned to emphasise 'a series of fatal flaws in the governance of the Third Republic': constitutional infirmities, defective bureaucratic machinery and institutionalised sectional self-interest were at the root of the state's failure to guarantee national security. Here, in turn, there was a degree of overlap with extreme right-wing writers such as Jacques Benoist-Méchin, a former Vichy junior minister, who also argued that the debacle 'illustrated the weaknesses of the Republic and an absence of leadership'. For these authors, however, the core problem lay in political culture, and they unfavourably contrasted democratic republicanism and parliamentarianism with the virtues of the experiment in authoritarian governance undertaken by Vichy. This illustrates that despite some areas of overlap there was no single homogeneous decadence interpretation in play. Moreover, while each variant lambasted the Third Republic and might therefore in a general sense be seen to give succour to the Fourth, they also functioned as subtly coded critiques of the existing regime advocating, respectively, extensive further progressive socio-political transformation, a more robust presidential republicanism and an anti-democratic turn.[57]

The positioning of authors with close ties to particular factions doubtless explains the particular tenor of their interpretations. But even when other historians did choose to explore this subject, in a country where university appointments and other honours were in the state's gift, 'scholars anxious to make a career under the Fourth and Fifth Republics were not noticeably intent on exonerating the Third'.[58] Beyond France historians also generally cleaved to the decadence framework. Anglo-American historians readily diagnosed a pathological malaise in pre-war France, reading the pursuit of appeasement and military collapse as ineluctable consequences of 'the failure of the *élan vital* of a great people'.[59] Although much of A. J. P. Taylor's classic 1961 text on war origins was maverick in its interpretation, his acerbic characterisation of the 'crippling enervation' of French policy was in tune with broader opinion.[60] Saturated with 'despairing cynicism', the feeble and irresolute French hampered British efforts to deal with Hitler, proving the truism that 'weakness is infectious'.[61] Peter Jackson has argued that British interpreters of France in this period – including such luminaries as Winston Churchill – were heavily influenced by personal memories and pervasive cultural stereotypes. On this reading, the scarring experience of a French surrender that left Britain standing alone against the Nazis, entrenched Francophobe preconceptions about 'an unscrupulous, excitable, and unstable people who cannot be relied upon', and a tendency to read the melodramatic, even hysterical, tone of French political rhetoric too literally, all combined to produce superficial interpretations of a weak and indecisive France on the brink of collapse in the 1930s.[62]

The notion that decadence had conditioned French foreign policy and fundamentally caused the defeat was firmly entrenched from 1940 through to the 1960s. This was not a single interpretation so much as a framework within which defeat was seen as inevitably determined by some profound fatal flaw – variously structural, spiritual or human – in the Third Republic. Decline and fall, according to the conventional operation of the emplotment in French political culture, implied the promise of renewal and rebirth. Thus, as exemplified by the findings of the parliamentary commission of inquiry, decadence served as the official reading of the Fourth Republic, grounding the regime ideologically as legitimate and entreating all segments of the nation to rally behind it. Yet the paradigm could also be put to work by opponents of the regime, as diagnoses of the frailties of the Third Republic simultaneously critiqued the Fourth; thus as it lapsed into dysfunction in its later years, apparently replaying 'the errors of the past', 'anti-system forces exploited the memories of 1940' while the parties of the republic 'had little incentive to dwell on the analogy'.[63] The advent of the Fifth Republic, more stridently distanced and distinguished from its predecessors, lessened this ambiguity and the decadent Third – 'condemned by governmental weakness and political cleavages to stagnation' – was therefore more readily available as rhetorical underpinning.[64] Since the resistance was emphatically the founding myth of de Gaulle's republic, the pre-existing tendency for the 1930s to recede to the margins of collective memory in favour of the occupation years persisted, and was even perhaps intensified; yet the defeat was nonetheless one of the subsidiary legitimating devices of the new regime.[65]

Rousso posits a significant turning point in the 'Vichy Syndrome' around 1954, as the polemics of 'unfinished mourning' gave way to repressive closure over a divisive past during the heyday of the 'myth of the resistance'. Given the persistent hegemony of the decadence paradigm over explanations of the defeat during the whole period considered here, it is difficult to map developments in this strand of collective memory cleanly onto Rousso's model. The idea of a specific and dramatic step-change is certainly hard to endorse, though it could be argued that disputes between advocates of different permutations of the decadence narrative constitute clashes of the kind characteristic of 'unfinished mourning', and that these did lessen in intensity as 1940 receded further into the past. The more telling point, however, is the fact that so many were disinclined to contemplate defeat and its causes at all – and that when they did they ubiquitously viewed it through the prism of decadence – which reinforces the notion that this was a period of evasion of the uncomfortable realities of the past. Although ostensibly searching and critical, sweeping condemnations of pre-war France in fact functioned as mechanisms to despatch the past perfunctorily in the name of ideological projects in the present, either applying the balm of narrative to internecine feuds, legitimating subsequent political arrangements and prescriptions, or fostering a new common sense about French unity and grandeur. In this respect, the decadence paradigm was a key part of the mnemonic architecture of 'repressions' whereby, in these years, France obstinately 'refused to look herself squarely in the face'.[66]

'A task ... both necessary and unattainable': the mirror breaks in international history

De Gaulle's authority was seriously threatened by the youth protests and general strikes which erupted in May 1968. Specific student grievances about a stultifying educational system soon mushroomed into widespread counter-cultural discontent amounting to 'an act of defiance against the older – wartime – generation'.[67] The trade unions' articulation of extensive social and economic demands challenged the validity of the whole Gaullist system, and chants of 'ten years is enough' made manifest that de Gaulle personally was also in the protestors' sights. Although the government eventually succeeded in drawing the revolutionary sting of the movement, de Gaulle's prestige was fatally tarnished and in April 1969 – after losing a referendum that was tantamount to a vote of confidence – he retired from active politics (dying the next year). The Fifth Republic itself weathered the storm and, indeed, in the longer run has 'enjoyed a period of unprecedented stability', its essentials accepted by left and right: witness, for example, how the Gaullist Georges Pompidou, the centrist Valéry Giscard d'Estaing and the socialist François Mitterrand successively followed de Gaulle as president. The election of the last in 1981 was something of a landmark, conjuring up echoes of the Popular Front, but over time socialist governments proved committed to relatively moderate policies. Indeed, the emergence of a broad measure of liberal consensus over economic and social policy caused the post-de Gaulle Fifth to be dubbed 'the republic of the centre'. This did not mean that these were easy or entirely harmonious years, however. France was very badly hit by the oil shocks of the early 1970s which brought 30 years of post-war growth to an abrupt halt, revealing significant underlying problems with the structure and competiveness of the national economy.[68] This gave impetus to a wider questioning of long-standing Gaullist verities about the internal and external dimensions of national identity, the first intimations of what would develop into 'acute anxiety about the decline of [French] culture, language, and way of life under the onslaughts of economic and cultural globalization'.[69]

The passing of de Gaulle also impacted decisively on French collective memory, as his 'carefully constructed myth' – his 'sacred and edifying history of the Resistance' – was shattered. In the generalised political, cultural and social ferment that precipitated and followed 1968, self-deluding evasion was challenged by a fresh eagerness to confront the murky realities of the war era candidly, and cosy consensus was supplanted by fierce contestation. Marcel Ophuls' controversial documentary film *Le Chagrin et La Pitié*, released in 1971, exposed the extent of collaboration, *attentisme* and anti-Semitism, and probed the ambiguous, unheroic facets of resistance.[70] Official attitudes here ran counter to a growing public hunger for openness. Pompidou and Giscard were not interested 'either in resuscitating the resistance myth and its fading glories or in leading the nation in a collective soul-searching over the realities of the Dark Years'. Rather, they 'fostered a kind of forgetfulness or "quietism" that sought either to put the past behind or defuse its more troubling ideological valences': hence Pompidou's famous 1972 declaration that it was time to 'draw a veil over the past' and Giscard's initiative in 1975 to downgrade the commemoration of VE Day. The outraged public reaction to Pompidou's surreptitious pardoning of Paul Touvier, a member of Vichy's paramilitary police who had been condemned to death *in absentia* in the post-war purges, demonstrated that these efforts were unavailing.[71]

Since the public had lost its appetite for forgetting, this no longer offered a route to national reconciliation. Instead, the war years acquired an unprecedented prominence across French culture in a so-called 'forties revival' and, even though some of the representations generated carried a pacificatory, depoliticising charge, the drive towards questioning received truths was unstoppable. From the mid-1970s, France entered – according to Rousso's categorisation – a phase of 'obsession' with the wartime past, its public life rent by a long succession of explosive political, cultural and judicial scandals. Crucial here was the awakening of Jewish memory, which led to the gradual uncovering of French complicity in the Holocaust, as part of the wider revelation of the full extent and implications of collaboration. That the significance of this legacy remained highly contested, however, (pointing to enduring cleavages within the nation) was illustrated at the close of the 1970s by the emergence of public expressions of Holocaust denial and protests against the indictment of Vichy officials for crimes against humanity.[72]

In part, this progressive shift in collective memory was instigated by the transnational phenomenon of the emergence of a heightened Jewish self-consciousness, with the demand for recognition of the Holocaust at its heart. In part, too, it was a consequence of generic factors such as generational change and the opening up of political space (here, after the demise of de Gaulle) which operated to similar effect in other countries during this period. Shifts in prevailing discourses of national identity constitute another such factor, and in this instance the imbrication of identity and memory is particularly marked: the efflorescence of compulsive memories of Vichy not only occurred 'alongside a general crisis of French identity', in the view of some authorities the former was an effect of the latter.[73]

Writing of the dissolution of 'a unified national consciousness' in France since the 'turning point' of the mid-1970s, Pierre Nora attributed it to three 'apparently unrelated upheavals'. First, the termination of the economic boom made 'the definitive end of the peasant world painfully apparent'; growth had transformed the nation's social composition, eliminating 'the very bedrock of a stability that had endured for a thousand years'. Second, the abandonment of Gaullism's mnemonic apparatus induced a 'period of historical weightlessness' and disorientating 'uprooting', just as brute international realities ensured that the French 'at last internalized their country's transition from the status of a great power to one of a middle-range power' (with the demise of empire and advance of European integration). Third, the waning potency of Marxism came to stand synecdochically for the exhaustion of all hopes for revolutionary change and left French political culture bereft; the loss of the idea of 'an end to history', of a sense of direction, amounted to the 'dissipation of the mirage in which the fatherland of revolution had so long wished to believe'. Collectively, these destabilising shocks marked 'the beginning of the end of French exceptionalism' and triggered a new era of introspective commemorative fever:

'a delving into the depths, a turning inward, a quest for familiar landmarks'.[74] (Other writers have adduced additional factors militating in the same direction, including the challenges posed to the traditional coherence of French identity by immigration and the consequent rise of multicultural diversity.[75])

The shift in collective memory towards a contested confrontation with Vichy can certainly be linked to the eruption of all-encompassing insecurity about national identity diagnosed by Nora (even if his account of the transformation of French consciousness of the past also has important ramifications beyond that national case[76]). Gaullism attempted to hegemonise a particular reading of the resistance in national memory in the service of a particular identitarian project. But with its passing this sense of national identity fragmented, formerly repressed historical subjects were opened up for investigation and plural contestation emerged as the mnemonic analogue of the triumph of sectional identities (in Nora's terms 'national identity was replaced by social identities'[77]). Thus Rousso describes the wider revolution in 'the way the French see their nation's history':

> The heroic reading of the past – the glue that held together French identity – has slowly been giving way to critical readings, 'plural' readings, readings with strong moralizing tendencies, and readings that do not lack a certain masochism ... These debates have been fueled by the ethical questioning of a new generation in search of a concept of citizenship different from the one defended by the wartime generations, imbued as it was with a Gaullist or Communist perspective, and even more by the weight of the tragedies that these generations lived through.[78]

Academic history was certainly implicated in the upheavals of the 1970s. In 1973 the publication of a French translation of a book on *Vichy France* by a young American historian Robert Paxton caused a sensation. Paxton argued that Vichy had enthusiastically collaborated with the Germans, demolishing the idea that Pétain had played some kind of double game; moreover, he contended that the National Revolution had been an ideological project of genuine substance, with authentically French roots (even in its anti-Semitism), and that Vichy had enjoyed considerable popularity until the war turned against the Axis.[79] These arguments directly contravened previously dominant readings of Vichy and provoked a 'firestorm of controversy', but they were in tune with the new critical atmosphere and have since become orthodox.[80] Paxton's positioning as a foreigner may have contributed to his ability to offer a novel perspective on Vichy, but many French historians were moving in the same direction. Although the *Annales* remained generally pre-eminent within French historiography, the 1970s witnessed a palpable blossoming of contemporary history writing: 'the study of World War II soon developed into a flourishing discipline'. This was partly facilitated by a series of legislative moves to liberalise archival access, meaning that theoretically a 30 year rule was in operation by 1979, though in practice here France still had 'a long

way to go compared with other western countries'. Important new work
began to be published on the Vichy regime and French society during the
occupation, and on Jewish policy and French fascism; moreover, its findings
began to filter through into educational curricula. (Writing on the resistance
was rather marginalised by these new preoccupations, though it continued, in
a less celebratory key than formerly).[81]

Writing on the defeat and its origins can also be incorporated into this
reading. As Vichy and the Holocaust became the focus of French collective
memory, 1940 remained overshadowed: Giscard's rousing warning in 1978
that the electoral victory of the left would usher in a new debacle was a rare
exception to this rule.[82] In the early 1970s, scholarship also remained stuck in
a similar and familiar mould. In general, French historians neglected it – 'very
little has been written about [the] leadership of France in the approach to
war' – preferring 'to leave the war of words to the memorialists and
publicists'.[83] In a rather circular fashion, the hegemony of the decadence
framework created the impression that the subject was not worth studying,
since it presupposed that French leaders were unwilling or unable to play a
significant role in international affairs. Commentators also speculated that the
tardy opening of archives, the product of political reserve and ingrained
bureaucratic habits of secrecy, underpinned this reluctance. Yet behind this,
there perhaps lurked lingering trauma: 'those going down to inglorious
surrender sustain wounds in the mind not easily healed ... Nerve endings
are still exposed'. When French historians did address the subject, the overwhelming tendency remained to vent bitter 'displeasure with the Third
Republic'. Anglo-American writers generally ploughed the same furrow,
perpetuating the 'legends' of a 'peculiarly rotten political regime' and a
'peculiarly decadent army', and in cruder accounts readily identifying 'idiots
and traitors'. These stereotypes were reinscribed in a clutch of high-profile
accounts of the debacle that appeared at the end of the 1960s from Guy
Chapman, Alistair Horne and William Shirer.[84] These were all suffused with
a fatalistic sense of 1940 as preordained by secular decay: hence Chapman's
conclusion that 'neither politically, nor militarily, nor psychologically,
was the French nation in a state to face the war into which ... it was
inveigled'.[85]

There had been intimations in earlier scholarship of alternative perspectives.
In 1956 Colonel Adolphe Goutard dubbed the campaign of 1940 'the war
of missed opportunities'. Rather than ascribing the defeat to ineluctable
'metaphysical causes', Goutard stressed instead the role of flawed doctrine and
command mistakes.[86] His emphasis on contingency was unusual, even if the
institutionalised failings of the military did also figure in conventional
renderings of decadence. Similarly, a Canadian scholar John Cairns mused in
the 1950s about the tendency of historians overwhelmingly to seek the causes
of defeat only in factors internal to France, neglecting the fact that it was
really an *Allied* defeat.[87] While specialists noted these pleas for a less
moralistic and more systematic contextualisation of French policy, however,

they scarcely dented decadence's grip on the wider historical imagination. Perhaps the most thoughtful body of work on the origins of the war in the 1950s and 1960s was produced by a group of historians at the Sorbonne headed by Pierre Renouvin. In response to the provocations of the *Annales* school, Renouvin, together with Maurice Baumont and Jean-Baptiste Duroselle, pioneered the transformation of narrow diplomatic history into an international history, one that took seriously the role of profound forces and structural factors (geographic, demographic, economic, ideological and psychological).[88] Apprising the 1930s through the lens of this thematically expansive practice, and interpreting them in a succession of general treatments of international relations between the wars, these historians were 'alive to the powerful constraints on French policy-making imposed by France's demographic and industrial inferiority in relation to its principal European rival as well as its lack of a great power ally willing to join in resisting Nazi revisionism'. Yet, as Peter Jackson has argued, this sensitivity to structural constraints did not necessarily entail a fully-fledged break with orthodoxy; locating the sources of French weakness in collective psychology, ideological division, elite self-interest, economic backwardness and an insidious lassitude 'was not far from the language of national decline'.[89]

There was other writing, especially outside France, which eschewed talk of decadence in trying to explain the deficiencies in French preparations for war, but until the 1970s it remained merely suggestive.[90] In that decade, however, there was both a palpable acceleration of scholarship on war origins and a flowering of revisionist approaches. Doubtless archival factors contributed to the construction of much more detailed and sophisticated readings. From 1963 volumes covering the 1930s in the official series *Documents Diplomatiques Français* began to appear (edited by Renouvin and his colleagues), though coverage would not be completed until the mid-1980s. More significantly, as noted above, crucial political, diplomatic and military archives began to be opened, even if for many years certain parts of certain collections were – sometimes for quite mysterious reasons – only available to favoured scholars who were granted exceptional access.[91] These materials provided the practical basis for a new wave of scholarship on French policy between the wars, beginning with innovative work exploring the complex interplay of economics, strategy and diplomacy in the aftermath of the First World War, crediting 'France's leaders with more imagination and flexibility than had previous studies'.[92] Yet there is scope to doubt how far the emergence of new sources actually drove revisionism: as one perceptive commentator observed, studies based on unprecedented access to a 'wealth of documentation' sometimes cleaved to 'old assumptions' whilst others with more slender material bases advanced original interpretations.[93] Due weight must also therefore be given to the broader context and ideational variables; the dissolution of former fixed coordinates of French national identity and collective memory created a normative environment conducive both to the generation and flourishing of alternative readings of the past on this subject too.

Within France, some scholars moved, albeit tentatively, to embrace new and more sympathetic interpretations. In 1975 Jacques Néré published a history of French foreign policy in the era of the world wars which argued that while France's leaders had certainly committed diplomatic and military errors, these were 'not on the whole greater than those which, since men are not infallible, are committed in even the healthiest and soundest political systems'. Moreover, he was refreshingly attuned to the constraints under which policy-makers laboured, and specifically to the responsibilities of other states. French policy-makers had perceived the dangers of Nazi revisionism and had tried to forestall it, but preserving the Versailles system proved impossible without adequate assistance from the other victorious powers, Britain and the United States; the tragedy was that French policy 'was faced with a task which was both necessary and unattainable'.[94]

Néré's work illustrated two central elements in revisionist thinking. First, talk of stupidity and incompetence gave way to an appreciation of the vigour and initiative that policy-makers had demonstrated in confronting the challenges of the 1930s. The notion of a decaying Third Republic drifting helplessly to defeat was challenged, for example, by analysis of the substantial progress made in rearmament from the mid-1930s, and of the perceptible national recovery that France experienced in the last year of peace, as public opinion rallied round the government and production of war materiel accelerated. Second, developing the earlier insights of the Sorbonne international historians, scholars elaborated a much more nuanced understanding of the dilemmas facing policy-makers; instead of blithely condemning their timidity, they elucidated the web of factors that circumscribed their freedom of action, including an unfavourable military balance, unreliable allies, limited industrial and financial resources, and the complexities of domestic politics and public opinion.[95] There was a slight tension between these two strands, since one seemed to point to the contingency of the French defeat (sometimes attributing great significance to short term developments like the erosion of confidence during the Phoney War) while the other could verge on determinism, suggesting that it was on balance highly probable given the formidable array of internal and external problems facing political leaders. But the locus of interpretation in either case was a world away from earlier denunciatory portrayals of doom foreordained by profound societal decay.

Foreign scholars often made somewhat bolder revisionists. In 1978 the Canadian Robert Young produced a thought-provoking study of the relationship between French foreign policy and military planning in the 1930s. Writing explicitly against caricatures of the French as 'directionless and defeatist, paralyzed by indecision' and 'malaise-ridden', Young argued that the men of the Third Republic evinced 'a seriousness of purpose toward the perils at hand, a determination to resist German attempts at hegemony, [and] a willingness to devote enormous care and effort to the cause of national defence'. The French consistently pursued a coherent security policy, carefully and rationally calibrated in light of diverse domestic and foreign constraints, premised on strong Franco-British cooperation and the fighting of 'a long war of attrition'. By the summer of 1939, with the hardening of British policy after the occupation of Prague, it appeared that this strategy had prevailed; contrary to 'the image of an inept and somnolent France draped on the arm of an alert and attentive Britain', the French had 'not only succeeded in winning their one indispensable ally but did so on the very terms which their vision of the next war proclaimed to be inevitable'. Granted, the defeat needed to be explained, but as Young opined 'edifices collapse for reasons other than rotten foundations just as death by violence or misadventure befalls more than the already infirm': contingent errors of military judgement and 'conceptual failure' in the campaigns of 1940 were primarily responsible. Young qualified his rehabilitation by conceding that pre-war French policy had not been 'sparkling or brilliant', but his overall aim was to 'restore to France a greater measure of independence, of rational and coherent motivation, of sensible planning, of dignity, than hitherto has been the case'.[96] Jeffrey Gunsburg defended French strategic policy even more vigorously, and developed Cairns' argument that France's allies (or putative allies) must bear a considerable share of the blame for 1940.[97]

Given the relatively low profile of the defeat in French collective memory, this strand of revisionist work did not arouse the same feelings as the parallel rethinking of the occupation years. Yet this did not mean that there was nothing at stake emotionally and politically. Colonel Pierre le Goyet found his career suffered as a consequence of his 'at best guardedly sympathetic' 1976 study of Gamelin, since he became *'persona non grata* at his place of work as a research archivist in the French army historical service'.[98] Moreover, revisionist work did not entirely displace the older framework, as was testified by the appearance in 1979 of Duroselle's authoritative study of French policy in the 1930s tellingly entitled *La Décadence*. Duroselle had succeeded Renouvin as chair of contemporary history at the Sorbonne in 1964 and was the dominant figure in French international history, with unparalleled access to the archives. Although Duroselle did not quite diagnose a thoroughgoing societal malaise, the political failings on which he focused – institutional deficiencies in the machinery of government ('the structural instability of executive power'), the sclerotic political culture of the Third Republic, a lack of imagination and a woeful irresponsibility in the governing elite – were familiar from the older literature. Duroselle depicted a France beset by political instability and division, an uncontrollable economic crisis and feeble leadership, its government buffeted by a 'pacifist tornado' in public opinion and unable to formulate long-range policy, drifting inexorably towards a tragic fate.[99] Specialists criticised Duroselle for failing to locate his work on an historiographical terrain and for leaving his central argument underdeveloped; for many, the very act of revivifying the dusty interpretive notion of decadence was unfortunate.[100] Yet this weighty intervention demonstrated that the tenacious Gaullist interpretation had certainly not been vanquished by the tidal wave of obsessive revisionings of the past.

Beyond France too there were scholars still more inclined to condemn than defend as the historiography fragmented and many diverse permutations were developed. For example, in an important 1977 study Anthony Adamthwaite catalogued the various structural circumstances that 'cabined and confined' policymakers. 'French diplomacy was crippled by internal divisions', the political institutions of the Third Republic were 'singularly ill-equipped' for contemporary challenges, while governing energies were 'almost wholly absorbed by the fight to save the franc and the search for economic recovery'; the 'continual shrinking of French power' and the absence of 'the inherent stamina needed to sustain a great power role' hampered efforts to cope with the Nazi menace. French policy-makers sought an agreement with Germany, but refused to pay the price of 'the liquidation of French interests in central and eastern Europe'. However, they also failed to devise a suitable military strategy or to concert a sufficiently robust Allied diplomatic front to defeat or deter Hitler. Despite his acknowledgment of French decline, Adamthwaite rejected the determinism of decadence: 'the dénouement of 1940 was not an inevitable one'. Yet he also distanced himself from the revisionist views that policy-makers acquitted themselves well or had no alternatives. 'Timidity was the dominant characteristic of the political leadership' and policy-makers 'did retain some freedom of manoeuvre'. Overall his judgement on French leaders was harsh; had they exerted themselves more 'to rebuild national unity in 1938–39 and to reshape military policy', had they behaved more firmly sooner with the British, then they 'might have averted the débâcle of 1940'.[101] This was a distinctive position, acknowledging constraints, but emphasising the contingency of events and the culpability of individual statesmen.

The historiography of France's fall decisively changed during this period. Having long been a 'Cinderella subject' dominated interpretively by decadence, the volume of serious scholarship burgeoned and a more diverse range of views came into play.[102] Revisionist arguments emerged, but the decadence framework was also refurbished and other judgemental perspectives were elaborated. Disentangling the causes of this transformation is problematic. The rise of a genuinely international history might seem to be an essential precondition, since by sensitising practitioners to political, economic, social and strategic constraints it often inclined them towards benign judgements on policy-makers. Yet *La Décadence* amply demonstrates that such an interpretive consequence is by no means guaranteed. Similarly, the opening of the archives certainly contributed to the emergence of more nuanced evaluations but this did not entail uniform approbation. Finally, some commentators stress how foreign scholars propelled revisionism forwards, implying that their physical and emotional distance from the passions of French politics and history facilitated their more measured assessments. Yet there were orthodox and revisionist scholars on both sides of the Channel and of the Atlantic (and Rousso himself in another context has rejected as a 'cliché' the idea that 'it took the arrival of foreign scholars … to generate scholarly interest' in the newly voguish subjects[103]). Moreover, foreign – and especially British – scholars are as often castigated for failing to transcend their stereotypical prejudices about the effete and excitable French as they peddle narratives of decadence. (This phenomenon received an additional boost in these years. The opening of the British archives long before the French saw the prejudicial musings of British observers in the 1930s being recycled and entrenched as historical truth; thus in Young's words, 'many of the recent works on British policy tend to reinforce and reproject the image of France as the sick man of Europe, ill at ease and lamentably prepared for war'.[104])

Supplementing these operative factors with consideration of the politics of identity and memory enables a fuller understanding. Certainly, it was not the case that scholarship blossomed because of a transformation in the wider French collective memory of 1940. The defeat continued to be obscured by what followed it, and this revisionist scholarship was never as controversial as writing on collaboration and the Holocaust. Yet it nonetheless seems plausible to link the emergence of revisionism with the wider shift to the 'obsession' phase in the 'Vichy Syndrome' and the general crisis of national identity that it connoted, since these processes occurred at precisely the same time. Although Gaullism did not make a particular representation of 1940 central to its mnemonic armoury, nonetheless the notion of a decadent Third Republic was an integral component of 'the Gaullist idea that the Fifth Republic has finally cured France's constitutional ills'.[105] Hence in the climate of the 1970s, defending decadence was a gesture that implied the defence both of Gaullism and of the established self-confident verities of French national identity, while challenging it through revisionism was in tune with the rising forces of fragmentation, dislocation and candid auto-interrogation.

'Obsession' signified a new willingness on the part of the French to pose difficult questions to themselves about their history and identity, and the opening up of what happened in and before 1940 to fresh scrutiny had a similar valence. Previously, the traumatic impact of defeat had been airbrushed through insistence on the rottenness of the past and the opportunities for renewal ultimately opened up by the disappearance of the Third Republic. But was greater temporal distance and a generalised loss of moorings at last permitting painful memories and troubling realisations to emerge, as implied by Rousso's invocation of the 'return of the repressed'? This is certainly one plausible reading of the slightly despairing concluding thoughts of the revisionist Néré:

> As far as France is concerned, she seems now to have recovered her material and her vital forces. Let us not deceive ourselves, however. This fall has injured even those who do not know the details of this past or who do not wish to remember them. Assurance, confidence in herself and in her free institutions, and even a certain *joie de vivre*, have vanished from France. Politically and morally, she has received a wound from which she has not recovered.[106]

'Hollow years' or 'best efforts'? Pluralism in an era of obsession

French political life since the early 1980s presents a somewhat paradoxical picture. On the positive side, constitutional stability was entrenched; the system survived prolonged periods of 'cohabitation' – a president co-existing with an assembly and government of different political complexion – under both Mitterrand and his post-1995 right-wing successor, Jacques Chirac. This testified to the endurance of a significant measure of consensus on key policy issues, indeed 'the displacement of totalizing ideologies by a pragmatic liberalism'. Yet on the negative side, both left- and right-wing blocs were periodically beset by internal division, powerful extra-systemic challenges to the established parties emerged on both flanks in the shape of the Greens and Jean-Marie Le Pen's National Front, and public disillusion and alienation from formal politics mushroomed.[107] Endemic structural economic problems and growing inequality fuelled social discontent, which intermittently erupted into violent protest. Thus in the autumn of 2005 French cities were convulsed by a wave of rioting, largely driven by French-born youths of African or Arab extraction incensed at police brutality, racial discrimination and unemployment. The scale of the threat to public order drove the government to declare a state of emergency, and triggered extensive soul-searching about France's relationship to its colonial past and the validity of its republican model of citizenship, which had apparently entirely failed to facilitate the integration of immigrants. For some commentators the crisis was so grave that it called the very legitimacy of the state into question.[108]

This demonstrated how the discourse of inquietude about French national identity that had emerged in the 1970s had only intensified in subsequent decades. Writing in the 1990s Julian Jackson asserted that national identity certainly constituted 'one of the current obsessions of French politics', citing in evidence the proliferation of an elegiac, 'mystically nationalist' historical literature on French identity, controversies over multiculturalism precipitated by the wearing of Muslim headscarves in (secular) state schools and the extended arguments about the meaning of the French Revolution stimulated by its bicentenary celebrations in 1989.[109] Negotiating the legacy of empire assumed an increasing prominence here from the 1990s, with multiple resonant interconnections between demands for recognition and apology for victims of colonial violence, especially during the Algerian war, and the disaffection of second-generation immigrant youth. Official responses embodied contradictory impulses; the attempted introduction in 2005 of a law requiring teachers to stress 'the positive role of the French overseas presence' proved hugely controversial at home and abroad, and the inauguration of a national day of remembrance for the victims of slavery in 2006 was in part an effort to repair the damage.[110]

National identity also figured prominently as a theme in the 2007 presidential elections. A coterie of intellectuals associated with the eventual victor, combative right-winger Nicolas Sarkozy, espoused a 'declinist' analysis of France's 'profound malaise', attacking the supposedly stultifying consensus born in the Mitterrand years.[111] Sarkozy himself had explicitly linked up the nation's political woes with its memory and identity during the history teaching controversy, condemning those who wanted 'to apologise for being French' and asserting that 'France is a great country because she has a great history'.[112] At his inauguration in May 2007 Sarkozy reiterated the theme, 'promising to create a new France, rooted in pride in the values of an "old France" of hard work, discipline, patriotism and self-sacrifice'.[113] Robust neo-liberal reform, an end to excessive repentance and reinvigorated national pride were here inextricably intertwined.

Collective memory of the Second World War was naturally implicated in all this. The shattering of established conceptions of national identity and the onset of the obsessive phase of the 'Vichy Syndrome' in the 1970s were constituent parts of the same shifting discursive structure, and over subsequent decades the crisis in national consciousness and proliferating critical histories were mutually sustaining. In the world of politics, the wartime past figured prominently in the rhetoric around the 1981 presidential election, and the emergence of a National Front that flirted with Holocaust denial and promoted a 'nationalistic, authoritarian and exclusionistic discourse', reminiscent of Vichy, ensured that this retained 'more than academic historical interest'.[114] In 1994 intense controversy erupted around Mitterrand when a biography revealed the full extent of his political and ideological entanglement with Vichy, and the expediency of his eventual move into the resistance; the return of the president's personal repressed was emblematic of the wider culture's trajectory.[115] There was also an important judicial strand to collective memory, with successive high profile trials of Lyon Gestapo chief Klaus Barbie in 1987, of Paul Touvier in 1994 and then of high-ranking Vichy bureaucrat Maurice Papon, responsible for deportations of Jews, in 1998. Convictions of collaborators for crimes against humanity underlined French responsibility for atrocities committed under Vichy.[116] (Since Papon had had a successful post-war administrative and political career, and as prefect of the Paris police in the 1960s was culpable for murderous brutalities inflicted on Algerian nationalist demonstrators, his case was multiply evocative of evasion and the imbrication of the 'Vichy Syndrome' with postcolonial guilt.[117]) These trials were often vaunted as cathartic but simply fuelled a compulsive, even masochistic, interest in uncovering the murky secrets of the wartime past.

Given the escalating global salience of Holocaust consciousness, it was scarcely surprising that Jewish memory continued to figure prominently. In 1995 Jacques Chirac made an unprecedented gesture when he spoke on the anniversary of the *Vélodrome d'Hiver* round-ups in Paris and admitted that 'the criminal insanity of the occupying forces was backed up by the French people and by the French State' in an act of 'collective sin'. (His predecessors including Mitterrand had always been markedly ambivalent about conceding official complicity in the Holocaust.)[118] Pressure for the state to confess full legal responsibility and grant compensation has continued unabated ever since, though resistance to the notion of any continuity between Vichy and the post-war republic lingers hard.[119] The inquisitorial gaze was directed not only at known collaborators but also at some sainted figures from the resistance: in 1997 Raymond and Lucie Aubrac were subjected to a round-table interrogation by historians, and made to answer accusations that they had been recruited by the Gestapo or had embellished and airbrushed their wartime activities in their memoirs.[120] Similarly, during the debates around the Papon trial, it often seemed as if Gaullism itself was in the dock, charged with having ignored the Holocaust and connived in the rehabilitation of Vichy criminals by crafting the 'myth of the resistance'.[121] The hysterical and hyperbolic tone of these indictments aroused anxieties that the juggernaut of reckoning had run out of control. Rousso, for example, came to deprecate the excess of sensationalistic scandal-mongering in the name of the 'duty to remember', arguing that the application of contemporary moral and historical perspectives to the past threatened anachronistic distortion. Moreover, fretting over Vichy had become 'just a substitute for the urgent demands of the present, or still worse, a refusal of the future'.[122]

Commentators regularly prophesy that the era of intense obsession must soon pass, and there is scope to debate whether 'by the late 1990s the haunting memory of Vichy was at last being put to rest'.[123] Yet in the new century war-related issues continue to provoke national controversy; witness, for example, the success of the 2006 film *Indigènes* about the forgotten contribution of North African soldiers in the fight against Nazism, which prompted the government finally to rectify a decades-old injustice and increase the pensions paid to former colonial troops to equal those of French veterans.[124] Moreover, Rousso's plea for measured and calm reflection to supplant frenzied self-flagellation was prone to exploitation for more dubious revisionist purposes.[125] Thus Sarkozy has demonstrated a keen awareness of the potential political utility of war memory. Defining himself against the penitent Chirac, he argued that repeated gestures of apology to minority activists militated against the transcendence of racial, ethnic and religious particularities and the cultivation of healthy identification with the nation. Indeed, Sarkozy has revived in modified form the Gaullist discourse of unity and grandeur that many thought long buried. This at any rate was one reading of his decision to pay homage on the day of his inauguration at a memorial to 35 young resistance fighters murdered by the Nazis in August 1944. This return to the practice of eulogizing heroic resistance martyrs as inspirational model citizens and patriots was pregnant with implications for French memory and identity.[126] Only time will tell whether this conservative reaction against recent dominant trends in collective remembering will succeed in launching an entirely new phase of the 'Vichy Syndrome'.

Academic history remained embroiled in these developments. The establishment in 1979 of the Institute for Contemporary History, with Rousso later its figurehead, drove forward the study of the recent past and helped to gain it unprecedented legitimacy. The continued accretion of documents facilitated the proliferation of diverse work on Vichy, and in the 1990s resistance historiography also enjoyed a palpable renaissance as the fading influence of the participant generation emancipated a young cohort of historians, opening up fruitful new perspectives.[127] Contemporary historians also began reflexive interrogation of collective memory, laying the foundations for Rousso's breakthrough analysis.[128] That the journal *Annales* dedicated a special issue to Vichy, the occupation and the Holocaust in 1993 demonstrated the enhanced status of this historical field within French intellectual life.[129] Although the thrust of much of this scholarship was to advance more complex and nuanced interpretations of these phenomena, substituting shades of grey for stark black and white, nonetheless simply by virtue of its existence it contributed to 'keeping Vichy in the public limelight'.[130] Hence Nora's observation that Rousso himself had unwittingly become a significant vector of the very syndrome that he had sought to critique.[131]

During this period, international history writing on the 1930s and the debacle also flourished as never before. Building on the innovations of the 1970s, scholarship accumulated and became more sophisticated and diverse. Again this did not reflect any drastic alteration in the place of 1940 in French collective memory; the defeat was more peripheral than ever during the most feverish phase of Vichy 'obsession', and was then further eclipsed by the eruption of the bitter legacy of Algeria. So this writing did not have the same public profile or cultural resonance as work on Vichy or the Holocaust. Yet international historians in France and abroad had now established the subject as a thriving field of inquiry, in the context of a larger transnational preoccupation with the origins of the Second World War; and given the quotidian scholarly dynamic of this robustly empiricist sub-discipline, continued archival releases continued to fuel research.

Different authorities taxonomise the main interpretations in different ways, but the astute French historiographer Pierre Grosser has identified four main approaches. The first, and most censorious, was the traditional emplotment that attributed France's feeble diplomacy and subsequent military defeat to profound failings in physical capabilities and willpower, in other words to the inexorable workings of decadence. The second denies this implication that France was doomed to catastrophe by her manifold difficulties, even though it accepts their existence, and recuperates contingency by focusing on failures of leadership and poor decision-making. Shifting to more charitable shades of interpretation, a third option seeks to explain French failure to adopt more resolute or effective policies in the 1930s, not by invoking an intrinsic malaise but rather by cataloguing in mitigation the formidable array of internal and external constraints impeding policy-makers. Finally, the strongest revisionist interpretation not only disputes that France was decaying, but spins the record of policy-making in the 1930s in a positive manner, stressing the nation's underlying strength and the sagacious choices that brought it to the brink of war in 1939 in a confident and united mood; on this reading, defeat must be explained by the contingencies – especially military – of the campaign of 1940.[132]

These categories are somewhat leaky, of course, but the schema offers a good rough guide to the interpretive terrain. In general, French historians remained more wedded than their foreign counterparts to 'readings of ineffectual pre-war French civil–military leadership, inept governmental diplomacy, and deepening national division'.[133] Duroselle's successor at the Sorbonne, René Girault, thus averred in 1984 that 'decay was in the air', adducing internal ideological fissures as the root cause of a fatal deficit in national will-power.[134] Other specialists concurred that defeat was a judgement rendered on a 'deliquescent' republic, the culmination of a long process of social and political decomposition of which Bloch's account might still stand as 'definitive'.[135] More general studies of France in the 1930s adopted the same explanatory framework; Serge Berstein, for example, argued that 'the sclerosis of ideologies and the fear of risk of a morally exhausted people' led the country 'ineluctably towards the tragedy of 1940'.[136] Not all French scholars were comfortable adopting this viewpoint, but there was nonetheless 'a noticeable reluctance to dispute the interpretive simplicity of decadence'.[137] This said, many scholars abroad remained of similar mind.[138] Eugen Weber dubbed the 1930s the 'hollow years', conjuring a picture of a nation in total disarray, divided, irresolute and 'no longer a great power'.[139] In his epic 1989 narrative of the last year of peace, Donald Cameron Watt was dismissive of a Third Republic 'in its penultimate stage of decay', its leaders congenitally chary of taking responsibility: 'passing the buck, like "Hunt-the-slipper", was central to the French system of government'.[140] Similar assumptions underpinned other denunciations such as Nicole Jordan's account of how the French sought to wage 'a cut-price conflict on the peripheries', compelling their East European allies to bear the main burden in the fight against Germany. While conceding a certain coherence to French strategy, Jordan was fired by moral indignation at its dishonesty and cynicism, and portrayed defeat in 1940 as an inevitable consequence of 'a tragic reluctance to shed French blood': 'by always attempting to fight the war elsewhere, Gamelin in effect made it impossible to fight at all'.[141]

Interpretations of this stripe merge into those in the second category, where the tone is still pejorative but the attribution of responsibility is rather more restricted. Work stressing the importance of French anti-communism offers a good illustration here. Michael Carley's study of the failure to forge a Grand Alliance in 1939 identified western anti-Soviet prejudice as the key operative factor. Conservative policy-makers were so blinded by their obsessive hatred and fear of Bolshevism that they failed to perceive the much larger threat to their national interest posed by Nazism, and refused to take up sincere Soviet offers of an alliance. Thus summarised, such a view might fit the paradigm of a decadent France, irretrievably plagued by ideological animosity, its leaders morally bankrupt, craven and paralysed in the face of the Nazi menace. Yet although Carley agreed that there was much rotten with the state of France, he distanced himself from this totalising perspective; resisting the notion that the course of events was predetermined, he called attention to the contemporary critics who advocated alternative policies in order to indict all the more forcefully his particular anti-communist 'villains and cowards'.[142] The quintessential exponent of this second position remains Anthony Adamthwaite, who expanded his analysis of French policy in a 1995 monograph covering the era of the two world wars. Adamthwaite stressed that the inter-war years did not constitute a preordained or inevitable 'slide to disaster', and that France 'was not as shabby and stagnant as traditionally portrayed'. There were undeniable constraints on French policy-making but defeat could not be seen as the inexorable product of 'deep-seated weaknesses' since it was a contingent outcome. 'Energetically led and supported by allies France could have warded off the German challenge and survived as an independent great power. Unhappily, the elements for success were wanting; decisive leadership, a revised grand strategy, self-confidence'. Ultimately, Adamthwaite was damning: 'if rulers and ruled had possessed the courage to say *merde* to Hitler before 1939 the story would have had a different ending'.[143]

This interpretation again shades into the next, which focuses squarely on the 'underlying structural causes' – 'political and economic weaknesses' – at work in the French defeat.[144] Here, policy-makers were not damnable but rather struggled creditably against adverse circumstances, or even had no choice but to act as they did. In a recent nuanced survey, Martin Thomas canvassed the diverse factors adduced to explain why (at least some) French policy-makers (at some points in time) advocated a policy of appeasement, including the shadow of the First World War and pacifist public opinion, the machinations of the political system, economic and financial difficulties, the military balance and the difficulties in securing reliable allies. Collectively these factors produced a decisive policy outcome at Munich: 'a faithful ally was betrayed owing to *realpolitik* calculations of limited financial reserves, insufficient momentum in rearmament, and well-founded doubts about the viability of an Eastern front without assured Soviet participation'. Yet for Thomas, the international dimension was crucial. 'The limitations of existing allies, the recalcitrance of some potential friends, the elusiveness of others, all were a powerful fillip to appeasement's proponents. France without a great power ally was a nation compelled to appease'.[145] This line of argument was often premised on an acceptance of French secular decline from great power status, without lapsing into the language of decadence. Thus according to Richard Overy, there was 'something grandly tragic about the French predicament between the wars': for 'a deeply conservative, defensive society, split by social conflict, undermined by a failing and unmodernised economy and [with] an empire in crisis', appeasement was 'a policy of realism'.[146] For this brand of revisionist, assessment of policy-makers must proceed from a recognition of 'the limits of French power and influence', and the 'acute constraints imposed by an unfavourable international balance of power and the need to work within a democratic political system and a capitalist system made fragile by the upheavals of the recent war'.[147] 'France's best efforts' ultimately 'failed to provide security'.[148] Yet since 'the challenges facing civilian and military policy makers were immense', this 'does not constitute evidence of corruption or moral decay'.[149]

It is often difficult to draw a clear distinction between this form of revisionism and the stronger version which constitutes Grosser's fourth category. Yet this last is characterised by an even more positive assessment of policy-makers, presenting them less as prisoners of circumstances than as figures responding with intelligence, creativity and a considerable measure of success to the challenges confronting them.[150] Biographical reinterpretations loomed large in the revisionist wave. Martin Alexander, for example, offered a measured defence of Gamelin, focusing on his role as 'architect of a programme of unprecedented peacetime defensive preparation'.[151] Similarly, Élisabeth du Réau provided a cautiously sympathetic defence of Daladier, stressing his 'industry and his unflinching patriotism', and the vital contribution he made to initiating French rearmament.[152] Together with studies of a range of thematic aspects of French policy, this scholarship presented a picture not 'of a society on the verge of implosion but instead of a nation preparing reluctantly' – but with some determination – 'to face the prospect of another bloodletting with its German neighbour'.[153]

These interpretations place great stress on developments in the last year of peace after Munich: 'in September 1938 the nation had been carried to the very brink of a war for which it was neither psychologically nor materially prepared. The brush with war was a dash of cold water to the face of a nation whose focus had been overwhelmingly inward. From this point onward the purse strings were opened for rearmament and public support began to coalesce for a *politique de fermeté*. French policy became more robust and assertive ... '.[154] Robert Young has summarised the crucial elements in this national resurgence: public opinion turned stoically to accept the need for resistance; industrial production accelerated and other economic indicators improved; rearmament steadily advanced so that the risk of war became at least thinkable; and French diplomacy towards Britain and other potential allies began to evince fresh vigour and initiative.[155] (Talbot Imlay amongst others has argued in this last respect that far from meekly following a lead, the French drove the Allied turn to resistance: 'it was the French and not the British who first decided that Germany had to be stopped, if necessary by war'.[156]) Although problems remained, 'in the summer of 1939 France was morally and materially ready to confront Nazi Germany'.[157]

Of course, it remains to explain why France nonetheless fell. In this endeavour, and against the occasionally determinist connotations of the previous revisionist mode, this strand emphasises contingency. Suggestions in the earlier military history literature that the outcome of the campaign in 1940 was not predetermined by French lassitude or weakness have now become utterly orthodox, certainly in the non-French literature.[158] On the one hand, this entails recognising the Allied nature of the defeat: 'the downfall of France can only be satisfyingly explained in the context of the destruction of an entire west European alliance'. On the other, it means focusing not on the alleged material inferiority of the Allied armies (a canard now 'conclusively interred') but rather on the more contingent matters of doctrine, tactics and generalship.[159] Although in many respects the French army was 'purposeful and not uninnovative', mistakes and misjudgements were evidently made.[160] In a recent large-scale study Ernest May identified intelligence failures rather than lack of moral fibre as crucial to the Allied defeat. In contrast to their complacent opponents, the Germans adroitly 'spied out and exploited the psychological and procedural weaknesses' of their enemies, allowing their comparatively weak forces to achieve the element of surprise and thus a decidedly *Strange Victory*.[161] Another means of restoring a sense of contingency to the defeat is to focus – as pioneering French work did – on the pernicious effects of the Phoney War in corroding morale and confidence in the war effort.[162] More recently, Talbot Imlay has also stressed how the situation in France deteriorated during the Phoney War as policy-makers were gripped by a rising sense of panic: 'growing political divisions and the real and perceived failure of economic mobilization fostered doubts about the country's ability to wage a long war, which in turn exacerbated the strategic crisis fuelled by the belief that time was an enemy'.[163]

In truth, it is slightly misleading to yoke Imlay together with this most assertive form of revisionism. Despite the sophistication of his conceptual apparatus, his doubts about the reality of French revival on the eve of war, criticism of policy-makers for lack of resolve and emphasis on the debilitating effects of endemic political polarization arguably align him more closely with other strands of interpretation. Of course, no classificatory system can entirely capture the variety and nuance of the arguments in play, and it is entirely salutary that scholars should seek to transcend the established parameters of interpretation. This was, for example, one of the signal virtues of Robert Young's stimulating 1996 invocation of ambivalence or ambiguity as the key to understanding French responses in the 1930s.[164] These qualifications do not, however, detract from the wider point that a plurality of views on the nature and causes of the fall of France flourished during these recent decades, the era of Vichy 'obsession'.

The loosening of Gaullist interpretive shackles in the 1970s allowed the revisionist dynamic inherent in professional disciplines to assert itself. Thereafter, international historians have generated a plurality of positive and negative interpretations by emphasising in different permutations the diverse variables of structure and agency, determinism and contingency, internal and external determinants and the ideational and the material. Peter Jackson has categorised orthodoxy as incarnating a stress on internal factors, agency and the ideational, whereas revisionism depends on external factors, structures and the material. This starkly dichotomised framework does not capture the nuances of the different variants in each tendency, which are produced through a more subtle and complex mingling of variables; yet the underlying point that the 'contending camps' are essentially animated by their 'contending approaches' to these interpretive alternatives is insightful and sound.[165]

Moreover, it is certainly more persuasive than viewing these interpretations as products of archival revelations. Viewed as story forms, and even leaving aside the issue of their possible correlation with generic narrative archetypes, these originate in the very events which they purport to describe. The emplotment of overarching and all-encompassing decadence is positively antique, while the variant in which degeneracy or enfeeblement is restricted to a particular class or group of leaders has been current since at least the immediate post-defeat recriminations; by the same token, the defence case at Riom was one of the first exercises in revisionism.

The defeat of 1940 has never been central in French collective memory, since it has been serially obscured by the great dramas of the occupation and latterly by postcolonial traumas. Yet it has nonetheless been consistently implicated in the fraught post-war negotiation of French national identity. Although it has exhibited some distinctive nuances, representations of it have broadly marched in step with the evolution of the 'Vichy Syndrome', from 'repressions' through to the current obsessive phase of pluralist contestation. Dilating on the historiographical manifestations of the 'national identity crisis' in France, Stefan Berger argues that it has 'produced multiple voices either discrediting or reclaiming particular versions of the national historical narrative, which had itself become the "broken mirror"'.[166] The continued debate around French national identity, manifest in Sarkozy's efforts to curtail destabilising interrogations and apologies and to resuscitate Gaullist grandeur, finds both an analogue and an expression in historiographical production, not just on Vichy but also on the origins of the war. The end of the interpretive hegemony of decadence and the fragmentation of the field thus both reflected and enacted this veritable 'existential crisis' in national identity.[167]

While the shape of the field itself thus carries an ideological valence, it is a less simple matter to divine the political import of individual interpretations. In a general sense, decadence arguments are in tune with traditional Gaullist attitudes while revisionist views chime rather with the disintegrative impulses in contemporary discourses on politics and memory, and the search for fresh ways of grounding national identity. More specifically, decadence interpretations focusing on the bankruptcy of the Third Republic and subsequent national rebirth can certainly be read as embodying 'a refusal, or a reluctance' to confront the waning of French power. If responsibility for the defeat could be assigned solely to a particular political regime and to its innate incapacities, then it was possible to deny 'that it had any significant implications for France's place in the world' and to recuperate conceptions of grandeur and independence. This is in palpable contrast to those iterations of revisionism that are premised on tallying the manifold constraints under which policy-makers chafed as a consequence of 'the geopolitical realities underlying France's decline'.[168] The emphasis of these revisionists on the dilemma of French policy-makers – suffering from a fatal want of allies, the diplomatic and geopolitical odds so heavily stacked against them that there was little they could do to repel Nazi Germany – is hardly compatible with de Gaulle's vaunted conviction that 'France is not really herself unless in the front rank'.[169] In this sense the historiographical revisionist turn can be interpreted as part of the process whereby France 'belatedly and obliquely' faced up to the trauma of 1940 and its implications for national identity.[170] With piquant irony, the trope of decadence long served as a screen to obfuscate the realities of decline.

Notes

1 Quoted in W. Fortescue, *The Third Republic in France, 1870–1940: Conflicts and Continuities* (London, Routledge, 2000), p. 213.

2 C. Fink, *Marc Bloch: A Life in History* (Cambridge, Cambridge University Press, 1989), pp. 205–40.

3 M. Bloch, *Strange Defeat: A Statement of Evidence Written in 1940* (New York, Norton, 1999, pb. edn), quotes at pp. 25, 174.

4 Fink, *Marc Bloch*, p. 321.

5 P. Jackson, 'Recent journeys along the road back to France, 1940', *Historical Journal*, vol. 39, no. 2, 1996, p. 497.

6 H. Rousso, *The Vichy Syndrome: History and Memory in France since 1944* (Cambridge, MA, Harvard University Press, 1991).

7 R. J. Young, 'A. J. P. Taylor and the problem with France', in G. Martel (ed.), *The Origins of the Second World War Reconsidered: A. J. P. Taylor and the Historians* (London, Routledge, 1999, 2nd edn), p. 85; J. Jackson, *The Fall of France: The Nazi Invasion of 1940* (Oxford, Oxford University Press, 2003), p. 188.

8 See, in particular, P. Jackson, 'Post-war politics and the historiography of French strategy and diplomacy before the Second World War', *History Compass*, vol. 4, no. 5, 2006, pp. 870–905.

9 J. Jackson, *France: The Dark Years, 1940–1944* (Oxford, Oxford University Press, 2001), pp. 602, 565, latterly quoting de Gaulle.

10 H. Rousso, quoted in J. Hellman, 'Wounding memories: Mitterrand, Moulin, Touvier, and the divine half-lie of resistance', *French Historical Studies*, vol. 19, no. 2, 1995, p. 483.

11 P. Lagrou, *The Legacy of Nazi Occupation: Patriotic Memory and National Recovery in Western Europe, 1945–1965* (Cambridge, Cambridge University Press, 2000).

12 Jackson, *France: The Dark Years*, p. 613.

13 Rousso, *The Vichy Syndrome*, p. 10.

14 For Rousso's subsequent thoughts, see É. Conan and H. Rousso, *Vichy: An Ever-Present Past* (Hanover, NH, University Press of New England, 1998); H. Rousso, *The Haunting Past: History, Memory, and Justice in Contemporary France* (Philadelphia, University of Pennsylvania Press, 2002).

15 A. Shennan, *The Fall of France, 1940* (London, Pearson, 2000), quotes at pp. 157, x.

16 S. Hoffmann, 'The trauma of 1940: a disaster and its traces', in J. Blatt (ed.), *The French Defeat of 1940: Reassessments* (Oxford, Berghahn, 1998), p. 357.

17 S. M. Osgood, 'Introduction', in S. M. Osgood (ed.), *The Fall of France, 1940: Causes and Responsibilities* (Boston, MA, D. C. Heath, 1965), p. viii; Rousso, *The Vichy Syndrome*, p. 279; Shennan, *The Fall of France, 1940*, pp. 156–61.

18 R. J. Golsan, 'The legacy of World War II in France: mapping the discourses of memory', in R. N. Lebow, W. Kansteiner and C. Fogu (eds), *The Politics of Memory in Postwar Europe* (Durham, NC, Duke University Press, 2006), p. 77.

19 H. Rousso, *Vichy: L'Événement, la Mémoire, l'Histoire* (Paris, Gallimard, 2001), pp. 9–51.

20 Jackson, *France: The Dark Years*, especially pp. 142–65.

21 Shennan, *The Fall of France, 1940*, p. 55.

22 Jackson, *France: The Dark Years*, pp. 354–81.

23 Pétain, quoted in P. Burrin, 'Vichy', in L. D. Kritzman (ed.), under the direction of P. Nora, *Realms of Memory: Rethinking the French Past: Vol. I: Conflicts and Divisions* (New York, Columbia University Press, 1996), p. 194.

24 A. Shennan, *Rethinking France: Plans for Renewal, 1940–1946* (Oxford, Oxford University Press, 1989).

25 Jackson, *France: The Dark Years*, p. 571.

26 Shennan, *The Fall of France, 1940*, pp. 35–39, quote at p. 35.

27 J-P. Sartre, *War Diaries: Notebooks from a Phoney War, November 1939–March 1940* (London, Verso, 1999, pb. edn), p. 175.

28 Jackson, 'Post-war politics and the historiography of French strategy and diplomacy before the Second World War', p. 872.

29 W. Schivelbusch, *The Culture of Defeat: On National Trauma, Mourning, and Recovery* (London, Granta, 2003), quotes at pp. 2, 30.

30 R. Gildea, *Marianne in Chains: In Search of the French Occupation, 1940–1945* (London, Macmillan, 2002), p. 3.

31 P. Pétain, 'Speech of October 11, 1940', in Osgood (ed.), *The Fall of France, 1940*, pp. 12–13.

32 Jackson, 'Post-war politics and the historiography of French strategy and diplomacy before the Second World War', p. 874.

33 Shennan, *The Fall of France, 1940*, p. 68, and more generally pp. 64–70.

34 R. J. Young, *France and the Origins of the Second World War* (London, Macmillan, 1996), p. 40.

35 Shennan, *The Fall of France, 1940*, p. 72, and pp. 70–75 for a broader discussion of Vichy's failure to negotiate the scapegoating/exculpation dynamic successfully.

36 Quoted in Jackson, *France: The Dark Years*, p. 397; Shennan, *The Fall of France, 1940*, p. 78.

37 Shennan, *The Fall of France, 1940*, pp. 75–82.

38 C. de Gaulle, *The Complete War Memoirs of Charles de Gaulle* (New York, Carroll and Graf, 1998, pb. edn), p. 998.

39 M. Agulhon, *De Gaulle: Histoire, Symbole, Mythe* (Paris, Plon, 2000), pp. 23–46.

40 A. von der Goltz and R. Gildea, 'Flawed saviours: the myths of Hindenburg and Pétain', *European History Quarterly*, vol. 39, no. 3, 2009, pp. 439–64.

41 'Pertinax' [A. Géraud], *The Gravediggers of France: Gamelin, Daladier, Reynaud, Pétain, and Laval* (New York, Doubleday, 1944, rev. edn), quotes at pp. 122, 33, 140, 163, 578–79.

42 R. Gildea, *France since 1945* (Oxford, Oxford University Press, 2002, 2nd edn), quotes at pp. 41, 51, 53.

43 Rousso, *The Vichy Syndrome*, pp. 15–59, quotes at pp. 16, 28.

44 Golsan, 'The legacy of World War II in France', p. 81.

45 Rousso, *The Vichy Syndrome*, pp. 60–97, quotes at pp. 94, 83; S. Hoffman, 'In the looking glass', in *The Sorrow and the Pity: A Film by Marcel Ophuls* (St Albans, Paladin, 1975), p. xiv. Lagrou, *The Legacy of Nazi Occupation*, cautions against ante-dating the emergence of the resistance myth, arguing that before the 1960s memories of suffering deportees were relatively more prominent. S. Farmer, *Martyred Village: Commemorating the 1944 Massacre at Oradour-sur-Glane* (Berkeley, CA, University of California Press, 1999) also stresses the theme of victimhood.

46 Shennan, *The Fall of France, 1940*, pp. 87–107, quotes at p. 100.

47 Young, *France and the Origins of the Second World War*, p. 41.

48 Rousso, *The Vichy Syndrome*, p. 17.

49 D. Chuter, *Humanity's Soldier: France and International Security, 1919–2001* (Oxford, Berghahn, 1996), especially pp. 214ff.; B. Heuser, 'Dunkirk, Diên Biên Phu, Suez or why France does not trust allies and has learnt to love the bomb', in C. Buffet and B. Heuser (eds), *Haunted by History: Myths in International Relations* (Oxford, Berghahn, 1998), pp. 157–74; Jackson, *The Fall of France*, pp. 239–47.

50 R. J. B. Bosworth, *Explaining Auschwitz and Hiroshima: History Writing and the Second World War, 1945–1990* (London, Routledge, 1993), pp. 94–117.

51 F. Braudel, 'Personal testimony', *Journal of Modern History*, vol. 44, no. 4, 1972, p. 454.

52 Jackson, *The Fall of France*, pp. 190–91; Rousso, *The Vichy Syndrome*, pp. 241–51.

53 J. C. Cairns, 'Along the road back to France 1940', *American Historical Review*, vol. 64, no. 3, 1959, pp. 583–603, quote at p. 586.

54 G. Bonnet, 'In defense of French policy', in D. E. Lee (ed.), *Munich: Blunder, Plot, or Tragic Necessity?* (Lexington, MA, D. C. Heath, 1970), pp. 13–27.

55 M. Baumont, 'French critics and apologists debate Munich', *Foreign Affairs*, vol. 25, no. 4, 1947, p. 690. Bonnet's memoirs have been characterised as 'a pretentious and windy far-rago of half-truths and evasions': 'forgetting that several excuses are always less convincing than one, Bonnet entangled himself in a web of contradictions' (A. Adamthwaite, *France and the Coming of the Second World War, 1936–1939* (London, Cass, 1977), p. 400).

56 Young, *France and the Origins of the Second World War*, p. 43.

57 H. Frey, *Representations of the Second World War: Ideological Currents in French History-Writing under the Fourth Republic*, unpublished PhD thesis, University of Surrey, 1998, pp. 105–36, quotes at p. 117, 126.

58 Young, *France and the Origins of the Second World War*, p. 44.

59 J. B. Wolf, 'The *élan vital* of France: a problem of historical perspective', in Osgood (ed.), *The Fall of France, 1940*, p. 9.

60 Young, 'A. J. P. Taylor and the problem with France', p. 85, and more broadly pp. 75–92.

61 A. J. P. Taylor, *The Origins of the Second World War* (London, Penguin, 1964, pb. edn), pp. 72, 209.

62 Jackson, 'Post-war politics and the historiography of French strategy and diplomacy before the Second World War'', pp. 875–77, quote at p. 876.

63 Shennan, *The Fall of France, 1940*, p. 102.

64 Quote from de Gaulle, *The Complete War Memoirs of Charles de Gaulle*, p. 8.

65 Shennan argues that as an essentially passive experience – of 'victimisation, loss of control, suffering' – the defeat was less suitable as the basis for grounding an active politics than memories of the 'actions, accommodations and choices' of the occupation years: *The Fall of France, 1940*, p. 107. Equally, some Gaullist historiography focused on Vichy rather than the Third Republic as the decadent foil for a new sense of national identity: H. Frey, 'Rebuilding France: Gaullist historiography, the rise-fall myth and French identity (1945–58)', in S. Berger, M. Donovan and K. Passmore (eds), *Writing National Histories: Western Europe since 1800* (London, Routledge, 1999), pp. 205–16.

66 J-P. Rioux, *The Fourth Republic, 1944–1958* (Cambridge, Cambridge University Press, 1989, pb. edn), p. 191.

67 Golsan, 'The legacy of World War II in France', p. 80.

68 Gildea, *France since 1945*, quotes at pp. 62, 205.

69 R. O. Paxton, 'Foreword', in Conan and Rousso, *Vichy*, p. xii.

70 For Rousso's 'broken mirror' phase, see *The Vichy Syndrome*, pp. 98–131, quotes at pp. 10, 100; M. Ophuls (dir.), *Le Chagrin et La Pitié* [*The Sorrow and the Pity*] (1969).

71 Golsan, 'The legacy of World War II in France', p. 81. For Giscard and VE Day, see G. Namer, *Batailles pour la Mémoire: La Commémoration en France, 1944–1982* (Paris, Papyrus, 1983), pp. 189–98.

72 For the 'obsession' phase, see Rousso, *The Vichy Syndrome*, pp. 132–216.

73 P. Ory, 'Why be so cruel? Some modest proposals to cure the Vichy Syndrome', in S. Fishman *et al.* (eds), *France at War: Vichy and the Historians* (Oxford, Berg, 2000), p. 283.

74 P. Nora, 'The era of commemoration', in L. D. Kritzman (ed.), under the direction of P. Nora, *Realms of Memory: The Construction of the French Past: Vol. III: Symbols* (New York, Columbia University Press, 1998), pp. 621–24.

75 P. Garcia, 'Politiques de la mémoire', *Eurozine*, July 2006, http://www.eurozine.com/articles/2006-07-03-garcia-fr.html (accessed 17 July 2007); B. Jenkins, 'Reconstructing the past: in search of new "national identities"?', in S. Blowen, M. Demossier and J. Picard (eds), *Recollections of France: Memories, Identities and Heritage in Contemporary France* (Oxford, Berghahn, 2000), pp. 13–21.

76 For an insightful discussion, see N. Wood, *Vectors of Memory: Legacies of Trauma in Postwar Europe* (Oxford, Berg, 1999), pp. 15–37.

77 P. Nora, 'Reasons for the current upsurge in memory', *Eurozine*, April 2002, http://www. eurozine.com/articles/2002-04-19-nora-en.html (accessed 2 December 2006). This formulation of course requires further interrogation and nuancing, in so far as it might suggest that national identity was ever entirely unitary.

78 H. Rousso, 'The historian, a site of memory', in Fishman *et al.* (eds), *France at War*, p. 287.

79 R. O. Paxton, *Vichy France: Old Guard and New Order, 1940–1944* (New York, Knopf, 1972). On French responses, see Fishman *et al.* (eds), *France at War*; and M. Temkin, '"*Avec un certain malaise*": the Paxtonian trauma in France, 1973–74', *Journal of Contemporary History*, vol. 38, no. 2, 2003, pp. 291–306.

80 S. Fishman and L. V. Smith, 'Introduction', in Fishman *et al.* (eds), *France at War*, p. 4.

81 Rousso, *The Vichy Syndrome*, pp. 251–71, quotes at pp. 259, 263. For the continued dominance of the *Annales*, witness the contents of J. Revel and L. Hunt (eds), *Histories: French Constructions of the Past* (New York, New Press, 1995).

82 Gildea, *France since 1945*, p. 211.

83 Adamthwaite, *France and the Coming of the Second World War*, p. xii.

84 J. C. Cairns, 'Some recent historians and the "strange defeat" of 1940', *Journal of Modern History*, vol. 46, no. 1, 1974, pp. 60–85, quotes at pp. 68, 72–73, 75, 78.

85 G. Chapman, *Why France Collapsed* (London, Cassell, 1968), p. 334.

86 A. Goutard, 'The war of missed opportunities', in Osgood (ed.), *The Fall of France, 1940*, pp. 30–42, quote at p. 30.

87 J. C. Cairns, 'The military collapse was European', in Osgood (ed.), *The Fall of France, 1940*, pp. 43–46. For further discussion, see P. M. H. Bell, 'John Cairns and the historiography of Great Britain and the fall of France', in K. Mouré and M. S. Alexander (eds), *Crisis and Renewal in France, 1918–1962* (Oxford, Berghahn, 2002), pp. 15–27.

88 J-B. Duroselle and M. Vaïsse, 'L'histoire des relations internationales', in F. Bédarida (ed.), *L'Histoire et le Métier d'Historien en France, 1945–1995* (Paris, MSH, 1995), pp. 351–58; A. Adamthwaite, 'Introduction', in J-B. Duroselle, *France and the Nazi Threat: The Collapse of French Diplomacy, 1932–1939* (New York, Enigma, 2004), pp. xi–xvii.

89 Jackson, 'Post-war politics and the historiography of French strategy and diplomacy before the Second World War', pp. 877–78.

90 Young, *France and the Origins of the Second World War*, pp. 44–48.

91 R. J. Young, *French Foreign Policy, 1918–1945: A Guide to Research and Research Materials* (Wilmington, DE, Scholarly Resources, 1981). For details on the published documentary series, see http://www.diplomatie.gouv.fr/fr/ministere_817/archives-patrimoine_3512/ publications_11473/documents-diplomatiques-francais_22237.html#sommaire_4 (accessed 2 February 2009). The period from 1932 to the outbreak of war in 1939 is covered in two series, comprising 32 volumes. Young notes that much important documentation was destroyed in the war; either because of these lacunae or because of the editors' commendably broad conception of international history, the published documents draw on the archives of many different ministries and on private papers (pp. 20–21).

92 Jackson, 'Post-war politics and the historiography of French strategy and diplomacy before the Second World War', p. 879. For a more detailed overview, see J. Jacobson, 'Is there a new international history of the 1920s?', *American Historical Review*, vol. 88, no. 3, 1983, pp. 617–45.

93 D. Johnson, 'Dwelling on the defeat', *Times Literary Supplement*, 4 January 1980, p. 15.

94 J. Néré, *The Foreign Policy of France from 1914 to 1945* (London, Routledge and Kegan Paul, 1975), quotes at p. 260.

95 Jackson, 'Post-war politics and the historiography of French strategy and diplomacy before the Second World War", pp. 879–81; Young, *France and the Origins of the Second World War*, pp. 48–51. As previously noted, incorporating structural constraints into an analysis did not necessarily generate a sympathetic interpretation. For example, the unfavourable strategic balance could be accepted as a tangible constraint limiting

French room for manoeuvre during some particular crisis, yet probing the earlier flawed decisions that produced it might lead to a diagnosis of political lassitude. In this respect, the revisionist turn involved less the 'discovery' of structural factors, and more of a shift from treating them as components of decadence to invoking them as mitigating factors. For further discussion see S. A. Schuker, 'France and the remilitarization of the Rhineland, 1936', reprinted in P. Finney (ed.), *The Origins of the Second World War* (London, Arnold, 1997), pp. 222–45, and the editorial commentary at pp. 200–202.

96 R. J. Young, *In Command of France: French Foreign Policy and Military Planning, 1933–1940* (Cambridge, MA, Harvard University Press, 1978), quotes at pp. 2–3, 245–46, 251, 258.

97 J. A. Gunsburg, *Divided and Conquered: The French High Command and the Defeat of the West, 1940* (Westport, CT, Greenwood, 1979).

98 M. S. Alexander, *The Republic in Danger: General Maurice Gamelin and the Politics of French Defence, 1933–1940* (Cambridge, Cambridge University Press, 1992), p. 8. In a later study of Munich, le Goyet adopted a more orthodox critical line on French policy.

99 Duroselle, *France and the Nazi Threat*, quotes at pp. xxx, 129. This is a (very inelegant) translation of *La Décadence, 1932–1939* (Paris, Imprimerie Nationale, 1985, 3rd edn).

100 Young', *France and the Origins of the Second World War*, pp. 51–52; Adamthwaite, 'Introduction', pp. xx–xxiv.

101 Adamthwaite, *France and the Coming of the Second World War, 1936–1939*, quotes at pp. 353–56, xiii, xi.

102 Quote from Adamthwaite, 'Introduction', p. xvii.

103 Rousso, *The Haunting Past*, p. 40.

104 Young, *In Command of France*, p. 6. On the 1930s stereotypes, see J. C. Cairns, 'A nation of shopkeepers in search of a suitable France, 1919–40', *American Historical Review*, vol. 79, no. 3, 1974, pp. 710–43; and M. Dockrill, *British Establishment Perspectives on France, 1936–40* (London, Macmillan, 1999).

105 Jackson, *The Fall of France*, p. 196.

106 Néré, *The Foreign Policy of France from 1914 to 1945*, p. 261.

107 Gildea, *France since 1945*, quote at p. 232.

108 P. Sahlins (ed.), *Riots in France*, October 2006, http://riotsfrance.ssrc.org/ (accessed 15 September 2007).

109 J. Jackson, 'Historians and the nation in contemporary France', in Berger, Donovan and Passmore (eds), *Writing National Histories*, pp. 241–49, quotes at p. 241.

110 J. Marshall, 'Liberté takes back seat as scholars told: think "positive"', *The Times Higher*, 6 January 2006, p. 19; 'Chirac plans to end colonial law', *BBC News*, 4 January 2006, http://news.bbc.co.uk/1/hi/world/europe/4580842.stm (accessed 6 January 2006).

111 A. Poirier, 'In the grip of declinology', *The Guardian*, 29 March 2006, http://www.guardian.co.uk/commentisfree/2006/mar/29/comment.france (accessed 3 April 2006).

112 Quoted in J. Thornhill, 'Confront our colonial past, urges Sarkozy', *Financial Times*, 11 December 2005, http://www.ft.com/cms/s/0/948d362e-6a74-11da-ba41-0000779e2340.html?nclick_check=1 (accessed 14 July 2009).

113 J. Lichfield, 'Patriotism and pride come first as Sarkozy takes power', *The Independent*, 21 May 2007, http://www.independent.co.uk/news/world/europe/patriotism-and-pride-come-first-as-sarkozy-takes-power-449162.html (accessed 21 May 2007).

114 Quotes from K. Munholland, 'Wartime France: remembering Vichy', *French Historical Studies*, vol. 18, no. 3, 1994, p. 820; Rousso, *The Vichy Syndrome*, pp. 178–99.

115 Golsan, 'The legacy of World War II in France', pp. 84–85. This was a complex affair, and since Mitterrand authorised the revelations it may be that he was seeking to make a point about the ambiguity of the past and the need to eschew moralistic, absolute judgement; if so, the hostile reaction suggested the public were not ready to take it (Jackson, *France: The Dark Years*, pp. 621–23).

116 Golsan, 'The legacy of World War II in France', pp. 94–98.

117 R. J. Golsan (ed.), *The Papon Affair: Memory and Justice on Trial* (New York, Routledge, 2000).

118 Conan and Rousso, *Vichy*, pp. 16–45, quoting Chirac at pp. 39, 41.

119 S. Hare, 'France's deported Jews deserve justice', *The Guardian*, 17 February 2009, http://www.guardian.co.uk/commentisfree/2009/feb/17/france-holocaust-war-crimes (accessed 23 February 2009).

120 D. Reid, 'Resistance and its discontents: affairs, archives, avowals, and the Aubracs', *Journal of Modern History*, vol. 77, no. 1, 2005, pp. 97–137.

121 N. Bracher, 'The trial of Papon and the tribulations of Gaullism', in Golsan (ed.), *The Papon Affair*, pp. 115–30. This charge echoes recent similar sentiments in the FRG about the political and moral failings of previous generations formerly commended for their efforts to master the past.

122 Conan and Rousso, *Vichy*, quotes at pp. 210–11.

123 Golsan, 'The legacy of World War II in France', p. 99. The literature is replete with suggestions that France has already entered such a 'post-obsession' phase: P. Carrier, '"National reconciliation?" Mitterrand, Chirac and the commemorations of Vichy, 1992–95', *National Identities*, vol. 2, no. 2, 2000, pp. 127–44; Munholland, 'Wartime France', p. 803.

124 S. Jeffries, '"They were heroes that history forgot"', *The Guardian*, 9 March 2007, http://www.guardian.co.uk/film/2007/mar/09/france (accessed 9 March 2007); R. Bouchareb (dir.), *Indigènes [Days of Glory]* (2006).

125 Rousso's claim that contemporary perspectives on Vichy are excessively and unhistorically 'Judeocentric' is especially pertinent here: Jackson, *France: The Dark Years*, pp. 618–20.

126 N. Bracher, 'Bruckner and the politics of memory: repentance and resistance in contemporary France', *South Central Review*, vol. 24, no. 2, 2007, pp. 54–70. Sarkozy's neo-Gaullism does not entail a wholesale return to the original, since it is more accepting of complexity and dark episodes in the past; but it does aspire to the construction of a more stable, unitary and unifying national narrative.

127 Jackson, *France: The Dark Years*, pp. 12–20. On contemporary history more generally, see Conan and Rousso, *Vichy*, pp. 46–73; and Rousso, *The Haunting Past*, pp. 25–47.

128 For example, Institut d'Histoire du Temps Présent (ed.), *La Mémoire des Français: Quarante Ans de Commémorations de la Seconde Guerre Mondiale* (Paris, Éditions du CNRS, 1986); Namer, *Batailles pour la Mémoire*; A. Wahl (ed.), *Mémoire de la Seconde Guerre Mondiale* (Metz, Centre de Recherche Histoire et Civilisation de l'Université de Metz, 1984).

129 L. Valensi (ed.), 'Présence du passé, lenteur de l'Histoire: Vichy, l'Occupation, les juifs', theme issue, *Annales ESC*, vol. 48, no. 3, 1993.

130 S. Berger, 'A return to the national paradigm? National history writing in Germany, Italy, France, and Britain from 1945 to the present', *Journal of Modern History*, vol. 77, no. 3, 2005, p. 668.

131 P. Nora, 'Le Syndrome, son passé, son avenir', and H. Rousso, 'Le Syndrome de l'historien', *French Historical Studies*, vol. 19, no. 2, 1995, pp. 487–93 and 525–26 respectively.

132 P. Grosser, *Pourquoi la Seconde Guerre Mondiale?* (Paris, Éditions Complexe, 1999), pp. 193–94, and more generally pp. 190–206. Grosser provides extensive bibliographical references, as do Jackson, 'Post-war politics and the historiography of French strategy and diplomacy before the Second World War', and Young, *France and the Origins of the Second World War*.

133 M. Thomas, 'Appeasement in the late Third Republic', *Diplomacy and Statecraft*, vol. 19, no. 3, 2008, p. 593.

134 Quoted in Young, 'A. J. P. Taylor and the problem with France', p. 84.

135 C. Levisse-Touzé, quoted in Jackson, *The Fall of France*, p. 196; J. Doise and M. Vaïsse, *Diplomatie et Outil Militaire, 1871–1991* (Paris, Seuil, 1992, rev. edn), p. 416.

136 Quoted in W. D. Irvine, 'Domestic politics and the fall of France in 1940', in Blatt (ed.), *The French Defeat of 1940*, p. 85.

137 Young, *France and the Origins of the Second World War*, p. 53.

138 Witness the varied contributions in Blatt (ed.), *The French Defeat of 1940*.

139 E. Weber, *The Hollow Years: France in the 1930s* (New York, Norton, 1994), quote at p. 145.

140 D. C. Watt, *How War Came: The Immediate Origins of the Second World War, 1938–1939* (London, Mandarin, 1990, pb. edn), p. 617.

141 N. Jordan, *The Popular Front and Central Europe: The Dilemmas of French Impotence, 1918–1940* (Cambridge, Cambridge University Press, 1992), quotes at pp. 301, 4.

142 M. J. Carley, *1939: The Alliance that Never Was and the Coming of World War II* (Chicago, Ivan Dee, 1999), quote at p. xiii. Elsewhere Carley has argued that Soviet ambassadors in Paris were essentially correct to perceive a 'divided French society destined to collapse': 'A Soviet eye on France from the Rue de Grenelle in Paris, 1924–40', *Diplomacy and Statecraft*, vol. 17, no. 2, 2006, pp. 295–346, quote at p. 337.

143 A. Adamthwaite, *Grandeur and Misery: France's Bid for Power in Europe, 1914–1940* (London, Arnold, 1995), quotes at pp. viii, 230–31.

144 Jackson, *The Fall of France*, p. 194.

145 Thomas, 'Appeasement in the late Third Republic', pp. 566–607, quotes at pp. 593, 591.

146 R. Overy, *The Road to War* (London, Macmillan, 1989), p. 142.

147 R. Boyce, 'Introduction: 1940 as end and beginning in French inter-war history and historiography', in R. Boyce (ed.), *French Foreign and Defence Policy, 1918–1940: The Decline and Fall of a Great Power* (London, Routledge, 1998), pp. 7–8.

148 R. A. Doughty, 'The illusion of security: France, 1919–40', in W. Murray, M. Knox and A. Bernstein (eds), *The Making of Strategy: Rulers, States, and War* (Cambridge, Cambridge University Press, 1994), p. 497.

149 P. Jackson, *France and the Nazi Menace: Intelligence and Policy-Making, 1933–1939* (Oxford, Oxford University Press, 2000), p. 2.

150 Boyce, 'Introduction', pp. 6–7.

151 Alexander, *The Republic in Danger*, quote at p. 379.

152 R. J. Young, review of É. du Réau, *Édouard Daladier, 1884–1970* (Paris, Fayard, 1993), in *American Historical Review*, vol. 99, no. 4, 1994, p. 1333.

153 Jackson, 'Post-war politics and the historiography of French strategy and diplomacy before the Second World War', p. 882.

154 Jackson, *France and the Nazi Menace*, p. 394.

155 Young, 'A. J. P. Taylor and the problem with France', pp. 85–88.

156 T. C. Imlay, 'Retreat or resistance: strategic re-appraisal and the crisis of French power in Eastern Europe, September 1938 to August 1939', in Mouré and Alexander (eds), *Crisis and Renewal in France, 1918–1962*, p. 125.

157 Irvine, 'Domestic politics and the fall of France in 1940', p. 95.

158 The distinctively favourable tone of foreign scholarship is the point of departure of M. Vaïsse (ed.), *Mai–Juin 1940: Défaite Française, Victoire Allemande, sous l'Oeil des Historiens Étrangers* (Paris, Autrement, 2000).

159 M. S. Alexander, 'The fall of France, 1940', in G. Martel (ed.), *The World War Two Reader* (London, Routledge, 2004), pp. 7–39, quotes at pp. 10, 26.

160 E. C. Kiesling, 'Illuminating *Strange Defeat* and *Pyrrhic Victory*: the historian Robert A. Doughty', *Journal of Military History*, vol. 71, no. 3, 2007, p. 882.

161 E. R. May, *Strange Victory: Hitler's Conquest of France* (New York, Hill and Wang, 2000), quote at p. 10.

162 For a recent French discussion, see F. Bédarida, 'Huit mois d'attente et d'illusion: la "drôle de guerre"', in J-P. Azéma and F. Bédarida (eds), *La France des Années Noires: Vol. 1: De la Défaite à Vichy* (Paris, Seuil, 2000, rev. edn), pp. 41–74.

163 T. C. Imlay, *Facing the Second World War: Strategy, Politics, and Economics in Britain and France, 1938–1940* (Oxford, Oxford University Press, 2003), quote at p. 364.

164 Young, *France and the Origins of the Second World War*.

165 Jackson, 'Post-war politics and the historiography of French strategy and diplomacy before the Second World War", pp. 890–93, quotes at p. 893; Jackson, 'Recent journeys along the road back to France, 1940", pp. 497–510.

166 Berger, 'A return to the national paradigm?', p. 670.

167 Quote from R. Kuhn, 'A narrative of decline?', *Modern and Contemporary France*, vol. 12, no. 3, 2004, p. 399.
168 Jackson, *The Fall of France*, p. 248.
169 Quote from de Gaulle, *The Complete War Memoirs of Charles de Gaulle*, p. 3; Jackson, 'Post-war politics and the historiography of French strategy and diplomacy before the Second World War', pp. 891–92.
170 Jackson, *The Fall of France*, p. 248.

5   On folly

Great Britain, appeasement and the romance of decline

> Without overlooking the assistance which we should hope to obtain from France, and possibly other allies, we cannot foresee the time when our defence forces will be strong enough to safeguard our territory, trade and vital interests against Germany, Italy and Japan simultaneously. We cannot, therefore, exaggerate the importance, from the point of view of Imperial defence, of any political or international action that can be taken to reduce the numbers of our potential enemies and to gain the support of potential allies.
>
> Committee of Imperial Defence, Report by the Chiefs of Staff Sub-Committee, 'Comparison of the Strength of Great Britain with that of certain other Nations as at January 1938', 12 November 1937[1]

British Prime Minister Neville Chamberlain returned to England from the Munich conference exhausted but exhilarated. At almost 70 years of age he had endured a fortnight of unprecedented shuttle diplomacy, wearying late night Cabinet meetings and lengthy sessions in the House of Commons, conscious all the while that the fragile peace of Europe was at stake. But he had emerged triumphant with the threat of war averted, the explosive Sudeten German question settled and Hitler's signature secured on an Anglo-German declaration in which the representatives of the two peoples resolved 'never to go to war with one another again'.[2] Basking in the acclaim of the cheering throng greeting his motorcade, an appreciative press and the congratulatory messages that subsequently deluged 10 Downing Street, Chamberlain seemed to have achieved a singular political success. Very soon, however, it turned to dust. Over the months that followed the international situation deteriorated and doubts accumulated about the moral ambiguities and *realpolitik* wisdom of his diplomacy; critics at the time of Munich had been a dissenting minority, but gradually a groundswell of opinion began to urge the abandonment of appeasement in favour of a more confrontational stance towards Nazi Germany, even at the risk of war. Less than a year after his exultant return, Chamberlain faced the House of Commons sadly to impart the news that Britain was at war with Germany: 'everything that I have worked for, everything that I have hoped for, everything that I have believed in during my public life has crashed into ruins'.[3]

From the very start, the meaning of the Munich settlement, and the appeasement strategy of which it was the apotheosis, was profoundly contested. Central to this debate were contrasting interpretations of what Chamberlain himself, on the basis of his not altogether consistent comments on the subject, believed he had achieved. Had he been a victim of his government's own propaganda, credulously trusting in the pledged word of the Führer and concomitant reality of the 'peace for our time' that he proclaimed from a Downing Street window?[4] Was he even criminally duplicitous in asserting the need to prepare for war whilst refusing to take the necessary military and diplomatic steps, whether through increased rearmament or the negotiation of a Grand Alliance with the Soviet Union? Or did his private words to his Foreign Secretary Lord Halifax – 'Edward, we must hope for the best and prepare for the worst' – rather reveal his strategic sagacity in leading a nation with limited options owing to its military, economic and political weakness through perilous circumstances?[5] Had he put Hitler on his word about future aggression with no great optimism but in order to engineer a situation in which war, if it proved unavoidable, might come in 1939 with the nation united behind a just cause and far better positioned militarily and diplomatically than a year before? Few questions in modern British political history have been as ferociously chewed over by historians as that of appeasement, but despite the processing of masses of pertinent government documents and Chamberlain's vast personal archive no settled judgement has been reached.

This historicisation of appeasement has occurred in the context of broader memory discourses on the Second World War. In certain respects, that conflict remains a peculiarly prominent reference point, almost an obsession, in British society. Reviewing a spate of innovative drama-documentaries produced around the sixtieth anniversary commemorations of 1945, one scholar opined that 'the further the Second World War recedes into history, the more ubiquitous it becomes on British television screens'.[6] The war is also constantly recycled in advertising images and slogans and the rhetoric of the popular press.[7] In 1999 the German Culture Minister Michael Naumann lamented with some bafflement that Britain seemed uniquely to have made it 'a sort of spiritual core of its national self, understanding and pride'; in 2005, another astute German observer deprecated 'official British triumphalism' and the continuous recycling of 'memories of grandeur' from the 1940s.[8] Undoubtedly, the flipside of this propensity is too often a crass Germanophobia. In 2006, the hosting of the football World Cup in Germany engendered anxious anticipation of 'the inevitable moment when the terraces or the press proudly vomit a surfeit of war-obsessed, Nazi-fixated anti-German excess on to our national living-room carpet'.[9] Not that such prejudice is restricted to the outré fringes of popular culture. Widespread British scepticism about European integration has its roots not only in residual suspicion of German hegemonic intentions but also in broader perceived lessons from the war; for continental Europeans the assertion of national sovereignty either resulted in humiliating defeat or – for Italy and Germany – was disastrously counter-productive; for the British who successfully stood alone it was triumphantly vindicated.[10] The glibly xenophobic import of these recollections – in stark contrast to the critical reflection on the war now entrenched in Germany – is commonly taken as indicative of a crippling post-imperial pathology. Having prevailed in the war, the British lost the peace and endured a long, slow ebbing of world power, prestige and prosperity; nostalgic and deluded fixation upon their last moment of unequivocal greatness thus functions as a 'security blanket' in a perpetually disappointing present.[11]

Against this stress on enduring pertinence, other accounts in the literature narrate a story of the waning and eclipse of the war's mythological potency. For several decades after 1945, 'World War II provided a template for the popular political imagination'; construed as the 'People's War', it formed 'the rhetorical binding of the postwar consensus'.[12] On this reading, amidst the hazardous exigencies of 1940, the nation united around common understandings of the past and the future. Reacting against the shabby failures of the 1930s, when an uncaring government had presided over the misery of 'the Slump' and the pusillanimous failed compromises of appeasement, the war was to be fought not just against fascism but for the establishment of a collectivist welfare state rooted in Keynesian economics and egalitarian values. This perception of the war and the socio-political arrangements that it supported broadly persisted until the 1960s when, in the context of economic decline and geopolitical contraction, it began to be challenged. At first, this was by politicians and historians on the left, angry that the revolutionary potential of the 'People's War' had been transmuted into timid reformism and urging the renewal of its radical democratic promise. From the 1970s, however, a more devastating attack was launched on this now destabilised consensus by a Thatcherite New Right. Historians reinterpreted the supposed 'devil's decade' of the 1930s in far more positive lights and began to question how far wartime had really engendered bipartisan concord over the desirability of a 'New Jerusalem'; meanwhile Margaret Thatcher overtly blamed the welfare state – and the moral laxity and economic profligacy of consensus-mongers – for the nation's woes. Consensus was thus written out of British history just as the Conservatives, after their return to power under Thatcher in 1979, set about dismantling the postwar domestic settlement and redefining British identity in a more assertive and individualistic vein. That Labour was only able to bring 18 years in the political wilderness to an end in 1997 by adopting a programme of 'Thatcherism with a human face' signified the definitive conclusion of the postwar era: 'thus 1940, for so long the birthday of "contemporary Britain"' had become 'a moment that moulded the present but which no longer underpins it'.[13]

These contrasting readings of the state of British war memory are not mutually exclusive, but simply testify that it is comprised of multiple intertwining and competing discursive threads. Despite the demise of one important understanding of the Second World War along with the socio-political order to which it was sutured, that war remains vividly alive in other respects, its memory constantly evolving and contested.[14] (Indeed, it may even be premature to proclaim the definitive passing of the 'People's War' myth: although now shorn of its former acute ideological valence, it has remained available for reworking, with many of its core elements continuing to resonate in the popular imagination.[15]) Even in 1940 the populist and collectivist myth of the 'People's War', founded specifically upon revulsion against the 1930s and oriented towards social justice, existed in tandem with a more nationalist 'Churchillian' myth that emphasised individual heroism and the glorious continuous history of a proud imperial race accustomed to standing alone against aggression.[16] To an extent the fates of these myths were intertwined, since both played a part in mobilizing the nation for war, and worked to bolster consensus through the 1940s and 1950s. But there were also significant tensions between them and their stories ultimately separated. So, the Churchill myth was one of the chief weapons wielded by Thatcher to deliver the *coup de grâce* to consensus, and though the 'People's War' may have faded, Churchillian visions of British history and grandeur retain their ideological magnetism.

Key texts on British collective memory of the war often marginalise appeasement, implying that the epochal events of 1940 and beyond – Dunkirk, the Battle of Britain and the Blitz – have overshadowed the antecedents of the war in the popular imagination. Conversely, discussions of the mnemonic afterlife of appeasement often treat it apart from wider trends in British collective memory, evincing interest in it primarily as a supposed source of more general lessons for the conduct of international relations.[17] The aim here is to explore the ongoing historicisation of appeasement in the context of the two core war myths but without entirely subsuming it within them, treating it as an additional strand in collective memory. Two broad interpretations are in play – the one critical and emphasising individual culpability and flawed perceptions, the other more sympathetic and focusing on objective structural constraints – and the debate between them needs to be related to the vicissitudes of British power and identity over six post-war decades.[18] In many respects, the British experience of the war was much less morally and politically ambiguous than that of the French, since despite the existential peril of the darkest days of 1940 Britain was never defeated or tainted by collaboration, and at war's end occupied an unchallenged place in the ranks of the victors.[19] Yet for all the seeming unequivocality of victory, in the long run the post-war period brought a steady slippage in strength and status and the erosion of traditional conceptions of national identity. So here too retrospectively negotiating the meaning of the conflict has entailed a dialogue with decline.

'A great empire, supreme in arms and secure in liberty': *Guilty Men*

The canonical point of departure for historical writing on appeasement is *Guilty Men*.[20] Conceived and written over a weekend in June 1940 by three radical Beaverbrook journalists – Michael Foot, Peter Howard and Frank Owen – under the pseudonym Cato, this polemical indictment proved immensely popular, and for a brief book has cast a long interpretive shadow. Its instant success was due to the vitriolic and accessible tone in which it offered a bewildered public a compelling explanation of the crisis facing the country at the time of its publication in early July 1940. This point marked the nadir of Britain's fortunes in the war, after the fall of France and debacle of Dunkirk but before the Battle of Britain which heralded at least a temporary respite. These precarious circumstances conditioned the book's savage critique of the appeasers, on whom blame for recent catastrophes was unequivocally laid. Prime Ministers Neville Chamberlain and Stanley Baldwin and their whole political clique, 'blind to the purposes of the criminal new Nazi war power', had consistently misjudged Hitler's intentions, capitulated to his escalating demands by proffering unilateral concessions in the vain hope of preserving peace, and so neglected Britain's armaments as to conduct 'a great empire, supreme in arms and secure in liberty' to 'the edge of national annihilation'. July 1940 lent a terrible retrospective clarity to the events of the 1930s which thus unfold in the pages of *Guilty Men* with the remorseless inevitability of Aeschylean tragedy; there was little point probing for rational motives behind appeasement since it could not but appear as an incomprehensible policy of utter folly, if not cowardice.

Issues of national identity suffuse *Guilty Men* both in terms of the assumptions that shaped the argument and what the text was avowedly designed to achieve. First, its critique of appeasement is fundamentally premised upon the idea of underlying British strength, greatness and capability. Cato takes it for granted that British policy-makers in the 1930s had the freedom to choose alternative, better, policies – of resistance and confrontation rather than conciliation – had they possessed the vision, intelligence and competence to do so: the essence of their culpability lies in the fact that they could and should have acted differently. Second, the authors' intention was to effect change in the government of the country. Despite Winston Churchill's assumption of the premiership in May 1940, many of the appeasers remained in office, including Chamberlain and Halifax, and Cato intended to rally the nation through a purging of those responsible for the calamity of 1940. Hence the closing words of the text: 'let the Guilty Men retire, then, of their own volition, and so make an essential contribution to the victory upon which all are implacably resolved'. The logic of *Guilty Men* is to personalise responsibility for the disaster by arraigning certain individuals in order by extension to exculpate the rest of the nation: the corollary of their guilt is the innocence of the general public. This is inscribed in the very structure of the text as the 'cast list' of elite villains in the frontispiece is immediately followed by the opening vignette of gallant ordinary soldiers marooned at Dunkirk, 'an Army doomed *before* they took the field'. Its further purpose is also future-oriented: after the departure of the culpable the mass of the nation – 'a people determined to resist and conquer' – could unite without further recrimination for the supreme effort of conducting total war, a war which given the assumed underlying vigour of the country could be prosecuted to victory.[21]

Guilty Men was thus a key text in the broad cultural movement of 1940, which enacted the collectivist and consensual identity that carried Britain through the 'People's War' and beyond. The public was mobilised to fight by the representation of the struggle to come as, on diverse fronts, a war against the 1930s.[22] (Even though the reality of the wartime consensus has now been convincingly called into question, there is good evidence that, whatever divisions remained amongst the British, appeasement did indeed become 'an object of universal revilement'.[23]) Its immediate context mandated a negative interpretation of appeasement that stressed enduring British strength and personal culpability rather than broader structural or impersonal factors. Yet while the text's ostensible purpose was to eliminate a coterie of individuals from power, it also contributed to an emerging discourse urging a wider transformation of domestic political, social and economic relations in the name of national renewal. By the same token, although it focused narrowly on issues of foreign policy, rearmament and supply, it came to be understood as a component of a larger critique of the failings of the Conservative establishment to meet the challenges of the 1930s. Politics, historiography and memory were here indissolubly bound together in forging the necessary myth of 1940. Most immediately, *Guilty Men* provided a reading of the past, linked to a particular characterisation of national identity (a powerful national 'us' which excluded the architects of appeasement), which offered a workable foundation for the waging of the war ahead.

Alternative readings of the 1930s were certainly possible on the basis of the information then in the public domain; but they failed to acquire similar contemporary authority or subsequent influence because they lacked this practical utility. Harold Nicolson's Penguin Special, *Why Britain is at War*, published in November 1939, advanced a cautious defence of the appeasers both implicitly by focusing much more on the iniquities of Adolf Hitler's foreign policy than on the democratic response to it, and explicitly by reference to the alleged determining influence of structural factors, and in particular pacific public opinion. This too was a text for its times, a product of the Phoney War when Britain was at but not really in war, and when Chamberlain remained in office as prime minister. In these circumstances patriotism, together with Nicolson's own solidly bourgeois temperament and position as a National Government MP, dictated a broadly sympathetic approach seeking to unite the country behind rather than against the appeasers. (Not that Nicolson abstained from all criticism: his pre-publication belief that sections of the book would 'annoy the Government terribly' was partially justified.[24]) W. N. Medlicott's scholarly accounts of the origins of the war similarly prefigured revisionist themes in evincing a sensitive perception of Britain's global strategic dilemma and the historical antecedents and determinants of appeasement, even while remaining critical of it as a departure from *realpolitik*.[25] In terms of literary elegance, coherence, logical consistency and scholarly rigour, the works of Nicolson and Medlicott were manifestly superior to *Guilty Men*, but in 1940 their interpretations were decisively marginalised. The disasters of Norway and Dunkirk rendered Nicolson's inclusive approach anachronistic and implausible, while Medlicott's treatment – with its Rankean detachment and preoccupation with the arcane subtleties of diplomacy – paled anaemically beside the passionate vigour of *Guilty Men*. Thus Cato effected a closure over other, more complex, explanations of the 1930s, by offering the only account which worked ideologically to provide a national history and present identity in tune with the new realities of the 'People's War'.[26]

From the outset, therefore, the scripting of a derogatory interpretation of appeasement followed from preconceived assumptions that Britain was inherently capable. Through the war years and into the immediate post-war period, the essential theses of *Guilty Men* were refined and developed into a dominant orthodoxy. The victory of the Labour Party in the 1945 general election ensured that post-war reconstruction was in tune with the collectivist vision of a 'New Jerusalem', as the new government embarked on a programme of nationalisation and the establishment of a comprehensive welfare state. Labour campaign rhetoric made much of 'the memory of the 1930s' as a negative foil, and so these domestic political developments only entrenched the essentials of the 'People's War' myth.[27] Moreover, the truth of the brutal indictment of appeasement seemed only to have been confirmed by revelation of the extent of Hitler's ambitions and the atrocities committed by his regime, and this was given a further judicial imprimatur by the Nuremberg war crimes trials. True, the imperative of maintaining unity between the prosecuting powers mandated an overriding focus during the proceedings on Germany's diplomatic and military initiatives and the veiling of British, French, American and Soviet reactions. Hence the picture of appeasement that emerged was somewhat anodyne, with the implicit suggestion that Hitler's expansionism had been so remorseless as to render opposition nugatory.[28] But the affirmation of a programmatic Nazi conspiracy to wage aggressive war was more widely understood as also condemning those in the democracies who had failed to perceive and foil it. A slew of historians working in this climate therefore recapitulated the notion of premeditated German aggression, the corollary of which was to damn appeasement as a product of 'political myopia';[29] a policy 'burdened ... with make-believe' and a lamentable 'failure of European statesmanship'. These authors did not require copious primary evidence to prove the truth of their interpretations. As Lewis Namier put it:

For who wants to read documents? And what are they to prove? Is evidence needed to show that Hitler was a gangster who broke his word whenever it suited him? That the British Government winked and blinked, and hoped against hope for appeasement?[30]

But the captured German documents amassed to support the Nureml indictments could nonetheless easily be read as confirming (and thus lending additional authority to) what had now become common sense.

The most emphatic and influential post-war articulation of this orthodox view was published in 1948 by Churchill in the first volume of his magisterial history of the Second World War, *The Gathering Storm*. His narrative scripted the 1930s in Manichean terms as a titanic confrontation between the 'English-speaking peoples' and 'the wicked'. The existence of a Nazi 'programme of aggression, nicely calculated and timed, unfolding stage by stage' was axiomatic. The appeasers had failed to grasp the essence of the German threat, and as a result of 'a long series of miscalculations, and misjudgements of men and facts' pursued a policy amounting to little more than 'complete surrender ... to the Nazi threat of force'. Appeasement was essentially a policy of one-sided concessions which proved both dishonourable – in that it entailed purchasing peace through betraying small states – and disastrous – in that it condemned Britain to fight the war against Germany in the most unfavourable circumstances. For Churchill the past conflict was 'the unnecessary war', and his narrative catalogued the lost opportunities – from the Disarmament Conference of 1932–34 through to the Anglo-Franco–Soviet negotiations of 1939 – for stopping Hitler. Failure to grasp these openings and to take concerted resolute action inexorably transformed an unnecessary war into an inevitable one, from which Britain was hard-pressed to emerge victorious.[31]

The Gathering Storm is a complex text that can profitably be read in many different ways. It of course represents a significant chapter in Churchill's almost ceaseless autobiographical self-construction: he was himself a participant in the events about which he wrote, and in vilifying the appeasers he also magnified his own heroic status, not only as the successor to Chamberlain who saved the nation from the consequences of his folly, but also as the Cassandra of the 1930s whose warnings and calls for resistance to Hitler were consistently ignored.[32] This also illustrates how, despite the tendency to regard *Guilty Men* as a foundational moment, the historiographical debate on appeasement developed almost seamlessly from the political polemic of the 1930s.[33]

Churchill's text can also be read through the lens of national identity, for it is laden with ideas and anxieties about Britain's role in the world. This critique was also premised upon an assumption of British strength: policy-makers not only should but could have rearmed more quickly and constructed a coalition to contain Hitler. Though Churchill's account is more sophisticated and characterises Chamberlain as merely inadequate rather than as a fool or a knave – his sins were 'hubris, illusions and mental rigidity' – the roots of appeasement are still located in erroneous individual choices rather than objective structural constraints.[34] In part, this reflected Churchill's general philosophy of history; the 'overriding theme' of the memoirs was that 'history was determined by the men at the top'.[35] Yet it was also a consequence of Churchill positioning appeasement in a longer-term context, identifying it as alien to the spirit of 'the wonderful unconscious tradition' of British foreign policy which from at least the Elizabethan age aimed at opposing 'the strongest, most aggressive, most dominating Power on the Continent', thereby to preserve British freedom and 'the liberties of Europe'. On this reading, appeasement was a sad aberration from a traditional policy that had laid the basis for imperial prosperity, by combining 'in natural accord' the protection of particular British interests ('our island security' and the growth of a 'widening Empire') with the furthering of the 'grand universal causes' of justice, democracy and freedom.[36] So a particular romanticised notion of British history and identity underpinned Churchill's critique.[37] Appeasement was a betrayal of that history which for him 'confirmed the particular genius of the English race and proved its right to be rich, Imperial and the guardian of human freedoms'.[38]

As these ideas constructed Churchill's interpretation of appeasement, so he intended that interpretation to influence British identity in the post-war period. Within his text he stressed his continued fidelity to the conception of Britishness which had informed his original hostility to appeasement – principles 'which I had followed for many years and follow still' – and his explicit allusions to the post-war situation make clear that those ideas entailed policy prescriptions. This is particularly apparent in those passages where he contributes to the promulgation of a foreign policy law of anti-appeasement, the notion that conciliating dictators was always disastrous and wrong. Repeatedly, he draws parallels between the Nazi threat in the 1930s and the alleged threat from Soviet Russia confronting the West 'in singular resemblance' at the time of writing, explicitly intending that 'the lessons of the past [might] be a guide' to ensure that the democracies did not repeat the mistake of appeasing totalitarianism in the Cold War.[39] Clearly, he felt Britain could and should continue to pursue its traditional foreign policy towards the continent, and take a leading role in opposing the machinations of a Stalin whom policy-makers were increasingly 'fitting ... to the Hitler model'.[40] By the same token, there was no sign that he had abandoned his belief that the British 'ought to set the life and endurance of the British Empire and the greatness of this Island very high in our duty'.[41] So Churchill's reading of the past, itself dictated by a particular sense of national identity, produced a prescription for present action designed to sustain that identity. It is true that Churchill's account was not devoid of anxieties about evolving geo-political realities: he acknowledged it would be no mean feat to negotiate a path through 'the awful unfolding scene of the future', and that Britain would have to exploit its vision and 'power of leadership' to punch above its weight in the post-war world.[42] So while *Guilty Men* had attempted to reconfigure national identity in a progressive sense, Churchill's text was a more conservative intervention, designed to protect a self that was now threatened. But it was nonetheless premised on a past and present ideal of British national identity rooted in imperial prestige, world power status and the identification of England with the advancement of universal human values.

There were undoubtedly tensions between Churchill's formulation of the orthodox critique and that of Cato.[43] Where *The Gathering Storm* was rooted in a conservative vision of imperial glory and prioritised *realpolitik* concerns, condemning the appeasers by the yardstick of the right, *Guilty Men* embodied a radical and internationalist assault on a decadent British establishment. Yet there was significant common ground at their heart in the substance of the charges against appeasement and its architects; read simply as an indictment of individual sinners to be purged, with the wider implied condemnation of an entire political class bracketed off, the essence of *Guilty Men* need not have been unpalatable to Churchillian sensibilities.[44] Moreover, focusing on the international rather than domestic perceived lessons of 1940 revealed a shared conviction about enduring British strength; thus there was a compatibility between them in a Cold War context of broad bipartisan agreement over the essentials of foreign policy and 'widespread belief in Britain's continuing role as a world power'.[45]

Indeed, in so far as Churchill modified the essential thesis of *Guilty Men* in a conservative direction, it is tempting to see this historiographical gesture as symbolic of the larger trajectory of British politics and war memory. In 1951 the Conservatives under Churchill returned to power, accepting the essence of the planned economy and welfare state but relaxing state controls. Tory reformers, especially during the premiership of Harold Macmillan from 1957 to 1963, presided over a period of economic boom. The Tories' vaunted 'true partnership between state, production, distribution and exchange' was intended as a 'middle way between the "devil take the hindmost" philosophy of the prewar years and the grim centralism that the crisis of war had made temporarily necessary but which Labour would have institutionalized'. The left reacted uneasily to this rightward turn, suspicious of populist consumerism but compelled to concede that in producing a better standard of living within the framework of consensus the Conservatives were delivering on some of the promises of the 'People's War'.[46] Similar developments were in evidence on the terrain of collective memory. For example, in British war films in the 1950s themes of collectivist egalitarian endeavour – the pulling together of classes and regions – were increasingly supplanted by stories of individual, elite, martial and masculine heroism.[47] 'These are the heroes of Churchill's war, of the few rather than the many, who impose their presence on British popular culture in the 1950s as much as do the values of the People's War'.[48] The dominance of Churchill's variant of the orthodox view of appeasement fits neatly within this context. To a significant extent collectivist and individualist thematics were complementary, and the basic discursive structure of the 'People's War' myth remained intact, but the change in emphasis was nonetheless noteworthy.

During the 1950s stirrings of British decline were already becoming apparent, as Churchill was himself forced to admit when making some hard choices during his final premiership. Decolonisation proceeded apace as Churchill's own faculties diminished and there was something particularly poignant about the image of the aged premier 'dressed in yet one more strange costume' at the coronation of Queen Elizabeth II in 1953, 'the indomitable embodiment of a once great empire now struggling, with great spirit and dignity, but in vain, against the ravages of time'.[49] World power status seemed to be slipping away as British autonomy was increasingly circumscribed by dependence on the United States, as was to be humiliatingly demonstrated over Suez in 1956. Yet perception for some time lagged behind reality and the orthodox interpretation of appeasement premised on the assumption of British power still seemed authoritative and was not subject to any serious challenge during the decade. Indeed, it was said that it 'satisfied everybody and seemed to exhaust all dispute', not least because the 'considerations of present day politics' which had originally conspired to construct the Nuremberg view largely remained in place, and other issues seemed more urgently to demand historical investigation.[50]

So the subject drifted out of scholarly fashion to such an extent that 'research and publication on the history of the 1930s ... seemed to have ceased': 'it was very difficult, if not impossible, to get anything published in England on the subject – at least in learned journals'.[51] The work which did appear followed the familiar narrative; the German documents 'conclusively proved the deliberate intention and plan of Hitler and a few of his leading coadjutors to start a second world war' and thus the appeasers had been wrong to pursue 'conciliation and tolerance to the point of failure to recognise evil, and in evil danger'.[52] Dissenting voices were largely confined to biographies of, or memoir accounts by, the appeasers themselves. Thus Samuel Hoare, a senior member of both Baldwin and Chamberlain governments, advanced a subtle defence of appeasement as a judicious blend of conciliation and rearmament aiming at 'peace upon reasonable terms ... [but] war in the last resort, when every attempt at peace had failed and the whole Commonwealth had been united in an unbroken front of resistance'.[53] But such accounts, from subjects tainted by Churchill's treatment, were dismissed as shameless, *ex parte* interventions and failed to detract from the plausibility of the orthodox view.

Throughout the 1950s, the amount of documentary material available relating to appeasement also steadily increased. The archives remained closed, of course, but much relevant material had become available through the Nuremberg process and in the volumes of German documents being published under Allied auspices; more to the point, the British government very early took a decision to publish selections from its archives and these began to appear in the edited collection *Documents on British Foreign Policy, 1919–1939* from 1946.[54] Confounding official hopes that these might counter polemical attacks on policy-makers, the published British materials consolidated existing arguments rather than triggering any radical revision. The early volumes focused on the execution rather than formulation of policy and so provided no basis for probing possible rational motives behind appeasement, leaving in place the existing superficial conclusion that it was misguided and foolish.[55]

By the same token, the staggered publication and patchy chronological coverage of the series — together with its geographical compartmentalisation of European, Far Eastern, Mediterranean and American affairs — precluded the construction of a rounded or dramatically reformulated picture of the problems facing British policy-makers in the 1930s.[56] Thus in reviewing the volumes on the Czech crisis and Munich in 1953, Bernadotte Schmitt concluded that despite:

> the difficult circumstances of the time, this record permits no doubt that British diplomacy suffered a defeat comparable only to the loss of the American colonies a century and a half before. That a subsequent British government should, eleven years later, publish this record was an act of high political courage and strengthens one's confidence in the objectivity of the entire publication.[57]

Although the parallel is not exact, the orthodox critique of appeasement performed a similar function to the decadence emplotment in France. It damned the pre-war past in order to provide an ideological foundation for the war effort and then for post-war reconstruction and renewal. The progressive variant was rather more thoroughgoing, implying that guilty individuals were also representative of a bankrupt political class and system; the conservative was more personalised and freighted with imperialist overtones. Yet the tensions between collectivist and individualist impulses were contained within the framework of a broad post-war consensus, in which the rectitude of a conflict fought by a united nation against fascism and for a fairer and more prosperous future went largely unquestioned. Moreover, the two variants were united in their assumption that the nation was fundamentally powerful and capable, and able to play a significant role in international affairs; even the more radical narrative, with its intimations of structural shortcomings, is premised on the belief that the appeasers had choices and should have acted differently. It was only in the 1960s that interpretations began to soften as the defence of appeasement that had previously been evident in embryo became generally sustainable; this shift occurred in tandem with a major realignment in understandings of British national identity, as the increasingly obvious fact of decline in the present triggered reassessments of this key episode in the national past.

'Massively overdetermined': the rise of a revisionist view

A. J. P. Taylor's *The Origins of the Second World War* is often characterised as essaying a pioneering defence of appeasement, but this interpretation is difficult to sustain. True, in denying that Hitler had a programme for aggression Taylor undermined a central tenet of the orthodox critique: 'after all, the British Government could hardly be blamed for not knowing what Hitler's plans were if he did not know them himself'.[58] Equally, he acknowledged that the appeasers were 'men confronted with real problems, doing their best in the circumstances of their time', beset by structural constraints such as pacific public opinion and the waning moral validity of the Versailles settlement. But Taylor had been a confirmed anti-appeaser in the 1930s, and despite his professed desire to allow 'the record, considered in detachment' to govern his conclusions, and his determination 'to understand what happened, not to vindicate or condemn', he remained convinced that that attitude had been justified.[59] Hence his characterisation of appeasement as driven by 'timidity; blindness; [and] moral doubts'; scarcely a revisionist sentiment.[60] Taylor may have redefined appeasement as an active rather than a purely passive policy, but since this elevated Chamberlain's restless determination 'to start something' – which presented Hitler with opportunities he gratefully seized – to the ranks of prime causes of the war, this hardly made appeasement wise, moral or right.[61] While it may therefore be difficult to pin down precisely what Taylor thinks of appeasement in a text so riven with paradoxes and contradiction, it requires some ingenuity to present him simply as a defender of Chamberlain.

The idiosyncrasies of Taylor's treatment can be linked to various factors, including his cavalier scholarship, the fragmentary nature of his sources and even generational experience.[62] But reading the text through the lens of national identity again proves fruitful, since it registers the discursive shift that was underway. One of Taylor's most notorious epigrams characterised Munich as:

> a triumph for all that was best and most enlightened in British life; a triumph for those who had preached equal justice between peoples; a triumph for those who had courageously denounced the harshness and short-sightedness of Versailles.[63]

Richard Bosworth has suggested that these phrases can be interpreted in starkly contrasting ways. Read literally they confirm that at Munich, British policy secured its professed objectives which were quite in tune with the dominant principles underlying it since 1919; read as sarcasm, they constitute a savage indictment of the betrayal of democratic Czechoslovakia by a 'British Establishment as shamelessly devoted to public plunder as it usually was'.[64] These readings connect with the ambivalence of Taylor's interpretation of appeasement as a whole, and thus to two different characterisations of British identity. The first betrays a measure of what was to become quintessential revisionist sympathy for the appeasers, struggling to enact an appropriate policy under severe constraints, not the least of which was the flawed nature of the settlement they were pledged to defend. The second, conversely, harks back to the leftist variant of the orthodox critique, insisting that policy-makers could and should have acted differently, as Taylor had himself argued in the 1930s. Taylor's well-documented and colourful life makes it tempting to elucidate his texts by recourse to the contradictions in his personality. Was the tension between these two sentiments expressive of a conflict between the Taylor of the 1960s and the Taylor of the 1930s, or between Taylor the supposedly objective scholar and Taylor the radical activist? Perhaps his ambivalent radicalism – which led him to crave approval from the establishment he affected to despise – generated a dilemma, never fully articulated or resolved: should the heroes in this critical episode in the national past be radical dissenting anti-appeasers like himself, or Tory establishment figures like Chamberlain whom 'the record, considered in detachment' seemed increasingly to vindicate?[65]

Alternatively, these tensions can be ascribed to the nascent reformulation of the British sense of self. The two perspectives on appeasement delineated above implied quite different views of British capability in the 1930s, conditioned by a budding equivocation at this point in the 1960s about Britain's place in the world. Taylor exemplified this uncertainty, as becomes evident upon developing the implications of the third reading of his Munich passage provided by Bosworth, which construes Taylor as warning against deriving simplistic anti-appeasement messages from the 1930s, and urging that 'in the post-Hiroshima world, the ability to sit down and reason together and not write off your present enemy as a madman was crucial to human survival'. Taylor knew that for contemporary Britain nuclear brinkmanship was not a viable option: 'he had become increasingly if sadly aware that England's moment of greatness had gone forever'.[66] Yet the alternative he espoused was ironically still predicated on British influence if not power: 'his exaggerated belief in Britain's central role in world affairs was as evident in the basic assumptions of his CND campaigning – that others would take note of a moral lead by Britain – as it was ... in *The Origins of the Second World War*'.[67] (Other critics have pointed out the fundamentally Anglocentric nature of the text and thus the misleading nature of its expansive title.[68]) Subsequently, Taylor confirmed the accuracy of this diagnosis, remarking of the failure of the Campaign for Nuclear Disarmament that 'we made one great mistake which ultimately doomed [it] to futility. We thought that Great Britain was still a great power whose example would affect the rest of the world'.[69] At this point the arch-patriot Taylor remained confused about this issue, but it is not fanciful to see ambivalences about national identity as a major ideological factor conditioning *The Origins of the Second World War*.

The incoherence of Taylor's interpretation of appeasement means that he can scarcely be labelled a revisionist. But to dwell on the inconsistencies of his account is to miss the essence of his achievement, which was destructive rather than creative. By the early 1960s existing interpretations were losing their suasive power, and Taylor's intervention comprehensively unsettled dominant ways of looking at the 1930s, opening up spaces for new narratives without itself offering a clearly articulated re-interpretation. So while his own arguments proved evanescent, *The Origins of the Second World War* nonetheless signposted the imminent coalescence of the revisionist view. Absolutely central to this process was growing sensitivity to the contemporary limitations of British power, as the national decline that Taylor had groped to comprehend appeared to gather pace. Where orthodox critics had assumed British strength and policy-makers' freedom of action, revisionists read back into the 1930s a sense of weakness, of a gulf between resources and commitments, which caused them to cast the appeasers in a much more favourable light. As Donald Cameron Watt presciently wrote in 1965, emerging sympathetic accounts of British policy predicated upon Chamberlain's limited room for manoeuvre had 'the ring of truth to men who live in the last stages of the contraction of British world power as we do today'.[70]

This rethinking coincided with a broader destabilising of established coordinates in British collective memory.[71] The return to power of Labour in 1964 might have been expected to presage a reaffirmation of the collectivist message of the 'People's War', but in fact the post-war consensus soon appeared to be in difficulties. 'By the late 1960s there were clear signs that Keynesianism was falling apart, as inflation gathered momentum and the trade balance soared'.[72] In the ensuing atmosphere of national malaise, the chief challenge to the settlement came from the left, with the 'cultural radicalisms' of the 1960s and 1970s 'angrily and exuberantly exposing its deficiencies and denouncing its congealing of values into a normalized resistance to change'. Historians and other cultural critics questioned the long-term achievements of consensus and urged a radical renewal of the vision of 'the democratic romance of 1945'. Such disparagement further undermined consensus, but never fully captured 'the political initiative in national-popular terms' and thus ultimately opened up space for the right 'to regroup' and mount its own 'culturalist backlash'.[73] From this perspective, the problem was not that consensus was too timid, but rather that its very existence had sapped national vitality: now the 'great crusade was ... to roll back the tide of state intervention, to free the people from the kind of central direction that could only be justified in emergencies such as that of 1940'.[74] It would take the consolidation of Thatcherism in power in the early 1980s for this indictment of consensus to achieve institutional supremacy, but throughout the 1970s these issues of politics and memory were raucously debated. Moreover, this occurred in the context of a generalised 'accumulation of national anxieties', with the growth of devolutionary nationalism, violence in Northern Ireland, economic crisis and 'panics over immigration and race'.[75] This climate of cultural disorder was propitious for the flowering of revisionist views of appeasement.

Other factors were also at work in prompting this historiographical turn. The debacle of Suez and the rise of détente had somewhat discredited simplistic Munich analogies.[76] The waning of Eurocentrism in a world dominated by superpower bipolarity and decolonisation encouraged scholars to conceive of the origins of the war as a global phenomenon, and thus to take a more synoptic view of the manifold problems confronting British policy-makers. Similarly, growing temporal distance from the war prompted increased consideration of the antecedents of immediate pre-war crises in the policies of previous administrations, thus placing them in longer-term perspectives. As elsewhere, the efflorescence of scholarly writing on the origins of the war in the 1960s was also facilitated by broader changes in the sub-discipline, as diplomatic history mutated into an international history attentive to profound and structural forces, the domestic determinants of policy and the role of economic, social and cultural factors. (This was in turn but one facet of shifts within the discipline *per se* as the rapid pace of social, economic and cultural change in the post-war world generated disenchantment with the explanatory power of traditional methodologies and encouraged a social turn.) These structural changes in the sub-discipline militated strongly in favour of analysis of the factors conditioning the appeasers' behaviour, precisely the issue upon which a revisionist defence was likely to depend.

Last, and in a sense least, came the 1967 Public Records Act which by reducing the closed period for British archives from 50 to 30 years almost instantly permitted access to the complete documentation of the inter-war period. Historians' 'professional ideology' dictates that this factor is usually identified as the critical one precipitating the rise of revisionism.[77] But while it was of course important – since it gave them access to the appeasers' own contemporary perceptions and justifications of their actions, and enabled much more detailed accounts – defences of appeasement along revisionist lines had always been possible, and had been growing increasingly plausible and numerous before the archives opened.

The 1960s were a transitional time, since interpretations of course did not become uniformly sympathetic at a stroke. In 1967, Christopher Thorne still focused on the 'considerable shortcomings' of British policy-makers, lamenting the fact that 'courage and ability were not abundant in public affairs', but he was fighting an explicit rearguard action against the advance of revisionism.[78] Even those accounts which still criticised Chamberlain for misjudging Hitler's intentions, even for being 'credulous and naive', now acknowledged how 'the country's resources were themselves under intense pressure' and 'how little these limitations on the sinews of policy were understood at the time and how much they have been overlooked since by critics of British policy'.[79] Some authors moved position rapidly, the most conspicuous example being Martin Gilbert's auto-revisionism between his co-authored (with Richard Gott) 1963 critique *The Appeasers* and his sympathetic 1966 delineation of *The Roots of Appeasement*.[80] By the end of the decade, revisionist sensibilities were dominant. In 1968 W. N. Medlicott's account of British policy in the period was premised on the notion of incipient imperial over-stretch, and it advanced a tentative defence of Munich as Chamberlainite *realpolitik*; moreover, he argued that such was the extent of consensus over the main lines of foreign policy in the 1930s that popular stereotypes drawing sharp distinctions between appeasers and resisters were now impossible to sustain.[81] In the same year, in one of the last major studies published before the opening of the archives, Keith Robbins catalogued the constraints under which Chamberlain had laboured before concluding that Munich had been 'the necessary purgatory through which Englishmen had to pass before the nation could emerge united in 1939'.[82] Appeasement was reassessed as 'a central episode in a protracted retreat from an untenable "world power" status'. On such an analysis, it 'was neither stupid nor wicked: it was merely inevitable'.[83]

Through the next two decades international historians worked on the mass of freshly available documents, exploring in a deluge of monographs and articles the thematic issues newly prominent in the sub-discipline, in order to bulk out a revisionist interpretation that fit the now dominant discourse of British decline. Accordingly, appeasement was redefined as a rational and logical response to imperial over-stretch, formulated by policy-makers who correctly perceived that the British Empire had inadequate resources to defend sprawling global commitments from the tripartite revisionist challenge of Germany, Italy and Japan. The interests of Britain, as a *status quo* power deriving prosperity from world trade, dictated the avoidance of war, but more to the point a host of objective constraints precluded the pursuit of any forceful policy. Britain had no dependable allies in Europe or across the Atlantic; the Dominions were chary of continental entanglements; at home, economic weakness and pacific public opinion in an age of mass democracy precluded large-scale rearmament to remedy the military deficiencies that had developed since 1919; the Versailles settlement was riven by contradictions, its moral validity irredeemably compromised; fear of the apocalyptic effects of modern warfare combined with the psychological scars left by the Great War further impelled British statesmen away from confrontation. In this context, appeasement was not a product of foolish individual whim, it was 'massively over-determined', the inevitable product of secular decline; the appeasers had no choice but to seek negotiations with the revisionists, aiming for general détente through the rectification of just grievances if it were achievable, otherwise buying time for rearmament and to create the most propitious circumstances for war.[84] Appeasement was thus incorporated into a new national narrative in which it was quite in keeping with tradition, indeed:

> a 'natural' policy for a small island-state gradually losing its place in world affairs, shouldering military and economic burdens which were increasingly too great for it, and developing internally from an oligarchic to a more democratic society in which sentiments in favour of the pacific and rational settlement of disputes were widely held.[85]

Appeasement thus became quintessentially British rather than a betrayal of the national heritage.

Any summary of the revisionist view necessarily presents it as rather more monolithic than it was. Although the constraints on policy-makers were now universally foregrounded, there remained significant debate as to precisely how far these had determined policy, as to the wisdom and skill demonstrated in prosecuting that policy in particular areas, and indeed as to the general verdict on appeasement and Chamberlain (some authors drawing a distinction between the two). On the fringes of revisionism lay Keith Middlemas who conceded that between 1937 and 1939 Chamberlain, 'aware of Britain's multiple weaknesses and the risks of war', attempted 'to bring commitments and power into alignment' and that he should be commended for this 'realistic acceptance of Britain's diminished estate in relation to the rest of the world'. But despite this, Middlemas still found a great deal to criticise in the formulation, execution and presentation of policy and argued that, particularly in the winter of 1938–39, Chamberlain pursued a *Diplomacy of Illusion* until external events forced the belated adoption of a coherent policy of deterrence.[86] In the heartland, conversely, stood David Dilks, who developed a strong interpretation that almost unreservedly defended Chamberlain as a masterly *realpolitiker* pursuing the best, if not only, policy possible given the 'substantial chasm' that separated 'Britain's commitments from her ability to fulfil them'.[87] Not only was this policy sensible, popular and of long-standing, it was also skilfully executed: at Munich Hitler was out-manoeuvred and put on his word, and when he proved in March 1939 that he could not be trusted, Chamberlain's policy became one of deterrence and resistance, his careful handling of affairs through his whole premiership ensuring that war came with the nation united and prepared.[88] (Looking to the historiography of France as a comparator, one could say that Dilks represented a 'strong' variant of revisionism, portraying appeasement as the product of Chamberlain's wise statecraft, whereas 'weaker' variants presented it as entirely determined by circumstances.)

Other discrete viewpoints within the revisionist tradition can also be identified. A significant minority opinion emphasised the imperialist dimension of British identity, arguing that Chamberlain's realistic policy was the only one 'which offered any hope of avoiding war – and of saving both lives and the British Empire'. According to this view, Chamberlain understood the limitations of British power far better than his critics, and his strategy of conflict-avoidance was best suited to the long run preservation of Britain's world role. Indeed, what was flawed about British policy was not Chamberlainite appeasement, but the decision to abandon it and resort to confrontation, which was forced upon Chamberlain by his Tory colleagues after Hitler's annexation of Prague. For John Charmley, a defence of Chamberlain was to be but a prelude to a thorough-going attack on Churchill, Chamberlain's most vociferous (and therefore most deluded) contemporary critic, whose over-estimation of national power and determination to confront Hitler eventually led to the sacrifice of British grandeur to colonial nationalists, Washington and socialism.[89] Different national perspectives were also evident. A signal contribution was made by German historians, coming to the subject with their own preoccupations and traditions and as some of the most devoted advocates of social science approaches. These scholars produced dense and massively documented structural analyses of the interaction between a huge range of domestic and international determinants of policy, demolishing criticisms of appeasement as 'illusionary and dilettantist' and powerfully contributing to the rise of revisionism.[90]

Differences of emphasis thus persisted between revisionists at the level of detail. But the new focus on structural constraints and the inexorable logic of decline transformed the terms of the debate, and this writing cumulatively consolidated a dominant revisionist sensibility. This was evident in Philip Bell's acclaimed, best-selling synthesis of 1986, and in the mass of works produced towards the end of the 1980s in connection with the fiftieth anniversary of the outbreak of war.[91] Donald Cameron Watt's monumental study of the last year of peace offered a not entirely flattering portrait of appeasement, but nonetheless doubted whether an alternative policy 'would have made any difference'.[92] Gerhard Weinberg, reflecting on the anniversary of the Munich crisis, presented the settlement as a defeat for Hitler and argued for the essential rationality, clarity and continuity of Chamberlain's strategy: 'if this Munich pact were broken, it was agreed, then the next German aggression that was resisted by the victim would bring on war'.[93] Finally, in a book accompanying a major BBC television series, Richard Overy synthesised the findings of two decades of research and concluded that no real alternative to appeasement had existed given that 'Britain's relative decline and her retreat from global power were evident already in the 1930s'.[94]

The factors identified above as precipitating revisionism had a persistent influence over much of the subsequent two decades. The reality of decline seemed to become ever more unquestionable: as one scholar observed, 'the onset of a new recession in Britain in the 1970s and 1980s' accelerated the growth of sympathy for the appeasers, fighting 'to save British society in its contemporary form, and to stabilize the decline in Britain's international position'.[95] In the post-war period in the context of consensus, the different variants of the orthodox critique had worked politically for both right and left, either 'validating the ascendancy in the Conservative party of Churchill's aristocratic paternalism over Chamberlain's Midlands business ethic, and thus help[ing to] support the "one nation" Toryism of Harold Macmillan', or serving as 'part of a left-wing critique of that patrician class'.[96] In the 1960s and beyond, as consensus faltered amidst general recognition of British decline (notwithstanding the fierce debate about its root causes), revisionism proved itself similarly supple and able to serve diverse political ends. A new generation of younger radical Tory historians emerged as amongst the staunchest advocates of revisionism, 'convinced by their instincts and their politics of the injustice done by the Tory critics of the Conservatives of the 1930s' and determined 'to bring the traditional *Guilty Men* of inter-war Conservatism out of the cold into the cosy warmth of the "central" British tradition as established by the Second World War'.[97] Conversely, for men of the left such as Taylor, questioning the verities of anti-appeasement was not simply a radical gesture in relation to the Cold War; problematising the hitherto bleakly monochrome picture of the 1930s on which consensus had been built was also a means of demanding whether the promises of the 'People's War' had really been fulfilled.[98]

The revisionist turn was a product of diverse disciplinary, political mnemonic factors. Changing perspectives on international history, the opening of the archives and the natural enthusiasm of each new generation of historians to confound the conventional wisdom established by their predecessors (especially in this era of university expansion) came together to produce a fresh sympathetic perspective focusing on structural constraints. Yet this also occurred in a broader political context where the meaning of the war and understandings of national identity had become profoundly contested; as Robert Skidelsky observed, 'a static society confirms its historical orthodoxies', whereas a dynamic one 'always rewrites its history'.[99] Although it is important not to drift into idealist determinism or monocausal fallacies, the shift in understandings of British national identity, with the acceptance across the political spectrum of the reality of decline, was central to this historiographical innovation. Although the general public remained rather resistant to the rehabilitation of the appeasers, the ideological thrust of this scholarship was to naturalise and rationalise a sense of decline. By rewriting appeasement in a heroic rather than shameful register, depicting Britain in the 1930s as in the present pluckily battling against adverse circumstances only finally to emerge victorious, the revisionists salvaged something positive for Britain from the wreck of empire, offering comfort to the nation as it adjusted to its more humble and restricted world role.

'Choices for conciliation rather than resistance': the counter-revisionist critique

If the historiography of appeasement had come to a full stop with revisionism, then it would have been plausible to argue that in the fullness of time interested, subjective explanations had simply given way to documented, objective ones. But that position is much harder to sustain given the further twist in the historiographical tale in the 1990s, which saw the coalescence of a self-styled counter-revisionist interpretation that reaffirmed, albeit with refinements, the orthodox position. Critical interpretations insisting on the primacy of agency and the necessity of harsh moral judgement never in fact disappeared, and as the context of research and writing changed, these views enjoyed a renaissance as the debate moved 'full circle'.[100]

Some of the criticisms levelled against revisionism during its years of dominance were methodological. The archives revealed the appeasers' own estimations of the constraints under which they were operating, and some alleged that the revisionists read these documents too literally, in a sense too sympathetic to the appeasers, simply reproducing rather than analysing their self-justifications. 'Mesmerised by the official memoranda, the forager in the Public Record Office may end up writing official history, perpetuating the Establishment's own reading of its problems and policies', concluding as ministers and officials had 'that nothing different could possibly have been done'.[101] It did not take 'postmodernists' to point out that while the factual record of British policy could now be reconstructed in greater detail than ever before, the documents could never decisively settle interpretive issues of motive or of the relative influence of different factors and interests in policy-making. The dominant literal reading of the documents reproduced the appeasers' own understanding of their actions as rational and logical, even inevitable, in the circumstances of the time. But arguably this begged the critical question: 'were the premises on which their policies were based correct?'[102]

So while the revisionist paradigm remained dominant, doubts about the contextual factors supposedly determining appeasement were constantly raised. On the one hand, it was argued that in many cases Chamberlain referred to alleged constraints 'only as an *ex post facto* justification of policies he had pursued for other reasons'.[103] A revisionist might contend that 'over Czechoslovakia Chamberlain saw the reluctance of the dominions to fight, and the consequent break up of the commonwealth, as decisive', but while this was certainly what Chamberlain had said in Cabinet, was it actually true?[104] After all, he issued the guarantee to Poland six months later in the teeth of continued Dominion hostility to continental entanglements: 'he did not consult them, but presented them with a "fait accompli"'.[105] On the other hand, the coercive reality of these 'determinants' was also open to question. For problems to become constraints they had first to be construed as such by the policy-making bureaucracy. But often during this process perceptions of the objective situation were flawed or inaccurate, the constraints magnified or invented by the particular ways 'in which the issues were perceived and tackled' reflecting 'a priori principles and choices'; indeed in some cases it seemed as if the so-called constraints were actively constructed by Chamberlain himself.[106] Thus methodological objections to revisionism shaded into substantive interpretive ones.

On each of the key thematic issues at stake, such alternative readings proved possible. Revisionists made much of the pessimistic prognoses the Chiefs of Staff tendered to Chamberlain throughout the later 1930s, but a trenchant case could be made that this advice was predicated upon a 'worst case analysis', and that delaying confrontation exacerbated rather than ameliorated the British strategic dilemma.[107] Similarly, it was obvious that economic difficulties were bound to limit rearmament to some degree, but the rearmament policy actually adopted depended upon the most conservative and cautious reading possible of the economic situation; revisionists might argue that policy-makers were constrained by economic orthodoxy, but if 'the Government was the prisoner of its own assumptions about the economy and society' were there not also in fact alternative choices available, and therefore some culpability to be borne?[108] In the case of potential allies, the preconception dictating that certain powers could not be relied on to assist in containing Germany arguably became 'a self-confirming conclusion'.[109] 'To be sure, there were special problems in Great Britain's relations with France, the Soviet Union, and the United States which would not have been easy to surmount. But no serious effort was made ... '.[110] Studies of propaganda also added grist to the sceptics' mill. Some research was predicated upon 'the realities of decline', and thus supported the revisionist case.[111] But damning evidence against Chamberlain came from work on his government's handling of the press. Far from being a helpless prisoner of a pacific public, the government had worked extensively to manage the media, to prevent the open airing of alternatives to appeasement and thus to fashion opinion to its own ends. Such research was doubly damaging. It cast doubt on the reality of the 'determinants' of appeasement, and also undermined Chamberlain's image as a sincere statesmen, occasionally forced to take tough decisions in the national interest, presenting him instead as a power-hungry autocrat, ready to manipulate public and colleagues alike and to use any means necessary to prosecute the personal policy that he was convinced was right.[112]

Through the heyday of revisionism such objections accumulated without displacing the 'authorized version'.[113] Arguments that policy had been poorly conceived or incompetently executed in a particular thematic or geographical area proved susceptible to incorporation into revisionist interpretations; alternatively, they could be disputed or ignored. Revisionism was, after all, a perspective that had arisen in advance of the detailed archival research that subsequently substantiated it; it was an act of faith as much as anything else and so long as the broad cultural forces and assumptions that had engendered it persisted, the edifice could survive the removal of numerous bricks. But towards the end of the 1980s the likely outlines of a comprehensive alternative interpretation could be discerned. Rather than seeing appeasement as a perspicacious response to the Nazi challenge, this would argue that the assumptions of the appeasers had been flawed and that their designs had not turned out as they anticipated:

> Appeasement, which was intended to conciliate, failed to pacify. Rearmament, which was meant to deter, failed to do so. War, which it was hoped to avoid, broke out on 3 September 1939, and the British Expeditionary Force proved inadequate for its task.[114]

If appeasement were redefined as a failure, then it would no longer be possible to discount its immoral dimension – the fact that it involved 'imposing sacrifices on the publics of countries who had looked to Britain as a model and a protector' – as revisionism had through its preoccupation with structural constraints and *realpolitik* logic.[115] This view would refocus attention on to personality and ideology, the subjective motives and contingent choices of individual statesmen. In 1986 Paul Kennedy, to a certain extent recanting his earlier revisionism, argued that it was necessary to re-emphasise:

> those very important personal feelings behind appeasement: the contempt and indifference felt by many leading Englishmen towards east-central

Europe, the half-fear-half-admiration with which Nazi Germany and Fascist Italy were viewed, the detestation of communism, the apprehensions about future war.[116]

The term 'counter-revisionist' was coined by R. A. C. Parker whose own elegant contributions played a crucial role in reorienting the debate in the 1990s back towards earlier critiques. For Parker, the appeasers were not fools or cowards, but they did fundamentally misunderstand the nature of Nazi expansionism and the menace it represented. Chamberlain in particular always entertained unrealistic hopes that a negotiated compromise agreement simultaneously satisfying Hitler (whom he judged rational and potentially sincere) and protecting British interests was possible. The dual policy of negotiation and rearmament that Britain pursued through the 1930s was in essence sensible and popular, but as prosecuted by Chamberlain after 1937 it comprised too much conciliation and not enough deterrence. Although decline limited British options, real alternatives to appeasement existed, but Chamberlain consciously rejected both large-scale rearmament and the construction of an anti-fascist coalition as potentially provocative and unnecessary, since limited defensive rearmament would prove sufficient to make Hitler see sense and come to terms: hence his decisions always entailed 'choices for conciliation rather than resistance'.[117]

Moreover, Chamberlain clung to appeasement long after it was drained of any *realpolitik* rationale, and when colleagues and country had abandoned any hope of agreement with Germany. After March 1939, British opinion had decisively moved in support of Churchill's policy prescriptions of increased rearmament and the negotiation of a Grand Alliance with Stalin; the guarantee to Poland and Chamberlain's increasingly blunt public rhetoric made it seem that appeasement was indeed dead, that 'confrontation had replaced conciliation'. But in fact Chamberlain was dissembling, offering the minimum concessions necessary in word and deed to appear 'sufficiently Churchillian to make it unnecessary for him to bring Churchill into the government', thus ensuring that he could continue his 'subtle manoeuvres' and 'furtive advances', exploring any possible avenue for compromise, even 'by stealth' through private channels of dubious constitutional legality, in order to avert the war he dreaded.[118] Appeasement was not 'a feeble policy of surrender and unlimited retreat', since Chamberlain intended to check German expansion and had a rational (though mistaken) strategy to achieve that goal; but he abandoned the traditional British method of containing threats through the balance of power, failing to see that Hitler could not be restrained by conciliation, and thus left Britain dangerously exposed and unprepared. 'Led by Chamberlain, the government rejected effective deterrence', which 'probably stifled serious chances of preventing the Second World War'.[119] This is not to say that Churchill's alternative strategy of resistance would certainly have forestalled Hitler, but Parker's 'tentative conclusion' reaffirms that this was indeed 'The Unnecessary War'.[120]

Parker's argument was far from entirely innovative: indeed, his detailed reconstruction of the parliamentary duel between Chamberlain and Churchill made crystal clear how the terms of the original political debate on the wisdom of appeasement remained central to the historiography. But he nonetheless mounted a formidable indictment. Though keen to distance himself from the 'posthumous libels' of earlier polemicists and tempering his own judgements with revisionist sensitivity to internal and external constraints, he evinced a basically orthodox sensibility, cogently adapting and synthesising the key criticisms made by anti-revisionist scholars from the 1960s onwards.[121] Chief amongst these was the argument that Chamberlain had a 'fundamental lack of grasp of what the Nazis really stood for': his rationalist worldview meant he could never comprehend Hitler or devise appropriate policies to deal with him.[122] Hence the assertion that the real roots of appeasement lay in Chamberlain's flawed perceptions, which led him to choose conciliation 'because he thought it correct': 'he was not the mere puppet of circumstantial constraints' (about whose insuperability Parker was naturally sceptical).[123] The claim that March 1939 marked no decisive turning point in Chamberlain's thinking similarly implied that individual convictions rather than objective factors 'must play a central part in ... explanation of British policy';[124] other counter-revisionists went even further, arguing that Chamberlain had to be dragged into war by his colleagues and clung to appeasement until May 1940, thus developing the thrust of earlier critical work.[125] Parker also echoed previous critics in distinguishing between appeasement in general and its Chamberlainite variant, the former being viewed much more positively than the latter. Keith Middlemas had argued that Chamberlain took British policy down a wrong turning in 1937, and later studies contended that other ministers – particularly Halifax – had played a key role after Munich in shifting British policy away from conciliation, even though Chamberlain's conversion was much less complete than theirs.[126] The upshot of all this is that Parker's verdict is in one sense even more severe than that of *Guilty Men*, in that it is Chamberlain almost alone rather than a whole political class that stands indicted:

> No one can know what would have happened in Europe if Mr. Chamberlain had been more flexible or if someone else had taken charge, but it is hard to imagine that any other foreign policy could have had a more disastrous outcome.[127]

The warm reception accorded Parker's *Chamberlain and Appeasement* suggested that a thoroughgoing reorientation was afoot. Apparent confirmation came from the way in which certain scholars seemed to have reconsidered their positions. For example, Sidney Aster – much more willing than Parker to present counter-revisionism as a return to the *Guilty Men* critique – had switched camps dramatically since writing his broadly revisionist 1973 study of *1939*.[128] Diverse other contributions, while not advancing identical interpretations, nonetheless gave credence to the notion of a nascent counter-revisionist school. Brian McKercher denounced appeasement as an unrealistic and disastrous departure from the British tradition of upholding a balance of power on the continent through robust alliance diplomacy: 'lacking a grounding in *realpolitik*' Chamberlainite appeasement entailed a 'fruitless search for compromises that were not there'.[129] Greg Kennedy delivered a devastating verdict on Chamberlain as 'an arrogant, narrow, vindictive man' – indeed, 'a petty dictator in his own right' – who 'was indeed guilty of being incapable of comprehending or defending the needs of Britain and the empire'. 'His goal was to use appeasement to provide time either for Britain to rearm to an adequate level, or to allow the aggressor states to come to the end of their demands and begin to take a more "conventional" role in European affairs. Neither option came to fruition'.[130] Erik Goldstein traced how at Munich, Chamberlain's 'initial ideal of action and courage had become pretence, then timidity and finally façade'.[131] General textbooks produced by scholars on both sides of the Atlantic similarly embraced more critical perspectives.[132]

Detailed monographic work in this vein undermined the alleged constraints on policy-makers and elucidated the potential alternatives to Chamberlainite appeasement. Revised interpretations of British defence policy disputed the view that the British economy could not sustain extensive rearmament, insisting that 'Chamberlain's government did not rearm because it did not want to'.[133] The constraining influence of Britain's want of reliable allies was also questioned by scholars arguing that antipathy to communism clouded government perceptions of the national interest, and decisively precluded meaningful Anglo-Soviet co-operation to contain Hitler.[134] Alternative policies that were actually advocated in the 1930s – such as Robert Vansittart's conception, as Permanent Under-Secretary at the Foreign Office, of a 'global strategy based on alliance diplomacy' and extended, conventional deterrence – were rehabilitated as genuine options, and the manner in which they were sidelined as Chamberlain established his ascendancy was traced.[135] There was even a left-wing variant of the counter-revisionist approach, harking back to earlier socialist critiques of appeasement as a product of the sinister capitalist intrigues of a decadent ruling class.[136] The generally lukewarm reception accorded by scholars in the early 1990s to a spate of critical biographies of Churchill, which rested in substantial part on revisionist interpretations of appeasement, was also telling.[137] This is not, of course, to say that revisionist works were entirely absent, for writing more inclined to defend than condemn could still be found both in general textbooks and detailed studies, but they were in a minority.[138] Although judgements about the shifting climate of opinion within scholarly fields are unavoidably subjective, it can nonetheless plausibly be argued that the 1990s witnessed the emergence of a powerful counter-revisionist sensibility.

In accordance with the sub-discipline's dominant conventions, counter-revisionists explained this by reference to empirical factors. Aster, for example, claimed that Chamberlain's private papers, neglected by the revisionists, decisively proved the counter-revisionist case.[139] This can hardly be true, however, since many key revisionist texts had been constructed using the very same documents from Chamberlain's papers that Aster deployed. Parker, conversely, implied that revisionists misinterpreted the available documentation, and that the balance of evidence now pointed towards counter-revisionist conclusions.[140] This at least had the virtue of making clear that what was actually at stake here was how a more or less given documentary record should be interpreted, but the implication that an entire generation of historians had lacked the intelligence and objectivity that permitted another to read the documents correctly was extremely Whiggish and implausible. Once more, it is necessary to attend to the broader cultural and ideological factors conditioning interpretation to acquire a nuanced understanding of this historiographical sea change.

Shifts in prevailing conceptions of British national identity were implicated in the rise of counter-revisionism. The view of British identity underpinning Parker's interpretation – namely that while there were certain limitations on British power the nation retained room for manoeuvre – was mirrored in contemporaneous writing on the theme of decline *per se*. The revisionist view was premised upon a determinist narrative of British history that scripted an inevitable, continuous, linear slide: 'Victorian grandeur, Edwardian sunset, Georgian decline, and Elizabethan disintegration'. This narrative flourished in general studies in the 1970s and 1980s, arguably reaching its apogee in Paul Kennedy's 1987 work on *The Rise and Fall of the Great Powers* which 'turned the tale of Great Britain as a great power into a paradigm: what was true of the British and their power has been true of all states at all times'. But a reaction against that position was already in train, and in the early 1990s British decline was widely reconceptualised, as it was argued that the decrease in British power was relative rather than absolute and that the onset of that process should not be antedated.[141] The result was the construction of a more nuanced narrative, 'not a history of inexorable decline, but an account of how a major power with intrinsic weaknesses *and* under-utilised potential tried to consolidate and retain its exposed position'.[142] In this paradigm, determinism gave way to an appreciation of the contingency of events and the role of subjective choices; how policy-makers played their hand became as important as the cards in it and 'certain decisions contributed substantially to the decline and almost resulted in national catastrophe'.[143] A negative interpretation of appeasement, emphasising flawed choices and Chamberlain's 'wishful thinking', thus featured as an intrinsic part of this new metanarrative of decline that had simultaneously underpinned Parker's re-interpretation.[144]

This, of course, simply poses a further question: why did 'declinist pathologies and their underlying "narratives"' become 'decreasingly potent' in the intellectual climate of the 1990s?[145] What forces impelled this academic rethinking of decline? Emphatically, they included the crafting of a more positive sense of British national identity in the years since Margaret Thatcher set out to transcend the troubled introspection of the gloomy 1970s and to instigate her own national renewal. Thatcherism as an ideological project combined diverse political and mnemonic elements in its reassertion of national grandeur, but specifically mobilised particular images and representations of the Second World War era to prise apart the structure of assumptions that had underpinned consensus. The post-war settlement had been erected upon a foundational opposition between the 1930s, characterised in unrelievedly negative terms and an implicitly superior present and future. The competing myths of the 'People's War' and Churchill's rugged individualist nationalism could just about co-exist within this structure, but Thatcherism posited a more nuanced reading of the 1930s, pointing up the contradictions between the two in order to consign collectivism to history. On the one hand, abetted by revisionist economic historians who had redefined the 1930s as years of stability and prosperity, Thatcher rehabilitated the non-interventionist, sound money, economic policies of the National Government and explicitly argued that 'what the country needed was a stiff dose of Victorian Values, transplanted from the … 1930s, when they had, allegedly, last held sway'.[146] On the other hand, she appropriated the orthodox critique of appeasement in its specifically right-wing variant as an integral element in her resurrection of the Churchillian vision of a proud island race beset by enemies (without and within); in vigorously reasserting a sense of national grandeur, she decisively exchanged 'ideals of social justice for a patriotism straight and pure'.[147]

The Falklands War was a critical moment in the successful consolidation of the Thatcherite project. On one level, this was because military victory served as a distraction from domestic troubles, thus facilitating the 1983 election triumph which inaugurated the period of high Thatcherism and 'the legislative and cultural undermining of the postwar domestic settlement'.[148] More profoundly, the rhetoric through which public support for the conflict was mobilised proposed a new basis for national unity and a new sense of national identity. It was saturated with references to the Second World War era portrayed in Churchillian terms; the post-war years of consensus – not coincidentally the years when Britain had declined – were a parenthesis, an aberration from those essential British traditions which had been dominant in the war and to which the nation – 'in exile from its authentic self' – was now urged to return. This interpretation replicated Churchill's narrative of British history in which a proud, heroic, resolute and strong nation had repeatedly stood firm against dictators in defence of democracy. This image of the national past might have been obscured during the collectivist years, but the war in the Falklands was represented as an ultimately successful quest for the recovery of that enduring identity: as Thatcher put it at the 1982 Conservative Party conference, "Britain found herself again in the South Atlantic and will not look back from the victory she has won".[149]

Thus Thatcher propagated a new sense of British identity, grounded in right-wing aggressively masculine values (presented as natural and traditional), and articulated through a particular representation of the Second World War. (Relatedly, this period also saw an upsurge in football hooliganism around the English national team, and the transformation of 'fairly humdrum' Germanophobia into 'a more violent chauvinism, greatly aided by the Thatcher governments' obsessive desire to identify enemies of Britain, whether they were domestic trade unions or foreign countries'.[150]) Admittedly, the precise circumstances in which the Falklands conflict came about made it difficult to draw direct parallels with the era of appeasement since in 1982 the guilty woman and men largely remained in office.[151] But 'potentially problematic comparisons with 1938 or with the collapse of Chamberlain's premiership in 1940 were quickly marginalised', and the focus was placed firmly on 1939, the last time Britain had embarked on a good war in defence of democracy and civilisation. 1982 offered an opportunity for the nation to rectify the mistakes of the past, to throw off the legacy of the shabby policies of compromise and retreat that had characterised the post-war years, and to be born again.[152] Thatcher redefined and simplified British collective memory, narrowing the range of acceptable readings down to an individualistic and patriotic Churchillian one, in order to ground her right-wing modernisation project. Contemporary critics easily grasped the thrust of this construction: 'Britain has fallen from "her" previous supremacy, but can be Great again. The Thatcher government is the self appointed heir of the glorious past'.[153]

This re-engineering of Britishness did not go uncontested, but more positive perspectives on national identity nonetheless persisted.[154] This was one of the more striking aspects of continuity between the Conservative governments of Thatcher and John Major and the New Labour administration of Tony Blair which came to power in 1997. Although some cosmetic reconfiguration of narratives of national history was required, at bottom Labour decided 'that the ideological codes of the Conservative Party are too powerful, too pervasive, to deconstruct'.[155] Specifically, it 'moved to accept the proposition that the 1980s had seen a reversal of "decline"'.[156] Hence one turn of the century commentator argued:

> The Falklands War may seem a geographically and historically distant conflict today, but ... it represents a critical space – physical, mythic and narrative – in the shaping of contemporary Britain. The brash, self-confident nationalism of later 1990s 'Cool Britannia' is built on the bones of what happened in the South Atlantic in the spring of 1982 and how these events were mediated, experienced and understood back in the United Kingdom.[157]

Explicit in this positive national redefinition was a reaffirmation of Churchillian themes in foreign policy rhetoric. This became manifest during the 1999 Kosovo crisis, when Blair took a leading role in scripting the conflict with Slobodan Milošević's Serbia as a replay of the Second World War, indeed as 'a battle between good and evil; between civilization and barbarity'.[158] The public war of words preceding the invasion of Iraq in 2003 was similarly saturated with the memory of appeasement. Blair drew the analogy explicitly, when he opined in impeccably counter-revisionist terms that 'when people decided not to confront fascism, they were doing the popular thing, they were doing it for good reasons, and they were good people ... but they made the wrong decision'.[159]

It would be an over-simplification to deem the emergence of counter-revisionism a direct effect of changing public memory of the war and dominant readings of national identity. For one thing, this would understate the extent to which politics, memory and historiography were bound up together as linked components of a larger discursive structure.[160] Equally, the persistence – albeit on the margins – of more sympathetic revisionist views demonstrated that even powerful ideological currents can be negotiated in diverse ways, suggesting that other factors are also operative. The turn to counter-revisionism could also be explained by reference to internal factors, such as the vicissitudes of methodological and interpretive fashion in the wider sub-discipline, or the simple disenchantment of appeasement scholars with revisionism's deterministic structuralism. Yet it is nonetheless striking that it should have emerged in this political and mnemonic climate, and there is a clear compatibility between this reading of appeasement and post-1970s efforts to revivify and reassert British national pride. Moreover, this neo-Churchillian narrative has further ideological implications in the real world, functioning as a 'regime of truth' that has helped to sustain recent Anglo-American foreign policy adventurism.[161]

Ever since its inception in the perceptions and rhetoric of the 1930s, the appeasement debate has revolved around two contrasting viewpoints, grounded in two of the most archetypal forms of narrative emplotment: a negative one emphasising contingency, agency and morality, and a positive one emphasising determinism, structural constraints and *realpolitik*. The public record of British diplomacy in the 1930s provides sufficient material to support either of these interpretations, and in the light of subsequent archival revelations historians have filled them out in ever-greater detail and nuance rather than supplanting them.[162] The literature tends to present particular iterations of these views as products of archival factors, but consideration of the broader political and mnemonic context helps to explain the relative salience or dominance of one interpretation at any given time, and is essential to grasp their ideological valence. The orthodox view prevailed during the post-war period of consensus, working to sustain reconstruction and a restored sense of national grandeur. Revisionism flourished from the 1960s as the realities of decline came home, and counter-revisionism emerged as the correlate of Thatcher's efforts to reverse decline by re-invoking a Churchillian narrative of national history. The very latest twist in the tale is an incipient revival of revisionist views, most notably in an authoritative new biography of Chamberlain from a scholar who has unrivalled knowledge of his personal archive.[163] It is too early to say whether this development presages another fully-fledged reorientation of the field, and powerful counter-revisionist sentiments certainly persist.[164] (Commentators also routinely preach the desirability of transcending these established oppositions through some form of methodological or interpretive innovation, even a cultural turn.[165]) It is also precarious to attempt to incorporate it into the broader reading essayed here, though it is tempting to observe that a revived revisionism might resonate uncannily with the downcast mood of a post-Blair Britain currently mired in disillusion and recession.[166]

How far collective memory of the war remains alive in contemporary Britain is much debated, with some claiming that 'the nation is witnessing the final manifestations of a national obsession that is about to pass into history'.[167] But various different elements in the complex amalgam of memory certainly retain an enduring presence and urgency. Despite seismic changes in Britain's place in the world and the internal coordinates of national identity, a Churchillian sense of British greatness and rectitude – in which the memory of the war figures prominently – maintains a tenacious foothold, exerting a baneful influence that is regularly decried; hence one recent German lament that 'New Labour increasingly philosophises about the blessings of being British, with no sense of there being a dark side, as with all other peoples'.[168] Although the great drama of the 'People's War' as the foundation of the post-war settlement has now been played out, elements of that mythological structure remain lodged in the public imagination, as was demonstrated after the London terrorist bombings of 7 July 2005 when in press coverage, public reaction and political rhetoric 'the memory of the Blitz pressed itself to the fore'.[169] It cannot be claimed that the historiography of appeasement has been as highly charged, contentious or salient a discourse of memory as these grand myths of the Second World War era (especially as it probably needs to be distinguished from the more generalised 'myth of Munich' in foreign policy discourse, which has had its own rhythm and has been relatively more static). Yet although its history is certainly intertwined with theirs, it deserves the dignity of a separate appraisal, having served as one distinctive means whereby the British and others have conducted an extended meditation on Britain's decline from world power status.

Notes

1 Quoted in A. Adamthwaite, *The Making of the Second World War* (London, Allen and Unwin, 1977), p. 177.
2 R. Overy, *The Origins of the Second World War* (London, Longman, 1998, 2nd edn), p. 113.
3 Quoted in S. Aster, '"Guilty Men": the case of Neville Chamberlain', in R. Boyce and E. M. Robertson (eds), *Paths to War: New Essays on the Origins of the Second World War* (London, Macmillan, 1989), pp. 255–56.
4 Quoted in J. W. Wheeler-Bennett, *Munich: Prologue to Tragedy* (London, Macmillan, 1963, rev. edn), p. 181.

5 D. Dilks, '"We must hope for the best and prepare for the worst": the Prime Minister, the Cabinet and Hitler's Germany, 1937–39', *Proceedings of the British Academy*, vol. 73, 1987, p. 333.

6 J. Chapman, 'Re-presenting war: British television drama-documentary and the Second World War', *European Journal of Cultural Studies*, vol. 10, no. 1, 2007, p. 13.

7 M. Connelly, *We Can Take It! Britain and the Memory of the Second World War* (London, Longman, 2004), especially pp. 280–97.

8 Quoted in P. J. Beck, 'The relevance of the "irrelevant": football as a missing dimension in the study of British relations with Germany', *International Affairs*, vol. 79, no. 2, 2003, p. 399; M. Matussek, 'My personal VE Day', *Spiegel Online*, 11 May 2005, http://www. spiegel.de/international/0,1518,355605,00.html (accessed 16 Feburary 2006). Some of the material drawn on in this chapter tends to conflate England and Britain; though this move elides important nuances, constraints of space preclude unpacking it here.

9 M. Kettle, 'The worst thing about this World Cup is it's in Germany', *The Guardian*, 3 June 2006, http://www.guardian.co.uk/commentisfree/2006/jun/03/comment.germany (accessed 31 July 2008). In fact, these fears were not realised and Anglo-German cordiality reigned during the competition itself: L. Harding, 'The war is over', *The Guardian*, 26 December 2006, http://www.guardian.co.uk/commentisfree/2006/dec/26/post839 (accessed 26 December 2006).

10 D. Reynolds, '1940: fulcrum of the twentieth century?', *International Affairs*, vol. 66, no. 2, 1990, p. 348; cf. A. Roberts, '1945 and all that', *The Spectator*, 11 February 1995, pp. 9–11. For a nuanced discussion see P. Ludlow, 'Paying the price of victory? Postwar Britain and the ideas of national independence', in D. Geppert (ed.), *The Postwar Challenge: Cultural, Social, and Political Change in Western Europe, 1945–58* (Oxford, Oxford University Press, 2003), pp. 259–72.

11 A. Beevor, 'Tommy and Jerry', *The Guardian*, 16 February 1999, http://www.guardian.co. uk/theguardian/1999/feb/16/features11.g22 (accessed 14 February 2006).

12 G. Eley, 'Finding the People's War: film, British collective memory, and World War II', *American Historical Review*, vol. 106, no. 3, 2001, p. 821.

13 M. Smith, *Britain and 1940: History, Myth and Popular Memory* (London, Routledge, 2000), quotes at pp. 9, 128.

14 Smith himself admits in *Britain and 1940* that 'the myth of 1940 and its contradictions continue to permeate British lives' (p. 9) especially in relation to attitudes towards Europe (pp. 130–48).

15 S. Nicholas, 'History, revisionism and television drama: *Foyle's War* and the "myth of 1940"', *Media History*, vol. 13, no. 2. 2007, pp. 203–19.

16 J. Baxendale and C. Pawling, *Narrating the Thirties: A Decade in the Making: 1930 to the Present* (London, Macmillan, 1996), especially pp. 127–29.

17 For example, respectively, Connelly, *We Can Take It!*; D. Chuter, 'Munich, or the blood of others', in C. Buffet and B. Heuser (eds), *Haunted by History: Myths in International Relations* (Oxford, Berghahn, 1998), pp. 65–79.

18 This claim is not entirely novel: decline figures in most historiographical overviews, albeit of course as a relatively marginal factor (e.g. D. C. Watt, 'The historiography of appeasement', in A. Sked and C. Cook (eds), *Crisis and Controversy: Essays in Honour of A. J. P Taylor* (London, Macmillan, 1976), p. 113).

19 This is not, of course, to deny that the British myth of a 'good war' is in some respects profoundly misleading: D. Cesarani, 'Lacking in convictions: British war crimes policy and national memory of the Second World War', in M. Evans and K. Lunn (eds), *War and Memory in the Twentieth Century* (Oxford, Berg, 1997), pp. 27–42.

20 'Cato' [M. Foot, P. Howard, F. Owen], *Guilty Men* (London, Penguin, 1998, rev. edn).

21 'Cato', *Guilty Men*, quotes at pp. 27, 17, 123, 14 (emphasis in original), 122.

22 Baxendale and Pawling, *Narrating the Thirties*, pp. 116–39.

23 J. Harris, 'Great Britain: the People's War?', in D. Reynolds, W. F. Kimball and A. O. Chubarian (eds), *Allies at War: The Soviet, American, and British Experience,*

1939–1945 (London, Macmillan, 1994), p. 245. For a recent disaggregation, see S. O. Rose, *Which People's War? National Identity and Citizenship in Wartime Britain, 1939–1945* (Oxford, Oxford University Press, 2003).

24 H. Nicolson, *Why Britain is at War* (London, Penguin, 1939); quote from N. Nicolson (ed.), *Harold Nicolson: Diaries and Letters, 1939–1945* (London, Fontana, 1971, pb. edn), p. 35.

25 W. N. Medlicott, *British Foreign Policy since Versailles* (London, Methuen, 1940); W. N. Medlicott, *The Origins of the Second Great War* (London, Bell, 1940).

26 R. J. Caputi, *Neville Chamberlain and Appeasement* (Selinsgrove, PA, Susquehanna University Press, 2000), pp. 15–33 details the range of wartime interpretations, including leftist critiques, high Tory hagiography and the subtle proto-revisionisms of J. F. Kennedy and E. H. Carr.

27 Quote from Smith, *Britain and 1940*, p. 115.

28 For example, see *The Judgement of Nuremberg, 1946* (London, TSO, 1999), pp. 41–43 on Munich.

29 Wheeler-Bennett, *Munich*, p. 437.

30 L. B. Namier, *Diplomatic Prelude, 1938–1939* (London, Macmillan, 1948), pp. xi, ix, 4. Cf. ch. 2, n. 26 above.

31 W. S. Churchill, *The Second World War: Vol. 1: The Gathering Storm* (London, Penguin, 1985, pb. edn), quotes at pp. xvii, 244, 292, 273, xiv.

32 D. Reynolds, *In Command of History: Churchill Fighting and Writing the Second World War* (London, Allen Lane, 2004) analyses the writing, contents and reception of the war memoirs.

33 Caputi, *Neville Chamberlain and Appeasement*, pp. 15–88; D. Dutton, *Neville Chamberlain* (London, Arnold, 2001) pp. 27–142. Note Dutton's observation that 'professional historians … did not sweep away these wartime polemics and start afresh' but rather 'built upon existing assumptions and prejudices, giving them in the process a considerable degree of academic respectability' (p. 87).

34 Quote from D. Reynolds, 'Churchill's writing of history: appeasement, autobiography and *The Gathering Storm*', *Transactions of the Royal Historical Society*, 6th series, vol. 11, 2001, p. 228.

35 Reynolds, *In Command of History*, p. 486.

36 Churchill, *The Gathering Storm*, pp. 186–89. These quotations are taken from a speech of March 1936 in which Churchill laid down the principles that should govern British policy towards Europe. Note also the assumption of enduring power: 'I know of nothing which has occurred to alter or weaken the justice, wisdom, valour, and prudence upon which our ancestors acted … I know of nothing which makes me feel that we might not, or cannot, march along the same road' (p.187); cf. J. Charmley, *Churchill: The End of Glory: A Political Biography* (London, Hodder and Stoughton, 1993), pp. 410–12, 418; R. A. C. Parker, *Churchill and Appeasement* (London, Macmillan, 2000), pp. 11, 50, 62.

37 A. Capet, 'Le thème de l'identité nationale dans les *Mémoires sur la Deuxième Guerre Mondiale* de Churchill et dans les *Mémoires de Guerre* de de Gaulle', *Revue Française de Civilisation Britannique*, hors-série, no. 1, 2001, pp. 84–98.

38 J. H. Plumb, 'The historian', in A. J. P. Taylor *et al.*, *Churchill: Four Faces and the Man* (London, Penguin, 1969), p. 122.

39 Churchill, *The Gathering Storm*, quotes at pp. 186, 38, 229; cf. Reynolds, *In Command of History*, pp. 133–35, 501, and *passim* for how Cold War concerns shaped Churchill's writing.

40 D. C. Watt, '1939 revisited: on theories of the origins of wars', *International Affairs*, vol. 65, no. 4, 1989, p. 690.

41 Churchill, *The Gathering Storm*, p. 188. Churchill's advocacy of continued post-war co-operation with the United States was also intended to help preserve Britain's great power status: D. Reynolds, *The Creation of the Anglo-American Alliance, 1937–41: A Study in Competitive Co-Operation* (London, Europa, 1981), p. 1.

42 Churchill, *The Gathering Storm*, p. xiv; Reynolds, *In Command of History*, p. 447.

43 In 'probably the nastiest review of any volume of the war memoirs', Michael Foot dubbed this one 'Churchill's *Mein Kampf*': Reynolds, *In Command of History*, p. 142.

44 Foot later argued that Churchill had formed a 'strange or interested alliance with the scurrilous *Guilty Men* authors', adopting their argument in his memoirs: '*Guilty Men* quoted Churchill on its cover, and he took a genial view of the exposition at the time' (M. Foot, 'Preface to the Penguin edition', in 'Cato', *Guilty Men*, pp. vi-vii).

45 Baxendale and Pawling, *Narrating the Thirties*, p. 151.

46 Smith, *Britain and 1940*, pp. 115–23, quotes at pp. 116.

47 J. Ramsden, 'Refocusing "The People's War": British war films of the 1950s', *Journal of Contemporary History*, vol. 33, no. 1, 1998, pp. 35–63.

48 Smith, *Britain and 1940*, p. 123.

49 K. Robbins, *Churchill* (London, Longman, 1992), pp. 164–65 (and p. 170 for Churchill's growing awareness of British decline).

50 A. J. P. Taylor, *The Origins of the Second World War* (London, Penguin, 1964, pb. edn), quotes at pp. 34, 36.

51 D. C. Watt, 'Appeasement: the rise of a revisionist school?', *Political Quarterly*, vol. 36, no. 2, 1965, p. 198; D. C. Watt, 'Setting the scene', in R. Douglas (ed.), *1939: A Retrospect Forty Years After* (London, Macmillan, 1983), p. 7.

52 P. A. Reynolds, *British Foreign Policy in the Inter-War Years* (London, Longmans, Green, 1954), quotes at pp. 164, 167.

53 Viscount Templewood [S. Hoare], *Nine Troubled Years* (London, Collins, 1954), quote at pp. 383–84.

54 See U. Bialer, 'Telling the truth to the people: Britain's decision to publish the diplomatic papers of the interwar period', in K. Wilson (ed.), *Forging the Collective Memory: Government and International Historians through Two World Wars* (Oxford, Berghahn, 1996), pp. 265–88. The collection, in three series (with one subdivided into two), eventually ran to 65 volumes, the last of which was published in 1986. For further information on documentary matters, see S. Aster, *British Foreign Policy, 1918–1945: A Guide to Research and Research Materials* (Wilmington, DE, Scholarly Resources, 1991, rev. edn), pp. 92–103.

55 T. D. Williams, 'The historiography of World War II', in E. M. Robertson (ed.), *The Origins of the Second World War: Historical Interpretations* (London, Macmillan, 1971), pp. 42–49, 61. Williams, in this 1958 essay, argued that the editorial principles at work presented the Foreign Office in a better light (as sceptical about appeasement) than diplomats abroad or other policy-makers in London. It is tempting to attribute the narrowly 'diplomatic' nature of the materials selected to prevailing sub-disciplinary norms, but Williams also noted that the comparable and contemporaneous collection of German documents was much more expansive in conception.

56 K. Robbins, *Appeasement* (Oxford, Blackwell, 1997, 2nd edn), pp. 3–4.

57 B. E. Schmitt, 'Munich', *Journal of Modern History*, vol. 25, no. 2, 1953, p. 180.

58 D. Marquand, quoted in W. R. Louis (ed.), *The Origins of the Second World War: A. J. P. Taylor and his Critics* (New York, Wiley, 1972), p. 68.

59 Taylor, *The Origins of the Second World War*, pp. 25, 40; cf. A. J. P. Taylor, *A Personal History* (London, Coronet, 1984, pb. edn), p. 298.

60 Taylor, *The Origins of the Second World War*, p. 9. Equally, in discussing rearmament and economics, Taylor identifies flawed choices as the key operative factors: pp. 152–55.

61 Taylor, *The Origins of the Second World War*, p. 172; P. M. Kennedy and T. C. Imlay, 'Appeasement', in G. Martel (ed.) *The Origins of the Second World War Reconsidered: A. J. P. Taylor and the Historians* (London, Routledge, 1999, 2nd edn). pp. 117–20 (a slightly revised version of the piece Kennedy wrote alone for the original 1986 edition of this collection).

62 D. C. Watt, 'Some aspects of A. J. P. Taylor's work as diplomatic historian', *Journal of Modern History*, vol. 49, no. 1, 1977, pp. 26–27.

63 Taylor, *The Origins of the Second World War*, p. 235.

64 R. J. B. Bosworth, *Explaining Auschwitz and Hiroshima: History Writing and the Second World War, 1945–1990* (London, Routledge, 1993), p. 42.

65 On Taylor's heroes, see C. Wrigley, 'A. J. P. Taylor: a nonconforming radical historian of Europe', *Contemporary European History*, vol. 3, no. 1, 1994, pp. 74–75.

66 Bosworth, *Explaining Auschwitz and Hiroshima*, p. 42; cf. A. Sisman, *A. J. P. Taylor: A Biography* (London, Sinclair-Stevenson, 1994), pp. 275–76, 288–89.

67 Wrigley, 'A. J. P. Taylor: a nonconforming radical historian of Europe', p. 75. Taylor was active in the Campaign for Nuclear Disarmament during the period when he was drafting *The Origins of the Second World War*. Bosworth, *Explaining Auschwitz and Hiroshima*, pp. 38–39.

68 E. Ingram, 'A patriot for me', in G. Martel (ed.), *The Origins of the Second World War Reconsidered: The A. J. P. Taylor Debate after Twenty-Five Years* (London, Unwin Hyman, 1986), pp. 250–52.

69 Taylor, *A Personal History*, p. 291. Taylor also reflected on decline in his later writings on Britain: J. D. Fair, 'A. J. P. Taylor as a "contemporary" historian', *International History Review*, vol. 23, no. 1, 2001, pp. 86–88.

70 Watt, 'Appeasement', p. 209.

71 Cf. G. D. Rosenfeld, *The World Hitler Never Made: Alternate History and the Memory of Nazism* (Cambridge, Cambridge University Press, 2005), pp. 50–70.

72 Smith, *Britain and 1940*, p. 124.

73 Eley, 'Finding the People's War', pp. 821–22.

74 Smith, *Britain and 1940*, p. 124.

75 Eley, 'Finding the People's War', p. 822.

76 Watt, 'The historiography of appeasement', p. 111. Watt argues that appeasement analogies were much less discredited in the United States than in Great Britain.

77 Baxendale and Pawling, *Narrating the Thirties*, p. 153; cf. Dutton, *Neville Chamberlain*, on 'the importance of evidence', pp. 155–88.

78 C. Thorne, *The Approach of War, 1938–1939* (London, Macmillan, 1967), pp. xiii–xiv, 22.

79 F. S. Northedge, *The Troubled Giant: Britain among the Great Powers, 1916–1939* (London, Bell, 1966), pp. 483, 628. The hysterical reaction that Northedge provoked from Anthony Eden, whose personal investment in the orthodox critique was unsurpassed, is telling: P. J. Beck, 'Politicians versus historians: Lord Avon's "appeasement battle" against "lamentably, appeasement-minded" historians', *Twentieth Century British History*, vol. 9, no. 3, 1998, pp. 396–419.

80 Caputi, *Neville Chamberlain and Appeasement*, pp. 95–105. The very titles of these works are revealing.

81 W. N. Medlicott, *British Foreign Policy since Versailles, 1919–1963* (London, Methuen, 1968, 2nd edn), pp. xiii–xix, 192–96 (though note the scepticism about too glib an invocation of decline at pp. 325–32); W. N. Medlicott, 'Britain and Germany: the search for agreement, 1930–37', in D. Dilks (ed.), *Retreat from Power: Studies in Britain's Foreign Policy of the Twentieth Century: Vol. 1: 1906–1939* (London, Macmillan, 1981), pp. 78–101 (in substance the 1968 Creighton Lecture).

82 K. Robbins, *Munich, 1938* (London, Cassell, 1968), p. 355.

83 Robbins, *Appeasement*, p. 5.

84 P. W. Schroeder, 'Munich and the British tradition', *Historical Journal*, vol. 19, no. 1, 1976, p. 242.

85 P. M. Kennedy, *The Realities Behind Diplomacy: Background Influences on British External Policy, 1865–1980* (London, Fontana, 1981, pb. edn), p. 301.

86 K. Middlemas, *Diplomacy of Illusion: The British Government and Germany, 1937–39* (London, Weidenfeld and Nicolson, 1972), quotes at pp. 411, 453.

87 D. Dilks, '"The unnecessary war"? Military advice and foreign policy in Great Britain, 1931–39', in A. Preston (ed.), *General Staffs and Diplomacy before the Second World War* (London, Croom Helm, 1978), p. 104.

88 D. Dilks, 'Appeasement revisited', *University of Leeds Review*, vol. 15, 1972, pp. 28–56; D. Dilks, '"We must hope for the best and prepare for the worst"', pp. 309–52.

89 J. Charmley, *Chamberlain and the Lost Peace* (London, Macmillan, 1991, pb. edn), quote at p. 212; Charmley, *Churchill*; M. Cowling, *The Impact of Hitler: British Politics and British*

Policy, 1933–1940 (Cambridge, Cambridge University Press, 1975); cf. the insightful discussion in A. Crozier, *The Causes of the Second World War* (Oxford, Blackwell, 1997), pp. 234–43.

90 P. M. Kennedy, 'The logic of appeasement', *Times Literary Supplement*, 28 May 1982, pp. 585–86. Quotation from B-J. Wendt, '"Economic appeasement" – a crisis strategy', in W. J. Mommsen and L. Kettenacker (eds), *The Fascist Challenge and the Policy of Appeasement* (London, Allen and Unwin, 1983), p. 171. G. Schmidt, *The Politics and Economics of Appeasement: British Foreign Policy in the 1930s* (Leamington Spa, Berg, 1986) is representative.

91 P. M. H. Bell, *The Origins of the Second World War in Europe* (London, Longman, 2007, 3rd edn). The 1986 first edition is slightly more sympathetic to appeasement.

92 D. C. Watt, *How War Came: The Immediate Origins of the Second World War, 1938–1939* (London, Mandarin, 1990, pb. edn), quote at p. 610.

93 G. Weinberg, 'Munich after fifty years', *Foreign Affairs*, vol. 67, no. 1, 1988, quote at p. 175.

94 R. Overy, *The Road to War* (London, Macmillan, 1989), p. 103.

95 M. Smith, *British Air Strategy between the Wars* (Oxford, Oxford University Press, 1984), quotes at pp. 308, 321.

96 Baxendale and Pawling, *Narrating the Thirties*, p. 152. On the Tory flight from Chamberlain's legacy, see Dutton, *Neville Chamberlain*, pp. 82–86

97 Watt, 'The historiography of appeasement', p. 120; R. Skidelsky, 'Going to war with Germany: between revisionism and orthodoxy', *Encounter*, vol. 39, no. 1, 1972, p. 58.

98 Bosworth, *Explaining Auschwitz and Hiroshima*, p. 43.

99 Skidelsky, 'Going to war with Germany', pp. 56, 58.

100 Caputi, *Neville Chamberlain and Appeasement*, p. 211.

101 Adamthwaite, *The Making of the Second World War*, p. 21; Skidelsky, 'Going to war with Germany', p. 58.

102 J. A. S. Grenville, 'Contemporary trends in the study of the British "appeasement" policies of the 1930s', *Internationales Jahrbuch für Geschichts-und Geographie-Unterricht*, vol. 17, 1976, p. 236.

103 L. Fuchser, *Neville Chamberlain and Appeasement: A Study in the Politics of History* (New York, Norton, 1982), p. 197.

104 R. Ovendale, *'Appeasement' and the English Speaking World: Britain, the United States, the Dominions, and the Policy of 'Appeasement', 1937–1939* (Cardiff, University of Wales Press, 1975), p. 319. To be fair, Ovendale states in the same passage that in general 'dominion opinion only confirmed Chamberlain on a course of action on which he had already decided'.

105 Grenville, 'Contemporary trends in the study of the British "appeasement" policies of the 1930s', p. 238.

106 A. Adamthwaite, 'War origins again', *Journal of Modern History*, vol. 56, no. 1, 1984, p. 106.

107 W. Murray, *The Change in the European Balance of Power, 1938–1939: The Path to Ruin* (Princeton, NJ, Princeton University Press, 1984). Murray's indictment of the strategic blunders of appeasement can be read as symptomatic of conservative opinion at the time of its publication, the height of the 'Second Cold War' chill.

108 B. Bond, review of G. C. Peden, *British Rearmament and the Treasury, 1932–1939* (Edinburgh, Scottish Academic Press, 1979), in *Journal of Strategic Studies*, vol. 2, no. 3, 1979, p. 363.

109 Adamthwaite, 'War origins again', p. 110.

110 W. Rock, 'Commentary: the Munich crisis revisited', *International History Review*, vol. 11, no. 4, 1989, p. 680. For another critique of the isolationism of British policy in the 1930s, see P. Ludlow, 'Britain and the Third Reich', in H. Bull (ed.), *The Challenge of the Third Reich: The Adam von Trott Memorial Lectures* (Oxford, Oxford University Press, 1986), pp. 141–62. Revisionists like Charmley, conversely, argued that British policy was insufficiently isolationist.

111 P. M. Taylor, *The Projection of Britain: British Overseas Publicity and Propaganda, 1919–1939* (Cambridge, Cambridge University Press, 1981), quote at p. 298.

112 R. Cockett, *Twilight of Truth: Chamberlain, Appeasement and the Manipulation of the Press* (London, Weidenfeld and Nicolson, 1989).

113 Adamthwaite, 'War origins again', p. 106.

114 Aster, '"Guilty Men"', p. 262.

115 Quote from D. C. Watt, 'Chamberlain's ambassadors', in M. Dockrill and B. J. C. McKercher (eds), *Diplomacy and World Power: Studies in British Foreign Policy, 1890–1950* (Cambridge, Cambridge University Press, 1996), p. 169. Watt's contribution over many decades to this historiography is vast: though here critical, elsewhere he has demolished the Churchillian anti-appeasement case in a rather revisionist manner: D. C. Watt, 'Churchill and appeasement', in R. Blake and W. R. Louis (eds), *Churchill* (Oxford, Oxford University Press, 1993), pp. 199–214.

116 Kennedy and Imlay, 'Appeasement', p. 128. Kennedy argues that both orthodox and revisionist views contain elements of truth which need to be appreciated to grasp appeasement 'as the complex, variegated, shifting phenomenon which it really was' (p. 129); a 'counter-revisionism' that sees appeasement as wrong but rational could constitute this kind of compromise synthesis, but in practice it is much closer to the orthodox view than to revisionism.

117 R. A. C. Parker, *Chamberlain and Appeasement: British Policy and the Coming of the Second World War* (London, Macmillan, 1993), quote at p. 343.

118 Parker, *Churchill and Appeasement*, quotes at pp. 212, 209, 239, 263.

119 Parker, *Chamberlain and Appeasement*, quotes at pp. 345, 347.

120 Parker, *Churchill and Appeasement*, quotes at p. 257.

121 Quotes from Parker, *Chamberlain and Appeasement*, p. 10. Parker's views are perhaps more firmly Churchillian in his second book. Viewed as a form of emplotment, counter-revisionism has affinities with the variant of orthodoxy advocated by Anthony Adamthwaite in the French case: it acknowledges the existence of constraints, but critiques policy-makers for poor choices and a failure of leadership. Interpretively, counter-revisionism fits with those sympathetic revisionist views of French policy that imply France was potentially available as an ally.

122 Grenville, 'Contemporary trends in the study of the British "appeasement" policies of the 1930s', pp. 242–43.

123 Quote from Parker, *Chamberlain and Appeasement*, p. 364.

124 Kennedy and Imlay, 'Appeasement', p. 129.

125 Aster, '"Guilty Men"', pp. 256–63; cf. Grenville, 'Contemporary trends in the study of the British "appeasement" policies of the 1930s', pp. 244–47; P. Ludlow, 'The unwinding of appeasement', in L. Kettenacker (ed.), *Das 'Andere Deutschland' im Zweiten Weltkrieg: Emigration und Widerstand in Internationaler Perspektive* (Stuttgart, Klett, 1977), pp. 9–47.

126 Pigeonholing scholars is obviously a somewhat futile task, but there is clearly some overlap between 'sceptical revisionists' like Middlemas and counter-revisionists: both accept the existence of certain constraints on policy, but also see reason to criticise Chamberlain for flawed decisions. On Halifax, see A. Roberts, *The Holy Fox: A Biography of Lord Halifax* (London, Weidenfeld and Nicolson, 1991).

127 Parker, *Chamberlain and Appeasement*, quote at p. 11; cf. Dutton's reading of *Guilty Men* in *Neville Chamberlain*, pp. 76–77.

128 Aster, '"Guilty Men"'; S. Aster, *1939: The Making of the Second World War* (London, Deutsch, 1973).

129 B. J. C. McKercher, 'Old diplomacy and new: the Foreign Office and foreign policy, 1919–39', in Dockrill and McKercher (eds), *Diplomacy and World Power*, pp. 79–114, quote at p. 114.

130 G. Kennedy, '"Rat in power": Neville Chamberlain and the creation of British foreign policy, 1931–39', in T. G. Otte (ed.), *The Makers of British Foreign Policy: From Pitt to Thatcher* (London, Palgrave, 2002), pp. 173–95, quotes at pp. 188–89.

131 E. Goldstein, 'Neville Chamberlain, the British official mind and the Munich crisis', *Diplomacy and Statecraft*, vol. 10, nos. 2/3, 1999, pp. 276–92, quote at p. 290.

132 For example, R. J. Q. Adams, *British Politics and Foreign Policy in the Age of Appeasement, 1935–39* (London, Macmillan, 1993); F. McDonough, *Neville Chamberlain, Appeasement and the British Road to War* (Manchester, Manchester University Press, 1998).

133 C. Price, *Britain, America and Rearmament in the 1930s: The Cost of Failure* (London, Palgrave, 2001), quote at p. xiii.

134 M. J. Carley, *1939: The Alliance that Never Was and the Coming of World War II* (Chicago, Ivan Dee, 1999); L. G. Shaw, *The British Political Elite and the Soviet Union, 1937–1939* (London, Cass, 2003).

135 M. L. Roi, *Alternative to Appeasement: Sir Robert Vansittart and Alliance Diplomacy, 1934–1937* (Westport, CT, Praeger, 1997). See also on the Liberal Party's alternative to appeasement, R. Grayson, *Liberals, International Relations and Appeasement: The Liberal Party, 1919–1939* (London, Cass, 2001).

136 S. Newton, *Profits of Peace: The Political Economy of Anglo-German Appeasement* (Oxford, Oxford University Press, 1996). Cf. ch. 1 n. 106.

137 E. H. H. Green, 'Churchill reappraised', *Parliamentary History*, vol. 13, no. 3, 1994, pp. 338–50; cf. J. Charmley, 'The price of victory', *Times Literary Supplement*, 13 May 1994, p. 8.

138 For example, P. Doerr, *British Foreign Policy, 1919–1939* (Manchester, Manchester University Press, 1998); J. Maiolo, *The Royal Navy and Nazi Germany, 1933–1939: A Study in Appeasement and the Origins of the Second World War* (London, Macmillan, 1998). Maiolo's study is primarily concerned to defend British naval policy rather than appeasement *per se*, though his argument that naval policy was based on realistic strategic incentives has broad revisionist implications. Dutton's verdict is nuanced, but in relative terms not unfavourable to Chamberlain: *Neville Chamberlain*, pp. 189–224.

139 Aster, '"Guilty Men"', pp. 240–41.

140 Parker, *Chamberlain and Appeasement*, pp. 347, 364–65.

141 G. Martel, 'The meaning of power: rethinking the decline and fall of Great Britain', *International History Review*, vol. 13, no. 4, 1991, pp. 662–94, quotes at pp. 663, 668; cf. J. McDermott, 'A century of British decline', *International History Review*, vol. 12, no. 1, 1990, pp. 111–24.

142 D. Reynolds, *Britannia Overruled: British Policy and World Power in the Twentieth Century* (London, Longman, 2000, 2nd edn), p. 31.

143 W. Murray, 'The collapse of empire: British strategy, 1919–45', in W. Murray, M. Knox and A. Bernstein (eds), *The Making of Strategy: Rulers, States, and War* (Cambridge, Cambridge University Press, 1994), p. 393.

144 J. Young, *Britain and the World in the Twentieth Century* (London, Arnold, 1997), quote at p. 120. See also B. J. C. McKercher, '"Our most dangerous enemy": Great Britain pre-eminent in the 1930s', *International History Review*, vol. 13, no. 4, 1991, pp. 751–83.

145 R. English and M. Kenny, 'British decline or the politics of declinism?', *British Journal of Politics and International Relations*, vol. 1, no. 2, 1999, p. 263.

146 Baxendale and Pawling, *Narrating the Thirties*, pp. 161–67, quote at p. 167.

147 Eley, 'Finding the People's War', p. 822.

148 Smith, *Britain and 1940*, p. 126.

149 K. Foster, *Fighting Fictions: War, Narrative and National Identity* (London, Pluto, 1999), quotes at pp. 25, 27. Thatcher's rhetoric echoed the oft-quoted verdict of C. L. Mowat in his seminal 1955 history of inter-war Britain, suffused with the spirit of consensus, that 1940 had been the moment at which the British people 'found themselves again, after twenty years of indecision' (quoted in Dutton, *Neville Chamberlain*, p. 103). Note that Thatcher's subject is the singular nation rather than the collective people.

150 Connelly, *We Can Take It!*, p. 286.

151 Connelly, *We Can Take It!*, p. 271–72.

152 L. Noakes, *War and the British: Gender, Memory and National Identity* (London, Tauris, 1998), pp. 109–10.

153 G. Dawson and B. West, 'Our finest hour? The popular memory of World War II and the struggle over national identity', in G. Hurd (ed.), *National Fictions: World War Two in British Films and Television* (London, BFI, 1984), p. 9.

154 This is obviously a very broad brush treatment: *inter alia*, it skates over the argument that a relatively unified British identity was in the process of fragmenting in these years under the impacts of immigration and devolution, as presented in R. Weight, *Patriots: National Identity in Britain, 1940–2000* (London, Macmillan, 2002).

155 S. Breese, 'In search of Englishness; in search of votes', in J. Arnold, K. Davis and S. Ditchfield (eds), *History and Heritage: Consuming the Past in Contemporary Culture* (Shaftesbury, Donhead, 1998), pp. 155–67, quote at p. 164.

156 J. Tomlinson, 'Thrice denied: "declinism" as a recurrent theme in British history in the long twentieth century', *Twentieth Century British History*, vol. 20, no. 2, 2009, p. 236.

157 Foster, *Fighting Fictions*, p. 2.

158 Quoted in P. Finney, 'On memory, identity and war', *Rethinking History*, vol. 6, no. 1, 2002, p. 1.

159 J. Ashley, 'No moving a prime minister whose mind is made up', *The Guardian*, 1 March 2003, http://www.guardian.co.uk/politics/2003/mar/01/iraq.interviews (accessed 2 February 2006).

160 Note however the general claim that 'the pattern has been for declinist narratives to be initiated in the political arena, then to be taken up by historians, to be followed in turn by historians' rebuttals of such arguments' (Tomlinson, 'Thrice denied', p. 227).

161 C. Layne, 'Security Studies and the use of history: Neville Chamberlain's grand strategy revisited', *Security Studies*, vol. 17, no. 3, 2008, p. 437.

162 W. Wark, 'Appeasement revisited', *International History Review*, vol. 17, no. 3, 1995, pp. 545–62.

163 R. Self, *Neville Chamberlain: A Biography* (Aldershot, Ashgate, 2006), especially pp. 295–96 for a discussion of constraints. There is an insightful review in D. Hucker, 'The unending debate: appeasement, Chamberlain and the origins of the Second World War', *Intelligence and National Security*, vol. 23, no. 4, 2008, pp. 536–51.

164 See, for example, the nuanced critical interpretations in B. J. C. McKercher, 'National security and imperial defence: British grand strategy and appeasement, 1930–39', *Diplomacy and Statecraft*, vol. 19, no. 3, 2008, pp. 391–442; and K. Neilson, 'The Defence Requirements Sub-Committee, British strategic foreign policy, Neville Chamberlain and the path to appeasement', *English Historical Review*, vol. 118, no. 477, 2003, pp. 651–84.

165 S. Aster, 'Appeasement: before and after revisionism', *Diplomacy and Statecraft*, vol. 19, no. 3, 2008, pp. 443–80.

166 Another important piece with revisionist implications is G. B. Strang, 'The spirit of Ulysses? Ideology and British appeasement in the 1930s', *Diplomacy and Statecraft*, vol. 19, no. 3, 2008, pp. 481–526.

167 Connelly, *We Can Take It!*, p. 301.

168 Matussek, 'My personal VE Day'.

169 R. Manthorpe, 'Spirit of the Brits', *The Guardian*, 1 July 2006, http://www.guardian.co.uk/books/2006/jul/01/featuresreviews.guardianreview29 (accessed 5 July 2006).

6 On liberty

FDR, American intervention and the empire of right

Ours has been a story of vigorous challenges which have been accepted and overcome – challenges of uncharted seas, of wild forests and desert plains, of raging floods and withering droughts, of foreign tyrants and domestic strife, of staggering problems – social, economic, and physical; and we have come out of them the most powerful Nation – and the freest – in all of history. Today in the face of this newest and greatest challenge of them all, we Americans have cleared our decks and taken our battle stations. We stand ready in the defense of our Nation and in the faith of our fathers to do what God has given us the power to see as our full duty.

Franklin Delano Roosevelt, President of the United States of America,
Navy and Total Defense Day address, 27 October 1941[1]

On 9 August 1941 the British battleship *Prince of Wales*, still scarred from its clash that May with the German behemoth *Bismarck*, steamed alongside the American heavy cruiser *Augusta* in Placentia Bay off Newfoundland. The ships were bringing together Winston Churchill, the British prime minister, and Roosevelt, the leader of a United States which was still technically neutral but nonetheless lending ever increasing aid short of war to the beleaguered island outpost of European democracy.[2] The so-called Atlantic Conference was to be the first of several epochal summits between the two statesmen; Roosevelt eagerly anticipated his meeting with the famous Churchill, who fully reciprocated: 'you would have thought he was being carried up into the heavens to meet God', an American observer opined of Churchill's demeanour.[3] If he was not quite a pious supplicant, Churchill's need was nonetheless greater than FDR's. Struggling to bear the burden of the war against the Axis, the very survival of the British empire was already dependent upon American Lend-Lease aid and indirect naval assistance, yet it was still in the balance. Churchill's over-riding goal was therefore to secure a declaration of war to bring the full weight of American moral and material resources into play. Roosevelt proved unable or unwilling to move this far yet, and Churchill would have to wait for the Japanese attack on Pearl Harbor in December to precipitate American belligerency. Instead, the main outcome of the conference was a joint declaration of war aims, the Atlantic Charter, which articulated the Anglo-American belief in self-determination, popular sovereignty, free trade, freedom from fear and want, and a permanent system of general security in international relations. If Churchill was disappointed to return home bearing just this paper commitment, and somewhat discomfited by the subversive implications for the empire of some of Roosevelt's principles, the charter was in retrospect a significant step towards war and represented 'the ideological basis of America's wartime globalism'.[4]

Churchill's persistent petitioning of Roosevelt for many months prior to Pearl Harbor dramatised the intersection of the very different historical trajectories of Britain and the United States. Whilst successfully standing alone against the Axis and then playing a significant part in its destruction may have constituted the British empire's finest hour, the Second World War was a chapter in a story of decline from international pre-eminence; hence much of the historiography of appeasement reading like a threnody for lost grandeur. In contrast, the conflict catapulted the United States to superpower status, constituting a vital stage in a long ascent to its current position as veritable hegemon enjoying 'more global power than any previous state'.[5] Accordingly, it is not unexpected that in debating the wisdom and efficacy of Roosevelt's foreign policy up to 1941, the historiography on American intervention is implicated in a series of larger questions about the roots, nature and consequences of the growth of American might.

If these historiographies are thus linked by shared preoccupations with meta-questions of national identity, a further point of comparison is that it is also slightly problematic in the case of the United States to map the international history literature against the landscape of war memory. Here, this is not so much because war memory has centred on more potent myths that have overshadowed or marginalised the issue of war origins: rather, it is because scholars have struggled to identify and chart the vicissitudes of any American 'Vichy Syndrome' or 'myth of the Great Patriotic War'. Although it is generally understood that the conflict has long been revered in the United States as a 'good war', several oft-quoted analyses are more concerned with unpicking the simplification, sanitization and romanticization entailed in this mythologizing – by drawing attention to the more ambiguous, unpleasant or pernicious dimensions of wartime reality – than with the myth's ongoing reproduction and the ideological work it has done.[6] Since the 1990s, scholarship dedicated to this latter explanatory task has indeed proliferated, but this has generally tended to focus on particular incidents and episodes (such as Pearl Harbor or Hiroshima), specific cultural genres (such as the World War II combat film), or discrete discourses (such as the operation in policy-making of the 'Munich analogy'), eschewing larger generalisations about the war as a whole and American society or culture.[7] It might be argued, of course, that this specialisation and fragmentation is simply reflective of the current moment in the broader scholarly field of war memory, but there does also seem to be something about the American case that has made it particularly difficult for scholars to readily discern or demonstrate an overall shape to its collective memory.[8]

Historical writing does not simply reveal reality, of course, yet it does seem plausible to relate the condition of the literature to the nature of the object of study. There is a strong *prima facie* case that American collective memory of the war actually has been strangely disparate and low-key, failing to cohere around an identifiable cluster of acute and ongoing ideological tensions; although representations of the war were endemic in cultural and political discourses in the US after 1945, they were not as ideologically radioactive or central in the national imagination as those in European countries.[9] Granted, these representations carried diverse political implications – for example, often rationalising militarised containment in the Cold War as common sense – and the generalised understanding of the conflict as a 'good war' obviously served in fundamental if diffuse ways to reaffirm positive understandings of the national self. Yet the war did not become the political and moral touchstone that it did elsewhere.

Three factors seem crucial here. First, there was the absence of widespread societal trauma from a conflict that was fought 'as far as most of the population was concerned, at arm's length'.[10] 'For a visceral experience of war', Richard Bosworth opined in 1993, 'the United States would have to await Vietnam'.[11] Second, the very fact that the conflict was almost universally accepted as having been fought against an evil enemy, for a noble purpose, and by legitimate means, meant that the ethico-political charge that might engender fierce mnemonic controversies was lacking. Third, and compounding the absence of a potent sense of collective suffering or a burden of guilt, after 1945 the Cold War and then Vietnam presented themselves as more obviously exigent preoccupations. So the war long figured in American cultural memory primarily as the conclusion to the indubitably traumatic times of post-1929 Depression or as the prologue to the Cold War rise to globalism, rather than as a meaningful episode in itself.[12] Thus in compiling his landmark 1984 collection of oral testimonies, Studs Terkel was explicitly writing against what he described as a lamentable and pervasive 'dis-remembrance of World War Two'.[13] This situation may have changed with the steadily increasing profile enjoyed by the war since the 1990s, but the prevalence of rhetoric about the 'rediscovery' of a forgotten conflict actually underscores the point.[14]

The peculiar nature of American war memory emphatically does not mean, however, that international historians writing on its origins escaped engagement with problematics of national identity. On one level, as already noted, the historiography of intervention has been haunted by anxieties over the longer term trajectory of American power. On another, Roosevelt himself raised the stakes by persistently framing American policy in relation to principles held to derive from a national essence. The case has been made that the United States is 'the imagined community *par excellence*', 'peculiarly dependent upon representational practices for its being'.[15] Myths of distinctiveness and inimitable virtue – derived from the complex historical circumstances of its founding – saturate American political culture, and foreign policy-making discourse certainly contributes to the ongoing imaginative labour of national self-fashioning. Thus when Roosevelt proclaimed in his 1941 Independence Day address that 'the fundamentals of 1776 are being struck down abroad, and definitely they are threatened here', he located himself squarely within a potent American diplomatic tradition, whereby foreign affairs were debated in terms of a heritage of national values.[16] As Michael Dunne has pointed out, in every single significant heated debate over foreign policy for more than two centuries, 'the protagonists invoked their ideal images of the American mission'.[17]

When historians come to represent these past debates and policies that are already freighted with these constitutive concerns, they bring to bear their own normative assumptions, which then create a further order of ideological content. Hence Anders Stephanson's argument that:

> the ideology of exceptionalism and the constant obsession with the world-historical role of the United States ... has served to accentuate in extraordinarily profound ways the meaning of ... the foundational distinction between inside and outside. To have an account of any given question of [US] foreign policy is by implication to have an account of what the United States is and ought to be. It is to take a personal position on a certain political terrain.[18]

The historiography of American diplomacy prior to the Second World War can certainly be read in this spirit; at stake, and at its heart, are the related issues of the proper role of the United States in the world and its nature as an ideological project.

'All I believed *was* America': struggles over intervention

The years leading up to intervention in the Second World War in 1941 witnessed a dramatic transformation in the external orientation of the United States. In the mid-1930s, beset by economic depression, it was a country 'turned in on itself', its foreign policy constricted by a series of Congressional Neutrality Acts, incarnating the dominant opinion that the nation must strictly confine itself to home defence and avoid enervating entanglement in foreign wars. Yet as the international crises of the later 1930s escalated, and especially after the dramatic fall of France in the summer of 1940, Roosevelt oversaw a succession of moves that inexorably engaged the United States in the struggle against the Axis. These included modification of neutrality legislation to permit arms sales on a cash and carry basis; a programme of accelerated rearmament; the destroyers for bases deal with Britain; the Lend-Lease Act of March 1941; the expansion of naval patrols and convoy escorts in the Atlantic; the extension of aid to the Soviet Union after the launch of Barbarossa; and the robust policy of containment and deterrence in the Pacific that ultimately culminated in Pearl Harbor. Although the precise character of American policy and Roosevelt's purpose remain contested, his expansive, Atlanticist, redefinition of what constituted national security was rooted in ideological as much as geopolitical calculation. Programmatic statements like the Atlantic Charter underlined that this was to be a conflict fought to make the world safe for a particular, American, conception of liberal capitalist democracy.[19] Momentously, the United States shifted 'from a strategy that had limited itself to controlling the western hemisphere to one aimed at winning a global war and managing the peace that would follow'.[20]

Roosevelt's policy was the subject of fierce domestic criticism from a heterogeneous but vocal coalition of anti-interventionists that coalesced in 1940 with the founding of the America First Committee. In part, the heat of this debate was due to the fact that prior to Pearl Harbor the United States was not compelled to become a belligerent as a consequence of direct aggression: rather, as Henry Luce put it in his famous editorial on 'the American century', 'we are faced with great decisions'.[21] Yet it was also crucially significant that the two camps rooted their preferred policies in conflicting conceptions of national identity, mission and destiny. Roosevelt's speeches were 'replete with statements of ideals and values', identifying the freedoms – of speech, of religion, of democratic government, of trade, and from war – that the United States was charged by its history to defend and which, moreover, were universally applicable.[22] He thus embodied a discourse that imagined the United States as 'a righteous nation opposing evil in the world' – 'effectively inscribing a hierarchy of good and evil onto the international order' – and mandated an active and transformative global belligerence.[23] Anti-interventionists shared the conviction of exceptional American virtue, but precisely feared that participation in the war would 'destroy the nation itself'. Externally, they were deeply suspicious of the corrupting influence of the Old World and warned that unrestrained globalism might precipitate perpetual war and transform the republic into an expansionist empire. Internally, they decried the erosion of civil liberties, the intensification of social and economic regimentation and the growth of executive power under the shadow of the war emergency, anxious that Roosevelt himself was succumbing to the totalitarian temptation.[24]

As Luce dramatised the matter, anti-interventionists sought to build up national defences and stay out of the European war, thus preserving the United States as a pristine and exemplary 'sanctuary of the ideals of civilization'. For Roosevelt, in contrast, it was essential to become 'the powerhouse from which the[se] ideals spread throughout the world and do their mysterious work of lifting the life of mankind from the level of the beasts to what the Psalmist called a little lower than the angels'.[25] Of course, to an extent these diverse prescriptions were premised upon contrasting political and geopolitical calculations about, for example, the reality of the Axis threat to American security; but suffusing such judgements were anxieties about the internal and external dimensions of American identity, and the national purpose. Hence anti-interventionist Anne Morrow Lindbergh's despairing comment in her diary after Pearl Harbor: 'I feel as if all I believed *was* America, all memories of it, all history, all dreams of the future were marching gaily toward a precipice – and unaware, unaware'.[26]

From December 1941 the exigencies of national unity during wartime largely stilled the political controversy over intervention. (That said, some 'old isolationists' did continue to agitate, for example in responding to successive official inquiries into the Pearl Harbor debacle.[27]) After victory, however, recrimination resurged with the replaying of the interventionist debate through a first wave of historiographical accounts of the road to war. These were often characterised by vituperative polemic, at least in part because their authors were generally personally implicated in the events that they were analysing. On the one hand, prominent 'traditionalist' defenders of Roosevelt's policy – such as Herbert Feis, William Langer and Everett Gleason – had held positions within his administrations or were otherwise personally intimate with key government figures. On the other, the key 'revisionist' critics – such as Charles Beard and Charles Tansill – had long records of activism within the anti-interventionist movement prior to Pearl Harbor.[28]

The context within which the controversy resumed was also significant. First, across a range of media the image assiduously nurtured in wartime propaganda of the 'good war' and its 'truly heightened sense of collective moral enterprise' was cemented in place.[29] (Notwithstanding that popular culture representations could often be searingly ironic, and quite candid about the war's brutality and capacity to wreak psychic damage.[30]) Second, with the transition to Cold War, intense ideological and political contestation ensued over the shape of the post-war American state and its external orientation. Roosevelt's policies prefigured many of the key characteristics of the national security state, including its Manichean worldview, expansion of executive authority, faith in 'technowar', military industrial complex and military Keynesianism, and globalist conception of American security. Yet if these features were 'already apparent in embryo' by the end of 1941, their precise configuration and extent were hammered out through post-war political and cultural negotiations.[31] These debates pitted believers in a new 'ideology of national security', advocating 'a more internationalist foreign policy and ... a supportive program of state making', against adherents of 'such received traditions as isolationism, antimilitarism, and antistatism'. The key issue was whether in the Cold War context, as partisans of the former position maintained, 'the United States had no choice but to assume the new role that history had thrust upon it – that of a great military power and defender of democracy globally'. There was considerable thematic continuity here with the debate over intervention and at stake again was 'the nation's political identity and postwar purpose'.[32]

There were important continuities, too, in the historiographical debate on intervention. Interpretations were now more complex and nuanced, and fortified by footnotes drawn from memoirs, the 40 volumes produced by the mammoth post-war Joint Congressional Committee inquiry into Pearl

Harbor, the documentation from the Nuremberg and Tokyo war crimes trials, and other official edited selections of American and foreign archival documentation. Yet for all that, these historians 'dealt with the same basic subject and issues' as had pre-war writings and speeches, and even 'used the same arguments, made the same fundamental assumptions, and advanced similar hypotheses'. Thus the terms of the original political debate were foundational for post-war historiographical treatments. In consequence, the competing accounts were also all hallmarked by a narrowness of chronological and thematic scope, and a determinedly 'intentionalist' focus upon the thinking and actions of key policy-makers to the detriment of wider structural factors. Interpretive absolutism was also strikingly evident: on both sides arguments were marked by 'the same emotional heat, the same ideological dogmatism, the same intolerance of conflicting views, and the same black-and-white portraits' as their forebears in the realm of politics.[33] Of course, the political and personal stakes here were high, but this was also in tune with the Cold War reassertion of the virtues of historical objectivity, after the American historical profession's inter-war dalliance with relativism. The Second World War also exerted a significant nationalising influence on American historians, in encouraging a resurgence of 'national political history' and a particular concern with 'wider issues of security, strategy, and diplomacy'. This is most apparent in the case of those 'traditionalist' diplomatic historians who enjoyed formal connections with the state, and whose arguments for the necessity of an activist foreign policy carried an obvious contemporary charge. Yet even their 'revisionist' antagonists were co-opted in a broader sense, in taking the nation and its essence as their explicit and implicit object of address.[34]

The interpretive positions of the two schools of thought can, in broad terms, be easily summarised. The 'traditionalists' located the fundamental causes of the war in developments external to the United States, and specifically in the 'extremely serious threats to American security and interests' posed by the Axis powers. Faced with this rising menace, Roosevelt hoped to keep the country out of hostilities, yet safeguard it by extending all aid short of war to victims of Axis aggression in Europe, and by containing and deterring the Japanese. While some 'traditionalists' argued that Roosevelt should have taken more vigorous action against the aggressors, their main criticisms were directed at his domestic, 'isolationist' opponents who hindered the implementation of a more robust policy until the 'genuine surprise' of Pearl Harbor compelled entry into the war. 'None of them believed that there were any alternatives available to President Roosevelt by 1940–41 which could have prevented American involvement in World War II without sacrificing American security and principles'. The 'revisionists', in contrast, emphasised internal factors and Roosevelt's agency in explaining the road to war. The Axis powers did not constitute a genuine menace to the western hemisphere, until 'shortsighted and provocative' American policies envenomed relations with them. Roosevelt entangled the United States with Nazi Germany through the extension of aid to Britain and exerted so much pressure on the Japanese that their vital interests were ultimately threatened. Whether this was by design or blunder was open to debate; in some variants Roosevelt engineered conflict with Japan as an Asiatic 'back door' to war with the whole Axis, either in the service of preserving the British empire or securing American economic expansionism. Roosevelt was additionally arraigned for persistently deceiving the American people about his intentions, for the militarisation of the nation and usurpation of executive power, and for contributing to the rise of global communism.[35]

These two narratives essentially represent expanded versions of the core emplotments that Emily Rosenberg has identified in the post-war debate on Pearl Harbor, the one depicting it as an act of infamy whereby an innocent, passive nation was roused in response to unprovoked aggression, the other portraying it as an act of presidential deception, the culmination of an activist campaign to manoeuvre the nation into an unnecessary war. The emergence of these two explanations was no accident since each drew on familiar, deep-rooted, narrative structures already circulating in American culture, the former grounding the story in 'a highly personalized and religiously tinged language of retribution', and the latter exemplifying a penchant for conspiracy theories and 'a pervasive cultural narrative of backlash against power wielders in Washington'. Moreover, each served readily identifiable political purposes rationalising particular policy options at home and abroad, in war and nascent Cold War alike.[36]

In any event, the 'traditionalist' interpretation prevailed in the post-war historiographical debate, and was enshrined 'in most college and high school textbooks' as the conventional wisdom.[37] This may have owed something to the insistent visibility in American culture in the inter-war years of the vision of (white) Americans as 'innocent victims of others' aggression'. In popular historical narratives and award-winning biographies, in state-sponsored memorials and commemorative jamborees (such as the fiftieth anniversary of the battle of the Little Big Horn in 1926), and in Hollywood films (such as 1939's *Drums Along the Mohawk*), individuals 'defended what was dear to them against invaders or usurpers or savages'. This 'national pageant' was 'a story built around sites of American defiance to those who sought to hinder the peaceful, progressive advance of democracy, capitalism, and Protestant moral values'. Thus when it actually occurred, Pearl Harbor 'fit into the popular narrative of American history ... like a key into the lock for which it had been cut'.[38] More pertinently, this explanation was manifestly more in tune with 'emotional, ideological, political, economic, and military conditions' in post-war America, particularly in relation to the dominance of the 'good war' paradigm and the triumph – albeit not unalloyed – of partisans of the new ideology of national security.[39] That said, the duplicity narrative had such a long historical and ideological lineage, and such political utility as a means for expressing isolationist and other oppositional sentiments, that it was never entirely vanquished. Rather it has retained a persistent if marginal presence – especially in relation to the narrower issue of Pearl Harbor – for all that it has been repeatedly declared discredited and empirically untenable.[40]

The stark divergence between these two opposed interpretations can obscure the fact that, at a deeper level, they continued to be linked by their shared preoccupation with national identity, and specifically about which policy option would best express the national essence. This is most explicit in the writings of the 'revisionists', in which passionate commitment conduces to florid rhetorical excess. To be sure, there are pragmatic arguments advanced about, for example, how far intervention actually enhanced American security; witness Tansill's charge that the supply of Lend-Lease goods to the Soviet Union 'eventually transformed her into the Frankenstein that now menaces the world'.[41] But the larger framework of the indictment yokes international developments – the nightmare prospect of fighting 'perpetual war for perpetual peace' – together with domestic ones: 'individual security is menaced by our unstable economy, by unprecedented inroads upon our civil liberties and personal rights and by the specter of universal military training and interminable war hazards'.[42] Moreover, these deleterious consequences followed from the abandonment of a 'policy of neutrality' that was 'in the highest tradition of George Washington and of the established pattern of American diplomacy'.[43] Through pursuing a policy of insulation from 'war and its evident evils', the United States 'had grown prosperous beyond the dreams of the founding fathers': 'it had escaped the recurring tides of conflict that had crumbled the walls of ancient civilizations and washed away the heritage men had earned through dauntless courage and high endeavour'.[44] In other words, 'isolation' had been the key to preserving American distinctiveness and virtue in the world.

This argument was put most eloquently and forcefully by Beard, the 'revisionist' camp's most accomplished historian, whose writings on American history had helped nurture isolationist sentiment in the 1930s.[45] Beard denounced the ends, means and outcomes of Roosevelt's diplomacy, charging him with both hypocrisy and deception. The 'noble principles' so often enunciated had been 'for practical purposes, discarded' in the post-war settlement which had also ensured the rise of 'Russia, one of the most ruthless Leviathans in the long history of military empires'. Moreover, having justified intervention on the grounds that an Axis victory would otherwise compel the transformation of the United States into 'a kind of armed camp for defense, with all the evils thereunto attached', Roosevelt had in fact presided over just such a revolutionary change. More seriously, the arrogation of power to the executive imperilled the very essence of the American democratic system. 'Since the drafting of the Constitution, American statesmen of the first order have accepted the axiom that militarism and the exercise of arbitrary power over foreign affairs by the Executive are inveterate foes of republican institutions'. Under current conditions, there was a real danger that 'constitutional and democratic government in the United States is at the end of its career'. External developments were equally pernicious. The notion that the president had 'the constitutional and moral right to proclaim noble sentiments of politics, economics, and peace for the whole world', or to 'emit grand programs for imposing international morality on recalcitrant nations', was both morally offensive and politically counterproductive in arousing the antagonism of foreign countries not disposed to accept American leadership. Similarly, the drive for external economic expansion was bound to 'bring on collisions with ... controlled or semicontrolled economies' abroad. In sum, Beard dreaded the consequences of American globalism: 'if wrecks of overextended empires scattered through the centuries offer any instruction to the living present, it is that a quest for absolute power not only corrupts but in time destroys'.[46]

These issues were generally engaged in a more muted fashion in the sober narratives of the 'traditionalists', their assumptions implicit in their endorsement of Roosevelt's estimation of the Axis threat and the response it called forth to defend American security and values. On this view, disruptive agency lay with what Feis termed the 'restless, sensitive, aggrieved' Japanese and the other Axis powers.[47] Struggling to manage their challenge in the national interest, Roosevelt was 'hogtied by the prevailing isolationist sentiment', and laboured mightily 'to arouse the American people from their dream of peace'.[48] So acute was his perception of the international crisis in comparison to his compatriots that, for some 'traditionalists', he was quite justified in indulging in 'nation saving duplicity': 'like the doctor who must temporarily lie to his patient, the president dared not inform the nation of either the extent or the implications of his commitments'.[49] At points, 'traditionalists' made their assumptions more explicit when sarcastically critiquing the anti-interventionist view that 'being not immediately menaced, the first duty of Americans is to maintain their unique civilization and protect it from foreign contamination'.[50] Anti-interventionists were simply wrong to believe it possible 'to keep ourselves pure, and therefore "100% American", by having no allies whatsoever', or that, thanks to 'the contagious power of example', the 'mere spectacle of a healthy American democracy might induce Adolf Hitler to abandon his policies of force and aggression'.[51] The rectitude of Roosevelt's policy was a matter not just of American interests, but of national 'duty'.[52]

This view was overtly propagated in the most authoritative 'traditionalist' account, two massive volumes – *Challenge to Isolation* and *Undeclared War* – by Langer and Gleason, produced with privileged access to classified archival material while the former was directing research at the Central Intelligence Agency and the latter was Deputy Executive Secretary of the National Security Council.[53] Their story, they averred, was of 'the tortured emergence of the United States of America as leader of the forces of light in a world struggle which even today has scarcely abated'. 'In response to the logic of events', an increasing number of the American people 'had come to feel that it was not merely their country's hapless fate but its bounden duty to enter the great conflict': 'without the elation of 1917, but surely with profounder understanding of the values it sought to preserve, the New World again advanced to the rescue of the Old'.[54]

The first phase of the historiographical debate on the origins of the war was conducted on much the same terms as the original political controversy over intervention, and in the context of a third debate on the Cold War substance and orientation of the American state, which lent interpretations a marked contemporary ideological pertinence. In all three debates, moreover, contentions about domestic and foreign policy choices were conditioned by conflicting conceptions of national mission and purpose. What is most striking, however, is that despite the polemical character of these controversies, all the participants were at a deeper level united in a basic assumption about the precious virtue and special calling of the United States; what divided them was what course of action was best calculated to protect and fulfil it. The debates manifested yet again the perennial tension, within a polity suffused with a conviction of 'manifest destiny', between 'two quite different ways of being in the outside world': 'the first was to unfold into an exemplary state *separate* from the corrupt and fallen world, letting others emulate it as best they can. The second, [Woodrow] Wilson's position, was to push the world along by means of regenerative *intervention*'. Hence, in Anders Stephanson's formulation, the drama of intervention: 'was this the Fall, the corruption of the United States by a corrupted world, or the beginning of the final redemption of that world?'[55] The fact of exceptionalism, and of the United States as a fundamentally benevolent ideological project with a unique historic role, was simply not called into question: at issue was whether intervention would traduce that virtue. This first generation of historians were thus as deeply invested in manifest destiny as the policy-makers and critics whose arguments they reproduced.

'Empire as a way of life': the tragedy of American diplomacy

The wide ranging political, social and cultural upheavals of the 1960s shattered the broad consensus over domestic and foreign policy that had coalesced in the United States in the 1950s, and inaugurated an era of national division and self-examination. At home, the civil rights movement and other ethnic and gender equality struggles called into question the extent to which supposedly universal American principles were actually honoured in practice. Simultaneously, the vicissitudes of Cold War foreign policy, and pre-eminently the increasingly disastrous course of the war in Vietnam, generated profound disquiet about the interventionist dimensions of containment and the very wisdom and legitimacy of the exertion of American power abroad. Dissent and bitter fragmentation accelerated as the decade wore on, fuelled by generic factors such as generational change as well as the specificities of the American experience. The more extreme hopes of the emergent 'New Left' for truly radical social transformation were ultimately thwarted as conservative forces regrouped – symbolised by Richard Nixon's decisive re-election in the 1972 presidential ballot – but these years nonetheless witnessed 'the most profound societal divisions since the Civil War'.[56] The conflicts of the period also invested with fresh urgency and nuance two concerns which had long lurked within foreign policy discourse. On the one hand, as 'brazen mendacity by the federal government increased in the course of the decade', suspicion of executive authority heightened, a process that culminated with the Watergate scandal.[57] On the other, the long agony of Vietnam sharpened anxieties about the imperialist tendencies immanent in the nation's rise to globalism and the beneficence of its broader purpose.[58]

These developments had a relatively marginal impact upon American collective memory of the Second World War, where the 'good war' myth persisted but remained low-key. True, in casting doubt on former Cold War verities, détente and Vietnam impaired the credibility of the Munich analogy.[59] Moreover, scepticism about the validity of deploying armed force abroad encroached on the myth to the extent that cynical, anti-patriotic representations of the absurdity and human costs of the Second World War – such as Joseph Heller's *Catch-22* or Kurt Vonnegut's *Slaughterhouse-Five* – proliferated and found a ready audience.[60] In a broader sense, it has been argued that 'the political disagreements and ideological wars related to Vietnam … eclipsed the memory of World War II'.[61] Renowned critical treatments can easily be read as not being especially 'about' the Second World War: rather, they seem more like generic anti-war narratives or Vietnam allegories.[62] That said, to conceive of a cultural preoccupation with Vietnam decisively displacing a concern with the earlier 'good war' is misleading, insofar as positive images of the latter also continued to have a pervasive if low-intensity presence. This period also witnessed, for example, a profusion of immensely popular, overblown filmic 'docu-cameo-epics' and 'big-war action adventures', sustaining the notion that the resilient 'good war' myth had 'shaken off all the challenges along the way'.[63] Moreover, it is not implausible to suggest that in the midst of an indubitably 'bad war', the need to retain the 'good war' as a positive and pristine foil may only have been strengthened: 'indeed, the war in Vietnam was often portrayed as bad in precise proportion to the goodness of America's fight against German fascism and Japanese militarism'.[64] Subsequently, to generate an additional layer of complexity, the 'good war' myth was available to suture the traumatic national wounds inflicted by the conflict in Indochina.[65]

Shifts in the structure and substance of historical writing in the United States mirrored the political and social tumult of the 1960s. The profession expanded as higher education boomed, but the discipline also fragmented with the proliferation of new forms of economic, social and minority history, often influenced by social science methodologies, and contestation of the repressive, 'depoliticising' norms of early Cold War objectivity.[66] These fresh perspectives had a potent significance in beginning to challenge 'the traditional triumphal and exceptionalist conception of American history', though their impact was felt very unevenly across the discipline and it would be some decades before it could be claimed with even tentative confidence that the exceptionalist tradition might be 'drawing to a close'.[67] Not surprisingly these tectonic shifts generated fierce controversy, much of it focusing on a broad constellation of emergent left-leaning scholars commonly demarcated as the 'New Left historians' (though the designation unfairly elides significant differences in generational perspective and political and intellectual commitments). They represented 'something hitherto unknown in the American historical profession': 'substantial and systematically "oppositional" historiographical tendencies'.[68]

In writing on the origins of the Second World War, the centre ground was held by scholarship that reflected these various developments, albeit in a rather muted fashion. There was a perceptible thickening of the literature as increasingly specialised monographs began to appear, often exploring thematic issues – 'ideological, economic, and psychological' – in line with the diversification of approaches across the discipline.[69] This was facilitated by the growing availability of source materials with the completion of the official documentary series *Foreign Relations of the United States* for the period and the gradual opening of the State Department archives and important collections of private papers, especially Roosevelt's.[70] Debate continued to focus, however, on the issue of Roosevelt's leadership. The dominant interpretation embodied considerable continuity with earlier 'traditionalist' defences, insofar as there was 'a massive scholarly consensus' evincing 'clear sympathy' with the policy of intervention.[71] That said, the suggestion that Roosevelt had been excessively timid was also further developed, lending this more 'mature' phase of scholarship a palpably critical hue. Given the obvious threat posed to the nation's security, 'the main question was and has remained, not why the United States entered the war against Germany, but why it did not do so earlier'.[72]

Extending an argument earlier adumbrated by Langer and Gleason, important works critiqued American policy prior to the war for being too passive and vacillating. For Robert Divine, Roosevelt was no perspicacious interventionist but rather a convinced isolationist who moved but hesitantly and indecisively towards the necessary war – withal, a most 'reluctant internationalist'.[73] The illusions of public opinion were partly responsible for this tardiness, but more significant was a fundamental 'failure of leadership'. 'By surrendering the initiative to Germany and Japan, the United States made itself the prisoner of events abroad' until it was eventually 'forced ... to adopt active policies of resistance'.[74] Arnold Offner went even further in his study of diplomacy towards Europe in the 1930s, indicting Roosevelt for the pursuit of an active policy of 'American appeasement': in this, the United States 'exhibited incredible political blindness'.[75] Although some authors continued to emphasise the constraints under which Roosevelt laboured, or even to stress his positive initiative, more critical treatments were 'increasingly in vogue among diplomatic specialists'.[76]

The experience of Vietnam exercised some influence over this literature. Criticism of Roosevelt's want of frankness, if not duplicity, in explaining foreign affairs to the public became more salient, and here 'disillusionment with the Vietnam War was the determining factor'.[77] To a certain extent, scepticism about foreign entanglements also conduced to a rehabilitation of the earlier isolationists, now dignified as possessing a coherent and rational worldview rather than dismissed as nationalist xenophobes.[78] Divine admitted in 1979 that in preparing the revised second edition of his *Reluctant Belligerent* he 'softened the wording' of his indictment, having become 'more understanding of the isolationist position' as a consequence of Vietnam.[79] However, as the substance of that text demonstrates, these modifications were essentially cosmetic and did not mar the predominant assumption that intervention was morally and politically warranted. Indeed the striking fact is that while foreign relations historiography in general came to be permeated in the shadow of Vietnam by disillusionment and doubt about past instances of 'twentieth-century American interventionism', the war against Hitler remained signally exempt.[80] As a sceptic noted in a text suffused with Vietnam-era anxieties that actually did question whether intervention was necessary on either security or moral grounds, 'participation in the war against Hitler remains almost wholly sacrosanct, nearly in the realm of theology'.[81] Yet such an isolated argument served merely as the exception to prove the rule as the 'good war' decisively trumped the 'bad'.

Premising their interpretations on the assumption that earlier intervention 'would have been desirable', and generally finding some fault with Roosevelt as a consequence, mainstream international historians overwhelmingly partook of and contributed to the perpetuation of the mythical status of the 'good war'.[82] Moreover, the terms in which American intervention was endorsed also had broader normative implications. When Divine castigated the United States for having 'refused to play its rightful role of world leader' and for passively 'reacting to events abroad rather than shaping viable alternatives in a troubled world', he implicitly sanctioned a pro-active globalist stance in the Cold War present, in a manner that cut across the wariness and hesitation of the Vietnam era.[83] Divine also, if subtly, engaged the issue of American exceptionalism. He described Roosevelt's initial attitude towards the international crisis of the 1930s as 'in the classic tradition of American isolationism', whereby the United States 'was to play a passive role as the beacon of liberty to mankind, providing a model for the world to follow'.[84] It was by now a commonplace in the literature debating America in the world that this form of exemplary isolationism existed in dichotomous tension with regenerative internationalism: competing means to realise 'the American purpose or mission of bringing the blessings of freedom to all men', 'both arose from the central conviction of the unique character and absolute significance of our experience'.[85] In lambasting one pole of this discursive dyad, Divine arguably not merely sanctioned the other policy preference but also intimated at sympathy with the underpinning supposition about the particular virtue of the American polity.[86]

The most potent challenge to this mainstream perspective on intervention came from the left, as part of a comprehensive revisioning of American foreign relations that gave direct expression to the political ferment of the Vietnam era (even if it originally pre-dated that conflict).[87] The 'great majority' of 'young radical historians entered one or another subdivision of social history'. Yet it was in the traditionally establishment field of diplomatic history that 'left dissidence had its greatest impact', largely through the agency of William Appleman Williams, as the intellectual figurehead of the so-called 'Wisconsin school'.[88]

Williams pioneered a critique of American foreign policy as consistently hallmarked by the pursuit of 'open door imperialism', in which economic and ideological expansionism intertwined to ensure global conditions that were congenial to American liberal capitalism, thus to safeguard a conservative domestic social and political order. Drawing on the heritage of Beard and other dissenting thinkers, this perspective shifted the locus of explanation away from the wisdom or culpability of individual policy-makers, and onto economic and ideological factors, tilting emphasis markedly from agency to structure (though there remained disagreement as to how far expansion was the product of objective structural necessity or subjective perceptions of such exigency).[89] In implying that the chief motive forces driving American foreign policy were domestic rather than external, it also challenged the cherished national metanarrative that posited an innocent, 'traditionally isolationist nation', 'overwhelmingly anti-imperialist' except for the odd 'aberrant spasm', being driven 'only slowly, reluctantly, and in self-defense' to take up the burden of world power.[90] The idea that the United States had pursued an inherently expansionist course for essentially selfish purposes was intellectual sacrilege in a climate wherein Samuel Flagg Bemis, doyen of American diplomatic historians, could extol its foreign policy as having been dedicated to defending and spreading 'the blessings of liberty'.[91] Moreover, the implications that Vietnam was the logical culmination of American expansionism rather than a tragic anomaly, and that American rather than Soviet hegemonic drives might have underpinned the very outbreak of the Cold War, were politically incendiary. As Peter Novick has argued, the ensuing debate struck at the heart of the United States' 'moral standing in the world' and self-perception: it 'was not just about what we should do, but about who we *were*'.[92]

For obvious reasons, the most hotly contested 'Wisconsin school' claims were those pertaining to the origins of the Cold War.[93] Yet in both wide-ranging surveys and more detailed monographic work, Williams and others also addressed the issue of intervention in the Second World War. In his landmark *The Tragedy of American Diplomacy*, first published in 1959, Williams described that conflict as 'the war for the American frontier'.[94] Contrary to the legend of isolationist innocence, he argued, 'the pattern of American expansion under the principles and procedures of the Open Door Notes came to maturity during the 1920s', and it was 'the threat posed to that program by the combined impact of the Great Depression and the competing expansion of Germany and Japan' – with their autarchic and exclusionary economic policies – 'which ultimately accounted for American entry into World War II'. Americans had come, he continued, 'firmly to believe that their own prosperity and democracy depended upon the continued expansion of their economic system under the strategy of the open door'. This 'sense of economic necessity' easily fused with a conviction that they were 'defending an anticolonial democracy charged with a duty to regenerate the world'. Indeed, the convergence of these beliefs laid the groundwork for the Cold War, transforming 'the traditional concept of open door expansion into a vision of an American Century', 'a utopian idea into an ideology'.[95]

Lloyd Gardner developed this argument in more detail. Faced with the economic crises of the 1930s, American policy-makers had to choose between a path of 'self-containment' and thoroughgoing domestic structural reform or an externally-oriented policy, continuing to seek commercial expansion in a free trade and open door world. The choice was made for the latter, so that these years came to demonstrate that 'the United States regarded the defense of its liberal trade system as central to the conduct of its foreign policy and the stem of that policy's ideology'. Gardner did not deny that Americans saw Germany ultimately 'as primarily a military threat', but did insist that 'it was not the existence of Nazism *per se* that made World War II and America's entrance into that struggle inevitable; rather, it was the expansion of the [Nazi] system'. American policy was not merely 'a reaction to German or Japanese militarism', but was rooted in economic considerations and a much longer term struggle to maintain an open door world.[96] Thus, 'the "National Orders" which replaced the Versailles system were at war economically long before September 1, 1939'.[97] Robert Freeman Smith seconded this point, identifying the prevalence from the mid-1930s of American anxieties about Axis economic aggression in Asia, Europe and Latin America: 'these arguments were repeated *ad infinitum*, and clearly indicate that the concept of security was thoroughly entangled with the belief that the preservation of private enterprise capitalism in the United States depended upon a world order in which this system was free to operate with few restrictions'.[98]

The 'Wisconsin school' critique dramatically redimensioned the interpretation of American intervention, shifting emphasis from intention to structure, from politics to economics, from external threats to internal drives, and from self-defence to self-interest. The argument that American diplomacy was hallmarked by an internally generated quest for (informal) imperial aggrandisement, and that liberal internationalism was not necessarily altruistic, confounded conventional assumptions about their moral and political rectitude. It also made these scholars more sceptical towards the dominant 'good war' myth than any diplomatic historians since Beard. When Williams decried the fact that 'empire as a way of life leads only to war and more war', and coupled this with a critique of how Roosevelt, through 'arbitrary' and 'dishonest' actions, 'committed the government to a war for America's imperial way of life', the critical intent seemed incontestable.[99]

That said, there was ambiguity here. Partly this arose simply from the ambition to 'normalise' the war by locating it within a longer term history of continuous expansion, rendering it in a sense a mere epiphenomenon (notwithstanding its significance in catapulting the United States towards global power); this had consequential implications, but it was less than the full-scale assault on the myth that Beard and earlier 'revisionists' had mounted.[100] Moreover, as a critical commentator noted, demonstrating the fact of intervention and of American interest in preserving an open door world did not in itself decisively prove that policy was not also motivated by 'the fear that a Eurasia controlled by hostile powers would ultimately pose a threat to America's physical security'. Even granted that American leaders defined national well-being – 'security in its greater than physical dimension' – in an expansive sense, it did not follow that the deleterious 'projected consequences to this country of an Axis victory could have been avoided if only American policy had not been committed to the expansionist goals of the Open Door'. Nor, he continued 'do radical historians seriously contend – let alone demonstrate – otherwise'.[101] This point seems supported by grudging and convoluted admissions – often obscured by the over-riding concern with the domestic dimension – that war was in fact ultimately warranted by the extent of Axis expansionist ambitions; hence Smith's concession that 'the actual defense of the United States' was an operative concern, with 'the restoration of the Open Door world order' merely 'of at least equal importance to the Roosevelt administration'.[102] In other words, the 'Wisconsin school' sought 'to attack America's motives for intervention in World War II rather than the intervention itself'.[103] As H. W. Brands has argued, Williams 'stopped short of declaring that the war had been unnecessary': given Pearl Harbor and Auschwitz, 'such a charge would have placed him entirely beyond the bounds of respectable opinion'. Nor 'did he believe American participation in the war had been entirely unjustified'. Rather he sought to 'question the high-mindedness with which Americans claimed to have fought and the purportedly selfless ends they pursued'.[104] In this sense, his challenge to the 'good war' myth was muted and partial.[105]

A similar tension pervades these scholars' relationship with American national identity. *Prima facie*, as Novick argued, this revisionist perspective posed searching, novel and profoundly critical questions about the virtue of the American self. Some sought explicitly to step outside of the framework of American exceptionalism which, they claimed, had structured both foreign policy rhetoric and diplomatic history. Thus Smith attacked patriotic historians who 'believe (and implicitly promulgate) the myth of the unique nation; a nation which is unselfish, unambitious, and whose world goals are good for all people'. Weighed down with 'the ideological baggage of Manifest Destiny', 'traditionalist' and mainstream scholars had produced 'briefs in support of an imperial role for the United States, whether this is euphemistically called world leadership or international responsibility'. Claiming to penetrate through to the deeper motives of policy, Smith rejected both exceptionalism and the exemplary separation/regenerative intervention dichotomy following from it, presenting the United States instead as 'a rather imperial-minded power with ambitions and goals which on the whole are rather similar to those of most other modern powers'.[106] The more extreme of the radical critics, especially those advocating a more dogmatically Marxian and determinist view in which overseas expansion was an inevitable outgrowth of American capitalism, tended in the same direction.[107] With the inexorable machinations of capitalism centre stage, 'America's professed ideals' became 'no more than empty rhetoric'. That said, there was also an irony here since some critics went so far in their condemnation of the evils of American aggression that one could be 'tempted to conclude, despite their protestations to the contrary, that they too share, though in inverted form, the belief in America's exceptionalism'.[108]

Arguably some radical scholars were in various ways just as invested in American exceptionalism as diplomatic historians of other persuasions (in addition to sharing in the pervasive sin of provincialism, through a mono-national focus and imputing decisive agency and influence in the international system to the United States).[109] This is especially true of Williams, who wrote in sorrow and anger 'from the standpoint of a bereaved patriot'.[110] Far from simplistically anti-American, he characterised his work as a 'candid and searching re-examination of [our] own mythology' rather than 'a tirade of useless self-damnation'. In his most famous formulation, 'the tragedy of American diplomacy' was 'not that it is evil, but that it denies and subverts American ideas and ideals'. Certainly he did not see the United States as an essentially pernicious ideological project, nor feel that hypocritical dissonance between rhetoric and reality was its inescapable existential condition. He ultimately eschewed economic determinism, making contingent perceptions of the necessity for expansion the crucial factor; his emphasis on *Weltanschauung* recuperated the possibility of agency as the ground of a manifesto for redemption.

The closing pages of *The Tragedy of American Diplomacy* outlined his views on how 'the specific tragedy of American diplomacy can be transcended in a creative, peaceful manner', through 'a radical but non-communist reconstruction of American society in domestic affairs' and the abandonment of the informal open door empire; in place of the latter he proposed 'an open door for revolutions', whereby 'having come to terms with themselves ... Americans could exhibit the self-discipline necessary to let other peoples come to terms with themselves', and to 'achieve their own aspirations in their own way'. America might set an example, but would not force others to follow it, and would 'no longer find it necessary to embark on crusades to save others'. American society would 'function even better on the basis of equitable relationships with other peoples' and this might also help carry 'the world on into an era of peace and creative human endeavor'.[111]

Commentators have characterised Williams as thus engaged in 'a struggle for America's very soul'.[112] For all the intellectual verve, explanatory novelty and political provocation of the 'Wisconsin school' approach, on the level of its engagement with national identity and the problematic of exceptionalism, the terms of the debate had not really changed at all. Williams' prescription 'for America to return to the path of right' and redeem its 'claim upon the admiration of the world' essentially entailed 'a shift from the vindicationism of the American empire to an exemplarism of true American democracy'.[113] The uncharitable might conclude that this was to partake of 'a discourse of dissent that revolved around the harm done *to* America through its foreign interventions instead of around the far greater harm done *by* America', with the risk of 'turning debates over foreign policy into an inward-looking distraction that [might] perpetuate the arrogance of which America is so often accused'.[114] At any event, 'it is well to remember that a central theme of the critique was liberal, even destinarian: the "perversion" of true Americanism'.[115]

'A major force for world prosperity and peace': a range of possible Roosevelts

The search to rediscover national purpose and pride was a prominent theme in American politics in the aftermath of Watergate and Vietnam. The bicentennial celebrations of the American Revolution in 1976 were conceived by many as an opportunity for 'a renewal of American consensus and patriotism'.[116] The ascendancy in the 1980s of Republican President Ronald Reagan accelerated the process, spinning it in an assertively conservative direction. 'Professing a vision of national renewal and collective redemption, Reagan promoted a project which was both political and religious to recover the golden age of American stability and prosperity and to reclaim the national greatness of the USA which was the holy birthright of the American people'.[117] Domestically, this entailed an assault on the evils of 'atheism, welfare liberalism, [and] government meddling', while externally it meant a return to a more 'vigorous prosecution of the cold war'.[118] The ground for a far less ambivalent attitude to the projection of American military power abroad was at least partly prepared by a revisionist rewriting of Vietnam as an act of heroic sacrifice in pursuit of a noble cause.[119] Victory in the Cold War ushered in a transitional era marked by cross currents. On the one hand, the collapse of Soviet communism generated a great deal of triumphalist rhetoric about the vindication by history itself of the American way of life; on the other, the disappearance of a defining enemy and the emergence of myriad unfamiliar threats engendered uncertainty, drift and a search for purpose. 'The absence of a story about where we are going and what our role is in the world' manifested itself in fierce 'culture wars' at home over political correctness, multiculturalism and history, and a somewhat tentative and shapeless foreign policy, albeit featuring recognizable themes such as the expansion of liberal capitalism and democracy promotion.[120]

The brutal shock of the terrorist attacks of 11 September 2001, however, engendered yet another vigorous and focused articulation of America's global mission.[121] President George W. Bush's 2002 National Security Strategy (NSS), as saturated with exceptionalist thinking as its distant predecessor NSC 68, specified the goals of 'defend[ing] the peace by fighting terrorists and tyrants' and 'extend[ing] the peace by encouraging free and open societies on every continent'.[122] This vision of the United States as a global champion of freedom against numerous fiercely demarcated others underpinned ongoing military campaigns in Afghanistan and Iraq that were castigated by critics as 'the most virulent expression of aggressive American nationalism since the Vietnam War'.[123] Unsurprisingly, the enunciation of a new variant of messianic Manicheanism, allied to a doctrine of preventative war to spread American values conceived as both 'absolutely good in themselves and identical with the good of the world', inaugurated a new phase of vociferous political and intellectual contestation about the imperialist drives putatively inherent in the American project.[124] For alarmed outsiders, this newly dominant 'aggressive interpretation' of exceptionalism embodied 'xenophobia', 'glorification of military power' and the 'demand of obeisance to a nationalist and anti-internationalist creed'.[125]

These developments were paralleled by a quantitative and qualitative transformation in American war memory. A palpable upsurge in the visibility of representations of the Second World War, an intensified tone of celebratory reverence and overt engagement with a set of contemporary ideological tensions all suggested that the United States had finally acquired a fully-fledged war myth. Reagan's speeches in Normandy in 1984 during the fortieth anniversary of D-Day offered an early portent, melding robust anti-Sovietism with eulogising of the veterans, thereby reminding 'a nation cynical after Watergate and Vietnam that America truly was still the shining city on the hill'.[126] The scale and intensity of the cycle of fiftieth anniversary remembrances which began in the early 1990s testified to the renewed prominence of the war. After an extensive round of commemorative events in 1991, cultural references to Pearl Harbor 'proliferated exponentially'.[127] The controversy that erupted in 1994 over the Smithsonian Institution's plans to mark the Hiroshima bombing was pregnant with significance. Academics and museum professionals were pitted against veterans and conservative politicians over the content of the proposed *Enola Gay* exhibition, with the latter ultimately prevailing in their insistence on sidelining critical analysis in favour of patriotic triumphalism. The new found cultural authority of veterans was underlined by a boom in media representations through the later 1990s lauding the achievements of *The Greatest Generation*.[128] This homage intersected with a relentless rise in Holocaust consciousness to reinscribe the virtue of the American cause in the war, as exemplified by the insistent presence of Holocaust thematics in Steven Spielberg's 1998 epic *Saving Private Ryan*.[129] The unveiling in 2004 of the National World War II Memorial in Washington confirmed both the ascendancy of this intensified 'good war' myth and – by its symbolic location between the Washington Monument and Lincoln Memorial – the strategic utility of the conflict within a vindicatory narrative of national history.[130]

Diverse factors combined to produce this frenzy of mnemonic labour. The memory activism of the fading veteran generation itself was not insignificant, and this chimed with a new eagerness on the part of baby boomers 'to honor and commemorate their parents and to rediscover a more glorious, less ambiguous time'. These impulses were interconnected with a broader cultural disposition towards *fin-de-siècle* nostalgic retrospection, and pervasive anxieties about an absence of existential challenges (at least prior to 11 September) and the secular waning of collective purpose and national unity.[131] Indeed, the 'return' of the Second World War has been characterised as 'a more or less thinly veiled conservative response to the contemporary crisis of national identity, to our failing sense of what it means to be an American and to do things the so-called American way'. On this view, heroicising and individualising popular culture representations of the war function as 'technologies of national cultural transformation', promoting social cohesion 'by manufacturing and embracing a particular *kind* of American, a certain idea of what it means to be a "good citizen"'.[132] 'Putting the recovery of the past to contemporary political use' could also be accomplished metaphorically, as in the 1996 sci-fi blockbuster *Independence Day*, freighted with Holocaust and Hiroshima allusions, which proposed a 'multicultural reuniting of America on violently exclusionary terms'.[133] This project carries both internal and external implications, as it links up with the recent rhetoric and practice of American foreign policy. The invocation of the Second World War as an epochal conflict fought by a united nation for altruistic purposes – the destruction of 'militarized nationalism, racial chauvinism, and imperialism' – fits very well with the reaffirmation of 'the providential, exceptional place of the United States in the course of world history': hence the ubiquity of references to it in efforts to justify American policy in the 'War on Terror' as historically sanctioned, righteous and benevolent.[134]

Within historical writing through these decades, numerous and increasingly vocal advocates of transnational approaches to the study of the American past stood in opposition to this resurgent exceptionalism.[135] The ongoing march of social history, the subsequent rise of cultural history, and the emergence of 'postmodernist' critiques of historical knowledge also conduced 'to dethrone many of the long-standing absolutisms about the nature of the American nation'. In consequence, the discipline of history itself figured prominently in the culture wars of the 1980s and 1990s, with educators attacked by conservatives for failing to tell 'an edifying national saga' and explicate 'transcendent Western values'.[136] That said, more traditional approaches persisted and in any event – as the *Enola Gay* controversy attested – it was doubtful how far critical academic perspectives on the national past gained any purchase in the popular imagination. Through much of this period international historians – 'traditional' in their preoccupation with the nation-state, elite policy-makers, diplomacy and war – tended to fret about their perceived marginalisation by a wider profession obsessed with the modish analytics of race, class and gender.[137] Arguably the subfield took something of a conservative turn as 'New Left' revisionism declined, partly mutating into milder if more sophisticated 'corporatist' and 'world-systems theory' approaches, and largely supplanted in Cold War studies by a 'post-revisionist' paradigm that essentially validated the exertion of American power.[138] From the 1990s, however, a new form of critical practice emerged as a significant minority of practitioners adapted cultural history methodologies to the historical study of international relations. These culturalist scholars subsequently made signal critical contributions to a newly thriving literature on the ideological nature of American foreign policy (with particular emphasis on exceptionalism and nationalism) and the fabric of American empire.[139]

The historiography of the origins of the war in this period was not marked by any major methodological innovations or fundamental interpretive controversies. (It would be too harsh to say that the field became a backwater, but the centre of gravity in the subdiscipline had decisively shifted towards the study of post-1945 international relations.[140]) The emergence of further archival and published sources facilitated the production of both general and specialised monographs, and in step with the expanding terrain of diplomatic history these dealt with a widening range of thematic topics, and offered ever more sophisticated accounts of policy-making. Yet to a remarkable degree the debate was dominated by a familiar question:

> What was Franklin Roosevelt's view of the world and of the United States' place in it? ... Most work since the late 1970s concerning the final phase of the interwar period has concentrated on the president: his thoughts, personality, and actions ... His towering presence forms the basis for this recent historiography, a development that has undercut the [Wisconsin school] tendency to downplay personality and policy.[141]

The heart of the historiography, then, featured the delineation of a range of possible Roosevelts.[142] The argument earlier advanced by Divine and Offner that the president was essentially an isolationist in the 1930s, even contributing to efforts to appease the revisionist powers, until the shifting geopolitical balance forced him towards an interventionist stance, remained in play.[143] Yet an alternative and much more favourable view came to prominence with Robert Dallek's landmark 1979 study of Roosevelt's diplomacy. For Dallek, Roosevelt was always a sincere internationalist, but was forced to manoeuvre and compromise in the face of multiple constraints: public opinion, a sceptical Congress and international circumstances. His 'caution and restraint' were praiseworthy rather than damnable, since he 'had to balance the country's desire to stay out of war against its contradictory impulse to assure the defeat of Nazi power'. Initially hoping to weave the two goals together through his policy of 'material aid to the Allies', even when Roosevelt came to see active belligerence as unavoidable in 1941 'he refused to force an unpalatable choice upon the nation by announcing for war' until 'a genuine provocation from abroad made the nation ready to fight'. Even his 'dissembling', while creating 'an unfortunate precedent for arbitrary action in foreign affairs', could be excused in the circumstances: 'it is difficult to fault Roosevelt for building a consensus by devious means'.

Overall, Dallek concluded that Roosevelt's 'appreciation that effective action abroad required a reliable consensus at home and his use of dramatic events overseas to win national backing from a divided country for a series of pro-Allied steps were among the great presidential achievements of [the twentieth] century'.[144] Others concurred, such as Waldo Heinrichs, writing in 1988, who depicted Roosevelt as 'an active and purposeful maker of foreign policy, the only figure with all the threads in his hands'. Over time, Roosevelt quite properly came to see that 'the defeat of Germany was essential for American security', and shifted from an initial attitude of prudent caution towards a more forceful diplomacy, 'impatient with delay, pressing upon events'. His robust diplomacy carried the risk of war, 'but the risks of inaction, in the global calculus, seemed greater'.[145] David Schmitz more recently presented a similarly glowing portrait of Roosevelt as a devoted and consistent internationalist, educating the public not only to accept the necessity of intervention in a just war but also to understand that 'only the spreading of American values and institutions would bring real security to the nation'.[146]

Yet other interpretations, whilst still approving intervention, found more to criticise in the coherence of Roosevelt's policy and the quality of his leadership. Warren Kimball noted that although his policy was hallmarked by underlying consistent assumptions, he 'often simply muddled through, sweeping obstacles under the rug in the hope that they would go away in time'.[147] Pushing this line of argument further, Mark Lowenthal characterised Roosevelt's diplomacy as 'a series of fits and starts'. He generally had a broad if vague understanding of 'what he wanted and what he hoped to avoid', but 'was disinclined to define his purposes or fundamental policy goals' to subordinates responsible for their implementation and execution. The result was 'a fundamental policy vacuum' on the twisted road to intervention.[148] While Lowenthal conceded the reality of domestic constraints on Roosevelt's freedom of action, others argued that he could have done far more to manage public opinion and forge a consensus for the pursuit of a more forceful foreign policy. Reviewing this question, J. Garry Clifford noted that Roosevelt 'played down his capacity to lead' and concluded that he 'led circuitously and deviously because he preferred it that way'.[149]

The most forceful critique in this vein was advanced by Frederick Marks. For Marks, incoherence, parochialism and a lack of vision were the hallmarks of Roosevelt's policy. Towards Japan, his diplomacy was equivocal and duplicitous, mingling 'misrepresentation, ambivalence, and prevarication'. Towards Europe, he disastrously combined the roles of 'crusader for democratic values and covert agent of appeasement', sending such mixed messages that he 'succeeded in simultaneously encouraging both sides to hold fast' and hastened the onset of war. In his first years in office he did much to nurture the 'extreme isolationist sentiment' that later constrained American policy, but as war loomed he actually lagged 'well behind Congress and the public' on matters such as rearmament; neglecting to integrate military and political factors, he failed to build up an effective deterrent, thereby both jeopardising national security and causing Hitler 'to view Western policy as a colossal bluff built upon a militarily defunct United States'. 'One is bound to be troubled', Marks adverted, 'by the president's apparent drifting, by his lack of any clearly defined strategy, and by his refusal to raise American military potential to a level commensurate with the nation's natural influence'. His indictment of the ultimate consequences of Roosevelt's failings is severe: 'grooming the image of crusader at home, he acted secretly as an agent of appeasement. In the end, he fueled optimism on both sides of the conflict until a peaceful solution gradually slipped beyond reach'.[150]

Many authors have invoked the personal opacity of 'the sly squire of Hyde Park' and the convoluted nature of the American policy-making process under him – a 'bureaucratic chaos' that 'emerged partly by design' – as explanations for this continued diversity of scholarly opinion.[151] Yet from another perspective what is actually striking is the narrowness of the parameters of debate, and the assumptions which are shared by the contributors to it.[152] This is not just a matter of the dominance of the 'presidential paradigm', and a consequent focus on 'means rather than ends', on 'the appropriateness of Roosevelt's actions in 1940–1941'; it is also about the related point that all participants tend to assume 'the essential rightness of U.S. belligerency against Germany and Japan'. As David Reynolds has observed, 'the debate keeps returning to Roosevelt, usually within the terms set by the orthodox consensus that this was a good war that the United States entered for justifiable ends, albeit by slightly dubious means'.[153] A partial exception to this generalisation exists in a strand of the literature that continues to advance 'Wisconsin school' style interpretations. Thus Patrick Hearden argued that 'American leaders were primarily concerned about the menace that a triumphant Germany would present to the free enterprise system', and that ultimately 'they chose to fight to keep foreign markets open for surplus American commodities and thereby to preserve entrepreneurial freedom in the United States'. Yet as with Williams these arguments critique conventional understandings of American motives for intervention, but generally fall short of explicitly contending that the war was wrong.[154] Overall, however, even the authors most critical of Roosevelt for inconsistency and drift have premised their accounts on the assumption that greater firmness in meeting the Axis threat would have been desirable; the elements of appeasement and isolationism, of 'shirking preparedness', are the crucial damnable faults in his diplomacy.[155]

American international historians writing on intervention thus continue to partake of the 'good war' myth. In his laudatory account David Schmitz implicitly endorsed the war as a battle to 'reshape the world in the U.S. image', laying the foundation for a post-war American role 'as a world leader, with its power and influence extended globally', and concluded insouciantly that this readily explained 'why World War II was seen as the "Good War" by so many Americans when it was fought and after'.[156] This may be an extreme example, but it is strongly suggestive of encapsulation by this hegemonic concept within American collective memory. Moreover, even when historians have themselves drawn attention to the dubious romanticising excess of that myth, they have nonetheless tended simultaneously to reiterate that 'the elimination of Hitler and the specter of Nazism was a necessity and a blessing'.[157] The point here is not to dispute that characterisation, or to argue that intervention was in no sense morally or politically justified. It is rather to highlight that expressing approbation for intervention in these conventional terms is to flirt with a larger set of ideological entanglements. This has been rendered all the more perturbing by the recent resurgence of the 'good war' myth in a more aggressive and politically pointed form, in parallel with a virulent new iteration of exceptionalism. Even if it is a retrospective co-optation (and thus hardly a matter of conscious intention for those writing years or decades ago), this scholarship now risks finding itself in discursive alignment and complicity with the simplistic pieties of 'greatest generation' triumphalism and the rhetorical underpinnings of the 'War on Terror'.

This is in no way to dissent from the contemporary near-global consensus concerning the unparalleled iniquity of Nazism. After all, as Anders Stephanson has observed, for all one might quibble about motives or the disparity between high-minded rhetoric and morally ambiguous practice in conducting the conflict, 'the Second World War as antifascism was necessity and it is hard to argue with necessity'.[158] The problem is rather with how the fact of Nazi evil is used as a foil to point up American virtue, in moves that are not logically entailed. Most egregious here is the now culturally pervasive notion of the war as having been fought against the Holocaust. This elides the negligible significance of the fate of the European Jews both in American decision-making over intervention and in subsequent military strategy: 'the celebration of World War II as a moral crusade obscures the actual Western nonresponse to genocide'.[159] The crusade emplotment further effaces complexity by tending to exaggerate the American contribution to victory: 'most Americans imagine their country to have won the war more or less on its own. Few know anything at all about the role played by the Soviet Union'.[160] Ironically, these moves are functionally extremely similar to those which occurred in the Soviet Union, where the waging of the Great Patriotic War against Nazism was construed as benevolent and morally justified, and then instrumentalised by generations of post-war historians in order to vindicate the Soviet system in its entirety. In like fashion, the insistent presentation of the Second World War as the 'good war' is inextricably entangled with the reinscription of the myth of America as uniquely benign.

More specifically, positive representations of American intervention against Nazism can function illicitly to legitimate the exertion of American power in the world in past, present and future. Here the implication of international historians is a subtle matter, since very few are unreflexive cheerleaders for

American empire. It is perhaps most obvious in the more favourable treatments, as when Dallek reproduces Roosevelt's estimation of the United States as 'a major force for world prosperity and peace' and approves his achievement in ensuring that 'the nation ended the war ready to shoulder substantial responsibilities in foreign affairs'; had Roosevelt lived beyond 1945, Dallek concludes, he would doubtless have embarked on a 'renewed struggle to make the world a better place in which to live'.[161] Even in more critical accounts, Roosevelt's exceptionalist thinking can be reproduced in ways that imply endorsement, as when Kimball discusses his particular ideology of 'Americanism', noting that 'it was the city-on-a-hill/an-example-for-all-the-world-to-follow approach that FDR preferred, even if coercion and force were sometimes legitimate means to the end' (which amounts to an intriguing blend of exemplarism and vindicationism). Roosevelt 'assumed the superiority and steady acceptance of American-style institutions' and sought a wider extension 'of American social, economic, and political liberalism'; this, Kimball avers, 'was not some kind of crude imperialism, but the normal, human impulse to convert the unenlightened in a practical, mutually beneficial way'.[162] It may not be entirely fair to equate description with prescription, but the fact remains that the more sceptical constructions of the American purpose are not considered here, and sympathetic interpretation of intervention furtively slides into a justification of global vindicationist activism with uncomfortable contemporary connotations.

Particular emplotments reinforce different components of the exceptionalism framework. For example, the choice to attribute decisive significance in precipitating intervention to the 'insatiable expansionist appetite' of Hitler and Japan's quest for 'imperial self-sufficiency and hegemony in East Asia' – the key factors in a 'different and dangerous world' that eventually 'made war inevitable sooner or later' – is an externalising move that forecloses full consideration of American agency. Witness Heinrichs' opening words: 'before war pounced on the United States on December 7, 1941, it crept up, stage by stage, over many years'.[163] Similarly, John Lamberton Harper has delineated a Rooseveltian exceptionalism, differently accented from Kimball's, that comprised a belief in 'the virtue and special destiny of America' as a 'sanctuary of civilised values' and morally superior to the Old World. This mandated an initial policy of 'Europhobic hemispherism', later transmuted into a partial internationalism, an interventionism founded on reluctant conviction that American participation was essential for victory and the shaping of a durable peace compatible with American interests: 'the only calamity worse than entanglement in Europe was the one likely to ensue from leaving the Europeans to their proverbial own devices'. Ultimately, Harper conjures up a profoundly tragic Roosevelt, weighed down as his death approached by realisation that thanks to the recalcitrance of Old Europe his ambition to enact a co-operative post-war settlement that would allow for the disengagement of America had been confounded. While Harper does not naively endorse what he terms Roosevelt's 'profoundly solipsistic nationalism', this is nonetheless a narrative that displaces abroad responsibility for the post-war expansion of American power.[164]

Whatever the empirical justification for these tropings (and they are not negligible), they also sustain a broader cultural metanarrative, about the innocence of a nation drawn reluctantly into global affairs, that has done very dubious political service. The United States, 'despite its long history of perpetrating violence, continues to see itself as an innocent victim of an unruly world that neither respects it nor seeks to emulate its democratic culture'. An amnesiac condition 'makes possible a constant rewriting of history in a manner that resonates with the narratives of the national self and facilitates the erasure of unpleasant memories'.[165] This notion of innocence is a central tenet of exceptionalism: 'the image of the United States as a country of pure intentions to which terrible things can happen, but which itself never provokes or initiates attack' enables an expansionist, even imperial, foreign policy, but needs 'constant maintenance in order to be sustained'.[166] Framed in particular ways, classically conceived renditions of the American road to intervention certainly participate in this ideological labour.

There is, of course, no way of purging historiography of ideology, but more explicit reflection on the imbrication of writing on intervention with 'good war' mythology and the rise to globalism would conduce to a scholarly practice more sensitised to its own entailments. Acts of reframing and contextualisation, for example, might reduce the danger of the purported legitimacy of one war being stealthily redeployed to justify other expansionist and aggressive actions abroad. The provocation of 'Wisconsin school' approaches – whatever their weaknesses – is pertinent here. Where mainstream accounts tended to view the 'good war' in isolation, focusing on the contingencies of perceived external security threats and moral challenges, revisionist readings emphasised its character as a chapter in a longer story premised on the continuous operation of internal expansionist drives. Narratives that were able to acknowledge simultaneously both the specificity and altruistic dimensions of the triumph over fascism, and its location within enduring processes of war making and imperialism (governed by less elevated motives), would have considerable explanatory power.

Granted, this prescription conflicts somewhat with calls for the war to be seen on its own terms – not, for example, 'submerged beneath the Cold War iceberg' – and with the disciplinary drivers that impel scholars to undertake detailed, narrowly conceived, specialised studies.[167] Yet the literature generated in response to the contemporary travails of American foreign policy already provides stimulating critical examplars, as it variously locates the Second World War as the opening act of the 'Long War' of the national security state, as a central episode in the unfolding of a twentieth century 'Faustian foreign policy' or the gradual traducing of precious 'core values' by the dominance of a 'security ethos', or as just another chapter in the secular imperialist expansion of 'the dominion of war', perpetually fighting for hegemony in the name of liberty.[168] If the 'tendency toward political, economic, and strategic dominance is not some aberration from our true nature but was imprinted in the nation's DNA', what are the implications for understanding intervention?[169]

Exceptionalism also demands more explicit interrogation. It is, after all, a claim about national identity that has unique global implications, given the contemporary capabilities of 'the redeemer nation committed to extending the domain of freedom and America's control over it'. ('Exceptionalism *was* the legacy of the Old World for the New, but exceptionalism *is now* the legacy of the United States for us all.')[170] Moreover, it is now commonplace in the literature that this 'capstone idea' of foreign policy ideology has long 'defined the American future in terms of an active quest for national greatness closely coupled to the promotion of liberty', with the more assertive, vindicationist, means to that end achieving decisive predominance in the twentieth century.[171] Consciousness of Americans' 'duty or destiny to lead the world' was certainly crucially influential from Roosevelt's time through to the promulgation of the NSS and beyond.[172] The source material underpinning writing on intervention is so manifestly saturated with exceptionalist justifications and assertions that historical narratives are inevitably freighted with cognate normative concerns. The dangers of unwitting reinscription would be mitigated if international historians explicated their own stance on these claims, and on the relative costs and benefits of the exemplarist and vindicationist policy options that flow from them. Such overt editorialising might jar with dominant sub-disciplinary sensibilities, but making the political valence of representation plain is surely preferable to implicit, surreptitious insinuation.

The critical possibilities here are demonstrated by Walter Hixson's recent work. Hixson argues that a particular conception of national identity – a 'Myth of America', affirming the nation 'as a manly, racially superior, and providentially destined "beacon of liberty", a country which possesses a special right to exert power in the world' – has driven 'a continuous militant foreign policy, including the regular resort to war'. Under the spell of this hegemonic myth, the United States '*chooses* to go to war, seizing opportunities to engage in militarism throughout its history' – indeed, it is 'a warfare state, a nation with a propensity for initiating and institutionalizing warfare'. As the myth 'enables the hegemony of a militant foreign policy', so the fruits of war reaffirmed the myth and a particular hegemonic identity, and 'paved the way for the next wave of pathological violence'. Hixson thus redimensions the problematic of exceptionalism using the tools of culturalism: 'I do not consider the United States uniquely evil, though I do consider its national identity unique and its foreign policy a critically important subject worthy of independent investigation'.

Three aspects of Hixson's critique are particularly germane here. First, his reframing offers a novel reading of intervention in the Second World War as a product of psychic instability and identity crisis: 'as the most economically advanced exemplar of modernity – racially superior, providentially destined, and determined to revivify its masculine strength – the United States went to war in an identity-driven quest to see its way of life prevail in Europe and Asia'. Second, he asserts the complicity of historical scholarship in the ongoing cycle of myth-making and violence, through its contribution to sustaining the 'good war' paradigm: 'the point is not that U.S. entry into World War II was necessarily wrong or mistaken but rather to unpack the hegemonic interpretation in order to broaden inquiry into the coming of the war, the war itself, and its profound consequences'; 'for decades, these narrative frames have empowered the U.S. warfare state at the expense of quests to advance an alternative hegemony of peaceful internationalism'. Third, Hixson has a practical political agenda, inspired by the tragedy of Iraq. 'The Myth of America and the pathologically violent foreign policy it inspires cannot remain unchallenged. The costs are too high, the consequences too great, both at home and abroad, to remain acquiescent'. Greater awareness of the pernicious consequences of this 'self-serving national mythology' might enable responsible citizens and scholars to take action to change it, and thus facilitate domestic reform and a 'genuinely cooperative internationalism' to 'make the world a safer and more humane place in which to live'.[173]

Hixson's reading is, of course, not definitive or uncontestable. Moreover, it remains an open question whether Barack Obama's Democratic administration will decisively transform the substance of American foreign policy and reconfigure the nation's sense of self. Yet Hixson underlines the manifest necessity of seeking to gain some critical distance within historiography from the enormously potent discursive structure of American exceptionalism and the patterns of behaviour that it has generated. It is evident that 'foreign relations were and are fundamental to US identity'.[174] For over six decades, international historians working on this topic – mediating and representing those relations – have been peculiarly implicated in both exceptionalism and the 'good war' myth, contesting and negotiating their nation's being in the world. Active effort is required here to avoid troubling associations and unwitting discursive complicity since 'when historians decline to deconstruct the nation's hegemonic foreign policy, they affirm the dominant narrative'.[175] If it be the case that in American foreign policy 'violent existential paroxysms, rooted in hypernationalist anxiety and discourse, reflect not only a continuous past but an ominous future as well', then the price of attempting to cling to a chimerical innocence within this scholarship may be extraordinarily high.[176] Thus one impassioned American critic has recently warned: 'our war-making', with all its 'sins of repression and barbarity', 'lies in our allegiance to the Myths of World War II'.[177]

Notes

1 N. Graebner (ed.), *Ideas and Diplomacy: Readings in the Intellectual Tradition of American Foreign Policy* (New York, Oxford University Press, 1964), p. 615.
2 F. Freidel, *Franklin D. Roosevelt: A Rendezvous with Destiny* (Boston, MA, Little, Brown, 1990), pp. 384–85.

3 R. Dallek, *Franklin D. Roosevelt and American Foreign Policy, 1932–1945* (New York, Oxford University Press, 1979), p. 282.

4 D. Reynolds, *From Munich to Pearl Harbor: Roosevelt's America and the Origins of the Second World War* (Chicago, Ivan Dee, 2001), pp. 144–49, quote at p. 148.

5 A. Lieven, *America Right or Wrong: An Anatomy of American Nationalism* (London, Harper Perennial, 2005, pb. edn), p. 1.

6 For example, P. Fussell, *Wartime: Understanding and Behavior in the Second World War* (New York, Oxford University Press, 1989); M. Adams, *The Best War Ever: America and World War II* (Baltimore, MD, Johns Hopkins University Press, 1994); K. Rose, *Myth and the Greatest Generation: A Social History of Americans in World War II* (London, Routledge, 2008).

7 See, for example, E. S. Rosenberg, *A Date Which Will Live: Pearl Harbor in American Memory* (Durham, NC, Duke University Press, 2003); M. J. Hogan (ed.), *Hiroshima in History and Memory* (Cambridge, Cambridge University Press, 1996); J. Basinger, *The World War II Combat Film: Anatomy of a Genre* (Middletown, CT, Wesleyan University Press, 2003, 2nd edn); Y. F. Khong, *Analogies at War: Korea, Munich, Dien Bien Phu, and the Vietnam Decisions of 1965* (Princeton, NJ, Princeton University Press, 1992).

8 Witness, for example, the attempt in P. Beidler, *The Good War's Greatest Hits: World War II and American Remembering* (Athens, GA, University of Georgia Press, 1998). A first putative single volume study of the whole long run of American war memory – V. Casaregola, *Theaters of War: America's Perceptions of World War II* (New York, Palgrave, 2009) – appeared as this book went to press. Casaregola makes some insightful observations but also inadequately acknowledges the existing literature, deals with a limited range of memory discourses and bafflingly overlooks numerous key issues. He posits an overall trajectory to American remembering, but the argument is underdeveloped and ultimately unpersuasive, especially in its reading of the more recent period.

9 Less helpful than it might be here is M. A. Stoler, 'The Second World War in US history and memory', *Diplomatic History*, vol. 25, no. 3, 2001, pp. 383–92.

10 D. Reynolds, 'World War II and modern meanings', *Diplomatic History*, vol. 25, no. 3, 2001, p. 470.

11 R. J. B. Bosworth, *Explaining Auschwitz and Hiroshima: History Writing and the Second World War, 1945–1990* (London, Routledge, 1993), p. 193.

12 G. K. Piehler, *Remembering War the American Way* (Washington D.C., Smithsonian Institution Press, 1995), p. 4; Reynolds, 'World War II and modern meanings', pp. 470–71; A. Stephanson, 'War and diplomatic history', *Diplomatic History*, vol. 25, no. 3, 2001, pp. 393–403.

13 S. Terkel, *'The Good War': An Oral History of World War Two* (New York, New Press, 1984), p, 3.

14 A. Schlesinger Jr, 'Searching for a heroic past: the rediscovery of World War II', *AARP Bulletin*, May 1999, http://www.aarp.org/bulletin/may99/wwii.html (accessed 6 June 2001).

15 D. Campbell, *Writing Security: United States Foreign Policy and the Politics of Identity* (Manchester, Manchester University Press, 1992), p. 105.

16 See http://www.ibiblio.org/pha/policy/1941/410704a.html (accessed 8 June 2006).

17 M. Dunne, 'The history and historiography of American diplomacy: principles, traditions and values', *International Affairs*, vol. 74, no. 1, 1998, p. 182.

18 Stephanson, 'War and diplomatic history', pp. 395–96.

19 Reynolds, *From Munich to Pearl Harbor*, quote at p. 31.

20 J. L. Gaddis, *Surprise, Security, and the American Experience* (Cambridge, MA, Harvard University Press, 2004), p. 48.

21 H. Luce, 'The American century', *Life*, 17 February 1941, reprinted in *Diplomatic History*, vol. 23, no. 2, 1999, quote at p. 162.

22 Reynolds, *From Munich to Pearl Harbor*, p. 180.

23 D. Zietsma, '"Sin has no history": religion, national identity, and US intervention, 1937–41', *Diplomatic History*, vol. 31, no. 3, 2007, pp. 531–65, quotes at pp. 534, 543.

24 J. D. Doenecke, *Storm on the Horizon: The Challenge to American Intervention, 1939–1941* (Lanham, MD, Rowman and Littlefield, 2000), quote at p. x.

25 Luce, 'The American century', p. 171.

26 Quoted in Doenecke, *Storm on the Horizon*, p. 328 (emphasis in original).

27 J. D. Doenecke, *Not to the Swift: The Old Isolationists in the Cold War Era* (Lewisburg, PA, Bucknell University Press, 1979), pp. 37–54, 91–95; Rosenberg, *A Date Which Will Live*, pp. 34–38.

28 W. S. Cole, 'American entry into World War II: a historiographical appraisal', *Mississippi Valley Historical Review*, vol. 43, no. 4, 1957, pp. 600–603.

29 Beidler, *The Good War's Greatest Hits*, quote at p. 3; S. A. Brewer, *Why America Fights: Patriotism and War Propaganda from the Philippines to Iraq* (Oxford, Oxford University Press, 2009), pp. 87–140.

30 J. Bodnar, '*Saving Private Ryan* and postwar memory in America', *American Historical Review*, vol. 106, no. 3, 2001, pp. 805–17; A. J. Huebner, *The Warrior Image: Soldiers in American Culture from the Second World War to the Vietnam Era* (Chapel Hill, NC, University of North Carolina Press, 2008). Casaregola, *Theaters of War*, stresses the existence from the beginning of an anti-war strand of representation in counterpoint to the mainstream 'good war' myth (pp. 159–84).

31 Reynolds, *From Munich to Pearl Harbor*, pp. 183–89, quote at p. 5.

32 M. J. Hogan, *A Cross of Iron: Harry S. Truman and the Origins of the National Security State, 1945–1954* (Cambridge, Cambridge University Press, 1998), quotes at pp. x, 19, 1.

33 Cole, 'American entry into World War II', pp. 595–617, quotes at pp. 600–601.

34 I. Tyrrell, *Historians in Public: The Practice of American History, 1890–1970* (Chicago, University of Chicago Press, 2005), pp. 185–207, quotes at p. 197; P. Novick, *That Noble Dream: The 'Objectivity Question' and the American Historical Profession* (Cambridge, Cambridge University Press, 1988), pp. 281–319. Beard had been a leading proponent of a brand of relativism, an epistemological position which Cold War objectivist critics aligned with totalitarianism, just as they claimed his pre-war anti-interventionist stance had encouraged appeasement.

35 Cole, 'American entry into World War II', pp. 603–10, quotes at pp. 603, 606–7; J. A. Combs, *American Diplomatic History: Two Centuries of Changing Interpretations* (Berkeley, CA, University of California Press, 1983), pp. 199–219.

36 Rosenberg, *A Date Which Will Live*, especially pp. 11–52, quotes at pp. 33, 51.

37 G. K. Haines, 'Roads to war: United States foreign policy, 1931–41', in G. K. Haines and J. S. Walker (eds), *American Foreign Relations: A Historiographical Review* (London, Pinter, 1981), p. 160.

38 F. Anderson and A. Cayton, *The Dominion of War: Empire and Liberty in North America, 1500–2000* (New York, Viking, 2005), pp. 375–84, quotes at pp. 378, 383.

39 Cole, 'American entry into World War II', p. 610.

40 Doenecke, *Not to the Swift*, pp. 106–7; Rosenberg, *A Date Which Will Live*, pp. 44–52, 126–39, 155–73.

41 C. C. Tansill, *Back Door to War: The Roosevelt Foreign Policy, 1933–1941* (Chicago, Regnery, 1952), p. 574.

42 H. E. Barnes, 'Summary and conclusions', in H. E. Barnes (ed.), *Perpetual War for Perpetual Peace: A Critical Examination of the Foreign Policy of Franklin Delano Roosevelt and its Aftermath* (New York, Greenwood, 1969, reprint edn), p. 654. This collection was first published in 1953.

43 F. R. Sanborn, 'Roosevelt is frustrated in Europe', in Barnes (ed.), *Perpetual War for Perpetual Peace*, p. 193.

44 Tansill, *Back Door to War*, p. 615.

45 H. W. Brands, *What America Owes the World: The Struggle for the Soul of Foreign Policy* (Cambridge, Cambridge University Press, 1998), pp. 109–43; C. Craig, 'The not-so-strange career of Charles Beard', *Diplomatic History*, vol. 25, no. 2, 2001, pp. 251–74.

46 C. A. Beard, *President Roosevelt and the Coming of the War, 1941: A Study in Appearances and Realities* (New Haven, CT, Yale University Press, 1948), quotes at pp. 576–78, 590–91, 593–96.

47 H. Feis, *The Road to Pearl Harbor: The Coming of the War Between the United States and Japan* (Princeton, NJ, Princeton University Press, 1950), p. 73.

48 R. E. Sherwood, *Roosevelt and Hopkins: An Intimate History* (New York, Harper, 1948), p. 127; S. E. Morison, *The Rising Sun in the Pacific, 1931 – April 1942* (Boston, MA, Little, Brown, 1948), p. 16.

49 J. D. Doenecke, 'Beyond polemics: an historiographical re-appraisal of American entry into World War II', *History Teacher*, vol. 12, no. 2, 1979, p. 219.

50 W. L. Langer and S. E. Gleason, *The Challenge to Isolation, 1937–1940* (London, RIIA, 1952), p. 13.

51 Sherwood, *Roosevelt and Hopkins*, p. 132; W. L. Langer and S. E. Gleason, *The Undeclared War, 1940–1941* (London, RIIA, 1953), p. 269.

52 Morison, *The Rising Sun in the Pacific, 1931 – April 1942*, p. 41.

53 Novick, *That Noble Dream*, p. 305.

54 Langer and Gleason, *The Undeclared War, 1940–1941*, pp. xvi, 941.

55 A. Stephanson, *Manifest Destiny: American Expansionism and the Empire of Right* (New York, Hill and Wang, 1995), pp. xii, 121 (emphasis in original). This dichotomous opposition also structures Brands, *What America Owes the World*; cf. the identification of four foreign policy traditions in W. R. Mead, *Special Providence: American Foreign Policy and How It Changed the World* (New York, Routledge, 2002, pb. edn).

56 R. J. McMahon, 'Contested memory: the Vietnam War and American society, 1975–2001', *Diplomatic History*, vol. 26, no. 2, 2002, quote at p. 160.

57 Novick, *That Noble Dream*, p. 416.

58 See, for example, R. W. Tucker, *Nation or Empire? The Debate over American Foreign Policy* (Baltimore, MD, Johns Hopkins University Press, 1968). In his foreword, Robert Osgood notes how Americans 'have continually examined, interpreted, questioned, and expounded the distinctive nature of their polity and its role in the world' (p. v), but the debate was nonetheless dramatically intensified by Vietnam. That said, Brands argued in 1998 that the literature 'on the history of the debate over the appropriate American role in world affairs' remained scant (*What America Owes the World*, p. 321).

59 Khong, *Analogies at War*, p. 6. Nonetheless, the analogy has endured: see, for example, K. M. Jensen and D. Wurmser (eds), *The Meaning of Munich Fifty Years Later* (Washington D.C., United States Institute of Peace, 1990).

60 J. Heller, *Catch-22, A Novel* (New York, Simon and Schuster, 1961); K. Vonnegut, *Slaughterhouse-Five; or, The Children's Crusade, a Duty-Dance with Death* (New York, Delacorte, 1969). Fussell, *Wartime*, stresses how such novels proposed an 'attractive alternative' – in his terms – to the myth (p. 180). See also R. D. Schulzinger, *A Time for Peace: The Legacy of the Vietnam War* (Oxford, Oxford University Press, 2006), p. xvii.

61 Rosenberg, *A Date Which Will Live*, p. 115. Casaregola, *Theaters of War*, favours a variant of this 'eclipse' interpretation.

62 M. Torgovnick, *The War Complex: World War II in Our Time* (Chicago, University of Chicago Press, 2005), pp. 95–96; Beidler, *The Good War's Greatest Hits*, pp. 150–71; Huebner, *The Warrior Image*, p. 243.

63 Beidler, *The Good War's Greatest Hits*, quotes at pp. 151, 3.

64 M. B. Young, 'Dangerous history: Vietnam and the "Good War"', in E. T. Linenthal and T. Engelhardt (eds), *History Wars: The Enola Gay and Other Battles for the American Past* (New York, Holt, 1996), p. 203.

65 A. S. Owen, 'Memory, war and American identity: *Saving Private Ryan* as cinematic jeremiad', *Critical Studies in Mass Communication*, vol. 19, no. 3, 2002, pp. 249–82; McMahon, 'Contested memory', pp. 159–84.

66 Novick, *That Noble Dream*, pp. 415–629 traces these developments and their subsequent evolution through to the later 1980s.

67 A. Molho and G. S. Wood, 'Introduction', in A. Molho and G. S. Wood (eds), *Imagined Histories: American Historians Interpret the Past* (Princeton, NJ, Princeton University Press, 1998), pp. 3–20, quotes at pp. 11, 17.

68 Novick, *That Noble Dream*, pp. 415–68, quotes at pp. 417–18.

69 Quote from Doenecke, 'Beyond polemics', p. 232.

70 A. A. Offner, *American Appeasement: United States Foreign Policy and Germany, 1933–1938* (Cambridge, MA, Harvard University Press, 1969), pp. 283–92. On the published documents, see R. W. Leopold, 'The *Foreign Relations* series: a centennial estimate', *Mississippi Valley Historical Review*, vol. 49, no. 4, 1963, pp. 595–612 and the details on the State Department website at http://www.state.gov/r/pa/ho/frus/c4035.htm (accessed 19 December 2007).

71 J. D. Doenecke, 'The United States and the European war, 1939–41: a historiographical review', in M. J. Hogan (ed.), *Paths to Power: The Historiography of American Foreign Relations to 1941* (Cambridge, Cambridge University Press, 2000), p. 227.

72 'Introduction', in D. Borg and S. Okamoto (eds), *Pearl Harbor as History: Japanese–American Relations, 1931–1941* (New York, Columbia University Press, 1973), p. xii. The necessity of war with Japan was always somewhat more contested: Doenecke, 'Beyond polemics', pp. 220–27.

73 R. A. Divine, *Roosevelt and World War II* (Baltimore, MD, Johns Hopkins University Press, 1969), quote at p. 23.

74 R. A. Divine, *The Reluctant Belligerent: American Entry into World War II* (New York, John Wiley, 1979, 2nd edn), quotes at p. x. The first edition was published in 1965.

75 Offner, *American Appeasement*, quote at p. 277.

76 Doenecke, 'Beyond polemics', p. 230.

77 Doenecke, 'United States and the European war, 1939–41', p. 227.

78 Haines, 'Roads to war', pp. 163–64.

79 Divine, *The Reluctant Belligerent*, p. ix.

80 Combs, *American Diplomatic History*, p. 383.

81 B. M. Russett, *No Clear and Present Danger: A Skeptical View of the United States Entry into World War II* (New York, Harper, 1972), quote at p. 12.

82 Quote from Combs, *American Diplomatic History*, p. 381.

83 Divine, *The Reluctant Belligerent*, pp. ix, 53.

84 Divine, *Roosevelt and World War II*, p. 8.

85 Tucker, *Nation or Empire?* p. 44.

86 This discussion marginalises the contribution of an influential 'realist' school, as pithily embodied in G. Kennan, *American Diplomacy, 1900–1950* (Chicago, University of Chicago Press, 1951). Critiquing generations of American foreign policy makers for naïveté and excessive moralism, the 'realists' charged that prior to World War II Roosevelt failed to grasp the essential power realities of international politics and to act expeditiously to forestall the Axis threat. That said, they approved of intervention as necessitated both by balance of power considerations and defensive self-interest (Haines, 'Roads to war', pp. 160–61); in this respect, they too endorsed the 'good war' myth. Moreover, although their frame of reference deprecated ideological crusading, or utopian missionary aspirations to regenerate the world, they did advocate activist intervention in support of the global balance of power. While in one sense the 'realists' thus side-stepped the exceptionalism problematic, it was also true that in general they 'were devoted to the American system' (Combs, *American Diplomatic History*, quote at p. 240, and more generally pp. 197–204, 216–42).

87 Demarcating 'leftist' approaches as non-'mainstream' has been critiqued as a politicised gesture of exclusion, but this is not my intent: see B. Cumings, '"Revising postrevisionism," or, the poverty of theory in diplomatic history', in M. J. Hogan (ed.), *America in the World: The Historiography of American Foreign Relations since 1941* (Cambridge, Cambridge University Press, 1995), pp. 32–33.

88 Novick, *That Noble Dream*, quotes at pp. 440, 445.

89 For overviews, see Combs, *American Diplomatic History*, especially pp. 252–57, 278–81, 313–16, 322–46; S. Hurst, *Cold War US Foreign Policy: Key Perspectives* (Edinburgh, Edinburgh University Press, 2005), pp. 29–60; J. M. Siracusa, *New Left Diplomatic*

Histories and Historians: The American Revisionists (Port Washington, NY, Kennikat, 1973); R. W. Tucker, *The Radical Left and American Foreign Policy* (Baltimore, MD, Johns Hopkins University Press, 1971).

90 Novick, *That Noble Dream*, p. 445. See also A. J. Bacevich, *American Empire: The Realities and Consequences of US Diplomacy* (Cambridge, MA, Harvard University Press, 2002), pp. 7–31.

91 S. F. Bemis, 'American foreign policy and the blessings of liberty', *American Historical Review*, vol. 67, no. 2, 1962, pp. 291–305.

92 Novick, *That Noble Dream*, pp. 447, 445 (emphasis in original).

93 For a critique, see R. Maddox, *The New Left and the Origins of the Cold War* (Princeton, NJ, Princeton University Press, 1973).

94 W. A. Williams, *The Tragedy of American Diplomacy* (New York, Norton, 2009, rev. edn), pp. 162–201. Williams expanded and hardened his argument through successive editions; this fiftieth anniversary edition reproduces the 1972 text.

95 Williams, *The Tragedy of American Diplomacy*, quotes at pp. 161, 201, 206.

96 L. C. Gardner, *Economic Aspects of New Deal Diplomacy* (Madison, WI, University of Wisconsin Press, 1964), quotes at pp. 3, 154, 98. This discussion also draws on Siracusa, *New Left Diplomatic Histories and Historians*, pp. 72–75.

97 L. C. Gardner, 'New Deal diplomacy: a view from the Seventies', in L. P. Liggio and J. J. Martin (eds), *Watershed of Empire: Essays on New Deal Foreign Policy* (Colorado Springs, CO, Ralph Myles, 1976), p. 101.

98 R. F. Smith, 'American foreign relations, 1920–42', in B. J. Bernstein (ed.), *Towards a New Past: Dissenting Essays in American History* (New York, Pantheon, 1968), p. 247.

99 W. A. Williams, *Empire as a Way of Life: An Essay on the Causes and Character of America's Present Predicament Along with a Few Thoughts about an Alternative* (New York, Oxford University Press, 1980), quotes at pp. 65, 164.

100 Beard, of course, was also concerned in his broader *oeuvre* with large scale interpretations of American history, and the economic underpinnings of foreign policy and expansionism: see Craig, 'The not-so-strange career of Charles Beard'.

101 Tucker, *The Radical Left and American Foreign Policy*, pp. 86–87.

102 Smith, 'American foreign relations, 1920–42', p. 251, and more broadly pp. 250–54. Note also the admission, referring to the rebuffing of Anglo–American pre-war attempts to offer 'the Germans an improved position in the existing world order', that 'perhaps the Germans would not have accepted these offers at any time' (p. 251); this conflicts with his earlier expressed scepticism about claims that the war was 'inevitable, realistic, and right' (p. 235).

103 Combs, *American Diplomatic History*, p. 382.

104 Brands, *What America Owes the World*, p. 246; cf. J. D. Doenecke, 'William Appleman Williams and the anti-interventionalist tradition', *Diplomatic History*, vol. 25, no. 2, 2001, pp. 283–91.

105 The parallel revisionist debate on the atomic bombing of Hiroshima more directly challenged the myth: see J. S. Walker, 'The decision to use the Bomb: a historiographical update', in Hogan (ed.), *America in the World*, pp. 206–33.

106 Smith, 'American foreign relations, 1920–42", pp. 235–37.

107 Brands, *What America Owes the World*, pp. 253–54.

108 Tucker, *The Radical Left and American Foreign Policy*, quotes at pp. 15, 10.

109 G. Lundestad, 'Moralism, presentism, exceptionalism, provincialism, and other extravagances in American writings on the early Cold War years', *Diplomatic History*, vol. 13, no. 4, 1989, pp. 527–45, especially pp. 533–39. On nationalist and exceptionalist tendencies within historical writing on American foreign policy, see also F. Costigliola and T. G. Paterson, 'Defining and doing the history of United States foreign relations: a primer', in M. J. Hogan and T. G. Paterson (eds), *Explaining the History of American Foreign Relations* (Cambridge, Cambridge University Press, 2004, 2nd edn), pp. 10–34; and Brands, *What America Owes the World*. The historiographical manifestations of exceptionalism deserve more systematic attention.

110 P. M. Buhle and E. Rice-Maximin, *William Appleman Williams: The Tragedy of Empire* (New York, Routledge, 1995), p. 99.

111 Williams, *The Tragedy of American Diplomacy*, quotes at pp. 20, 291, 309–11.

112 Bacevich, *American Empire*, p. 24.

113 Brands, *What America Owes the World*, quotes at pp. 242, 249.

114 A. McPherson, 'Americanism against America empire', in M. Kazin and J. A. McCartin (eds), *Americanism: New Perspectives on the History of an Ideal* (Chapel Hill, NC, University of North Carolina Press, 2006), p. 170.

115 Stephanson, *Manifest Destiny*, p. 126.

116 J. Bodnar, *Remaking America: Public Memory, Commemoration, and Patriotism in the Twentieth Century* (Princeton, NJ, Princeton University Press, 1992), p. 227.

117 B. Cauthen, 'Covenant and continuity: ethno-symbolism and the myth of divine election', *Nations and Nationalism*, vol. 10, nos. 1/2, 2004, p. 28.

118 Stephanson, *Manifest Destiny*, pp. 129–30.

119 McMahon, 'Contested memory', pp. 164–71.

120 Quote from F. FitzGerald, 'American foreign policy and the rhetoric of history and morality', in L. Kramer, D. Reid and W. L. Barney (eds), *Learning History in America: Schools, Cultures, and Politics* (Minneapolis, MN, University of Minnesota Press, 1994), p. 189. On foreign policy, see J. Dumbrell, 'America in the 1990s: searching for purpose', in M. Cox and D. Stokes (eds), *US Foreign Policy* (Oxford, Oxford University Press, 2008), pp. 88–104.

121 Earlier roots are fruitfully explored in Bacevich, *American Empire*, and T. Smith, *A Pact with the Devil: Washington's Bid for World Supremacy and the Betrayal of the American Promise* (New York, Routledge, 2007).

122 Quoted in Gaddis, *Surprise, Security, and the American Experience*, p. 83.

123 W. L. Hixson, 'The war in Iraq and American freedom', *The Arab World Geographer*, vol. 6, no. 1, 2003, http://users.fmg.uva.nl/vmamadouh/awg/ (accessed 14 February 2008).

124 Quote from Lieven, *America Right or Wrong*, p. 73.

125 G. Hodgson, *The Myth of American Exceptionalism* (New Haven, CT, Yale University Press, 2009), quotes at pp. 188, xiii.

126 D. Brinkley, *The Boys of Pointe du Hoc: Ronald Reagan, D-Day, and the U.S. Army 2nd Ranger Battalion* (New York, Harper, 2006, pb. edn), p. 9.

127 Rosenberg, *A Date Which Will Live*, p. 99.

128 Paradigmatically, T. Brokaw, *The Greatest Generation* (New York, Random House, 1998).

129 P. Ehrenhaus, 'Why we fought: Holocaust memory in Spielberg's *Saving Private Ryan*', *Critical Studies in Media Communication*, vol. 18, no. 3, 2001, pp. 321–37.

130 N. Mills, *Their Last Battle: The Fight for the National World War II Memorial* (New York, Basic, 2004), pp. 217–18; E. Doss, 'War, memory, and the public mediation of affect: the National World War II Memorial and American imperialism', *Memory Studies*, vol. 1, no. 2, 2008, pp. 227–50. Casaregola, *Theaters of War*, properly stresses that this resurgent 'good war' myth did not go uncontested (pp. 213–38).

131 Rosenberg, *A Date Which Will Live*, pp. 113–25, quote at p. 113; D. H. Noon, 'Operation enduring analogy: World War II, the war on terror, and the uses of historical memory', *Rhetoric and Public Affairs*, vol. 7, no. 3, 2004, pp. 348–52.

132 B. A. Biesecker, 'Remembering World War II: the rhetoric and politics of national commemoration at the turn of the 21st century', *Quarterly Journal of Speech*, vol. 88, no. 4, 2002, pp. 393–409, quotes at pp. 406, 394, (emphasis in original).

133 M. Rogin, *Independence Day, or How I Learned to Stop Worrying and Love the Enola Gay* (London, BFI, 1998), quotes at p. 15.

134 Noon, 'Operation enduring analogy', pp. 339–66, quotes at pp. 345–46.

135 See, for example, T. Bender (ed.), *Rethinking American History in a Global Age* (Berkeley, CA, University of California Press, 2002).

136 J. Appleby, L. Hunt and M. Jacob, *Telling the Truth about History* (New York, Norton, 1994), pp. 198–99. See also G. B. Nash, C. Crabtree and R. E. Dunn, *History on Trial: Culture Wars and the Teaching of the Past* (New York, Knopf, 1997).

137 R. J. McMahon, 'Toward a pluralist vision: the study of American foreign relations as international history and national history', in Hogan and Paterson (eds), *Explaining the History of American Foreign Relations*, pp. 35–50.

138 Hurst, *Cold War US Foreign Policy*, pp. 61–139; R. Buzzanco, 'What happened to the New Left? Toward a radical reading of American foreign relations', *Diplomatic History*, vol. 23, no. 4, 1999, pp. 575–607.

139 For a recent survey of culturalism see T. W. Zeiler, 'The diplomatic history bandwagon: a state of the field', *Journal of American History*, vol. 95, no. 4, 2009, pp. 1053–73. For recent orientations in the now vast, and theoretically and politically disparate, literatures on these topics, see D. Deudney and J. Meiser, 'American exceptionalism', and C. Rowley and J. Weldes, 'Identities and US foreign policy', in Cox and Stokes (eds), *US Foreign Policy*, pp. 24–42 and 183–209 respectively, and P. K. MacDonald, 'Those who forget historiography are doomed to republish it: empire, imperialism and contemporary debates about American power', *Review of International Studies*, vol. 35, no. 1, 2009, pp. 45–67. Note also the seminal culturalist contribution of M. H. Hunt, *Ideology and U.S. Foreign Policy* (New Haven, CT, Yale University Press, 1987).

140 Doenecke, 'United States and the European war, 1939–41', p. 264.

141 B. J. C. McKercher, 'Reaching for the brass ring: the recent historiography of interwar American foreign relations', in Hogan (ed.), *Paths to Power*, pp. 176–223, quotes at pp. 216, 210.

142 The following draws particularly on the discussion in Doenecke, 'United States and the European war, 1939–41', pp. 229–38.

143 For example, D. G. Haglund, *Latin America and the Transformation of US Strategic Thought, 1936–1940* (Albuquerque, NM, University of New Mexico Press, 1984).

144 Dallek, *Franklin D. Roosevelt and American Foreign Policy, 1932–1945*, quotes at pp. 530–31, 289.

145 W. Heinrichs, *Threshold of War: Franklin D. Roosevelt and American Entry into World War II* (New York, Oxford University Press, 1988), quotes at pp. vii, 179, 145.

146 D. F. Schmitz, *The Triumph of Internationalism: Franklin D. Roosevelt and a World in Crisis, 1933–1941* (Washington D. C., Potomac, 2007), quote at p. xxii.

147 W. F. Kimball, *The Juggler: Franklin Roosevelt as Wartime Statesman* (Princeton, NJ, Princeton University Press, 1991), quote at p. 8.

148 M. M. Lowenthal, 'Roosevelt and the coming of the war: the search for United States policy, 1937–42', *Journal of Contemporary History*, vol. 16, no. 3, pp. 413–40, quotes at pp. 413–14, 434.

149 J. G. Clifford, 'Both ends of the telescope: new perspectives on FDR and American entry into World War II', *Diplomatic History*, vol. 13, no. 2, 1989, p. 229.

150 F. W. Marks III, *Wind over Sand: The Diplomacy of Franklin Roosevelt* (Athens, GA, University of Georgia Press, 1988), quotes at pp. x–xi, 149, xii, 167, 281.

151 Kimball, *The Juggler*, p. 7; S. Casey, 'Franklin D. Roosevelt', in S. Casey and J. Wright (eds), *Mental Maps in the Era of Two World Wars* (London, Palgrave, 2008), p. 217.

152 Witness the 'debate' between a measured critic and guarded defender in J. D. Doenecke and M. A. Stoler, *Debating Franklin D. Roosevelt's Foreign Policies, 1933–1945* (Lanham, MD, Rowman and Littlefield, 2005).

153 Reynolds, *From Munich to Pearl Harbor*, pp. 7, 9.

154 P. J. Hearden, *Roosevelt Confronts Hitler: America's Entry into World War II* (DeKalb, IL, Northern Illinois University Press, 1987), quotes at p. x. Hearden focuses overridingly on the alleged American quest to construct a liberal capitalist world system and hegemonic *Pax Americana*, devoting relatively scant discussion to the military threat posed by Nazi Germany; he does tend to discount this, which implies that the war might have been unnecessary, but this is the least developed and convincing aspect of his case.

155 Quote from Marks, *Wind over Sand*, p. 166.

156 Schmitz, *The Triumph of Internationalism*, quotes at pp. 93, xix.

157 Kimball, *The Juggler*, p. 13.

158 Stephanson, 'War and diplomatic history', p. 396.
159 W. L. Hixson, *The Myth of American Diplomacy: National Identity and U.S. Foreign Policy* (New Haven, CT, Yale University Press, 2008), p. 190. See also D. B. MacDonald, 'Bush's America and the new exceptionalism: anti-Americanism, the Holocaust and the transatlantic rift', *Third World Quarterly*, vol. 29, no. 6, 2008, pp. 1101–18.
160 M. B. Young, 'The age of global power', in Bender (ed.), *Rethinking American History in a Global Age*, p. 284. Cf. Hodgson, *The Myth of American Exceptionalism*, pp. 118–22.
161 Dallek, *Franklin D. Roosevelt and American Foreign Policy, 1932–1945*, quotes at pp. 58, 538.
162 Kimball, *The Juggler*, pp. 185–200, quotes at pp. 186, 198, 187.
163 Heinrichs, *Threshold of War*, quotes at pp. 4–6, 8, 3.
164 J. L. Harper, *American Visions of Europe: Franklin D. Roosevelt, George F. Kennan, and Dean G. Acheson* (Cambridge, Cambridge University Press, 1996, pb. edn), quotes at pp. 64, 60, 76, 131. The issue of whether Roosevelt's death pushed American foreign policy in a new direction remains contested. Some scholars stress that Roosevelt hoped for a cooperative post-war international system, under the joint tutelage of his 'Four Policemen', and that his passing contributed decisively to the descent into Cold War conflict. In such cases, the claim that approval of Roosevelt's interventionism in effect entails complicity in Cold War exceptionalism is slightly problematised; but it can still be argued that 'globalism' brought 'conceptual continuity' across the Roosevelt–Truman divide (W. O. Walker III, *National Security and Core Values in American History* (Cambridge, Cambridge University Press, 2009), p. 123).
165 S. Philpott and D. Mutimer, 'The United States of Amnesia: US foreign policy and the recurrence of innocence', *Cambridge Review of International Affairs*, vol. 22, no. 2, 2009, pp. 301–17, quotes at pp. 315–16.
166 M. Sturken, *Tourists of History: Memory, Kitsch, and Consumerism from Oklahoma City to Ground Zero* (Durham, NC, Duke University Press, 2007), quotes at pp. 15, 18.
167 Quote from W. F. Kimball, 'The incredible shrinking war: the Second World War, not (just) the origins of the Cold War', *Diplomatic History*, vol. 25, no. 3, 2001, p. 365.
168 See, respectively, A. J. Bacevich (ed.), *The Long War: A New History of U.S. National Security Policy since World War II* (New York, Columbia University Press, 2007); J. Hoff, *A Faustian Foreign Policy from Woodrow Wilson to George W. Bush: Dreams of Perfectibility* (Cambridge, Cambridge University Press, 2008); Walker, *National Security and Core Values in American History*; Anderson and Cayton, *The Dominion of War*. Anderson and Cayton note *à propos* World War II: 'in no other war has the American mission to extend the empire of liberty been less controversial; in no other has the American rhetoric of liberation seemed more perfectly suited to circumstances'; yet they insist that both America's 'imperialist military adventures' and its 'wars of liberation' need to be seen 'as enmeshed in a larger contingent narrative of a continent's development through half a millennium' (pp. 392, 421).
169 R. Kagan, 'Dangerous nation', *International Politics*, vol. 45, no. 4, 2008, pp. 403–12, quote at p. 407. Kagan differs from the authors listed in the previous footnote in essentially approving of the thrust of American foreign policy, though he too advocates reflexive discussion of its underpinnings.
170 Quotes from D. L. Madsen, *American Exceptionalism* (Edinburgh, Edinburgh University Press, 1998), pp. 165–66 (emphasis in original).
171 Hunt, *Ideology and U.S. Foreign Policy*, p. 17. Hunt does take an overt position on the deleterious influence of American nationalism both domestically and internationally in an extensive conclusion (pp. 171–98).
172 A. A. Offner, 'Liberation or dominance? The ideology of U.S. national security policy', in Bacevich (ed.), *The Long War*, pp. 1–52, quote at p. 4.
173 Hixson, *The Myth of American Diplomacy*, quotes at pp. 1–2, 14 (emphasis in original), 10, 14, 16, 161–62, 306–8. Even sophisticated critical work like Hixson's sometimes flirts with exceptionalist fallacies by focusing on the 'matrixes, causes, and motives' of US actions in the world, paying 'little or no attention to the role and traits of that larger

world': M. Del Pero, 'On the limits of Thomas Zeiler's historiographical triumphalism', *Journal of American History*, vol. 95, no. 4, 2009, p.1080.

174 D. Ryan, *US Foreign Policy in World History* (London, Routledge, 2000), p. 10.

175 W. L. Hixson, 'Response from Walter Hixson', *Passport: The Newsletter of the Society for Historians of American Foreign Relations*, vol. 39, no. 3, 2009, p. 16.

176 W. L. Hixson, 'Leffler takes a linguistic turn', *Diplomatic History*, vol. 29, no. 3, 2005, p. 421.

177 E. W. Wood, *Worshipping the Myths of World War II: Reflections on America's Dedication to War* (Washington D.C., Potomac, 2006), quotes at pp. 158, 172.

7 On tragedy

The dark valley of Imperial Japan

The United States demanded complete and unconditional withdrawal of troops from China, withdrawal of our recognition of the Nanking Government, and the reduction of the Tripartite Pact to a dead letter. This not only belittled the dignity of our Empire and made it impossible for us to harvest the fruits of the China Incident, but also threatened the very existence of our Empire ... Under the circumstances, our Empire has no alternative but to begin war with the United States, Great Britain, and the Netherlands in order to resolve the present crisis and assure survival ... At the moment, our Empire stands at the threshold of glory or oblivion.

Tojo Hideki, Prime Minister of Japan, address to
Imperial Conference, 1 December 1941[1]

On the morning of 27 September 1945 Emperor Hirohito, attired in formal morning dress, visited the American embassy in Tokyo for his first meeting with General Douglas MacArthur, the Supreme Commander for the Allied Powers in occupation of Japan. MacArthur, dressed casually in an open-necked uniform without tie or medals, received him in an audience that lasted almost 40 minutes. No official record of the conversation was kept, but a hugely symbolic photograph was published to sensational effect soon after in the Japanese press. It depicted the two men standing together staring straight into the camera, the bespectacled Hirohito in a stiff pose with his hands by his sides whilst MacArthur loomed over him, with hands placed on his hips behind his back, eminently assured and imposing. For the Japanese public this image drove home the reality of their nation's plight, at the mercy of a United States that had recently mounted an awesome display of its economic, technological and military superiority in dropping atomic bombs on Hiroshima and Nagasaki. 'The emperor they saw there was not a living god but a mortal human beside a much older human to whom he now was subservient. Hirohito perfectly exemplified the defeated nation; MacArthur stood completely relaxed and projected the confidence that comes from victory'.[2]

With three million war dead, nine million homeless and one third of its national wealth destroyed, Japan was certainly in a parlous state at the close of hostilities. Moreover, hardships such as food shortages, mass unemployment, black marketeering and rampant inflation persisted through much of the occupation. In the longer run, however, exhaustion and despair dissipated as Japan rose almost miraculously from these depths to become a signal success story of the post-war era.[3] The Allies initiated an extensive programme of democratisation, reform and reconstruction which provided the basis for an extended post-war economic boom that transformed the country into a prosperous industrial and technological powerhouse. Moreover, Japan's international reputation was also rehabilitated as it simultaneously emerged as the United States' key Asian ally in the global Cold War. This enduring partnership with a former enemy was central to Japan's stunning post-war revival, an irony that could scarcely have been anticipated as Japanese policy-makers plunged along the road to Pearl Harbor. Indeed, in retrospect the more subtle and significant message of the famous MacArthur–Hirohito snapshot was that the Americans were 'hospitable to the emperor, and would stand by him' – and, by implication, his people.

The process of post-war reconstruction necessarily entailed some form of negotiation with the wartime past. Like other defeated peoples, the Japanese were somewhat preoccupied with their own distress. The traumatic nature of defeat, the fact that Japan alone experienced atomic bombardment and the palpable misery of the post-war years ensured that 'a pervasive victim consciousness took root, leading many Japanese to perceive themselves as the greatest sufferers from the recent war'.[4] Such sentiments inevitably marginalised consciousness of the things which the Japanese had inflicted on others: the launching of aggressive wars in China, South East Asia and the Pacific in which some 20 million people were killed, the commission of atrocities like the 1937 Nanking massacre, and systematic barbarities such as the brutal exploitation of slave labour, the biological and chemical warfare experiments carried out on human subjects by Unit 731 of the Imperial Japanese Army, and the enforced military prostitution of the so-called 'comfort women'. The apparent persistence of sentiments of self-pity together with a concomitant sanitisation or relativisation of Japanese war crimes and responsibilities has burdened Japan with a reputation as the most relentlessly amnesiac of the former Axis powers. In 2005, for example, foreign journalistic commentary on Prime Minister Koizumi Junichiro's refusal to desist from visiting the Yasukuni shrine where major war criminals are enshrined along with other war dead, and his government's approval of school history textbooks downplaying Japanese aggression, reiterated the view of a nation still singularly unwilling to accept responsibility for its wartime actions.[5] Similar interpretations suffuse much of the memory literature, which castigates Japan for its secular inability to muster sufficient contrition and its preference instead for denial, a wilful erasure of an uncomfortable history.[6]

In certain respects, 'there are solid grounds for such criticism'.[7] Japan's conservative political elite have long evinced at best a very ambiguous attitude towards the darker aspects of the wartime past, as illustrated by the muted and equivocal terminology in which various 'apologies' have been delivered.[8] Moreover, since the 1990s vociferous neo-nationalist pressure groups – such as the Japanese Society for History Textbook Reform – have indeed acquired a disturbing prominence in public debates over war memory. Yet, while scholarly judgements on the shape and trajectory of Japan's collective memory remain diverse, the most nuanced writing now cogently argues that to focus attention merely on official government narratives or the sensational pronouncements of 'Japan's most bombastic nationalists' is 'to misread the tenor and complexity of popular Japanese recollections of World War II'.[9] On this view, surveying the whole range of memory discourses within Japanese society actually reveals a wide diversity of perspectives, with nationalist apologists constituting merely one extreme on a spectrum that also features searchingly critical progressive elements, with many other voices in between. Far from the popular stereotype of a monolithic disposition towards denial, war memory within Japan has long been a site of acute contestation – even if much of it was not immediately visible to foreign observers – and geopolitical developments since the end of the Cold War together with the global turn to memory and human rights have fostered an even more intense and impassioned engagement with this profoundly problematic heritage: 'the war maintains a powerful grip on the modern Japanese psyche ... The war has not been forgotten. Quite the opposite, the Japanese seem unable to let it go'. Moreover, while a politically influential conservative lobby maintains control over official narratives it actually now represents a minority opinion according to polling data; the hysterical vociferousness of neo-nationalist polemic betrays paranoia that purportedly unpatriotic views of Japan's wartime past are becoming ever more firmly entrenched in public consciousness.[10]

Japanese war memory is then complex and multi-faceted.[11] From the very beginning, the question of war origins has naturally figured within it. MacArthur's meeting with Hirohito testified to the United States' pragmatic decision to retain the emperor on his throne, albeit deprived of his divinity and constitutional power, as a focal point for democratic reconstruction and the concomitant reengineering of Japanese national identity. This necessitated the parallel elaboration of a narrative in which guilt for precipitating the war was located squarely with a 'cabal of conspiratorial militarists' held to have manipulated the emperor, who was thus personally absolved of war responsibility. This strategic move had deleterious long term consequences in obfuscating the extent of pre-war complicity in aggression, but also demonstrates how 'the soft-pedaling of Japan's war responsibility was an American *policy*, and not merely a peculiarly Japanese manifestation of nationalistic forgetfulness'.[12] Subsequently, arguments about the origins and nature of Japan's wars evolved as one thread within a more complex tapestry of war memory. Their progress and politics can be charted by exploring two sets of inter-related questions on which competing positions have been staked out along the spectrum, from the progressive to the stridently nationalist.

The first concerns the nature of Japanese expansion in China and South East Asia. Should this be conceived of as naked imperialist aggression, fired by a conviction of racial superiority over Asian others that also legitimised the commission of criminal atrocities? Or did Japan merely act in much the same way as every other power in the chaotic and brutal circumstances of the 1930s, seeking to protect its legitimate interests on the continent as they were threatened by rising Chinese nationalism, communist subversion and western economic protectionism? Was it even perhaps the case that the war-time ideology of 'Asia for the Asians' underpinning the establishment of the 'Greater East Asia Co-Prosperity Sphere' had real validity, with Japan's leaders engaged in 'a genuinely moral campaign to liberate all Asia from the oppressive Europeans and Americans, and to simultaneously create an impregnable bulwark against the rising tide of Communism'?[13] The second relates rather more to the motives behind Japan's confrontation with the United States in the Pacific. Was this an integral part of a broader campaign of aggression, launched as a desperate gamble to preserve the new empire in Asia, and expressive of a pathological militarism produced by profound structural deformities in Japanese society? Or was it a tragic accident, the result of disastrous misunderstandings between Japanese and American policy-makers that could have been avoided by more skilful diplomacy? Was it even sincerely defensive, a justifiable response to encirclement by the United States and other western powers which were impinging on vital Japanese interests through a campaign of economic strangulation as they sought to preserve existing imperialist structures in Asia?

This presentation of the interpretive options somewhat elides nuance.[14] (There are also further additional variables, such as the fact that commentators of different political stripes have given greater or lesser attention to either the Asian or Pacific components of the war). Yet it provides a workable frame-work to explore how readings of international history – in both strictly historical writing and less formal mnemonic discourses – have participated in contestation over Japanese collective memory and national identity.

'A common plan for the achievement of a common object': conspiracy and beyond

The Allied occupation lasted until April 1952 and had a profound effect on Japan's post-war history. Its ambitious and unprecedented agenda entailed 'remaking the political, social, cultural, and economic fabric of [the] defeated nation, and in the process changing the very way of thinking of its popu-lace'.[15] The constitution enacted in 1947 embodied demilitarisation and democratisation, as it vested sovereignty in the people, guaranteed a wide range of civil and political liberties and – in article nine – renounced the use of force in international affairs. This was complemented by extensive moder-nising reforms to landownership and the legal and educational systems, the disestablishment of Shinto as a state religion and attacks on monopolistic big business. These changes were eagerly embraced by many sectors of Japanese society, and especially the progressive left which revelled in new-found freedoms of expression in the early post-war period. However, the decision to retain the emperor as figure-head of the new democracy testified to the limits of reform, and these became more pronounced when in the context of the nascent Cold War the occupation authorities embarked on the so-called 'reverse course'.

Radical policies were retrenched or abandoned, the purging of militarists and ultranationalists gave way to the purging of communists, rearmament began and conservative political and economic elites reacquired predominant influence. Essentially, the goal of thoroughgoing transformation was subordinated to the imperative of making Japan a regional bulwark against communism. In the 1950s, politics stabilised with the conservative Liberal Democratic Party (LDP) firmly in the ascendant, and foreign relations dominated by the bilateral relationship with the United States which to an extent insulated Japan from engagement with its Asian neighbours.[16] Powerful progressive voices were still part of the fabric of political life. These included the pacifist movement fired by memories of atomic atrocity, the vocal activists of the leftist Japan Teachers Union and the diverse vehement protesters against the 1960 renewal of the US–Japan security treaty. Yet while 'the ideals of peace and democracy' underpinning initial occupation policy had taken firm root, ultimately the post-war political settlement was staunchly conservative in character.[17]

War memory was heavily influenced by American mnemonic imperatives. The initial strategy of the occupation authorities was to compel the Japanese to confront their nation's responsibility for aggression and war crimes head on, whilst also restricting the attribution of serious guilt to a vaguely-specified militarist clique.[18] This narrative originated in wartime propaganda that had sought to sow dissension between people and state, and was disseminated widely through the press and radio in early occupation publicity campaigns.[19] Similarly, approved school history texts stipulated that Japan (together with Germany) must 'accept the greatest responsibility for World War II', yet averred that 'the Japanese people suffered terribly from the long war. Military leaders suppressed the people, launched a stupid war, and caused this disaster'.[20] (Whether the 'disaster' was the war, the defeat or the suffering remained tantalisingly ambiguous.[21]) Such two-fold formulations had a clear pragmatic rationale in grounding democratic reconstruction. Inevitably, however, they also foreclosed broader questions of complicity and fostered Japanese tendencies to regard themselves as victims rather than victimisers. 'In the postwar narrative, the Japanese people, as well as the emperor, were seen as having been hoodwinked by the evil militarists into going to war – a plausible contention, but not unproblematic given the overwhelming public support for the war at its beginning'.[22]

Japanese collective memory was, however, far from monochromatic. Certainly, there was considerable solipsism, as the majority of Japanese defined their personal experiences 'predominantly in terms of bereavement, hunger, air raids and defeat'. Yet as the occupation authorities circulated information about atrocities, many experienced a genuine sense of revulsion, even if the venting of fury against those in the military deemed responsible for crimes could simultaneously serve as a mechanism of self-exculpation. Leftist intellectuals also directly challenged the limitations of the American narrative, calling on the whole nation to engage in deeper self-criticism about war responsibility, for a more thoroughgoing break with the imperial system and for investigation of the deeper structural roots of Japanese imperialism and militarism.[23] Conservative political elites had quite different reservations about the new orthodoxy. While they shared the agenda of protecting the emperor and diverting blame onto the military, they were less comfortable with blunt admissions that Japan had been an aggressor and sought to preserve discursive space for more positive readings of the wartime past.[24]

The changed circumstances of the 1950s were propitious for such inter-pretations. After all, the political and bureaucratic elite that had led the country before and during the war effectively returned to power. This was symbolised when Kishi Nobusuke, who had spent three years awaiting trial as a suspected major war criminal, became prime minister in 1957.[25] In this climate a conservative politician could publicly declare (though admittedly not without sparking controversy) that the 'rightness or wrongness' of the war might be a matter of opinion.[26] While the United States did not endorse revanchism, the exigencies of the Cold War alliance meant it had little incentive to insist on frank reckoning with the past (not least since China, Japan's chief victim, was now in the communist camp). So in this period 'downplaying prewar Japanese militarism, sanitizing Japanese atrocities, [and] minimizing the horror of war in general' came to constitute 'a bilateral agenda'.[27] Moreover, an alternative to the militarist conspiracy narrative had always been available, if subordinate, within American discourse on Japan, one which construed it as an unmodern and almost child-like nation. Thus MacArthur told a 1951 senate hearing that while the 'mature' Germans had breached 'the standards of modern morality' quite deliberately in going to war, the Japanese had 'stumbled into it to some extent', leaving open the possibility of viewing the Pacific War as a tragic accident.[28] The 1950s con-sequently witnessed a 'swing to the right in ... popular representations of the war'. Nostalgic films and war memoirs flourished and school textbooks were revised, with more progressive sentiments being expunged. Critical repre-sentations continued to appear in all genres of film and literature, but apologetic and victim-mentality perspectives were 'gaining the upper hand'.[29]

The chief mechanism through which the Allies initially sought to assign war guilt was the International Military Tribunal for the Far East (IMTFE). In the wake of the war almost six thousand individuals were indicted throughout the region for conventional war crimes and crimes against humanity. The centre piece of the retributive and didactic judicial endeavour was the tribunal held in Tokyo between May 1946 and November 1948 of the so-called Class A war criminals who were also charged with crimes against peace. Twenty-five of the most prominent pre-war Japanese military and civilian leaders were found guilty by a majority verdict, receiving either long prison terms or – in seven cases – death sentences.[30] The central charge was that the accused had from 1928 to 1945 been involved in 'pursuance of a common plan for the achievement of a common object ... that they should secure Japan's domination by preparing and waging wars of aggression'. Specifically, it was alleged that they had conspired:

> that Japan should secure the military, naval, political and economic domination of East Asia and of the Pacific and Indian Oceans, and of all countries and islands bordering therein or bordering thereon, and for that purpose should, alone or in combination with other countries having similar objects, wage a war or wars of aggression against any country or countries which might oppose that purpose.[31]

This charge imposed a dramatic clarity on the complexity of pre-war international politics, marginalising structural factors and the initiative of other actors and assigning interpretive priority to the unprovoked conspiratorial agency of the clique. Moreover, while firmly fixing war guilt in this way, the trial also intentionally exculpated the mass of the nation. Thus the prosecution's opening statement affirmed that the Japanese people 'were utterly within the power and forces of these accused, and to such extent were its victims'.[32]

The Tokyo proceedings are generally adjudged much more flawed than those of Nuremberg.[33] One line of critique stresses the limitations of the trial as a reckoning with the past. In a qualifying opinion, the Australian tribunal president lamented that Hirohito, 'the leader in the crime, though available for trial, had been granted immunity'.[34] Progressives likewise argued that by focusing on the military elite and largely excluding bureaucrats, the military police, industrialists, financiers and ultranationalist agitators from prosecution, the trial obscured the deeper structural origins of aggression and the full extent of culpability.[35] Furthermore, the Tokyo indictment overwhelmingly prioritised crimes against peace over crimes against humanity, which obfuscated the horrors inflicted by the Japanese on their Asian neighbours and retarded widespread self-critical reflection.[36] (This process was merely compounded by the *realpolitik* decision to exclude certain crimes from consideration altogether, most notably the operation of Unit 731, the research findings of which the Americans had appropriated.[37]) This trial was more generally preoccupied with the confrontation between Japan and the United States to the neglect of Japan's wars in Asia. Only three of the eleven judges were Asian, and the trial was 'fundamentally a white man's tribunal'.[38] Although the whole history of Japanese aggression was recounted the climax of the narrative was Pearl Harbor, and the interpretive centrality of the Japanese–American war was reinforced by the overwhelming attention given to Tojo as putative leader of the conspiracy.[39] Under the occupation the Americans had banned the use of the name 'Greater East Asia War' – because it was a 'term associated with Japan's ideological justification of its expansion in Asia to liberate it from Western colonialism' – and insisted instead on 'Pacific

War'.[40] This too marginalised Japanese depredations in Asia and gave succour to a relativising narrative. Incarnating 'a neat moral calculus', this set the attack on Pearl Harbor off against Hiroshima and Nagasaki, climaxing with the supreme instances of Japanese suffering, and turning 'atomic memory into imperial denial'.[41]

A converse line of criticism holds that the trials were a hypocritical exercise in victors' justice. One core claim here is that the notion of a consistent 18 year conspiracy imposes a false coherence on policy that lacked any underpinning blueprint and was often the product of factional struggle or improvisation.[42] Moreover, the defence consistently maintained that Japan's wars had been launched in self-defence – against the threats of Chinese nationalism, communist subversion and western economic protectionism – and did not contravene international law or the norms of statecraft prevalent at the time. The Indian judge Radhabinod Pal, a staunch anti-colonialist, concurred and declared all the defendants not guilty in a scathing dissenting opinion. Pal denied that the conspiracy concept derived from the Nuremberg precedent was applicable to Japan, given the very different contingencies of state structure, ideological motivation and government personnel. He also averred that it was generally 'more plausible to see Japan's leaders engaged in ad hoc responses to what they perceived as threats to their nation's security', a claim at least partly rooted in his own anti-communism and intensified by consciousness of the rising communist menace in post-war Asia, which the United States was vigorously countering in the present. Concerning the road to Pearl Harbor, Pal rejected the notion of a conspiracy, asserting instead that Japan ' "was driven by the circumstances that gradually developed to the fatal steps taken by her" '. He also highlighted Allied double standards, noting an equivalence between Japan's alleged imperialism and the earlier western acquisition of overseas possessions, suggesting that when placed in proper context Japan's actions were far from unique. He further argued with lofty acerbity that a nation which had unleashed the indiscriminate destruction of the atom bomb was in no position to arraign another for crimes against humanity.[43]

It is perhaps not surprising that proceedings susceptible to such diverse readings only rendered 'the many-sided problem of war responsibility … more intractable'.[44] The 'stark narrative of culpability' they offered actually reinscribed the innocence of the mass of the nation, whilst their doubtful legitimacy nourished angry resentment.[45] That said, by the time the verdicts were handed down the moment of intense preoccupation with the past was already waning. In contrast to Nuremberg the Allies did not publish the documentary record of the trials and all the surviving defendants were to be released by the end of the 1950s. An ultranationalist fringe was implacably critical of the tribunal, while progressive opinion lamented it as a lost opportunity for frank and profound confrontation with the past. Mainstream conservative opinion, on the other hand, preferring as the 1950s progressed to focus on the present as a displacement strategy, 'tried to ignore the trial, put it out of mind, [and] block the transmission of any positive political and cultural lessons'.[46]

The early historiography of Japan's road to war incarnated a similar spectrum of responses. The most important development in post-war Japanese historical writing was the revival of Marxism which, released from the shackles of war-time censorship, initially established a near 'intellectual hegemony'. The occupation authorities generally regarded the Marxists benignly because of their anti-war stance, and there was a considerable degree of collusion between Marxist critiques of 'emperor-system fascism' and the Allied demo-cratisation agenda. It is a striking contrast with the West German case – where a largely conservative discipline took refuge in apologetic formulations deeming Nazism an aberration – that the most potent post-war explanations in Japan embodied a form of *Sonderweg* analysis, whereby the absence of a fully-fledged bourgeois revolution at the time of the Meiji restoration in 1868 ensured the persistence of semi-feudal structures that had spawned militarism, imperialism and war.[47] Despite the considerable overlap between this para-digm and the Tokyo trial view of history insofar as 'both put the war guilt solely on the Japanese', there was also tension between them since the ulti-mate logic of one was collectivising or structural whilst that of the other was individualising.[48] After the advent of the 'reverse course' – a truncation of reform whereby in Marxist eyes 'the evil old system of Japan ... survived and thrived as a prop of U.S. imperialism' – the more conservative climate of the 1950s was much less hospitable to Marxist analyses. Marxist accounts of the *Showa* period (that since Hirohito's accession in 1926) still found a size-able audience, but they were increasingly challenged by nationalist, liberal–conservative and competing leftist interpretations (such as Maruyama Masao's alternative characterisation of Japanese fascism).[49] More and more out of step with a dominant conservative political culture, Marxist historical writing flourished in the academy but was in broader terms confined in 'a gilded and permanent opposition'.[50]

Fired by a sense of moral and political urgency, Marxist historians were in the vanguard in seeking to explain Japan's aggressive past. A landmark work here was a five volume *History of the Pacific War* published under the aegis of the Historical Science Society of Japan in 1953–54, which sought to integrate military and diplomatic history with political, economic and cultural devel-opments. This cast blame for the war on the whole (allegedly unified) Japanese ruling class – 'the military, bureaucrats, monopoly capitalists, land-lords, and others' – whilst also offering a long term perspective in which deformed modernisation drove these rulers to indulge in aggression. 'Given the domestic imperatives, that is, the narrowness of the Japanese home market and the scarcity of natural resources, Japan had no alternative but to expand on the Asian continent to survive the age of imperialism ... Militarism, in addition to diplomacy, was thought to be an effective way to make up for the weakness which handicapped a late starting nation like Japan'.[51] A further characteristic of Marxist approaches was to insist that the various phases of

Japanese military activity from Manchuria to Pearl Harbor constituted a coherent, aggressive whole, with an essentially unbroken if not always openly avowed war on China at its heart: hence the coining of 'Fifteen-Year War' in 1956 as the preferred progressive sobriquet.[52]

To the chagrin of the left, however, 'favorable evaluations of the war began to recover the ground they had lost in the early years of defeat'.[53] For example, a 1952 collection of documents pertaining to the end of the Pacific War published by the foreign ministry 'was criticized as a subterfuge to avoid responsibility for the war' because of the stress it placed on the peace efforts of wartime leaders.[54] Under the occupation, the Americans had co-opted former military figures to assist in the collation of historical records and the production of basic military histories, and after 1952 these efforts were continued independently by the Japanese. In 1953 a four volume *Complete History of the Greater East Asia War* was published by a team under Colonel Hattori Takushiro; while undoubtedly 'a valuable historical source as a detailed record of combat operations', this was viewed by the left as an implicit justification of the Japanese war effort (and the conduct of its forces) and as portending a resurgence of militarism.[55] The quantity of archival material available gradually increased through the 1950s, with various documentary publications supplementing the records gathered by the IMTFE and partial opening – to at least some favoured scholars – of the foreign ministry archives and the military records in the custody of the defence agency (some of which had also been microfilmed by the Americans). The left, however, argued that the official or semi-official publications produced on the basis of privileged access to these archives were inherently reactionary, since in purporting to offer a neutral rendering of newly discovered facts they failed to engage larger issues of war responsibility.[56]

Some of this scholarship did explicitly present itself as refuting Marxist interpretations. The 'empirically oriented' authors of a 1953 volume produced by the Association for the Study of Japanese Diplomacy entitled *The Origins of the Pacific War* claimed to clarify Japan's real intentions in the war against the supposedly misleading theses of the Marxists and the Tokyo tribunal. To this end they devoted considerable attention to the constraints and provocations facing Japanese policy-makers, including anti-Japanese boycotts in China and the issue of oil resources.[57] This interpretive focus pointed to one way in which the lexicon of exculpation generated by the Tokyo trial defendants crossed over into serious post-war scholarship. Similarly, some historians began to argue that Japan had acted within the bounds of existing international law – essentially, in self-defence – in advancing in Manchuria and China, and that in opposing it a moralising United States had made demands resting on an entirely new construction of that law. On this view, the clash between these competing and irreconcilable approaches to international affairs eventually made the Pacific War inevitable. In 1961 Ueyama Shunpei 'stressed the interaction of nationalism, power politics, the communist menace, and the tendency of the United States to approach these issues ... through a naïve identification with the Nationalist government of China'. Progressives responded that it was illegitimate and apologetic to locate the causes of that war 'in the realm of international politics' rather than in 'the internal pressures and contradictions of Japanese society, in the realms of Japanese capitalism and militarism' – and in the aggressive schemes of policy-makers in Tokyo.[58] By the close of the 1950s, interpretations seeking more or less strongly to offer some form of justification for Japan's war were clearly in evidence. While the more egregiously nationalist failed to win widespread legitimacy – 'beaten back in part by the energy of the progressives' – moderate conservative scholarship was nonetheless challenging both Tokyo tribunal and Marxist assertions of war responsibility.[59]

Scholarship beyond Japan exhibited not dissimilar tendencies. Undoubtedly, the Tokyo tribunal thesis that Japan had unleashed 'an unprovoked series of wars of aggrandisement' culminating in Pearl Harbor remained prominent: indeed, arguably it reigned for two decades as 'the orthodox interpretation of war origins and responsibility'.[60] Yet even as a work like Robert Butow's 1961 *Tojo and the Coming of the War* narrated 'the decade of violence and aggression which had begun in 1931' after a militaristic clique secured control of the government, it nuanced the notion of a fully-fledged conspiracy by observing that Tojo and his colleagues often 'took things as they came and preferred to pass from one imminent problem to another'.[61] Similarly, Richard Storry's study of Japanese nationalism accepted that the plots and incidents of the period 'conformed very broadly ... to the same general design' but maintained that 'it would be a distortion' to conceive of 'a single grand conspiracy'.[62] A British historian writing as early as 1954 advanced more fundamental objections, denying that Japanese foreign policy represented 'the steady unfolding of a master-plan, aimed at securing the hegemony of East Asia and devised by a coolly calculating and united band of conspirators'; instead, he emphasised factionalism, 'opportunism and blundering', whereby the Japanese 'got themselves into a position in which they [had to] choose either humiliation or disgrace, or else embark upon the dread gamble of war'.[63] The Tokyo verdict was especially vulnerable to revisionism because of the widespread qualms about the politicised and simplistic character of its historical narrative, and the alternative interpretive options which had always been available were soon put into circulation.

In writing on Japan, 'attention ... gravitated toward the motivation of the Japanese, in place of their guilt; toward the unique process of decision-making, in place of plot; toward the historical roots of Japanese attitudes, in place of hastily sketched denunciation of Japanese national character'.[64] Budding exploration of the economic, social and structural context of policy – and especially of the impact of the problems generated by the Great Depression – sharply contrasted with the Tokyo prosecution's fixation on spontaneous aggressive agency, and inclined historians to 'levy fewer indictments' but rather to attempt 'to understand Japan's predicament'.[65] Heightened sensitivity to factionalism amongst both civilian and military elements in Japanese politics problematised the assumption that coherent policy flowed smoothly from the will of a unified leadership; the same was true of scrutiny of the relative significance of the initiative of field officers, presenting the Tokyo government with a series of *faits accomplis* in Manchuria and China.[66] Competing arguments were adumbrated on each of these themes, and their political implications were not always readily discernible; for example, if rogue elements on the periphery did contribute significantly to the course of policy, did that intensify war responsibility, spreading it more widely throughout Japanese society than had the Tokyo judgement, or dilute it by supporting the notion that Japan had blundered its way into war as rational policy-making was in abeyance? Yet either way the interpretive terrain became thornier.

Writing on American policy also had implications for understandings of Japanese responsibility. The 'traditionalist' defence of Roosevelt's policy which portrayed it as a relatively prudent reaction to an external threat tended to fit with the Tokyo tribunal paradigm, whereas 'revisionist' critiques which castigated him for exerting unwarranted and over-bearing pressure on the Japanese were in tune with emergent 'patriotic' views within Japan.[67] Japanese authors seeking to challenge established interpretations of the conflict drew eagerly on this latter literature.[68] Even if the 'revisionist' view failed to gain a dominant position, American historians were early and remained far more ready to question the necessity of the war in the Pacific than in Europe. Thus in 1958 Paul Schroeder advanced a provocative argument that the Japanese had been willing in 1941 to make significant concessions, abandoning their obligations to Germany under the Tripartite Alliance and withdrawing from southern Indochina, but that negotiations foundered because of an unreasonable American insistence on an evacuation of China itself as the price for ending economic sanctions. For Schroeder, American policy ignored power realities in its 'uncompromising adherence to moral principles and liberal doctrines', and thus hastened on 'an unnecessary and avoidable war'. Pearl Harbor was 'an act of desperation': 'Japan fought only when she had her back to the wall as a result of America's diplomatic and economic offensive'.[69] Schroeder's vision of a potentially moderate Japan was not entirely novel; a similar argument had been advanced by America's pre-war ambassador in Tokyo, Joseph Grew, both at the time and later in his memoirs.[70] Its specifics were fiercely contested, but it was expressive of a persistent sentiment amongst some American scholars that 'the United States was at least partly responsible for the Pacific War'.[71]

The inspiration for these interpretations was manifold. Many commentators invoke the 'fading of wartime passions and the advent of a generation of scholars trained in Japanese language and culture' as contributing to the emergence of more benign views.[72] Arguably, a quotidian internal scholarly dynamic was also in play, as the excessively agent-centred Tokyo verdict was challenged by scholars more inclined to structural and systemic approaches. However, this historiography must also be located in the context of the broader ideological endeavour through which the Japanese–American Cold War partnership was cemented. A great deal of cultural work was required on both sides to manufacture representations suitable for transforming erstwhile antagonists into intimate friends. Yet by 1960, through the propagation of 'new narratives for promoting amity with the Japanese', 'a confluence of geo-political, consumerist, and domestic concerns had helped Americans accept their former enemy as a worthy recipient of their nation's largesse, protection, and guidance'.[73] Much of the historical writing considered here conduced towards this rapprochement. However, in so doing, it also gave succour to conservative elements within Japan seeking to downplay Japanese war responsibility in the interests of promoting a more placid and harmonious collective memory of the wartime past.

'To shift war responsibility away from Japan': diplomatic history 'in the classical sense'

Through the 1960s and 1970s the national political hegemony of the LDP remained generally secure, largely as a consequence of its skilful economic management. Ideological issues were downplayed in favour of 'pragmatic "economism"': 'nationalistic sentiment was still cultivated, but the promotion of national prestige was now identified with the conspicuously high rate of economic growth achieved during this period'. Japan's relative success in smoothly overcoming the disruptive effects of the 1973 oil crisis cemented its positive reputation 'both at home and abroad as an "economic superpower" and "Number One" in management skills'.[74] Japan's reintegration into the international community also proceeded apace. The hosting of the Olympic Games in Tokyo in 1964 both 'symbolized Japan's commitment to international peace and friendship and demonstrated its possession of financial, logistical, and technological capabilities on a par with those of any modern industrial nation'.[75]

Equally pertinent were the restoration of normal diplomatic relations with many of the Asian neighbours that had suffered from Japanese aggression, and especially South Korea in 1965 and the People's Republic of China (PRC) in 1972. Negotiations here mandated some attention to the past and carefully formulated expressions of regret by Japanese officials. However, given the domestic imperatives driving the South Korean and PRC governments towards a settlement and in the interests of reconciliation, neither pressed the Japanese for fulsome apologies and both renounced their rights to demand reparations in return for promises of economic aid.[76] Thus while in one sense these agreements heralded a new 'internationalization of Japanese war memory and responsibility issues', in another Japanese conservatives were able to interpret them as a final settlement of accounts. The reversion of Okinawa to Japanese sovereignty in 1972 could similarly be read as marking a final step in the process of consolidating Japan's transition to post-war. Formal con-servative political dominance did not, however, mean that oppositional and progressive voices were stilled. In particular, the Vietnam War – and Japanese complicity in the American war effort – stimulated an enormous popular protest movement, 'using the pacifist language of both the constitution ... and anti-nuclear and antiwar rhetoric within the Hiroshima narrative'. While on one level these protests were simply anti-American, the Vietnam imbroglio could not but raise uncomfortable questions amongst Japanese about their own colonial wars in Asia decades before.[77]

Contrary to the amnesia stereotype, war memory continued to be characterised by cross currents and contestation. True, 'conservatives and nationalists remained strong within cultural life and maintained their grip on the official narrative'.[78] Successive LDP governments refused 'to take an explicit, representative, "official" stance on the meaning of the war'. With rare exceptions, 'cabinet members publicly neither condoned Japan's war efforts nor denied war atrocities directly', 'but statements of apology or remorse ... also remained few and far between'. The elaborate 1968 ceremonies around the centennial of the Meiji restoration were symptomatic, 'celebrating a century of "Japan in the world" by lightly skipping over the imperial and colonial quality of much of that history' in order to promote patriotic identification. That said there were also a range of efforts to shape public memory actively in a conservative sense, often directed through the central bureaucracy. Thus school textbook screening continued, and in 1978 government ministries connived with the Yasukuni authorities to arrange the clandestine enshrinement of 14 convicted Class A war criminals, including Tojo.[79]

Conservative representations also flourished in the broader culture. The atomic bombings became more insistently visible, and by a subtle shift Hiroshima gradually became less part of 'the iconography of left-wing pacifism' than 'a national symbol of victimhood'. The 'ageing and passing of the war generation' led to a boom in published testimonies, the majority of which 'focused on Japanese victimhood (such as air raids and Siberian internment) and there was continued interest in military memoirs'.[80] Hugely popular films and novels proliferated, generally eschewing explicit moralising in favour of 'good entertainment, focusing on famous battles for maximum visual effect' and 'swashbuckling narrative': thus the war was 'de-historicized and de-politicized', if not indeed beautified and glorified.[81] In a similar vein, the 1970s witnessed a vogue for a 'businessman's war literature' that drew positive and negative lessons in management technique from wartime campaigns. 'The self-sacrifice of the military for their country ... became an inspirational metaphor for the self-sacrifice of salarymen for their companies'.[82]

Conservative narratives only constituted part of a wider picture, however, since as time went on they came to be 'fighting a rearguard action against growing popular acknowledgement of an "aggressive war"'.[83] Leftist politicians and citizen's activist groups vigorously contested official efforts to propagate apologetic sentiments, protesting the 1965 treaty with South Korea, for example, 'precisely for its lack of contrition or remorse'. Similarly, when the LDP premier visited Yasukuni to pay his respects to the war dead in April 1979 he needed bodyguards for protection 'so great was public outrage at [the] matter-of-fact resurrection of convicted war criminals'.[84] The reversion of Okinawa was also a double-edged development, since it inserted into national collective memories the horrific treatment of Okinawans forced to commit mass suicide by the Japanese military during the climactic stages of the 1945 battle there.[85] Awareness of Japanese atrocities in Asia also mounted. Writing on the 'comfort women' began to emerge, while damning revelations about the operations of Unit 731 were aired in television documentaries.[86] The publication in 1971 of journalist Honda Katsuichi's series of articles *Travels in China*, which offered graphic new eyewitness testimony on the Nanking massacre and other war crimes, was a particular landmark. In subsequent polemical debates nationalists sought to minimise the extent of Japanese malfeasance or deny it altogether, but the general public became more and more inclined to adopt a 'victimizer consciousness'.[87] Progressive intellectuals also began to ponder more reflexively on mnemonic politics, 'coining the term "postwar responsibility"'. Hence the chief dynamic of war memory increasingly pitted 'liberal, responsible citizens' against 'an undemocratic and (scandalously) unapologetic government'.[88]

New approaches to historical writing continued to emerge. In the late 1950s and 1960s a range of liberal critics attacked Marxist approaches to the *Showa* period, decrying their over-schematised fixation on class struggle and calling for more nuanced appreciation of the role of human agency and non-material factors.[89] The importation of American modernization theory in the early 1960s posed a more profound challenge, as it was explicitly anti-Marxist in its conceptualisation of 'modernization without revolution as historical norm'.[90] Delivering a positive verdict on industrial and social development since the Meiji restoration, it even reassessed the significance of so-called feudal remnants by 'arguing that traditional values such as the goal-oriented ethical view and sense of duty and responsibility gave rise to progressive vitality and entrepreneurial spirits'. The Cold War utility of arguments that adopted 'a much more positive and uplifting teleology about the country's past' was manifest, as was their appeal in a booming nation sloughing off post-war pessimism. However, they also entailed interpreting the years of militarism as but a temporary aberration, in a manner amenable to conservative sensibilities.[91] Marxism responded but lost some influence within the academy, not least to the innovative and fertile non-Marxist leftist approaches that were more prominent through into the 1970s. Influenced by the *Annales* school, practitioners of 'people's history' turned to the social and cultural to explore the history of everyday life and mentalities at a grass-roots level, often using oral and local history methodologies.[92] While these historians did engage with popular attitudes during the war, deftly teasing out histories of both collaboration and resistance at a micro-level, they arguably 'tended to put into the background the juggernaut of the war machine'. 'A "human approach", in an effort to transcend the Cold War frame, side-stepped the fundamental questions raised and argued by their predecessors: which war, how, and why?'[93]

This is not to say that as the discipline diversified war and diplomacy went unaddressed. Traditional approaches here remained strong, but diplomatic historians also diversified their concerns in parallel with colleagues in other countries, in particular through borrowings from analytical frameworks in social science. These included theories of decision-making and bureaucratic politics, psychological approaches to leadership, the role of images and perceptions, systems theory, and the linkages between domestic politics, public opinion and foreign policy. Multi-archival scholarship also flourished, competing with and complementing more conventional mono-national approaches.[94] Writing about the origins of the war also continued to be a site of ideological contestation as existing competing perspectives were further elaborated.

The boom years of the 1960s gave a significant fillip to the right, and the 'mass media began publishing a glut of articles and books that relegitimized Japan's war cause – to liberate Asia from the yoke of Western colonialism'.[95] Notoriously, 'the first major academic defence of Japan's wars' was Hayashi Fusao's *Affirmation of the Greater East Asian War*, published serially from 1963–65, which portrayed the conflict as the culmination of a 100 year war against western imperialist domination of East Asia that had begun with the first American attempts to open up Japan.[96] The war was thus in essence defensive against a western threat, and while it ended in defeat nonetheless it objectively facilitated Asian liberation. Harking straight back to wartime propaganda, this interpretation was tendentious in the extreme (not least because for much of the period concerned Japan had co-operated with the western powers in the Anglo–Japanese alliance and the Washington treaty system), yet it was influential with a popular audience.[97] Indeed, the basic argument that the Japanese occupation of parts of Asia, its 'destructive and barbaric side' notwithstanding, 'made positive contributions and proved enlightening in the historical perspective' through catalysing Asian nationalist independence movements, became established in the scholarly literature.[98] (Even some progressive adherents to the 'Fifteen-Year War' view were susceptible to ambiguity here; whilst denouncing Hayashi's apologetics and affirming and condemning Japanese aggression, they could feel that the Pacific War against western imperialists had a somewhat different character to that in East Asia, and also acknowledge that the latter had some positive anti-imperialist consequences.[99]) Hayashi's strident revisionism was intensely controversial, but his raising of 'bold questions' had 'a strong impact on Japanese specialists in contemporary diplomatic history'.[100]

By far the most significant – arguably 'epoch-making' – development in mainstream scholarship in this period was a seven volume collection of lengthy monographic essays on *The Road to the Pacific War*, published in 1962–63 by the Japan Association of International Relations.[101] Based on privileged access to unpublished materials from military, naval and foreign ministry archives, as well as personal papers and interviews, these essays contained dense and richly documented reconstructions of the making of Japanese foreign policy from the later 1920s through to 1941.[102] The empirical achievement of the authors in unearthing new data was universally recognised, and the collection remains a canonical reference point. Substantial portions of it were translated for a five volume English edition, and a second Japanese edition was published at the end of the 1980s, indicating that its findings 'retain[ed] their scholarly value'.[103] Although individual essays by the 14 authors varied somewhat in emphasis, this was a remarkably 'well-knit and organised' collaborative endeavour. A consensus on underpinning philosophy helped secure cohesion, as the contributors agreed to cleave strictly to an objectivist approach refraining from the use of supposedly loaded terms such as militarism and imperialism.[104] The last editor in chief of the project, Tsunoda Jun – a 'participant-observer' in the road to war as a prime ministerial aide and activist in nationalist think-tanks – prescribed a defiantly traditional methodological approach: to write 'straightforward historical accounts solidly based on primary source materials – narratives of diplomatic history (leading to the war) in the classical sense'.[105]

Summarising the interpretive thrust of such a voluminous work is not easy, and its particular mode of narration, tightly focused on the chronological unfolding of action and event with extreme 'restraint in analysis and interpretation', compounds the problem.[106] Thematically, the volumes overwhelmingly prioritised military affairs and tracing the process of decision-making through various military, political and bureaucratic structures in painstaking detail; yet this achieved, they eschewed 'generalisations on the nature of Japan's foreign relations', systematic engagement with the broader context of policy-making, or consideration of the wider interpretive issues entailed in the problematic of war responsibility. One sympathetic commentator characterised the volumes as leaving these ultimate issues of interpretation open, arguing that they were best regarded as 'documentary collections, on the basis of which old theories could be revised and new interpretations drawn'.[107] Yet this judgement belied how the volumes collectively did offer an overarching vision of the period, and how framing the subject in this particular narrow way was far from an innocent move. Making a virtue of the desire 'to search tenaciously for the facts of history on a positivist basis, avoiding value judgements as far as was possible' was explicitly intended as a riposte to Marxist scholarship. Technical, deracinated reconstruction of the minutiae of decision making and illumination of the 'complex realities of the 1930s' was to trump the supposedly over-neat, schematic and politically motivated arguments of progressives.[108] This would correct the excessive stress on war responsibility which, according to one of the project's editors, was apt to 'produce a guilt-ridden nation'.

Little wonder that progressives vigorously attacked *The Road to the Pacific War* as 'an unmistakeable effort to shift war responsibility away from Japan'.[109] Overall, it embodied a sophisticated and subtly modulated nationalist apologia, combining exculpatory tropes visible in the cases of both the Tokyo defence – relating to the external threats and pressures faced by

Japan – and prosecution-stressing the influence of military extremists. On the one hand, in so far as the authors dealt with the rationalisations, justifications and world views of policy-makers, they tended to reproduce them without critical comment, seeing events 'through the eyes of … its most direct participants' and letting them 'speak for themselves'. This form of empathetic reconstruction could easily seem to imply approbation for policy-makers' claims to be acting chiefly in the name of imperial self-sufficiency and national self-defence.[110] On the other hand, the collection placed great emphasis on the actions of 'precipitate and irresponsible military officers', both acting autonomously 'at the periphery of the Japanese empire' and at the heart of government.[111] To be sure, this second strand of argument stood in certain tension with the first, but the search for exemplary villains is not incompatible with broader exculpatory intent, and overall the collection flexibly combined the topoi of 'external "pressures" and a handful of "wrong-headed" extremists' as the basic causes of war. If the admission of some guilt illustrated the distance between this moderate conservative argument and that of Hayashi, nonetheless the point of the progressive criticism was clear.

According to one critic's characterisation, the authors argued that both the Manchurian incident and Sino-Japanese conflict were 'wars of self-defense to protect Japan's vested interests in China', which were constantly threatened by external forces such as Comintern agitation, Chinese obstinacy and American 'moralism and formulism'. Yet both were also engineered by a small clique of army radicals. Japan then came to be involved in war with the United States because of the manoeuvrings of influential navy die-hards in Tokyo and the pressurising machinations of Roosevelt: 'irresolute and irresponsible Japanese political and military leaders, who held misconceptions about the world situation, not only misjudged American moves, but also succumbed to the pressure of the Navy extremists'. Thus the road to the Pacific War was complex, 'a story full of surprises and miscalculations'.[112]

Progressives and subsequent commentators detected numerous other defects. One corollary of the refusal to offer 'systematic and consistent discussion on how to evaluate and characterize the Pacific War as a whole', together with the tremendously detailed micro-reconstruction of specific episodes, was the depoliticising disaggregation of the left's 'Fifteen-Year War' into a long succession of separate incidents. Even when connections were drawn, the left complained that the wars in China and Asia were viewed 'largely within the narrow framework of the origins of the Japanese–American war'.[113] Thus in concluding his essay on the Manchurian incident, Seki Hiroharu observed how, 'in the name of national defense, that sacred slogan of the twentieth century, Japan entered the long road that would ultimately end at the outbreak of the Pacific War'.[114] This treatment, it was alleged, tended to elide 'the larger questions of why Japanese forces were in Manchuria and then China proper in the first place'.[115] Obscuring these essential issues, 'positing Japanese vested interests in China as the givens, [these] historians hardly criticized Japanese aggression on the Asian continent and in South

East Asia'.[116] The preoccupation with diplomacy and decision-making also militated against any serious consideration of the crimes committed by the occupying Japanese there.

The neglect of profound forces, ideological drives and domestic political and economic structures also conduced at points to a narrative that emphasised contingency, 'blunders and misjudgments', and lost opportunities.[117] This was particularly apparent in Tsunoda's own treatment of the final stages of the road to Pearl Harbor which stressed chances missed on both sides to avoid the escalation of conflict. Downplaying the bellicosity of Japanese popular and official opinion and the stubborn intransigence of the military, Tsunoda laid the responsibility for war on the contingent choices and errors of a handful of policy-makers on either side. (While he offered nothing 'by way of criticism of Japan's mission in Asia', he did chide the United States for a Sinophilia grounded in '"sentimentality, idealism, ignorance, and self-interest"'.)[118] Marginalising the ideological thrust of Japan's imperialist policy, he portrayed the outbreak of the war as 'the result of disastrous misunderstanding' – a move which not only effaced Japanese war responsibility but also naturalised the notion of cordial Japanese–American relations as the norm.[119] A contrasting reading of the moral of the collection is that it depicted Japanese policy-makers caught up in the unfolding of 'a massive Greek tragedy', struggling 'to avoid the disaster of total war' but caught up in the playing out of an inexorable fate; even if Japan's continental policy was presented as the root cause of the chain reaction, this emplotment too performed an act of absolution.[120]

This discussion necessarily underplays the empirical achievement of *The Road to the Pacific War*. Yet the point remains that this form of objectivist scholarship can be meticulous and scrupulous, vastly extending factual knowledge, and yet still convey dubious political messages because of the things that it fails to do or, indeed, the mnemonic context in which it intervenes. Choices of subject matter and focus shape the ideological valence of a text just as much as its overt emplotment, and in this case an orthodox form of diplomatic history that refused to raise its sights above the narrowly-framed reconstruction of decisions proved to be highly compatible with concurrent apologetic tendencies within Japanese society. This is not to suggest that the contributors, or all mainstream Japanese international historians, evinced a unanimous interpretive outlook or political orientation. Despite the rapturous reception accorded the collection, parts of it – and especially those authored by Tsunoda – have been criticised by other Japanese scholars as 'ambiguous, uneven in coverage, and scattered with questionable value judgments'.[121] Equally, other academic and political interventions by some of the authors were of quite different import; for example, in 1995 Hosoya Chihiro resigned from a commission advising the government on the founding of a new war museum because of fears that it would be used to justify Japanese aggression.[122] Yet what is at issue here is the intimacy between a particular mode of representation and wider desires to evade confrontation with war responsibility.

Scholarship on the origins of the war proliferated through the remainder of this period, abetted by ever more documentary publications and increasing access to archives.[123] Japanese historians produced work on a very wide range of thematic issues, relating both to internal determinants and processes of Japanese policy and also the wider context of international relations.[124] A predilection for detailed monographic work over interpretive synthesis meant that the thrust of this literature in relation to war responsibility was not always readily apparent, but diverse political messages were evident. In writing on the ideology of pan-Asianism, for example, some authors took a 'positive view' of the search 'for a doctrine of Asian solidarity that would reject traditional Western colonialism and at the same time satisfy Chinese nationalism', while others interpreted it as having provided 'fundamentally a rationale to justify the Japanese invasion of China'.[125] That said, the key organising tropes of *The Road to the Pacific War* also continued to be deployed, while the application of theories of decision-making and bureaucratic politics introduced a fresh nuance. Emphasising 'institutional malfunctionings and deficiencies in Japan's policymaking process' and the 'spiral of mutual misperceptions and distrust', this tended to sustain a 'drift toward war' framework, exaggerating the prospects for the avoidance of hostilities.[126]

In contrast, progressives simultaneously maintained their 'Fifteen-Year War' thesis castigating Japan for aggression. Ienaga Saburo became a household name through his indefatigable mnemonic activism, fighting a series of legal battles with the government from the 1960s through to the late 1990s, disputing the constitutionality of school textbook screening.[127] His 1968 book *The Pacific War* explicitly aimed 'to stimulate reflection and self-criticism about the war' and to guard against the threat of revanchist militarism: 'only the determination not to ever repeat "the horrors of war" described in this book sustains the pacifism and democracy of the Japanese Constitution'. Ienaga aspired 'to reach the core of the war' and sought its roots in Japan's domestic circumstances, structures and history. Principally, he identified three key factors underpinning the 'abject slide into aggression'. First, there was racism, or the 'irrational Japanese contempt for their Asian neighbors fostered over several decades and the imperialist policies sanctioned by that attitude'. Second, government thought control and indoctrination inculcated militarist values and incorporated the populace into an imperialist project. Third, the 'authoritarian and irrational' military, imbued with a brutal and illogical mind-set, had secured a privileged institutional position within the state. 'The Pacific War was a mirror image of that gestalt: recklessness, absurd persistence beyond the point of no return, and innumerable acts of savagery. That kind of war did not just happen. It was not the result of accident or loss of control'.

Ienaga's treatment also squarely implicated the other 'agencies of the Japanese state' which, 'some enthusiastically, others passively, joined the cabal'. Political repression notwithstanding, his innovative discussion of the relatively few 'intrepid individuals' who 'resolutely refused ... to kowtow to the authorities' also highlighted the culpability of the masses who had failed to resist. Ienaga refuted claims that Japan was acting in self-defence, and even when he acknowledged the influence of perceived external threats such as Soviet communism it tended only to compound guilt: 'if one fundamental distinction between bourgeois democracy and fascism was the latter's attempt to destroy communism not by ideological but by military means, Japan's protracted aggression was assuredly a Fascist war'. Insisting on the integrity of the 'single conflict' fought by Japan from 1931, he repeatedly reiterated that 'aggression against China was at the heart of the fifteen-year war'. Despairing of a decisive result there, Japanese militarists 'sought victory by expanding the conflict' which ultimately led to the stark choice between capitulation over China or the gamble of war with the western powers. 'They plunged the country into war with America and England in the hope of cutting the Gordian knot in China'. Ienaga here departed from the Tokyo tribunal view that Pearl Harbor was the culmination of a blueprint for war, but in so doing he fixed responsibility even more firmly upon bellicose Japanese imperialism.

Ienaga's synthetic work perforce offered but a fraction of the information about diplomacy and decision-making that was available in *The Road to the Pacific War*.[128] Equally, his omission of detailed treatment of the roles of other powers and the denser context of international relations – in line with his overriding focus on Japanese agency – meant that inevitably he covered 'at best one part of a very complicated story'.[129] Yet in other ways he provided a much more total history than his liberal conservative competitors, since he integrated a narrative of politics and war-making with discussion of the ideologies of imperialism and militarism, the linkages between domestic and foreign policy, patterns of collaboration and resistance, brutal occupation methods and atrocities such as the 'comfort women' and Unit 731. Moreover, through skilful deployment of personal vignettes he imparted a sense of the human tragedies inherent in aggression and defeat. Writing with a texture and thematic range that prefigured later much more sophisticated treatments of Axis war-making, Ienaga mounted a profound indictment of Japan's 'disgraceful and bloody rampage' and brought into focus the contemporary moral and political urgency of attending assiduously to the responsibility it imposed.[130]

In North America, scholars continued to place 'more and more blame for the Pacific War upon the United States'.[131] To be sure, some still posited the existence of a fully fledged *Imperial Conspiracy*, while others remained adamant that 'the Japanese military establishment was primarily responsible for the Pacific war'.[132] Yet James Crowley adopted a much more representative position, deprecating the ideas of a civilian–military split in Tokyo or of policy being forced by renegade field officers, and instead positing that 'national policy was, throughout the 1930s, technically and legally formulated by the cabinet' in pursuit of coherent and not damnable goals. Whilst Japan had certainly sought a hegemonic position in East Asia, this was done in the name of 'the enhancement of national security and the enhancement of the economic well-being of the state'; ultimately this *Quest for Autonomy* had resulted in aggression and a disastrous war, but these goals were a rational response to external circumstances. Moreover, it ill-behoved any western historian 'to label the garnering, defense, and extension of an empire as an illegitimate form of state action'. Crowley thus drew attention to the double standards that had allegedly permeated previous accounts, and urged a more empathetic understanding of the dilemmas facing Japanese policy-makers.[133] Reacting to events, Japan forged an association with Germany and drifted into antagonism with the western colonial powers and the United States as it extended the conflict, vainly hoping that '"just one more victory" would allow her to extricate herself from the Chinese quagmire'.[134]

American policy was also the subject of ongoing critique. 'Wisconsin school' interpretations stressing the consistent pursuit of open door imperialism obviously tended to lay primary blame for the Pacific War on the United States, and to support the notion that Japanese policy had been primarily defensive. Indeed, Noam Chomsky's notorious iteration of this view came close to replicating Hayashi's polemic.[135] (Some Japanese progressives advanced their own 'New Left' interpretations of American imperialism, even though this created some tensions over the issue of Japanese war responsibility.[136]) Other international historians diagnosed diverse faults in American diplomacy: inconsistency in defining vital interests in Asia and devising policies to protect them, excessive passivity, maladroit handling of negotiations, bureaucratic infighting and lack of coordination, ignorance and a miscalculated and self-defeating application of deterrence. If much of this work was closely focused on bilateral relations, and tended to stress American responsibility for forcing the Japanese towards war, a somewhat contrasting perspective placed the Japanese–American relationship in a broader international context. Rather than seeking the causes of the stiffening of American policy in specific acts of the Japanese, this tended to emphasise Washington's global calculus. Focusing above all on the Nazi threat in Europe, Roosevelt hoped to contain the Japanese and prevent them from attacking either the Soviets or the British, animated by a conviction that Tripartite Pact cooperation presaged a concerted assault on freedom and civilisation. Interlocking with concurrent writing on Japan that emphasised the tenuous and contingent nature of the connection with Berlin, the sincere sentiments of self-defence prevailing in Tokyo, and the piecemeal and desperate nature of Japan's forward moves, this conduced to a narrative stressing dissonance of mutual perceptions, wishful thinking and the avertibility of war rather than naked Japanese desire for aggrandisement.[137]

The broad compatibility in the thrusts of their scholarship facilitated fruitful exchanges between Japanese and western historians. The proceedings of a 1969 bi-national conference published in English as *Pearl Harbor as History* presented tightly focused parallel studies of the role of bureaucratic agencies, political institutions and interest groups in Japan and the United

States. Yet again, the focus here was on bilateral decision-making processes, with a thematic emphasis upon how misunderstanding, mutual distrust and organisational deficiencies contributed to eliminate all possibilities of compromise and eventually render war inevitable (even if there were significant differences of opinion as to when the point of no return was reached).[138] Rather than 'Japan forcing war on America', the picture here was of 'two sides blundering their way towards a cataclysm'.[139] Urging attention to complexity and the need for 'deeper understanding', the participants concluded that 'blame for the war could not be attributed primarily to either the United States or Japan'.[140] Japanese and British scholars convened a similar conference in 1979. In one sense, there was a greater stress on the inevitability of conflict since Japanese aspirations to carve out a sphere of influence in Asia impinged much more directly upon British economic, political and imperial interests than they did on those of the United States. To an extent, this underscored Japanese war responsibility even if it remained an issue whether 'have not' powers should bear more blame in such cases than 'haves'. Yet in a wider sense, by pointing again to how this confrontation only escalated into a Pacific War because of the way in which Britain and the United States came to see their own fates as interdependent on a wider global canvas, the extent to which this outcome was primarily the result of the specific contingencies of Japanese thought and deed was called into question.[141]

The oft-enunciated hopes in this literature that measured perusal of the past would assist in working out how 'future relations' between Japan and her former enemies 'should take shape' had, to be sure, a bromidic quality.[142] Yet a past in which conflict had been a tragedy of accident and mutual misunderstanding was undeniably conducive to the ongoing maintenance of amicable Japanese–American relations, as Iriye Akira – perhaps tellingly, a Japanese scholar translated to American academe – made manifest in his prize-winning 1979 study of *The Japanese–American War*. Iriye stressed the aberrant nature of Pacific War era discord given the existence of deeper common assumptions about the international system, 'an undercurrent of shared interests and outlooks'; the end of the war and subsequent partnership demonstrated that 'Japanese–American cooperation and interdependence were a more desirable framework than rivalry and conflict'.[143] Historians persistently enjoined the necessity of removing the 'blanket of vaporous stereotypes' produced by '"the praise and blame" approach to history' of the Tokyo trials in order to intensify this post-war amity.[144] Contemporary politics intruded here in other ways too. When historians characterised the American deterrent policy of 1941 as counter-productive since it had led the 'irrational' Japanese to escalate the conflict, it was hard not to read their work as a product of the vicissitudes of détente.[145] Similarly, Richard Minear's 1971 attack on the Tokyo trial was explicitly underpinned by revulsion at the criminal activities of the United States in contemporary South East Asia.[146] Sympathising with Japan's plight, trapped in an imbroglio from which it could not extricate itself without imperilling its perceived vital interests, was a natural impulse in the Vietnam era. 'The intervening years have made us realize', Mark Peattie wrote in 1975, 'that Japan has not been the only power whose sense of mission against a hostile ideology in Asia had led to the profoundest contradictions of national purpose and integrity'.[147]

Such interpretations placed quite coherent and plausible constructions upon the empirical evidence. Moreover, if the protean past can be emplotted in diverse ways, historiographies calculated to encourage harmonious rather than discordant international relations in the present might in some senses have a superior ethical value. Yet these developing understandings of the origins of the Pacific War – with Japanese policy aimless and inconsistent, 'opportunistic' and 'ambiguous', the Americans the active agents trying to coerce Japan back into its older role as a responsible member of the international community, and events in Asia essentially contingent on developments elsewhere – flirted with palpable political dangers too.[148] While viewed from an American perspective these interpretive moves might be benignly regarded as politically progressive, their ideological valence as transnational interventions was quite different. Although their tenor was not outrageously apologetic, they nonetheless converged with mainstream conservative scholarship in Japan in relativising and mitigating Japanese war responsibility in ways which the left there deemed unacceptably exculpatory. In a discursive terrain of complex contestation, as they encouraged a premature neutralisation of the past, these arguments threatened to lend sustenance to the disposition of denial that refused to confront the reality of Japanese aggression or acknowledge the atrocities perpetrated during the war.[149]

'Japan ... stumbled into the Second World War': walking fine lines in a contested terrain

Over the next three decades, the shifting contingencies of domestic and international politics profoundly unsettled many of the verities of the Japanese post-war. Although the LDP long remained the dominant political force, it lost its former hegemony when it briefly fell from power in 1993 amidst unprecedented economic troubles. Subsequent LDP governments grappled laboriously with the implementation of the economic, social and structural reforms necessary to revitalise the nation to meet the challenges of globalisation.[150] Political instability in the mid-1990s reflected a wider reconfiguration of allegiances that came in the wake of the death of Hirohito in 1989; the symbolic landmark of the passing of the *Showa* era generated intense reflection about the nature of the national community and Japan's place in the world. This in turn was further fuelled by the end of the Cold War, which removed much of the rationale for Japan's domestic post-war settlement and external orientation, indeed the 'clearcut framework within which all events were endowed with political meaning'.[151] One obvious consequence was the onset of strained relations between Japan and the United States through much of the 1990s, exacerbated by economic frictions and disputes over the Japanese contribution to the Gulf War.[152]

More profoundly, this waning of geopolitical bipolarity intensified a process of regional integration in East Asia whereby Japan became more closely enmeshed economically, politically and culturally with her near neighbours. This restructuring generated new complexities, threats and responsibilities for Japanese policy-makers; it also created a dramatically changed environment for debating the national purpose.[153] That said, the turn to Asia did not entirely occlude older ties, and in the new century the Japanese–American alliance was rejuvenated as the Koizumi government lent staunch support to Washington's policy in the 'War on Terror'. The more hawkish elements of the LDP saw this new environment as 'conducive to their plans to remake Japan into a nation capable of playing a global political and military role', pressing with renewed vigour against strenuous popular opposition for constitutional revision to permit freer deployment of troops overseas and campaigning to secure a permanent seat on the United Nations Security Council.[154]

These developments impacted heavily on the terrain of war memory. There was 'a massive increase in discussions about the wartime past, and the emergence of new actors in these debates', which together rendered them more complex and contested than ever before.[155] Moreover, issues of Japan's war and post-war responsibility were ever more overtly 'tied to the politics of redefining its position in the world'.[156] The 'deluge of retrospectives' precipitated by Hirohito's death largely focused on the wartime past, as formerly marginalised critiques of his war responsibility 'exploded into a public debate of unprecedented proportions – what came to be known as the lifting of the "Chrysanthemum taboo"'.[157] This coincided with the global upsurge in war memory triggered *inter alia* by the cycle of fiftieth anniversary commemorations, the aging and consequent new vocality of the wartime generation and the emergence of new discourses of victimhood and restitution.[158] Within Japan subsequent discussions ranged very widely across war crimes and war responsibility, and their reflexive character was further intensified, often with explicit comparison to the German case.[159] This was not the only sense in which Japan's war memory was internationalised. For domestic political reasons, and as part of the working out of a new configuration of regional relationships, the Chinese and South Korean governments began to express more active interest in Japan's 'history problem', vociferously protesting allegedly sanitised textbooks and prime ministerial visits to Yasukuni, and insisting on the elaboration of a more inclusive transnational memory of the war. The new exigencies of economic and political power in the region compelled the Japanese government to pay some heed to these demands (as did the fact that some American politicians, scholars and activists, freed from Cold War constraints and increasingly attentive to the politics of reparation, often vigorously seconded them). The voices of individual victims also began to be heard as former slave labourers and 'comfort women', aided by international networks of civil society activists, launched an avalanche of compensation law suits against the Japanese government and corporations.[160]

Unprecedented detail about Japanese war crimes and atrocities thus entered the public domain, and in this climate the previous trend whereby the majority of Japanese accepted that their country had conducted a war of aggression for which it should make proper repentance and restitution was consolidated.[161] Progressive intellectuals and grass-roots activists engaged in ceaseless endeavour to raise consciousness about war memory issues and to promote reconciliation with Japan's Asian neighbours, evidenced for example by the convening of the Women's International War Crimes Tribunal for the Trial of Japanese Military Sexual Slavery in Tokyo in December 2000 which 'tried' – and 'convicted' – Hirohito and the Japanese state over the 'comfort women'.[162] For such progressives, a positive national identity could only be premised upon candid acknowledgement of dark chapters in the national past.

That said, from the mid-1990s neo-nationalist intellectuals and cultural commentators mounted a vigorous backlash against the advancing discourse of war responsibility. Fired by determination to maintain more roseate views of national history, and resentment at incessant foreign demands for apology and compensation, these critics asserted that dwelling masochistically on alleged historical misdeeds was profoundly inimical to the cultivation of a healthy nationalism.[163] Insecure and frustrated amidst a widespread social and economic malaise, 'conservatives were increasingly nostalgic about the war days and the economic miracle, when there were clear national missions, every citizen had a role to play, and hardships were endured as a self-sacrifice for the greater good of the nation'.[164] One important front in this campaign was the historiography of the Nanking massacre, which proponents of this so-called 'liberal historic' view either minimised or denied.[165] They also exercised pressure against the trend through the 1990s towards franker treatment of war atrocities in school textbooks, and authored their own startlingly revisionist alternative, airbrushing crimes and affirming the liberationist virtues of Japanese imperialism, which was approved by the education ministry in 2001. This official approbation, coinciding with Japanese assertiveness in foreign affairs and incremental rearmament, not surprisingly caused consternation in the PRC and South Korea.[166] The neo-nationalist view struck a chord with significant conservative elements of public opinion and the mass media, and it was also widely disseminated in popular form through the best-selling *manga* of Kobayashi Yoshinori.[167] The cleavages in collective memory were illustrated by the diverse nature of Japan's proliferating state and private war museums; some frankly depicted Japanese aggression and brutalisation of other Asian peoples, while others either explicitly justified the war effort or emphasised Japanese suffering through a depoliticising focus on the hardships of daily life on the home front.[168]

Buffeted by these conflicting domestic and foreign pressures, Japanese governments were forced to articulate more explicit positions on the 'history problem' than ever before. From the 1980s, politicians issued a whole series of official apologies. A high point came in August 1993 when (non-LDP) Prime Minister Hosokawa Morihiro referred publicly to Japan's 'aggressive war'; in 1995 a parliamentary resolution expressed 'deep remorse' and 'sincere condolences' for the 'pain and suffering' Japan had inflicted; and in 2005 Koizumi offered a 'heartfelt apology' to victims of 'its colonial rule and aggression'.[169] The putative addressees of these apologies, however, generally deemed them inadequate owing to their evasive terminology, itself partly a product of the domestic political horse-trading that accompanied their enunciation.[170] Moreover, contradictory gestures and interventions undermined their claims to sincerity. These included continued prime ministerial visits to Yasukuni, revisionist outbursts – indeed, 'apology sabotage' – by nationalist politicians, and a niggardly legalistic stubbornness towards the payment of compensation to individual victims, whose claims official Japan regarded as definitively settled by previous inter-state treaties.[171] Back-sliding also reinforced the idea that past apologies had been grudging rather than manifestations of genuine repentance: thus although the government formally apologised to the 'comfort women' in the early 1990s, in March 2007 Prime Minister Abe Shinzo implicitly resiled from this by denying state responsibility for military prostitution, and even that it had involved coercion.[172] There are serious doubts about the legitimacy of the normative criteria in play in holding Japanese governments to account on the apology and compensation issues.[173] Yet nonetheless the suspicion died hard that Japanese governments were indulging pragmatically in ambivalent apologies to close off the issue of war responsibility, adopting a '"future-facing" apologetic stance' devoid of authentic sympathy for victims.[174] Their most recent position, indeed, raised the stakes by maintaining that Japan's whole post-war history – from its acceptance of the Tokyo trials verdicts, through peace education to its exceptionally generous overseas aid policy – had consistently incarnated remorse for the war. When this allegedly positive record was rhetorically linked to 'Japan's current *right* and *duty* to assume a leadership role in regional and global affairs', it was not difficult to see why the issue of war responsibility continued to envenom international relations in East Asia.[175]

The most contentious topics within collective memory during this period related to the atrocities visited on the victims of Japanese aggression, yet the issue of war origins was also still salient. Indeed, an enduring strand in conservative rhetoric sought to keep open the issue of whether Japanese foreign policy in the years before the war could even fairly be characterised as aggressive. The debates around apologies in the mid-1990s encompassed repeated interventions in this sense by prominent conservative politicians, including some cabinet members dissenting from the government line. They tended to disparage the continued unhelpful obsession with the war-era, insisting that 'it makes little sense to keep harping on the past and apologizing for one particular incident after another'. Yet while thus preaching the virtues of transcendence they also advanced substantive historical claims. One core theme here was liberationist, as in the refrain that 'it was thanks to Japan that most nations in Asia were able to throw off the shackles of colonial rule under European domination and to win independence'. Another stressed the defensive nature of Japanese policy, opining that 'because Japan was in danger of being crushed, the country rose up to ensure its survival'. A further relativising move invoked the issue of double standards: 'doesn't it take two to wage a war, that is, mutual use of aggression?'[176] The persistence of these tropes was illustrated in 2007 when Nitta Hitoshi, professor of literature at Kogakkan University, defended prime ministerial visits to Yasukuni as expressions of respect and gratitude 'to our ancestors': 'for it was they who sacrificed their lives to ensure independence; they who, with military force, broke down the global colonial system in order to lay the foundations for resource-scarce Japan to engage in free trade'.[177]

These claims were naturally contested by the memory partisans of the progressive left. They insisted ever more vociferously on the fact of Japanese aggression, its location in the longer term trajectory of 'the imperialism and colonialism of the modern Japanese nation-state', and the imperative to recognise the 'war responsibility' not just of Class A war criminals but also of the emperor, 'the mass media, intellectuals, religious leaders, and educators', indeed of 'all levels of society'.[178] Yet these apologetics were also contested in different terms from the centre and centre right. Even in these segments of the political spectrum the 'nationalistic reassertion of pride in Japan's past' aroused anxieties through its airbrushing of the horrors of war and deleterious impact on intra-Asian relations.[179] In one of the major publishing events coinciding with the sixtieth anniversary of the end of the war, right of centre newspaper the *Yomiuri Shimbun* launched a year-long inquiry into war responsibility which presented itself as 'the first of its kind taken up by Japanese themselves'. This concluded by reaffirming the prime guilt of Japan's leaders – principally Tojo and other Class A war criminals, but also some individuals not indicted by the Tokyo tribunal – for 'starting the reckless war' and bringing 'unspeakable suffering to Japan and neighboring countries'. The inquiry's treatment was conventionally (that is, narrowly) framed and somewhat problematic by the progressive yardstick. Thus it exonerated Hirohito, failed to address either the longer history of Japanese colonialism or the full gamut of war crimes, and insinuated that the Americans and Soviets had also committed atrocities. Similarly, the recapitulation of the course of Japanese aggression was somewhat superficial in its discussion of ideological motivation, being couched rather in terms of blunders, misjudgements and myopia, and the reckless behaviour of maverick factions.[180] These tropes served somewhat to dilute any sense of aggressive, consistent and culpable Japanese agency. That said, in context the inquiry was a stark rebuttal of 'liberal historic' efforts at whitewashing war responsibility, pointedly warned about the past and present dangers of 'nationalistic posturing', and stimulated a vital and engaged public debate; indeed, arguably the deployment of this conservative framework 'helped to make critical discussion of war responsibility "respectable", and encouraged participation ... by those who might otherwise have feared to approach such a sensitive topic'.[181]

To a significant extent, the *Yomiuri* inquiry's conclusions replicated views current in the mainstream of Japanese international history. During this period, assisted by the ever-growing availability of documents, historians increasingly located Japanese foreign policy in a wider international context, developing 'a relatively comprehensive regional coverage of Japan's war' with greater emphasis particularly upon the Chinese and Soviet dimensions.[182] By the same token, international historians continued to expand their thematic compass, especially through engagement with cultural history, which conduced to 'increasing awareness of the importance of social forces and popular opinion'.[183] This also entailed more systematic treatment of war crimes, though it was historians of other stripes, and scholars in media and cultural studies, who were in the vanguard here.[184] There remained, of course, significant disagreements between practitioners. Some, notably Hata Ikuhiko, became associated with the 'liberal historic' neo-nationalist position.[185] Other conservatives talked freely of how a Japan 'surrounded by great powers ... tried to become an empire that could uphold its own values vis-à-vis the United States, the Soviet Union and China but failed in the attempt'.[186] More progressive scholars, conversely, wrote explicitly to reaffirm against neo-nationalist encirclement apologetics that 'in the history of modern Japan, the will to go to war had never been so clearly and deliberately defined' as in 1941.[187] This strand in the sub-discipline was also exemplified by the leftist scholarship on Hirohito that proliferated after his death, indicting him for his active and bellicose influence as commander in chief.[188]

The dominant position, however, fell between these two poles. In the case of Hirohito, it argued that he must 'share some sort of responsibility for the war, moral if not legal', yet essentially endorsed the Tokyo tribunal view that he was personally against war but that his constitutional position precluded the exercise of decisive opposition to the militarists.[189] More generally, this scholarship recognisably built upon the foundations of earlier work such as *The Road to the Pacific War*, and continued to stress vacillation, miscalculation, perceived threats and extremist factions. Yet in tune with the generally enhanced recognition of past malfeasance across society in this period, international historians were now more inclined to affirm the integrity and consistently aggressive purpose of Japanese imperialism in the age of what was increasingly and tellingly referred to as the Asia–Pacific War.[190]

Foreign scholarship similarly comprised diverse strands purveying contrasting messages regarding war responsibility. Of more critical hue was work like Michael Barnhart's study of the emergence of a 'total war' faction in Japan dedicated to the pursuit of geopolitical security through autarky, to be achieved by external expansion to secure markets and raw materials and domestic reform. Although their programme proved fraught with contradictions and unravelled in practice, Barnhart persuasively delineated how internal factional rivalry over the dictates of this ideological matrix impelled Japan towards war with the West.[191] Similarly Louise Young's study of Japanese imperialism in Manchuria illustrated not only how 'the maturation of modern institutions' (rather than 'incomplete modernization') 'set forth a certain logic of expansionism' and thus the deep roots of 'the turn to total empire', but also how many sectors of Japanese society were implicated in the imperial project, including the media, capitalists, political parties, voluntary associations and the intelligentsia, and not just an all-powerful military cabal.[192] On the other hand, the ongoing tendency to level 'stinging indictments' at US policy-makers for inflexibility or incompetence in their dealings with the Japanese continued to imply that Washington was primarily responsible for the 'drift toward war'. The intensified stress on diplomatic strategising on the widest international plane and the emphasis on 'the construction of coalitions, one successful, one not', could also divert attention from the drives behind Japanese policy in a potentially exculpatory manner.[193] The same could be said for the well-established relativising emplotment that construed the Japanese–American confrontation as one between two 'diametrically opposed conceptions of a global economic system', with Japan seeing herself as 'a "have-not" surrounded by richer and stronger powers', struggling to carve out a self-sufficient bloc under her hegemony, opposed by a United States determined to preserve 'a world-wide free trade system'. As before, while the effort to spread war responsibility and draw attention to western double standards embodied here might seem critical and progressive, it also flirted with a pernicious and long standing apologetic discourse in Japan.[194]

Given this interpretive heterogeneity, it would be wrong to indict international history as inherently doomed to generate stories palatable to a conservative politics, even though it demonstrably has the capacity to do so. Yet the interpretations that now stand centre stage do need to be formulated with extreme care to avoid an unhealthy complicity with the neo-nationalist sentiments flourishing in the contested terrain of Japanese collective memory. In a succinct recent essay summarising the state of the literature, Antony Best demonstrated how to walk this fine line. After summarising the internal and external determinants of Japanese expansion, Best traced how the notion of a conspiratorial design for aggressive expansion had given way to a more complex picture, emphasising the agency of diverse powers and the convoluted contingencies through which the China war degenerated into a quagmire and escalated into the Asian–Pacific conflict. On the central issue of war responsibility, he concluded that there were some affinities between Japan and its European Tripartite Pact partners, in that it was 'a highly nationalistic and militaristic state that sought redemption through expansion', and possessed an ideological vision to construct an Asian new order that would 'cement its leadership over the region'. Yet there was a crucial difference in the matter of agency; Japan 'seems to have had little control over its own destiny' and was increasingly forced to react to events:

> The impression generated ... is that Japan blundered into its wars due to a mixture of hubris and the misplaced hope that one more victory would confound its enemies and solve all of its problems. Reinforcing this relentless drive forward into uncharted territory was the knowledge that retreat would only exacerbate the internal tensions created by its too rapid modernisation. Rather than a conspiracy to wage aggressive war, therefore, Japanese policy from 1937 constituted a series of disastrous and largely short-term reactions to the waxing and waning of its international position.

Whereas Germany willed destruction on the world, 'Japan ... stumbled into the Second World War through its own ineptitude and propensity for favouring military solutions over compromise'. Crucially, however, with careful and necessary nuance Best stressed that 'to state that there was no real design to Japan's aggression' was absolutely not 'to exonerate it': 'the fact that Japan chose to react in the way it did to events in the 1930s was not accidental, for it clearly had a thirst for war and was capable of the most appalling and barbaric acts'.[195]

War origins remain an object of fierce contestation with direct political import in contemporary Japan. In October 2008 the Air Self-Defence Force Chief of Staff General Tamogami Toshio was sacked after publishing an essay defending Japan's colonialism as humane, legal and conducive to racial equality and denying that it had been an 'aggressor nation'. Tamogami asserted that the escalation of conflict in Asia was due to 'frequent acts of terrorism' by Chinese nationalists and the machinations of the Comintern; then 'Japan was ensnared in a trap that was very carefully laid by the United States', forced to take 'the first shot' rather than submit to humiliating demands that might ultimately have rendered it 'a white nation's colony'. Urging the nation to 'take back the glorious history of Japan' and reject the 'mind control' of the Tokyo tribunal view, Tamogami used his historical narrative to ground a call for relaxation of the constitutional restrictions that denied Japan the right of 'protecting itself through its own power'.[196] The outrage that greeted Tamogami's essay demonstrated how he had 'placed himself at odds with the political sense of most educated Japanese people' who overwhelmingly rejected his 'fringe ideas'. Yet his dismissal notwithstanding, significant elements in the LDP shared his 'shallow nationalistic sentiments' and his agenda of inculcating a more robust patriotism in the young and of abrogating article nine to facilitate offensive military operations.[197] The shattering historic defeat of the LDP in the general election of August 2009 has doubtless retarded the prospects of such changes, but the close connections between understandings of war origins and these fundamental issues of politics and national identity nonetheless remain. Scholarship on this subject is unavoidably entangled in these ideological thickets. Although Tamogami's narrative was a crude iteration and demonstrably factually incorrect in places, many of the tropes it employed were not unfamiliar from the mainstream international history literature.

Notes

1 N. Ike (ed.), *Japan's Decision for War: Records of the 1941 Policy Conferences* (Stanford, CA, Stanford University Press, 1967), pp. 263, 283. Japanese names in the text are given in Japanese style, with family name preceding given name; the style in footnote references follows the format of publication.

2 H. P. Bix, *Hirohito and the Making of Modern Japan* (London, Duckworth, 2001), pp. 543–51, quote at p. 550.

3 J. Dower, *Embracing Defeat: Japan in the Aftermath of World War II* (London, Penguin, 2000, pb. edn), figures at pp. 45–48.

4 Dower, *Embracing Defeat*, quotes at pp. 293, 119.

5 For diverse views on Yasukuni, see J. Breen (ed.), *Yasukuni, the War Dead and the Struggle for Japan's Past* (London, Hurst, 2007).

6 For example, E. Paris, *Long Shadows: Truth, Lies and History* (London, Bloomsbury, 2001), pp. 122–63.

7 J. Dower, 'Three narratives of our humanity', in E. T. Linenthal and T. Engelhardt (eds), *History Wars: The Enola Gay and Other Battles for the American Past* (New York, Holt, 1996), p. 63.

8 Wakamiya Y., *The Postwar Conservative View of Asia: How the Political Right has Delayed Japan's Coming to Terms with its History of Aggression in Asia* (Tokyo, LTCB International Library Foundation, 1999).

9 J. Dower, '"An aptitude for being unloved": war and memory in Japan', in O. Bartov, A. Grossmann and M. Nolan (eds), *Crimes of War: Guilt and Denial in the Twentieth Century* (New York, New Press, 2002), p. 220.

10 P. A. Seaton, *Japan's Contested War Memories: The 'Memory Rifts' in Historical Consciousness of World War II* (London, Routledge, 2007), quote at p. 7; see also another excellent recent detailed study F. Seraphim, *War Memory and Social Politics in Japan, 1945–2005* (Cambridge, MA, Harvard University Asia Center, 2006).

11 For a comparison of Japan and Germany, reflecting the recent trend to judge the former more benignly and the latter more harshly, see T. Berger, 'Dealing with difficult pasts: Japan's "history problem" from a theoretical and comparative perspective', in T. Hasegawa and K. Togo (eds), *East Asia's Haunted Present: Historical Memories and the Resurgence of Nationalism* (Westport, CT, Praeger, 2008), pp. 17–41.

12 Dower, 'Three narratives of our humanity', p. 68 (emphasis in original).

13 Dower, '"An aptitude for being unloved"', quote at p. 223.

14 Cf. the sketch of five positions presented in Seaton, *Japan's Contested War Memories*, pp. 20–24.

15 Dower, *Embracing Defeat*, p. 78.

16 'Unlike West German leaders, who found official apologies for Nazi crimes politically necessary in order to integrate Germany into the European Community, the Japanese government saw no political reason to make amends for its colonial past. Reconciliation with Communist China and war-shattered Korea was not called for under alliance agreements with the United States, which allowed Japanese leaders instead to focus single-mindedly on economic growth': Seraphim, *War Memory and Social Politics in Japan, 1945–2005*, p. 19.

17 Dower, *Embracing Defeat*, quote at p. 23; on the 'reverse course', see J. Dower, *Japan in War and Peace: Essays on History, Culture and Race* (London, Harper Collins, 1995), pp. 155–207.

18 The post-war purging of militarists in various sectors of society and imposition of structural reforms obviously indicated that blame was not entirely limited to the restricted elite cadres that were put on trial (J. W. Morley, 'Introduction: choice and consequence', in J. W. Morley (ed.), *Dilemmas of Growth in Prewar Japan* (Princeton, NJ, Princeton University Press, 1971), pp. 10–11); but these processes were far less extensive than in Germany (S. Conrad, 'Entangled memories: versions of the past in Germany and Japan, 1945–2001', *Journal of Contemporary History*, vol. 38, no. 1, 2003, p. 88).

19 J. Orr, *The Victim as Hero: Ideologies of Peace and National Identity in Postwar Japan* (Honolulu, HI, University of Hawaii Press, 2001), pp. 14–35; T. Yoshida, *The Making of the 'Rape of Nanking': History and Memory in Japan, China, and the United States* (Oxford, Oxford University Press, 2006), pp. 48–49.

20 Quoted in S. Ienaga, *The Pacific War, 1931–1945: A Critical Perspective on Japan's Role in World War II* (New York, Pantheon, 1978), p. 255.

21 C. Gluck, 'The past in the present', in A. Gordon (ed.), *Postwar Japan as History* (Berkeley, CA, University of California Press, 1993), p. 68.

22 N. Shibusawa, *America's Geisha Ally: Reimagining the Japanese Enemy* (Cambridge, MA, Harvard University Press, 2006), p. 133.

23 Seaton, *Japan's Contested War Memories*, p. 39; on progressive voices see Dower, *Embracing Defeat*, especially pp. 185–87, 233–39, 507.

24 Bix, *Hirohito and the Making of Modern Japan*, pp. 557–59. Another element in conservative discourse was to urge the whole nation to accept responsibility for the war, the intention being to dilute responsibility for apologetic ends rather than, as with the progressive trope, to heighten it.

25 Wakamiya, *The Postwar Conservative View of Asia*, pp. 24, 49–58.

26 Quoted in Ienaga, *The Pacific War, 1931–1945*, p. 252.

27 Dower, 'Three narratives of our humanity', p. 68.

28 Quoted in Shibusawa, *America's Geisha Ally*, p. 95.

29 Seaton, *Japan's Contested War Memories*, p. 45, and more broadly pp. 42–47.

30 Dower, *Embracing Defeat*, pp. 446–50.

31 B. V. A. Röling and C. F. Rüter (eds), *The Tokyo Judgement: The International Military Tribunal for the Far East (I.M.T.F.E): 29 April 1946 – 12 November 1948: Vol. 1* (Amsterdam, APA–University Press, 1977), pp. 441, 439.

32 Quoted in M. Futamura, *War Crimes Tribunals and Transitional Justice: The Tokyo Trial and the Nuremberg Legacy* (London, Routledge, 2008), p. 57.

33 See, for example, Futamura, *War Crimes Tribunals and Transitional Justice*; and R. H. Minear, *Victors' Justice: The Tokyo War Crimes Trial* (Princeton, NJ, Princeton University Press, 1971). Y. Totani, *The Tokyo War Crimes Trial: The Pursuit of Justice in the Wake of World War II* (Cambridge, MA, Harvard University Asia Center, 2008), is more sympathetic.

34 Röling and Rüter (eds), *The Tokyo Judgement: Vol. 1*, p. 478; Dower, *Embracing Defeat*, pp. 467–68.

35 Dower, *Embracing Defeat*, pp. 464–65, 474–84.

36 Futamura, *War Crimes Tribunals and Transitional Justice*, pp. 64–66; cf. Totani, *The Tokyo War Crimes Trial*, pp. 151–89. The imbalance was even more pronounced than at Nuremberg.

37 Dower, *Embracing Defeat*, p. 465.

38 Dower, *Embracing Defeat*, p. 469.

39 Shibusawa, *America's Geisha Ally*, pp. 122–33; Dower, *Embracing Defeat*, pp. 510–11.

40 Orr, *The Victim as Hero*, p. 31.

41 C. Gluck, 'The "end" of the postwar: Japan at the turn of the millennium', in J. K. Olick (ed.), *States of Memory: Continuities, Conflicts, and Transformations in National Retrospection* (Durham, NC, Duke University Press, 2003), pp. 293–94.

42 Minear, *Victors' Justice*, pp. 127–34.

43 Dower, *Embracing Defeat*, pp. 458–59, 463–64, 469–74, 629, 632–33, quotes at pp. 463, 629 (in the second instance from Pal's opinion). On the issue of self-defence, see also Minear, *Victors' Justice*, pp. 149–59.

44 Bix, *Hirohito and the Making of Modern Japan*, p. 618.

45 Quote from Gluck, 'The past in the present', p. 83.

46 Bix, *Hirohito and the Making of Modern Japan*, pp. 612–18, quote at p. 618; Dower, *Embracing Defeat*, pp. 453–54, 472, 474–76, 485–521; Futamura, *War Crimes Tribunals and Transitional Justice*, pp. 68–76.

47 Conrad, 'Entangled memories', pp. 87–91, quote at p. 90.

48 Hatano S., 'Japanese foreign policy, 1931–45: historiography', in S. Asada (ed.), *Japan and the World, 1853–1952: A Bibliographic Guide to Japanese Scholarship in Foreign Relations* (New York, Columbia University Press, 1989), p. 218.

49 Y. Koshiro, 'Japan's world and World War II', *Diplomatic History*, vol. 25, no. 3, 2001, p. 431. The intricacies of the fascism debate are beyond the scope of this chapter.

50 R. J. B. Bosworth, *Explaining Auschwitz and Hiroshima: History Writing and the Second World War, 1945–1990* (London, Routledge, 1993), p. 185.

51 Hatano, 'Japanese foreign policy, 1931–45', quote at p. 219; T. Matsuda, 'The coming of the Pacific War: Japanese perspectives', *Reviews in American History*, vol. 14, no. 4, 1986, pp. 630–33, 648, quote at p. 630.

52 L. Yoneyama, *Hiroshima Traces: Time, Space, and the Dialectics of Memory* (Berkeley, CA, University of California Press, 1999), p. 220. This assertion of coherence was not incompatible with awareness that different elements of the conflict had different characters: Hatano, 'Japanese foreign policy, 1931–45', p. 219.

53 Ienaga, *The Pacific War, 1931–1945*, p. 252.

54 Hatano, 'Japanese foreign policy, 1931–45', p. 220.

55 Quote from Ienaga, *The Pacific War, 1931–1945*, p. 252; I. Hata, 'Japanese historical writing on the origins and progress of the Pacific War', in D. C. S. Sissons (ed.), *Papers on Modern Japan 1968* (Canberra, Australian National University, 1968), pp. 85–87.

56 Hosoya C., 'Introduction: an overview', in Asada (ed.), *Japan and the World, 1853–1952*, pp. 3–5. Hosoya's view of the accessibility of materials in the 1950s may be somewhat rosy: cf. J. B. Crowley, 'Japan's military foreign policies', in J. W. Morley (ed.), *Japan's Foreign Policy, 1868–1941: A Research Guide* (New York, Columbia University Press, 1974), pp. 108–9; and Ohata T., Asada S. and Hatano S., 'Guide to documents, archives, encyclopedias, and reference works', in Asada (ed.), *Japan and the World, 1853–1952*, pp. 25–27, 32–34.

57 Hatano, 'Japanese foreign policy, 1931–45', p. 220.

58 Crowley, 'Japan's military foreign policies', pp. 112–13, quotes at p. 113. Particular approaches could be deployed to contrasting effect. Thus a progressive 'structural' argument might focus on deformed modernisation and 'emperor-system fascism' to bring the war responsibility of the Japanese ruling class into clear focus, while a more conservative one might stress external determinants such as the communist menace to abstract responsibility onto impersonal forces for apologetic purposes. Similarly, arguments that the Pacific War was inevitable owing to the aggressive impulses inherent in 'emperor-system fascism' had a quite different ideological valence to those that deemed inevitability a consequence of the clash of two morally equivalent imperialisms.

59 Quote from Gluck, 'The past in the present', p. 84.

60 A. Best, 'Imperial Japan', in R. Boyce and J. A. Maiolo (eds), *The Origins of World War Two: The Debate Continues* (London, Palgrave, 2003), p. 52.

61 R. J. C. Butow, *Tojo and the Coming of the War* (Princeton, NJ, Princeton University Press, 1961), quotes at pp. 226, 155.

62 R. Storry, *The Double Patriots: A Study of Japanese Nationalism* (London, Chatto and Windus, 1957), quotes at pp. 298–99.

63 F. C. Jones, *Japan's New Order in East Asia: Its Rise and Fall, 1937–45* (London, Oxford University Press, 1954), quotes at pp. 450–51.

64 G. Totten *et al.*, 'Japanese imperialism and aggression: reconsiderations I', *Journal of Asian Studies*, vol. 22, no. 4, 1963, p. 469.

65 J. D. Doenecke, 'Beyond polemics: an historiographical re-appraisal of American entry into World War II', *History Teacher*, vol. 12, no. 2, 1979, p. 221.

66 Crowley, 'Japan's military foreign policies', pp. 109–16.

67 L. Morton, '1937–41', in E. R. May and J. C. Thomson (eds), *American–East Asian Relations: A Survey* (Cambridge, MA, Harvard University Press, 1972), pp. 267–79.

68 Hata, 'Japanese historical writing on the origins and progress of the Pacific War', p. 89; A. Iriye, 'Japan's policies towards the United States', in Morley (ed.), *Japan's Foreign Policy, 1868–1941*, p. 458.

69 P. W. Schroeder, *The Axis Alliance and Japanese–American Relations, 1941* (Ithaca, NY, Cornell University Press, 1958), quotes at pp. 203, 201.

70 J. C. Grew, *Turbulent Era: A Diplomatic Record of Forty Years, 1904–1945*, 2 vols (Boston, MA, Houghton Mifflin, 1952).

71 Totten *et al.*, 'Japanese imperialism and aggression', p. 469. The enduring influence of Schroeder's work is demonstrated in M. Trachtenberg, *The Craft of International History: A Guide to Method* (Princeton, NJ, Princeton University Press, 2006), pp. 79–139.

72 Doenecke, 'Beyond polemics', p. 221.

73 Shibusawa, *America's Geisha Ally*, p. 288.

74 G. Hicks, *Japan's War Memories: Amnesia or Concealment?* (Aldershot, Ashgate, 1997), pp. 23, 39.

75 Seraphim, *War Memory and Social Politics in Japan, 1945–2005*, pp. 191–92.

76 Seraphim, *War Memory and Social Politics in Japan, 1945–2005*, pp. 189–90, 202–14.

77 Seaton, *Japan's Contested War Memories*, pp. 47–51, quotes at pp. 51, 48.

78 Seaton, *Japan's Contested War Memories*, p. 53.

79 Seraphim, *War Memory and Social Politics in Japan, 1945–2005*, pp. 24, 226–57, quotes at pp. 226, 24. Previously the LDP had sponsored a bill to bring the shrine back under state management, but this had been defeated.

80 Seaton, *Japan's Contested War Memories*, pp. 47, 49.

81 N. Shimazu, 'Popular representations of the past: the case of postwar Japan', *Journal of Contemporary History*, vol. 38, no. 1, 2003, pp. 112–13.

82 Hicks, *Japan's War Memories*, p. 39; Seaton, *Japan's Contested War Memories*, p. 53.

83 Seaton, *Japan's Contested War Memories*, p. 53.

84 Seraphim, *War Memory and Social Politics in Japan, 1945–2005*, pp. 205, 227. Annual prime ministerial visits to the shrine had occurred almost without interruption since 1951.

85 Seaton, *Japan's Contested War Memories*, p. 48.

86 Ueno C., 'The politics of memory: nation, individual and self', *History and Memory*, vol. 11, no. 2, 1999, p. 136; F. R. Dickinson, 'Biohazard: Unit 731 in postwar Japanese politics of national "forgetfulness"', *Japan Focus*, 12 October 2007, http://japanfocus.org/-Frederick%20R.-Dickinson/2543 (accessed 15 October 2007).

87 Yoshida, *The Making of the 'Rape of Nanking'*, pp. 81–89.

88 Seraphim, *War Memory and Social Politics in Japan, 1945–2005*, pp. 25, 230.

89 Matsuda, 'The coming of the Pacific War', pp. 633–34.

90 Conrad, 'Entangled memories', pp. 92–93.

91 Matsuda, 'The coming of the Pacific War', pp. 634–36, quote at p. 635; G. G. Iggers, Q. E. Wang and S. Mukherjee, *A Global History of Modern Historiography* (London, Pearson Longman, 2008), pp. 325–27, quote at p. 326.

92 Iggers, Wang and Mukherjee, *A Global History of Modern Historiography*, pp. 325–26, 331–33. Though note the claim from 1978 that 'most historians of all generations remain squarely in the tradition of Japanese Marxist historiography': C. Gluck, 'The people in history: recent trends in Japanese historiography', *Journal of Asian Studies*, vol. 38, no. 1, 1978, p. 26.

93 Koshiro, 'Japan's world and World War II', p. 434.

94 Hosoya, 'Introduction', pp. 8–14.

95 Koshiro, 'Japan's world and World War II', p. 432.

96 Seaton, *Japan's Contested War Memories*, pp. 45–46.

97 Hicks, *Japan's War Memories*, pp. 29–30; Seraphim, *War Memory and Social Politics in Japan, 1945–2005*, pp. 196–97.

98 Akashi Y., 'Japan and "Asia for Asians"', in H. Wray and H. Conroy (eds), *Japan Examined: Perspectives on Modern Japanese History* (Honolulu, HI, University of Hawaii Press, 1983), pp. 323–30, quotes at pp. 323, 329.

99 Morley, 'Introduction', pp. 15–17. In a further irony, in the shadow of Vietnam, progressive calls for Japanese solidarity with anti-American Asian independence movements often uncannily echoed the wartime rhetoric of 'Asia for Asians': Koshiro, 'Japan's world and World War II', pp. 433–34.

100 Hatano, 'Japanese foreign policy, 1931–45', p. 223.

101 Quote from A. Iriye, 'Japan's foreign policies between world wars: sources and interpretations', in E. M. Robertson (ed.), *The Origins of the Second World War: Historical Interpretations* (London, Macmillan, 1971), p. 262.

102 In terms of access to documents held by the defence agency, the series was evidence of 'some degree of successful co-operation between the military "old boys" and academic historians': Hata, 'Japanese historical writing on the origins and progress of the Pacific War', p. 87.

103 Hosoya, 'Introduction', p. 5. The English language volumes, in chronological order of contents, are J. W. Morley (ed.), *Japan Erupts: The London Naval Conference and the Manchurian Incident, 1928–1932* (New York, Columbia University Press, 1984); J. W. Morley (ed.), *The China Quagmire: Japan's Expansion on the Asian Continent, 1933–1941* (New York, Columbia University Press, 1983); J. W. Morley (ed.), *Deterrent Diplomacy: Japan, Germany, and the USSR, 1935–1940* (New York, Columbia University Press, 1976); J. W. Morley (ed.), *The Fateful Choice: Japan's Advance into Southeast Asia, 1939–1941* (New York, Columbia University Press, 1980); J. W. Morley (ed.), *The Final Confrontation: Japan's Negotiations with the United States, 1941* (New York, Columbia University Press, 1994).

104 A. Iriye, 'Japanese imperialism and aggression: reconsiderations II', in Robertson (ed.), *The Origins of the Second World War*, pp. 247–48.

105 Quoted in Hatano, 'Japanese foreign policy, 1931–45', p. 224; D. A. Titus, 'Introduction', in Morley (ed.), *The Final Confrontation*, p. xxxiv.

106 Quote from M. B. Jansen, 'The Manchurian incident, 1931: introduction', in Morley (ed.) *Japan Erupts*, p. 122. There are disagreements in the historiographical literature about the interpretive import of this collection.

107 Iriye, 'Japanese imperialism and aggression', pp. 256–57.

108 Hata, 'Japanese historical writing on the origins and progress of the Pacific War', p. 88; Hatano, 'Japanese foreign policy, 1931–45', p. 225.

109 Ienaga, *The Pacific War, 1931–1945*, p. 253, in the first instance quoting Kamikawa Hikomatsu.

110 Quotes from A. Iriye, 'The extension of hostilities, 1931–32: introduction', in Morley (ed.), *Japan Erupts*, pp. 234–35. Iriye further notes that according to Shimada Toshihiko there was 'an almost total absence of ideology as a driving force behind military action', with the army apparently believing that their acts were simply 'logical expressions of a rational strategy, designed to carry out what to them was a legitimate goal of national policy' (p. 238).

111 L. Young, 'Japan at war: history-writing on the crisis of the 1930s', in G. Martel (ed.), *The Origins of the Second World War Reconsidered: A. J. P. Taylor and the Historians* (London, Routledge, 1999, 2nd edn), p. 172.

112 Matsuda, 'The coming of the Pacific War', pp. 636–38. Compare Bosworth's characterisation of the basic plot of convicted Class A war criminal and former Foreign Minister Shigemitsu Mamoru's memoirs, in which all blame is cast on 'the militarists, bad luck and the encirclement of Japan': *Explaining Auschwitz and Hiroshima*, p. 247.

113 Hatano, 'Japanese foreign policy, 1931–45', p. 225; see also Young, 'Japan at war', pp. 165–72.

114 Seki H., 'The Manchurian incident, 1931', in Morley (ed.), *Japan Erupts*, p. 230.

115 Titus, 'Introduction', p. xxii (but see pp. xix–xxiii for a wider critical discussion of the progressive position).

116 Matsuda, 'The coming of the Pacific War', p. 638.

117 Quote from D. Lu, 'The Marco Polo Bridge incident, 1937: introduction', in Morley (ed.), *The China Quagmire*, p. 236; Matsuda, 'The coming of the Pacific War', pp. 637–38.

118 Titus, 'Introduction', pp. xx–xxxv, quotes at p. xxxiv. Although rejecting Tsunoda's apologetics, Titus agrees that the *status quo* western powers do bear some responsibility for failing to grant Japan equality as a great power (pp. xxxv–xxxviii).

119 Koshiro, 'Japan's world and World War II', p. 431.

120 R. A. Scalapino, 'Southern advance: introduction', in Morley (ed.), *The Fateful Choice*, p. 118.

121 Hatano S. and Asada S., 'From the Sino-Japanese War to the Pacific War', in Asada (ed.), *Japan and the World, 1853–1952*, p. 325.

122 N. D. Kristof, 'Japan's plans for a museum on war mired in controversy', *New York Times*, 21 May 1995, http://query.nytimes.com/gst/fullpage.html?res=990CEFDE1530F932A15 756C0A963958260& partner = rssnyt& emc = rss (accessed 23 May 2008).

123 On empirical matters see Iriye, 'Japanese imperialism and aggression', pp. 262–71; Ohata, Asada and Hatano, 'Guide to documents, archives, encyclopedias, and reference works', pp. 21–69; and Hatano S. and Asada S. 'Notes on basic sources, 1931–45', in Asada (ed.), *Japan and the World, 1853–1952*, pp. 240–61.

124 This discussion is based primarily on the contributions to Asada (ed.), *Japan and the World, 1853–1952*.

125 Hatano and Asada, 'From the Sino-Japanese War to the Pacific War'', p. 309.

126 Hatano and Asada, 'From the Sino-Japanese War to the Pacific War'', pp. 319–20; Hatano, 'Japanese foreign policy, 1931–45', p. 226.

127 For his life and work, see Ienaga S., *Japan's Past, Japan's Future: One Historian's Odyssey* (Lanham, MD, Rowman and Littlefield, 2001).

128 Ienaga, *The Pacific War, 1931–1945*, quotes at pp. xi, 245, xv, 3, 12, 33, 46–47, 63, 203, 84, 70, 135, 129, 140. Ienaga entitled his book as he did somewhat reluctantly, on the grounds that the Japanese public was unreceptive to the usage 'Fifteen-Year War' (p. xiii).

129 R. H. Minear, 'Translator's introduction', in Ienaga, *Japan's Past, Japan's Future*, p. 8.

130 Ienaga, *The Pacific War, 1931–1945*, quote at p. 180.

131 Doenecke, 'Beyond polemics', p. 227.

132 D. Bergamini; *Japan's Imperial Conspiracy* (London, Heinemann, 1971); S. E. Pelz, *Race to Pearl Harbor: The Failure of the Second London Naval Conference and the Onset of World War II* (Cambridge, MA, Harvard University Press, 1974), quote at p. 5.

133 J. B. Crowley, *Japan's Quest for Autonomy: National Security and Foreign Policy, 1930–1938* (Princeton, NJ, Princeton University Press, 1966), quotes at pp. 394, xv, 395.

134 Doenecke, 'Beyond polemics', p. 222, quoting J. H. Boyle.

135 Young, 'Japan at war', pp. 172–73.

136 Matsuda, 'The coming of the Pacific War', pp. 640–41.

137 Doenecke, 'Beyond polemics', pp. 220–27; M. A. Barnhart, 'The origins of the Second World War in Asia and the Pacific: synthesis impossible?', in M. J. Hogan (ed.), *Paths to Power: The Historiography of American Foreign Relations to 1941* (Cambridge, Cambridge University Press, 2000), pp. 268–78.

138 D. Borg and S. Okamoto (eds), *Pearl Harbor as History: Japanese–American Relations, 1931–1941* (New York, Columbia University Press, 1973). For critical commentary, see Hatano, 'Japanese foreign policy, 1931–45', pp. 226–29; Hatano and Asada, 'From the Sino-Japanese War to the Pacific War'', pp. 318–20; and Matsuda, 'The coming of the Pacific War', pp. 641–46.

139 Best, 'Imperial Japan', p. 57.

140 'Introduction', in Borg and Okamato (eds), *Pearl Harbor as History*, p. xiv.

141 I. Nish (ed.), *Anglo-Japanese Alienation, 1919–1952: Papers of the Anglo-Japanese Conference on the History of the Second World War* (Cambridge, Cambridge University Press, 1982). For critical commentary, see Barnhart, 'The origins of the Second World War in Asia and the Pacific', pp. 277–78; and Hatano and Asada, 'From the Sino-Japanese War to the Pacific War', pp. 320–22. In two separate contributions, Hosoya Chihiro demonstrated some

ambivalence on the issue of inevitability: compare 'Britain and the United States in Japan's view of the international system, 1937–41', pp. 73–74 and 'Some reflections on the conference from the Japanese side', p. 284, in Nish (ed.), *Anglo-Japanese Alienation, 1919–1952*.

142 Hosoya, 'Some reflections on the conference from the Japanese side', p. 284.

143 First published in Japanese, the English edition is A. Iriye, *Power and Culture: The Japanese–American War, 1941–1945* (Cambridge, MA, Harvard University Press, 1981), quotes at pp. 1, 265. For the wider issues, see C. Gluck, 'House of mirrors: American history-writing on Japan', in A. Molho and G. S. Wood (eds), *Imagined Histories: American Historians Interpret the Past* (Princeton, NJ, Princeton University Press, 1998), pp. 434–54.

144 M. R. Peattie, *Ishiwara Kanji and Japan's Confrontation with the West* (Princeton, NJ, Princeton University Press, 1975), p. vii.

145 Morton, '1937–41', pp. 284–85.

146 Minear, *Victors' Justice*, especially pp. x–xiv, 177–79.

147 Peattie, *Ishiwara Kanji and Japan's Confrontation with the West*, p. 370.

148 Iriye, *Power and Culture*, pp. 1–35, quotes at p. 13.

149 Admittedly, the criteria being brought to bear in this chapter and the previous one make it difficult for American historians to escape censure, since if they place blame for the Pacific War on Japan they are criticised for reinscribing American exceptionalism whereas if they blame the United States they are charged with incipient endorsement of Japanese nationalist apologetics. Further exploration of such issues through more properly transnational methodologies would undoubtedly prove fruitful.

150 N. Onishi, 'Departing Japanese leader shook up politics as usual', *New York Times*, 19 September 2006, http://www.nytimes.com/2006/09/19/world/asia/19koizumi.html?_r=1&oref=slogin (accessed 15 June 2008).

151 Conrad, 'Entangled memories', pp. 95–96, quote at p. 95.

152 Seaton, *Japan's Contested War Memories*, pp. 54–55.

153 S. M. Jager and R. Mitter, 'Introduction: re-envisioning Asia, past and present', in S. M. Jager and R. Mitter (eds), *Ruptured Histories: War, Memory, and the Post-Cold War in Asia* (Cambridge, MA, Harvard University Press, 2007), pp. 1–14.

154 Seaton, *Japan's Contested War Memories*, pp. 61–62, quote at p. 61.

155 Conrad, 'Entangled memories', p. 94.

156 Seraphim, *War Memory and Social Politics in Japan, 1945–2005*, p. 26.

157 Seaton, *Japan's Contested War Memories*, p. 53; Seraphim, *War Memory and Social Politics in Japan, 1945–2005*, p. 274.

158 C. Gluck, 'Operations of memory: "comfort women" and the world', in Jager and Mitter (eds), *Ruptured Histories*, pp. 47–77.

159 Seraphim, *War Memory and Social Politics in Japan, 1945–2005*, pp. 263–70.

160 Gluck, 'Operations of memory'; F. Seraphim, 'Relocating war memory at century's end: Japan's postwar responsibility and global public culture', in Jager and Mitter (eds), *Ruptured Histories*, pp. 15–46.

161 Gluck, 'Operations of memory', pp. 55–56; Futamura, *War Crimes Tribunals and Transitional Justice*, p. 140; Dower, '"An aptitude for being unloved"', p. 241; Seaton, *Japan's Contested War Memories*, p. 61.

162 Seraphim, *War Memory and Social Politics in Japan, 1945–2005*, pp. 306–09.

163 G. McCormack, 'The Japanese movement to "correct" history', in L. Hein and M. Selden (eds), *Censoring History: Citizenship and Memory in Japan, Germany, and the United States* (Armonk, NY, M. E. Sharpe, 2000), pp. 53–73.

164 Seaton, *Japan's Contested War Memories*, p. 59.

165 Yoshida, *The Making of the 'Rape of Nanking'*, pp. 89–101, 129–53.

166 C. Schneider, 'The Japanese history textbook controversy in East Asian perspective', *Annals of the American Academy of Political and Social Science*, no. 617, 2008, pp. 107–22. Seaton notes that this text was only actually adopted in a minute proportion of Japanese

schools, but that the balance of content in some other textbooks did shift to the right in response to nationalist agitation (*Japan's Contested War Memories*, pp. 59, 100–102, 144–47).

167 B. Kushner, 'Nationality and nostalgia: the manipulation of memory in Japan, Taiwan, and China since 1990', *International History Review*, vol. 29, no. 4, 2007, pp. 793–820.

168 R. B. Jenas, 'Victims or victimizers? Museums, textbooks, and the war debate in contemporary Japan', *Journal of Military History*, vol. 69, no. 1, 2005, pp. 149–95.

169 Seraphim, *War Memory and Social Politics in Japan, 1945–2005*, pp. 270–86, quotes at pp. 275, 278, 284; Seaton, *Japan's Contested War Memories*, pp. 87–92.

170 Wakamiya, *The Postwar Conservative View of Asia*, pp. 9–29.

171 Seaton, *Japan's Contested War Memories*, pp. 65–70, 92–96, quote at p. 95. A fund was established in 1995 to compensate former 'comfort women', but this was largely provided by private donations and was thus criticised as embodying state refusal to admit legal responsibility.

172 A. Dudden and K. Mizoguchi, 'Abe's violent denial: Japan's prime minister and the "comfort women"', *Japan Focus*, 2 March 2007, http://japanfocus.org/-K-MIZOGUCHI/2368 (accessed 5 March 2007).

173 Seaton elucidates these, even as he underlines that most Japanese also regard the official stance as unsatisfactory: *Japan's Contested War Memories*, pp. 65–106.

174 A. Dudden, 'Apologizing for the past between Japan and Korea', in M. P. Friedman and P. Kenney (eds), *Partisan Histories: The Past in Contemporary Global Politics* (New York, Palgrave, 2005), pp. 39–54, quote at p. 41.

175 Seraphim, *War Memory and Social Politics in Japan, 1945–2005*, pp. 284–86, quote at p. 286 (emphases in original).

176 Shimamura Y., Sakurai S. and Okuno S., quoted in Wakamiya, *The Postwar Conservative View of Asia*, pp. 12–13. Similar claims appear in the *New History Textbook* published by the 'liberal historic' Japanese Society for History Textbook Reform; a partial translation of the 2005 edition is available on the society's website at http://www.tsukurukai.com/05_rekisi_text/rekishi_English/English.pdf (accessed 6 June 2009).

177 Nitta H., 'And why shouldn't the Japanese prime minister worship at Yasukuni? A personal view', in Breen (ed.), *Yasukuni, the War Dead and the Struggle for Japan's Past*, pp. 141–42.

178 Takahashi T., 'Legacies of empire: the Yasukuni shrine controversy', in Breen (ed.), *Yasukuni, the War Dead and the Struggle for Japan's Past*, pp. 114–16.

179 T. Morris-Suzuki, 'Who is responsible? The Yomiuri project and the enduring legacy of the Pacific War', *Japan Focus*, 19 June 2007, http://www.japanfocus.org/-Tessa-Morris_Suzuki/2455 (accessed 25 June 2007).

180 J. E. Auer (ed.), *Who Was Responsible? From Marco Polo Bridge to Pearl Harbor* (Tokyo, Yomiuri Shimbun, 2006), quotes at pp. 287, 377. The concept of Asian co-prosperity is said to have 'focused too much on ideology' (p. 271).

181 Morris-Suzuki, 'Who is responsible?'.

182 Koshiro, 'Japan's world and World War II', p. 435, and for a wider discussion pp. 434–41.

183 A. Best, 'Economic appeasement or economic nationalism? A political perspective on the British empire, Japan, and the rise of intra-Asia trade, 1933–37', *Journal of Imperial and Commonwealth History*, vol. 30, no. 2, 2002, p. 77.

184 Seaton, *Japan's Contested War Memories*, p. 55.

185 D. McNeill, 'Japan's history wars and popular consciousness', *Japan Focus*, 27 April 2007, http://www.japanfocus.org/-David-McNeill/2413 (accessed 1 May 2007). I. Hata, 'Continental expansion, 1905–41', in P. Duus (ed.), *The Cambridge History of Japan: Vol. 6: The Twentieth Century* (Cambridge, Cambridge University Press, 1988), pp. 271–314 offers an earlier, more balanced, mainstream analysis.

186 S. Kitaoka, 'Diplomacy and the military in Showa Japan', in C. Gluck and S. R. Graubard (eds), *Showa: The Japan of Hirohito* (New York, Norton, 1992), p. 168.

187 Fujiwara A., 'The road to Pearl Harbor', in H. Conroy and H. Wray (eds), *Pearl Harbor Reexamined: Prologue to the Pacific War* (Honolulu, HI, University of Hawaii Press, 1990), p. 151.
188 This is surveyed and summarised in H. P. Bix, 'War responsibility and historical memory: Hirohito's apparition', *Japan Focus*, 6 May 2008, http://www.japanfocus.org/-Herbert_P-Bix/ 2741 (accessed 14 May 2008).
189 N. Kawamura, 'Emperor Hirohito and Japan's decision to go to war with the United States: reexamined', *Diplomatic History*, vol. 31, no. 1, 2007, pp. 51–79, quote at p. 54.
190 For example, Kibata Y., 'Anglo-Japanese relations from the Manchurian Incident to Pearl Harbor: missed opportunities?', in I. Nish and Y. Kibata (eds), *The History of Anglo-Japanese Relations, 1600–2000: Vol. II: The Political-Diplomatic Dimension, 1931–2000* (London, Macmillan, 2000), pp. 1–25. For a discussion of Japanese scholarship since 1980, see Aruga T., 'Japanese scholarship in the history of U.S.–East Asian relations', in W. I. Cohen (ed.), *Pacific Passage: The Study of American–East Asia Relations on the Eve of the Twenty-First Century* (New York, Columbia University Press, 1996), pp. 36–87.
191 M. A. Barnhart, *Japan Prepares for Total War: The Search for Economic Security, 1919–1941* (Ithaca, NY, Cornell University Press, 1987).
192 L. Young, *Japan's Total Empire: Manchuria and the Culture of Wartime Imperialism* (Berkeley, CA, University of California Press, 1999, pb. edn), quotes at p. 435. See also an important recent study of the 'ideological' bases of Japanese expansion, E. Hotta, *Pan-Asianism and Japan's War, 1931–1945* (London, Palgrave, 2007).
193 Barnhart, 'The origins of the Second World War in Asia and the Pacific', pp. 280–95, quotes at pp. 285, 295. Cf., for example, the critique of American 'hardliners' in Hosoya C., 'Miscalculation in deterrent policy: U.S.–Japanese relations, 1938–41', in Conroy and Wray (eds), *Pearl Harbor Reexamined*, pp. 51–64.
194 W. Rahn, 'Japan's road to war', in Militärgeschichtliches Forschungsamt (ed.), *Germany and the Second World War: Vol. VI: The Global War* (Oxford, Oxford University Press, 2001), p. 241.
195 Best, 'Imperial Japan', pp. 52–69, quotes at p. 66.
196 Tamogami T., 'Was Japan an aggressor nation?', available at http://www.apa.co.jp/ book_report/images/2008jyusyou_saiyuusyu_english.pdf (accessed 10 November 2008).
197 H. P. Bix, 'Tamogami's world: Japan's top soldier reignites conflict over the past', *Japan Focus*, 9 November 2008, http://www.japanfocus.org/-Herbert_P – Bix/2945 (accessed 10 November 2008).

Conclusion

History, identity, memory

> Impartiality is either a delusion of the simple-minded, a banner of the opportunist, or the boast of the dishonest.
>
> Gaetano Salvemini[1]

The seventieth anniversary of the German invasion of Poland in September 1939 was marked by a considerable flurry of scholarly publications, as the historiography of the origins of the war marched on.[2] It was also the object of formal commemorations, such as the elaborate day of ceremonies on 1 September attended by dignitaries from 20 former combatant countries in Gdansk, where the first German shells fell. A simultaneous outbreak of historical and political polemic testified to the enduring significance of the war within various national narratives of identity and memory. Polish President Lech Kaczynski spoke of how resistance to aggression was proof of his nation's 'unbreakable spirit', and lauded the glorious heroes who had 'fought in World War Two against German Nazism, and against Bolshevik totalitarianism'. This attempt to posit an equivalence between Germany and the Soviet Union as joint aggressors was furiously denounced by Moscow, where officials pointed out that Poland had itself collaborated with the Nazis in destroying Czechoslovakia prior to the Nazi–Soviet pact. The Russian government sanctioned the release of fresh documents on pre-war diplomacy which implicitly defended the pact as a product of necessity and a response to Anglo-French efforts to turn Hitler's aggression eastwards. Vladimir Putin did apologise to the Poles for this 'morally unacceptable' document, but underlined that many other states had indulged in similar appeasement during the 1930s and reaffirmed the pre-eminent Soviet contribution to the liberation of Europe.[3] The apparent rawness of these seventy-year-old wounds underlined the wisdom of one commentator's rumination that 'this is one war that has not gone away'.[4]

Against the backdrop of this ongoing contestation over the meaning and significance of the war, this book has explored how international history writing on its origins has been imbricated with wider discourses of national identity and collective memory. The chapters have essayed necessarily partial readings, intended to be suggestive rather than definitive. Moreover, the structure adopted means that the book perhaps offers a series of interlinked parallel case studies rather than a systematically comparative treatment. Nonetheless, similarities between cases are readily apparent. It is instructive, for example, to compare the historicisation of the origins of the war in the three defeated Axis powers; in each case, without necessarily (for the most part) indulging in extreme apologetics, international historians devised explanations of their nation's pre-war aggression that were less than entirely candid and thereby contributed to the reconstruction of broadly conservative senses of national identity. The cases of Britain and France are notable for the cognate manner in which, despite the diverse nuances of trajectory and structure in their historiographical fields, coming to terms with decline from imperial grandeur shaped both broad collective memory and the specific historicisation of the road to war. In contrast, in the Soviet Union/Russia and the United States – and again allowing for significant variations in timing and intensity – the origins of the war have been narrated in wider mnemonic contexts that were markedly similar in so far as the experience of contributing to the victory over fascism was instrumentalised to reinscribe the virtue of broader national ideological projects.

Thinking across the cases about the structural features of these historiographical debates also proves fruitful. Of course, any meaningful comparison entails the identification of differences as much as similarities, and the former are significant in the sense that varying numbers of interpretive options have been in contestation across time in different countries. (Although it can be debated how far competing interpretations actually constituted discrete viewpoints as opposed to positions on an interpretive spectrum.) A more striking commonality, however, is evident in the manner in which the various narrative options constituting the scholarly fields often originated in the political and cultural debates of the 1930s and 1940s.[5] Granted, they were initially often only visible in embryo and consequently acquired substantial fresh nuances, complexities and depth as they were iterated through the decades; but if they are viewed as story forms what is striking is how little interpretive innovation has occurred. There was often, indeed, remarkable continuity at this level even through the transition from contemporary commentary to mature, archive-based scholarship in the 1960s and 1970s. Although the advent of disciplined international history did lead to the significant thickening of interpretations and often contributed to one competing interpretation supplanting another as dominant, the basic parameters of the interpretive field were usually not fundamentally transformed. (Where theoretical resources from beyond the sub-discipline were brought into play, as with 'New Left' scholarship in the United States, more dramatic innovation was sometimes possible; though even in that case there was significant underlying continuity around the problematic of exceptionalism.) This does suggest that it is rather problematic to posit too sharp a distinction – as many practitioners are wont to do – between the 'para-historical' realm of political polemic and the 'realities of the historical record'.[6]

Previous commentators on, for example, the historiography of British appeasement have lamented the inability of historians to escape from familiar tramlines of debate, but without connecting the case to others or drawing out its potential theoretical implications.[7] Writing about quite different controversies in the historiography of pre-Soviet Russia, however, Kevin Platt has suggested that scholars were:

> heir to a tradition of storytelling about [historical actors] – a tradition which has its origins in the political milieu of the events themselves and in the works of early commentators who are generally implicated in this milieu. For later historians, this inherited tradition presents a set of options for narration and interpretation which come already equipped with specific political implications. The historian may expand upon these options in various ways, but the overall map of possibilities remains linked together as a part of an established cultural system devoted to representation of the national past ... I want to emphasize that I am not arguing for the impossibility of innovation in historical interpretation. Yet I do think that innovation in telling a given story is contingent upon the versions of that story that have already been told: each new interpretationmust 'fit' into a pre-existent political and narrative universe.[8]

The cases explored here do not entirely bear out Platt's observations; the political implications of particular narrative options, for example, can shift as they are deployed or consumed in different contexts. Nonetheless, the basic insight about how historians operate within a prefigured field and deploy rather than generate emplotments is sound.

In many instances, moreover, the narratives in play within contemporary political discourse were themselves but iterations of more generic emplotments already in circulation within particular cultures. Obvious examples include the 'triumph over alien forces' schematic narrative template in Russia, the 'infamy' and 'conspiracy' narratives in the United States and the 'decadence' emplotment in the French Third Republic. By the same token, the emplotments that became attached to the origins of the war and the tropes that recurred in historical explanations in the various defeated states – involving, for example, the scapegoating and damning dismissal of former leaders, notions of parenthesis and rebirth, or moral victory – often matched those identified by Wolfgang Schivelbusch as the dominant modes of rationalisation in defeated states *per se*.[9] Even more broadly, the literature on nationalism has of course identified particular historiographical stereotypes that commonly figure in the stories nations in general tell themselves – myths of suffering and redemption, decline and rebirth, and dark ages followed by golden ages – which can also be found in some of the cases considered here.[10] Although this treatment has not attempted a fully-fledged tropological analysis *à la* Hayden White, the various interpretations prevalent within the international history literatures could doubtless also be read as historiographical expressions of even more basic story forms. It would be too much to claim that this way of thinking about the tales that international historians tell definitively supports a Whitean epistemological position, but it surely suggests that an historiographical discourse focusing overwhelmingly on empirical issues somewhat misconstrues the nature of history writing as cultural intervention.

A related issue thrown up across numerous cases is the role of foreign – as opposed to indigenous – historians in writing about particular national roads to war. In certain instances, notably France and Italy, foreign historians appear to have pioneered revisionist approaches or to have offered a distinctively contrasting perspective in ways that might suggest they were helpfully detached from the political and mnemonic passions conditioning indigenous scholarship. This point is difficult to push too far, however, since while it might hold as a generalisation about broad propensities, on closer inspection it transpires that, to take the case of France, not all foreign historians were revisionists and not all revisionists were foreign. Indeed, foreign historians are perhaps as likely to be the prisoners of derogatory stereotypes of another nation as in a position of privileged objectivity. Moreover, in some cases, such as that of the Soviet Union, foreign historians were divided into sharply contrasting schools along more obviously (Cold War) ideological lines, illustrating how national identity is just one of the variables of positioning that determines historians' perspectives. In other instances, foreign historians were led by their own methodological predilections to produce interpretations that chimed with the dominant view of indigenous historians; this was so, for example, in the case of British appeasement with the attachment to social science approaches of German structural revisionists of the 1970s and 1980s. Perhaps the most interesting case here is that of Japan, where mainstream international historians in Japan and the United States were long driven by different and multiple indigenous imperatives to produce compatible relativising interpretations of Japan's responsibility for the Pacific War; thus both participated in a bi-national project of post-war reconciliation. Often, foreign historians seem to form a coherent transnational community with their indigenous counterparts, sharing ideas, research findings and assumptions, and often fully conversant with their national political, cultural and mnemonic debates. More to the point, the two may operate within the same narrative universe, trammelled by the same framework of politically charged possibilities in constructing their arguments.[11]

One core purpose underpinning the insertion of this international history scholarship onto the terrain of memory was to thicken our understanding of the diverse ways in which the war was negotiated and instrumentalised across post-war decades. Admittedly, the case studies testify that the origins of the war was seldom the most high profile or radioactive topic in national collective memory; rather, it was often overshadowed by the traumatic dramas and atrocious crimes of the war period itself, and is perhaps increasingly so in a contemporary age marked by heightened sensitivity to human rights, restitution and the Holocaust. Nonetheless, this issue and this historiography did constitute important and distinct filaments in collective memory. Given the myriad diverse specificities of each case, it would be imprudent to make any broad cross-national generalisations about the shape and trajectory of these debates, though it is notable how frequently the 1960s and 1970s witnessed the conjuncture of critical shifts in collective memory, turbulent crises in dominant perceptions of national identity and revisionist turns in writing on the origins of the war. By the same token, in most cases, the incorporation of international history into collective memory tends to confirm rather than decisively transform our existing sense of the various phases in broad national reckonings with the past. It also proves compatible with the recent thrust of scholarship in levelling, for example, a more critical judgement on the frankness of memory in Germany and Italy, and in advancing a more finely drawn picture of the complex contestation over the wartime past in Japan. That said, it does also sometimes – as with Britain and to a lesser extent France – suggest important new nuances about the timing and substance of recognised phases, or indicate that some strands of memory were not entirely subordinated to them but followed their own rhythm. Moreover, with the outlier case of the United States, it contributes to the as yet inchoate work of mapping a general trajectory at all. Finally, even where it simply demon-strates the existence of yet one more cultural conduit for contestation, this is by no means insignificant in enhancing our sense of the breadth and depth of collective memory, especially since fundamental and urgent issues of national identity and political orientation have frequently been and remain at stake therein.

The other core ambition here was to add an extra dimension to historio-graphical debates about the origins of the war by demonstrating the need to take a range of cultural and ideological factors much more seriously within them. Repeatedly across numerous cases, and especially those of Germany, Italy and Japan, international history has appeared as a rather conservative discourse, often aligned with evasive apologetics and ranged against the struc-tural critiques of progressive historians. The case can certainly be made that there was something about the particular conjunctures of professional sociol-ogy, personal positioning and intellectual preference in these cases that led these historians into an unfortunate intimacy with nationalist discourse. His-toricist traditions, a predilection for mimetic and empathetic reconstruction of policy-making discourse, and a focus on the narrow minutiae of diplomacy and decision-making that excluded larger issues of ideological motivation, and the commission of criminal atrocities, might all be adduced here. This might seem to lend credence to the charges often levelled against the sub-discipline that it peddles 'court history', unwilling to appraise critically the 'great men who make decisions', and is inherently unsuited to the propaga-tion of radical messages.[12] Yet this argument too cannot be pushed too far. In the case of Italy, for example, foreign historians plying precisely the same methodologies as De Felicean apologists produced interpretations purveying a staunchly anti-Fascist message. Indeed, far from constantly figuring as a conservative pole in a wider mnemonic spectrum, international history just as often – witness the case of the more recent historiography in France – manifested considerable internal heterogeneity and reproduced within itself a full spectrum of positions with diverse political entailments.

In any event, whether international history always evinces a particular political valence is not the key point at issue here; delineating the intertwining of history, identity and memory is rather intended to raise awareness of the fact that it always has *some kind* of political valence. Against a dominant tendency to prioritise the role of empirical factors in precipitating interpretive shifts, these cases have demonstrated that often revisionist turns began in advance of major archival releases and in any event essentially entailed the filling out of narrative options that were already in existence; moreover, given bodies of documents have repeatedly proved susceptible to interpretation in starkly contrasting and even contradictory ways. So while the empirical dimension to scholarly production is, of course, not negligible, due attention must also be paid to the role of shifting discourses of identity and memory in precipitating explanatory step changes and rendering alternative narratives newly plausible within particular interpretive communities. The case studies strongly suggest that neither scrupulous objectivity, nor the conventions and procedures of a professional discipline, nor formidable arrays of archival sources, can provide any sort of safeguard against implication in ideological contestation. The relationships between international history and wider discourses of national identity and collective memory have certainly differed from case to case. In some instances, such as within the Soviet Union and in France during the heyday of decadence, international history was almost totally in thrall to them. Sometimes, as with the De Feliceans in Italy, international historians have figured as active propagators of interpretations that also buttressed wider narratives of the wartime past and contemporary sectional political identities. At others, as with much of the scholarship in the United States, it was more the case that international history was subtly underpinned by unacknowledged normative assumptions about the status of the war and visions of national identity. At yet others, this scholarship simply provided a vocabulary and vehicle for meditation and contestation, as choices made about subject matter, framing and emplotment carried political implications in their wider mnemonic context. Regardless of these variations, however, the fact of mutual entwinement – and consequently of political inspirations and entailments – was a constant.

The main claim to flow from this recognition of the ideological nature of international history representation is simply that interrogation of that politics ought to occupy a much more prominent place in our historiographical discourse. It would be disingenuous, however, to pretend that this treatment has not also brought to bear more specific normative criteria within the discussions of individual historiographies. A marked authorial preference for certain kinds of politics over others, and for interpretations that embody scepticism towards nationalist projects and candid engagement with responsibility for past crimes and aggression, should have become manifest. To an extent, the narratives discussed here are constructed through the differential combining of a range of binarised interpretive options: structure versus agency; ideology versus *realpolitik*/national traditions; continuity versus discontinuity; determinism versus contingency; and conspiracy versus systemic failure. (Indeed, revisionist turns often seem to embody less the transformation of understanding through new empirical discoveries than a simple methodological or interpretive shift in preferences from amongst these terms.) Although the cases discussed here offer much food for thought on the point, it is not possible to generalise about the political valence of the two sides of these binaries; after all in the German case continuity arguments were generally coded as frank and critical while in the Italian context they are exculpatory, and in the Japanese case 'structural' arguments could be found at both ends of the political spectrum. Moreover, it sometimes appears to be the case – for example, with the German 'intentionalist'–'functionalist' debate – that none of the interpretive options in play have been entirely free of dubious or problematic implications. Such cases perhaps suggest the need to reconfigure how international history explains the world through the importation of theoretical resources that can assist in transcending these binaries. The form of historical representation, after all, is itself a highly ideological matter.[13]

This treatment also aspired to provide material for further reflection on the nature of historiographical change and, indeed, of history, *per se*. Here it is probably wise not to be too ambitious, since there is an obvious risk of circular argument in using a set of theoretical ideas to ground an exercise in critical historiography and then proclaiming that it 'proves' the validity of those ideas. By the same token, just as historiographical works by 'practical realists' have been appropriated for this treatment, so it seems probable that its argument about the ideological nature of historical representation could be incorporated in dilute form into a 'practical realist' world view without great difficulty. Yet the findings of these case studies nonetheless do suggest that certain powerful and prevalent understandings of how historiographical change happens are deficient, even misleading. Without denigrating the crucial empirical dimensions of historical practice, this treatment suggests that the role of 'new data' or 'disconfirming evidence' in precipitating interpretive shifts is far less important than internal disciplinary factors and changes in external context.[14] This is not necessarily to attribute a simple causative power to discourses of identity and memory, or to see them as the direct progenitors of historical interpretations. Rather, history, identity and memory are bound up together in a shifting discursive relationship, constantly feeding off and speaking to each other. The realisation that 'collective memory and history writing cannot easily be delineated from one another' offers a corrective to historians' self-congratulatory delusion that disciplined scholarship necessarily functions to counteract myth.[15] Such a characterisation also, of course, chimes with the critical ideas about history and theory adumbrated in the introduction to this book.

If these contentions about the politics of international history representation hold good, then a reflexive recalibration of the terms of our historiographical discussions is certainly warranted. If the documentary record is capable of supporting a range of contrasting interpretations, and if those interpretations carry diverse ideological charges, then historians incur a political and ethical responsibility in making a choice to propagate one rather than another. It would surely be preferable for this choice to be as witting as possible. After all, as Hayden White puts it:

> if historians were to recognize the fictive element in their narratives, this would not mean the degradation of historiography to the status of ideology or propaganda. In fact, this recognition would serve as a potent antidote to the tendency of historians to become captive of ideological preconceptions which they do not recognize as such but honor as the 'correct' perception of 'the way things *really* are'.[16]

Notes

1 G. Salvemini, *Prelude to World War II* (London, Gollancz, 1953), p. 9.

2 For example, R. Overy, *1939: Countdown to War* (London, Allen Lane, 2009).

3 L. Glendinning and L. Harding, 'Poland marks second world war anniversary', *The Guardian*, 1 September 2009, http://www.guardian.co.uk/world/2009/sep/01/poland-second-world-war-anniversary (accessed 2 September 2009); I. Traynor and L. Harding, 'Poland and Russia row over second world war marks Gdansk day', *The Guardian*, 1 September 2009, http://www.guardian.co.uk/world/2009/sep/01/russia-poland-second-world-war-stalin (accessed 2 September 2009).

4 R. McCrum, 'The Second World War: six years that changed this country for ever', *The Guardian*, 23 August 2009, http://www.guardian.co.uk/world/2009/aug/23/second-world-war-mccrum (accessed 23 August 2009).

5 This point is also touched on in D. Reynolds, 'How the Cold War froze the history of World War Two', Annual Liddell Hart Centre for Military Archives Lecture, 2005, available at http://www.kcl.ac.uk/lhcma/info/lec05.htm (accessed 8 February 2006).

6 D. C. Watt, 'Could anyone have deterred him?', *Times Literary Supplement*, 22 December 2000, p. 9.

7 Why 'write a history of British foreign policy based primarily on a study of the political leadership? ... Great men performed their scripts; we have studied their parts for a half-century. We now have their characters in hand; we know their parts': W. Wark, 'Appeasement revisited', *International History Review*, vol. 17, no. 3, 1995, pp. 545–62, quotes at pp. 547, 561.

8 K. M. F. Platt, 'History and despotism, or: Hayden White vs. Ivan the Terrible and Peter the Great', *Rethinking History*, vol. 3, no. 3, 1999, pp. 262–63.

9 W. Schivelbusch, *The Culture of Defeat: On National Trauma, Mourning, and Recovery* (London, Granta, 2003).

10 J. Coakley, 'Mobilizing the past: nationalist images of history', *Nationalism and Ethnic Politics*, vol. 10, no. 4, 2004, pp. 531–60.

11 These issues – and especially the disproportionate influence of English language authors on 'foreign' historiographies – are further unpacked in R. J. Evans, *Cosmopolitan Islanders: British Historians and the European Continent* (Cambridge, Cambridge University Press, 2009).

12 P. Finney, 'Still "marking time"? Text, discourse and truth in international history', *Review of International Studies*, vol. 27, no. 3, 2001, p. 303, quoting R. Buzzanco.

13 Cf. the argument that conventional forms of historical representation cannot do justice to the phenomenon of Nazism in D. Stone, *Constructing the Holocaust: A Study in Historiography* (London, Vallentine Mitchell, 2003).

14 Cf. the similar argument in S. Fitzpatrick, 'Revisionism in Soviet history', *History and Theory*, vol. 46, no. 4, 2007, pp. 77–91, quotes at pp. 89–90.

15 S. Berger, 'On the role of myths and history in the construction of national identity in modern Europe', *European History Quarterly*, vol. 39, no. 3, 2009, p. 492.

16 H. White, *Tropics of Discourse: Essays in Cultural Criticism* (Baltimore, MD, Johns Hopkins University Press, 1978), p. 99 (emphasis in original).

Index

CPSIA information can be obtained
at www.ICGtesting.com
Printed in the USA
FSOW02n1804140816
23721FS